AMERICAN NATIONAL BIOGRAPHY

AMERICAN
NATIONAL BIOGRAPHY

Published under the auspices of the
AMERICAN COUNCIL OF LEARNED SOCIETIES

General Editors

John A. Garraty

Mark C. Carnes

VOLUME 24

OXFORD UNIVERSITY PRESS

New York   1999   Oxford

OXFORD UNIVERSITY PRESS

Oxford   New York
Athens   Auckland   Bangkok   Bogotá
Buenos Aires   Calcutta   Cape Town   Chennai
Dar es Salaam   Delhi   Florence   Hong Kong   Istanbul
Karachi   Kuala Lumpur   Madrid   Melbourne   Mexico City
Mumbai   Nairobi   Paris   São Paulo   Singapore
Taipei   Tokyo   Toronto   Warsaw
and associated companies in
Berlin   Ibadan

Published by Oxford University Press, Inc.,
198 Madison Avenue, New York, New York 10016
http://www.oup-usa.org

Funding for this publication was provided in part by
the Andrew W. Mellon Foundation, the Rockefeller Foundation,
and the National Endowment for the Humanities,
a federal agency.

Library of Congress Cataloging-in-Publication Data

American national biography / general editors, John A. Garraty, Mark C. Carnes
p.   cm.
"Published under the auspices of the American Council of Learned Societies."
Includes bibliographical references and index.
1. United States—Biography—Dictionaries.   I. Garraty, John Arthur,
1920–   .   II. Carnes, Mark C. (Mark Christopher), 1950–   .
III. American Council of Learned Societies.
CT213.A68   1998   98-20826   920.073—dc21   CIP
ISBN 0-19-520635-5 (set)
ISBN 0-19-512803-6 (vol. 24)

Printing (last digit): 9 8 7 6 5 4 3 2 1

Printed in the United States of America
on acid-free paper

CONTINUED

WRIGHT, Alice Morgan (10 Oct. 1881–8 Apr. 1975), sculptor and suffragette, was born in Albany, New York, the daughter of Henry Romeyn Wright, a merchant, and Emma Jane Morgan. Following her graduation from Smith College in 1904, she moved to New York City to begin her sculpture studies at the Art Students League, where her teachers included well-known sculptors Hermon Atkins MacNeil and James Earle Fraser. Although women art students confronted greater obstacles in their training (for instance, women were not permitted to sketch from the male nude, a circumstance Wright circumvented by attending boxing and wrestling matches to study anatomy), she did well, and in 1909 the league awarded her both the Gutzon Borglum and Augustus Saint-Gaudens prizes in recognition of her work. That same year she exhibited her work publicly for the first time at the National Academy of Design.

Wright sailed for Europe in the fall of 1909 to study in Paris. She enrolled in classes at the Académie des Beaux-Arts and at the Académie Colarossi, both popular with foreign students and more accessible than the state-run École des Beaux-Arts. One of her major instructors was Jean Antoine Injalbert. While she was in France, Wright's work was shown at the Paris Girls Club (1910), the Salon (1912), the Salon d'Automne (1913), and in London at the Royal Academy (1911). She also sent pieces back to the United States for exhibition at the National Academy of Design, the Pennsylvania Academy of the Fine Arts, and the Art Institute of Chicago. During vacations from the atelier, Wright traveled throughout Europe to broaden her art education. Sometimes her parents accompanied her, and on another occasion Bessie Berenson, the sister of Italian Renaissance art scholar Bernard Berenson, invited her to visit Settignano.

Although Wright had been involved with the Collegiate Equal Suffrage League in New York, it was during her European sojourn that she became actively involved in the woman suffrage movement, organizing meetings and attending public protests in both Paris and London. By 1911 Wright had joined the National Women's Social and Political Union, and in 1912 she met its founder, Emmeline Pankhurst. When Pankhurst ·organized the English Militant Campaign for Suffrage in 1912 she asked Wright to participate; Wright eagerly left Paris for London. In March 1912 she was one of many who were arrested and subsequently sentenced to two months in Holloway Prison for "willful damage." Her fellow inmates included suffragettes Emmeline Pethick-Lawrence, Zoe Proctor, and Mabel Tuke. The story of Wright's arrest and imprisonment was reported in newspapers all over the United States, and throughout her ordeal her parents remained supportive. Wright and her companions also participated in a hunger strike during their incarceration, and she was able to avoid the humiliation of forced feeding. More unusual was Wright's successful smuggling of art materials into her cell; she used these to model a small head of Pankhurst (1912, Sophia Smith Collection), of whom she later made two other busts.

When Wright returned to the United States in late April 1914 she established her studio in New York in MacDougal Alley, a Greenwich Village location popular with artists. Once back in New York she became acquainted with several members of the artistic avant-garde. When Marius de Zayas showed Wright's work at his Modern Gallery in 1916, it was displayed with pieces by Modernist sculptors Amedeo Modigliani and Constantin Brancusi and by modernist American sculptors Adelheid Lange Roosevelt and Adolf Wolff. In this exhibit Wright showed one of her most advanced pieces, *Wind Figure* (1916, Hirshhorn Museum and Sculpture Garden), a small bronze of an abstracted, twisting human figure, which subsequently entered the collection of Arthur B. Davies, one of the organizers of the 1913 Armory Show, the first large-scale introduction of modernism to the American public. Wright never aligned herself with a particular group or gallery. She was a founder of the Society of Independent Artists in 1917 and remained an active member until the mid-1930s.

Wright's commitments to art and to the woman suffrage movement were strongly connected during her time in Europe, and she continued her political activism once back in the United States. In 1913 she sent a figure titled *Weeping* to a benefit exhibition at the Macbeth Gallery for the cause of suffrage. Linking her art and her politics, she designed a 1916 medal celebrating Harvest Week of the New York State Woman Suffrage Party. Wright was also a member of the organization Women Painters and Sculptors, with which she regularly exhibited.

Wright continued her work for suffrage until the Nineteenth Amendment granted women the right to vote in 1920. After the successful passage of this landmark legislation Wright, sharing the views of many of her contemporaries, believed that one of the most important goals for women had been achieved. In about 1920 Wright gave up her New York studio and moved back to her parents' home in Albany, where she continued to sculpt, though little new work can be documented after about 1930. Thereafter she focused her energies on causes relating to animal rights, including the Humane Education Society. She was active in the World Federation for the Protection of Animals, and in 1960 she was named Humanitarian of the Year by the Humane Society of America. She became internationally famous for her efforts, which she continued until a few years before her death. Wright never married or had children. Her lifelong companion was Edith J. Goode, whom she had met at Smith. Wright died in Albany.

The themes and style of Wright's sculpture (all works cited are in private collections unless otherwise indicated) reveal a wide range of inspirations and influences. Some are conservatively academic, such as *Faun* (1915, examples at Harmanus Bleecker Library, Albany and the National Museum of American Art). Others show the strong impact of French sculptor Auguste Rodin in their passionate themes and powerful style; these include *The Wayfarers* (1909), *Force* or *The Mountain* (1910), and *The Flesh Lusteth against the Spirit* (1912). Wright's love of literature inspired several pieces, including *Lady Macbeth* (1918, examples at the Newark Museum and the Folger Shakespeare Library), *Medea* (1920), *I Am the Captain of My Soul* (c. 1920, Brookgreen Gardens, Murrells Inlet, S.C.), and *Ophelia* (1926). Modern dance also fascinated her, and dancers Isadora Duncan, Ruth St. Denis, and Vaslav Nijinsky inspired *Renaissance* (c. 1915), *Off Shore Wind* (1916), and *Lyra* (1919). The theater provided the source for *Yvette Guilbert* (1917) and *Trojan Women* (1927). While most of Wright's work is three-dimensional, in the mid-1920s she produced a series of paintings in a sleek art moderne style titled *The Golden Apples*.

It is Wright's modernist sculpture that comprises her most significant work. She was one of a small group of independent artists who, although they enthusiastically embraced avant-garde styles, only produced a small body of advanced work. Among Wright's most adventurous pieces are *Wind Figure* and *The Fist* (1921, Albany Institute of History and Art), both of which reveal the influence of cubism.

• Many of Wright's papers are in the Sophia Smith Collection at Smith College in Northampton, Mass., while others remain with her cousin Elinor Wright Fleming. The rediscovery of Wright began in 1975 with an entry by Betsy Fahlman, "Alice Morgan Wright," in the exhibition catalog *Avant-Garde Painting and Sculpture in America 1910–25* (Delaware Art Museum, Wilmington, 1975), pp. 152–53. The definitive work is an exhibition catalog by Fahlman, *Sculpture and Suffrage, the Art and Life of Alice Morgan Wright (1881–1975)* (Albany Institute of History and Art, 1978). Several subsequent publications have drawn on this catalog and have served to place Wright's work in its larger art historical context, notably Roberta K. Tarbell, "Figurative Interpretations of Vanguard Concepts," in *Vanguard American Sculpture* (Rutgers University Art Gallery, 1979), pp. 29–44; Charlotte Streifer Rubinstein, *American Women Artists* (1982); and Rubinstein, *American Women Sculptors* (1990). An obituary is in the *Albany Times-Union*, 10 Apr. 1975.

BETSY FAHLMAN

WRIGHT, Arthur Williams (8 Sept. 1836–19 Dec. 1915), physicist, was born in Lebanon, Connecticut, the son of Jesse Wright, a state legislator and justice of the peace, and Harriet Williams. He received his early education in Lebanon, at the Bacon Academy at Colchester, and at Kinne's private school in Canterbury. He entered Yale in 1855 and excelled in Latin, astronomy, and mathematics. Upon receiving his A.B. in 1859, he elected to remain at Yale, which was then organizing its graduate school and was to offer the first doctoral program in the United States. In 1861 Wright and two others were awarded the first American Ph.D. degrees. His dissertation, "Having Given the Velocity and Direction of Motion of a Meteor on Entering the Atmosphere of the Earth, to Determine the Orbit about the Sun Taking into Account the Attractions of Both These Bodies," was on astronomy and mathematics and was directed by Elias Loomis, professor of astronomy and natural philosophy.

From 1860 to 1863 Wright served as an assistant in the Yale College Library and a librarian of the Linonian Library. He then joined the Yale faculty as a tutor (instructor), first in Latin (1863–1866) and then in natural philosophy (1866–1867). In 1864, and later in 1890, he was a major collaborator in the revisions of Webster's dictionary, participating in the preparation of manuscripts for press, proofreading, and providing definitions of terms in chemistry and physics. Unsure of making a career in academia, he also studied law; he was admitted to the Connecticut bar in 1866, although he never practiced. To augment his credentials in chemistry and physics, he spent the years 1868 and 1869 in Germany, where he studied with Robert W. Bunsen and Gustav Kirckhoff at the University of Heidelberg and with August W. von Hoffmann and Heinrich G. Magnus at the University of Berlin.

Upon returning to the United States, Wright became professor of physics and chemistry at Williams College (1869–1872). He returned to Yale in 1872 as professor of chemistry and molecular physics; after 1887 his position was professor of experimental physics. He retired in 1906.

On 6 October 1875 Wright married Susan Forbes Silliman; they had two daughters and one son. Wright was elected a member of the National Academy of Sciences in 1881 and was active in several governmental advisory committees connected with it. In particular, from 1881 to 1886 he was a consulting specialist for the U.S. Signal (later Weather) Service (Bureau); in 1887 he was chairman of the Committee of Weighing on the Assay Commission to test the quality of gold and silver coins produced at the U.S. Mint in Philadelphia.

Wright's research never involved any startlingly new discoveries in either chemistry or physics; however, by the standards of the time—particularly in the United States—his work was well regarded, and he was respected as an investigator. His research produced about thirty scientific papers, the majority of which were published in the *American Journal of Science and the Arts*, established by Benjamin Silliman, Wright's wife's grandfather, in 1818. This journal was an ideal outlet for American Scientists and typified Yale's commitment to scientific growth. Wright's most notable work included a study of electrical discharges between poles of a machine (1870, 1871), invention of an apparatus to produce ozone (1872, 1874), the polarization of light from comets and its spectrum (1874), and the extraction of gases from stony meteorites and its relation to the observed spectra in comets (1875–1876). In 1896 he was one of the first Americans to confirm Wilhelm K. Roentgen's recent discovery of X-rays. All of this experimental work, except that on X-rays, was carried out under rather primitive conditions and with very meager equipment. Much of the equipment and facilities at Yale dated back to the first quarter of the nineteenth century, having been acquired and used by Silliman. Wright set out to remedy the situation, and through his efforts the Sloane Physical Laboratory was opened at Yale in 1883. This was planned, equipped, and built under his supervision, and it is claimed to be the first building in the United States exclusively designed as a physical laboratory. It is likely that Wright also played a crucial role in financing the project; the two principal benefactors, the brothers Henry T. and Thomas C. Sloane, were his close friends. The laboratory was a major boost for both Yale and American physics, because its existence encouraged competing universities to devote resources to developing similar facilities. After Wright's retirement, when plans were being laid for a new Sloane Laboratory, Wright may again have played a major role in arranging its financing. The new laboratory was opened in 1912 under the directorship of Wright's successor, Henry A. Bumstead. In a 1903 poll conducted by *American Men of Science* of the leaders of science in America, Wright was ranked thirty-sixth (out of 150) in physics.

Wright's major contribution to American physics lies in his devotion and service to Yale, leading to the construction of the Sloane Physical Laboratories. Under his guidance these became a reality, and he was also at least partially responsible for the creation of a professorship of experimental physics at Yale. His research likewise served to capture the imagination of the public and in doing so advanced the cause of science in the United States. Wright died in New Haven following a protracted illness.

• A detailed biographical notice of Wright appears in National Academy of Sciences, *Biographical Memoirs* 15 (1932): 241–57, with a portrait and a bibliography of his most important scientific papers. An obituary is in the *New York Times*, 19 Dec. 1915.

JOSEPH D. ZUND

WRIGHT, Austin Tappan (20 Aug. 1883–18 Sept. 1931), law professor and author, was born in Hanover, New Hampshire, the son of John Henry Wright, who served as dean of the Graduate School of Arts and Sciences at Harvard University, and Mary Tappan, a novelist. In his youth Wright engaged some of the finest legal minds of his day, attending Harvard College from 1901 to 1905, studying at Oxford from 1906 to 1907, and returning to Massachusetts to graduate cum laude from Harvard Law School in 1908 with an LL.B. During his final year at Cambridge, Wright's top-ten class standing earned him a position as editor of the *Harvard Law Review*, examining the works of Learned Hand, Roscoe Pound, and others. On at least one occasion his close affiliation with Harvard faculty freed the young man from personal legal difficulties. One story recalls how James Barr Ames represented Wright in a Boston police court against charges of trespassing and won compensation for wrongful arrest. From graduation until 1916 Wright worked in the Boston office of Louis Brandeis until the latter accepted a position on the Supreme Court.

Wright married Margaret Garrad Stone in 1912; they had four children. The family moved west after Wright received a teaching position at the University of California School of Jurisprudence. At Berkeley Wright began to build an impressive body of scholarship in the fields of corporation law and admiralty. During the First World War he took a position as assistant counsel to the U.S. Shipping Board and U.S. Shipping Board Emergency Fleet Corporation in San Francisco. He returned to his faculty position upon the conclusion of hostilities and began practice at a San Francisco law firm. In 1924 Wright took a position at the University of Pennsylvania, where he taught until 1931, when he died from injuries suffered in a car accident outside Santa Fe, New Mexico. In an obituary that appeared in the *University of Pennsylvania Law Review*, a colleague noted Wright's love of sailing, thoughtful legal mind, and impatience for the details of school administration.

Eleven years after Wright's death, Farrar and Rinehart published the meticulously detailed 1,013-page novel *Islandia* and revealed a side to Austin Wright that had been hidden from all but his family. This utopian novel depicts in vivid detail a mythical island in the South Pacific whose population of preindustrial farmers confronts economic and cultural colonialism in the beginning of the twentieth century. The protagonist, John Lang, is very much like Wright—a Harvard-educated New Englander who struggles to reconcile the promise and pressures of modern life with the simplicity of a distant island. An oft-described fact of Islandian life is the absence of a word for love. Members of this society have four words associated with various forms of attachment, ranging from simple friendship (*amia*) to love for family and place (*alia*). Writing on and off from 1908 onward, Wright indulged in his private *alia* by charting the geography, outlining the literature, exploring the religion, and even defining the peerage of his imaginary locale.

After her husband's death, Margaret Wright transcribed 2,300 pages of manuscripts and sought the assistance of Leonard Bacon, a member of the English department at Berkeley, to secure a publisher. After Margaret's death in 1937, daughter Sylvia Wright edited the manuscript with the aid of Mark Saxton (who went on to complete three sequels to *Islandia*). The book achieved critical acclaim but lukewarm sales of about 30,000 copies in 1942. Despite Wright's corpus of law review articles and even the appearance of a short story in the *Atlantic Magazine* in 1915, colleagues reacted with surprise to his literary endeavors. In his introduction to *Islandia*, Bacon recalls, "In spite of my affection for him and what I supposed to be my knowledge of him I hadn't the faintest inkling that he had left something behind him outside of his professional publications." Out of Wright's voluminous collection of notes related to his utopian island, Farrar and Rinehart also published a promotional booklet in 1942 called *An Introduction to Islandia*, written by Basil Davenport. Sadly, many more of the documents left behind were lost or stolen during rail shipment from a Philadelphia book fair to New York. Sylvia Wright once suggested that, in the hurry of troop and supply movement during the Second World War, the documents might have been accidentally sent to Iceland. What remains is *Islandia*'s compelling vision of an elegant civilization, uncluttered by modern philosophy and sympathetic to the conflicting roles of women. This vision propelled Austin Wright from relative obscurity as a legal philosopher to that pantheon of utopian novelists whose universal aspirations endure.

• Harvard's Houghton Library maintains a collection of papers associated with Islandia (MS AM 1605). Biographical information on Wright can be found in two obituaries: William H. Lloyd, *University of Pennsylvania Law Review* 80 (Nov. 1931): 1–4, and Orrin K. McMurray, *California Law Review* 20 (Nov. 1931): 60–61. Useful essays on the significance of *Islandia* include Norman Cousins, "The Anniversary of 'Islandia,'" *Saturday Review*, 11 Apr. 1942, p. 7; Kenneth Oliver, "Islandia Revisited," *Pacific Spectator* 9 (Spring 1955): 178–82; Lawrence C. Powell, "All That Is Poetic in Life," *Wilson Library Quarterly* 31 (May 1957): 701–5; "Talk of the Town: Vanished," *New Yorker*, 23 Aug. 1958, pp. 18–19; Verlyn Flieger, "Wright's Islandia: Utopia and Its Problems," in *Women and Utopia: Critical Interpretations*, ed. M. Barr and N. D. Smith (1983), pp. 96–107; David N. Samuelson, "Islandia," in *Survey of Modern Fantasy Literature*, ed. Frank N. Magill (1983), pp. 781–86; and Naomi Jacobs's superb "Islandia: Plotting Utopian Desire," *Utopian Studies* 6 (1995): 75–89. Wright's other published work of fiction, "1915?," appeared in the *Atlantic Monthly*, Apr. 1915, pp. 453–63.

ANDREW FRAZIER WOOD

WRIGHT, Beals Coleman (18 Dec. 1879–23 Aug. 1961), tennis player, was born in Boston, Massachusetts, the son of George Wright, a baseball player and cofounder of Wright & Ditson Sporting Goods Company, and Abbie H. Coleman. Wright was named for Tommy Beals, his father's teammate on the Boston Red Stockings, and belonged to a sports-oriented family—his grandfather a cricket professional; his uncles Harry Wright and Sam Wright expert cricketers and major league baseball players; and his younger brother Irving Cloutman Wright a prominent tennis player. George Wright and Harry Wright were elected to the Baseball Hall of Fame in 1937 and in 1953.

Taught by his father, Wright began playing tennis in 1894. Representing Hopkinson's School of Boston, he reached the finals in his first tournament, the 1897 Harvard Interscholastics. The next two years he won both the Harvard and the National Interscholastic

championships. With his father as mentor, Wright, Dwight Davis, Holcombe Ward, and Malcolm Whitman traveled to the Pacific states during late 1899 to play team matches against the best male players on the West Coast. The trip inspired Davis to donate what became known as the Davis Cup. That autumn Wright entered Harvard University, but he left during his freshman year and joined Wright & Ditson. He enjoyed enough latitude there to be able to pursue his tennis career for the next dozen years, during which time he never held a U.S. singles ranking poorer than fourth. He also became one of the world's best doubles players.

Wright gained the semifinals in 1900 and the finals in 1901 of the U.S. singles championships, each time losing to Bill Larned. In 1904 he won the singles and doubles titles at the Olympic Games in St. Louis; most important, he formed a partnership with Ward to win the U.S. doubles crown. The next year, 1905, became Wright's banner year. In Davis Cup ties against France, Australasia, and Great Britain, Wright and Ward won two doubles matches and almost toppled Reggie and Hugh "Laurie" Doherty, the world's best pair. In singles, Wright upset Norman Brookes, the Australian who had just won the all-comers final at Wimbledon before losing to Laurie Doherty in the challenge round, and Wright easily defeated Tony Wilding, the New Zealand star. At home, Wright and Ward successfully defended their U.S. doubles championship, and Wright captured his only national singles title by downing seven skilled opponents, including Bill Clothier, Larned, Clarence Hobart, and, in the challenge round, Ward. Just before the 1906 U.S. Davis Cup team embarked for England, Wright severely cut the fingers of his right hand. Infection followed, which kept him out of the cup matches and hampered his play for the rest of the year. Clothier defeated him decisively in the singles challenge round, although Wright performed well enough in the doubles challenge so that he and Ward won their third consecutive title, after which Ward retired.

The 1907 U.S. Davis Cup players Wright and Karl Behr lost to Australasia in London. In the matches, Wright won from Wilding but lost to Brookes, and he and Behr dropped a five-setter to Brookes and Wilding. After a year's absence from the singles championships, Wright captured the 1908 all-comers tournament but lost to Larned in the challenge round. After the nationals, Wright lost ignominiously to M. J. G. Ritchie of the visiting British Davis Cup team, but he recovered to eke out a victory against Cecil Parke of Ireland as the U.S. team won the tie. The two-man team of Wright and Fred Alexander in November lost to Australasia, 3–2. Wright scored over Wilding and finally closed out a long, classic struggle with Brookes at 12–10 in the fifth set under extremely hot, windy conditions. Wright, who, unlike his opponents, played bareheaded, suffered sunstroke, the effects of which caused him to forgo competition throughout 1909.

Wright resumed tournament play impressively in 1910. Although he had lost in early rounds at Wimbledon in 1905 and 1907, he reached the 1910 all-comers final and extended Wilding to five exciting sets before losing. At home, he gained the all-comers final again, but he could not contain the net rushing of Tom Bundy. The next year, 1911, became his last in major competition. One last time he progressed to the U.S. all-comers final, only to lose to the rising California star Maurice McLoughlin. Later that year in Australia for a Davis Cup challenge, he lost to Brookes in singles, and he and McLoughlin were defeated by Brookes and Alf Dunlop in doubles.

Wright continued with Wright & Ditson until the mid-1910s when he bought an apple ranch. After operating the ranch for several years, he returned to the family concern, now the Wright & Ditson–Victor Company, in 1918. He became a partner of the firm and remained in that capacity until he retired almost thirty years later. In 1917 he married Dorothy Mullins of Cleveland; they had two children. Wright died in Alton, Illinois, where he had moved in old age to be near his children.

At 5′11″ and 180 pounds, the left-handed Wright possessed an exceptionally powerful physique, tireless legs and lungs, an even temperament, determination, and an acute tennis mind. A master of angles rather than speed, he carefully plotted his attack or defense and then executed precisely. Lacking an all-court game, he outlasted, outthought, and outfought opponents, frequently turning apparent losses into wins. At the baseline, instead of using drives, he chopped on both sides with short backswings, accurately varying length, pace, and well-disguised direction to catch net rushers off balance, to pass them, or to lob over their heads. He could win from backcourt, but against the better players he consistently charged the net, where he possibly was the best of his era in dispatching overheads and putting away volleys of all types. His easy, rhythmic, straight serves, kept low and well-placed, allowed receivers no liberties. Although his singles record was impressive, he was held in even higher regard as a doubles player. Gus Touchard, a perceptive critic and former doubles champion, rated Wright and his right-handed partner, Ward, the best of all the pre–World War I American doubles teams, especially praising their phenomenal volleying abilities and court generalship. Wright was elected to the International (then National Lawn) Tennis Hall of Fame in 1956.

• No biographies of Wright have been published. Beals C. Wright, "The Chop Stroke Wins a Championship" and "Some Famous American Teams," in U.S. Lawn Tennis Association, *Fifty Years of Lawn Tennis in the United States* (1931), furnish his own accounts of his victories. S. Wallis Merrihew, *The Quest of the Davis Cup* (1928), describes his play in Davis Cup matches. Perceptive analyses of Wright's game are given in Edward C. Potter, *Kings of the Court* (1936, rev. ed. 1962); Arthur S. Pier, "Some Tennis Champions," *American Magazine*, Apr. 1910, pp. 466–76; and Gustave F. Touchard, "Ten Great American Doubles Players," *American Lawn Tennis*, 15 Apr. 1916, pp. 18–20, and "Our Five Greatest Doubles Teams," *American Lawn Tennis*, 15 May 1916, pp. 55, 92–93. Obituaries appear in the *Boston Herald* and the *New York Times*, both 24 Aug. 1961.

FRANK VAN RENSSELAER PHELPS

WRIGHT, Benjamin (10 Oct. 1770–24 Aug. 1842), civil engineer and surveyor, was born in Wethersfield, Connecticut, the son of Ebenezer Wright and Grace Butler, farmers. He displayed an interest in mathematics as a student, and in his mid-twenties he was sent to live with his uncle, Joseph Wright, in Plymouth, Connecticut. There he had access to surveying instruments and was able to study both surveying and law. In 1789 he and his family moved to Fort Stanwix (now Rome), New York. Soon Wright began work as a surveyor, setting boundaries and subdividing tracts for newly sold lands on the frontier. During 1792–1796 he plotted 500,000 acres in Oneida and Oswego counties and surveyed an additional 2 million acres in parts of northern New York. In 1798 he returned to Plymouth to marry Philomela Waterman. They settled in Fort Stanwix and eventually had nine children, eight of whom survived their parents. In 1830 the family relocated to New York City, where Philomela died in 1835.

Wright began his lifelong association with canal building during his years as a surveyor. He was initially hired in the late 1790s by William Weston, the English engineer who worked for the Western Inland Locks Navigation Company. In 1802 he was hired to perform a survey of Wood Creek, and the next year he was asked to survey the Mohawk River from Fort Stanwix to Schenectady and propose a plan for navigation improvements.

Over the next several years Wright turned his attention to politics and pursued other business dealings. He was elected to the New York State Assembly, and in 1808 he offered a resolution calling for a canal survey from the Hudson River to Lake Erie, adding to the growing calls for federal and state development of the region. Wright also acted as an agent for large landowners in the area, for whom he had done earlier survey work. In 1811–1812 he continued the canal survey, this time for the state canal commissioners, ranging from Albany to Seneca Lake.

In 1813 Wright was appointed a judge for Oneida County. His background in surveying was as important for the position as his political experience and knowledge of law, as judges commonly ruled on cases involving land title and boundary disputes. Although he resigned his position in 1816, he continued to be referred to as "Judge Wright" for the remainder of his life.

Wright was hired as one of three principal engineers for the Erie Canal in 1816. He and James Geddes, another judge/surveyor, were on good terms with the faction of the canal commission that wanted Americans, despite their lack of formal training, to oversee canal construction rather than European engineers. Soon, Wright was placed in charge of the middle section of the canal, from Utica to the Seneca River. The canal commissioners were initially dissatisfied with Wright because he devoted much time to private business dealings, but they later publicly praised him for both his performance and competence. In 1819, when the middle section of the canal was completed, he moved to the more topographically challenging eastern portion, from Utica to the Hudson River. Wright proposed a route along the Mohawk River to the Hudson near Troy, and then south to Albany. Albany business leaders and local engineer John Randel, Jr., attacked Wright and his proposal publicly, offering a more direct route to Albany, which bypassed the rival Troy, but Wright's route was adopted. Disagreements—with Randel again on the Chesapeake & Delaware Canal, and with other engineers elsewhere—would punctuate his career in the future.

The Erie Canal and its offshoots became a major field school for early American civil engineers, in the absence of formal training. Wright and Geddes hired John Jervis, Canvass White, and many others who worked their way up the ranks on the Erie Canal and then went on to become prominent engineers themselves. Before completing the Erie Canal, Wright had begun to work on other canal projects, often as a consultant. They included the Farmington Canal in Connecticut, the Blackstone Canal in Rhode Island, the Chesapeake & Delaware Canal in New York, the Delaware & Hudson Canal in Delaware, and the Chesapeake & Ohio Canal in Virginia. In most of these cases, consultancy led to appointment as chief engineer. He often brought assistant engineers with him from New York and, after the Erie Canal was completed, contractors and crews as well. Much of the rest of Wright's career may be described as a series of overlapping projects on which he was either chief or consulting engineer.

Wright was chief engineer of the Delaware & Hudson Canal until 1827 and then of the Chesapeake & Ohio Canal until 1831. At the age of sixty-two, he decided to retire from the canal business to spend time with his family in New York City, but this arrangement did not last long. In New York he was appointed street commissioner, although he resigned after one year. He was involved in a study of the New York City water supply and also became a corporate member of the New York & Albany Railroad in 1832. He became chief engineer on the New York & Harlem Railroad project and also consulted on the Welland Canal in Ontario during this time. In 1834 the governor of New York appointed him to survey a route through southern New York for the New York & Erie Railroad, and Wright later became chief engineer for that project. He also took the job of chief engineer for the James River & Kanawha Canal project in Virginia in 1835. Wright's most distant consultancy also came in 1835, when he worked on the Havana-Guines Railroad project in Cuba, subsequently engineered by his son, Benjamin H. Wright.

In 1836 Wright resigned from the New York & Erie to become chief engineer on the smaller Tioga & Chemung Railroad. During his final working years, he acted as an adviser on the Chicago & Illinois River Canal and was involved in a variety of projects for the state of Virginia. He died in New York City.

Wright's career has been described as that of a "political engineer," one who identified more with his employers than with the engineering requirements of the project. He quarreled with engineers of the other variety, worked well with politicians and boards, and was a politician himself. However, Wright's importance in the field of engineering is the result not of these things, nor of his technical abilities, but of his leadership on the Erie Canal and involvement with so many of the canals and early railroads in eastern North America. In 1968 the American Society of Civil Engineers named him the Father of American Civil Engineering.

• Many of Benjamin Wright's letters are found in the papers of his fellow engineers and of those for whom he worked: the John B. Jervis Papers, Jervis Public Library, Rome, N.Y.; the David Thomas Papers and the Georg Scriba Papers, New York State Library, Albany; the Charles Ellet Papers, Transportation Library, University of Michigan; and the Philip Schuyler Canal Papers, New York Public Library. Other letters may be found at the Oneida County Historical Society Library, Utica, N.Y. Early survey maps and field notes from the 1790s for Oneida, Oswego, Jefferson, and Lewis Counties are at the New York State Library. Most of Wright's publications are technical reports and progress reports for the various companies and commissions who employed him. Other sources that contain significant information on Wright are "Benjamin Wright: Surveyor and Civil Engineer," in Charles B. Stuart, *Lives and Works of Civil and Military Engineers of America* (1871); "Conflict and Trend: The Progress of Benjamin Wright," in Daniel H. Calhoun, *The American Civil Engineer: Origins and Conflict* (1960); Noble E. Whitford, *History of the Canal System of the State of New York* (1906); and Ralph D. Gray, *The National Waterway: A History of the Chesapeake and Delaware Canal, 1769–1985*, rev. ed. (1989). An obituary is in the *New York Tribune*, 25 Aug. 1842.

JEFF WANSER

WRIGHT, Charles (29 Oct. 1811–11 Aug. 1885), botanical explorer, was born in Wethersfield, Connecticut, the son of James Wright, a carpenter and farmer, and Mary Goodrich. He entered Yale College in 1831 and graduated in 1835. He may have developed a serious interest in botany while at Yale, although at that time the college offered no specific instruction in that subject. He trained as a land surveyor in a course at Yale when he was a junior, but his first position was as tutor to the children of a wealthy family in Natchez, Mississippi. He continued in this post until financial reverses in the family caused them to let him go.

Wright then migrated to the eastern part of the new Republic of Texas in 1837 and earned his living by teaching school and surveying, botanizing during his free time. In 1844 he sent a collection of plants with his first letter to the famed botanist Asa Gray at Harvard. Texas was a geographical area of interest to Gray, and an exchange of letters and specimens began. Gray supplied whatever assistance he could to Wright in the form of books and herbarium supplies, in return for the dried plants. The duplicate specimens were eventually sold to other herbaria for Wright's financial benefit. Mosses and liverworts were sent to William Sullivant, and lichens to Edward Tuckerman.

In 1845 Wright moved to central Texas and earned a living as a tutor and schoolmaster while continuing his fieldwork. After returning from the wilds in September 1848, he found a letter from Gray offering him the opportunity to spend the winter in Cambridge as a curator and the chance to learn advanced botany. Wright accepted and the two finally met, but it was soon obvious that Wright wanted to return to Texas to continue his explorations. In 1849 he accompanied U.S. troops from San Antonio to E1 Paso and was able to collect a large number of plants, many of them new species. These were published by Gray in "Plantae Wrightianae I" (*Smithsonian Contributions to Knowledge* 3 [1852]). After another stint as a Texas schoolmaster, Wright was appointed botanist with the U.S.-Mexico boundary survey; this trip yielded material mostly from New Mexico and Arizona. The new species became the basis for Gray's "Plantae Wrightianae II" (1853) and "Botany of the Mexican Boundary Survey" (1859). The end of this survey in 1852 marked the end of Wright's fifteen-year residence in Texas.

Wright's next collecting position was as botanist for the North Pacific Exploring and Surveying Expedition. In June of 1853 the ships sailed from Virginia across the Atlantic and stopped at Madeira and the Cape Verde Islands before sailing to the Cape of Good Hope, where the group stayed for six weeks. The expedition then headed for Sydney, went on to a prolonged stay in Japan, and visited the Bonin Islands and Ryukyu Islands. They also spent time in Hong Kong, visited the Bering Strait, and then headed to San Francisco. William Stimpson was zoologist on the expedition, and it was probably while with Stimpson, when he was collecting invertebrates, that Wright became interested in mollusks. There are several references to shell-collecting in his letters. In 1865 Wright gave the Museum of Comparative Zoology at Harvard 955 specimens of shells from Hong Kong, which he probably collected on the voyage.

In February 1856 Wright received permission to leave the expedition after having spent the previous months collecting in the San Francisco area. One condition for his leaving was that plants he collected in Nicaragua, on his way home, were to be counted as part of the expedition materials. Unfortunately, many of the manuscripts based on the plants collected on this expedition were never published.

After spending the summer of 1856 in Cambridge and Wethersfield, Wright embarked for Cuba in November to begin eleven years in the botanical exploration of the island. In addition, he continued to collect shells, some of which were new to science. In 1871 Wright accompanied a U.S. commission to Santo Domingo.

When he was not on collecting trips, Wright divided his time in his later years between Cambridge and his family home in Connecticut. He spent the last ten years of his life working on his farm in Wethersfield, where he died. He never married. Asa Gray was the earliest to realize that a keen eye for subtle differences in plants and a love of travel and adventure made Wright one of the best plant collectors of his time.

• The Wright and Gray letters, plant lists, and unpublished manuscripts based on his collections are at the library of the Gray Herbarium, Harvard University; the letters between Wright and George Engelmann, botanist, physician, plant taxonomist and collector, are in the library of the Missouri Botanical Garden. S. W. Geiser, "Naturalists of the Frontier VI," *Southwest Review* 15 (1930): 343–78, gives a detailed account of Wright's life including his years in Texas and a brief summary of the rest of his life. M. K. Jacobson, "Charles Wright (1811–1885) in Cuba as Revealed by His Letters," *Sterkiana* no. 53 (1974): 1–5, is an account of his conchological collecting. T. H. Thatcher, *Biographical and Historical Record of the Class of 1835 in Yale College* (1881), pp. 178–81, and *Obituary Record of Graduates of Yale College* (1886) are accounts written by a classmate. Another obituary is Asa Gray, "Botanical Necrology of 1885," *American Journal of the Sciences* 31 (1886): 12–17. D. H. Pfister, ed., "Cryptogams of the United States Exploring Expedition, 1853–1856, Unpublished Manuscripts (Fungi, Lichens and Musci)," Farlow Reference Library and Herbarium, Harvard University (1978), contains a detailed itinerary and map of the territory covered and details of the dates Wright was at various collecting sites.

ANNA M. M. REID

WRIGHT, Charles Barstow (8 Jan. 1822–24 Mar. 1898), financier and railroad executive, was born in Wysox, Bradford County, Pennsylvania, the son of Rufus Wright, a currier, and Elizabeth (maiden name unknown). His father, a Quaker, had moved in 1814 from Connecticut to the upper Susquehanna River, where he established the first tannery in the area. In 1830 the family moved a few miles upstream to Tioga Point (now Athens), Pennsylvania. Charles attended the Athens Academy until he was fifteen.

In 1837 Wright became a clerk in a general store at Le Raysville, Pennsylvania, and four years later was a partner in the firm. In 1843, at the age of twenty-one, Wright was commissioned by banker C. L. Ward of Towanda, Pennsylvania, to investigate the land holdings of several eastern capitalists in the Chicago area. He moved to Chicago and in the next two years not only accomplished his mission but also engaged in extensive land purchases of his own, especially in the vicinity of Chicago. The rapid arrival of immigrants into northern Illinois and southern Wisconsin in 1845–1846 permitted Wright to lay the foundation of a considerable fortune.

Wright returned to Pennsylvania, and in 1848 entered into the mercantile business with James H. Williams in Erie, Pennsylvania. Three years later the partners also established a bank in Erie. When Williams retired in 1855, Wright opened a branch bank in Philadelphia under the name C. B. Wright & Co. After spending several months in Europe in 1857, Wright gave up his bank in Erie and moved to Philadelphia. He became interested in railroad development in the late 1850s. Wright was elected a director of the Sunbury and Erie Railroad (later the Philadelphia and Erie) and supervised the completion of the line. The bulk of this 287-mile road, running from Sunbury on the upper Susquehanna River to northwestern Pennsylvania, was built between 1859 and 1864. In 1862 the Philadelphia and Erie was taken over by the Pennsylvania Railroad with a long-term lease. Shortly after oil was discovered in western Pennsylvania in 1859, Wright was busy promoting and constructing several short railroads to serve the growing petroleum industry. He was a director of the 96-mile Oil Creek and Allegheny River Railroad.

As a Philadelphia banker, Wright naturally was acquainted with Jay Cooke, the investment banker. In 1870 Cooke and his bank became interested in the projected Northern Pacific Railroad. This railroad had been granted a charter in 1864 and the largest federal land grant ever given to a railroad. Before 1870 only a few miles of the line had been constructed because of inadequate financial support. In 1870 Wright was one of several financiers who supported Cooke's $5 million syndicate that hoped to build the Northern Pacific. Wright was elected to the board of directors of the road in 1870 and was also a member of the executive committee. In 1872 he was a member of the committee sent to the Pacific Coast to select the line's terminal on Puget Sound; the small settlement of Tacoma was chosen, and the Tacoma Land Company was founded to sell lots and wharf rights in the new terminal. Wright was a major investor in the land company, took an active role in the founding of the city, and remained involved in the affairs of Tacoma until his death.

In December 1872 Wright was made chairman of the finance committee of the Northern Pacific board and in the spring of 1873 was elected vice president of the railroad, which was headquartered in New York City. During the early 1870s the Northern Pacific had been built westward from Duluth to Bismarck, Dakota Territory, a distance of over 500 miles. The failure of Jay Cooke & Co. in September 1873, made it impossible for the Northern Pacific to meet its obligations, and construction stopped. In April 1874 Lewis Cass, the road's president, was appointed receiver, and Wright was elected president to succeed Cass. A reorganization plan for the troubled Northern Pacific permitted the conversion of the mortgage bonds into preferred stock. Wright quieted the other creditors and operated the line with rigid economy.

By 1876 the Northern Pacific was showing a small surplus. Using his own credit, Wright purchased a cargo of railroad iron in the East, shipped it around Cape Horn to Tacoma, and used it to build a line east from Puget Sound. In 1877 an agreement with the St. Paul & Pacific and construction of a short connecting line gave the Northern Pacific an entrance into St. Paul, Minnesota. In 1878 Wright resumed the construction of the main line west of Bismarck, North Dakota, toward the Yellowstone River in eastern Montana Territory. Because of ill health Wright resigned the presidency of the Northern Pacific in May 1879 but continued as a director. After a short trip to Eu-

rope Wright returned to the railroad as chairman of the finance committee, which was responsible for obtaining funds to complete the line to the Pacific. He ended all connections with the Northern Pacific Railroad in 1893 and turned his full attention to his banking and financial interests in Philadelphia. Wright had become a member of the Philadelphia Stock Exchange in May 1892.

With an enduring faith in the Northwest and its future, Wright had made highly profitable investments in the region served by the Northern Pacific and endeavored to give some of his wealth back to society. His gifts to Tacoma were so numerous that he was often called "the father of Tacoma." He was a major investor in the beautiful Tacoma hotel and donated the money to build the St. Luke's Episcopal Church. He also founded in Tacoma the Annie Wright Seminary for Young Ladies, in memory of his wife and daughter. Wright was twice married, first in 1848 to Cordelia Williams of Erie. In 1858 he married Susan Townsend of Sandusky, Ohio, with whom he had four children. Wright died in Philadelphia.

• Some of Wright's letters are in the archives of the Northern Pacific Railroad, St. Paul, Minn. Material on his railroad career is in Thomas C. Cochran, *Railroad Leaders, 1845–1890: The Business Mind in Action* (1953). Wright's relations with Jay Cooke are briefly noted in Ellis P. Oberholtzer, *Jay Cooke: Financier of the Civil War* (1907). E. V. Smalley, *History of the Northern Pacific Railroad* (1883), and Louis T. Renz, *The History of the Northern Pacific Railroad* (1980), both review Wright's career with the railroad. Obituaries are in *Railroad Gazette*, 1 Apr. 1898, and *Railway World*, 26 Mar. 1898.

JOHN F. STOVER

WRIGHT, Chauncey (20 Sept. 1830–12 Sept. 1875), philosopher and mathematician, was born in Northampton, Massachusetts, the son of Ansel Wright, a grocer and deputy sheriff, and Elizabeth Boleyn. He graduated from Harvard College in 1852 and excelled in mathematics and science. From 1852 to 1872 he was a mathematician in the employ of the *American Ephemeris and Nautical Almanac*, a forerunner of later publications emanating from the Harvard Observatory. Owing to his mathematical skill, Wright was able to condense his yearly calculations for the *Ephemeris* into three months a year and hence was left free to become the Socratic sage of Old Cambridge. His "salon," beginning in 1855, was attended by his former classmates and *Ephemeris* colleagues and later by younger friends like C. S. Peirce, William James, Oliver Wendell Holmes, Jr., Nicholas St. John Green, and Henry Holland. Wright and his younger friends met regularly in the early 1870s as an informal club, meeting at their various homes. As before, Wright was the whetstone on which his friends continued to sharpen their philosophical wit. Peirce, James, and Holmes thought of him as their intellectual "boxing master" and early mentor.

In 1860 Wright was elected a fellow of the American Academy of Arts and Sciences and from 1863 to 1870 was its recording secretary. In the academy debates during these years Asa Gray, Harvard botanist, defended Charles Darwin's views on the mutability of species against Louis Agassiz, Harvard zoologist, and Wright was a staunch defender of Gray. In later years Darwin was so much impressed by Wright's defense of his views that he reprinted Wright's *North American Review* article on "The Genesis of Species" as a pamphlet and at his own expense had it widely distributed in England. Wright visited Darwin at Down in 1872, perhaps the highlight of his life. To Sara Sedgwick he wrote, "If you can imagine me enthusiastic,—absolutely and unqualifiedly so, without a *but* or criticism,—then think of my last evening's and this morning's talks with Mr. Darwin as realizing that beatific condition. . . . I was never so waked up in my life, and did not sleep many hours under the hospitable roof" (*Letters*, p. 248).

From 1864 to 1875 Wright contributed numerous essays and reviews to the *North American Review* and the *Nation*, many of which were published posthumously by C. E. Norton as *Philosophical Discussions*. These writings constituted the first technically proficient philosophy of science written in the United States. Wright's *Letters*, published by J. B. Thayer, contains not only important theoretical discussions of utilitarian moral philosophy but also makes specific applications of it to practical issues such as women's rights, the abuse of wealth, the decline of political liberty, and the rearing of children.

Wright's philosophical development is not difficult to trace. At Harvard Dr. James Walker influenced him along the lines of Thomas Reid's commonsense philosophy. According to Reid, any philosophical system that denies the truths of everyday life must be false, and the task of the critical philosopher is to discover and eliminate the faulty premises that yield these denials. During the first five years after college Wright adopted the maverick commonsense views of William Hamilton, and for several years his relation to Hamilton's philosophy was like that of a devout Christian to the Bible. But John Stuart Mill's critique of Hamilton convinced Wright to become an adherent of British empiricism, particularly that variety espoused by Mill and Alexander Bain. Wright agreed with Mill that basic sensory propositions like "this rock is hard" are summaries of experience and have no hypothetical element. However, he modified Mill's view considerably by rejecting Mill's claim that laws and scientific theories are summaries of particular experiences and by interpreting them instead as working hypotheses from which new data can be inferred and experientially tested.

Wright's pragmatist friends were influenced by his forward-looking, consequence-oriented empiricism and his rejection of the backward-looking, summary views of the British tradition. The pragmatists later developed Wright's "working hypothesis" interpretation of general propositions into a hypothetical interpretation of all propositions, including basic sensory ones. For them, "this rock is hard" was not a summary

of experiences but rather a hypothesis with many consequences to be tested. While Wright's articulation of the concept of forward-looking empiricism influenced the pragmatists, he rejected the pragmatists' generalization of his theme to sensory experiences and thus was not himself a pragmatist.

Wright's personality was unusually attractive but not without faults. He was congenial and considerate, and men were quickly drawn to him. "He was certainly catholic in his taste among men," observed E. W. Gurney, "but, as I run over in my mind the women who found a place in his regard, I am struck with the sureness of his instinct for what is charming, refined and feminine" (*Letters*, p. 383).

On 11 September 1875 Wright suffered a stroke while writing at his desk in Cambridge. He was discovered the next morning, but another stroke came and Chauncey—as everyone affectionately addressed him—died at the age of forty-five. No doubt his personal habits hastened his untimely death. He smoked constantly, was irregular in his sleeping and eating habits, and twice during his life had a serious drinking problem. Henry James, the novelist, was his only friend not away from Cambridge on holiday, and he rushed through the deserted Sunday morning streets, arriving within minutes of his friend's death. James always remembered Wright's penetrating blue eyes, fair complexion, and the splendid shape of his head, handsome not only in a surface way but for representing the capacity for great thought. James also recalled his friend's gentle nature and his "bachelor" attitude toward life, an attitude, one should add, that often caused him lonely moments even amidst friends.

Wright's major contributions to science and philosophy are his defenses of Darwinism, highly valued by Darwin himself, his emergence as the first technically proficient philosopher of science in the United States, and his departure from classical British empiricism by turning attention from antecedent meanings of propositions to their experiential consequences and thereby preparing the way for the appearance of pragmatism. His application of utilitarian moral philosophy to specific social problems, specifically his defense of women's rights and his criticism of the excesses of capitalism, have been of increasing interest in recent times.

• The two most important sources on Wright's philosophy are *Philosophical Discussions*, ed. C. E. Norton (1877), and *Letters of Chauncey Wright*, ed. J. B. Thayer (1878). Thayer added much useful biographical information and included biographical information by other authors, the most important of which is E. W. Gurney. Some of Wright's articles and reviews are not reprinted in *Philosophical Discussions* and are available only in the journals in which they originally appeared. *Chauncey Wright and the Foundations of Pragmatism* by Edward H. Madden (1963) is a full-scale examination of Wright's life and thought and provides bibliographical references to all that he wrote and all secondary literature about him. Of the many excellent essays about Wright, two deserve special attention, the chapters on Wright in Morton White's *Science and Sentiment in America* (1972), and Joseph Blau's *Men and Movements in American Philosophy* (1952). For a comprehensive review and evaluation of the literature about Wright, see Robert Giuffrida, "The Philosophical Thought of Chauncey Wright," *Transactions of the Charles S. Peirce Society* 24 (1988): 33–64.

EDWARD H. MADDEN

WRIGHT, Eliphalet Nott (3 Apr. 1858–10 Jan. 1932), physician, politician, and businessman, was born near Armstrong Academy, Choctaw Nation, in Indian Territory (now southeastern Oklahoma), the son of Allen Wright, a Choctaw civil and religious leader and scholar, and Harriet Mitchell, a white Presbyterian mission teacher. Wright attended school fourteen miles southwest of Atoka at Boggy Depot, Choctaw Nation, when it was a Confederate post during the Civil War. He was in Washington, D.C., briefly, when his father represented the Choctaw Nation to treat with the U.S. government. Wright attended classes for one year at Westminster College, Fulton, Missouri, and three years at Spencer Academy near Doaksville in Choctaw Nation. In 1878 he entered Union College in Schenectady, New York, but discontinued his classical course of study there in 1881 to enter the Albany Medical College, New York. He earned necessary money by practicing back home in the summer of 1883 and then returned to Albany, where he received an M.D. early in 1884. He went home to Boggy Depot to begin a career combining medicine, politics, and business.

Early in 1884 Wright opened a successful medical practice in and near Boggy Depot. In 1888 he married Ida Belle Richards, a Presbyterian teacher in the Atoka mission; they had two children who survived infancy. In 1885 Wright was appointed chief surgeon and physician for the Missouri-Pacific Coal Mines in Lehigh, Choctaw Nation, where he and his family made their home until 1894. He undertook postgraduate studies at the College of Physicians and Surgeons, New York City, in the fall and winter of 1894–1895, after which he and his family moved to Atoka to establish his practice there. In 1903 he was elected president of the Indian Territory Medical Association. He addressed members at the annual meeting in Tulsa in 1904 and advocated a merger with the Oklahoma Medical Society to unify activities. This was accomplished two years later. In subsequent years Wright was often called on by Indian and white physicians in the Five Civilized Tribes—that is, Cherokee, Chickasaw, Creek, Seminole, and Choctaw—to share his surgical and diagnostic expertise. Years later, when the 1917–1918 influenza epidemic hit oil fields in the southern United States, Wright generously answered the call for physicians and went to Avery, Texas, to care for scores of patients and advise numerous overworked doctors and nurses throughout the community.

Wright's political career began in October 1884, when he accompanied his father to a meeting of the General Council at Tuskahoma, the new (and last) capital of Choctaw Nation. While there, he helped prepare a law regulating the Choctaw medical profession, then weakened by ill-trained and even quack physicians in its midst. Also while at Tuskahoma, he became interested in developing Choctaw Nation oil for the financial betterment of his people. In 1890 the Choctaw principal chief appointed Wright as agent to try to enforce contracts to develop stone, oil, and timber resources and be appropriately paid for them. His skillful work for the next four years resulted in unprecedented, if short-lived, Choctaw prosperity. In 1894 Wright was a representative at meetings in Checotah, Choctaw Nation, of the Dawes commission of the federal government and the Five Civilized Tribes to consider dissolving Indian territorial governments and allotting their communally held lands in severalty. The Dawes commission intended to distribute parcels to private developers—Indians and whites alike—so that much-vaunted "American" initiative and individualism might take root and flourish there. At first Wright favored severalty, lost out, and was called a traitor by his constituents. A bill to fine and jail Indian advocates of severalty, and to execute repeat offenders, was sponsored by Indian legislators but failed to become law. In the spring of 1896 Wright was named chair of the Indians' Republican party convention at Muskogee, Choctaw Nation, and supported William McKinley's bid for the presidency. When in November 1896 the Dawes commission demanded immediate deeding of Indian lands to the federal government, Wright opposed it as contrary to the intent of the negotiating process. In December 1896 and early 1897 he conferred in vain with president-elect McKinley in Canton, Ohio, and with Department of the Interior officials in Washington, D.C., for redress of ongoing grievances. In 1897 he sought to meet with Dawes commissioners in Atoka but was told to stay away; thereafter he played no role in the negotiations. In 1900 Wright ran unsuccessfully to become Choctaw Nation principal chief. In 1902 he fought in vain against federal officials demanding terms more advantageous to purchase coal and asphalt resources held by the Choctaw and Chickasaw nations.

Wright opposed the creation of two states, one out of the Oklahoma Territory, the other out of Indian Territory, and was pleased that Oklahoma was admitted as one state in 1907. (In 1866 his father had suggested the name Oklahoma, from the Choctaw *okla*, "people," and *humma* or *homma*, "red.") Thereafter, the focus of Wright's political activities changed. In 1908 the governor of Oklahoma named him Choctaw Nation resident delegate in Washington, D.C., charging him to do what he could to protect Choctaw lands and resources. Although he was eminently successful in preventing further exploitation at this time, the office of resident delegate was abolished in 1910. In 1912 Wright was a delegate to the Progressive party's national convention in Chicago and was involved in party concerns for a full decade thereafter. In 1922 he attended a Choctaw convention in Albion, Oklahoma, and was asked anew to help settle tribal affairs. The inefficient Indian Bureau in Washington, with outmoded and crippling regulations, had been allowing

Choctaw businesses and schools to deteriorate. Wright led a fight to settle money owed the Choctaws in accord with relevant treaties and to force the Interior Department to buy Choctaw coal and asphalt deposits or let Choctaw companies handle such sales to private companies. The Choctaws called their quiescent General Council into action again, with Wright as a major leader. After four fruitless years of conventions, resolutions, and delegations to Washington, he decided to exert direct political pressure. In 1926 he helped organize the Tuskahoma League, of which he was first chair. Nonpartisan in nature and staffed by Indians from all the Oklahoma tribes, its purpose was to elect those politicians who vowed to favor Indian rights. Results were generally positive. In 1928 Wright was a Republican party state committeeman and helped Herbert Hoover gain a sizable majority in Oklahoma. A year later, hearing that the Indian Bureau was turning more sympathetic, Wright sought to become principal Choctaw chief; he was unsuccessful, however, and thereafter was less directly involved in politics.

Over the years Wright's medical and political work blended with his many commercial activities. While at the 1884 Tuskahoma council meeting, he was elected first president of the Choctaw Oil and Refining Company, serving to 1889. An oil-drilling crew, financed in part by Wright, found oil and natural gas just west of Atoka in 1887, but work was abandoned after Dr. H. W. Faucett, the principal promoter and the driller, became ill and soon died. In 1901, when the Rock Island Railroad was building a line in southeastern Oklahoma Territory, Wright persuaded company officials to place a station close to Clear Boggy and his farm. His plan was to set up a nearby town, which he named Olney, and to lease adjacent land and develop businesses there. Soon after organizing a Presbyterian church in Olney, Wright in 1906 helped establish and then became director of a bank there. Beginning in 1916 he participated in developing the oil field near Avery, Texas, which was soon hit by influenza. By the end of his life Wright was tired alike of medicine, diplomacy, and commerce. He died in an Oklahoma City hospital of influenza and pneumonia. Insufficiently singled out for praise by later historians, he was a major force—often behind the scenes and not always successful, to be sure—for the improvement of Oklahoma's perennially mistreated Native Americans.

• Papers concerning Wright are filed in the History of Medicine Collection, University of Oklahoma Health Sciences Center Library, Oklahoma City. "A Brief Review of the Life of Eliphalet Nott Wright," *Chronicles of Oklahoma* 10, no. 11 (June 1932): 265–86, by his granddaughter Muriel H. Wright, is the best biography. Angie Debo, *The Rise and Fall of the Choctaw Republic* (1934), places Wright in context. Roy Gittinger, *The Formation of the State of Oklahoma, 1803–1906* (1939), and Arrell Morgan Gibson, *Oklahoma: A History of Five Centuries*, 2d ed. (1981), provide Choctaw historical data. C. B. Glasscock, *Then Came Oil: The Story of the Last Frontier* (1938), mentions H. W. Faucett's work. An obituary is in the *Indian Citizen-Democrat* (Atoka, Okla.), 14 Jan. 1932.

ROBERT L. GALE

WRIGHT, Elizur (12 Feb. 1804–21 Nov. 1885), abolitionist and life insurance reformer, was born in South Canaan, Connecticut, the son of Elizur Wright, Sr., and Clarissa Richards, farmers. In 1810 the family moved to the Western Reserve of Ohio to obtain cheaper farm land and also to spread the Congregational faith. Wright was the first son of his father's second marriage, and his parents' high expectations and exhortation to act on moral principles undergirded his long reform career. Circumstances and youthful ambivalence conspired to bar him from his intended career as a minister. After graduation in 1826 from Yale College (his father's alma mater), he taught school in Groton, Massachusetts, from 1826 to 1828, where he met his future wife, Susan Clark, whom he married in 1829. They eventually had eighteen children. In lieu of the ministry, the pious young man served four months between 1828 and 1829 as an agent for the American Tract Society in western Pennsylvania before accepting a professorship of mathematics and natural philosophy at Western Reserve College in Hudson, Ohio.

Although Wright had a strong commitment to do good works in the spirit of the ongoing Second Great Awakening, his inclination was increasingly toward secular pursuits rather than a purely sacred calling. For example, while at Western Reserve College in 1833, Wright was persuaded by the impassioned writings of William Lloyd Garrison in Boston that the gradual emancipation program of the American Colonization Society was a moral fraud. In a consistent extension of the evangelical belief that sin must readily be abandoned, Wright embraced the crusade of immediate abolition, making him one of the first Garrisonians in the West. In 1833 he accepted a call from the philanthropist Lewis Tappan in New York City to help organize the American Anti-Slavery Society and then served as its national secretary until 1839. Responsibility for the daily operation and many publications of the nation's premier abolitionist society tempered his youthful euphoria that the millennium was at hand.

The inefficacy of voluntary change in abolishing slavery and eradicating racism convinced Wright that political action and legislative mandates were essential to compel right conduct. His commitment to the formation of what by 1840 became the Liberty party alienated him from the Garrisonian camp, which after 1837 embraced a form of Christian anarchism—nonresistance—and opposed political action. As editor of the *Massachusetts Abolitionist* in Boston (1839–1840), Wright was a major critic of Garrisonian nonresistance. In addition, he was alienated from Tappan and his evangelical circle in New York City, which at the time opposed the creation of an antislavery party because they wished to concentrate on a church-oriented abolitionism. Disillusioned with the failure of the major Protestant denominations to condemn slavery, Wright came out of the church and emerged as a vocal critic of what he regarded as Christian hypocrisy on the issue of racial equality. He positioned himself as a maverick among the abolitionists, becoming increasingly isolated after 1840 from a leadership role in a movement he had pioneered.

Following the schism with the abolitionists, Wright faced insecure employment, debts, growing family responsibilities, and a period of hardship and self-doubt. During 1844 he went to England to market his translation of La Fontaine's *Fables* (1842). After returning to the United States he secured financial backing from Liberty Men and Conscience Whigs to publish in 1846 his own Boston newspaper, the *Chronotype*. An outspoken and irreverent journalist, his editorials called for a series of reforms that included vehement opposition to the Mexican War. Moderate political abolitionists in Boston, who disliked Wright's intemperate evangelical style, pressured him to create a disciplined Free Soil party organ; because he refused to succumb, he was forced to sell the financially ailing paper in 1850. By mid-century, he was estranged from his former immediatist colleagues, only to be accepted superficially by another generation of pragmatic antislavery politicians coalescing about the Free Soil party and subsequently the Republican party.

No longer in an influential role in the abolitionist movement and needing a stable income, after 1844 Wright applied his mathematical talents to consulting work with life insurance companies such as the Massachusetts Hospital Life Insurance Company and the New England Mutual Life Insurance Company. His efforts on behalf of the policyholder provided a continuity with his earlier commitment as an abolitionist to the quest for social justice. Wright's contribution to the development of life insurance and to the protection of the policyholder was to reform and regulate business practices. His contributions were manifold: in 1853 he published valuation tables that laid the mathematical foundation for the financial liability of life insurance companies; in 1858 he lobbied successfully for a Massachusetts law that required life insurance companies to maintain an adequate capital reserve, subject to state supervision; in 1861 he was instrumental in securing another state law that prevented forfeiture of a life insurance policy because of nonpayment of a premium; and in 1880 the Massachusetts legislature enacted his concept of a cash-surrender value for retiring policyholders.

His life insurance work, unlike his early abolitionist crusade, was without overt religiosity, an indication of his growing secularization. He was searching for rational solutions to social problems bred by a dynamic capitalist economy. To place the growing business on a financially precise basis while making it safe and secure for, in his words, "the widow and orphans," Wright introduced actuarial innovations in the compilation of accurate valuation tables. He also sponsored landmark regulating legislation and served as Massachusetts commissioner of life insurance from 1858 to 1867. As the century's leading life insurance reformer, his achievement was no less than an economic discernment of death. He led governmental efforts to regulate powerful corporations, anticipating the twentieth-century Progressives who sought to hold corporate capitalism publicly accountable. He advocated national supervision of life insurance companies, a philosophy akin to his support of a participatory federal government role during the Civil War and Reconstruction on behalf of the slaves and freedmen, most notably in advocating the confiscation and redistribution of land.

No other aspect of his long reform career presents such a seeming disparity as Wright's embrace of atheism. He had left the church during the 1830s in moral indignation over organized religion's opposition to abolitionism. His rejection of conventional theistic assumptions was based on a skepticism derived from scientific evidence. His controversial election in 1878 to the presidency of the National Liberal League (an organization dedicated to the separation of church and state and the right of free speech) was highlighted by a rancorous debate over the issues of obscenity and free speech. He advocated repeal of the Comstock Law based on the belief that the federal government did not have the right to suppress unpopular opinions through censorship of the mail.

After 1880 Wright turned his attention as doggedly as he had previously to abolitionism and insurance reform to the preservation of the Middlesex Fells, a forested region of glaciated hills and ponds that is now a Boston park. He died at his home in Medford, Massachusetts, after suffering a stroke while working at his desk on the Middlesex Fells project.

In the context of the fundamental social and economic transformation of the United States during the nineteenth century, Wright's commitment to social change was rooted in republican principles of government, Enlightenment rationalism, and the secularized religious ideals of the Second Great Awakening.

• Wright's manuscripts are in the Library of Congress. His most important work on abolitionism is *The Sin of Slavery* (1833). The *Valuation Tables on the Combined Experience Rate of Mortality, for the Use of Life Insurance Companies* (1853) and *"The Bible of Life Insurance"* (repr. 1932), which contains his annual reports as Massachusetts commissioner of life insurance, are his pivotal writings on this subject. One important biography is Lawrence B. Goodheart, *Abolitionist, Actuary, Atheist: Elizur Wright and the Reform Impulse* (1990).

LAWRENCE B. GOODHEART

WRIGHT, Fielding Lewis (16 May 1895–4 May 1956), governor of Mississippi and vice presidential candidate, was born in Rolling Fork, Mississippi, the son of Henry James Wright, the sheriff of Sharkey County, and Fannie Clements. Wright attended elementary school in Rolling Fork and in 1911 left home to attend the Webb School at Bellbuckle, Tennessee. Wright entered the University of Alabama in 1912 and graduated with a degree in law in 1915. After passing the Mississippi bar examination in 1916, Wright became a full partner in his uncle's law practice in Rolling Fork. Wright married Nan Kelly, his childhood sweetheart, in 1917; the couple had one child and adopted another.

Wright's budding law career was sidetracked by World War I. He served as a private in the U.S. Army in France from September 1918 to July 1919. From 1919 to 1922 Wright played baseball for semiprofessional teams in the Mississippi Delta area and also resumed his law practice. He organized Company B of the 106th Engineers of the Mississippi National Guard in 1925 and served as its captain for three years. He resigned his post in 1928 after being elected to the Mississippi Senate.

Wright served in the state senate for four years (1928–1932), aligning himself with the conservative Delta interests. He was prevented from running for reelection because his home county, Sharkey, shared its senator with another county. Instead, Wright announced his candidacy for the Mississippi House of Representatives. He was elected without opposition.

Like the rest of the country, Mississippi faced serious financial difficulties in 1932. Wright was among those who worked to pass a sales tax that would help alleviate the state's $10 million budget deficit. Wright was reelected to the house in 1936 and continued to be active during his second term. He was one of the sponsors of a highway bill designed to "lift Mississippi out of the mud," and he worked closely with the governor to ensure passage of the Balance Agriculture with Industry Program, a plan designed to encourage new industry in the state. Wright helped secure passage of the Homestead Exemption Act, legislation designed to enable more citizens to purchase and keep their own homes. During Wright's second term Speaker of the house Horace Stansel died, and house members unanimously elected Wright to fill the vacancy.

In 1938 Wright was considered by some to be a promising candidate for lieutenant governor, but instead of seeking higher office, he chose to retire from politics at the end of his second term. Wright returned to his legal practice, becoming a partner in a Vicksburg law firm. But his hiatus from politics was short-lived. In 1943 Wright was elected lieutenant governor on the same ticket with his old friend and former Mississippi Speaker of the house Thomas Bailey. Early in 1946 Governor Bailey became ill, and Wright stepped in as acting governor. When Bailey died on 2 November 1946, Wright became the governor of Mississippi.

Not long after becoming governor, Wright and the state of Mississippi became the focus of national attention. In March 1947 Wright called a special session of the legislature soon after the U.S. Supreme Court ruled the white primary unconstitutional. In an attempt to circumvent the Court's decision and thus prevent black Mississippians from voting, the legislature decreed that to vote in a primary, a voter "must be in accord with the statement of the principles of the party holding such a primary." In other words, the Mississippi Democratic party would have sole authority in determining the eligibility of voters.

Wright served out the remainder of Bailey's term and was elected to the governorship for a full four-year term in 1947. In his inaugural address of January 1948, Wright once again became the focus of national attention when he established himself as an early and vocal opponent of President Harry S. Truman's civil rights program, which advocated federal antilynching and anti–poll tax legislation and the establishment of a permanent Fair Employment Practices Committee. Wright issued an open threat that Mississippi would bolt the Truman ticket or any other Democratic ticket unless the president's civil rights program was left out of the party platform. He considered Truman's civil rights agenda a form of political harassment "deliberately aimed" at the South and warned the national party not to take Dixie for granted. Wright regretted the day when Mississippi or the South should break with the Democratic party in a national election, "but vital principles and eternal truths transcend party lines," he said, "and the day is now at hand when determined action must be taken."

Wright and other southern leaders convened the States' Rights Conference in May 1948 in Jackson, Mississippi, where the conferees drew up plans to block the inclusion of a civil rights plank in the Democratic party platform. At the Democratic National Convention held in Philadelphia in July, the States' Rights Democrats, or Dixiecrats, as they came to be called, were unable to prevent the incorporation of the civil rights plank; nor could they block the nomination of President Truman. In protest, Wright led the Mississippi delegation out of the convention hall. The States' Rights Democrats reconvened in Birmingham, Alabama, on 17 July to nominate candidates of their own. The convention nominated South Carolina governor J. Strom Thurmond for president and Wright for vice president. Although Truman's civil rights program had been the impetus for the southern bolt, the Dixiecrats claimed that their campaign was not about race. Rather, Truman's civil rights proposals were only part of what the Dixiecrats identified as a general tendency toward centralized government and federal intervention in activities usually left to the states.

The Dixiecrats' strategy was quite simple. They hoped to upset Truman's reelection bid by capturing the 127 electoral votes of the solid South. This would prevent either major party candidate from winning a majority, thus throwing the election into the House of Representatives. It was in the House that the Dixiecrats sought to exact concessions favorable to the South. Ultimately, they were unsuccessful. When it was all over, the Dixiecrats carried only four southern states and received thirty-nine electoral votes.

Fielding Wright returned to his Vicksburg law practice in 1952. Two years later he again announced his candidacy for governor but was defeated in the primaries. Wright died of a heart attack at his home in northeast Jackson.

While many former Dixiecrats eventually returned to the Democratic party, the 1948 presidential election and subsequent southern political defection initiated by Fielding Wright marked the beginning of the political realignment of the South, from solidly Democratic to predominantly Republican in presidential voting.

Although the transformation would take twenty years to complete, the first fissures in the solid South appeared with the Dixiecrat bolt. Furthermore, the 1948 presidential election was the first national election since the late nineteenth century in which the status of black Americans was an issue. While President Truman's civil rights proposals were modest, Wright and other southern leaders felt sufficiently threatened to leave the Democratic party—the traditional party of segregation in the South—and create an alternative political party. Wright and the Dixiecrats, then, were the harbingers of southern "massive resistance" to desegregation that would erupt in the mid-1950s.

• The majority of Wright's gubernatorial papers were destroyed in a fire. The few documents that do exist concern pardons, paroles, and suspensions granted by Wright. These are located at the Mississippi Department of Archives and History in Jackson. The States' Rights Democrats Vertical Files and States' Rights Scrapbooks at the Mississippi Department of Archives and History provide information on the 1948 campaign. Also see Elbert R. Hilliard, "A Biography of Fielding Wright: Mississippi's Mr. States' Rights" (master's thesis, Mississippi State Univ., 1959); Richard D. Chesteen, "'Mississippi Is Gone Home!': A Study of the 1948 Mississippi States' Rights Bolt," *Journal of Mississippi History* 32 (1970): 43–59; Richard C. Ethridge, "Mississippi's Role in the Dixiecratic Movement" (Ph.D. diss., Mississippi State Univ., 1971); and Emile Ader, *The Dixiecrat Movement—Its Role in Third Party Politics* (1955). An obituary is in the Jackson (Miss.) *Daily News*, 5 May 1956.

KARI FREDERICKSON

WRIGHT, Frances (6 Sept. 1795–13 Dec. 1852), reformer and author, was born in Dundee, Scotland, the daughter of James Wright, a linen merchant, and Camilla Campbell. Wright's father was an ardent supporter of Thomas Paine, and although "Fanny" was younger than three when her parents died, she later remarked on "a somewhat singular coincidence in views between a father and daughter, separated by death when the first had not reached the age of twenty-nine, and when the latter was in infancy" (Eckhardt, pp. 5–6). After her parents' death, she and her siblings were parceled out to various relatives, and Wright went to live with her aunt and maternal grandfather in England. She and her sister Camilla were reunited in Dawlish around 1806, only to suffer the death of their brother and their grandfather three years later.

Although Wright was, by her own account, surrounded by "rare and extensive libraries" as a child, her practical education came from the streets of London, where she had seen thousands of beggars whom her grandfather, an idle socialite, said were too lazy to work. She also witnessed enclosures by wealthy lords in Dawlish who ruthlessly forced peasants from their land. Such injustices left indelible marks on Wright's psyche, causing her to "wear ever in her heart the cause of the poor and helpless," a promise she would spend the rest of her life trying to keep (Eckhardt, p. 11).

Wright and Camilla left Dawlish in 1813, moving to Scotland to live with their uncle James Mylne, a professor at the University of Glasgow whose staunch opposition to the slave trade also made a lasting impression on Wright. In Scotland she began to explore her talents as a writer, completing her first version of *Altorf*, a tragedy about the Swiss fight for self-rule, as well as a historical fantasy about a young female disciple of Epicurus, which she eventually published in 1822 as *A Few Days in Athens*.

By the time Wright turned twenty-one, her sights were firmly set on America. Eager to test the new republic's commitment to liberty, she and her sister set sail for the New World in August 1818, a portentous trip that would begin Wright's controversial relationship with a country whose ideals were more noble in theory than in practice. Initially staying in New York, Wright fell in love with America, a country that seemed characterized by neither extreme wealth nor extreme poverty.

During Wright's two-year stay, *Altorf* was staged in New York (1819) and in Philadelphia (1820) with modest success, although its publication went largely unnoticed. Wright then set out to see the "real" America, traveling throughout the Northeast and collecting observations that would eventually become *Views of Society and Manners in America* (1821), a memoir constructed from a series of letters to a Scottish friend. Published after her return to England, the book was warmly received by Americans who liked her romantic portrait, which naively asked, "What country before was ever rid of so many evils?" (Eckhardt, p. 45).

Despite a patronizing reception in England, the text also won Wright the support of European reformers like Jeremy Bentham and the marquis de Lafayette. Wright's friendship with the latter was particularly intimate, and in 1824 she returned to the United States as part of his entourage amidst rumors that the two were lovers. Although Wright suggested that Lafayette either marry or adopt her, the general did neither, and by the time he returned to France in 1825, his young protégée's attentions were fixed elsewhere.

Wright had become consumed with the issue of slavery. In 1825, after visiting Robert Owen's utopian society in New Harmony, Indiana, she purchased 640 acres near Memphis, Tennessee, named the settlement "Nashoba," and began her grand effort to confront the country's most painful dilemma. After acquiring several slaves, Wright set out to prove that the institution was unprofitable. She argued that if slaves were given an education and a goal—the promise of freedom in approximately five years—they would not only work harder but in the end the settlement would undersell its competitors. Although radical in its inception, Wright's proposal was tentatively endorsed by Thomas Jefferson, who thought her plan had "its aspects of promise," and hesitantly supported by James Monroe.

Ultimately, Wright's experiment was destroyed by alleged improprieties. In addition to lean harvests and overwhelming debt, her health failed, and during her brief return to Europe the *Genius of Universal Emancipation* (1827) printed excerpts from Nashoba overseer James Richardson's journal, which described the "free love" practiced at the colony. Suggestions of miscegenation angered even abolitionists, and Wright did little to refute the contents of the journal. Upon her return to the United States she printed a full account of her views in the *Memphis Advocate* and embarked on a crusade against organized religion. This final affront to morality cost the settlement its financial backing, and by 1828 all of the other free members, including Camilla, had abandoned the project. Keeping her promise to her thirty slaves, Wright nevertheless secured their freedom a year later, personally escorting them to Haiti.

First, however, Wright joined Robert Dale Owen as coeditor of the *New Harmony Gazette*, making her one of the first women to edit a widely circulated paper in the United States. Likewise, in July 1828 Wright shocked Americans by becoming one of the first women to speak publicly in front of a mixed audience. Traveling from Boston to New Orleans, Wright blasted religion, capital punishment, and the treatment of women while simultaneously promoting equality and tolerance. Despite her rhetorical brilliance, in some cases her "strengths and virtues, themselves, became primary offenses" (Kissel, p. 8), and in several cities mob violence erupted during her lectures.

Settling outside of New York City, Wright in 1829 purchased a church near the Bowery, converting it into a "Hall of Science," a building that served as a lecture hall as well as a publishing house for the *Free Enquirer* (formerly the *New Harmony Gazette*). Although a vehement supporter of women's rights (the promotion of birth control earned her the title of "The Great Red Harlot of Infidelity"), she increasingly fixed her attention on public education, calling for free state boarding schools funded by a graduated property tax. Wright's push for educational reform eventually led to her leadership of the free-thought movement in New York and her involvement in the Workingman's party, which the opposition facetiously dubbed "the Fanny Wright party."

Wright returned to Europe in 1830 with her sister. After a brief stay in Paris, Camilla died, and in 1831 Wright married William Phiquepal, a French physician with whom she had traveled to Haiti in 1829. The couple had one child, and Wright spent several years in Paris away from the limelight. Unfortunately, her efforts in America collapsed without her presence. The Hall of Science was converted into a Methodist church, public interest in education waned, and the *Free Enquirer* ceased publication in 1835. Nevertheless, when she returned to America with her husband, Wright resumed her role as lecturer, joining Democrats on the campaign trail in both 1836 and 1838. Although she valiantly argued against the Bank of the United States in 1836 and continued to support both an independent treasury and gradual emancipation, she became discouraged by the public's lack of interest in her increasingly Comtean view of social ills. She left the United States in 1839 for France and spent the next decade embroiled in financial struggles, traveling from America to Europe five times. She and her husband divorced in 1850, and Wright lost custody of her child. She died in Cincinnati.

A controversial figure, Wright dared to hold America to its promise of "liberty and justice for all." Equally hated and adored, she paved the way for later social reforms, and ultimately her life reflects the story of America's resistance to change, of "how much people love the rhetoric of equality and how little they are inclined to make equality possible" (Eckhardt, p. 4).

• Although there is no complete collection of Wright's papers, many of her letters are in the Robert Owen Papers at the University of Illinois; the library of the Working Men's Institute in New Harmony, Ind.; the Percy Bysshe Shelley Papers at Duke University; and the Lafayette papers at the University of Chicago. Rutgers University and Cornell University also house files of the *Free Enquirer*. Additional information on Wright is in the Theresa Wolfson Papers at Cornell's Martin P. Catherwood Library and in the Garnett letters at Harvard University's Houghton Library. For a sample of one of Wright's public lectures see *Address on the State of the Public Mind* (1829). A useful biography is Celia Morris Eckhardt, *Fanny Wright: Rebel in America* (1984). Older, but also useful, is A. J. G. Perkins and Theresa Wolfson, *Frances Wright: Free Enquirer* (1939). For a comparison of Wright with her contemporary Frances Trollope see Susan S. Kissel, *In Common Cause: The "Conservative" Frances Trollope and the "Radical" Frances Wright* (1993). For a feminist perspective of Wright, as well as other early female reformers, see Elizabeth Ann Bartlett, *Liberty, Equality, Sorority* (1994). An obituary is in the *Cincinnati Daily Gazette*, 15 Dec. 1852.

DONNA GREAR PARKER

WRIGHT, Frank Lloyd (8 June 1867–9 Apr. 1959), architect, was born in Richland Center, Wisconsin, the son of William Cary Wright and Anna Lloyd Jones. The middle name given to him at birth was Lincoln, but he adopted the name Lloyd in 1886, an indication of his strong identification with the Lloyd Joneses, the Welsh family of his mother. She had been a schoolteacher; his father worked at various times as a lawyer, preacher, school superintendent, and music teacher and was known as a distinguished orator. After ten years of peripatetic life, the family returned to Wisconsin in 1877 to live in Madison near relatives of Anna Wright who were farmers outside Spring Green. Sent to his relatives' farms to labor during the summers, Wright acquired a lifelong appreciation of nature. From his father he learned piano and musical structure; from his mother, the lessons of the Froebel kindergarten system, which involved the manual handling of simple geometric shapes, and thus developed a perception of geometric forms. His father left his mother in 1885 and filed for divorce.

Though Wright did not finish high school and his college education was a brief stint in 1885 at the University of Wisconsin, he was well read, absorbing in particular the ideas of Emerson, in whose writings Wright saw the unity of beauty and use as well as the primacy of the individual. Like that of many of his contemporaries, Wright's architectural training occurred through apprenticeship, beginning in 1885 in Wisconsin with Allen Conover, a professor of engineering.

After moving from Madison to Chicago in 1887, Wright worked for Joseph Lyman Silsbee, who introduced many East Coast architectural styles to Chicago, and for Beers, Clay and Dutton. In 1888 Wright entered the firm of Dankmar Adler and Louis Sullivan, where he worked for five years and eventually became chief draftsman for the entire office and the principal designer of residences. Sullivan was instrumental in shaping Wright's aesthetics, methods of design, and social vision of architecture. Along with their immediate circle, Sullivan and Wright championed a fresh architecture meant to represent the young democracy of America while breaking with European architectural traditions. Secure in his employment, Wright married Catherine Lee Tobin in 1889, and they acquired a home in the Chicago suburb of Oak Park. Having six children required Wright to launch a series of architectural enlargements and experiments on their home.

Wright's moonlighting on residential projects outside the firm of Adler & Sullivan created a rift with his mentor that resulted in Wright's departure and the opening of his own practice in 1893. For three years he shared an office with Cecil Corwin, a colleague from the Silsbee firm. In 1894 Wright lectured on the relationship of architecture to technology and had the first exhibition of his recent work at the Art Institute of Chicago.

Wright's first major commission after leaving Sullivan's office was for William H. Winslow, a successful supplier of ornamental ironwork. Built in 1894 in River Forest, Illinois, the Winslow house showed the influence of Sullivan's ornament in the use of abstracted vegetal forms to cover building surfaces and details. But the house also exhibited the cool geometry and clear functional division of interiors that would characterize Wright's own approach to design and announce the beginnings of his principles of "organic" architecture, eventually published under the title "In the Cause of Architecture" (*Architectural Record* 23 [Mar. 1908]: 155–221). Synthesized by 1901, those principles were implemented in the Ward Willits House (Highland Park, Ill.), which expressed an architectural vocabulary aimed at unifying interior and exterior with a building's site and its occupants' lifestyle. His subsequent early commissions encompassed a broad range of residential designs for both people of modest income and the well-to-do, including the expansive Susan Lawrence Dana House (Springfield, Ill.; 1902–1904).

Wright's design method used a unit system to generate grids and a governing module that was combined with overhanging cantilevers to provide shelter. He associated the resulting long, low-pitched roofs and horizontality of his buildings with the prairies of the Midwest, and these designs became characteristic of his so-called Prairie period. The interiors and exteriors were increasingly integrated through the use of terraces and walls used as glazed screens. Moldings emphasized visual continuities and produced an unprecedented spatial openness. No mere formal gesture, such spatial openness had in Wright's view a metaphysical and psychological impact on people, which would help liberate them from oppressive conformity to past norms.

Wright also designed two monumental buildings, Unity Temple (Oak Park, Ill.; 1904) and the Larkin Company Administration Building (Buffalo, N.Y.; 1903–1906, demolished 1950), which demonstrated his techniques of formal integration and spatial flow. At Unity Temple, Wright celebrated the use of concrete—chosen for its economy as a building material—by emphasizing the mass of its wall and surface finishes. While the thick walls sheltered the congregation from the noise of the street, the glazed coffers of the ceiling flooded the worship space with light. Concrete, the use of the structural cantilever, and the intrinsic expression of building materials such as glass, steel, and wood provided Wright with the essential signs of his modern vocabulary. Those elements defined the spatial complexities that he, beyond all other contemporaries, explored. He later stated that Unity Temple showed that the reality of architecture was the space within.

Wright's building for the Larkin Company, a mail-order business selling soap and related products, consisted of a main ground-floor workroom in a floor-to-ceiling skylit atrium, an annex with auxiliary facilities, and numerous technical innovations, including large plate glass, metal furniture, and an early version of air-conditioning. This example of form fitting function included sculpture and carved sayings that reflected the owner's intentions of ennobling the value of work and the goodness of commerce.

In the midst of this productive period, Wright traveled in 1905 to Japan, where he began to collect Japanese wood block prints, an art form previously of interest to him. The trip marked his beginnings as a serious connoisseur and eventually a dealer of Japanese prints. Unlike his contemporaries in the United States who saw European architecture as their legacy and a European Grand Tour as their goal, Wright viewed Japan and Japanese culture as the model for his aesthetics. He mounted his first exhibition of Japanese prints, works by Hiroshige, at the Art Institute of Chicago in 1906.

On his return from Japan, Wright designed an estate for Avery and Queenie Fairy Coonley in Riverside, Illinois (1907). His design of the Robie House (Chicago; 1906–1910) ultimately drew the attention of European modernists because of its shifting planes and abstract masses. They saw it as presaging the modern movement in architecture; Wright himself viewed it as extending his explorations of the abstraction of natural form into pure geometry. To many, the Robie House was the culmination of what the architectural scholar Grant Manson has labeled Wright's First Golden Age.

Despite his success as a regional architect poised for increasing recognition, Wright experienced around 1908 a midlife crisis. He not only felt creatively exhausted from an intensive decade of work; he was emotionally drained, having fallen in love with Mamah Borthwick Cheney, who, with her husband, had been Wright's client in Oak Park. Wright's temporary solution to his dilemma was to take the opportunity to publish his work in Germany, departing in 1909 with Mrs. Cheney as his companion. The Wasmuth Verlag of Berlin produced for him *Ausgeführte Bauten und Entwürfe von Frank Lloyd Wright*, a two-folio monograph summarizing his buildings and designs, and *Frank Lloyd Wright: Ausgeführte Bauten*, a small picture book showing executed work. The two publications are said in every standard architectural history to have had an immediate influence on the exponents of modernism in Europe, in particular Walter Gropius and Ludwig Mies Van Der Rohe; but whatever success they had in Europe was incidental to his purposes. Not only did Wright pay to have them published; he intended to sell them via direct mail as primers for a new democratic American architecture.

Ironically, Wright's exposure to Europe at this time had more of an impact on him than he had on European modernism. While he was able to reconcile himself to Western traditions of art and architecture that originated in the Renaissance, he perceived in the work of some European contemporaries an effort to find a modern language in pure archaic and non-Western sources of art and architecture. He felt a particular affinity, in this regard, to artists and architects of the Secession movements, who had renounced the stale precepts of academic teaching and theory. Wright's turn to sophisticated primitivistic sources in Asian, Amerindian, and Mesoamerican art and architecture "confirmed," as he described it, his long-standing interest in archetypal forms and marked the beginnings of an experimental primitivist period in his work.

When Wright returned to the United States in 1910, he told his wife Catherine that their separation was permanent and reiterated his desire for a divorce; she refused to accommodate him. Wright immediately began designing for himself Taliesin, a country house outside Spring Green. In 1911 he moved there with Mamah Borthwick, who had resumed using her maiden name upon divorcing her husband that same year. Over the next three years Borthwick and Wright published a series of translations of the Swedish feminist Ellen Key, who argued that love alone sanctioned intimate relationships and that the liberation of children—freedom to be themselves and discover their own identities—was the hope of the future. Wright's defense of love outside the bounds of accepted social mores brought down on him intense public and private criticism.

Wright resumed his practice in his studio at Taliesin, while keeping an office in Chicago. Although he continued to use the rectilinear aesthetics of his Prairie period, his new experimental designs explored surface patterns, figural sculpture, and universal iconography. Over the next decade he undertook a major evolution in the language of his ornament, which would influence the rest of his career. Moving from the limits of rectilinear geometry, he started to emphasize diagonal visual forces and use the primary forms of circles, squares, and triangles in unique combinations. The Midway Gardens (1913–1914), an entertainment complex in Chicago, was the first major achievement of his primitivist phase. At the same time, he began work on the Imperial Hotel in Tokyo, the largest and most complex commission of his career. Wright's designs for the A. D. German Warehouse (Richland Center, Wis.; 1915) appeared on the surface to resemble Maya motifs, but they represented for him a universal iconography of abstract form. He applied the same complexity of meaning to the Hollyhock House (1917–1929), a courtyard residence for Aline Barnsdall in Los Angeles, California; although it too superficially recalls Maya motifs, its mass consists of archetypal forms found in many primitivist cultures, and its canted walls were intended to be constructed of poured concrete (but were built with conventional wood framing).

Wright was engaged in his primitivist experiments both before and after the tragic events of August 1914, when a deranged servant set Taliesin on fire and murdered Mamah Borthwick, her two children, and four others. While he was still in mourning, Wright was contacted by Miriam Noel, a self-described artist, who became his companion. She accompanied him on his prolonged stays in Japan over the next seven years while he designed the Imperial Hotel.

Following his return from his final trip to Japan on 1 August 1922, Wright confronted the prospect of reestablishing his career in his own country. Even though his work had begun to assume importance in European debates about the future of modern architecture, most of his designs remained unbuilt in the United States. At the same time, his life continued to be in turmoil. In November 1922 Wright and his wife Catherine were finally divorced after a twelve-year separation. Despite the foundering of his relationship with Miriam Noel, he married her in 1923; but a year later she left him. In 1924 Wright met Olgivanna Lazovich Hinzenberg, a married 26-year-old woman of Montenegran origin. She divorced her husband in 1925 and moved into Taliesin with her daughter, Svetlana. Their domestic life was disrupted by a second fire at Taliesin in April 1925, which destroyed their living quarters but spared Wright's studio and drawings. Wright and Olgivanna had a daughter, Iovanna, in December 1925. Threats of financial foreclosure on Taliesin and harassment by Miriam Noel sent Wright and his new family into hiding until his arrest for alleged violation of the Mann Act; the charges were later dropped. A year after Wright and Noel were divorced in August 1927, he married Hinzenberg and then adopted Svetlana.

During this period of domestic chaos, Wright had restarted his practice in 1923 by opening an office in Los Angeles, where his first commissions involved construction using concrete blocks, a continuation of his efforts to find economical means of building middle-class houses. Termed by Wright "textile blocks," the masonry units were to be cast on site, eliminating the need for professional masons and creating an aesthetic expressed by the surface patterns on the block. Others had been experimenting with modular block systems, but Wright's surface patterns were unique and sustained the experiments in diagonal geometry that he had started a decade earlier at the Midway Gardens and the Imperial Hotel. While he was able to build the Ennis, Freeman, Storrer, and Millard houses in and around Los Angeles in 1923, he also proposed his system for other residences, speculative developments, and community buildings that were not built. He might have worked in relative obscurity in the United States but for an act of nature that gave him unexpected recognition. When the great Kanto earthquake demolished much of Tokyo and Yokohama in September 1923, the Imperial Hotel survived with only minor damage, a victory over nature that was widely noticed in the press.

Wright's unbuilt projects of the period showed a uniquely individual development of building types precisely at the time the modern movement was becoming less open to innovation. Explored at first in ornament, his use of the diagonal started appearing in his floor plans during the 1920s. In the western United States, he saw the great expanses of the desert as a vast canvas on which to carry forward his experiments in diagonal planning, resulting in such projects as a desert compound and shrine for Albert M. Johnson (Grapevine Canyon, Calif.; 1924). For the same client Wright also designed the National Life Insurance Company office building (Chicago; 1924), a tall structure that used copper sheathing on its skin to deflect the sun. Wright continued to design large-scale projects of complexity, including a resort in Arizona, San Marcos-in-the-Desert for the veterinarian Dr. Alexander Chandler, and two projects for Reverend William Norman Guthrie: a 2,100-foot Steel Cathedral and St. Mark's-in-the-Bouwerie, an apartment tower intended to produce income for its New York City congregation; none of these was executed.

The lack of recognition at home contrasted sharply with the significance given to Wright's work by Europeans. The appearance of Heinrich de Fries's *Frank Lloyd Wright: Aus dem Lebenswerk eines Architekten* (1926) and a compilation of essays edited by Dutch architect H. Th.Wijdeveld, *The Life-Work of the American Architect Frank Lloyd Wright* (1925), refocused attention on Wright's earlier work and introduced some of his latest projects from the 1920s. Overall, the European reaction was mixed: some critics saw him as a decadent romantic individualist and enemy of collective action; others considered him an artist who poetically celebrated the forces of nature and the individual. While it was difficult to grasp his true innovations—few in Europe having seen his work at firsthand—it was clear that his use of ornament, central to his organic concepts, was anathema to rationalizing European modernists.

When the stock market crash of 1929 halted any possibility of constructing Wright's projects, he entered a new phase of his work through writings, lectures, and exhibitions that gave him a more public profile. His lectures at Princeton University were published in 1931, and his *Autobiography* appeared in 1932. The latter charmed many readers and inspired young people to come work with Wright. The timing was propitious: curious students could join the new communal enterprise that he and his wife launched in October 1932. The Taliesin Fellowship was a realization of his long-standing interest in the education of youth that built on the earlier apprenticeship model of his studio. At the farm complex at Taliesin, the fellows set about repairing and expanding the old Hillside Home School buildings that had formerly belonged to Wright's aunts. In a comprehensive approach to architectural education, apprenticeship in the drafting studio was combined with practical work, including gardening, repairs, construction, and cooking. The members of the fellowship not only became the educational charges of the Wrights; they also formed the office that would produce all his subsequent designs.

In 1934, with an eager workforce at hand, Wright launched his synthetic vision of America with a model: Broadacre City. Meant to be four square miles of land, Broadacre City represented both an ideological attack on the norms of urban development and a proposal for settling the American countryside, where individuals would have their own piece of land. Wright's social, economic, and technical programs, along with the model and related designs, were published in 1935 in such journals as *Architectural Record* and *American Architect*. Put on tour throughout the United States was an ensemble composed of the main model and subsidiary models of houses, buildings, and highway overpasses, as well as placards with slogans and explanations of the program of Broadacre City. For the rest of his career, Wright used Broadacre City as a repository of ideal designs; he deemed it the characteristic settlement in the decentralized America that he envisioned, "Usonia" (a name derived partly from the "United States of North America").

Wright intended to fill Usonia with new building types for an American democracy that championed individuals, connected them to nature, and provided modern comfort through economical means. His designs for Usonian houses proliferated in one of the most productive periods of his career. Using simple geometric forms of circles, squares, and polygons, he produced nearly endless variations, which ranged from the very economical to the lavish. While the Broadacre City model circulated throughout the United States, Wright had the opportunity of building four major works in 1936 that demonstrated his Usonian ideas. The house for the Herbert Jacobs family (Madison, Wis.) showed Wright's ongoing commitment to finding economical solutions to housing the middle class. Using a modular grid and L-shaped floor plan,

Wright designed the brick, wood, and glass house to embrace a vegetable garden. A masterpiece of simplicity, the house originally cost $5,500. Wright's design of Fallingwater, a weekend house at Mill Run, Pennsylvania, for the Edgar Kaufmann family, became internationally celebrated as a monument of modern architecture, a structure notably warmer and richer than contemporary examples of European modernism. With its dramatic cantilevers over a stream, it balanced the benefits of technology with an embrace of nature mirrored in the layering of facade stones, which recalled ledges of rocks nearby. Wright's design of the S. C. Johnson & Company Administration Building (Racine, Wis.) illustrated his own interpretation of streamlined design in a continuation of his explorations of a suitable environment for the workforce of corporate America. Honeycomb House, the residence designed for Jean and Paul Hanna on the edge of the Stanford University campus, showed how Wright's system of polygonal modules could provide the openness that he associated with freedom of movement while gracefully integrating the house with its sloping topography. The hexagonal modules of the floor plan gave the appearance of a honeycomb; hence the name of the house.

In 1936 the seventy-year-old Wright had emerged on the national scene not only as an architect but also as a cultural personality. In this year of great success, however, Wright contracted pneumonia at Taliesin; he therefore traveled to Phoenix in 1937 to recuperate. Familiar with the desert landscape and appreciating the warm climate, Wright purchased land in 1938 on Maricopa Mesa, east of Phoenix, and started construction of a winter headquarters in the desert. From this point on, Wright and the Taliesin Fellowship would make an annual journey from Taliesin in Wisconsin to Taliesin West in Arizona for the winter.

The solidification of his practice was reinforced by the establishment in 1940 of the Frank Lloyd Wright Foundation. Intended as a tax-exempt organization, it was created by a group of friends and supporters who wanted to stabilize Wright's financial situation, which he had never managed well. The foundation became the owner of Wright's work and intellectual property, thus freeing him of personal financial liabilities.

In addition to his gain in national prominence, underscored by an exhibition of designs at the Museum of Modern Art in 1940, Wright received increasing international recognition. As American involvement in World War II approached, Wright was a vocal pacifist, and during the years 1941–1945 his designs were again more anticipated than realized. In the immediate postwar years he was primarily concerned with the elaboration of his designs ideas rather than with innovation. His use of the circle was particularly prolific. At the residential scale, Wright continued to develop the various types of the Usonian home, culminating with a do-it-yourself version called the Usonian Automatic. He was also involved in several large-scale projects, including ones in Pittsburgh, Washington, D.C., and Madison, Wisconsin, the last a civic center rede-signed over several decades and built in an altered version in 1977. Like Broadacre City, those projects hovered between realistic proposals and polemical critique.

The best realization of Wright's artistic achievements and urban critique is the Guggenheim Museum (1943–1959). Solomon R. Guggenheim, relying on the artistic guidance of Baroness Rebay, commissioned Wright to design a museum in New York City for his collection of "non-objective art." Wright's original design of 1943 showed a ziggurat that would house a Museum of Non-Objective Painting. The central design concept was a spiral ramp, Wright's symbol of organic process; later the spiral would be inverted and capped with a shallow glazed dome. It took years to satisfy the New York City building code requirements. In 1952 the museum trustees changed the name of the building to the Solomon R. Guggenheim Museum, and sculpture was added; but Wright's concept for a fixed collection remained unaltered. The building opened shortly after Wright's death, and—despite curators' complaints that the curving space was not well suited for exhibiting art—the Guggenheim became internationally recognized as a major icon of modern architecture. The design indissolubly united spatial drama and the fabric of its construction into a poetic metaphor for experiencing both architecture and art.

During the 1950s Wright's stature continued to increase throughout the world. In 1951 the major retrospective of his work, Sixty Years of Living Architecture, opened in Philadelphia and went on tour for three years in Europe, elsewhere in the United States, and in Mexico City. His designs were featured in numerous magazines—including *Life*, *Look*, *House Beautiful*, *Newsweek*, and *Time*—which introduced his ideas to the upwardly mobile American middle class, while his architectural idiom trickled down into the stock of split-level and "ranch-style" houses that began to define many American suburbs. Wright recycled numerous design ideas, and several of his publications incorporated previously published material, creating some confusion for his readers. When the H. C. Price Company office tower and apartments were erected in Bartlesville, Oklahoma, in 1952, he achieved the long-held desire of seeing one of his skyscrapers built. In light of his distaste for urban settings, he produced a remarkably sensitive design (not executed) for the Masieri Memorial, a student library and dwelling intended for a site on the Grand Canal in Venice. Large-scale civic projects continued to preoccupy Wright, as seen in the elaborate designs he proposed for a new Arizona State Capitol in Phoenix. His drawings were filled with adults and children, as well as plants and aquaria, showing that his goal for envisioning a vital American life through architecture had not diminished. His designs for an opera and cultural center in Baghdad, Iraq, exemplified the full scale of his cultural and social programs. Having solidified his early career with the major design of a religious structure, the Unity Temple, Wright arrived at a suitably symbolic terminus to his work with designs for the

Beth Sholom Synagogue (Elkins Park, Pa.; 1954), one of his most successful collaborations with a client, and the Annunciation Greek Orthodox Church (Wauwatosa, Wis.; 1956). They reaffirmed the outlook of an architect who saw spiritual issues not so much as elements of formal religion but rather as emanations from the human heart.

Wright died in Phoenix. His wife Olgivanna directed the Taliesin Fellowship until her death in 1985, and the fellowship continued an architectural practice dedicated to organic architecture. Of the thousand structures Wright designed, more than four hundred were built.

As an architect, author, and social critic, Wright combined the reformist ideals of nineteenth-century America with a prescient sense of the possibilities of modernism. His artistic genius showed an extraordinary capacity to synthesize precedents in new solutions, creating architectural space and an architectural vocabulary that drew inspiration from nature, technology, and the inherent qualities of building materials and structural systems. Never a formalist, he wedded his architectural language to a social vision for an ideal democratic American life. He championed an organic architecture that in principle needed no architect to express the innate qualities of nature and humanity. Never a populist, he paradoxically searched for the true collective expression of American democracy and yet always saw the architect, rather than everyman, as the central figure in American culture. Creating buildings of spatial drama, he became the best-known architect of the United States and one of the most important architects in the world. A figure almost larger than life, Wright had an impact on American culture and global architecture of a magnitude that posterity has only begun to grasp.

• Wright's drawings and papers (including much of his art collection) are the Frank Wright Archives, Taliesin West, Scottsdale, Ariz. *An Autobiography* (1932), which deals more with his upbringing and social views than his architecture, was enlarged in a second edition (1943); the third edition was published posthumously (1977). The original editions of his many publications often show Wright's own layouts and attention to graphics, which were not preserved in the otherwise convenient compendium of his own publications, *Frank Lloyd Wright: Collected Writings*, ed. Bruce Brooks Pfeiffer (5 vols., 1992–1995). An excellent visual survey of Wright's built and unbuilt work can be found in *Frank Lloyd Wright*, ed. B. B. Pfeiffer and Yukio Futagawa (12 vols., 1984–1988). The definitive guide to his built structures is William Allin Storrer, *The Frank Lloyd Wright Companion* (1993). For a pioneering critical biography, see Robert Twombly, *Frank Lloyd Wright: His Life and His Architecture* (1979). Brendan Gill, *Many Masks: A Life of Lloyd Wright* (1987), provides a provisional, if sensationalist, study of the architect's life. For the history of Wright's famous Wasmuth publications, his first travels to Europe, and his primitivist phase from 1910 to the early 1920s, see Anthony Alofsin, *Frank Lloyd Wright: The Lost Years, 1910–1922* (1993). The seminal early treatments of Wright's work are Grant Manson, *Frank Lloyd Wright to 1910: The First Golden Age* (1958), and Henry-Russell Hitchcock, *In the Nature of Materials: The Buildings of Frank Lloyd Wright, 1887–1941* (1942); both are limited in their chronological coverage but still provide worthwhile insights. For an interpretation of Wright's innovative use of architectural space, see Bruno Zevi, *Frank Lloyd Wright* (1947). The insights of a former apprentice and lifelong scholar of his work can be found in Edgar Kaufmann, Jr., *9 Commentaries on Frank Lloyd Wright* (1989). Numerous monographic studies of individual buildings have enhanced our appreciation and understanding of his work, including studies of the Larkin Company Administration Building, Fallingwater, Unity Temple, the Robie House, the Johnson Wax Administration Building, the textile block houses built in California, and the Hollyhock House. Some clients wrote of their experiences with Wright, and these testaments often provide insight into the complex architect-client relationships. An accessible, well-illustrated general overview is Robert McCarter, *Frank Lloyd Wright* (1997).

ANTHONY ALOFSIN

WRIGHT, George (28 Jan. 1847–21 Aug. 1937), baseball player and sporting goods entrepreneur, was born in New York City, the son of Samuel Wright, a cricket professional, and Ann Tone. When Wright was about ten, his father moved the family across the Hudson River to Hoboken, New Jersey, where the senior Wright had been named groundskeeper, coach, and bowler for the St. George Cricket Club. Here, Wright learned to play cricket; he also learned baseball at nearby Elysian Fields. He excelled in both sports. At age fifteen he was promoted from the junior to the senior nine of the Gotham Base Ball Club of New York. About the same time he was hired as assistant cricket professional for the St. George club. In 1865 he performed professionally for the Philadelphia Cricket Club, and on Wednesdays he played baseball with the Olympics, one of Philadelphia's leading teams. That same year he played for an American all-star cricket team that defeated the Canadian team in Toronto.

Wright returned to New York and the Gothams in 1866, but he deserted the club in July for the Unions of Morrisania (now a section of the Bronx). He left that club for a season with the Nationals of Washington, D.C., but he returned to Morrisania in 1868. Playing shortstop, he earned a gold medal from the *New York Clipper* as baseball's leading batsman at his position.

In 1869, when the Cincinnati Base Ball Club (nicknamed the Red Stockings) decided to field baseball's first openly all-professional team, Wright was hired to play shortstop for $1,400, the club's top salary. There he joined his elder brother, Harry, the team's manager and pitcher. With Wright starring as the team's—and the nation's—leading hitter, the Red Stockings remained undefeated throughout 1869, inspiring the expansion of professional baseball to other clubs the next year. Cincinnati lost six games to the improved competition in 1870, however, causing a drop in attendance that persuaded the club's officers to disband its professional team after the season had ended.

In 1871 Wright was the first of several Cincinnati players hired by Boston's new professional baseball club, which was organized to compete for the championship of the National Association, baseball's first professional league. Harry Wright managed the club, which adopted Cincinnati's red stockings and team nickname. Wright starred at shortstop, but he missed much of the season with a leg injury as Boston finished second to Philadelphia's Athletics in the first pennant race. That same year Wright opened a sporting goods store in Boston; eight years later he joined Henry A. Ditson to form the sporting goods firm of Wright & Ditson. In 1872 Wright married Abby Anna Coleman of Boston; they had four children.

Wright's play helped Boston teams win four consecutive National Association championships from 1872 through 1875 and National League titles in 1877 and 1878. In 1879 he signed to manage and play shortstop for Providence. In this, his only season as a baseball manager, he led his club to the National League championship by five games over Harry Wright's Boston.

In large part because Wright deserted Boston for Providence in 1879, National League owners secretly conspired to "reserve" five players from each team, effectively preventing them from leaving one club for another. (A reserve clause was soon added to all player contracts, restricting ballplayers' freedom of movement between clubs for nearly a century, until a series of adverse court rulings led to its modification in 1976.) Providence reserved Wright and forbade his return to Boston in 1880 when he wished to be nearer his sporting goods business. Wright announced his retirement from ball playing but evaded the reserve agreement to play one game for Boston in 1880 and seven games in 1881. When Harry Wright was hired away from Boston to manage the Providence club in 1882, Wright returned to Providence, but after suffering the poorest season of his career he retired for good.

In 1884 Wright helped organize a baseball club for Boston in the Union Association, and Wright & Ditson supplied the association with scorecards and baseballs. But when the Union Association—and its Boston club—expired after a single season of play, Wright turned the attention of Wright & Ditson increasingly to other sports. Although A. G. Spalding's sporting goods company acquired Wright & Ditson in 1891, Wright's firm retained its corporate identity, and Wright remained associated with it until his death.

Playing baseball gave Wright enduring fame, and his sporting goods company brought him fortune, but his pioneering efforts at introducing and promoting golf and tennis (and, to a lesser degree, hockey) form his most lasting influence on American life.

Wright & Ditson was reportedly the first company to sell tennis equipment in the United States, and Wright delighted in telling how he brought golf to Boston in 1890 at Franklin Park. It required six years, however, for the city's parks commission to approve construction of New England's first nine-hole golf course there.

Around 1895 Wright took an American "ice polo" team to Montreal to compare the sport with Canada's ice hockey. Ice hockey was deemed the superior game, and it was promptly brought back to the United States.

In 1899 Wright shepherded a group of young eastern tennis champions (including his son Beals Wright) on a West Coast tour, where their superior play stimulated Californians' interest in the game. On this trip one eastern player, Dwight Davis, conceived the idea of holding the international tournament for the prize cup that bears his name. Wright in 1908 led another group of young tennis standouts (including son Irving Wright) to California, where they were humiliated by the now-dominant westerners. While on the West Coast, Wright persuaded the parents of young Hazel Hotchkiss to permit her to come to Philadelphia for the national grass court championships. For three straight years (1909–1911) Hotchkiss won national titles in women's singles and doubles and in mixed doubles.

Wright took part in 1907 on the commission that—despite a lack of credible evidence—declared Abner Doubleday the inventor of baseball in Cooperstown, New York; in 1935–1936 Wright served on baseball's centennial committee that helped plan Cooperstown's Baseball Hall of Fame. He died at his home in Boston.

As a baseball player, Wright participated in the first tour of the Midwest by an eastern team in 1867, the first transcontinental tour by a baseball team (Cincinnati) in 1869, and the introduction of baseball to England in 1874. In 1888–1889 he accompanied baseball's first around-the-world tour, and in 1912 he umpired a demonstration game of baseball in Oslo as a sidelight to the Olympics.

In 1937 Wright was elected to the Baseball Hall of Fame, and two years later he was inducted posthumously.

• The George Wright file at the National Baseball Library, Cooperstown, N.Y., contains newspaper articles and clippings, chiefly concerning Wright's career in baseball. Articles by William D. Perrin in the *Providence Journal* in 1928, reprinted as *Days of Greatness: Providence Baseball 1875–1885* (1984), provide detail of Wright's Providence years and the effect on Wright of the reserve agreement. Dwight Davis and Helen Hotchkiss Wightman discuss Wright's tennis tours to California in *Fifty Years of Lawn Tennis in the United States* (1931), and Pete Cava confirms Wright's trip to the 1912 Olympics in "Baseball in the Olympics," *National Pastime* 12 (1992). Informative obituaries can be found in the *Boston Post* and *Boston Herald*, and a biographical essay by W. S. Barnes, Jr., accompanies the brief obituary in the *Boston Globe*, all 22 Aug. 1937.

FREDERICK IVOR-CAMPBELL

WRIGHT, George Ernest (5 Sept. 1909–29 Aug. 1974), archaeologist and biblical theologian, was born in Zanesville, Ohio, the son of the Reverend Ernest Johnson Wright, a Presbyterian pastor, and Caroline L. Shedd. Wright and his family moved frequently during his childhood, following his father's service as pastor of numerous small-town congregations throughout Pennsylvania and Ohio. He received his B.A. from the College of Wooster (Ohio) in 1931 and his B.D. from McCormick Theological Seminary in Chicago, Illinois, in 1934, where he studied with Ovid

R. Sellars. Wright was ordained a Presbyterian minister in April 1934 and had his first archaeological field experience as a member of Kyle Memorial Expedition to Bethel, Palestine, that summer. He entered Johns Hopkins University in the fall of 1934 to study under William F. Albright. Wright also served as supply pastor of several Baltimore area churches while he completed his A.M. (1936) and Ph.D. (1937).

His dual interests in archaeology and the Bible are reflected in his early publications, which include his dissertation on the morphology of Palestinian pottery, *Pottery of Palestine from Earliest Times to the End of the Early Bronze Age* (1937), and his article, "Exegesis and Eisegesis in the Interpretation of Scripture" (*Expository Times* [May 1937]: 353–57). He spent the summer and fall of 1937 organizing reports on the Beth-Shemesh excavations in Palestine as research assistant to Professor Elihu Grant of Haverford College. He married Emily E. DeNyse in July 1937; they had four children.

In January 1938 Wright moved to New Haven, connecticut, to become the field secretary of the American Schools of Oriental Research (ASOR) under the direction of Millar Burrows. Charged with publicity and fundraising, Wright founded the *Biblical Archaeologist* as a vehicle to bring ASOR's work to the attention of a larger, nonspecialized audience. The journal's inaugural four-page issue contained the first of thirty-six articles and countless book reviews and columns that Wright would eventually contribute to the journal during his twenty-five years as its editor (1938–1959) or coeditor (1959–1963).

In 1939 Wright became instructor in Old Testament at McCormick Theological Seminary, rising to the rank of professor in Old Testament history and theology by 1945. In his efforts to integrate archaeological findings and biblical theology, he published *The Challenge of Israel's Faith* (1944), *The Westminster Historical Atlas to the Bible*, coedited with Floyd V. Filson (1945; rev. 1956), *The Old Testament against Its Environment* (1950), and *God Who Acts: Biblical Theology as Recital* (1952) and served among the founding editors of Studies in Biblical Theology (1950–1972) and The Old Testament Library (1961–1974). Wright's understanding of biblical faith and its view of history as the arena of "the redemptive handiwork of God" was a cornerstone of the biblical theology movement in America, a movement that shared significant characteristics with Karl Barth's neoorthodoxy.

Wright was active in ecumenical and denominational affairs. He was an observer at the first assembly of the World Council of Churches (WCC) in 1948 and later wrote several articles about the WCC and coauthored *The Biblical Doctrine of Man in Society* (1954) for the WCC's study department. In 1958 his denomination, the United Presbyterian Church in the U.S.A., named Wright to the committee that drafted its *Confession of 1967*. His ecumenical interests bore fruit in a 1963 colloquium at Harvard, whose proceedings were edited and published by Wright and Samuel Miller as *Ecumenical Dialogue at Harvard: The Roman Catholic-Protestant Colloquium* (1964).

Later in his career, Wright gave increasing attention to archaeology. From 1956 to 1964 he served as archaeological director for the Drew-McCormick ASOR Research Expedition to Shechem, Israel. In 1957 he published *Biblical Archaeology* (rev. 1962), which became the standard textbook in its field for more than two decades. To teach future scholars as well as to continue to train pastors, he became Parkman Professor of Divinity at Harvard Divinity School (1958–1974). He adapted features of Joseph Caldwell's interdisciplinary "New Archaeology" to biblical archaeology when he added a geologist to the Shechem dig in 1960. In 1961 he assumed additional duties at Harvard as curator of its Semitic Museum, where he gradually purchased significant acquisitions, sponsored overseas research, and reinstituted the museum's education programs for schoolchildren. In 1964 he published *Shechem: The Biography of a Biblical City* and relinquished his responsibilities for the Shechem excavation to his associates. During a 1964–1965 sabbatical year in Israel, he began excavations at Gezer and served as visiting director of the Hebrew Union College Biblical and Archaeological School. From 1966 until his death, he served as president of the American Schools of Oriental Research. After the 1967 Six-Day War severed relations between excavations in Arab and Israeli territories, Wright's diplomatic reorganization of ASOR into separately incorporated centers in Amman (the American Center of Oriental Research) and Jerusalem (the W. F. Albright Institute of Archaeological Research) allowed ASOR's work to continue uninterrupted. When Wright became director (1971–1974) of the Joint American Archaeological Expedition to Idalion, a Phoenician site in Cyprus, he was able to implement his interdisciplinary vision of archaeology by adding an agronomist, geologist, metallurgist, paleontologist, physical anthropologist, artist, and conservator to his staff.

Wright died in Jaffrey, New Hampshire. After his death, colleagues and students praised his humility, zeal, vision, versatility, and teamwork. With his death, said Wright's former student Philip King, "American biblical scholarship lost one of its most devoted and distinguished contributors."

• Wright's field notes, photographs, and ASOR records are in Harvard University's Semitic Museum. His memorial festschrift, *Magnalia Dei: The Mighty Acts of God* (1976), includes a complete bibliography of his works. Wright's relation to his mentor Albright is treated in Burke O. Long, *Planting and Reaping Albright: Politics, Ideology, and Interpreting the Bible* (1997), and his work with ASOR is covered in Philip J. King, *American Archaeology in the Mideast: A History of the American Schools of Oriental Research* (1983). An important critique of Wright's biblical theology is Langdon Gilkey, "Cosmology, Ontology, and the Travail of Biblical Language," *Journal of Religion* 41 (1961): 194–205. Later assessments of Wright's contributions to the biblical theology movement include Brevard S. Childs, *Biblical Theology in Crisis* (1970), and James Barr, "Biblical Theology," in *Inter-*

preter's Dictionary of the Bible, Supp. vol. (1982), while James D. Smart, *The Past, Present, and Future of Biblical Theology* (1979), disputes the existence of such a movement. Biblical theology and the *Confession of 1967* are discussed in Edward A. Dowey, Jr., *A Commentary on the Confession of 1967 and an Introduction to the Book of Confessions* (1968), and in the Spring 1983 issue of the *Journal of Presbyterian History*.

Other evaluations of Wright's significance include William G. Dever, "Biblical Theology and Biblical Archaeology: An Appreciation of G. Ernest Wright," *Harvard Theological Review* 73 (Jan.–Apr. 1980): 1–15; R. Lansing Hicks, "G. Ernest Wright and Old Testament Theology," *Anglican Theological Review* 58 (Apr. 1976): 158–78; and Philip J. King, "The Influence of G. Ernest Wright on the Archaeology of Palestine," in *Archaeology and Biblical Interpretation: Essays in Memory of D. Glenn Rose*, ed. Leo G. Perdue et al. (1987). The March 1987 issue of *Biblical Archaeologist* contains a fiftieth-anniversary tribute to founding editor Wright, including an interview with his widow Emily Wright. The *American Schools of Oriental Research Newsletter* (Winter 1994) printed several appreciations of Wright on the twentieth anniversary of his death. An obituary is in the *New York Times*, 31 Aug. 1974.

DAVID B. MCCARTHY

WRIGHT, George Frederick (22 Jan. 1835–20 Apr. 1921), theologian and geologist, was born in Whitehall, New York, the son of Walter Wright and Mary Peabody Colburn, farmers. He was reared in a deeply religious home in rural New York. His early education was in a country school; he later attended Castleton Academy in Vermont. His father became attracted to the thought of Charles Finney, and when Finney was named president of the new Oberlin College, Walter Wright sent five of his children, including George, to Oberlin. George Wright received his bachelor's degree from Oberlin in 1859 and his divinity degree from its Theological Seminary in 1862. Under Finney's influence Oberlin became a center for abolitionist activity, and when the Civil War broke out, Wright volunteered in a company comprised of Oberlin students. During training he contracted pneumonia, in part from exposure, and was exempted from war duty. Instead, on completion of his divinity degree he accepted a call to a small Congregational parish in Bakersfield, Vermont. In 1862 Wright married Huldah Day; they had four children, all of whom graduated from Oberlin. She died in 1899, and Wright married Florence Bedford in 1904.

Wright had little formal scientific training, since at Oberlin students studied six different sciences in a period of five semesters. During his ten years in Bakersfield he had the time and opportunity to read the current scientific literature and explore the Vermont countryside. He read Darwin's *On the Origin of Species* as well as Lyell's *The Geological Evidences on the Antiquity of Man*. These readings and the presence of extensive glacial deposits in the area led him to develop considerable interest, and eventual expertise, in glacial geology and paleoarchaeology.

In 1872 Wright accepted a call to the Free Church in Andover, Massachusetts, the home of the conservative Calvinist Andover Seminary and its journal, *Bibliotheca Sacra*. As a result of his relationship with both the school and the journal and with the Boston scientific community, Wright began to emerge as a significant scientist and theologian. He met Asa Gray, the famous botanist, a leading U.S. adherent of Darwinism, and a devout Presbyterian. Their interests meshed, and together they developed an apologetic for Darwinism, known as Christian Darwinism, which was instrumental in Darwinism's acceptance in the United States. At Wright's urging, Gray published *Darwiniana: Essays and Reviews Pertaining to Darwinism* (1876), while Wright developed a five-part series of articles, "Recent Works Bearing on the Relation of Science to Religion," which later formed the core of his book *Studies in Science and Religion* (1882).

In the Andover area Wright found more striking glacial deposits, including a series of eskers. He was among the first to provide a plausible explanation for these eskers as deposits from ice-walled channels of streams associated with receding ice sheets. This work culminated in four papers, including "Indian Ridge and Its Continuations" (*Bulletin of the Essex Institute* 7 [1875]: 165–68).

As a result of this work, Wright and a colleague were appointed in 1881 by the Second Geological Survey of Pennsylvania to trace the terminal moraine through Pennsylvania and western New York. He subsequently traced the glacial drift border through Ohio, Kentucky, Indiana, and Illinois, the last under the auspices of the U.S. Geological Survey. This work was published as USGS Bulletin 58, *The Glacial Boundary in Western Pennsylvania, Ohio, Kentucky, Indiana and Illinois* (1890).

At this time Wright also began to study and publish on human artifacts found in these glacial deposits. In 1886 he studied the Muir glacier in Alaska as well as glacial deposits in the western United States. This work culminated in a lecture series at the Lowell Institute and in his best-known book, *The Ice Age in North America and Its Bearings on the Antiquity of Man* (1889), which went through six editions. Between 1892 and 1908 Wright took four trips to study the glaciers of Europe and Asia; he visited the Greenland Icefields in 1894. These studies became the basis for two books, *Man and the Glacial Period* (1892) and, with Warren Upham, *Greenland Icefields and Life in the North Atlantic* (1896).

In 1881 Wright left the Free Church to accept the chair of New Testament language at Oberlin College, where he remained for the rest of his life. In 1892 he accepted the Professorship of Harmony of Science and Revelation, a position created for him, which he held until he was granted emeritus status in 1907. In 1883 *Bibliotheca Sacra* was transferred from Andover Seminary to Oberlin; Wright served first as its associate editor, and then as editor from 1900 until his death. He died in Oberlin.

Wright was an original fellow of the Geological Society of America; with his son, Frederick, he edited the archaeological journal *Records of the Past*; and he was president of the Ohio Archaeological and Historical

Society. In his lifetime he was a successful minister, geologist, archaeologist, teacher, editor, and musician, but above all he was a person of faith. He demonstrated great competence as a field geologist and archaeologist, able both to describe and to explain. He was, however, a cautious investigator who always sought the middle ground, especially when it came to reconciling his scientific understandings and his religious beliefs. Some of his theories—such as his insistence on a single glacial episode with only local advances and retreats, as well as his late date for the introduction of humans—show heavy influences from his faith. By the end of his career this influence became even more evident, as seen in the creed that ends his autobiography, *Story of My Life and Work* (1916), and in two articles he wrote for *The Fundamentals* (1916): "The Passing of Evolution" and "Testimony of the Monuments to the Truths of the Scriptures." Though controversial, his work by its scope and depth influenced not only his generation but later ones as well.

• Wright's collected works and many papers are in the Oberlin College Archives. In addition to his conventional scientific treatises, his sixteen books include *Origins and Antiquity of Man* (1912) and *Scientific Confirmation of Old Testament History* (1906). He edited thirty volumes of *Bibliotheca Sacra* and fourteen of *Records of the Past* (merged with *Art and Archaeology* in 1914). He also wrote many articles for popular magazines. Examples of the breadth of his nearly 600 articles are "Ground of Confidence in Inductive Reasoning," *New England* 30 (1871): 601–15; "Paleolithic Man in New Jersey," *The Independent*, Dec. 1880; "Unity of the Glacial Epoch," *American Journal of Science* 44 (1892): 351–73; and "Origin and Distribution of Loess in Northern China and Central Asia," *Bulletin of the Geological Society of America* 13 (1901): 127–38. A biographical sketch is Warren Upham, "Memorial of George Frederick Wright," *Bulletin of the Geological Society of America* 33 (1922): 14–30. On Wright and Darwinism see Michael McGiffert, "Christian Darwinism: The Partnership of Asa Gray and George Frederick Wright" (Ph.D. diss., Yale Univ., 1958); William J. Morison, "George Frederick Wright: In Defense of Darwinism and Fundamentalism" (Ph.D. diss., Vanderbilt Univ., 1971); and Ronald Numbers, "George Frederick Wright: From Christian Darwinist to Fundamentalist," *Isis* 79 (1988): 624–45, the core of a chapter in Numbers, *The Creationists* (1992). Obituaries are in the *New York Times*, 21 Apr. 1921, and the *Cleveland Plain Dealer*, 22 Apr. 1921.

WILLIAM S. FALLA

WRIGHT, Harold Bell (4 May 1872–24 May 1944), novelist, was born on a farm near Rome, New York, the son of William A. Wright and Alma T. Watson. His father, a Civil War veteran, became an alcoholic, was an itinerant carpenter, and in time settled with his impoverished family in Sennett, New York. Wright attended public school and Presbyterian Sunday school in Sennett, learned a little about art and literature from his mother, and was grief-stricken when she died of tuberculosis (1883) and the family began to disintegrate. He lived with relatives and worked for farmers in the region, moved to Ohio (c. 1887), and became a house painter. Joining the Disciples of Christ, he attended Hiram College in Hiram, Ohio (1892–1894), to prepare for the ministry, but pneumonia prevented him from continuing to work in a stone quarry for tuition money, and he began to paint landscapes for sale. Threatened by tuberculosis, he canoed 500 miles down the Mahoning and Ohio rivers to improve his health, hiked to the Ozarks near Notch, in southwestern Missouri, and joined relatives there. While doing farm work he sketched, painted, and regularly attended church. He chanced one day to substitute for a pastor in a log schoolhouse in the mountains (1897). Though untrained to do so, he proceeded to serve as a Christian church minister in Pierce City, Missouri (1897–1898), Pittsburg, Kansas (1898–1903), Kansas City (1903–1905) and Lebanon, Missouri (1905–1907), and Redlands, California (1907–1908). In 1899 Wright married Frances Elizabeth Long, whom he had met at Hiram College.

Wright's first fiction was in the form of story chapters he read to his Pittsburg congregation on successive Sundays. These chapters grew into his first novel, *That Printer of Udell's: A Story of the Middle West* (original title: *Practical Christianity*), published in 1903 by the Book Supply Company, a Chicago mail-order firm, which advertised it well and sold an astounding 450,000 copies. The hero is an ex-alcoholic hobo who finds work, practices frugality, marries a Christian woman, finds faith, and becomes a church leader and a successful politician. The twin morals? Social unconcern in churches aggravates snobbery, unemployment, alcoholism, and crime; and practical work is more important than theoretical faith. Wright was living in Lebanon when he wrote his second novel, *The Shepherd of the Hills* (1907). Its runaway sales encouraged him to devote himself to writing didactic fiction. Moving to a ranch near Holtville, in California's Imperial Valley, he produced another bestseller, *The Calling of Dan Matthews* (1909).

Enormous success followed, partly because of high-pressure promotion by the Book Supply Company but mainly because Wright wrote what mainstream America wanted: fiction criticizing urban evil, praising nature's open spaces, and flooded with sweetness and light. Not long after the publication of his next bestseller, *The Winning of Barbara Worth* (1911), a California hotel, country club, junior high school, and road were all christened "Barbara Worth." Soon after he published *The Eyes of the World* (1914), which takes citified artists and effete critics to task, he moved to a desert camp in Arizona to write *When a Man's a Man*. In 1916 he was hit and almost killed by a speeding car while he was riding one of his horses along a road. Although he had broken ribs and suffered a recurrence of tuberculosis, he completed his paean to masculinity on time, and it was published in 1916. The Book Supply Company spent $100,000 advertising it and sold 600,000 advance copies. Wright continued to publish but never again did so well. Still, total sales of his twenty-one novels exceeded ten million copies.

After World War I Wright made changes in his personal and professional life. He and his wife, with whom he had had three children, were divorced in 1920. Later that same year he married Mary Potter Duncan. The couple had no children. He also changed publishers, to D. Appleton and Company (1921–1932). With *God and the Groceryman* (1927) he sought but failed to capitalize on characters from *The Shepherd of the Hills* and *The Calling of Dan Matthews*. He then moved his business to Harpers, which published his unsuccessful *Ma Cinderella* (1932); his self-serving autobiography, *To My Sons* (1934); and his final novel, a failure with the prophetic title *The Man Who Went Away* (1942). Meanwhile, Wright had turned to Hollywood. In addition to writing fifteen original screenplays, he sold five of his novels to moviemakers (1926–1941). Particularly notable are *The Winning of Barbara Worth* (1926), starring Gary Cooper, and *The Shepherd of the Hills* (1941), starring John Wayne. Wright died in La Jolla and was buried in San Diego under a large, memorabilia-filled glass case.

The Calling of Dan Matthews is representative of Wright's successful sentimental romances. The first printing was 100,000 copies in 1909; second printing, another 100,000 in 1910. In the story, Dan is the son of "Young Matt" Matthews and "Sammy" Lane, hero and heroine of *The Shepherd of the Hills*, a healthy Adam-and-Eve couple whose love was nurtured by Daniel Howitt, the ministerial "shepherd" in Missouri's Ozarks. In his story, Dan Matthews is a pure, mountain-grown young clergyman with a church in Corinth, a town of middle-class working people. He is distressed that the railroad has just penetrated the Edenic hills nearby and is bringing changes for the worse. His congregation, becoming more interested in money than in Christianity, begins to gossip about his sincere kindness to two unfortunate women—one the good daughter (named Grace) of a bad criminal, the other a poor Irish Catholic widow with a crippled son. Dan concludes that organized churches are hypocritical, especially when Judge Strong, an elder, proves to be crooked. So Dan heads for the hills with his wife (named Hope), who was sickly Grace's nurse, to practice his true calling: he will work a mineral-rich mine that Howitt found on Dan's parents' property and use this God-given wealth properly—for the betterment of humankind.

It is easy to agree with adverse critics of Wright's works. From the start they complained that Wright created wooden characters often standing for abstract virtues and vices, used shameless sentimentality and stilted dialogue, concocted melodramatic plots and distracting subplots, and stridently criticized healthy aspects of progress—for example, electricity, railroads, automobiles, immigration, and labor unions. It is even easier, however, to understand the appeal of his novels in a period of increasing secularization and commercialism. They dramatize the dangers of corrupt city life, godless science, institutionalized churches, and alcoholism and the likely damnation of moneygrabbers. At the same time, they comfortably preach about the healing character of the great outdoors, the value of patriotism and self-reliance, the joys of decent family life and neighborliness, the virtues of following Christ's example, and the tangible—not abstract—rewards of hard work.

• The Lilly Library, Indiana University, has scrapbooks on Wright as well as an author file on him from the records of D. Appleton Century Co. Lawrence V. Tagg, *Harold Bell Wright* (1994), offers a solid general treatment, stressing Wright's West-oriented works. Frank Luther Mott, *Golden Multitudes: The Story of Best Sellers in the United States* (1947; repr. 1960), and James D. Hart, *The Popular Book: A History of America's Literary Taste* (1950; repr. 1963), survey and account for Wright's popularity. A fine comparative treatment is John P. Ferré, *A Social Gospel for Millions: The Religious Bestsellers of Charles Sheldon, Charles Gordon, and Harold Bell Wright* (1988). Scathing critiques of Wright's poor style and lack of verisimilitude are in Frederic Taber Cooper, "The Popularity of Wright," *Bookman* 40 (Jan. 1915): 498–500, and Grant C. Knight, *The Strenuous Age in American Literature* (1954). Most temperate and balanced is Edward Ifkovic, "Harold Bell Wright and the Minister of Man: The Domestic Romancer at the End of the Genteel Age," *Markham Review* 4 (Feb. 1974): 21–25. An intriguing comparison study is Dale B. J. Randall, "The 'Seer' and 'Seen' Themes in *Gatsby* and Some of Their Parallels in Eliot and Wright," *Twentieth Century Literature* 10 (July 1964): 51–63, which relates Wright's *The Eyes of the World* to F. Scott Fitzgerald's "The Jellybean" and *The Great Gatsby* and to T. S. Eliot's *The Waste Land*. A detailed obituary is in the *New York Times*, 25 May 1944.

ROBERT L. GALE

WRIGHT, Hendrick Bradley (24 Apr. 1808–2 Sept. 1881), congressman and Pennsylvania Democratic leader, was born in Plymouth, Luzerne County, Pennsylvania, the son of Joseph Wright, a schoolteacher, merchant, and farmer, and Ellen Hendrick. His father's family had migrated from England in 1681 with William Penn's first group of settlers. Wright said his mother was a forceful and determined woman who insisted on a "thorough education of her children. . . . [B]y her determined character" Hendrick and his "brothers Caleb and Harrison were all educated and prepared for the law." Wright began his education by attending the schools in the community. In 1829 he enrolled in Dickinson College in Carlisle, Pennsylvania. He left there the following year to study law in the office of John N. Conyngham and was admitted to the bar on 8 November 1831. His legal business prospered, as his younger brother Caleb observed: "It is not usual, for young lawyers to succeed as rapidly in practice as you." Wright confirmed this assessment when he asserted that he was "entirely confident with . . . his . . . lot."

Shortly after undertaking the practice of law, Wright entered the political arena, where he was to remain for most of his life. In 1835 he married Mary Anne Robinson, the granddaughter of Colonel Zebulon Butler of revolutionary war fame and a descendant of William Bradford, second governor of Plymouth. They had ten children, five of whom survived Wright.

That year he also realized one of his ambitions, when he was commissioned and elected colonel of the Wyoming Volunteer Regiment of the Second Brigade, Eighth Division, Pennsylvania Militia.

One of Wright's dominant character traits was his ambition, and he used politics throughout his life to further this end. After a brief fling with the Anti-Masonic movement, he switched to the Democratic party, where he remained until his death. He was not an orthodox Democrat. Like most Democrats he believed in states' rights, was sympathetic toward the South, and detested abolitionism, but he differed from the consensus view by favoring, like other Pennsylvanians, protective tariffs, internal improvements, and certain reform movements. Soon he became the leader of the conservative Democrats in his district, who favored a tariff for Pennsylvania staples, coal and iron. In 1833 he was appointed Luzerne County district attorney. He began his elective political career in the general assembly in 1841, serving three terms, the last as Speaker. In the legislature he labored tirelessly to complete the North Branch span of the Pennsylvania Canal system, led his party in debate against the Whigs, and worked successfully for the repeal of imprisonment for debt. He tried unsuccessfully to abolish the company store system, which had been recently introduced into the anthracite region, his own bailiwick, and he tried to eliminate capital punishment. He achieved the passage of a stay law, which prevented the collection of collateral for debt nonpayment.

In 1844 Wright achieved national prominence when his party picked him as chairman of the Democratic National Convention for that year. At the meeting held in Baltimore, he sided with other opponents of Martin Van Buren and helped pass the two-thirds rule for a nomination, thereby eliminating the former president as the party's standard-bearer for a third time and paving the way for the first dark horse, James K. Polk.

In 1848, 1850, and 1854 Wright was unsuccessful in his attempts to gain a seat in Congress because of Democratic factionalism, but in 1852 he succeeded when the party unified. In Congress he was a staunch administration man who had little trouble choosing between loyalty amd political ideology. Warned early that "any Northern man who supports the Kansas-Nebraska Bill is dead and buried as a politician," Wright plunged ahead. He boldly endorsed the measure, declaring that he cared little whether or not he was returned to the House, since it was "a matter of no earthly importance" to him. His district agreed. Voters rejected him decisively in his bid for reelection.

During the tumultuous years of the 1850s, Wright's leadership position in the state councils of the Democracy became recognized. Thrice during that decade he chaired the state conventions. After 1844 he attended every convention of the national party, always serving in a major capacity. At the 1856 gathering he helped hold the New York and Pennsylvania delegations faithful to James Buchanan, thereby enabling Buchanan to win the nomination.

When the Civil War erupted, Wright received the joint nomination to Congress of both major parties. As a Union man, he served with distinction, achieving national recognition and commendation for his unswerving loyalty to the North and for his opposition to the peace faction within the Democracy. While in Congress he focused his concerns again on the Homestead Act, a measure he had backed and fought for in his previous congressional term. He referred to it as "a people's measure."

During the 1863 session Wright made a speech, much quoted and widely printed in the North, in reply to resolutions advocating peace offered by the Peace Democrat Clement L. Vallandigham. Wright opposed any peace that would destroy the integrity of the Union, and in the conclusion he referred to his son, Captain Joseph Wright, who died in defense of the Union, saying, "I can truly close my remarks with a quotation from an ancient philosopher, uttered over the dead body of his son, slain in battle: 'I should have blushed if Cato's house had stood secure and flourished in a Civil War.'"

With the expiration of his term in 1863, Wright declined to run again, preferring to retire from public life for personal and financial reasons. His retirement lasted six years. By careful speculation and prudent investment in coal lands, he became a wealthy man, and in 1869 he resumed his political career as the chief spokesman for a large labor constituency in Luzerne and other counties in Pennsylvania. It was not long before he again became a state leader within the ranks of not only the Democratic party but also the newly established Greenback Labor party. During the decade of the 1870s he presided over the state conventions of the Democracy. He became campaign manager for the state Democratic party in 1875, he headed the Horace Greeley campaign for the presidency in Pennsylvania in 1872, and he was one of the Pennsylvania leaders backing Samuel Tilden in the 1876 election. In 1876 he returned to Congress, this time as a Democrat-Greenback-Labor man, remaining until his retirement in 1881. During this four-year span he was under active consideration as a vice presidential candidate for the Democrats and as a presidential prospect for the Greenback Labor ticket.

In Congress during these last four years of his life he labored long and unsuccessfully for a proposal to correct a defect in the Homestead Act of 1862 that barred the destitute from participation. He proposed that the federal government finance the settlers with a $500 loan to be used for transportation, occupation, and development of the free land, most of which lay in the region west of the Mississippi River. Public reaction was overwhelmingly condemnatory, and the *New York Times* denounced him as a demagogue for holding out to the destitute "the unattainable." One of the news media referred to him as "the old-man-not-afraid-to-be-called-a-demagogue," to which the aged legislator responded proudly that he was "just that man. I am not afraid to be called a demagogue when the employment of men at fair wages" is the issue.

Wright championed other measures in Congress. He wanted the income from the sale of public land to be disbursed to the states for educational purposes, he pleaded for a gigantic government-sponsored public works program to help the unemployed, he supported a graduated income tax, and he embraced the eight-hour day. Debilitated by advancing years and declining health, branded, as he said in a letter of 20 November 1880 to Terence Powderly, "a fool, a demagogue, and a lunatic in the chamber of the House of [Representatives]," Wright lost heart and abandoned politics, passing on the burden of reform to his younger contemporaries. Broken in spirit and exhausted by his active labors, he died in Wilkes-Barre, Pennsylvania, shortly after retiring from Congress.

Wright was the author of two books, *A Practical Treatise on Labor* (1871) and *Historical Sketches of Plymouth, Luzerne County, Pennsylvania* (1873). He was a Quaker, a spokesman for ethical progress, a reformer in a time of reaction, and a humanitarian in an era of squalid laissez-faire dehumanism. He was a voice of prophecy and of hope, a political leader fighting for the defenseless and exploited, and a man with a vision beyond his generation. Above all, he was a conservative leader who passionately believed in an American democratic system that could resolve societal problems through the electoral process.

• For further information on Wright see Daniel J. Curran, "Hendrick B. Wright: A Study in Leadership" (Ph.D. diss., Fordham Univ., 1962); and George B. Kulp, *Families of the Wyoming Valley*, vol. 1 (3 vols., 1885–1889). Obituaries are in the *Wilkes-Barre Daily Union-Leader*, 2 Sept. 1881, the *Wilkes-Barre Daily Record*, 3 Sept. 1881, and the *Philadelphia Press*, 3 Sept. 1881.

DANIEL J. CURRAN

WRIGHT, Henry (2 July 1878–9 July 1936), architect and town planner, was born in Lawrence, Kansas, the son of Francis Alfred Wright, an English-born certified public accountant, and Mary Hulda Chace. Shortly after the family moved to Kansas City, Missouri, Wright was sent to the Friends' School in Westtown, Pennsylvania, outside of Philadelphia. He returned to Kansas City for his high school education, graduating with honors in 1896. He had already developed a strong interest in architecture and worked as a draftsman in the Kansas City office of the architectural firm of Root and Siemens. In 1899 he began a special two-year course in architecture at the University of Pennsylvania, graduating in 1901. When Wright returned to Kansas City his firm was involved in work on the Louisiana Purchase Exposition to be held in St. Louis in 1904. After the fair Wright began to work for landscape architect George E. Kessler, designing parks in Kansas City, Denver, Cincinnati, and other cities. Kessler, a former student of Frederick Law Olmsted, passed on to his new colleague many of the ideas of late nineteenth-century urban planning, eventually enabling Wright to open his own office in 1909. His early work involved planning three subdivisions in St. Lou-

is (Brentmoor, West Brentmoor, and Forest Ridge), reflecting Olmsted's influence and illustrating Wright's own concern for comprehensive community planning that integrated domestic, recreational, and civic needs in the areas of both design and function. In 1903 Wright married Eleanor Niccolls, and the couple had four children.

During World War I Wright worked as a planner and landscape architect for the U.S. Shipping Board and then the Emergency Fleet Corporation, under the direction of Robert Kohn, both of which were responsible for constructing workers' residences near East Coast shipyards. From 1920 to 1923 Wright served as an architectural adviser to the St. Louis City Planning Commission. Wright's wartime work led, in 1923, to his move to New York City, where he began an association with Clarence S. Stein. Under the auspices of the City Housing Corporation, a limited dividend company headed by real estate mogul Alexander M. Bing, the two architect-planners developed a pair of housing projects. The first, a 77-acre site in Sunnyside, Queens (1924–1928), provided living space for 1,200 families as well as numerous parks and playgrounds and parking areas on the perimeter of the community. Because they had to conform to a preexisting grid street pattern, Wright and Stein arranged the row houses to face either the streets or inner green spaces. Elliot Willensky and Norval White in the *AIA Guide to New York City* (3d ed. [1988]) observe, "Walk under umbrellas of London plane trees along the paths that penetrate each block, an urban delight, where the architecture is unimportant—even insipid—but the urban arrangements a source of great community delight" (p. 743).

In suburban Fair Lawn, New Jersey, about twenty miles from midtown Manhattan, Wright and Stein created an even more innovative planned community called Radburn (1928–1929), promoted as a "Town for the Motor Age." With both houses and apartments for moderate-income families, plus recreational areas, schools, and shopping precincts, the designers made sure that pedestrians did not have to cross busy streets. Each dwelling was reached by car from a dead-end road off of the main traffic artery or by foot along an interconnected network of pleasant sidewalks. The residential units were thus secluded from the noise of traffic and other public activities. All elements underscored the designers' concern for the safety and health of the residents. The depression of the 1930s prevented Wright and Stein from carrying out their plans in full; nevertheless, Radburn influenced scores of integrated communities in the United States and around the world.

In 1931 Wright began work by himself on a section of Chatham Village about two miles from the business center of Pittsburgh, Pennsylvania. Only a third of Wright's site was devoted to housing, arranged in rows with two to eight dwellings in each unit, separated by terraces. Here Wright avoided even the stereotyped look of a planned community, striving to give aesthetic integrity to a multiuse environment that was economically feasible for families with limited financial resources. Architectural critics generally concur that Wright's work in Chatham Village represents the finest expression of his pragmatic but humanistic vision.

Wright also left his mark as a thinker, writer, and teacher. The 1926 final report of the New York State Housing and Regional Planning Commission, titled *A Plan for the State of New York*, reflects many of Wright's attitudes. He was a frequent contributor to architectural journals. In 1931 Wright established a summer school near his Mount Olive, New Jersey, home to teach the principles of community planning. Two years later, with Alfred Mayer, he organized the Housing Study Guild to instruct young planners and builders in the new concerns of community housing. He was also a consultant to the federal Public Works Administration (1933–1934) and a visiting lecturer at a number of colleges and universities. In 1935 his book *Re-Housing Urban America* was published. The following year he accepted a special professorship at Columbia University's School of Architecture a few months before his sudden death in Newton, New Jersey, from arteriosclerosis. Lewis Mumford summed up Wright's achievement when he wrote: "He recognized the necessity of both lowering the cost of housing and doing a better job of it; and his analysis led him to emphasize the way in which control over the over-all pattern could contribute to both ends" (introduction to Stein, *Toward New Towns*).

• In addition to those mentioned above, Wright's publications include "Cottage and Tenement in the U.S.A.," in *Papers of the International Housing and Town Planning Congress* (1926); "The Modern Apartment House," *Architectural Record* 65 (Mar. 1929); "The Autobiography of Another Idea," *Western Architect* 39 (Sept. 1930); and "Housing Conditions in Relation to Scientific Machine Production," *Journal of the Franklin Institute* (Oct. 1934). Clarence S. Stein, *Toward New Towns for America* (1951; rev. ed., 1957), is invaluable in understanding his collaboration with Wright. Also of note are Roy Lubove, *Community Planning in the Nineteen-Twenties* (1964), and Daniel Schaffer, *Garden Cities for America: The Radburn Experience* (1982). Obituaries are by Lewis Mumford, *New Republic*, 29 July 1936, and Stein, *American Architect and Architecture* 149 (Aug. 1936).

ANDREW RUBENFELD

WRIGHT, Henry Clarke (29 Aug. 1797–16 Aug. 1870), reformer and abolitionist, was born in Sharon, Connecticut, the son of Seth Wright, a farmer and house-joiner, and Miriam Wright, who had the same surname as her husband but was unrelated to him before marriage. The family moved to Hartwick in the "western country" of New York when Wright was four. In his autobiography, *Human Life* (1849), Wright described his father as stern and powerful, a revolutionary veteran, militia leader, and Federalist. His mother, who died when he was six, was skilled in spinning, weaving, knitting, and sewing.

In 1814 Wright was apprenticed to a hatmaker in Norwich, New York. His endeavors in that trade were wrecked, however, by the influx of British goods after the War of 1812. In Norwich he experienced an emotional religious conversion during a revival and went on to study for the ministry, first with a local minister in Hartwick, and then at Andover Seminary (1819–1821, 1822–1823). At Andover he felt his rural religious faith undermined by the scholarly approach to theology and biblical study, but he moved on to a clergyman's life and served first as a supply minister in West Newbury, Massachusetts, then had temporary pastorates in New Hampshire. In 1826 he was settled as Congregationalist pastor in West Newbury.

In 1823 Wright married a wealthy widow, Elizabeth LeBreton Stickney; she was forty-three years old and the mother of four children, while he was twenty-six. Elizabeth Wright's interest in reform movements preceded his own. She encouraged his decisions to turn away from the parish ministry and enter the field of missionary work and reform in the 1830s. In the long term, however, his wife and stepchildren came to resent his absences and his handling of the family's financial affairs. He later reflected bitterly on a loveless marriage with no children of his own.

Wright moved from the ministry to reform through a series of brief assignments: he was a fundraiser for evangelical Amherst College in 1832, an agent of the American Home Missionary Society and the American Sunday School Union in 1833, and from 1834 to 1836 an employee of Boston's Presbyterian and Congregational churches, with responsibilities to set up Sunday schools, preach to children, and give guidance to mothers. In the meantime he adopted radical positions on two reform issues that were breaking up evangelical consensus. In the peace movement, he sided with radical pacifists who denied the legitimacy of national defense and promoted an ethic of nonviolence in all forms of conflict. In 1836 he was appointed an agent of the American Peace Society, but the moderate officers reprimanded him for his radical views, and he immediately resigned. In the antislavery cause, after much soul searching, he offended evangelical colleagues by siding with William Lloyd Garrison and other champions of immediate abolitionism.

When his peace assignment fell through, Wright found employment with the American Anti-Slavery Society, assigned first to Maine, next to New York City (where his special responsibility was to form children's antislavery societies), and then to Essex County, Massachusetts. His Newburyport home served as headquarters in summer 1837 for Angelina and Sarah Grimké, daughters of a South Carolina slaveholding family, when they began to create controversy as women speaking in public on behalf of the slaves. Not only was Wright accused of encouraging the Grimkés to take too bold a stand on woman's public role, but by publishing two accounts of conversations with them he showed that he was extending his radical pacifist views to question all forms of domination in the family. At times he challenged whether coercive civil government was consistent with Christian faith. Some critics used Wright as an example of the anarchy let loose by immoderate abolitionist attacks on traditional institutions. In August 1837 the board of managers of the antislavery society reassigned him to Philadelphia. In September they fired him as too great a liability to the cause.

Disagreements over the links between abolitionism and other radical reforms led to a schism in the American Anti-Slavery Society in 1840. Wright, who was now a hero to radical reformers, was employed as traveling representative, unsalaried and unmuzzled, of a new organization—the New England Non-Resistance Society. The group was anchored in the New Testament injunction not to return evil for evil. Wright and other nonresistants were often called "no-governmentists." They were also strongly anticlerical, insisting that ministers adulterated the true nonviolence of Jesus. During this period Wright wrote *A Kiss for a Blow* (1842), a collection of stories about what happened when people, especially boys, treated each other either violently or lovingly, which the abolitionist Wendell Phillips called "the best book for children ever written."

In 1842 the Non-Resistance Society sent Wright on a mission to Great Britain and Ireland. While overseas he lectured widely and wrote a major antiwar book, *Defensive War Proved to Be a Denial of Christianity and of the Government of God* (1846), and numerous antimilitary tracts. He participated vigorously in campaigns urging Scottish and English churches to sever ties with American churches that included slaveholders. Exhausted and nearly dying of consumption, he was sent by British reformers to Graefenberg, a famous water-cure establishment in Silesia. Some of his best writing appeared in a long series of letters describing for readers of Garrison's newspaper, *The Liberator*, the scenes of military, ecclesiastical, and aristocratic rule he witnessed on the Continent. In *Six Months at Graefenberg* (1845) Wright began to speak as an expert on health.

After returning to the United States in 1847, Wright spent the rest of his life as a freelance author and lecturer, especially in the Midwest. Criticizing traditional Christianity, he voiced certainty that progress would occur in the world when loving, considerate couples, who avoided excessive sexual intercourse, gave birth to healthy, peaceful children. *Marriage and Parentage* (1854) and *The Unwelcome Child* (1858) are representative of his numerous books during this period. Throughout his life, in writings published and unpublished, Wright labored over memories of childhood. Much of his work as a reformer was devoted to children, and he gained a public reputation as an expert on marriage. He remained an abolitionist, and as sectional animosities intensified he found it possible to justify violence and celebrate the heroism of John Brown. He was a steadfast supporter of Abraham Lincoln and the Republicans against the criticisms of other abolitionists.

Wright died in Pawtucket, Rhode Island. In a much publicized incident, Garrison received instruction from Wright's spirit, via two different mediums, on the precise spot in Swan Point cemetery where he wished to be buried. In the years after the Civil War, when abolitionists were praised in the North as paragons of morality, divisive figures like Wright were forgotten. He was rediscovered in the twentieth century, often by those who echoed his critics of the 1830s and dismissed him as a fanatic. With changes in historical curiosity, Wright's speeches and books on marriage, sexuality, and therapeutic behavior have gained scholarly importance as illustrations of changing attitudes toward sex and gender.

• Wright's diaries are in the Harvard College Library and the Boston Public Library. His life is studied in detail in Lewis Perry, *Childhood, Marriage, and Reform: Henry Clarke Wright, 1797–1870* (1980). Wendell Phillips Garrison and Francis Jackson Garrison, *William Lloyd Garrison* (4 vols., 1885–1889), contains much information on Wright. His role in the peace movement is analyzed in Valarie Ziegler, *The Advocates of Peace in Antebellum America* (1992). Peter F. Walker, *Moral Choices: Memory, Desire, and Imagination in Nineteenth-Century American Abolition* (1978), has a sensitive chapter on Wright. Wright's life is interpreted as an instance of the transition to modernity in Perry, *Boats against the Current: American Culture between Revolution and Modernity, 1820–1860* (1993).

LEWIS PERRY

WRIGHT, Horatio Gouverneur (6 Mar. 1820–2 July 1899), soldier and engineer, was born in Clinton, Connecticut, the son of Edward Wright and Nancy (maiden name unknown). He entered the U.S. Military Academy in 1837, graduated second in his class in 1841, and was commissioned a second lieutenant in the Corps of Engineers. In 1841 and again from 1844 to 1846 he served as assistant to the army's Board of Engineers. He taught French and engineering at West Point from 1842 to 1844. In 1842 Wright married Louisa M. Bradford, with whom he had two children. In 1845 he accompanied Secretary of War William L. Marcy on a tour of inspection.

From 1846 to 1856 Wright's principal duty was as superintending engineer of the building of Fort Jefferson, Florida. In this period he also oversaw repairs of the St. Augustine sea wall, directed the improvement of the St. Johns River, supervised the lighthouses in Florida, and was superintending engineer for the construction of Fort Taylor and the navy coal depot at Key West. He was promoted to first lieutenant in 1848 and to captain in 1855. From 1856 to 1861 he was assistant to the chief engineer in Washington, D.C., and served on boards for arranging details of iron carriages and platforms for seacoast guns and for testing the fifteen-inch gun.

Wright's early Civil War service was also in an engineering capacity. He was chief engineer of the expedition to destroy the Norfolk Navy Yard, where he was captured and released. As an aide on the staff of General Samuel P. Heintzelman, he participated in the seizure of heights opposite Washington and was engineer for the construction of defenses in the Washington area. At the first battle of Manassas, he was chief engineer of Heintzelman's division. He became a major of engineers in August 1861.

Wright was raised to the rank of brigadier general of volunteers in the following month and led combat troops for the remainder of the war. As chief engineer and brigade commander in the South Carolina expedition (Oct. 1861–Apr. 1862), Wright conducted a reconnaissance of the Confederate works at Port Royal and was present at the capture of Hilton Head. He was the leader of the land forces of the Florida expedition that captured Fernandina, Jacksonville, and St. Augustine. Wright led a division at the unsuccessful assault against Secessionville, South Carolina, in June 1862. Promoted to major general of volunteers, he assumed command of the Department of the Ohio (Aug. 1862–Mar. 1863) and the District of Western Kentucky. The Senate failed to confirm his promotion, so he reverted to brigadier general but retained command of the District of Western Kentucky.

Wright again commanded a division with the Army of the Potomac (VI Corps, First Division) in the Pennsylvania campaign of 1863. Reaching Gettysburg after a forced march of thirty-five miles, his division served in reserve at the battle there. In the Rapidan campaign (Sept.–Dec. 1863) he led the VI Corps in the seizure of the Confederate works at Rappahannock Station and participated in the operations at Mine Run. Briefly in early 1864 he was a member of the board to reorganize the system of seacoast fortifications. At the Wilderness he led a division, and at Spotsylvania, where he was wounded, he succeeded John Sedgwick (who was killed) as commander of the VI Corps, with the rank of major general. His corps next fought in the battles of North Anna, Totopotomoy, and Cold Harbor. After arriving at Petersburg, Wright was sent to Washington, where he conducted the successful defense against Jubal Early's raid on the capital city. In command of the VI Army Corps (Aug.–Dec. 1864), he joined Philip Sheridan's Shenandoah campaign and saw action in several skirmishes and at Fisher's Hill. At Cedar Creek, where he was again wounded, Wright was temporarily in command and was surprised by a Confederate attack, but Sheridan returned in time to lead the Union forces to victory.

Wright returned with the VI Corps to the Army of the Potomac and engaged in numerous actions at the siege of Petersburg, where his troops spearheaded the final assault. At Sayler's Creek he captured Richard Ewell's corps. After the surrender of the southern forces at Appomattox, Wright marched south to participate in the operations against Joseph E. Johnston.

During the war Wright had been brevetted to lieutenant colonel, colonel, brigadier general, and major general in the regular army. The Connecticut legislature voted him the thanks of his native state. His postwar duties included command of a provisional army corps, the Department of Texas, and the District of Texas.

Mustered out of the volunteer army in 1866, Wright resumed engineering duty with the regular rank of lieutenant colonel. Again he served on a series of boards. His other responsibilities included service as senior officer on the Sutro Tunnel Commission in 1872 and overseeing the completion of the Washington Monument. He was promoted to colonel in March 1879, and in June he became the army's chief of engineers with the rank of brigadier general, a position he held until his retirement in 1884. Wright died in Washington, D.C., and is buried in Arlington National Cemetery.

Wright had not commanded troops of the line before the Civil War and, unlike most of his generation of West Pointers, had not participated in the war with Mexico. Despite this, he emerged as one of the Union army's most capable corps commanders. He was also an exceptionally able military engineer.

• Details of Wright's career before and after the Civil War are in George W. Cullum, *Biographical Register of the Officers and Graduates of the U.S. Military Academy at West Point, N.Y., from Its Establishment, March 16, 1802, to the Army Reorganization of 1866–67* (1868). A good sketch of his life is "Horatio Governeur [sic] Wright," *Professional Memoirs. Corps of Engineers, United States Army and Engineer Department at Large* 4 (1912): 88–90. Shelby Foote, *The Civil War: A Narrative* (1958–1974), covers the actions in which Wright figured prominently.

MICHAEL J. BRODHEAD

WRIGHT, James (8 May 1716–20 Nov. 1785), colonial governor of Georgia, was born in London, England, the son of Robert Wright, a lawyer, and Isabella Pitts. Wright evidently came to South Carolina about 1730, when his father was appointed chief justice of the colony. In South Carolina, beginning at about the age of twenty, Wright held several legal appointments and practiced law. He entered Gray's Inn in London on 14 August 1741 and was called to the bar. He married Sarah Maidman in February 1742; they had eight children. He then returned to South Carolina and began serving as attorney general. He was officially appointed from London in 1747. In 1757 he was selected as South Carolina's agent in London and returned to that city for three years.

Wright was appointed lieutenant governor of Georgia in 1760 and governor a year later. In terms of background knowledge and willingness to work at the job, Wright was by far the best of Georgia's three colonial governors. Having lived in South Carolina, he understood conditions in the southern colonies, and his experience in London provided him an understanding of the British imperial system. Wright took the oaths as lieutenant governor in Savannah on 31 October. After a slow start, Georgia was ready for rapid growth. With the cession of Florida to England in 1763 and the departure of the French from the Alabama country, Georgia no longer needed to worry about unfriendly neighbors. The land between the Altamaha and St. Mary's rivers was added to western Georgia by the royal proclamation of 1763. On 10 November 1763, at the Treaty of Augusta, the Creek Indians ceded some 2.4 million acres of land down the coast from the Altamaha to the St. Mary's and between the Ogeechee and

Savannah rivers from Ebenezer Creek to the Little River above Augusta.

Wright was conservative, favoring small- to medium-sized grants to farmers who would settle and cultivate their own land rather than large grants to speculators. He believed this to be the only effective way to settle the area and protect it against Indians. Wright also worked for approval in England of a second Treaty of Augusta in 1773, which ceded more land behind the coastal cession of 1763 and a sizable amount north of the 1763 cession between the Savannah and Ogeechee rivers. Wright favored justice to the Indians according to existing treaties, and he had no serious Indian troubles during his governorship.

Although Wright aided the small settlers in Georgia, he did not oppose large planters if they cultivated their land and secured it legally by bringing in substantial numbers of settlers under the Georgia headright system. Wright was one of the largest planters in Georgia by 1775, owning eleven plantations comprising 25,578 acres and worked by 523 slaves. He always picked good land and was noted as being one of Georgia's better planters. By the 1770s he shipped two to three thousand barrels of rice a year from his plantations.

Most Georgians approved of his actions as governor until the Stamp Act troubles of 1765. Thereafter, there was always an American rights group that opposed him. Most Georgians, however, were still willing to work with him on ordinary matters. Wright, who had lived in America a long time and had all of his personal wealth in Georgia, was more American than British. Yet as the king's representative he felt that he must carry out his orders from London, even if he did not approve of them. In 1765 he was able through positive action and his good reputation in the colony to protect the stamp agent sent to Georgia to sell stamps to clear the vessels in the harbor at Savannah. These were the only stamps sold in any colony that later rebelled.

After the Stamp Act troubles in 1765, whenever the assembly was not in session, Wright's relations with the Commons House of Assembly were varied. In the November and December 1768 session, the Commons House approved the Massachusetts and Virginia circulars against the Townshend Revenue Acts. From this action, Wright carried out his instructions from London, of which he had warned the assembly, and dissolved it. There were several other dissolutions by Wright before the rebellion in 1775.

From July 1771 to February 1773 Wright was on leave in England, where he was created a baronet as a reward for his services in Georgia. He also received royal approval for the Indian land cession, which was secured at Augusta in May 1773. Wright was welcomed by both houses of the assembly on his return and had no trouble with the Commons House for the next two years. This cooperation was ended in February 1775 when Wright prorogued the assembly to keep it from approving the actions of the First Continental Congress. Wright was able to delay revolutionary activity in Georgia, but he could not prevent it. By July 1775 Wright was convinced that Georgia was lost to British control, said he could not bear the daily insults by then being heaped on him, and requested leave to return to England as he was powerless in Georgia.

The royal government in Georgia was replaced by a Whig organization, consisting of a council of safety and a provincial congress. In mid-January 1776 several British men-of-war arrived at Savannah hoping to purchase provisions for British troops in America. The council of safety refused to have any dealings with these vessels and arrested Wright and other leading Tories. On the night of 11 February Wright broke his parole and boarded one of the men-of-war. Wright's departure ended any pretense of royal government in Georgia.

Almost as soon as Wright and Governor Lord William Campbell of South Carolina arrived in London in 1776, they began to agitate for the recapture of their colonies. After a British expedition in December 1778 had captured Savannah, Wright, Lieutenant Governor John Graham, and Chief Justice Anthony Stokes arrived there in July 1779 to reinstate royal government. But Wright soon discovered that there were not as many Loyalists in Georgia as he had believed. He continually called for more British troops to return all of Georgia to its "proper loyalty" but never received them. The only part of Georgia under royal control was the area held by the British military. A state government, usually operating from Augusta, competed with the royal government in Savannah for public favor. Wright continued to head the royal government, but rather than the Commons House of Assembly, Wright's biggest troubles were with the British army, which usually ignored his proposals. He was especially unhappy that the commanding officer in Savannah, Lieutenant Colonel Friedrich von Porbeck, a Hessian, did not understand British government and law.

From the summer of 1780 to the summer of 1781, when the Whigs regained control of Augusta, all of Georgia except Wilkes County (the 1773 Indian cession) was under British control. By early 1782 the British had lost all of Georgia except the Savannah area. In July they evacuated Savannah, despite Wright's protests that a few more troops would make Georgia entirely loyal to Britain.

Back in London, Wright became the head of a board of American Loyalists seeking compensation for their losses as a result of the war and the confiscation of their American property. Wright claimed personal losses of £33,000, plus his office of governor, which had paid £1,000 a year. He was awarded an annual pension of £500. He died at his house in Westminster.

• For further information about Wright, see Kenneth Coleman, "James Wright," in *Georgians in Profile*, ed. Horace Montgomery (1958); Coleman, *Colonial Georgia: A History* (1976); and Coleman, *The American Revolution in Georgia, 1763–1789* (1958). See also W. W. Abbot, *The Royal Governors of Georgia, 1754–1789* (1959); Allen D. Chandler et al., eds., *The Colonial Records of the State of Georgia* (32 vols., 1904–1989); other volumes are in manuscript form at the

Georgia Department of Archives and History, Atlanta; and the letters of James Oglethorpe and James Wright in *Collections of the Georgia Historical Society*, vol. 3 (1873).

KENNETH COLEMAN

WRIGHT, James Arlington (13 Dec. 1927–25 Mar. 1980), poet, was born in Martins Ferry, Ohio, the son of Dudley Wright, a factory worker, and Jessie (maiden name unknown). Although he was enrolled in the local high school's vocational training program, Wright was encouraged by two of his teachers to pursue a study of English and Russian literature. After graduating from high school, however, he entered the army, serving two years with the occupation force in Japan.

In 1948, aided by the GI Bill, Wright enrolled at Kenyon College, where he came under the influence of John Crowe Ransom, the neoclassic southern poet. Graduating in 1952, he married Liberty Kardules, with whom he had two children, and won a Fulbright Scholarship to study for a year at the University of Vienna. Upon his return from abroad, Wright attended the University of Washington, earning an M.A. and a Ph.D. and working with another distinguished faculty poet, Theodore Roethke. His teaching career, which included positions at Macalester College in St. Paul, Minnesota, and the University of Minnesota, would never involve any poetry workshops, although his first collection, *The Green Wall* (1957), was a Yale Younger Poet title, selected and introduced by W. H. Auden.

As Auden's foreword indicated, the verses in *The Green Wall*, formal and ironic in the manner of the times, evinced strong empathy with "social outsiders" of all kinds, including the convicted Ohio rapist and murderer George Doty, and a traditional reliance on nature imagery. The language, however, was vividly contemporary, conversationally so, reflecting Wright's conscious allegiance to the modernist examples of Robert Frost and Edwin Arlington Robinson. The same could be said for his second collection, *Saint Judas* (1959), although a return to Doty, "At the Executed Murderer's Grave," attempted to defuse criticism of the prior romanticizing of the criminal. But another poem, "American Twilights, 1957," was equally sympathetic toward Caryl Chessman, another notorious criminal, and the title poem canonized Judas by imagining him pausing to comfort a mugging victim before moving on to his suicide.

Wright's marriage ended in divorce in 1962. According to Richard Hugo's memoir, the break up climaxed with "Libby" undergoing shock treatments and Wright experiencing a nervous breakdown, the first of six, abetted by his addictive drinking. The next year, however, he published *The Branch Will Not Break*, his single most potent collection and a dramatic change from the conventional ways of his first two volumes. Influenced by the "deep image" poetics of Robert Bly, with whom he had worked on translating Georg Trakl, Wright had evolved a flexible free-verse style ideally suited to dreamlike, even surreal explorations of a continuing Wordsworthian fascination with natural phe-

nomena and of society's anguished outcasts, as in "A Blessing" and "Two Hangovers," two memorable signature performances.

In 1966, after not being rehired by the University of Minnesota, Wright moved to New York to join the English faculty at the City University of New York's Hunter College, where he would remain until his death. A year later, his marriage to Edith Anne Runk (which was childless) inaugurated a new era in his life and art. His wife would help Wright curb his excessive drinking and smoking, but her effect on his poetry was less felicitous as her metaphoric role as Muse and Beatrice encouraged a release of sentimentality that had always lain just beneath the surface of his identification with America's marginalized misfits, whom he knew so well from his Martins Ferry childhood.

As a result, *We Shall Gather at the River* (1968) rarely achieved the resonating impact of *The Branch Will Not Break* collection, although the poems still ostensibly probed the Jungian depths of a "deep image" technique with easy vulgate directness. In "Speak," Wright defined his artistic quest as speaking "of flat defeat / In a flat voice" while pursuing an apparently absent godhead. Pathos, not transfiguring tragedy, dominated, as in "I Am a Sioux Brave, He Said in Minneapolis" and "In Terror of Hospital Bills," a pair of poems devoted to articulating the sad plight of Native Americans ravaged by a rejecting culture. Reviews, however, were generally positive, sympathetic to the poems' social conscience and expressionist style.

The publication of *The Collected Poems* (1971), which won a 1972 Pulitzer Prize, represented the zenith of Wright's public recognition, although only two of the thirty-three new poems in the book ("To the August Fallen" and "Small Frogs Killed on the Highway") were unqualified successes in their inventive manipulation of familiar nature imagery. Too many of the others pursued the kind of sentimental extremes that had marred *Shall We Gather at the River*.

But it was *Two Citizens* (1973) that seemed to signal a complete collapse of Wright's aesthetic control. Structured on a trip through Italy and France with his wife, "a beautiful woman who loved me," the collection approached self-parody, midwestern stereotypes replaced by European counterparts. Terse declarative stabs at ambiguous wisdom had deteriorated into glib pseudoprofundities, as at the end of "To the Creature of the Creation," when the speaker avows, "I will die on the wing, / I love you so." Wright himself subsequently dismissed *Two Citizens* as "a bust" in an interview with Dave Smith, but in the same interview he also referred to his next collection, *To a Blossoming Pear Tree* (1977), as "the best book that I have ever published." Hugh Kenner's *New York Times* review was less kind, if more accurate, deeming it "an unexpectedly weak book."

The last decade of Wright's life was relatively serene and productive as he taught, traveled with his wife, worked on translations, and continued to explore the possibilities of the prose poem, a number of which appeared in *To a Blossoming Pear Tree*. Two chapbooks of prose pieces written during the European trips with his wife were published, *Moments of the Italian Summer* (1976) and *The Summers of Annie and James Wright* (1981), which contained entries by him and Anne Wright. In addition, he put together two volumes of translations for works by Herman Hesse, *Poems* (1970) and *Wanderings: Notes and Sketches* (1972), the latter done with his son, Franz Wright.

Wright was awarded a Guggenheim grant in 1978 and spent most of his leave in Europe, completing the bulk of *This Journey* (1982) and planning a book of personal and critical essays. The fruits of literary fame included a January 1980 invitation to the White House, where he revealed to Richard Hugo that he was suffering from the throat cancer that killed him two months later in New York City.

• Wright's papers are at the University of Minnesota Library in Minneapolis. Incorporating some prose pieces and translations, James Wright's *Above the River: The Complete Poems* was published in 1990. Edited by Anne Wright, his *Collected Prose* (1983) includes essays, reviews, memoirs, and four interviews. See also Dave Smith, ed., *The Pure Clear Word: Essays on the Poetry of James Wright* (1982), and Andrew Elkins, *The Poetry of James Wright* (1991). Richard Hugo's memoir, *The Real West Marginal Way* (1986), provides scattered references to Wright. An obituary is in the *New York Times*, 27 Mar. 1980.

EDWARD BUTSCHER

WRIGHT, John Joseph (18 July 1909–10 Aug. 1979), Roman Catholic cardinal and theologian, was born in Dorchester, Massachusetts, the son of John Joseph Wright, a clerk, and Harriet Cokely. He received his early education in Boston public schools and was awarded a prestigious scholarship to Boston Latin School. As a boy, Wright worked as a page at the Boston Public Library, where he began his great love for books. Over time he acquired a large personal library, collecting over 5,000 volumes and manuscripts relating to Saint Joan of Arc alone. He donated this huge corpus to the library, where it was housed in a room dedicated to Wright's memory.

Upon graduation Wright went on to Boston College, a Jesuit institution, where he earned a B.A. in 1931. He began studies for the priesthood at St. John's Seminary, Brighton, and then attended the North American College in Rome, Italy, to complete his theological training. He was ordained a priest for the archdiocese of Boston on 8 December 1935. He continued postgraduate studies in Rome at the Pontifical Gregorian University and received a doctorate in theology in 1939. Upon completion of his studies, he was appointed to the faculty of St. John's Seminary in Brighton. In 1943 he was named secretary to Cardinal William O'Connell, archbishop of Boston, and remained in this position with O'Connell's successor, Archbishop (later Cardinal) Richard Cushing.

Wright quickly rose up the clerical ranks in Boston and on 30 June 1947, at the age of thirty-seven, was ordained an auxiliary bishop. On 28 January 1950 he was named the first bishop of the newly created dio-cese of Worcester, Massachusetts. He soon became known for his witty and gregarious personality and was active in the American Catholic church beyond Worcester. In 1954–1955 he was president of the "National Liturgical Weeks," which were annual meetings of liturgists, theologians, and priests to discuss renewal of the liturgy and to argue for its intrinsic relationship to social justice. In 1956 he gave support to the liturgist Hans Ansgar Reinhold, inviting him to live and work in Pittsburgh, when the German emigré priest was at odds with his bishop. Wright was also active in ecumenical affairs and race relations. In 1967 he angered many who supported America's role in Vietnam when he questioned whether the just war theory had meaning in view of the state of modern warfare. In 1956 he wrote a piece supporting Monsignor John Tracy Ellis's controversial essay, "American Catholics and the Intellectual Life," in which Ellis criticized the dearth of Catholic scholarship in America in all academic disciplines, including theology, despite the large number of Catholic colleges and universities.

On 28 January 1959 Wright was named the eighth bishop of Pittsburgh, a larger and more important diocese than Worcester. During the preparations for the second Vatican Council (1963–1965), Wright served as a member of the Theological Commission. At one of the conciliar sessions he strongly championed the role of the laity in the church, acknowledging "the place, dignity, and vocation of the laity in the Church of Christ." Subsequently, many of the conciliar and post-conciliar documents embodied this new vision by granting the laity greater participation in church affairs.

On 23 April 1969 Pope Paul VI named Wright prefect of the Congregation for the Clergy and created him a cardinal. After moving to Rome to take up this new position, Wright's health deteriorated seriously, and he suffered from chronic arthritis and circulatory problems that confined him to a wheelchair. Wright grew increasingly disenchanted with what he considered the misinterpretation of the decrees of the recent council. He criticized, for example, those religious sisters who had discarded their distinctive garb and abandoned traditional ministries such as teaching and nursing. He also complained about the huge number of priests who sought dispensations from celibacy in order to marry.

Although he had earned a doctorate in theology, Wright produced little in terms of original research or scholarship. Rather, he wrote widely on more pastoral topics including marriage and the family, social justice, peace and ecumenism. He was a complex churchman who often stood on the opposite side of public opinion. Both an advocate for and a critic of change in the church, he rarely hesitated to speak his views and to work in support of his firmly held convictions. Ellis, the one-time dean of American Catholic church history, lamented that a man who had once been so "forward looking" had become the object of scorn by those in the American church who believed that the directives of the Vatican Council were being properly implemented. Wright died in Cambridge, Massachusetts.

Wright's warnings against changes too quickly enacted and too poorly thought out went largely ignored. However, his words seemed prescient at the end of the twentieth century as leaders in the Catholic church attempted to reverse much that was brought about by the Second Vatican Council.

• Wright's papers are at Duquesne University in Pittsburgh. His works include: *National Patriotism in Papal Teaching* (1942), *The Christian and the Law: Selected Red Mass Sermons* (1962), and *The Church: Hope of the World*, ed. D. W. Wuerl (1972). A collection of his talks was published in three volumes under the title *Resonare Christum* (1982). See also John Tracy Ellis, *Catholic Bishops: A Memoir* (1983), and Vincent T. Mallon, "Resonare Christum," *the Homiletic and Pastoral Review* 82 (1982): 64–68. An obituary is in *L'Osservatore Romano*, 20 Aug. 1979.

ANTHONY D. ANDREASSI

WRIGHT, Jonathan Jasper (11 Feb. 1840–18 Feb. 1885), politician and jurist, was born in Luzerne County, Pennsylvania. Little is known of his parents except that his father was a farmer and that the family moved to Susquehanna County, Pennsylvania, during Wright's childhood. Wright attended Lancasterian University in Ithaca, New York, and later studied law at the offices of Bently, Fith, and Bently in Montrose, Pennsylvania. He also taught school and read law in the office of Judge O. Collins of Wilkes-Barre, Pennsylvania. Wright attended the 1864 national black convention in Syracuse, New York, that opposed slavery, supported universal manhood suffrage, and endorsed equality before the law.

At the end of the Civil War in April 1865, the American Missionary Association sent Wright to Beaufort, South Carolina, where he taught adult freedmen and soldiers of the 128th U.S. Colored Troops. In November 1865 he served as a delegate to the Colored Peoples' Convention in Charleston. Disappointed that the state's recent all-white, all-male constitutional convention relegated the black population to second-class status through a series of measures known as the black code, the forty-five delegates to the Charleston convention supported the enfranchisement of black men and the abolition of the black code and appealed for "even handed justice." Seven years later, in a speech assessing black political progress, Wright denounced the code as an attempt to keep blacks virtually enslaved by depriving "the colored people of all and every opportunity of being elevated an iota above their former condition. They were left totally at the mercy of the white man."

In 1866 Wright returned to Pennsylvania, where he became the first black admitted to the state bar. A few months later he was back in Beaufort as a legal adviser for the Freedmen's Bureau, representing the interests of former slaves and offering legal advice to the bureau's commanding officer in South Carolina, General Robert K. Scott. Though some bureau agents were accused of cooperating closely with white planters and ignoring the needs of the freedmen, Wright insisted that he would not do the bidding of white men. "Had I been contented to settle down, and been what the masses of white persons desired me to be (a bootblacker, a barber, or a hotel waiter) I would have been heard of less."

When Congress authorized the reorganization of the southern states and adopted universal manhood suffrage in the 1867 Reconstruction Acts, Wright promptly joined in organizing the Republican party and speaking on its behalf. At a rally in July 1867, he urged the party to nominate a black man for U.S. vice president in 1868. He resigned from the Freedmen's Bureau in 1868 and was elected to represent Beaufort at the state constitutional convention.

Wright played a prominent part in the convention, serving as one of two black vice presidents (of five total vice presidents) and as a member of the Judiciary Committee. He persuaded the convention to support the legislative election of judges to fixed terms rather than to permit gubernatorial appointment of judges for life. Wright was also deeply concerned about education. Like most of the convention's delegates (black and white), he showed little interest in integrated public schools, claiming that he did "not believe the colored children will want to go to the white schools, or vice versa."

Wright was involved in a major controversy when he supported the adoption of a $1 poll tax, the proceeds of which would be devoted to education. Wright and Francis L. Cardozo believed the tax was necessary to finance the establishment of public schools, while other black delegates led by Robert Brown Elliott feared the failure to pay the tax would disfranchise large numbers of black voters. The tax was not included in the constitution.

In 1868 Wright, Elliott, and William Whipper were the first three black men admitted to the South Carolina bar. Shortly thereafter Wright was elected to the South Carolina Senate, representing Beaufort County. In 1869, while traveling through Virginia, Wright was removed from a first-class, all-white coach on the Richmond and Danville Railroad. He subsequently won a $1,200 lawsuit against the railroad.

On 1 February 1870 the general assembly elected Wright to the state supreme court to fill the unexpired term of Solomon L. Hoge, who had been elected to Congress. The following December Wright was elected to a full six-year term. Wright's elevation to the court was part of a larger effort by South Carolina black leaders to secure the election of more black men to major political offices. In 1870 black men were elected lieutenant governor, treasurer, Speaker of the house, and to three seats in Congress.

Wright's seven-year tenure on the three-member court was largely uneventful. Only his most biased critics considered him less than competent and effective. Wright participated in 425 cases; he wrote eighty-seven opinions and dissented on just one occasion. Wright's judicial career ended in controversy in 1877 during the prolonged dispute involving the results of the 1876 gubernatorial election, when Democratic candidate Wade Hampton (1818–1902) and Republican incumbent Daniel Chamberlain each claimed victory. In a supreme court case testing Hampton's authority as governor, Wright and Associate Justice A. J. Willard upheld a pardon issued by Hampton. (Chief Justice Franklin Moses, Sr., was ill.) Two days later Wright attempted to reverse his decision as well as the order releasing the prisoner.

The revocation of the order was not accepted, and rumors circulated that black Republicans bribed Wright or had gotten him drunk to compel him to change his position. Counter rumors contended that black Republican legislator Thomas E. Miller was offered a bribe by Democrats to testify that Wright was drunk. Other reports claimed that Wright was threatened by one party or the other. A month later Hampton's claim to executive authority was supported by Republican president Rutherford B. Hayes, and the Republican party lost political control of South Carolina. Though a special legislative committee under Democratic control recommended the impeachment of Wright for misconduct for allegedly accepting a bribe to uphold Hampton's pardon, no formal charges were presented. Wright resigned from the court on 6 August 1877.

Wright resumed his career as a lawyer. He supported Hampton's reelection in 1878, and in 1879 he moved to Charleston and opened a law practice on Queen Street. In 1881 the Board of Trustees of Claflin University in Orangeburg, South Carolina, authorized Wright to teach law courses for the university. He offered the courses in Charleston on behalf of Claflin until his death. Wright never married. He died of tuberculosis in Charleston.

Wright was one of the vanguard of black men who rose to political power in the 1860s and 1870s and is noteworthy as the only black state supreme court justice in the nineteenth century. Moderate in his political views and restrained in his legal decisions, he nevertheless persistently sought expanded political influence for African Americans while defending the rights they so recently had gained. His life and career illustrate both the possibilities and the limitations that black men encountered in the post–Civil War era.

• A number of Wright's letters are contained in the American Missionary Association collection at Tulane University. His supreme court opinions can be found in *Reports of Cases Heard and Determined in the Supreme Court of South Carolina*, vols. 2–9 (1872–1879). There is no biography. The most useful accounts of his life and career are Robert H. Woody, "Jonathan Jasper Wright, Associate Justice of the Supreme Court of South Carolina, 1870–1877," *Journal of Negro History* 18 (Apr. 1933): 114–31; Joel Williamson, *After Slavery: The Negro in South Carolina during Reconstruction, 1861–1877* (1965); Thomas Holt, *Black over White: Negro Political Leadership in South Carolina during Reconstruction* (1977); George B. Tindall, *South Carolina Negroes, 1877–1900* (1952); J. R. Oldenfield, "A High and Honorable Calling: Black Lawyers in South Carolina, 1868–1915," *Journal of American Studies* 23 (1989): 395–406; and George C. Rogers, Jr., *Generations of Lawyers: A History of the South Carolina Bar* (1992). There is an uncomplimentary obituary in the Charleston *News and Courier*, 20 Feb. 1885.

WILLIAM C. HINE

WRIGHT, Joseph (16 July 1756 or 1757–13 Sept. 1793), painter and sculptor, was born and raised in Bordentown, New Jersey, the son of Joseph Wright, a cooper, and Patience Lovell. Historian William Dunlap, based on information provided by Wright's daughters, gives the year of his birth as 1756, whereas the register of the schools of the Royal Academy of Arts in London states that he turned seventeen in 1774, meaning he was born in 1757. His father possessed considerable property in Philadelphia and New Jersey, and his mother, who gave him his first lessons in art, would become an internationally known sculptor. Wright entered the Academy of Philadelphia (now the University of Pennsylvania) in 1769 and studied there until 1772, probably the year that he and two of his four sisters crossed the Atlantic to join their mother, now a widow, in London, where she had established a waxworks, which they all presumably helped her operate.

In April 1775 Wright became the first native-born American to be admitted to the school of the Royal Academy of Arts, where he remained until 1881. He must have been fairly proficient as a draftsman in order to pass the tests for admission, but no work by him from this period has been located. That autumn he received his first published notice as an artist; *London Magazine* (Nov. 1775), in an article on Patience Wright, observed that her one son "has an amazing turn to the liberal arts, and from a most promising beginning he gives assurances of arriving at great perfection in painting." He received a medal in 1778 from the Royal Academicians for his model of an academy figure (probably a plaster copy of an antique statue). Among his fellow students was John Hoppner, who would become a leading British artist of the 1780s and 1790s, and who in 1781 married Wright's sister Phoebe.

Wright began his professional career as an artist in 1780. His *Portrait of a Gentleman* was no. 304 in that year's exhibition of the Society of Artists of Great Britain. This painting is otherwise unidentified but may have been the portrait of Major Peter Labilliere (unlocated), of which a mezzotint was published by H. Kingsbury later in 1780. Wright also submitted a portrait of his mother to the Royal Academy's exhibition for 1780. Entitled *Mrs. Wright Modeling a Head in Wax* (no. 202 in the academy's catalog), it depicted Patience Wright modeling a head of King Charles I while the reigning monarchs, King George III and Queen Charlotte, observed her at work. The blatantly pro-American sentiments of the painting, unfortunately unlocated and never engraved, proved to be so controversial that Wright never again submitted a painting to a Royal Academy exhibition. The uproar appears to have inspired his first recorded engraving, which is also his earliest-known likeness, a self-portrait etching—and defiant reply to his critics—entitled *Yankee*

Doodle, or the American Satan (impressions are owned by the National Portrait Gallery, Washington, D.C., and the John Carter Brown Library, Providence).

Wright remained in London for another year, but by the end of 1781 he was in Paris, where his mother was at work modeling wax portraits. She returned to London the following spring, but he stayed in Paris, where he painted a portrait of Benjamin Franklin, then the chief American representative to the French court. The portrait (versions owned by the Royal Society, London; the Corcoran Gallery of Art, Washington, D.C.; and elsewhere) was not done from life but rather was based on a pastel (New York Public Library) by the French artist Joseph Siffred Duplessis, to whom Franklin had sat in 1778. Wright was acquainted with Franklin, however, and was able to incorporate his own knowledge of Franklin's physiognomy into his portrait, thus raising it above the level of a mere copy. His portrait was a popular one, and he made several replicas of it.

After having been away from his native land for a decade, Wright was eager to return to the now-independent nation, and in the late summer of 1782 he sailed for America. By the spring of 1783 he had returned to Philadelphia and opened a studio. Later that summer he journeyed to the Continental army's headquarters at Rocky Hill, New Jersey, in order to do a portrait of General George Washington. Congress had passed a resolution calling for the creation of an equestrian statue, and Charles Thomson, the secretary of Congress, wrote a letter introducing Wright to Washington. The general was agreeable, and Wright went to work. He not only painted a small portrait from life, but he also took a life mask and modeled a clay bust of the general; he is said to have painted a portrait of Martha Washington as well. Congress never followed through on its plan to raise an equestrian statue, but it did pay Wright 50 guineas for the bust. Neither the bust nor the life mask are located today, but a plaster bas-relief and a smaller wax relief (both now owned by the Mount Vernon Ladies' Association) and another wax relief (Henry Francis duPont Winterthur Museum, Winterthur, Del.), all in right profile, must derive from either the mask or the bust. The painting that Wright did from life (Historical Society of Pennsylvania, Philadelphia) was highly regarded by the general's contemporaries. Washington himself wrote that Wright "is thought . . . to have taken a better likeness of me, than any other painter has done" (quoted in Fabian, p. 100). From the life portrait Wright began a replica (Massachusetts Historical Society, Boston) for Thomas Jefferson but completed only the head before Jefferson departed in June 1784 for a diplomatic assignment in France; it was completed by John Trumbull in Paris in 1786. Jefferson, pleased with his replica, commented on it and a portrait of Washington by Charles Willson Peale, which he also owned, thusly: "the one by Peale, better painted; but the other by Wright, more resembling the general" (quoted in Fabian, p. 104). Wright also painted replicas for Mrs. Samuel Powel of Philadelphia (Historical Society of Pennsylvania) and the Graf zu Solms of Saxony (unlocated).

Wright moved to New York City in 1786, the year after it became the nation's capital. Portraits that he painted between 1784 and 1793, either in Philadelphia or New York, include paintings of James Giles (National Museum of American Art, Washington, D.C.), Mrs. James Giles (née Hannah Bloomfield) (private collection), Charles Thomson, Mrs. Charles Thomson (both Tudor Place Foundation, Washington, D.C.; these portraits were formerly attributed to Matthew Pratt), Baron von Steuben (private collection), and George Clinton (unlocated). In New York, Wright painted portraits of John Jay (New-York Historical Society), his son Peter Augustus Jay (owned by a Jay descendant), Lewis Pintard (private collection), and Benjamin Goodhue, a congressman from Massachusetts (New York Society Library, New York City). He also made a drypoint etching of Washington in right profile (examples are owned by the Metropolitan Museum of Art and the New York Public Library), based on either the life mask or the bust he had done in 1783. In New York Wright evidently lived in the home of Mrs. Peter Vandervoordt, and he soon won the hand of his landlady's daughter Sarah, whom he married in Philadelphia on 5 December 1789. They had three children.

The U.S. capital moved back to Philadelphia in 1790, and the following year Wright also returned. In this last period of his career he became much occupied with work for the U.S. Mint. Congress had awarded a gold medal to Major Henry Lee in 1779, but it had never been executed. Thomas Jefferson, then secretary of state, commissioned Wright to design the medal and oversee its production, but as Jefferson reported, Wright "would not agree to warrant against the quality of the steel" (quoted in Fabian, p. 135). Wright's doubts were well-founded; the quality of the steel used to make the dies was poor, and at least one of them cracked during post-engraving processing. (A bronze example of the Lee medal with a cracked obverse die is owned by the National Museum of American History, Washington, D.C.) Wright also engraved the dies for a quarter-dollar coin in 1792. The coin was never put into circulation, but several sample strikes exist. (One of these is in the National Museum of American History.) Wright, who has been called the mint's first engraver, submitted bills for all of his work for the mint to the government, indicating that he worked on contract rather than as an employee. Although there is no evidence that he ever received an official appointment, Washington's and Jefferson's letters clearly indicate that they regarded him as such. It was also during this period that Wright took on his only known pupil, William Rush, who became an important sculptor in the early nineteenth century.

Wright died in Philadelphia during an epidemic of yellow fever a few days after his wife. His last-known painting, a group portrait of his own family (Pennsylvania Academy of the Fine Arts, Philadelphia), evidently begun in 1793 and brought close to completion, was left unfinished. Besides the group portrait and his early self-portrait etching, Wright drew a self-portrait in chalk (unlocated). A posthumous terracotta bust by Rush, executed probably around 1810, belongs to the Pennsylvania Academy of the Fine Arts.

Had he lived longer, Wright likely would have been recognized as the equal of such "American Old Masters" as Charles Willson Peale and John Trumbull. He was certainly a better painter than Matthew Pratt, Ralph Earl, or Edward Savage, to each of whom paintings by Wright have occasionally been misattributed. (He also has sometimes been confused with the British artist Joseph Wright of Derby, to whom he was not related.) The skill evident in his surviving bas-reliefs of Washington indicates that Wright might have become esteemed as the most important American sculptor of the late eighteenth and early nineteenth centuries. Only about fifty of his works are recorded. Probably more are waiting to be discovered, but not many more; according to his sister Phoebe Hoppner, Wright was "inclined . . . to be idle," and Washington himself reported that Wright was "said to be a little lazy" (quoted in Fabian, pp. 33 and 100). In spite of his indolence, Wright was an artist of considerable talent held in high regard by his contemporaries.

• There is no collection of his papers, but letters by Wright are in the Library of Congress and the National Archives in Washington and at the American Philosophical Society in Philadelphia. His friend and fellow artist William Dunlap included a short biography of Wright in his *A History of the Rise and Progress of the Arts of Design in the United States* (1834). The best account is Monroe H. Fabian, *Joseph Wright: American Artist, 1756–1793* (1985), the catalog of an exhibition held at the National Portrait Gallery, Smithsonian Institution, Washington, D.C.; it includes a biography of the artist, a catalog of his works, and a complete bibliography.

DAVID MESCHUTT

WRIGHT, Joseph Albert (1809/1810?–11 May 1867), governor of Indiana, congressman, and diplomat, was born in Washington County, Pennsylvania, the son of John Wright, a merchant, and Rachel Seaman. In 1819 his family moved to Bloomington, Indiana, where Wright attended the common school and worked in his father's brickyard until 1823 when his father died. He paid his way through the Indiana seminary (now Indiana University) for the next two years by working as a janitor and by doing odd jobs. He studied law with Craven P. Hester, and after being admitted to the bar in 1829 he moved to Rockville, Indiana, where he set up a practice. In 1831 he married Louisa Cook; they had one child before her death in 1852.

Wright affiliated with the Democratic party and was elected to the Indiana House of Representatives in 1833 and again in 1836; then in 1839 he served one term in the state senate. He was elected to the Twenty-eighth Congress in 1842 but failed in his bid for reelection in 1844. In the House of Representatives he advocated building a transoceanic canal across Central America and argued for a low protective tariff.

Wright was a states' rights Democrat who emphasized decentralization of power, but he also asserted his devotion to the Union. In the gubernatorial campaign of 1849, Wright, the Democratic party candidate, soundly defeated the Whig candidate John A. Matson. Wright was elected by a majority of 9,778 votes under the old state constitution for the term of three years and was reelected in 1852 under the new state constitution for four years. In his message to the state legislature after the adaptation of the Compromise of 1850, Wright urged Indianans to reject both northern and southern extremists.

Governor Wright revolutionized the public school system by recommending the establishment of a state board of education and by urging cities and towns to authorize taxes to pay for schools. His administration was marked by the passage of a new temperance law regulating the sale of liquor and by the adjustment of state statutes to conform with the state constitution of 1850. Although Wright was not a farmer by occupation, he was an eager advocate of scientific farming and the use of new technology to increase agricultural production. To this end he urged the development of local and county agricultural societies for the purpose of diffusing practical use and scientific information among farmers. A bill embodying these ideas was passed by the legislature on 14 February 1851, and as a result the State Agricultural Society and the State Board of Agriculture were established. In 1854 he married Harriet Burbridge, with whom he had two children and adopted a third; she died in 1855.

On the issue of slavery Wright embraced colonization as a solution. Like many of his fellow citizens, Wright simultaneously deplored slavery but was convinced of the innate inferiority of African Americans. During the Civil War, as a senator and a member of the Union party, Wright continued to insist that the answer to the race problem was to colonize African Americans outside of the United States.

When Governor Wright's term ended in 1857, he was appointed minister to Prussia by President James Buchanan. In this capacity Wright encouraged the exchange of American and German seeds and the distribution of German agricultural literature in the United States. His efforts to protect naturalized U.S. citizens of German origin from Prussian conscription laws met with stiff opposition from the Prussian government.

In 1861 Wright had just returned from Prussia when his longtime political foe, Jesse Bright, was expelled from the Senate because of his alleged sympathy for the Confederacy. The Republican governor, Oliver Morton, appointed Wright to complete Bright's term of office. Wright served in the U.S. Senate from 24 February 1862 to 14 January 1863.

As a prerequisite for his appointment, Wright promised Morton that he would support the unconditional prosecution of the war, he would support the confiscation of rebel property, including slaves, and he would not support the ticket and platform adopted by the Democratic State Convention in January 1862.

With this appointment, Wright severed his ties with the Democratic party and became a Unionist supporter of President Abraham Lincoln.

The Civil War intensified the conflict between the Democrats and the Unionist Republicans in Indiana. The military reversals, the arbitrary arrests, and the suspension of the writ of habeas corpus turned Indianans against the Lincoln administration and resulted in a sweeping victory of the Democratic victory of the election of 1862. Wright did not stand for reelection to the Senate; instead Lincoln appointed him commissioner to the Hamburg Exposition in 1863. That same year Wright married Caroline Rockville. In 1865 President Andrew Johnson returned him as minister to Prussia. He died at his post of duty in Berlin.

Raising the standard of education by recommending the establishment of a state board of education and improving the standard of living for the farmers of Indiana by urging the development of local and county agricultural societies were Joseph Albert Wright's most lasting contributions.

• Wright's papers are at the Indiana State Library. There is one work on Wright: Philip Crane, "Governor Jo Wright: Hoosier Conservative" (Ph.D. diss., Indiana Univ., Bloomington, 1963). A biographical sketch of Wright is in the *Biographical Dictionary of Governors of the United States*, vol. 1. For a general history that also treats Wright see Emma Lou Thornbrough, *Indiana in the Civil War Era, 1850–1880*, vol. 3 (1965). Information on his diplomatic career may be found in *Papers relating to Foreign Affairs, 1861–67* and instructions and dispatches in the Prussia MSS at the State Department. An obituary is in the *Indianapolis Daily Journal*, 13, 14 May 1867.

MARGARET HORSNELL

WRIGHT, Joseph Jefferson Burr (27 Apr. 1801–14 May 1878), military physician, was born in Wilkes-Barre, Pennsylvania; his parents' names are unknown. He received an A.B. from Washington (Pa.) College in 1821 and attended the University of Pennsylvania School of Medicine from 1825 to 1826. He married Eliza Jones, with whom he had three children; the year of the marriage is unknown.

In 1826 Wright opened a general medical practice in Luzerne County, Pennsylvania. In 1833 he closed the practice to join the U.S. Army as an assistant surgeon and spent the next seven years at frontier outposts, among them Fort Gibson, Indian Territory. Between 1840 and 1841 he served in Florida during the Second Seminole War, perhaps the most costly Indian conflict for the United States in terms of lives and money. Like other army medical officers, he found service in tropical Florida particularly difficult. The dispersal of American troops throughout the northern peninsula forced him to shuttle back and forth among several posts without an escort and at times under enemy fire, while the tropical climate contributed to bug-infested dispensaries and widespread dysentery and fever. In 1843, the year after the Seminoles surrendered, Wright was dispatched to Florida a second time to treat the occupying troops for malaria, which he succeeded in doing by administering dosages of quinine sulfate far in excess of what was considered normal.

In 1846 Wright was made surgeon of the Eighth Infantry Regiment, at the time part of General Zachary Taylor's Army of Observation in Texas. When the Mexican War broke out, Wright served with the regiment at the battles of Palo Alto and Resaca de la Palma, after which he established and administered the military hospital in Matamoros, Tamaulipas. The next year he joined General Winfield Scott's staff as medical purveyor and accompanied his army on its campaign from Veracruz to Mexico City. During the campaign, more than one-quarter of Scott's troops was hospitalized with either diarrhea or typhus. Because wagons could not be spared to ship the sick and wounded back to the army hospital in Veracruz, Wright improvised hospitals en route at Jalapa, Perote, and Puebla, which he staffed with soldiers detailed from the line. Of the many surgical procedures he performed during the campaign, the most difficult one involved digging out with a knife each ball of a charge of enemy grape-shot from the chest of the unanesthetized General James Shields, who survived.

After the war Wright was stationed in San Antonio, Texas, where in 1849 he contended with a particularly virulent outbreak of cholera. In 1857 he was stationed in Kansas and the following year accompanied an army expedition to Utah. When the Civil War broke out in 1861 he was made medical director of the Union army's Department of the Ohio, which included Ohio, Indiana, and Illinois, and assumed responsibility for organizing a military hospital in Cincinnati. As senior medical officer on General William Rosecrans's staff during his advance into western Virginia, Wright established field hospitals immediately following the battles of Rich Mountain and Carrick's Ford and a general hospital near Rosecrans's headquarters in Beverly, Virginia. Later that year he transferred to the Department of the Missouri in St. Louis, where he became General Henry W. Halleck's medical director.

In 1862 the aging Wright was appointed surgeon at the Carlisle (Pa.) Barracks, where he served until his retirement. After 1863, when the barracks became a cavalry recruiting depot, he spent much of his time setting broken bones and performing orthopedic surgery. He was promoted to brevet colonel in 1864 and brevet brigadier general in 1865.

After the war, the barracks was converted into a training center for the Army Hospital Corps, and Wright became one of its medical instructors. One of his pupils was George Martin Kober, who became active in the public health campaign against tuberculosis. Wright retired in 1876 at the rank of colonel and died in Carlisle.

Wright's successful experimentation with quinine therapy contributed directly to the increased survivability of U.S. troops stationed in tropical theaters. His skillful performance as a senior medical administrator during the Mexican War helped to sustain the level of morale necessary for Scott's army to achieve victory and bring the war to a speedy end.

• Wright's papers have not been located. His Civil War career is discussed in Robert E. Denney, *Civil War Medicine: Care and Comfort of the Wounded* (1994); and in *The War of the Rebellion: A Compilation of the Official Records of the Union and Confederate Armies* (128 vols., 1880–1901). Obituaries are in the *Carlisle Herald* and the *Philadelphia Press*, 16 May 1878.

CHARLES W. CAREY, JR.

WRIGHT, J. Skelly (14 Jan. 1911–6 Aug. 1988), jurist, was born James Skelly Wright in New Orleans, Louisiana, the son of James Edward Wright and Margaret Skelly. Wright was raised in a working-class neighborhood. His father was a city building superintendent and plumbing inspector who at times secured minor contracting work. Following his education in the New Orleans public schools, Wright enrolled in Loyola University, where he received his bachelor of philosophy degree in 1931 and his LL.B. in 1934.

Wright taught mathematics and English at Fortier High School from 1931 to 1935 and was a lecturer in English at Loyola from 1936 to 1937. In 1936 his uncle Joseph P. Skelly, a member of the city commission, used his influence with Allen E. Ellender, Louisiana's newly elected U.S. senator, to secure his nephew a job as assistant U.S. attorney in New Orleans. During World War II Wright left the U.S. attorney's office for service as a Coast Guard officer from 1942 to 1945, first commanding a sub-chaser in the North Atlantic and then serving as an attaché at the American embassy in London. In 1945 he married Helen Mitchell Patton, an admiral's daughter working at the embassy. The couple had one son.

After military service Wright returned briefly to New Orleans as senior assistant to U.S. Attorney Herbert Christenberry. But in the spring of 1946 he moved to Washington, D.C., and opened a law office. The next year he entered a partnership with two other attorneys. Wright's practice was devoted largely to maritime and shipping matters, but during this period he also made his first appearance before the Supreme Court in *Louisiana ex rel. Francis v. Resweber* (1947), one of the most bizarre civil liberties cases ever to reach the high bench. Wright's role in this case, involving an African-American defendant, foreshadowed his later efforts on behalf of desegregation and African-American civil rights. The case involved Willie Francis, a young black man sentenced to death for murder. When Louisiana's portable electric chair failed to electrocute Francis, the defendant's father retained a Louisiana lawyer in an effort to block further efforts to carry out Francis's death sentence. Securing no relief for his client in Louisiana's courts, Francis's counsel contacted Wright, asking that he present an appeal to the Supreme Court. Although Wright filed an unusually weak brief on Francis's behalf, he made what Justice Harold Burton would later term a "good" oral argument before the justices, but to no avail. In a five to four vote, the justices "assumed," without holding, that the Fifth and Eighth Amendment guarantees against double jeopardy and cruel and unusual pun-

ishment were binding on the states through the Fourteenth Amendment's due process clause; yet they also held that the case involved no violation of either guarantee but only a mechanical malfunction that the state was entitled to correct. Francis was then executed.

In 1948 Wright returned to New Orleans as U.S. attorney, replacing Herbert Christenberry, whom President Truman had appointed to a federal district judgeship. Somewhat ironically, given his later judicial record, the new U.S. attorney's agenda included an investigation of communism in labor unions. But his tenure in the office was to be brief. In the summer of 1949 a vacancy developed on the Court of Appeals for the Fifth Circuit. As a friend of President Truman's attorney general, Tom Clark, and one of the few Truman supporters in Louisiana during the 1948 election campaign (when most of the state's Democrats bolted from the party for Strom Thurmond's Dixiecrat ticket), Wright stood a good chance of securing the appointment. In fact, his nomination was prepared for submission to the Senate. But at the urging of Fifth Circuit Chief Judge Joseph Hutcheson, who expressed concern about Wright's relative youth, the administration appointed Wayne Borah to the circuit seat and selected Wright to replace Borah on the federal district court for Louisiana's eastern district. At age thirty-eight Wright became the youngest judge on the federal bench.

Shortly after his appointment, the National Association for the Advancement of Colored People (NAACP) began the attack on segregated public schools that would culminate in the Supreme Court's 1954 and 1955 decisions in *Brown v. Board of Education*. Even before *Brown*, however, Wright had ordered the admission of black students to the law school at previously all-white Louisiana State University (LSU) on the grounds that the law school for blacks at Southern University was not equal to the white institution. Later, he ordered a black undergraduate admitted to LSU and mandated desegregation of New Orleans's buses and parks. His efforts to desegregate city buses and parks raised little furor. But Wright's decisions desegregating the New Orleans public schools made him the most despised man in the state.

Bush v. Orleans Parish School Board first arose in 1952, but both NAACP lawyers and the school board agreed with Judge Wright's decision to delay a ruling in the case until after the Supreme Court had decided *Brown*. By 1956, when the suit was reactivated, Louisiana and other Deep South states had embarked upon an assortment of "massive resistance" stratagems designed to maintain complete segregation in the schools, including adoption of complicated pupil placement laws. In February of that year, Wright and other members of a three-judge district court panel struck down Louisiana's pupil placement laws and made clear their opposition to any further such attempts to circumvent *Brown*. Sitting alone, Wright then forbade the New Orleans school board to perpetuate segregation in the city's schools, becoming the first judge of the Fifth Circuit to issue such an order.

The intransigence of state politicians and the NAACP's preoccupation with other cases delayed the beginning of actual desegregation in New Orleans another four years. In May 1960 Wright issued an order requiring the schools to begin desegregating the following September. However, Eisenhower administration officials, privately concerned about the impact of a "second Little Rock" on Republican chances in the November elections, persuaded Wright to delay the order until the beginning of the second term of the school year. Finally, on 14 November 1960, four black first-graders entered two white schools.

By this point, "Smelly," "Judas Scalawag" Wright had become a pariah in his native state. Federal marshals guarded his home and escorted him to and from his chambers. Crosses were burned on his lawn, the judge was hanged in effigy, most of his old friends no longer spoke to him, he and his wife were the regular targets of vile telephone calls, and state politicians denounced him and urged white citizens to defy his orders. At one rally Leander Perez, Louisiana's most rabidly racist political boss and Wright-hater, exhorted his audience, "Don't wait for your daughter to be raped by these Congolese. Don't wait until the burr-heads are forced into your schools. Do something about it now!" (Bass, p. 129). But with the backing of the new Kennedy administration now behind the judge's orders, the resistance effort collapsed.

In 1962 President Kennedy considered appointing Wright to the Fifth Circuit, but fearing opposition from southern senators he chose the judge instead for a seat on the court of appeals for the District of Columbia. Wright served on the circuit bench twenty-five years, retiring in 1987. As senior judge in terms of service, he was the court's chief judge from 1978 to 1981. In 1982 he was also made chief judge of the Temporary Emergency Court of Appeals. Wright died at his home in Westmoreland Hills, Maryland.

During his lengthy tenure in Washington, Wright heard a wide variety of cases dealing with contract law, the scope of the Environmental Protection Act, the rulemaking authority of the Federal Trade Commission, and other sorts of administrative law issues that form an important part of the D.C. circuit's caseload. In the summer of 1971, moreover, he was the sole dissenter on a three-judge panel that issued a temporary restraining order halting the *Washington Post*'s publication of portions of the "Pentagon Papers." He saw his position vindicated eleven days later when the Supreme Court upheld freedom of the press against Nixon administration efforts to prevent the papers' publication. As in New Orleans, however, his most controversial decisions during his Washington years were those issued when he was designated in the 1960s to sit as a district judge to hear *Hobson v. Hanson*, the protracted challenge to de facto segregation in the District of Columbia schools. Emphasizing the detrimental effects of racial segregation, whatever its source, on educational attainment, Wright found little constitutional difference between de jure and de facto segregation and also treated racial and wealth classifications as equivalents.

While a U.S. attorney, Wright had once watched from a window of his office as blind people arrived at the Lighthouse for the Blind across the street for a Christmas Eve party. Sightless whites were escorted into the front of the building, while their black counterparts were led to the rear. That experience had an enormous impact on Wright. An avowed liberal-activist who considered himself fortunate to be able to "make a contribution" toward eliminating such practices, he possessed what one admirer termed a "capacity for outrage" against injustice of every sort. That quality, clearly reflected in his many opinions and off-the-bench writings, was his greatest legacy.

• The J. Skelly Wright Papers are in the Library of Congress. For a quasibiographical study, see Arthur S. Miller, *A "Capacity for Outrage": The Judicial Odyssey of J. Skelly Wright* (1984). Jack Bass, *Unlikely Heroes* (1981), examines Wright's role in the New Orleans desegregation controversy; Donald L. Horowitz, *The Courts and Social Policy* (1977), is a critical analysis of his involvement in school desegregation in the District of Columbia.

TINSLEY E. YARBROUGH

WRIGHT, Louis Tompkins (22 July 1891–8 Oct. 1952), surgeon, hospital administrator, and civil rights leader, was born in La Grange, Georgia, the son of Ceah Ketcham Wright, a physician and clergyman, and Lula Tompkins. After his father's death in 1895, his mother married William Fletcher Penn, a physician who was the first African American to graduate from Yale University Medical School. Raised and educated in Atlanta, Wright received his elementary, secondary, and college education at Clark University in Atlanta, graduating in 1911 as valedictorian of his class. His stepfather was one of the guiding influences that led to his choice of medicine as a career.

Wright graduated from Harvard Medical School, cum laude and fourth in his class, in 1915. While in medical school he exhibited his willingness to take a strong stand against racial injustice when he successfully opposed a hospital policy that would have barred him (but not his white classmates) from the practicum in delivering babies (obstetrics) at Boston-Lying-In Hospital. Despite an early record of publications, because of restrictions based on race, Wright completed an internship during 1915–1916 at Freedmen's Hospital, the teaching hospital at the Howard University School of Medicine in Washington, D.C., one of only three black hospitals with approved internship programs at that time.

While he was an intern at Freedmen's Wright rejected a claim in the medical literature that the Schick test for diptheria could not be used on African Americans because of their heavy skin pigmentation. A study he conducted proved the validity of the usefulness of this test on dark-skinned people and was the basis of his second published paper, "The Schick Test, with Especial Reference to the Negro" (*Journal of Infectious Diseases* 21 [1917]: 265–68). Wright returned to Atlanta in July 1916 to practice medicine. In Atlanta he launched his civil rights career as a founding member of the Atlanta branch of the National Association for the Advancement of Colored People (NAACP), serving as its first treasurer (1916–1917).

With the onset of World War I, Wright applied for a military commission and became a first lieutenant in the U.S. Army Medical Corps. A month before going overseas in June 1918, he married Corrine M. Cooke in New York City. They would have two daughters, both of whom would become physicians: Jane Cooke Wright and Barbara Penn Wright.

While Wright was in France, his unit was gassed with phosgene, causing him permanent lung damage. Because his injury (for which he received a Purple Heart) imposed physical limitations, he served out the rest of the war in charge of the surgical wards at three field hospitals. As a medical officer he introduced the intradermal method for smallpox vaccination ("Intradermal Vaccination against Smallpox," *Journal of the American Medical Association* 71 [1918]: 654–57), which was officially adopted by the U.S. Army.

In 1919, when Wright settled in Harlem to start a general medical practice, Harlem Hospital, a municipal facility with a 90 percent black patient population, had no African-American doctors or nurses on staff. With an assignment effective 1 January 1920 as a clinical assistant (the lowest rank) in the Out-Patient Department, he became the first African American to be appointed to the staff of a New York City hospital. His steadfast and successful efforts during the 1920s working with hospital administrators and with city officials led gradually to appointments for other African Americans as interns and attending physicians. His push for greater opportunities for African-American professionals at Harlem Hospital culminated in a reorganization mandated in 1930 by William Schroeder, commissioner of the Department of Hospitals for the City of New York. The result was the first genuine effort to racially integrate the entire medical staff of a major U.S. hospital. By then Wright had risen to the position of visiting surgeon, and in October 1934 he became the second African American to be admitted to the American College of Surgeons (established in 1913). In 1938 he was appointed to a one-year term as the hospital's director of surgery. In 1929 he had achieved yet another breakthrough, as the first African American to be appointed as a police surgeon through the city's competitive civil service examination. He retained the position until his death.

In 1935 Wright was elected chairman of the national board of directors of the NAACP, a position he held until 1952. As a civil rights leader he opposed the establishment of hospitals exclusively for black people, and in the 1940s he argued for national health care insurance; he also challenged discriminatory policies and practices of the powerful American Medical Association. In a published open letter (dated 28 Jan. 1931) in response to an offer from the Julius Rosenwald Fund to build a hospital for blacks in New York City, Wright wrote: "A segregated hospital makes the white person feel superior and the black person feel inferior. It sets the black person apart from all other citizens as being a different kind of citizen and a different kind of medical student and physician, which you know and we know is not the case. What the Negro physician needs is equal opportunity for training and practice—no more, no less."

Treating common injuries in the surgical wards of Harlem Hospital led Wright to develop, in 1936, a device for handling fractured and dislocated neck vertebrae. In addition to this neck brace, he also designed a special metal plate to treat certain fractures of the femur. He became an expert on bone injuries and in 1937 was asked to write the chapter on head injuries for Charles Scudder's monumental textbook *The Treatment of Fractures* (1938), this being the first contribution by an African American to a major authoritative medical text.

Wright became ill with tuberculosis in 1939 and for nearly three years was confined to Biggs Memorial Hospital in Ithaca, New York. In 1939, while hospitalized, he was elected a diplomate of the American Board of Surgery. The year before, *Life* magazine had recognized him as the "most eminent Negro doctor" in the United States. In 1940 he was awarded the NAACP's prestigious Spingarn Medal for his achievements and contributions to American medicine.

In 1942, after returning to Harlem Hospital, Wright was appointed director of surgery, a position he held until his death. In 1945 he established a certified four-year residency program in surgery, a first for a black hospital. In 1948 he led a team of resident doctors in the first clinical trials of the antibiotic aureomycin with human beings. This pioneering testing at Harlem Hospital and subsequently at other hospitals paved the way for the approval of this drug and eventually other antibiotics by the U.S. Food and Drug Administration. In 1948 he established and became director of the Harlem Hospital Cancer Research Foundation, funded by the U.S. Public Health Service. Perhaps his crowning achievement was his election, that year, as president of the hospital's medical board.

Over the course of his long career at Harlem Hospital, Wright welded together into a harmonious whole the various white and black groups within the hospital. He recognized and confronted directly the problems faced by other ethnic professionals, particularly Jewish and Italian-American physicians, so that shortly before his death, at the dedication of the hospital's Louis T. Wright Library, he said, "Harlem Hospital represents to my mind the finest example of democracy at work in the field of medicine."

Wright died in New York City. His presence at Harlem Hospital and on the national civil rights scene, and his voice and actions in public and private health forums and debates, had significant consequences on American medicine in three areas: it led to a rapport between black and white doctors that generated scientific and clinical research yielding important contributions in several areas of medicine; it dispensed with myths regarding black physicians that excluded them from any hospital staff on grounds other than those related to individual competence and character; and it led to the admittance of qualified physicians who were African American into local and national medical and scientific societies.

• Wright published eighty-nine scientific articles in leading medical journals: thirty-five on antibiotics, fourteen in the field of cancer, six on bone trauma, and others on various surgical procedures on the colon and the repair of gunshot wounds. For additional information on Wright and a list of his publications, see William Montague Cobb, "Louis Tompkins Wright, 1891–1952," *Journal of the National Medical Association* 45 (Mar. 1953): 130–48. For more on his tenure at Harlem Hospital, see Aubre de L'Maynard, *Surgeons to the Poor: The Harlem Hospital Story* (1978). An obituary is in the *New York Times*, 9 Oct. 1952.

ROBERT C. HAYDEN

WRIGHT, Lucy (5 Feb. 1760–7 Feb. 1821), first Elder of the United Society of Believers in Christ's Second Appearing (the Shakers), was born in Pittsfield, Massachusetts, the daughter of John Wright and Martha "Molly" Robbins. John Wright is characterized by Shaker historian Calvin Green as a "respectable plebian." Though her mother died when Lucy Wright was still a child, her biographer notes that she "acquired an uncommon education for those times" (Green, "Memoir of Lucy Wright," p. 2).

Lucy Wright was married at age nineteen to Elizur Goodrich, a young merchant who, within a few months, joined the small Shaker church at Niskeyuna, New York (near Albany). At this time, the Shakers were a small band of pious, celibate English immigrants, known for their "strange" primitive Christian ecstatic religious behavior (for which they were originally named in derision the "Shaking Quakers," or Shakers). They testified that Christ had made the promised second appearing, ushering in a new millennialistic era. Their leader, the illiterate charismatic Englishwoman Ann Lee, held that confession of sins to a Shaker elder and celibacy were the beginning of a life of earthly salvation from sin.

Lucy Wright joined the Shakers several months after her husband (resuming her maiden name at about this time because she was now "married to the lamb"). When Ann Lee and some of her closest associates left for an itinerant missionary tour through southeastern New England in May 1781, Wright remained in charge of the Sisterhood at Niskeyuna (later called Watervliet). After Ann Lee died in 1784, the remnant of the Shaker church was headed for a brief period by Lee's English successor, James Whittaker (1784–1787). Later Joseph Meacham, the Connecticut Baptist convert who emerged as the next heir to Lee, had the "Mother gift"—the revelation that future Shaker church organization required a parallel male and female leadership structure, a "joint parentage." Wright was selected by Meacham to be his partner in spiritual and political governance, and she assumed her office in 1788. In the year of his death in 1796, Meacham explicitly appointed her his successor, affirming his

view of her "as one whom I esteem my Equal in order & Lot according to thy sex."

During the nine years in which Lucy Wright and Joseph Meacham were joint leaders of the United Society, the eleven eastern Shaker communities were organized. Though specific documentation for this period is scanty, Wright probably played a major role in helping choose male and female leaders for the communities forming in New York, Massachusetts, Connecticut, New Hampshire, and Maine. After Meacham's death, Wright and her subordinates in the central ministry at New Lebanon sent missionaries to the Kentucky Revival (1805–1806), thus "reopening the testimony" and again seeking new converts after a period of separatist withdrawal from "the world." Six new Shaker communities were founded in Ohio and Kentucky in the first two decades of the nineteenth century as a result of this decision.

Meacham and Wright together had resisted publishing a full account of Shaker beliefs, fearing that persecution would increase if Shaker enemies had access in writing to the Believers' unconventional doctrines. When the missionary venture to the west required a clear and complete exposition of Shakerism for potential converts, however, Wright agreed to authorize the publication of a series of major foundational, theological, and historical writings. These included *The Testimony of Christ's Second Appearing* (1808), in which Benjamin S. Youngs first articulated publicly the Shaker doctrine of the dual-gender godhead (by which the father aspect of the creator god was balanced by Holy Mother Wisdom, just as the male aspect of the Redeemer, in Jesus, had been balanced and completed by the "second appearance" in the female form of Ann Lee); and *Testimonies of the Life, Character, Revelations and Doctrines of Our Ever Blessed Mother Ann Lee* (1816), a remarkable collection of oral-historical testimonial in which early Shaker history and memories of founder Ann Lee are embodied. Wright's other innovations included the choreographed symbolic religious dancing that was to distinguish Shaker worship for nearly a century and a school system established with her active support, after over a decade of rejection of worldly book learning.

Wright's authority as a female first Elder was questioned repeatedly during her administration, but she weathered all such challenges. Her male supporters rebuked one prominent critic of the United Society's "petticoat government" in 1816 with a letter asserting her right as a woman to head the society: "Whether Christ governs us through the medium of man, or woman, it is the same unction from the Holy One, and we are equally satisfied," they wrote.

Wright died in Watervliet, New York, and was revered after her death as Shakerism's "second Mother." Manuscript collections of her sayings have remained in continuous use by Ann Lee's spiritual descendants down to the present day.

• Wright's correspondence and sayings are to be found in the Western Reserve Historical Society's Shaker manuscript collection (Cleveland, Ohio). Important primary sources illuminating her activities as a Shaker first Elder include Angell Matthewson's "Reminiscences" (New York Public Library Shaker collection); Calvin Green's "Memoir of Lucy Wright" (1864), "Biographic Memoir of Calvin Green," and biography of Joseph Meacham (all in Western Reserve); and the seceder Thomas Brown's *An Account of the People Called Shakers* (1812). A modern selection of her correspondence and sayings is included in Jean M. Humez, *Mother's First Born Daughters: Early Shaker Writings on Women and Religion* (1993).

Assessments of her influence from a Shaker point of view include Anna White and Leila Taylor, *Shakerism: Its Meaning and Message* (1904), and Frances Carr, "Lucy Wright: the First Mother in the Revelation and Order of the First Organized Church," *Shaker Quarterly* 15, nos. 3 and 4 (1987): 93–100 and 128–31. See also Edward Deming Andrews, *The People Called Shakers* (1953); Priscilla J. Brewer, *Shaker Communities, Shaker Lives* (1986); Stephen A. Marini, *Radical Sects of Revolutionary New England* (1982); Jean M. Humez, "'Ye Are My Epistles': The Construction of Ann Lee Imagery in Early Shaker Sacred Literature," *Journal of Feminist Studies in Religion* 8, no. 1 (1992): 83–103, and "'Weary of Petticoat Government': The Specter of Female Rule in Early Nineteenth-Century Shaker Politics," *Communal Societies* 11 (1991): 1–17; and Stephen J. Stein, *The Shaker Experience in America: A History of the United Society of Believers* (1992).

JEAN M. HUMEZ

WRIGHT, Mabel Osgood (26 Jan. 1859–16 July 1934), naturalist and author, was born in New York City, the daughter of Samuel Osgood, a Unitarian minister, and Ellen Haswell Murdock. Her father, a member of William Cullen Bryant's literary circle, was the pastor of the Church of the Messiah in New York City from 1849 to 1869, after which he entered the Episcopal ministry. Susanna Haswell Rowson, author of *Charlotte Temple* (1791), was a grandaunt.

Wright was raised in a large house in lower Manhattan at a time when much of New York City was still rural. She was educated at home and at Miss Lucy Green's school for girls at Number One Fifth Avenue in Greenwich Village. Her early interest in nature was encouraged by her father and developed during long vacations at "Mosswood," the family summer home in Fairfield, Connecticut. In 1884 she married James Osborne Wright, a British bibliographer and rare book dealer, and divided her time between Fairfield and New York City. She had no children.

Apart from a few poems she published at age sixteen in the *New York Evening Post*, Wright's first printed work was a nature essay titled "A New England May-Day," published in the *Evening Post* in 1893. This and ten other essays, some of which appeared in the *New York Times*, were reprinted in 1894 as *The Friendship of Nature*, her first major book. According to Frank Chapman, curator of birds at the American Museum of Natural History, the book "records a loving intimacy with birds and flowers and seasons with the charm of one who sees keenly, feels deeply, and writes eloquently and sincerely" (*Bird-Lore*, July–Aug. 1934). *Birdcraft* (1895), Wright's second book, was one of the

earliest inexpensive field guides to birds. Reprinted nine times, it was the leading guide to bird identification until the appearance of Roger Tory Peterson's *Field Guide to the Birds* (1934). *Flowers and Ferns in Their Haunts* (1901) is a companion guide to plant life.

An outspoken advocate of bird preservation, Wright founded the Audubon Society of the State of Connecticut in 1898 and served as its first president until 1925. She also served on the board of directors of the National Association of Audubon Societies (now the National Audubon Society) from its organization in 1905 until 1928 and was named an associate member of the American Ornithologists' Union in 1895 and a member in 1901.

Wright contributed many articles to *Bird-Lore* magazine (now *Audubon*), which was edited by Chapman for thirty years and was published, like all of Wright's books, by Macmillan. For the magazine's first seven years, from 1899 to 1906, Wright served as editor of the Audubon department, writing opinion pieces in support of bird conservation and contributing articles about the habits and haunts of various species. From 1907 to 1910 she edited the school department, where she developed an ambitious campaign to educate young people about birds—preparing pamphlets, sponsoring contests, and encouraging teachers to organize Audubon chapters in their schools.

Wright's efforts at nature education extended beyond the pages of *Bird-Lore* to her eight children's books, two of which—*Tommy-Anne and the Three Hearts* (1896) and *Wabeno, the Magician* (1899), a sequel—together constitute "one of the most ambitious works of nature fiction for children published in the nineteenth century," according to Robert Welker. *Citizen Bird* (1897), a bird book for beginners written with naturalist Elliott Coues, features the first major series of drawings by Louis Agassiz Fuertes, and *Four-footed Americans and Their Kin* (1898), a sequel, was edited by Chapman and illustrated by artist-naturalist Ernest Thompson Seton. *Gray Lady and the Birds* (1907) is a teaching guide to birds.

In addition to her books for children, from 1901 to 1913 Wright produced ten works of fiction for adults, the most popular of which were the semiautobiographical "Barbara" books, beginning with *The Garden of a Commuter's Wife* (1901), a chatty how-to manual containing plant lists, diary entries, letters, and sketches. Though she seemed to value these books more than her nature writing, Wright never fully mastered the novel form, and her romances in particular feature contrived circumstances, undeveloped characters, and stilted speech. Nevertheless, many of these works address the effects of urbanization on society and reveal Wright's views on suburban life, marriage, and the proper role of women.

After 1913 Wright devoted most of her time to the development of Birdcraft Sanctuary, a ten-acre plot of land near her home in Fairfield. Established in 1914, Birdcraft was the first songbird sanctuary to be established by a state Audubon society. The sanctuary is "an oasis in a desert of material things," Wright wrote in *Bird-Lore* (July–Aug. 1915). "In it the bird may lead its own life for that life's sake, and the joy of many of such lives overflows all arbitrary boundaries in its ethical benefit to the community and state." Still an active facility of the Connecticut Audubon Society, Birdcraft was named a National Historic Landmark in 1993.

Following her husband's death in 1920, Wright produced three more books, including *My New York* (1926), her autobiography. Though a charming portrait of mid-nineteenth-century Manhattan, *My New York* is limited as an autobiography, revealing little of Wright's personal life and covering only the years prior to her engagement. Wright died at her home in Fairfield.

Part of the first generation of American women nature writers, Wright counted among her contemporaries Olive Thorne Miller, Florence Merriam Bailey, and Neltje Blanchan Doubleday, and her books helped to introduce thousands of Americans to the pleasures of natural history. As the title of her book *Citizen Bird* suggests, Wright was also "an early exponent of the doctrine that all living creatures, not just human beings, had their natural rights" (Brooks, p. 168), and she deserves to be remembered as much for her active role as a conservationist as for her achievements as a writer and editor.

• Wright's papers are housed in Connecticut at the Bridgeport Public Library, the Fairfield Historical Society, the Fairfield Public Library, and the Birdcraft Sanctuary and Museum, and in New York City at the American Museum of Natural History. Wright's own *My New York* (1926), her semiautobiographical novels, and her contributions to *Bird-Lore* through July–Aug. 1934 provide valuable information. Frank M. Chapman describes his encounters with Wright in *Autobiography of a Bird-lover* (1933). Her life and work are discussed in Robert Henry Welker, *Birds and Men* (1955); Paul Brooks, *Speaking for Nature* (1980); Felton Gibbons and Deborah Strom, *Neighbors to the Birds* (1988); and Frank Graham, *The Audubon Ark* (1990). Examples of Wright's literary criticism can be found in *The Critic* 42 (Apr. 1903): 308–11, and the *New York Times Book Review*, 9 Dec. 1905, p. 872. Obituaries are in the *Auk*, Oct. 1934; *Bird-Lore*, July–Aug. 1934; and the *New York Times*, 18 July 1934 (which gives an incorrect death date of 17 July).

DANIEL J. PHILIPPON

WRIGHT, Martha Coffin Pelham (25 Dec. 1806–4 Jan. 1875), women's rights advocate, was born in Boston, Massachusetts, the daughter of Thomas Coffin, a ship captain, merchant, and factory owner, and Anna Folger. Martha's father died in 1815 after losing his nail factory to creditors, leaving her mother with four young children. Anna Coffin opened a small shop and ran a boardinghouse, soon paying off her late husband's remaining debts and educating her children in private Quaker boarding schools. In part, Wright's mother survived this ordeal with help from the Philadelphia Quaker community that the Coffins had joined when they moved to that city in 1811. However, it was also Anna Coffin's personal strength that sustained her, a strength her youngest daughter shared.

In 1824, a month before her eighteenth birthday, Martha Coffin defied her mother and married one of the boarders. Peter Pelham was an army captain, and he soon moved his young bride to Florida. Two years later Martha Coffin Pelham was a widow herself, living again in Philadelphia with her mother and her infant daughter. In 1827 she moved to Aurora, New York, to teach in a school Anna Coffin had just opened. She married a local lawyer, David Wright, in 1829 and over the next nineteen years had six more children, five of whom lived to adulthood. In 1848, the same year that Martha Coffin Wright gave birth to her seventh and last child, she joined her more famous sister, Lucretia Coffin Mott, in the cause of women's rights.

Lucretia and her husband, James Mott, were Quakers as well as prominent abolitionists. In the summer of 1848, when the Motts were visiting the Wrights in their Auburn, New York, home, Jane Hunt, a local Quaker woman, invited Martha Wright and her visiting sister to tea. Also invited was Elizabeth Cady Stanton, another active abolitionist who lived in nearby Seneca Falls. This tea party on 13 July gave birth to the Seneca Falls Convention, at which the nineteenth-century women's rights movement began. The convention itself, organized by these same women, was held only six days after their initial meeting. Those in attendance heard speeches from Lucretia Mott and Frederick Douglass, an escaped slave turned ardent abolitionist. For her part, Wright injected some satire into the gathering by reading several articles that looked humorously at the status of women in mid-nineteenth-century America.

It was that status—the lack of property rights, lack of rights in marriage, and especially the lack of voting rights—that Wright devoted the rest of her life to changing as she met the demands of motherhood at the same time. Throughout the 1850s she led convention after convention devoted to gathering more support for the rights of women. At the time, demanding these rights was seen as an extremely radical position, and Wright knew that achieving those rights meant a long struggle. In 1855, after presiding over women's rights conventions in Albany and Saratoga, New York, and in Cincinnati, Ohio, she wrote fellow activist Susan B. Anthony that "people are getting a little more accustomed to the demand for the Right of Suffrage, and will soon cease to ridicule."

While advocating the rights of women, Wright was also deeply involved in the fight against slavery. Although many abolitionists were also ardent supporters of the cause of women, they felt it most expedient to concentrate on gaining the freedom of millions of enslaved African Americans as the crisis over slavery accelerated toward the Civil War. Wright agreed with this tactic, but once the war had ended she split with those who felt that tying woman suffrage to the fight to gain the vote for the newly freed African-American males would jeopardize that cause. Instead, she sided with her old friends Anthony and Stanton, who refused to support any constitutional amendment that would guarantee the right to vote for African-American men but omitted women of any race. The women's movement would be divided over this issue for the next twenty years.

Those women who supported the Fifteenth Amendment, which gave all men the right to vote regardless of color, formed the American Woman Suffrage Association in 1869. That same year, Wright joined Anthony and Stanton in forming the National Woman Suffrage Association (NWSA), a more radical organization that put forward the controversial Victoria Woodhull as its own presidential candidate in 1872. The NWSA frequently resorted to direct action, encouraging members to vote in local elections and, when denied that right, to place their ballots in a special protest box. Wright's love of satire, evident in her letters to family members and the poems she wrote for special occasions, shaped much of the level of protest the NWSA engaged in during its early years. Although she usually played a secondary role to her more famous sister, Mott, as well as to the more outspoken Anthony and Stanton, Wright's tireless dedication to the cause of women's rights earned her the presidency of the NWSA in 1874. Forty-five years after her death in Boston, her goal of woman suffrage finally became a reality. In 1920 the passage of the Nineteenth Amendment was achieved in part because of the efforts of Martha Coffin Wright.

• Wright's papers are part of the Garrison Family Papers, Sophia Smith Collection, Smith College. While many secondary sources discuss the women's rights movement during the nineteenth century, the standards remain Ellen Carol Dubois, *Feminism and Suffrage: The Emergence of an Independent Women's Movement in America, 1848–1869* (1978), and Eleanor Flexner, *Century of Struggle: The Woman's Rights Movement in the United States*, rev. ed. (1975).

KATHLEEN BANKS NUTTER

WRIGHT, Mary Clabaugh (25 Sept. 1917–18 June 1970), sinologist and historian, was born Mary Oliver Clabaugh in Tuscaloosa, Alabama, the daughter of Samuel F. Clabaugh, a businessman and the publisher of the *Tuscaloosa News*, and Mary Duncan. Mary received an A.B. in languages from Vassar College in 1938. She then studied European history and Chinese civilization at Radcliffe, receiving her M.A. in 1939.

Mary married sinologist Arthur F. Wright in 1940 in Washington, D.C., before leaving to do research in Japan and China; they had two sons. Wright and her husband were in Beijing, China, conducting research when Japan declared war on the United States in 1941. Subsequently, they were interned by the Japanese in a Shantung prisoner of war camp. Her studies of the Taiping Rebellion (1849–1865) were thus interrupted, but she was able to refine her language facility in Chinese, Japanese, and Russian. At the end of World War II Wright remained in China to gather documents and accounts of the Nationalist Revolution for the Hoover Institute at Stanford University. In 1946 she met and interviewed Mao Tse-Tung (Mao Zedong) in Yenon. Returning to the United States in 1947, she served as a faculty member and the curator of the Chinese collection at the Hoover Institute until 1959. She received her doctorate from Radcliffe in 1951.

In the early 1950s Wright became a critic of Senator Joseph McCarthy's investigations into government spying. She also defended Owen Lattimore's academic freedom to criticize the China policy of the United States after the defeat of the Nationalist government in the civil war (1947–1949). In the presidential elections of 1952 and 1956 she was an active supporter of Democrat Adlai Stevenson, and as early as the 1950s she was already a critic of U.S. policies in Vietnam. Wright's position was not based on ideology but the right of academics to disagree with established State Department policies based on historical and objective evaluations of the political state of affairs in Asia.

Wright's first book was published in 1957. Based on her Radcliffe dissertation, *The Last Stand of Chinese Conservatism: The T'ung Chih Restoration, 1862–1874* (1957) examined the failed Confucian revival after the Taiping Rebellion and chronicled the efforts of the Ch'ing government to play foreign powers off against each other. Drawing on her research into more than 4,000 volumes of documents, Wright succeeded in showing a Chinese society that tried to preserve the stabilizing elements of tradition while reaching for segments of Western science, technology, and culture designed to modernize Chinese civilization and preserve its independence from Western political imperialism. In the end, Ch'ing leadership was incapable of effecting significant change and was overthrown.

With the growth of her reputation as a scholar, Wright was invited in 1959 to become the first tenured woman faculty member in the College of Arts and Sciences at Yale University. In 1961 she was named the director of the Chinese Studies Program. Respected for her work as a scholar and her courage and strength of character, she was appointed a trustee of Wesleyan College in 1969. Sadly, she died the following year of lung cancer in Guilford, Connecticut. Wright is considered a leader among American sinologists who studied the Nationalist Revolution. She was called by John King Fairbank, the "dean" of China experts, "most daring . . . ambitious . . . a major historian" (*American Historical Review* [Oct. 1970]: 1885).

As the founder of the Society of Ch'ing Studies and its publication, the *Ch'ing-Shih Wen-T'i*, Wright provided the major vehicle for Chinese scholars to publish their work on the 300-year-old Ch'ing period. Of special interest was the nineteenth-century spirit of nationalism that grew in China against the Manchu dynasty. The role of secret societies throughout many Chinese cities and the provincial countryside played a major role in attracting followers who expressed a belief in antiforeign efforts to rid China of undue Western influence and the alliances between foreign states and the Ch'ing government. Eventually many of these secret groups joined in the Nationalist political movement for a modern Chinese state.

• Some of Wright's materials and records, including letters, are in the Stanford University and Radcliffe College library archives. Her other publications include "The Adaptability of Ch'ing Diplomacy: The Case of Korea," *Journal of Asian Studies* 18 (1958): 363–81, concerning the Manchu use of alliances and the balance of power; "From Revolution to Restoration: The Transformation of Kuomintang Ideology," *Far Eastern Quarterly* 14 (Aug. 1955): 515–32, an analysis of political reactionism within the Nationalist movement; *Approaches to Modern Chinese History* (1967), edited with Albert Feuerwerker; and *China in Revolution: The First Phase, 1900–1913* (1968), the edited proceedings of the Ch'ing Society's research conference of 1965. Obituaries are in the *New York Times*, 19 June 1970, and the *American Historical Review* 75 (Oct. 1970).

SALVATORE PRISCO

WRIGHT, Muriel Hazel (31 Mar. 1889–27 Feb. 1975), historian and Choctaw activist, was born in Lehigh, Choctaw Nation, Indian Territory, the daughter of Eliphalet Nott Wright, a doctor, and Ida Belle Richards, a Presbyterian missionary teacher. Wright's one-fourth Choctaw descent was through her paternal grandfather, the Reverend Allen Wright, principal chief of the Choctaw Nation from 1866 to 1870, who proposed the name of Oklahoma for Indian Territory. Her father practiced medicine in the Choctaw Nation and served as company physician for the Missouri-Pacific Coal Mines. Throughout Wright's youth, her father held several influential positions as a Choctaw delegate to the U.S. government during the allotment and disposition of Indian lands and the abolition of tribal governments prior to Oklahoma statehood in 1907.

Wright's early childhood education came from Presbyterian and Baptist elementary schools and home schooling from her mother when adequate schools were unavailable. The Wright family traveled frequently to Washington, D.C., New York City, St. Louis, and Canada, and Wright was inspired by a visit from her maternal aunt and uncle, Dr. and Mrs. James Dixon, when they returned from an assignment as Presbyterian missionaries to Japan. In 1906 Wright entered Wheaton College in Norton, Massachusetts, but left in December 1908 to accompany her parents to Washington, D.C. The family lived in a hotel, and Wright studied history and the classics privately. Upon her return to Oklahoma in 1911, she entered East Central State College in Ada to pursue a teaching degree, and she graduated in 1912. She hoped to earn a master of arts degree in history and English at Barnard College, which she attended in 1916, but World War I ended her opportunity for further education. An intense spirit of patriotism and her father's exhaustive efforts to develop a new oil field drew her back to Oklahoma to serve the needs of her family and her state.

Wright held a number of teaching and administrative positions in the rural schools of southeastern Oklahoma. She taught history, English, and Latin, often serving as girls basketball coach, class play director, and principal as well. School facilities and sup-

plies proved the greatest challenge. Wright generally instructed the higher grades, sometimes in a one-room school separated from grades one through four by a curtain. She organized her students into a mutual benefit league that performed the janitorial chores for the school. The ten dollars per month the school board provided for janitorial service the students invested in a bank account, drawing upon it to purchase necessary supplies so that all students at the school had adequate materials.

Wright's family background, her academic training and love of history, and her awareness of the ignorance of most Americans regarding the significance of Native Americans in the history of her home state and the nation propelled her life work in two directions. Never married, Wright devoted her time and energy to both activism in Indian affairs and historical research and writing. Wright participated in Choctaw tribal business, first as an aide to her father and, after his death, on her own. From 1922 to 1928 she served as secretary to the Choctaw Committee and from 1934 to 1944 as secretary to the Choctaw Advisory Council; both groups were concerned with the resolution of conflicts over Choctaw lands and resources. In this capacity she kept tribal records, compiled reports, prepared correspondence, and mediated among interest groups. She published articles in the *Tuskahoman*, the official Choctaw newspaper, and became the driving force behind the preservation of the original Choctaw Council House at Tuskahoma. Wright was also instrumental in founding the National Hall of Fame for Famous American Indians in Anadarko, Oklahoma, in 1952 and served on its board of officers until 1974.

Extensive research projects she began in the 1930s and 1940s led to the reproduction and publication of the official seals and banners of the Five Civilized Tribes and the creation of the "Fourteen Flags over Oklahoma" exhibit illustrating the history of the area and the various international claims to it. The display appeared as the Oklahoma theme at the New York World's Fair in 1964–1965 and later was moved to the south entrance to the Oklahoma Capitol Complex in Oklahoma City. Throughout her life Wright traveled across Oklahoma researching, mapping, and marking historic sites. Serving on the Historic Sites Committee, Wright identified, wrote descriptions of, and published information about more than 600 locations significant to Oklahoma history.

Between 1929 and 1974 Wright wrote or coauthored twelve books on Oklahoma and Indian history, including three history textbooks with accompanying workbooks for public school classroom use. Remembering her own lifelong pursuit of education, Wright believed that "maximum truth as revealed through study is the strength of intellectual development" (Fischer, p. 19). She published her most significant book, *Guide to the Indian Tribes of Oklahoma*, in 1951, and it continues to be a useful reference source. Wright accomplished her most valuable work, however, as editor of the *Chronicles of Oklahoma*, a journal of scholarly studies published by the Oklahoma Historical Society. From 1943 to 1973 Wright directed the quarterly publication, insisting on high standards of scholarship, critical evaluation of issues, a diversity of articles from all periods of Oklahoma history, and an emphasis on primary sources. She made the "Notes and Documents" section an ongoing source of exciting primary materials inviting further investigation, and she captured biographical and oral history sources that would otherwise have been lost to historians. During her tenure she wrote or edited ninety-five articles for the journal and reviewed twenty-nine books. Wright's work emphasized the intelligence, dignity, and integrity of Native Americans and their positive contributions to the development of the state. Indeed, her unfavorable review of *The Rise and Fall of the Choctaw Republic* created a lifelong rivalry with its author, Oklahoma's nationally known female historian, Angie Debo. When Debo suggested the complicity of Native American leadership with white corruption in land dispossession, Wright accused her of prejudice, error, and faulty research.

Wright received numerous awards both during her lifetime and posthumously. She was inducted into the Oklahoma Hall of Fame in 1940; received citations from the American Pen Women, the Oklahoma City Business and Professional Women's Club, and Soroptimist International; and in 1971 the North American Indian Women's Association honored her as the outstanding Indian woman of the twentieth century. She died in Oklahoma City. Recognizing her many contributions to the preservation of Oklahoma history, the Oklahoma Historical Society named her one of the first inductees to the newly created Oklahoma Historians Hall of Fame in 1993.

• The largest repository of information on Muriel Wright is at the Oklahoma Historical Society in Oklahoma City, but her life must be constructed from several collections: the Muriel Wright Collection, Minutes from the Choctaw Council and Choctaw Advisory Council, Records of the National Hall of Fame for Famous American Indians, and Records and Minutes of the Oklahoma Historical Society. Angie Debo's conflict with Wright is explored in the Angie Debo Collection at Oklahoma State University, Stillwater. Wright published an article about her father, "A Brief Review of the Life of Doctor Eliphalet Nott Wright (1858–1932)," in *Chronicles of Oklahoma* 10 (June 1932): 267–86. The best profile of Wright's career is LeRoy H. Fischer, "Muriel H. Wright, Historian of Oklahoma," *Chronicles of Oklahoma* 52 (Spring 1974): 3–29. It includes a comprehensive bibliography of Wright's publications. A brief tribute, Ed Montgomery, "Keeping Our History Bright," is in *Orbit: Magazine of the Sunday Oklahoman*, 26 May 1968, pp. 4–6.

LINDA W. REESE

WRIGHT, Orville. *See* Wright, Wilbur, and Orville Wright.

WRIGHT, Richard (4 Sept. 1908–28 Nov. 1960), author, was born Richard Nathaniel Wright on Rucker's Plantation, between Roxie and Natchez, Mississippi, the son of Nathaniel Wright, an illiterate sharecropper, and Ella Wilson, a schoolteacher. When Wright was five, his father left the family and his mother was forced to take domestic jobs away from the house. Wright and his brother spent a period at an orphanage. Around 1920 Ella Wright became a paralytic, and the family moved from Natchez to Jackson, then to Elaine, Arkansas, and back to Jackson to live with Wright's maternal grandparents, who were restrictive Seventh-day Adventists. Wright moved from school to school, graduating from the ninth grade at the Smith Robertson Junior High School in Jackson as the class valedictorian in June 1925. Wright had published his first short story, "The Voodoo of Hell's Half-Acre," in three parts in the *Southern Register* in 1924, but no copies survive. His staunchly religious and illiterate grandmother, Margaret Bolden Wilson, kept books out of the house and thought fiction was the work of the devil. Wright kept any aspirations he had to be a writer to himself after his first experience with publication.

After grade school Wright attended Lanier High School but dropped out after a few weeks to work; he took a series of odd jobs to save enough money to leave for Memphis, which he did at age seventeen. While in Memphis he worked as a dishwasher and delivery boy and for an optical company. He began to read contemporary American literature as well as commentary by H. L. Mencken, which struck him with particular force. As Wright reveals in his autobiography *Black Boy*, he borrowed the library card of an Irish co-worker and forged notes to the librarian so he could read: "Dear Madam: Will you please let this nigger boy have some books by H. L. Mencken?" Determined to leave the South before he would irretrievably overstep the bounds of Jim Crow restrictions on blacks, Wright took the train to Chicago in December 1927.

In Chicago Wright worked at the post office, at Michael Reese Hospital taking care of lab animals, and as an insurance agent, among other jobs. There, in 1932, he became involved in the John Reed Club, an intellectual arm of the Communist party, which he joined the next March. By 1935 he found work with the Federal Negro Theater in Chicago under the Federal Writers' Project. He wrote some short stories and a novel during this time, but they were not published until after his death. In 1937 Wright moved to New York City, where he helped start *New Challenge* magazine and was the Harlem editor of the *Daily Worker* as well as coeditor of *Left Front*. Wright's literary career was launched when his short story collection, *Uncle Tom's Children* (1938), won first prize for the *Story* magazine contest open to Federal Writer's Project authors for best book-length manuscript. Harper's published this collection with "Fire and Cloud," "Long Black Song," "Down by the Riverside," and "Big Boy Leaves Home"; in 1940 the story "Bright and Morning Star" was added, and the book was reissued. *Native Son* followed in 1940, the first bestselling novel by a black American writer and the first Book-of-the-Month Club selection by an African-American writer. It sold 215,000 copies in its first three weeks of publication. *Native Son* made Wright the most respected and wealthiest black writer in America; he was awarded the National Association for the Advancement of Colored People's prestigious Spingarn Medal in 1941. After *Uncle Tom's Children*, Wright declared in "How Bigger Was Born" that he needed to write a book that bankers' daughters would not be able to "read and feel good about," that would "be so hard and deep that they would have to face it without the consolation of tears"; *Native Son* is uncompromising.

In *Native Son*, Wright presents his guilt-of-the-nation thesis. His main character, Bigger Thomas, is a nineteen-year-old edgy small-time criminal from Chicago's South Side ghetto. The novel races with no stops in between the three parts: Book I, Fear; Book II, Flight; and Book III, Fate. When Bigger is offered a job as a chauffeur for a wealthy white family, he imagines himself in various fanciful scenarios, including sexual ones with the daughter. Lines that referred to Bigger's sexual interest in Mary Dalton were taken out in 1940 and only restored fifty-three years later in the 1993 Library of America edition, edited by Arnold Rampersad and copyrighted by Wright's second wife, Ellen Wright. Bigger's first driving job requires him to take Mary to pick up her communist lover, Jan Erlone, then eat with the couple in a black diner on the South Side. They drink themselves into oblivion on the ride home and invite Bigger to join them. Jan leaves, and Bigger must take Mary home and put her in bed. Terrified to be in Mary's bedroom and afraid to be caught as he is kissing her, he puts a pillow over her face when her blind mother walks in. Realizing he has accidentally murdered her, he drags her in a trunk to the basement and burns her in the furnace. Bigger rationalizes, correctly for a while, that the whites will never suspect him because they will think he is not smart enough to plan such a crime.

As it begins to snow, Bigger leaves the Dalton house and returns to his mother's tenement feeling like a new man. Bigger now sees that everyone he knows is blind; he himself is filled with elation for having killed a white girl, the ultimate taboo, and gotten away with it. To seal his guilt, Wright has Bigger murder his girlfriend Bessie in a brutal and premeditated way, in Book II. As the snowfall becomes a blizzard, Bigger is surrounded by the white world, whose search closes in and captures him. At the trial in Book III Bigger is never convicted for Bessie's murder, but only for the assumed rape of Mary, deemed to be a more serious crime than even Mary's murder. Boris A. Max, a Communist party lawyer, undertakes Bigger's defense because Bigger has implicated Jan and the party in a kidnap note to the Daltons.

While Wright made blacks proud of his success, he also made them uncomfortable with the protagonist, Bigger, who is a stereotype of the "brute Negro" they had been trying to overcome with novels of uplift by the "talented tenth" since the Gilded Age. Wright's argument is that racist America created Bigger; therefore, America had better change or more Biggers would be out there. At the end, when Max fails to understand Bigger, who cannot be saved from the electric chair, Wright is faulting the Communist party for not comprehending the black people it relied on for support. (Personally disillusioned with the party, Wright left it in 1942 and wrote an essay published in *Atlantic Monthly* in 1944 called "I Tried to Be a Communist," which was later reprinted in *The God That Failed* (1949), a collection of essays by disillusioned ex-Communists.) *Native Son* continues to be regarded as Wright's greatest novel and most influential book. As a result, he has been called the father of black American literature, a figure with whom writers such as James Baldwin had to contend.

To divest himself of Wright's influence, Baldwin wrote a series of three essays criticizing Wright's use of naturalism and protest fiction. In "Everybody's Protest Novel," published in *Partisan Review* in 1949, Baldwin concludes, "The failure of the protest novel lies in its rejection of life, the human being, the denial of his beauty, dread, power, in its insistence that it is his categorization alone which is real and which cannot be transcended." On the other hand, Wright has been credited with presaging the Black Arts Movement of the 1960s, particularly in his protest poetry, much of which was published in Chicago in the 1930s. As Irving Howe said in his 1963 essay "Black Boys and Native Sons," "The day *Native Son* appeared, American culture was changed forever. No matter how much qualifying the book might later need, it made impossible a repetition of the old lies . . . [and] brought out into the open, as no one ever had before, the hatred, fear, and violence that have crippled and may yet destroy our culture."

As Wright was rising to prominence, his personal life was going through changes as well. In 1939 he had married Dhimah Rose Meadman, a Russian-Jewish ballet dancer. Wright moved her, her son, her mother, and her pianist to Mexico for a few months and then realized the marriage was not a success. He returned to New York and divorced Dhimah in 1940. On the trip back to New York, Wright stopped to visit his father for the first time in twenty-five years. In *Black Boy*, he describes his father during this visit as "standing alone upon the red clay of a Mississippi plantation, a sharecropper, clad in ragged overalls, holding a muddy hoe in his gnarled, veined hands . . . when I tried to talk to him I realized that . . . we were forever strangers, speaking a different language, living on vastly distant planes of reality." In 1941 he married Ellen Poplar, a white woman and Communist party member with whom he had worked and been in love before he married Dhimah. A year later their first daughter was born. Their second daughter was born in Paris in 1949.

During 1940–1941 Wright collaborated with Paul Green to write a stage adaptation of *Native Son*. It ran on Broadway in the spring of 1941 and was produced by John Houseman and staged by Orson Welles. Simultaneously, Wright published his sociological-psychological treatise *Twelve Million Black Voices: A Folk History of the Negro in the United States* (1941), with photographs collected by Edwin Rosskam; the book was well received. His autobiography, *Black Boy*, came out in 1945, again a bestseller and Book-of-the-Month Club selection, although the U.S. Senate denounced *Black Boy* as "obscene." The later section about his life in Chicago and experience with the Communist party was not published until 1977 under the title *American Hunger*. Wright's publishers in 1945 had only wanted the story of his life in the South and cut what followed about his life in the North. There have been numerous biographies of Wright, but all must begin with *Black Boy*, Wright's personal and emotional account of his childhood and adolescence in the Jim Crow South. In a famous passage in the autobiography that has bothered critics and set Wright apart from the African-American sense of community, he asserts the "cultural barrenness of black life": " . . . I used to mull over the strange absence of real kindness in Negroes, how unstable was our tenderness, how lacking in genuine passion we were, how void of great hope, how timid our joy, how bare our traditions, how hollow our memories, how lacking we were in those intangible sentiments that bind man to man, and how shallow was even our despair." He found an "unconscious irony" in the idea that "Negroes led so passional an existence": "I saw that what had been taken for our emotional strength was our negative confusions, our flights, our fears, our frenzy under pressure." Statements like these are contradicted by others that describe a caring community. For example, when Wright's mother suffers a paralytic stroke, "the neighbors nursed my mother day and night, fed us and washed our clothes," and Wright admits to being "ashamed that so often in my life I had to be fed by strangers."

In 1946 Wright was invited to France. After he returned to the United States he decided he could no longer tolerate the racism he experienced even in New York City. Married to a white woman and living in the North, he still was not able to buy an apartment as a black man; furthermore, he hated the stares he and his family received on the streets. And he was still called "boy" by some shopkeepers. So in 1947 he moved permanently to France and settled in Paris. Wright never again saw the United States. He worked during 1949–1951 on a film version of *Native Son*, in which he himself played Bigger. Wright, forty years old and overweight, had to train and stretch verisimilitude to play the nineteen-year-old Bigger. During filming in Buenos Aires and Chicago, the production was fraught with problems. The film was released briefly but was unsuccessful. European audiences acclaimed it, but the abridged version failed in the United States and the film disappeared.

Wright did not publish a book after *Black Boy* until 1953 when his "existential" novel, *The Outsider*, was published to mixed reviews. Cross Damon, the main character, is overwhelmed by the demands of his wife, his mother, and his mistress. Seizing a chance opportunity during a train crash, he leaves his identity papers with a dead man and disappears. He ends up committing three murders to save himself, then is himself murdered by the Communist party in the

United States for his independence. *Savage Holiday* followed in 1954, a "white" novel whose main character, Erskine Fowler, exemplifies the dangers of repressed emotion. Fowler has been obsessed with desire for his mother. He marries a prostitute, then murders her; the graphic murder scene disturbed some readers. The novel is an exception to Wright's work in that it has no black characters. *Savage Holiday* was not even a mild critical success.

During the mid-1950s Wright traveled extensively—to Africa, Asia, and Spain—and wrote several nonfiction works on political and sociological topics. He had helped found *Présence Africaine* with Aimé Césaire, Leopold Senghor, and Alioune Diop during 1946–1948. He spent some time in Ghana and in 1954 published *Black Power* (a term coined by Wright) to mixed reviews. *Black Power* concerns itself with the color line in Africa and the new "tragic elite," the leaders of the former colonies. Ghanaian writer Kwame Anthony Appiah said later that Wright failed to understand Africans when he urged Africa to leave tribal custom behind and join the technological era. In April 1955 Wright attended the Bandung Conference in Indonesia, the first meeting of twenty-nine new nations of Africa and Asia. He published his account as *The Color Curtain* in 1956 (after the French edition of 1955).

Throughout his international political activities, Wright knew correctly that he was being shadowed by the Central Intelligence Agency; his paranoia was later justified when evidence about his surveillance was made available under the Freedom of Information Act. After Wright made two trips to Franco's Spain, he published a book of his observations, *Pagan Spain* (1956); here Wright with his "peasant" understanding exposes the dark side of violence and moral hypocrisy beneath the national adherence to Catholicism. In 1957 he put together a collection of his lectures given between 1950 and 1956 in Europe, *White Man, Listen!*, which includes "The Literature of the Negro in the United States," an important overview. Wright's books published during the 1950s disappointed some critics, who said that his move to Europe alienated him from American blacks and thus separated him from his emotional and psychological roots. During the 1950s Wright grew more internationalist in outlook. While he accomplished much as an important public literary and political figure with a worldwide reputation, his creative work did decline.

The last work Wright submitted for publication during his lifetime, *The Long Dream*, a novel, was released in 1958. Here he portrays his strongest black father, Tyree Tucker, and treats the black middle class in the setting of Clintonville, Mississippi. This was the first novel in a planned trilogy about Tyree Tucker and his son Fishbelly. Wright did finish the second novel, "Island of Hallucinations," about Fishbelly's escape to Paris, but it was not published. *The Long Dream*, taking place in the long-gone South of the 1940s, seemed out of date to readers; critics faulted Wright for being away from the source of his material for too long, and *Time* magazine criticized him for "living amid the alien corn." Subsequent critics, however, have regarded his late fiction more seriously. In 1959 Wright's *Daddy Goodness* was staged in Paris in collaboration with Louis Sapin, and a 1960 Broadway stage version of *The Long Dream*, produced by Ketti Frings, was unsuccessful.

During his last year and a half, Wright suffered from amoebic dysentery acquired during his travels to Africa or Asia, and he died suddenly of an apparent heart attack while recuperating at the Clinique Eugène Gibez in Paris. There have been recurrent rumors that Wright was murdered, but this has not been substantiated. After his death, his wife Ellen submitted for publication his second collection of short stories, *Eight Men* (1961), which Wright had completed eight years earlier. She then published his novel *Lawd Today* in 1963, generally considered to be the least powerful of Wright's works, although William Burrison has argued for its sophistication and artistic merit ("Another Look at *Lawd Today*," *CLA Journal* 29 [June 1986]: 424–41). *Lawd Today*, clearly influenced by James Joyce's *Ulysses*, presents one day in the life of Jake Jackson in Chicago. Wright had finished this manuscript in 1934, titled it *Cesspool*, and had had it repeatedly rejected by publishers before *Native Son* was released.

The unexpurgated 1993 edition of *Native Son* saddles readers with an even less sympathetic Bigger Thomas, ensuring this novel's role in confronting future generations of complaisant Americans about the scourge of race and fulfilling W. E. B. Du Bois's prophecy in *The Souls of Black Folk* (1903) that "the problem of the twentieth century is the problem of the color line."

• The largest collection of Wright's papers is at the Beinecke Rare Book and Manuscript Library, Yale University, but there are also materials in the Fales Collection of the New York University Library and in the Firestone Library at Princeton University. Private papers and letters are housed at the Beinecke and at the Schomburg Library in New York City.

Of the numerous biographies, early ones include John A. Williams, *Richard Wright* (1969), and Constance Webb, *Richard Wright: A Biography* (1968). Webb, a friend of Wright's, had access to his personal papers, and after Wright's death she spoke at length with Ellen Wright, who made available to Webb all of her husband's files. More recent biographies are Margaret Walker, *Richard Wright: Daemonic Genius* (1988), which has a questionable psychological focus, and Michel Fabre, *The Unfinished Quest of Richard Wright* (1973; rev. ed., 1993), a more literary account of the writer's life. The 1993 edition of *The Unfinished Quest* includes an excellent bibliographical essay, but much of Fabre's biographical material relies on Webb's book. Addison Gayle, *Richard Wright: Ordeal of a Native Son* (1980), focuses on Wright's surveillance by the CIA and the FBI during his life.

Book-length studies of Wright's work include Robert Bone, *Richard Wright* (1969); Keneth Kinnamon, *The Emergence of Richard Wright* (1972); Evelyn Gross Avery, *Rebels and Victims: The Fiction of Richard Wright* (1979); Joyce Ann Joyce, *Richard Wright's Art of Tragedy* (1986); and Jean Fran-

co Goundard, *The Racial Problem in the Works of Richard Wright* (1992). Among the abundant collections of critical essays are Henry Louis Gates, Jr., and Kwame Anthony Appiah, eds., *Richard Wright: Critical Perspectives Past and Present* (1993); Richard Abcarian, *Richard Wright's "Native Son": A Critical Handbook* (1970); C. James Trotman, ed., *Richard Wright: Myths and Realities* (1988); and Kinnamon, ed., *New Essays on "Native Son"* (1990). For primary materials, see Charles T. Davis and Fabre, *Richard Wright: A Primary Bibliography* (1982); for secondary sources, see Kinnamon, *A Richard Wright Bibliography: Fifty Years of Criticism and Commentary, 1933–1982*. An obituary is in the *New York Times*, 30 Nov. 1960.

ANN RAYSON

WRIGHT, Richard Robert, Sr. (16 May 1855–2 July 1947), educator and banker, was born in Whitfield County, Georgia, the son of Robert Waddell and Harriet (maiden name unknown), both slaves. His father, of mixed African and Cherokee descent, was the coachman on a plantation where his mother was a house servant. When Richard was two years old, his father escaped to free territory. Richard and his mother were taken by their slave owner to Cuthbert, Georgia, where she married Alexander Wright and had two children. After emancipation Harriet Wright moved with her three children to Atlanta to take advantage of the recent opening of a Freedman's Bureau School for Negroes. While she supported the family by running a boarding house, Richard entered Storrs School, which was run by the American Missionary Association. In 1866 General Oliver Otis Howard, then current commissioner of the Freedmen's Bureau, visited the Sunday school at the Storrs Church and asked the students what message he should tell the children of the North about them. The young Wright stood up and said, "Tell them we are rising." This incident inspired the poem "Howard at Atlanta" by the great abolitionist John Greenleaf Whittier. Wright attended Atlanta University where he received a B.A. and was valedictorian of the university's first graduating class in 1876. Wright married Lydia E. Howard in 1869, and they had nine children.

After graduation from Atlanta University, Wright became the principal of a primary school in Cuthbert, Georgia. In Cuthbert, he helped organize local farmers into cooperatives and coordinated the state's first county fair for blacks. In 1878 he organized the Georgia State Teachers' Association (for black educators), served as its first president, and began publishing the association's *Weekly Journal of Progress*, later called the *Weekly Sentinel*. Wright represented Georgia at the 1879 National Conference of Colored Men of the United States, held in Nashville, Tennessee, which sought primarily to assist in the plight of African Americans.

In 1880 Wright was asked to set up and direct Ware High School in Augusta, Georgia, which became the state's first public high school for blacks. His political activities definitely aided his career in education. Wright was an alternate delegate in 1880 to the Republican National Convention in Chicago, a participant at the conference of the Afro-American League in Minneapolis (1881), a member of the State Republican Central Committee (1882), a special agent for the U.S. Department of the Interior Development in Alabama (1885), and a delegate for Georgia to the Republican National Convention through 1896. In return for his political influence with the black voters, Wright was appointed by President William McKinley to the position of paymaster in the army with the rank of major during the Spanish-American War.

In October 1891 the Georgia legislature established the Georgia State Industrial College for Colored Youth in Savannah. Wright, an obvious candidate to lead the school because of his long experience in teaching and administration, remained president for thirty years, until his retirement in 1921. One of the members of his faculty was Monroe Nathan Work, who later wrote the well-known *Bibliography of the Negro in Africa and America.*

Wright's tenure as president was troubled by the control of an all-white board of trustees for the college that objected to higher education for blacks. Especially controversial were Wright's efforts to include classical education in the curriculum. Early in his presidency, he organized the Negro Civic Improvement League in Savannah. This political organization proved to be very unpopular with the college trustees, and, under much pressure from them, Wright withdrew from the organization and politics in general. He decided to follow the emphasis placed by many black scholars and leaders of the day, such as Booker T. Washington, on programs of self-help and cooperative efforts with whites. It was during this time that Wright wrote *A Brief Historical Sketch of Negro Education in Georgia* (1894), which addressed his inability to obtain sufficient support for an adequate curriculum at the college.

In 1921 Wright retired as president of the Georgia State Industrial College for Colored Youth and began a new career as a banker and elder statesman. Along with a son, Richard R. Wright, Jr., and a daughter, Lillian W. Clayton, Wright founded in Philadelphia in 1921 the Citizens and Southern Bank and Trust Company. Wright's reputation as an honest and well-qualified man provided the kind of stability needed to survive such economic crises as the 1929 stock market crash and the Great Depression of the 1930s. The fact that Wright managed to maintain banking operations during the depression can be credited to both the diversity of his investment portfolio and the conservative policy of his bank.

In 1945 he attended the conference in California that organized the United Nations. A banquet was held at the conference in recognition of his long career, which included the presidency of the National Association of Presidents of A & M Colleges (1906–1919) and the presidency of the National Association of Teachers of Colored Schools (1908–1912). He helped to establish the National Freedom Day Association, supported a 1940 commemorative stamp for Booker T. Washington, and gathered information for the Georgia Archives about African Americans who fought in the First World War. In 1946, a year before his death, Wright accepted the Muriel Dobbin's Pioneers of Industry Award from the business community of Philadelphia. He died in Philadelphia.

• Wright's papers are held by his family, the majority with Emanuel C. Wright of Philadelphia and others with Wright's daughter Harriet B. S. Hines of Glenarden, Md. Noteworthy sources about Wright's life include Elizabeth Ross Haynes, *The Black Boy of Atlanta* (1952); Horace Mann Bond, *The Black American Scholars—A Study of Their Beginnings* (1972); and Rayford W. Logan, *The Betrayal of the Negro* (1965). An important monograph, Clyde W. Hall, ed., *One Hundred Years of Educating at Savannah State College, 1890–1990* (1990), contains a wealth of information about Wright's early leadership of that institution. August Meier, *Negro Thought in America, 1888–1915* (1963), also gives useful material. An obituary is in the *New York Times*, 3 July 1947.

ROBERT C. MORRIS

WRIGHT, Robert (20 Nov. 1752–7 Sept. 1826), U.S. senator, U.S. representative, and governor of Maryland, was born in Queen Annes County, Maryland, the son of Solomon Wright, an attorney, judge, and politician, and Mary Tidmarsh (or Tidmarch). After a local private elementary education, Robert studied law at Washington College and was admitted to the bar in 1773. Early that same year he served as one of three clerks to Maryland's lower house, of which his father was a member. Wright resigned his clerkship in late June 1773 to practice law at Chestertown and continued his practice until February 1776, when he marched with a company of Minutemen against Loyalists in Virginia. In 1777 he served his first term in the Maryland House of Delegates but remained active in the patriot military. On 27 May 1777 he was warranted a captain of a company in Colonel William Richardson's battalion of the Maryland line and immediately began to sign for supplies and direct the company. His official appointment came through on 7 July 1777. Like other revolutionary war officers, Wright struggled to keep his men paid and provisioned as they fought the British in battles such as Paoli and Brandywine. He was mustered out in October 1777.

In 1780 Wright married Sarah DeCourcy, daughter of Colonel William DeCourcy. Though Sarah died soon after their marriage, they had one son. Wright later married a Miss Ringgold of Kent County; they had a son and a daughter. In 1784 the constituents of Queen Annes County elected Wright a member of the Maryland House of Delegates. Queen Annes did not reelect Wright in 1785, but the following year Kent County elected him to the House of Delegates in a bitter contest that led to several abortive duel attempts between Wright and his electoral opponent, General James Lloyd. Wright also served a year in the state senate in 1787. Though Wright, who also cultivated a 2,000-acre estate and bred fine horses, did not return to the state legislature for over a decade, he remained active in local politics. During the Independence Day celebrations of 1794, for example, he accused his old nemesis General Lloyd of cowardice and perfidy in order to block his taking command of a brigade and to punish him for supporting George Washington's policy of neutrality in the European war. Lloyd responded with a long pamphlet that insinuated Wright served in the Revolution and in public office solely to enrich himself. He directly accused Wright of serving a "worthless junto" intent on violence of the deadly French variety.

In 1801 Wright was again elected to the state senate. That body elected him to serve in the U.S. Senate, where he was a strong and vocal supporter of Thomas Jefferson's policies, including the purchase of Louisiana, the war against the Barbary pirates, and the repeal of the Judiciary Act of 1801. He later voted for Samuel Chase's acquittal, because he believed in the independence of the judiciary and desired to embarrass John Randolph, the leader of the impeachment forces. A strong orator, Wright also delved deeply into the wording of prospective bills, suggesting changes designed to make laws clearer, more exact, and fairer. A good example of this was his report on an act *For the Relief of Insolvent Debtors, within the District of Columbia* in 1803. Also in 1803 Wright served as a delegate to the Board of Agriculture. In 1806 he communicated to the Senate the Maryland House of Delegates' resolves to seek a constitutional amendment to end the importation of slaves into the United States.

Wright resigned his Senate seat after the 1806 session, because the Maryland legislature elected him governor. He was inaugurated on 12 November 1806 and was reelected twice. As governor, he continued to support Jefferson, convening the meeting in 1808 in Annapolis that endorsed Jefferson's trade restriction policies and urged him to run for a third term. He also ordered Maryland's militia to stop violations of the embargo. Wright's popularity sank as the economic effects of the embargo were increasingly felt, and he opted to resign as governor in May 1809 to become a candidate for the Maryland Court of Appeals. His bid failed, but in 1810 he served as clerk of Queen Annes County and later that year was elected to fill a vacancy in the U.S. House of Representatives. Wright strongly opposed the rechartering of the Bank of the United States in 1811 and just as strongly supported measures for the vigorous prosecution of the War of 1812. In April 1812, for example, he caused a ruckus on the floor of the House to stop a clerk from reading a Boston antiwar petition. In the postwar years he served on important committees, including the Committees on the Judiciary (1815–1817) and Foreign Affairs (1821–1823).

Though some of Wright's positions, such as his 1812 attempt to pass a bill for the indemnification of American seamen, met little support, even from his own party, his positions and actions must have met some approbation at home, as he won several reelections, serving from 3 December 1810 until 4 March 1817. In March 1816 he and his Maryland colleague Samuel Smith sought to fix the headquarters of the Second Bank of the United States at Baltimore and to increase its capital to $45 million. Though they failed

on both accounts, their agitation probably helped to move the proposed headquarters from New York to Philadelphia. Wright also took a strong stand on the tariff issue. In seeking a 21 percent ad valorem tariff on woolens, he proposed that "those members interested in any manufactory of cloth" should not be allowed to vote on the tariff bill. Wright withdrew his motion the next day on Smith's insistence. Though defeated in his reelection bid in November 1816, Wright regained his seat in 1820, serving one term (Mar. 1821 to Mar. 1823). He finished his career as judge of the district court for Kent County (1822–1826). He died at "Blakeford," his estate in Queenstown.

Wright is significant because he helped the commercial wing of the Democratic-Republican party plot its course between the economic backwardness of the agrarian Republicans and the political backwardness of many Federalists. Wright and other commercially minded Republican patriots, such as William Few, were essential to the creation of a vigorous and democratic Republic.

• Bernard Steiner et al., eds., *Archives of Maryland* (70 vols., 1883–1964), is the best source for the official colonial and revolutionary activities of Wright and his father, especially vols. 11, 16, 18, and 63. For a negative view of Wright's role in the Revolution, see General James Lloyd, *Address to the Citizens of Kent and Queen Anne's Counties, In Answer to the Late Calumnious Charge Made against Him by Robert Wright* (1794). For Wright's meticulousness in the Senate, see U.S. Congress, Senate, *Mr. Wright, from the Committee to Whom Was Referred the Act "For the Relief of Insolvent Debtors, within the District of Columbia,"* 7th Cong., 2 Feb. 1803, Evans 2d ser. 5300. For Wright's communication of the Md. slave importation resolves, see U.S. Congress, Senate, *Mr. Wright Communicated the Following Resolution of the Legislature of the State of Maryland*, 9th Cong., 7 Apr. 1806. Richard E. Ellis, *The Jeffersonian Crisis: Courts and Politics in the Young Republic* (1971), provides the best analysis of Wright's role in the Judiciary Act repeal and the Chase impeachment. A good source for his role in state politics is Richard Walsh and William Fox, *Maryland: A History, 1632–1974* (1974). Wright's exploits in the House during the war can be followed in the *New York National Advocate*, 8 Apr. 1816, and the *New York Herald*, 13 May 1812 and 20 Mar. 1816. For reaction to his seamen indemnification bills, see Samuel Taggart to John Taylor, Washington, 26 Mar. 1812, "Letters of Samuel Taggart," ed. George Henry Haynes, *Proceedings of the American Antiquarian Society* 33 (1923): 113–226, 297–438. The *New York National Advocate* is a good place to follow Wright's stance on the tariff in 1816.

ROBERT E. WRIGHT

WRIGHT, Russel (3 Apr. 1904–22 Dec. 1976), industrial designer, was born in Lebanon, Ohio, the son of Willard Wright, a local judge, and Harryet Morris Crigler. Wright began his artistic career with a brief period of study at the Cincinnati Art Academy. In the autumn of 1920 he moved to New York City and enrolled at the Art Students League. The following fall he entered Princeton University. Indifferent to academic life, Wright left Princeton in 1924 intent on a career in the theater. During the early 1920s he worked as an assistant and apprentice to Norman Bel

Geddes and Aline Bernstein studying set design. From 1925 to 1927 he held a number of posts with New York and regional theater companies.

In 1927 Wright met and married Mary Small Einstein; they had one adopted daughter. Mary Wright, who worked with her husband as a close collaborator throughout their marriage, encouraged Russel to put his experience designing theatrical properties to work making and marketing decorative accessories for retail sale. After some initial experimentation with different materials, Wright was soon producing a large line of spun aluminum bun warmers, ice buckets, cheese servers, "sandwich humidors," spaghetti sets, and the like. Although the shapes of these pieces were at least partially determined by the capabilities of the aluminum spinning process, they also reflected Wright's developing preference for rounded and somewhat exaggerated forms. From the start his designs, neither streamlined nor Bauhaus inspired, were distinctive and impossible to confuse with those of other designers either European or American.

Wright's designs were not only formally arresting, but they were marketed with unusual flair. Added to the novelty of his inventive specialized pieces, Wright developed and skillfully used the press to present a design philosophy that stressed the suitability of his designs to the growing informality of modern life. Working as a team, the Wrights exploited social connections to keep Russel and his work before the public. By the end of the 1940s his name was a virtual household word in much of America, synonymous with all that was up to date.

As Wright's celebrity grew, so did opportunities for diversification. In the early 1930s Wright was engaged by firms such as Wurlitzer and Chase Brass to work on product designs. Throughout the 1930s Wright also worked on commercial interiors (offices, restaurants, showrooms, etc.) while simultaneously designing for himself and Mary a series of increasingly elaborate apartment and townhouse interiors.

In 1934 Wright's first line of mass-produced furniture was introduced. The 64-piece group unveiled that year by the Heywood-Wakefield Company was notable for both its use of contrasting veneers and the flexibility of its modular components. The following year, this time working with Conant-Ball Furniture, Wright introduced his much more successful "Modern Living" line. Using solid native maple in what the designer called "full, hardy, craftsmanlike forms," the new furniture was clean, open, and functional in appearance.

In 1935 Wright sought to follow up on the success of his Modern Living furniture with a complementary line of ceramics. "American Modern" dinnerware was simple and organically modeled in soft, rimless forms and was glazed in unusual, mottled colors. In both shape and color American Modern was almost without stylistic precedent. Each color was designed to harmonize with all of the others. Wright encouraged buyers to create mixed settings. Food service, Wright believed, could be "dramatized" by presenting each dish on the color plate most flattering to it.

The designs for American Modern were complete by late 1937, but because of the unusual shapes and colors used, it took two full years to locate a manufacturer. The dinnerware finally reached the stores in 1939. Success built rapidly, and Wright added coordinated accessories—glassware, table linens, flatware—to the line. Production of American Modern continued through 1959, by which time the design had become the most successful line of dinnerware in history.

In 1939 Wright embarked on an extended cross-country trip to organize a network of some sixty-five artists, craftsmen, and manufacturers to produce, under his direction, a complete line of home furnishings. Wright hoped that this project, marketed nationally through major department stores under the name "The American Way," would simultaneously make well-designed home furnishings available to a broad spectrum of Americans while helping to overcome what he saw as the country's lingering aesthetic inferiority complex. Timing was not propitious, however, and wartime shortages and distribution difficulties led to liquidation of the American Way in 1942.

Exempted from military service in World War II, Wright used the war years to conduct with his wife a study of American housekeeping and entertaining practices. The result was *Mary and Russel Wright's Guide to Easier Living*, published in 1951. The book is a blend of manifesto and helpful hints designed to assist Americans in adapting their style of life to the realities of the postwar world. In connection with party-giving the Wrights offered such "work-saving" ideas as asking guests to help with party cleanup; drastically reducing the number of your possessions to make maintenance easier; replacing sit-down meals with "family cafeteria" service; using only throw-away paper plates for most meals; and redecorating the home, replacing old-fashioned fabrics and surfaces with easy-care plastic.

This preoccupation with functionality is reflected in Wright's "Casual China," introduced in 1946. The Casual line was designed to make the durability of restaurantware available for home use. Other lines of dinnerware were to follow, including "Highlight" (1951), "White Clover" (1951), "Esquire" (1956), and two lines in melamine. While some of these designs were distinctive, none achieved the level of popular acceptance accorded to American Modern.

Wright was acutely disappointed by his lack of postwar success. His wife's death in 1952 was also a major blow, and in the following years Wright withdrew more and more from his New York design practice, spending increasingly large amounts of time at "Dragon Rock," his country home outside of Garrison, New York. During this period Wright continued to do consulting work on a reduced basis, designing, among other things, a line of metal school furniture, folding tables and chairs, packaging for Proctor and Gamble, and a line of "Easier Living" wooden furniture.

In 1955 Wright was invited by the International Cooperation Administration of the U.S. State Department to survey handicraft industries in Southeast Asia and to make recommendations for stimulating international trade in these handicraft items. Wright was deeply impressed by much of what he saw, particularly in Japan, and returned to the United States determined to put Asian design ideas into use at Dragon Rock. Wright had acquired this eighty-acre estate (also known as "Manitoga") in 1941 as a weekend retreat. In subsequent years he increasingly saw Dragon Rock both as a home and as a laboratory for his ideas, as the living embodiment of his emerging philosophy of total design. At Dragon Rock Wright worked to "dramatize" both nature and his built environment, to link them into a seamless whole. Highlighting natural contours and features, he sculpted the landscape, laying out trails, adding ponds, and moving natural features, to choreograph a series of vistas, each with its own mood and style. In the midst of this controlled and dramatic environment Wright built his house. He blended in its design a wide range of natural materials from the site (including the living rock, still in its original place) and the latest in synthetic plastics. Construction began in 1957 and was completed four years later.

Dragon Rock is maintained today as a nature and design center where the public can experience Russel Wright's most complete and ambitious creation while learning more about this pioneering designer who did so much to bring comfort, efficiency, and beauty within the reach of modern Americans. He died in New York City.

Russel Wright was among the pioneers in the first generation of American industrial designers. A marketing innovator with a dramatic flair developed through years of work in the theater, he demonstrated that good contemporary design did not have to be cold, mechanical, or European in origin. Through his highly successful furniture and dinnerware he not only brought innovatively styled products within the reach of Americans of even modest means but also made well-designed articles a virtual necessity for any up-to-date young family.

Although Wright consistently stressed the functionality of his designs—their suitability for the increasingly informal style of American entertaining—his work grew from an essentially sculptural sensibility. Throughout his career Wright repeatedly showed himself willing to sacrifice functionality to achieve a dramatic and arresting form. He took pains to identify himself not with the intellectual theorists of contemporary design, whom he saw as essentially foreign, but with a native American crafts tradition.

• Wright's papers (seventy-nine boxes) are housed in the Arendt's Research Library at Syracuse University. Additional files are preserved at Wright's former home, Manitoga, outside of Garrison, N.Y. The most complete study of Wright and his work to date is William Hennessey, *Russel Wright: American Designer* (1983). Wright is mentioned in most histories of American twentieth-century design, including Jeffrey Meikle, *Twentieth Century Limited: Industrial Design in America, 1925–39* (1979); Donald Bush, *The Streamlined Decade* (1975); and Arthur Pulos, *American Design Ethic* (1983). A number of good articles also discuss and illustrate Wright's work; see Diane Cochrane, "Designer for All Seasons," *Industrial Design* 23 (Mar.–Apr. 1976): 46–51; J. Watson, "American Way," *Magazine of Art*, Nov. 1940, pp. 626–29; Olga Geuft, "Dragon Rock," *Interiors*, Sept. 1961, pp. 100–111; and Farrell Grehan, "A Wonderful House to Live In," *Life*, 16 Mar. 1962, pp. 74–83. Also see three unsigned articles, "Designers Today: Russel Wright," *London Studio* 109 (June 1935): 311–23; "Russel and Mary Wright: Snapshot," *Interiors*, Dec. 1944, pp. 56–66; and "Idyll on 48th Street," *Interiors*, Sept. 1949, pp. 88–95.

WILLIAM J. HENNESSEY

WRIGHT, Sela Goodrich (21 July 1816–9 July 1906), educator and missionary, was born in Pompey, New York, the son of John Wright and Betsy Goodrich, farmers. The family moved to Medina, Ohio, after 1830. Wright enrolled in the preparatory department of Oberlin College in 1840 but left three years later, before completing a degree. He went to northern Minnesota to become one of the first members of the "Oberlin Band," a group of evangelical missionaries working with the Ojibwa (Chippewa) tribe. The mission was sponsored originally by Oberlin College students, then was adopted, in 1847 or 1848, by the American Missionary Association (AMA), a predominantly Congregationalist body. The members of the mission worked without compensation other than donations of used clothing, food, and tools.

Except for a brief trip to Oberlin in 1846, during which he married Emeline Farnsworth, Wright worked among the Ojibwa continuously from 1843 to 1862, serving at Red Lake, Lake Winnibigoshish, and Leech Lake. The Wrights had eight children, two of whom died in childhood. The mission sought to evangelize the Ojibwa directly through didactic teaching in classrooms and in religious services, and by providing examples of nonnomadic industry such as farming and lumbering. Wright participated in the latter, but his primary obligation originally was school teaching. After his ordination in 1849 he added ministerial duties to his work in the schoolhouse. The mission dissolved in 1859, having made few converts, but Wright remained in the area with his family as a government teacher among the Native Americans. He continued privately to work toward evangelization, preaching on weekends.

After the Sioux uprising in 1862 Wright settled his family in Oberlin, Ohio, and began a five-year career in the South, working for the AMA among the slaves freed by the Civil War. He established schools and churches and superintended teachers in Mississippi and Virginia, but he was frequently at odds with his superiors and teachers due to weak administrative skills and conflicts over ends and means. In 1867, with his family still in Ohio, Wright returned to government service in Minnesota as teacher to the Ojibwa, establishing a boarding school at Leech Lake in order to reduce the influence of family and tribe on the Native American students. With one interruption, he remained among the Ojibwa of Minnesota until 1883, and he served for a brief time in the late 1880s as a missionary to members of the tribe living in Wisconsin. In all, Wright spent forty-one years working with the Ojibwa, far longer than any of his contemporaries.

The Ojibwa people appear to have tolerated the intrusion of Wright and other AMA missionaries while largely rejecting their message. Wright's work among them constantly foundered on unresolved contradictions in his attitudes and beliefs. He mastered the Ojibwa tongue, a feat accomplished by few of the missionaries, and developed a profound appreciation for the richness of the language. Yet he was contemptuous of the culture from which the language had sprung and was blind to the language's embeddedness in the nomadic, subsistence life of the Ojibwa. Simultaneously, he excoriated the incursion of white settlers and the demoralizing influence of unscrupulous traders and government agents. Yet he clung to rigid cultural prejudices, insisting that the Ojibwa repudiate their traditional ways of life in favor of the culture of those same white settlers, traders, and agents. In his last years Wright spoke bitterly of the greater success of the Episcopal mission among the Ojibwa, failing to recognize the denomination's greater cultural tolerance. He died in Oberlin, Ohio.

• Many of Wright's letters dealing with his work after 1843 are housed in the American Missionary Association Archives, Amistad Research Center, Tulane University, New Orleans; the Oberlin College Archives, Oberlin, Ohio; and the Minnesota Historical Society Collections, St. Paul. Particularly informative is Wright's own "Reminiscences," which he dictated in 1890, housed in the Oberlin College Library, Special Collections. No biographies of Wright have been published, though he is mentioned in studies of the Oberlin Band and the Ojibwa, including Henry W. Bowden, "Oberlin and Ojibwas: An Evangelical Mission to Native Americans," in *The Evangelical Tradition in America*, ed. Leonard I. Sweet (1984). The obituary in *Congregational Yearbook* (1907) is unreliable.

RONALD E. BUTCHART

WRIGHT, Sewall (21 Dec. 1889–3 Mar. 1988), mathematical geneticist, was born Sewall Green Wright in Melrose, Massachusetts, the son of Philip Green Wright and Elizabeth Quincy Sewall. In 1892 the Wright family moved to Galesburg, Illinois, where Wright's father accepted a position at Lombard College, a small Universalist school, teaching a variety of subjects, including mathematics, astronomy, economics, and writing. Philip Wright was a polymath whose diverse interests included the running of a printing press. Using this press, Sewall and brother Quincy helped their father publish the poems of Carl Sandburg, who had been a student in their father's composition class.

Sewall Wright was a precocious child who manifested an early interest in physical events and phenomena that could be expressed mathematically. He also de-

veloped an interest in natural history, as a result of reading widely and of his mother's influence. Because his parents educated their children at home, Wright entered public school only in 1897, where his quantitative talents became even more apparent; he completed the usual eight years of grade school in only five and then attended Galesburg High School, from which he graduated in 1906. In his final year, he read Charles Darwin's *Origin of Species*, which he thought presented a sensible argument.

From 1906 to 1911 he attended Lombard College, where he took some courses with his father in mathematics and surveying. One summer he worked as a surveyor in South Dakota on the Chicago, Milwaukee & St. Paul Railroad, using his mathematical skills to calculate rail curvature. His interest in biology was sparked his senior year by Lombard biology professor Wilhelmine Entemann Key, one of the first women to have received a Ph.D. from the University of Chicago. With her encouragement, Wright spent the summers of 1911 and 1912 at the Carnegie Institution of Washington Station for Experimental Evolution at Cold Spring Harbor, which was run by Key's former mentor, Charles Benedict Davenport. Wright was especially inspired there by the lectures of biologists like George Harrison Shull, who reported on his research on inbreeding.

Following his first summer at Cold Spring Harbor, Wright returned to Illinois, where with the aid of a fellowship he entered the University of Illinois for graduate work in biology. In 1912 Wright met Ernest William Castle from the Bussey Institution at Harvard University, who was visiting the Agricultural College at the University of Illinois. Castle's lectures explaining his work on selection experiments in hooded rats proved so stimulating that Wright decided to leave Illinois to study mammalian genetics with Castle at Bussey. He completed a master's degree at Illinois on the anatomy of the trematode *Microphallus opacus* in 1912. At Harvard, Wright received a Ph.D. in 1915 for research on the inheritance of coat colors in guinea pigs, for which he developed novel mathematical methods to measure inbreeding.

In 1915 Wright accepted a position as a senior worker in animal husbandry at the U.S. Department of Agriculture in Washington, D.C. There he continued research on inbreeding and factor interaction in guinea pigs and livestock and developed the quantitative method known as path analysis. Much of this work was so unusual for his position that he had some difficulty publishing it in the standard publications of the Bureau of Animal Industry and the Department of Agriculture. Wright married Louise Williams, a teacher of genetics at Smith College, in 1921; they had three children. In 1926 Wright left for the University of Chicago, where he trained several graduate students while continuing his research on guinea pigs. He retired from the University of Chicago in 1955 at the age of sixty-five and took an appointment at the University of Wisconsin as Leon J. Cole Professor of Genetics until a second retirement five years later. He remained at the University of Wisconsin as emeritus professor for another twenty-five years, until his death.

Wright's publication career, which began in 1912 and spanned seventy-six years, was distinguished in several respects: for developing statistical and quantitative methods, especially in the practice of animal breeding; for providing understanding of mammalian genetics, especially within the new field of physiological genetics; in pioneering the new field of mathematical population genetics; and in contributing to modern evolutionary theory. He became best known in statistics for his development of path analysis. Originally applied to the solutions of problems in genetics, the method was later applied to analyzing such problems in the social sciences as the contributions of heredity vs. the environment in determinations of the "Intelligence Quotient." Wright also made important contributions to understanding the complex genetics of animal breeding through firsthand observations of the crosses in guinea pigs. His detailed observations and exact recordkeeping of various pedigrees of guinea pigs for generations helped him to derive an algorithm that could be used to compute a coefficient of inbreeding. Later extended by Jay L. Lush (c. 1922–1925), Wright's methods helped to transform animal breeding into a more exact science. Wright's original mind was also apparent in his research on the interactive effect of genes, especially at the more fundamental biochemical and enzymatic level. This led him to become one of the earliest workers in physiological genetics, a new area of research.

Finally, in the field of modern evolutionary biology, Wright was recognized as one of the foremost evolutionary theorists and mathematical population geneticists, ranking alongside R. A. Fisher, and J. B. S. Haldane. More than any of their contemporaries, these three scientists explored Darwinian evolutionary theory by constructing various mathematical models that studied the parameters of evolutionary change. In addition to demonstrating the efficacy of natural selection as an agent of evolutionary change, they integrated Mendelian genetics within their mathematical studies of populations in a way that gave rise to mathematical population genetics. In the early 1930s the combined work of Wright, Fisher, and Haldane helped lead to what was then termed the Neo-Darwinian synthesis of evolution (or the "Modern Synthesis of Evolution"), a synthesis between Darwinian selection theory and Mendelian genetics; this served as the grounding for modern evolutionary theory.

One of Wright's most important and widely read papers, "Evolution in Mendelian Populations" (*Genetics* 16: 97–159), appeared in 1931. Growing out of his extensive knowledge of livestock inbreeding patterns, especially in Shorthorn cattle, the paper articulated Wright's famous shifting balance theory of evolution, a theoretical attempt to understand populational parameters of evolutionary change. In his own twist to modeling evolution, Wright differed from his colleagues Haldane and Fisher by stressing the role that the structure of small, subdivided populations had on evolutionary change. The specific features of Wright's theory and its general applicability subsequently drew considerable discussion from evolutionists, and questions regarding the general interpretation of Wright's theory still remain.

In the early 1930s Wright further influenced the direction of twentieth-century evolutionary biology by collaborating with the field biologist and geneticist Theodosius Dobzhansky. The interaction between the two brought Wright's mathematical and theoretical insights within the purview of Dobzhansky's experimental and field observations. The result was a large-scale study on understanding the genetics of natural populations of *Drosophila pseudoobscura*, a study—manifested in a series of papers—critical to consolidating the field of evolutionary genetics.

Wright's magnum opus, the four-volume work collectively titled *Evolution and the Genetics of Populations*, appeared in 1968, 1969, 1977, and 1978. More than just a summary of the development of his ideas, the work synthesized much of the current literature and understanding in mathematical evolutionary theory that had developed over the century.

In addition to his scientific pursuits, Wright also engaged in serious philosophical studies. He developed a philosophy termed "panpsychic dualism," which integrates mind and matter in such a way that consciousness pervades even the most elementary particles. While philosophical colleagues like Charles Hartshorne appreciated his views, other scientific colleagues remained largely unaware of Wright's idiosyncratic philosophy.

Although he was known as a rather modest, shy, and diffident individual, Wright demonstrated a tenacity and determination in defending his work in intellectual circles. This trait was apparent in a notorious dispute with his British colleague R. A. Fisher. Their theoretical differences over the mechanism and importance of natural selection, which began in the late 1920s with their dispute over dominance, culminated in a personal rift that lasted until Fisher's death in 1962. Despite his visible falling-out with Fisher, which had the unfortunate effect of dividing the community of evolutionists, Wright remained a highly regarded colleague, who gave generously of his time and frequently served as a referee for difficult theoretical papers.

During his unusually long and productive career, Wright received numerous awards, including the Darwin Medal of the Royal Society of London (1980), the National Medal of Science (1966), the Weldon Medal of the Royal Society of London (1947), the Elliott and Kimber Awards from the National Academy of Sciences (1947 and 1956, respectively), and the Lewis Prize from the American Philosophical Society. He received several honorary degrees and belonged to more than a dozen professional societies, serving as president of the American Society of Zoologists in 1944, the Genetics Society of America and the American Society of Naturalists in 1952, and the Society for the Study of Evolution in 1955. Because his novel mathematical methods had widespread applicability to the social sciences, especially economics, he was also elected a fellow of the Econometric Society.

Wright died in Madison, Wisconsin. Although he was ninety-eight at the time of his death, his colleague in genetics at the University of Wisconsin, James F. Crow, was not alone in feeling it an untimely end; Wright was intellectually alert, healthy, and made important contributions to science until the end.

• Many of the papers and correspondence of Wright are in the possession of William B. Provine, Professor of Ecology and Systematics and of History at Cornell University. This collection includes more than 120 hours of tape-recorded interviews with Provine. Other material can be found in the genetics collection at the library of the American Philosophical Society. Wright's scientific publications primarily before the 1950s are in *Evolution. Selected Papers*, ed. William B. Provine (1986). The most comprehensive historical treatment of the life and work of Wright is Provine, *Sewall Wright and Evolutionary Biology* (1986). For additional historical and scientific assessment of Wright, see, all by James F. Crow, "Sewall Wright, the Scientist and the Man," *Perspectives in Biology and Medicine* 25 (1982): 279–94; "Sewall Wright and Physiological Genetics," *Genetics* 115 (1987): 1–2; with W. R. Engles and C. Denniston, "Phase Three of Wright's Shifting Balance Theory," *Evolution* 44 (1990): 233–47; "The Third Phase of Wright's Theory of Evolution," in *Population Biology of Genes and Molecules*, ed. N. Takahata and J. F. Crow (1990); and "Sewall Wright's Place in Twentieth Century Biology," *Journal of the History of Biology* 23 (1990): 57–89. On the Fisher-Wright controversy, see Provine, "The R. A. Fisher-Sewall Wright Controversy," and M. J. S. Hodge, "Biology and Philosophy (including Ideology): A Study of Fisher and Wright," in *The Founders of Evolutionary Genetics*, ed. Sahotra Sarkar (1992). Biographical sketches include James F. Crow, "Sewall Wright," National Academy of Sciences, *Biographical Memoirs* 64 (1994): 439–69. An obituary is in the *New York Times*, 5 Mar. 1988.

VASSILIKI BETTY SMOCOVITIS

WRIGHT, Silas (24 May 1795–27 Aug. 1847), U.S. senator and governor of New York, was born in Amherst, Massachusetts, the son of Silas Wright, a shoemaker, and Eleanor Goodale. In 1796 the family moved to Weybridge, Vermont, where they prospered moderately as farmers. Silas Sr. served several terms in the Vermont legislature.

In 1811 Wright enrolled at Middlebury College, where, he later recalled, he "supported a kind of mediocrity." After graduating in 1814, he studied law in the offices of two lawyers in Sandy Hill, New York, where he was admitted to the bar in 1819. He then began to practice in Canton, a village near the Canadian border.

Being the only lawyer in Canton, Wright soon became involved in local politics. He held several offices, including surrogate of St. Lawrence County, postmaster of Canton, and inspector of highways and schools. In 1823 he was elected to the state senate as a member of the Bucktails, a faction led by U.S. Senator Martin Van Buren. (With Van Buren in Washington, his New York associates became known as the Albany Regency.) The Bucktails were essentially Jeffersonian agrarians, favoring majority rule but suspicious of policies that required the expenditure of large amounts of public money. Their point of view was more local than national, and their primary loyalty was to their own organization. "Love the State and let the nation save itself," Wright wrote in 1827. "When our enemies accuse us of feeding our friends instead of them, never let them lie in telling the story."

In 1826 Wright was elected to the House of Representatives, where as a member of the Committee on Manufactures he drafted the so-called tariff of abominations of 1828, which raised rates on many items. He had no objection to protective tariffs on manufactured goods such as woolen cloth, but insisted that farm products, especially wool, an important product in his part of New York, also be protected. Northern woolens manufacturers protested bitterly. Southern free-trade congressmen voted to maintain the high tariff on wool in the expectation that this would lead New England congressmen to vote against the bill, but their strategy failed and the bill was passed. It was later claimed that Wright and other members of the committee actually had wanted the bill to be defeated so as to mollify southern Democrats without angering their own constituents, but it is clear that this was not the case.

Wright was reelected to Congress in 1828 but was appointed New York State comptroller in January 1829 as part of a general reorganization of Albany Regency management after newly elected President Andrew Jackson appointed Van Buren secretary of state. The comptrollership involved ministering to the financial operations of the state and overseeing a considerable staff, but the comptroller was also a key figure in the Albany Regency organization. Wright, who was by this date Van Buren's closest associate, was admirably suited to fulfill this aspect of the position. In 1832, however, the legislature elected him U.S. senator.

In September 1833 he married Clarissa Moody, whom he had known from his earliest days in Canton. They had no children. She was a shy person uncomfortable among the "great statesmen" of Washington, and their marriage marked the beginning of Wright's desire to retire from politics.

In the Senate, Wright served on the Finance Committee, becoming chairman after Van Buren was elected president in 1836. Suspicious of all banks, he faithfully supported the Jackson and Van Buren administrations' policies. He favored strict state regulation of banks and opposed rechartering the Second Bank of the United States. He supported both Jackson's 1836 Specie Circular, which required that purchases of government lands be paid for in coin, and the Independent Treasury plan, which called for keeping all government funds in sub-treasuries in cities scattered across the country. "I had rather repose any degree of confidence connected with our monied affairs in the worst executive . . . than in the best bank," he told Van Buren in 1837.

Wright's position on the slavery question was similar to that of many northern congressmen in the 1830s and 1840s. He opposed the gag rule banning the reception of antislavery petitions by Congress, but hoped to keep the issue out of national politics. He resisted efforts to outlaw slavery in the District of Columbia on the ground that such a measure would not "give freedom to a single slave."

Wright campaigned hard for Van Buren's reelection in 1840 and after his friend's defeat, for his renomination by the Democrats in 1844. He cordially approved Van Buren's arrangement with the likely Whig candidate, Henry Clay, to keep the slavery issue out of the campaign by agreeing to oppose the annexation of slave-holding Texas. He was so bitter when the Democratic national convention in Baltimore nominated James K. Polk of Tennessee, a supporter of annexation, that when the convention nominated him for vice president in an attempt to mollify Van Buren's supporters, he refused to run. "WILL SUPPORT MR. POLK CHEERFULLY, BUT CAN NOT ACCEPT THE NOMINATION FOR VICE-PRESIDENT," he informed the delegates over Samuel F. B. Morse's newly invented "magnetic electric telegraph." The delegates were forced to reconvene and nominate another candidate.

Wright voted to reject a treaty annexing Texas, but he did support Polk for president because he did not blame him for Van Buren's defeat at the convention. When pressured to run for governor of New York to help carry the state for Polk, he reluctantly agreed. The strategy succeeded. Wright defeated the Whig candidate, Millard Fillmore, by 10,000 votes, twice the margin by which Polk carried the state.

Wright's term as governor was vexed by conflicts in the Democratic party between a conservative Hunker faction and the so-called Barnburners. He successfully vetoed Hunker attempts to resume what he considered an unwise expansion of the state system of canals, but destroyed his administration by using the militia in the so-called Anti-Rent war of 1845. About 1.8 million acres in the Hudson valley were held by small farmers under long-term leases dating back to the seventeenth century. The rent, in most cases in the form of produce, was owed to large landowners whose ancestors had obtained large grants under the Dutch Charter of Freedoms and Exemptions of 1629. Much of it was unpaid; the tenants, having farmed the land for generations, considered themselves by right owners and the "rent" a form of feudal dues. In 1844–1845 irate farmers disguised as Indians resisted sheriffs' efforts to serve warrants and in one instance killed a deputy who was trying to seize the cattle of a defaulting farmer. Wright ordered militia into the region to preserve order, and while he called for legislation putting an end to the outmoded system, he insisted that the rents were legal and that rioters must be punished. This cost him heavily in the affected district, and—combined with the defection of the Hunker faction because of his opposition to canal construction—it resulted in his defeat when he ran for reelection in 1846.

Wright then retired to his farm in Canton, much to the satisfaction of his wife, who had never accustomed herself to life in Washington or Albany. During the spring and summer of 1847 he became a full-time farmer, working daily in the fields. Like many of his contemporaries, he had been a heavy drinker; now he became, in the words of an amazed friend, "a most *abstinent teetotaller*!" The combination of hard physical labor and the sudden abandonment of alcohol undoubtedly contributed to the fatal heart attack he suffered while picking up his mail one day in the Canton post office.

Silas Wright was not an original thinker or a particularly radical person. During his early career his inclinations were Jeffersonian, and he tended to consult with close associates before taking a position on new issues. He did not change fundamentally as time passed, but his views evolved; in his last years he lost interest in protectionism and showed an increasing concern about the spread of slavery in the territories. He came to reject the political expediency he had learned and admired as a member of the Albany Regency. He opposed the annexation of Texas in 1844 even though accepting it would probably have insured Van Buren's election as president. Despite a fondness for alcohol advertised by his florid complexion, his fundamental integrity and stern honesty won him the nickname "the Cato of the Senate."

• Wright left no collection of his correspondence; thus letters written to him are rare. There are, however, hundreds of his own letters in the papers of his associates, the most important being the Azariah C. Flagg Papers in the New York Public Library; the Martin Van Buren, Andrew Jackson, William L. Marcy, and James K. Polk Papers in the Library of Congress; and the George Bancroft Papers in the Massachusetts Historical Society. There is also a small collection of Wright material at St. Lawrence University in Canton, New York. Ransom H. Gillet, *Life and Times of Silas Wright* (2 vols., 1874), contains many Wright letters not available elsewhere, and Jabez D. Hammond's *Life and Times of Silas Wright* (1848), part of his *History of Political Parties in the State of New-York* (1842–1848), is full of valuable material. The only modern biography is John A. Garraty, *Silas Wright* (1949).

JOHN A. GARRATY

WRIGHT, Sophie Bell (5 June 1866–10 June 1912), educator and humanitarian, was born in New Orleans, Louisiana, the daughter of William H. Wright, a planter and former Confederate soldier who had been impoverished by the Civil War, and Mary S. Bell, daughter of a planter from St. Mary Parish, Louisiana. Permanently crippled by a fall at age three and immobilized for some six years, Sophie was educated at home until about 1875. An apt pupil, she attended elementary and secondary schools at Franklin, St. Mary Parish, Louisiana, until she was fourteen. Two years later, recognizing the inadequacy of her education, Wright arranged to teach mathematics at Peabody Normal Seminary in New Orleans, in exchange for the privilege of attending other classes there.

In 1881 Wright opened a "Day School for Girls" in one room of her mother's home at Race and Constance streets in New Orleans, serving a rapidly growing enrollment. Chartered in 1883 as the Home Institute, the school was expanded in 1885 to accommodate female boarders and to provide free classes in the evening for male students who were employed during the day. Like most southern schools of its day, the Home Institute enrolled only white pupils. Impetus for establishing the night school came from a circus acrobat who appealed for help in preparing for a civil service examination. Teaching the girls during the day, Wright tutored him in the evening and soon recognized the desire for learning among many New Orleans men and boys whose formal education had been curtailed by economic necessity. Hers was, at the time, the only free night school in New Orleans. Proceeds from the Home Institute and volunteer teachers sustained the night school, where courses of study ranged from the basics of reading and writing to shorthand and mechanical drawing. Many evening students went on to careers in business, sales, transportation, printing, and other trades.

By 1897, with a night enrollment of 300, Wright had incurred considerable debt to acquire a more spacious building at 1440–1446 Camp Street. A severe epidemic of yellow fever that year necessitated closing schools and suspending all nonessential activity. Jeopardizing her own less than robust health, Wright converted the school into a dispensary for medicines, food, and clothing. With the help of volunteers, she cared for the sick and the destitute, explaining, "It was so lonesome, and I was afraid to think of the debt, and there was so much to do and so many needed help" (quoted in Matthews, p.11).

With the Home Institute closed and no tuition coming in, Wright's financial situation remained grim even after the epidemic subsided. Fortunately, the benefactors prevented foreclosure, funded renovations, and helped to purchase better furnishings and equipment. Reopened in December 1897 with 300 students, within a year night school enrollment had increased to 1,000; several years later registration peaked at nearly 1,600. Expanded courses of study included algebra, geometry, calculus, bookkeeping, and other subjects. The faculty of forty included teachers conversant in French, German, Italian, and other foreign languages who were able to communicate with non-English-speaking students. In 1904, as women increasingly entered the business world, 200 female students were admitted to certain departments of the night school. A Public Evening School operated by the city school system opened in 1905, and in 1909 Wright closed the night school. During its twenty-five years of existence, it educated more than 25,000 pupils. According to the New Orleans Picayune, "The result [of her dedicated efforts] is that her army of scholars fairly idolize her, and throughout the community she is held in the highest esteem and respect" (1 May 1904). After Wright's death her sisters continued to operate the Home Institute until 1928.

Wright also authored a series of inspirational articles for youth, published first in the New Orleans Picayune and then collected in a monograph entitled Heart to Heart Talks (1908; reissued 1910), in which she exhorted her readers to be honorable and virtuous. An excerpt from the essay "Our Girls and Boys" exemplifies her philosophy and the attitude she sought to instill in her students: "O, for the manly boy that respects girlhood and old age and for the refined girl who is ready to show the same courtesy to the poor woman as to the woman of wealth, just because she is somebody's mother" (1910 ed., p. 24).

The plight of a crippled orphan alerted Wright that no public institution for disabled children then existed in Louisiana. In 1904 she petitioned the Home for Incurables in New Orleans for permission to build an annex to that institution to house crippled youngsters. Within a year she had raised the requisite $10,000, and soon the annex was operating. Among other charitable and civic accomplishments, Wright was instrumental in founding Rest Awhile, a vacation center at Mandeville, Louisiana, for working women and girls. She also helped to expand the facilities of the Eye, Ear, Nose, and Throat Hospital. Wright held state office in the International Order of the King's Daughters and Sons, served as president of the Woman's Club of New Orleans from 1897 to 1898 and the Home for Incurables from 1908 to 1912, and was active in the Prison Reform Association, the Young Women's Christian Association, and the Traveler's Aid Society.

A grateful citizenry bestowed many honors upon Wright. In 1904 she became the third person and the first woman to receive the Picayune Loving Cup, awarded to the person who rendered the greatest service to the community during the past year. According to effusive newspaper accounts, the presentation occasioned an outpouring of "the admiration and love of an entire city to its most valued citizen" in "the most remarkable tribute of affection almost ever laid at the feet of a woman" (Picayune, 30 Apr. 1904). Wright taught until just a few days before she died in New Orleans of valvular heart disease. She had never married or had children. The Picayune acclaimed her as a "saint of common weal," and she is remembered in association with the New Orleans street and public school that bear her name.

• No corpus of Wright's papers has been located. Most sketches of her life are based on John L. Matthews, The Story of a Noble Life (c. 1906), and an obituary in the New Orleans Picayune, 11 June 1912. See also Rodney Cline, Pioneer Leaders and Early Institutions in Louisiana Education (1969), and Robert Meyer, Jr., Names over New Orleans Public Schools (1975).

FLORENCE M. JUMONVILLE

WRIGHT, Susanna (4 Aug. 1697–1 Dec. 1784), frontierswoman and writer, was born in Lancashire, England, the daughter of Patience Gibson and John Wright, of Warrington and, later, Manchester, England. John Wright trained as a physician, became a practicing Quaker minister, and made his living variously as a tradesman, a farmer, and a ferry master. The Wright family immigrated to Pennsylvania in 1714, bringing a certificate of good standing from

Hartshaw Monthly Meeting in Lancashire that John Wright presented to Chester (Pa.) Monthly Meeting later that year together with a certificate from Philadelphia Monthly Meeting, indicating a brief residence in Philadelphia. The family later became members of New Garden Monthly Meeting and Sadsbury Monthly Meeting. John Wright purchased land below Chester in an area then known as Chamassungh or Finland.

Sometime between c. 1726 and 1728 the Wrights moved to the Susquehanna River Valley, at that time the westernmost Pennsylvania frontier, to establish Wright's Ferry (later Columbia) and provide a Quaker presence in an area where Indian tribes were leaving and communities of Germans and Scots-Irish were already established. Susanna Wright lived the rest of her long life in that area, by c. 1741 in the house that became known as Wright's Ferry Mansion and after 1757 (possibly earlier) in a larger house to which she had been given a life interest in 1745 by Samuel Blunston, longtime companion and friend. She never married, but she assumed responsibility for managing her father's extensive household when her mother died in 1722, and later she helped to care for the family of her brother James.

In addition to the arduous work associated with maintaining a frontier household, particularly one located at a major intersection for travelers, Wright pursued a variety of scientific and civic activities. She experimented with the cultivation of silkworms, at one point winning a prize in Philadelphia for raising the best cocoons. Local and family traditions maintain that Wright explored the medicinal uses of herbs, acted as an unpaid apothecary and physician for her neighbors, and served her community as an informal arbiter of disputes and drafter of deeds, wills, and indentures. Leonard W. Labaree suggests that Wright, and perhaps her brother James, contributed to Benjamin Franklin's pamphlet narrative denouncing the massacre of the Conestoga Indians.

These accomplishments and Wright's widely appreciated hospitality would have been enough to make her well known in her region. But it was her remarkable education and literary accomplishment that earned her a reputation in a much larger circle of Pennsylvania citizens. Wright maintained an extensive correspondence with James Logan from 1718 until his death in 1751 and exchanged several letters with Benjamin Franklin in the 1750s. She was part of a network of Pennsylvania poets, exchanging verse with Hannah Griffitts and Deborah Logan. Her Philadelphia connections, including Charles Norris and Isaac Norris, loaned her books from their well-stocked libraries. She was fluent in French, was competent in Italian and Latin, and studied extensively in natural philosophy. Shortly before her death in Columbia, Pennsylvania, she confided to physician Benjamin Rush "that she still retained her relish for books—'that she could not live without them.'" Enjoying her learned conversation, Franklin, Rush, and historian Robert Proud made her home a stopping place in their travels. Rush notes in his journal when he met "the famous Suzey

Wright a lady who has been celebrated Above half a Century for her wit—good Sense & valuable improvements of mind" (Butterfield, p. 455).

Wright apparently wrote prolifically. Some two dozen letters are presently recoverable, and Joshua Francis Fisher noted in his nineteenth-century account that her poems were "dated in almost every year of the last century" (p. 177). More than thirty have been located, most of which are in Milcah Martha Moore's eighteenth-century commonplace book, now held at Haverford College. The Moore collection suggests Wright's range as a poet: neoclassical meditations on subjects such as time or labor, occasional verses on birthdays and deaths, an imitation of Racine, biblical paraphrases and devotional pieces, and verse letters and exchanges. Two long pieces in the Historical Society of Pennsylvania—"To Eliz^a Norris at Fairhill" and "The Grove"—reveal a skilled poet at work. "To Eliz^a Norris," probably written before Norris's death in 1779, redirects the fire of revolutionary rhetoric to women's independence. After tracing the conventional Christian basis for male authority back to Eden, Wright uses Enlightenment assumptions to take that authority apart:

> But womankind call reason to their aid,
> And question when or where that law was made,
> That law divine (a plausible pretence)
> Oft urg'd with none, & oft with little sense.

"The Grove" skillfully builds heroic couplets around the controlling image of a decimated forest, a figure recalling Edenic nature and the consequences of its destruction for human culture, and in the process developing a powerful meditation on mortality and memory, power and waste, myth and history:

> For mortal man, mistaken Adam's son,
> Completes the draught his hapless sire begun,
> Must drink—but drinking deeply is undone.

Almost certainly other poems remain to be found, though a contemporary biographical sketch, possibly by Deborah Logan, explains that "as she wrote not for fame, she never kept copies, and it is to be feared but little is at this time recoverable" (Knapp, p. 486).

• Wright's extant correspondence and poetry are at the Historical Society of Pennsylvania, Haverford College, and the Chester County (Pa.) Historical Society. Other materials that may develop this outline of Wright's life and works are held in the Wright's Ferry Mansion archive, but scholars have been denied access. The texts of two of Wright's poems have been published in Pattie Cowell, *Women Poets in Pre-Revolutionary America, 1650–1775: An Anthology* (1981). "To Eliz^a Norris" is available in Cowell, "'Womankind Call Reason to Their Aid': Susanna Wright's Verse Epistle on the Status of Women in Eighteenth-Century America," *Signs* 6 (1981): 795–800. The Moore commonplace book has been edited by Catherine Blecki and Karin Wulf, *Milcah Martha Moore's Book: A Commonplace Book from Revolutionary America* (1997). This archival material for reconstructing Wright's life is supplemented by two nineteenth-century accounts, both of which draw on a contemporary sketch by Joshua Francis Fisher, "Some Account of the Early Poets and Poetry of

Pennsylvania," ed. Samuel Hazard, *Register of Pennsylvania* 8 (17 Sept. 1831): 177–78, and Samuel Knapp, *Female Biography* (1836). Wright's correspondence with Franklin has been published in *The Papers of Benjamin Franklin*, ed. Leonard W. Labaree et al. (1959–). Lyman H. Butterfield's text of "Dr. Benjamin Rush's Journal of a Trip to Carlisle in 1784," *Pennsylvania Magazine of History and Biography* 74 (Oct. 1950): 455, outlines Rush's impression of Wright. More recent sketches are available in Marion Reninger, "Susanna Wright," Lancaster Co. (Pa.) Historical Society *Papers*, 63 (1959): 183–89, and Karin Wulf, "A Marginal Independence: Unmarried Women in Colonial Philadelphia" (Ph.D. diss., Johns Hopkins Univ., 1993). Lorett Treese provided copies of important archival materials for shaping this sketch of Wright's life.

PATTIE COWELL

WRIGHT, Theodore Paul (25 May 1895–21 Aug. 1970), aviation administrator and educator, was born in Galesburg, Illinois, the son of Philip Green Wright, a college professor, and Elizabeth Quincy. Wright grew up in a financially secure family; his father taught mathematics at Galesburg's Lombard College and imbued his sons with a sense of social duty. Wright's two older brothers excelled in their professions, Sewall as a geneticist and Quincy as a scholar of international law, and their achievements motivated young Ted to succeed as well. Wright graduated from Lombard with a B.S. in 1915 and studied architectural engineering at the Massachusetts Institute of Technology (MIT), where he received a second B.S. in 1918, the year he also married Margaret McCarl. They had two children.

During the military preparedness movement that preceded U.S. entry into World War I, Wright enrolled in the U.S. Navy Reserve Flying Corps at MIT in 1917 and learned to fly. After graduating, he became a naval aircraft inspector after eight weeks of additional studies in aeronautical engineering. Among his responsibilities was certification of a trio of flying boats (NC-1, NC-3, and NC-4) to fly across the Atlantic, successfully completed in 1919 by the Curtiss NC-4. After his discharge in 1921, he landed a job with the Curtiss Aeroplane and Motor Company as an engineer. He remained at Curtiss for nearly two decades, in 1930 rising to the rank of corporate vice president of one of the world's largest aircraft manufacturers at the time.

Wright spent many years at Curtiss as its chief engineer, presiding over design and construction of pacesetting aircraft such as a series that won Pulitzer race honors as well as the prestigious Schneider International Cup contests. There were famous military designs like the Hawk, Falcon, and Helldiver, as well as civil personal planes like the prize-winning Tanager, which won the Guggenheim Safe Aircraft Competition in 1929. Wright presided over development of the classic Curtiss Robin light plane of the 1930s, along with the Condor airliner and C-46 Commando twin-engine transport of World War II. This catholic experience yielded the practical knowledge that led Wright to develop the "project engineer" system of design, development, and manufacture, which gave one individual comprehensive authority for all phases so that continuity never lagged. He also developed a statistical procedure to predict the curve of variable production costs.

After World War II convulsed Europe in 1939, President Franklin D. Roosevelt tapped Wright to join the National Defense Advisory Commission to plan the rational expansion of industrial production for national defense. After Pearl Harbor, Wright resigned his several posts with Curtiss-Wright Corporation (renamed after a 1929 merger involving the pioneer firm affiliated with Orville Wright and Wilbur Wright) to become a wartime administrator. He was appointed assistant chief for aircraft manufacture within the national organization that eventually became the Office of Production Management. He served concurrently on several key wartime boards, including the Anglo-American committee that scheduled aircraft deliveries from both sides of the Atlantic. By all accounts, he played a key role in accomplishing the unprecedented record of some 100,000 planes produced annually in the United States.

In 1944 Wright accepted a presidential appointment as administrator of the Civil Aeronautics Administration (CAA), a position of great influence in shaping the development of aeronautics in postwar America. During nearly four years as head of the CAA, Wright wisely guided its transition into peacetime operations. He proved especially helpful in promoting private flying, expanding modern radio and electronic navigational systems, and equipping major airports with instrument landing systems. At the same time, he served as technical secretary of the International Civil Aviation Conference, which convened in Chicago at the end of 1944. His international negotiating skills and personal acquaintance with numerous delegates (acquired during his wartime production work with allied personnel from other nations) helped successfully draft the basic rules for safety on postwar global airline routes.

Tired of political battles and bureaucratic conflicts involving Congress and various aviation lobby groups, Wright resigned in 1948 and joined Cornell University as its president for research and director of the Cornell Aeronautical Laboratory. The laboratory became a center for studies in aviation safety and also won millions of dollars in contracts for military research on airplanes, helicopters, missiles, and related systems.

Wright was active in many aviation organizations, serving in an executive capacity with leading groups like the Flight Safety Foundation and the National Advisory Committee for Aeronautics, and he was president of the Institute of Aeronautical Sciences (now the American Institute of Aeronautics and Astronautics).

In addition to Wright's influence on manufacturing procedures, wartime management, and educational leadership, he published a number of articles on the social and economic aspects of aviation. More than others in his position, Wright took a long view on the social consequences of aviation. For the Wilbur Wright Memorial Lecture, delivered for the Royal

Aeronautical Society in London in 1945, he chose the topic "Aviation's Place in Civilization," noting the destructiveness of aerial warfare as well as the promise of global air travel. His final publication, on population and the environment, appeared only months before he died, in Ithaca, New York.

• There is a collection of Wright's papers in the archives of Cornell University Library, Ithaca, N.Y. Many of Wright's own observations about engineering and aviation technology have been collected in T. P. Wright, *Articles and Papers of Theodore P. Wright* (1969–1970). There is a useful summary of his life in *Current Biography* (1945). Wright's career in the CAA is discussed in John R. M. Wilson, *Turbulence Aloft: The Civil Aeronautics Administration amid Wars and Rumors of Wars, 1938–1953* (1979). For commentary on manufacturing concepts and wartime industry, see Irving Brinton Holley, *Buying Aircraft: Materiel Procurement for the Army Air Forces* (1964). An obituary is in the *New York Times*, 22 Aug. 1970.

ROGER E. BILSTEIN

WRIGHT, Theodore Sedgwick (1797–25 Mar. 1847), black Presbyterian minister and reformer, was born in New Jersey and brought up in Schenectady, New York, the son of R. P. G. Wright, an early opponent of the American Colonization Society's program of returning American blacks to Africa. (His mother's name is unknown.) He was named after a distinguished Massachusetts jurist, Theodore Sedgwick, (1746–1813), whose defense of a slave woman against her master's claim of ownership had effectively abolished slavery in that state.

Wright received a good education in spite of rejection by a number of colleges to which he applied. After several years at New York's African Free School, he was admitted into Princeton Theological Seminary in 1825 at the age of twenty-eight. Well treated there by both fellow students and faculty, he graduated in 1828, thus becoming the first American of his race to complete a theological seminary program. That same year Wright was chosen to be pastor of New York City's First Colored Presbyterian Church, which had been founded some years earlier by pioneer black journalist Samuel Cornish. Wright devoted the remaining two decades of his life to building this church into a large (more than 400 members) and socially concerned black congregation.

Angered by the oppression of his race, Wright became a social activist on many fronts. He and Cornish were charter members of the largely white American Anti-Slavery Society, founded in 1833. They served for several years with white radicals Arthur and Lewis Tappan on the society's executive committee. Both of them withdrew from the Presbytery of New York because of its opposition to censuring southern Presbyterian slave owners and joined the abolition-inclined Third Presbytery. When the New York Vigilance Committee was founded in 1835 to combat the kidnapping of free blacks off the streets of Manhattan into slavery, and to help fugitive slaves, Wright became its first chairman. In 1839, when the American Anti-Slavery Society's founder and chief staff member, William Lloyd Garrison, denounced political activity as a means of reform, Wright withdrew from the AASS. He had become a strong supporter of the most extensive African-American political effort to date: the New York State campaign to recover full voting rights for black males by securing signatures on petitions to the state legislature and by lobbying individual legislators.

Wright's blend of spiritual fervor, clarity of thought, anger over racial discrimination, and political activism helped to influence young black pastors such as Charles Ray, Henry Highland Garnet, and Amos Beman, who later became leaders of the drives for reenfranchisement in New York State and Connecticut. Wright's speeches to gatherings of mostly white abolitionists denounced slavery, the American Colonization Society, and prejudice against free blacks and commanded their rapt attention.

Bitter personal experience lay behind Wright's denunciation of prejudice. During an alumni gathering at Princeton, he had been publicly humiliated by being called "nigger" and kicked several times by a Princeton alumnus. Several years later, in excoriating discriminatory treatment of black passengers on shipboard, Wright cited three cases of black people whose deaths had resulted from the exposure forced on them when, refused cabins, they had had to stay on deck through a cold and stormy night. One of those casualties had been his young wife, whom he probably married in 1828 and who had died in 1829, a few months after such exposure on a boat from Brunswick, New Jersey, to New York City and again on her passage up the Hudson to Schenectady. Wright had suffered in less dramatic ways, too, by being made to feel like a pariah at presbytery meetings when white clergy entered the pew where he was sitting at prayer, saw that he was black, and hastily withdrew looking for another pew.

For Wright the exclusion of blacks from equal education was, next to slavery, American society's greatest crime against his race. "They keep us down," he agonized, "drive us out of their schools, mob and break down our schools and then point at us in scorn as an inferior race of men. 'Can't learn anything.' Why don't they let us try?" (1836). Wright was a central figure in the founding of the Phoenix Society, a many-faceted educational enterprise for blacks in New York City. Begun in 1833, the society aimed to provide basic schooling for children and assistance to young men toward apprenticeships and long-term employment as "mechanics." That same year Wright, Cornish, and black Episcopal priest Peter Williams, Jr., opened a private high school for black males; they established one for women three years later. But by 1838 both schools had to close for lack of funds.

In May 1837 Wright married Adeline T. Turpin of New Rochelle, New York. There is no record of children borne by either of his wives.

Wright died in New York City. His death at age fifty was said to have been hastened by overwork and by undue exposure to the elements in covering a huge parish on foot—blacks risked humiliation and physical injury if they tried to board the "horse cars." Thousands attended his funeral or joined in an extended funeral march through the streets of lower Manhattan. William Lloyd Garrison, setting aside earlier bitter disagreement with Wright over political action, published a lengthy and generally laudatory obituary in his weekly, the *Liberator*.

• Wright's published works include *A Pastoral Letter Addressed to the Colored Presbyterian Church, in the City of New York, June 20th, 1832* (1832); "The Progress of the Anti-slavery Cause" and "Prejudice against the Colored Man" (Sept. 1837), reprinted in Carter Woodson, ed., *Negro Orators and Orations* (1925), pp. 86–95; with Samuel E. Cornish, *The Colonization Scheme Considered, in Its Rejection by the Colored People—in Its Tendency to Uphold Caste—in Its Unfitness for Christianizing and Civilizing the Aborigines of Africa, . . .* (1840); with Charles B. Ray and James McCune Smith, *An Address to the Three Thousand Colored Citizens of New York Who Are the Owners of One Hundred and Twenty Thousand Acres of Land in the State of New York, Given to Them by Gerrit Smith, Esq. . . .* (1846).

Wright also contributed to *The First Annual Report of the New York Committee of Vigilance* (1837). Useful information can be found in Bella Gross, "Life and Times of Theodore S. Wright, 1797–1847," *Negro History Bulletin* 3 (1939–1940): 133–38, 144. The most detailed account of Wright's life is in David E. Swift's collective biography of six black ministers, *Black Prophets of Justice: Activist Clergy before the Civil War* (1989).

DAVID E. SWIFT

WRIGHT, Wilbur (16 Apr. 1867–30 May 1912), and **Orville Wright** (19 Aug. 1871–30 Jan. 1948), inventors of the airplane, were born, respectively, near Millville, Indiana, and in Dayton, Ohio, the sons of Milton Wright, a clergyman, and Susan Catherine Koerner. Their father, who rose from circuit preacher to bishop of the Church of the United Brethren in Christ, and their mother presided over a loving home where children were encouraged to think for themselves and support one another. "From the time we were little children," Wilbur remarked just before his death, "my brother Orville and myself lived together, played together, worked together, and in fact, thought together. . . . nearly everything that was done in our lives has been the result of conversations, suggestions and discussions between us."

Wilbur Wright enrolled in college preparatory classes at Dayton's Central High School with the intention of entering Yale and studying for the clergy. His plans were shattered that winter when he was struck in the face while playing "shinny," a kind of free-form ice hockey, on a neighborhood pond. The facial injuries led to physical and psychological complications. He remained at home for the next three years, reading widely in his father's extensive library; nursing his mother, who was dying of tuberculosis; and keeping house for his father, younger brother, and sister.

The Wright family passed through a series of crises in the spring and summer of 1889. In May of that year, Bishop Wright ended two decades of struggle over

church doctrine when he led a small group of followers to establish a new Brethren organization. Susan Wright died on 4 July. Orville, who had completed the eleventh grade, decided not to return to school that September. Instead, he and Wilbur established themselves as job printers. It was the beginning of a lifelong business partnership.

The Wright brothers, neither of whom ever married, enjoyed a modest prosperity as printers, producing everything from church tracts to business cards and advertising circulars. From May 1889 to August 1890 they also published two neighborhood newspapers, the *West Side News* and the *Evening Item*. The brothers branched out in 1892, hiring help to assist with the print shop and establishing a bicycle repair and sales business. Within four years they had begun the small-scale manufacture and sale of bicycles. It was clear, however, that Wilbur, far from satisfied with his life as a small businessman, was in search of a challenge against which to measure himself. He found it in the airplane.

The Wrights dated the origin of their interest in flight to 1878, when their father had presented them with a toy helicopter. News accounts of the death of the German gliding pioneer Otto Lilienthal in an August 1896 glider crash reawakened their interest and led to a search for trustworthy information on aeronautics. On 30 May 1899, having exhausted the resources of the local public library, Wilbur wrote to the Smithsonian Institution requesting advice on additional readings. "I am an enthusiast," he acknowledged, "but not a crank in the sense that I have some pet theory as to the proper construction of a flying machine. I wish to avail myself of all that is already known and then if possible add my mite to help on the future worker who will attain final success."

The Wrights concluded that the construction of a mechanical flying machine would require the solution of problems in aerodynamics, propulsion, and control. Reasoning that earlier experimenters had designed wings capable of flight and engines with enough power to propel a craft through the air, the brothers focused their attention on devising a mechanical system that would enable the operator to maneuver a flying machine in all three axes of motion: pitch, roll, and yaw. Wing-warping, the notion of achieving control in roll by twisting the wing across the span to increase lift on one tip while decreasing it on the other, was their first in a series of key intellectual breakthroughs.

Encouraged by the successful test of the new system on a small biplane kite flown near Dayton in the summer of 1899, the Wrights designed and built a kite/glider large enough to carry a human being aloft. After consulting U.S. Weather Bureau publications and corresponding with a local resident, they selected the little fishing village of Kitty Hawk, North Carolina, as a suitable test site where they would find isolation from prying eyes, tall sand dunes from which to launch their machine, and the high steady winds required to keep it aloft.

Tested from 3 to 18 October 1900, the first full-scale Wright glider had 165 square feet of wing area, weighed some 112 pounds, and featured an elevator placed in front of the wings for pitch control. The control system seemed satisfactory, but the wings generated much less lift than predicted by calculation. Most of the tests were made with the unmanned craft flown as a kite while a careful record was kept of wind speed, the amount of lift generated, and the angle of attack at which the machine flew.

From 17 July to 16 August 1901 the brothers conducted a new series of tests at Kitty Hawk with a second glider featuring 290 square feet of wing area. The larger wing enabled Wilbur, who did all of the flying prior to 1902, to spend more time in the air, but the performance of the machine remained disappointing.

Discouraged but determined to preserve a record of their two years of experience, Wilbur accepted the invitation of his friend, the civil engineer and aeronautical pioneer Octave Chanute, to address a meeting of the Western Society of Engineers in Chicago. That talk, "Some Aeronautical Experiments," presented on the evening of 18 September 1901 and published in the journal of the society, indicated the extent to which the Wrights, in spite of their disappointments, had already moved far beyond all other flying-machine experimenters.

The brothers knew that the disappointing performance of their machines could be explained only by assuming an error in the experimental data published by their predecessors. They set out to collect accurate information with a wind tunnel constructed in the back room of the bicycle shop. Nowhere is the genius of the Wright brothers so clear as in the design and operation of their wind tunnel balances, the instruments set inside the tunnel to measure the forces operating on small model airfoils. Constructed of bicycle spoke wire and hacksaw blades, the balances enabled Wilbur and Orville to gather those precise bits of information required to design the wings of a flying machine.

The Wrights tested their third glider near Kitty Hawk from 15 September to 24 October 1902, completing more than 250 flights during which they covered distances of up to 622.5 feet and remained in the air for up to twenty-six seconds. With the major aerodynamic and control problems behind them, they pressed forward with the design and construction of their first powered machine. The brothers built a four-cylinder engine with the assistance of Charles Taylor, a machinist whom they employed in the bicycle shop. The design of the twin pusher propellers puzzled them until they realized that an efficient propeller was a rotary wing in which the lifting force was vectored as thrust.

Success came on the morning of 17 December 1903, with four powered flights made from a strip of level sand four miles south of Kitty Hawk. Orville made the first flight, covering 120 feet in twelve seconds. Wilbur was in control during the fourth and best flight of the day: 856 feet in fifty-nine seconds. For the first time in history, a heavier-than-air flying machine had taken off from level ground under its own power and had flown far enough to demonstrate beyond any doubt that it was operating under the control of the pilot.

Determined to move from marginal success to a practical airplane, the Wrights built and flew two more powered aircraft from a pasture eight miles east of Dayton in 1904 and 1905. They continued to improve the design of their machines during this period, gaining skill and confidence in the air. By October 1905 they were remaining in the air for up to thirty-nine minutes at a time. No longer able to hide the extent of their success from the press, and afraid that the essential features of their machine would be understood and copied by knowledgeable observers, the Wright brothers decided to cease flying until their invention was protected by patents and they had negotiated a contract for its sale.

The claim of the Wrights to have flown was widely debated during the years 1906 to 1908. A handful of European and American pioneers struggled into the air in machines designed on the basis of an incomplete understanding of Wright technology, while the brothers, confident that they retained a commanding lead over their rivals, continued to negotiate with financiers and government purchasing agents on two continents.

Finally, in February 1908 the Wrights signed a contract for the sale of an airplane to the U.S. Army. For a price of $25,000, they agreed to deliver and demonstrate an airplane capable of flying for one hour with a pilot and passenger at a speed of at least forty miles per hour. The following month they negotiated a second agreement with a group of French investors interested in building and selling Wright machines.

Not having flown since October 1905, the brothers would have to brush up their flying skills. With the new aircraft that they would fly in Europe and America under construction, they returned to the Outer Banks of North Carolina in May 1908, where they made twenty-two flights with the 1905 machine, modified with upright seating and new hand controls. On one of those flights, Wilbur carried aloft their first passenger, mechanic Charles Furnas.

Wilbur immediately left for France, where he made his first public flight from a racetrack near Le Mans on 8 August. All of the doubts of the Wright claims were immediately swept away. Overnight Wilbur became the toast of Europe. Kings, queens, and prime ministers, the elite of the continent, came to Le Mans, Pau, and to Centocelle, near Rome, to watch him fly. The new century had produced its first hero.

Orville began the U.S. Army trials at Fort Myer, Virginia, with a flight on 3 September 1908. Nine days later he was flying with a passenger, Lieutenant Thomas E. Selfridge, when a propeller split. Orville survived the resulting crash, but Selfridge became the first human being to die in the crash of a powered aircraft. During the course of his recovery, Orville and his sister Katharine joined Wilbur in Europe. Together the brothers returned to Fort Myer in 1909, completed the trials, and concluded the sale of the first airplane to the U.S. Army.

Increasingly Wilbur focused his energies on business and legal activities. As president of the Wright Company, organized in 1909, he was associated with a board of directors that included August Belmont, Cornelius Vanderbilt, and Robert J. Collier. The new company maintained offices in New York City, a factory in Dayton, and a flying field and training school on the spot where the brothers had flown in 1904 and 1905. As chief flight instructor, Orville selected and trained the members of the Wright exhibition flying team, whose aerial performances thrilled millions of spectators across the nation. Other pupils included Lieutenant John Rogers, the first U.S. naval aviator; and Lieutenant Henry H. Arnold, who commanded the U.S. Army Air Forces in World War II.

After 1910 Wilbur took the lead in bringing legal suits against rival aircraft builders in America and Europe whom the brothers believed had infringed on their patent rights. The cases were bitterly contested over a period of seven years. In Germany the Wrights claims were disallowed on the basis of prior disclosure. Even in France and America, where the brothers were awarded interim judgments, the defendants were able to avoid a definitive verdict and substantial legal penalties.

On 2 May 1912 Wilbur returned home to Dayton following a series of legal meetings and court appearances. He was exhausted and suffering from what the family doctor diagnosed as typhoid fever. He died at home. "A short life, full of consequences," Bishop Wright reported in his diary that evening. "An unfailing intellect, imperturbable temper, great self-reliance, and as great modesty, seeing the right clearly, pursuing it steadfastly, he lived and died." With the death of his brother, Orville assumed leadership of the Wright Company. He was primarily responsible for designing new types of Wright aircraft between 1909 and 1915 and was awarded the prestigious Collier Trophy in 1913 for the development of an automatic stabilizer for aircraft.

In 1915 Orville Wright sold his shares in the company to a group of financiers. He worked as an aeronautical engineer and consultant during World War I, helping plan the production of foreign aircraft designs by the Dayton-Wright Company and playing a role in the development of a pilotless aircraft bomb. He retired from active involvement in the aircraft industry following the war but remained a major figure in American life for the next half century. His continued service to aviation included membership on both the National Advisory Committee for Aeronautics and the board of the Daniel and Florence Guggenheim Fund for the Promotion of Aeronautics.

Shy and retiring, Orville avoided public ceremonial occasions, preferring to spend his time with family and friends or working in his private laboratory in Dayton. He devoted considerable attention to defending his position as coinventor of the airplane against the claims of those said to have flown prior to the Wrights. He loaned the 1903 Wright airplane to the London Science Museum in 1925, vowing that the world's first airplane would not return to the United States until the Smithsonian Institution repudiated its claim that a craft designed by Samuel P. Langley had been capable of flight before the Wright brothers'. The Wright-Smithsonian feud continued until 1944, when Smithsonian secretary Charles Abbot finally agreed to Orville's conditions. Orville Wright died in Dayton.

The Wright brothers were the inventors of the airplane in a much truer sense than Samuel Morse can be said to have invented the telegraph, Alexander Graham Bell the telephone, or Thomas Edison the incandescent lamp. They attacked an enormously difficult set of technical problems that had baffled great minds for over a century and achieved enormous conceptual leaps that carried them far beyond any of their contemporaries. Their work stands as the very definition of engineering excellence.

• The bulk of the papers of Wilbur and Orville Wright are held by the Manuscript Division of the Library of Congress. The Wright State University Archive maintains a collection of family papers and photographs. Orville Wright, *How We Invented the Airplane* (1953), is a good first-person description of the events surrounding the invention of the airplane; together, *The Papers of Wilbur and Orville Wright*, ed. Marvin W. McFarland (2 vols., 1953), and *Miracle at Kitty Hawk: The Letters of Wilbur and Orville Wright*, ed. Fred Kelly (1951), contain most of the documents relating to the invention. Arthur G. Renstrom, *Wilbur and Orville Wright: A Bibliography* (1968), remains the best available bibliography of printed materials by and related to the brothers. Other useful reference tools are Renstrom, *Wilbur and Orville Wright: A Chronology* (1975) and *Wilbur and Orville Wright: Pictorial Materials, a Documentary Guide* (1982), and Patrick A. Noland and John Zamonski, *The Wright Brothers Collection: A Guide to the Technical, Business, and Legal, Genealogical, Photographic and Other Archives at Wright State University* (1977). Kelly, *The Wright Brothers* (1943), the authorized biography, is dated. Tom D. Crouch, *The Bishop's Boys: A Life of Wilbur and Orville Wright* (1989), and Fred Howard, *Wilbur and Orville: A Biography of the Wright Brothers* (1987), are good current biographies. Peter Jakab, *Visions of a Flying Machine* (1990), and Howard Wolko, ed., *The Wright Flyer: An Engineering Perspective* (1987), offer insight into the details of Wright technology. Charles Harvard Gibbs-Smith, *The Wright Brothers and the Rebirth of European Aviation, 1902–1908* (1974), and Alfred Gollin, *No Longer an Island: Britain and the Wright Brothers* (1984), describe the impact of the Wrights on European aviation.

TOM D. CROUCH

WRIGHT, Willard Huntington (15 Oct. 1888–11 Apr. 1939), editor, novelist, and critic, was born in Charlottesville, Virginia, the son of Archibald Davenport Wright, a hotel proprietor, and Annie Van Vranken. In 1900 the Wrights moved to Santa Monica, California, a crucial move, for a good part of Wright's early professional development occurred in southern California. Both Wright and his brother Stanton were regarded as precocious by their parents, and both gravitated toward the arts. Stanton Wright early settled on a painting career, but Willard Wright vacillated, experimenting with painting and music before concentrating on literature.

Though widely read, Wright did not adjust well to formal education. He spent a year (1900–1901) at New York Military Academy at Cornwall-on-the-Hudson and then drifted through a series of colleges, finally spending a few months as a special student at Harvard, beginning in 1906. In the summer of 1907, on a roundabout trip home from Harvard, he stopped in Seattle, where he married Katherine Belle Boynton, who also was nineteen and whom he had known only two weeks. Wright and his wife moved in with his parents. By late 1908, after holding a variety of unsatisfactory jobs, he was hired as a book review writer for the *Los Angeles Times*. His marriage was weakened from the outset by his interest in other women, although his first involvement, unlike many later ones, did not include sexual infidelity. The birth of his daughter, his only child, in the second year of marriage further strained the relationship. The Wrights lived together only six years of their marriage, which ended in divorce in 1930 because Wright wished to marry Eleanor Rulapaugh, a newspaper editor whose pseudonym was Claire de Lisle.

Wright became successful at the *Los Angeles Times* and, through a recommendation from his friend H. L. Mencken, was made editor of the *Smart Set* in January 1913, whereupon he moved to New York City, leaving his wife behind. With Mencken, book reviewer for the *Smart Set*, Wright shared a taste for the works of Friedrich Nietzsche, Theodore Dreiser, and Joseph Conrad and an ambition to introduce the American public to emerging modern literature. As an editor he published then-innovative and daring work by Ezra Pound, Floyd Dell, D. H. Lawrence, Joseph Conrad, and Ford Madox Ford, among others. Publisher John Adams Thayer, disturbed by the magazine's direction and by public reaction, and angered because Wright had used *Smart Set* funds to pay for a dummy issue of a new magazine, fired him in December 1913.

In March 1914 Wright, accompanied by his brother Stanton and financed by his mother, left for a year of writing and studying in Europe. Stanton gave his brother an introduction to modern art, which spurred him to write *Modern Painting: Its Tendency and Meaning* (1915), an influential if financially unrewarding work. In it he defended Stanton's theory, synchromism, which asserted that art need not be representational and that form itself should be developed through color. Wright's anthology, *What Nietzsche Taught*, published earlier in the same year, was another commercial failure. In spite of his monetary embarrassments, Wright had become established as a major critic in New York, often publishing his views on art in *The Forum*. In 1916 he published two more financially unsuccessful works, a novel, *The Man of Promise*, and *The Creative Will: Studies in the Logic and the Syntax of Aesthetics*. A passage from the latter work embodies Wright's aesthetic theories:

Merely to *feel* art is to sink to the plane of the primitive savage: to *recognise* art, by an intellectual process, attests to the highest degree of culture to which man has attained. . . . Genius is the alliance of a pure sensitivity with a generating intelligence; and it can be discerned only by those who bring to it the faculties which enter into its making. (p. 251)

Wright's pro-German sympathies made him unpopular when the United States entered World War I, and in December 1917 he retreated to the West Coast, where he wrote first for the *Los Angeles Times* and then for the *San Francisco Bulletin*. Returning to New York in 1920, he eked out a living writing for movie magazines under pseudonyms. Overwork or professional frustration at times threw Wright into moods of extreme depression during which he used drugs, including, according to varying reports, cocaine, opium, and marijuana. His drug experimentation had begun during his trip to Europe in 1914. Following his return to New York Wright was, understandably, very depressed, and he followed the advice of his friend Jacob Lobsenz, an obstetrician. Lobsenz, who was probably trying to curb Wright's drug habit as well as cure his depression, suggested that Wright avoid serious literature for six months and read nothing but detective fiction. By 1924 Wright had begun a systematic study of detective fiction that resulted in a highly successful series of detective stories published under the pseudonym S. S. Van Dine. Philo Vance, Wright's erudite, erratic, Wildean, high-society detective, made his debut in *The Benson Murder Case* (1926) and remained phenomenally popular through the mid-1930s. Some of his stories were adapted for the screen. For the first time in his adult life Wright was well off financially, but he never reconciled himself to the role of popular novelist, and only gradually did the identity of S. S. Van Dine become generally known. By the late 1930s, however, Philo Vance's popularity was being overshadowed by that of the tougher heroes of Dashiell Hammett and the more colorful creations of Agatha Christie and Dorothy L. Sayers.

Wright died of a heart attack in New York City almost immediately after completing a draft for another Philo Vance novel, *The Winter Murder Case*, published in 1939. Although it is unlikely that he will ever recapture a large popular readership, Wright will likely always have a following among connoisseurs of detective fiction. A revival of interest in synchromism in the 1980s led to renewed interest in his art criticism. In addition, Wright will almost certainly be remembered as an early champion of modernism. As his biographer John Loughery has aptly noted, Wright's life, though "not a tale of undeterred accomplishment and impeccable aspirations," is nonetheless "a very American story of ambition, struggle, and 'success' on a large scale." It is also a record of the personal and professional costs that may be incurred in the pursuit of recognition matching one's own self-regard.

• Collections of Wright's papers are at the Princeton University Library, the Alderman Library at the University of Virginia, and the Beinecke Library at Yale. John Loughery, *Alias S. S. Van Dine* (1992), includes a good bibliography. Under his own name, Wright also published *Europe after 8:15*, with H. L. Mencken and George Jean Nathan (1914); *The Forum Exhibition of Modern American Painters* (1916); *The Great Modern French Stories: A Chronological Anthology* (1917); *Misinforming a Nation* (1917); *Informing a Nation* (1917); *The Future of Painting* (1923); and *The Great Detective Stories: A Chronological Anthology* (1927), in the introduction of which he expatiates on his theory of detective fiction. Under the pseudonym S. S. Van Dine, in addition to the two Philo Vance novels mentioned above, Loughery lists thirteen additional books published between 1927 and 1938. Of these mysteries, only *The "Canary" Murder Case* (1927) and *The Bishop Murder Case* (1929) have much interest for modern readers. Jon Tuska deals with Wright's detective works and their film adaptations in *Philo Vance: The Life and Times of S. S. Van Dine* (1971), *The Detective in Hollywood* (1978), and *In Manors and Alleys: A Casebook on the American Detective Film* (1988). Wright's aesthetic theories are treated in Elizabeth Hertz, "The Continuing Role of Stanton MacDonald Wright in Modern Art" (Ph.D. diss., Ohio State Univ., 1968), and Marilyn Baker, "The Art Theory and Criticism of Willard Huntington Wright" (Ph.D. diss., Univ. of Wisconsin, 1975). An obituary is in the *New York Times*, 13 Apr. 1939.

MARYJEAN GROSS
DALTON GROSS

WRIGHT, William. *See* De Quille, Dan.

WRIGHT, William Hammond (4 Nov. 1871–16 May 1959), astronomer and fifth director of Lick Observatory, was born in San Francisco, California, the son of Selden Stuart Wright, a lawyer and judge, and Joanna Shaw. Wright attended public schools in San Francisco and graduated in 1893 from the University of California with a B.S. in civil engineering. He then spent two years as a graduate student at Berkeley, where, with Armin O. Leuschner as his teacher, Wright's interest shifted to astronomy. He volunteered at Lick Observatory on Mount Hamilton in the summer of 1895 and then spent 1896–1897 at the University of Chicago. There he worked with George Ellery Hale at Yerkes Observatory, just before its forty-inch refractor was completed and put into operation. In the fall of 1897 Wright returned to Lick Observatory as an assistant astronomer, and he remained a member of its staff until his final retirement in 1944, two years after he had given up its directorship. In 1901 he married Elna Leib, the daughter of a judge; they had no children.

At Lick Observatory Wright at first worked in stellar spectroscopy on W. W. Campbell's radial-velocity program. Campbell became director in 1901 and had built a 36-inch reflecting telescope and a spectrograph, which he intended to take to Chile in order to establish a Lick Southern Hemisphere observing station. In the process of testing the telescope in California, however, he was badly injured and Wright went in his place, with Harold K. Palmer as his assistant. They sailed from San Francisco in February 1903, landed in Valparaiso a month and a half later, located a site in Santiago, erected the telescope and the dome they had brought with them, and were taking data within six months of their arrival in Chile. Wright stayed for three years and established the observing and reduction procedures that were continued by a series of Lick astronomers after him, until this D. O. Mills–financed expedition ended in 1926.

After his return to Mount Hamilton in 1906, Wright declined the opportunity to become Campbell's chief assistant on the radial-velocity program. Prizing his independence, Wright preferred to work on his own on the spectra of gaseous nebulae and novae. An extremely skilled observer, he knew how to get the most out of the Lick telescopes and spectrographs. In his studies of novae he analyzed and described in detail the progression of stages through which these objects evolve as they throw off a shell that expands into space. In planetary nebulae Wright measured accurately the wavelengths of the then unidentified nebular emission lines and studied the spatial distributions in the nebulae of the gases that emit them. These data were later used by Ira S. Bowen in identifying the nebular emission lines as forbidden transitions among energy levels of ions of oxygen, nitrogen, neon, and other elements. The spatial distributions that Wright had observed confirmed that the highest stages of ionization occurred closest to the central star in a planetary nebula, the source of the radiation that ionizes it. He also found that many of the central stars have broad emission-line spectra, similar to those of the previously known, higher-luminosity Wolf-Rayet stars.

Wright had designed and built a spectrograph that was especially efficient in the ultraviolet spectral region. With it and Lick Observatory's newly aluminized Crossley (36-inch) reflector, he was able to obtain ultraviolet spectrograms of several planetary nebulae, on which he identified spectral lines of doubly ionized oxygen that showed a most unusual excitation pattern. Wright speedily communicated these results to Bowen, who identified the excitation process as resonance fluorescence, driven by the strongest (far-ultraviolet) emission line of ionized helium, confirming the paramount importance of high-energy radiation in these objects.

In the 1920s and 1930s Wright pioneered in large-scale photography of the planets, especially Venus, Mars, Jupiter, and Saturn, in different colors and in ultraviolet and infrared light. On these photographs he was able to identify various cloud features and atmospheric scattering phenomena, but his results have been completely superseded by images obtained from space vehicles from the 1960s on.

Wright was director of Lick Observatory from 1935 to 1942. During this period he broke down some of its scientific isolation by bringing visiting astronomers such as Ejnar Hertzsprung, Bowen, and Pol Swings to Mount Hamilton for extended stays; by vigorously supporting the younger, astrophysically oriented Lick staff members and graduate students, making it possible for them to present research papers at national scientific meetings in the East; and by switching the dissemination of Lick scientific papers from in-house publication to the national *Astrophysical Journal.* Wright's own research contributions over the years covered an unusually wide range of fields of astronomy.

Wright's final contribution was starting the long-term program to measure the "proper motions" (minute angular motions in the apparent plane of the sky) of stars with respect to a reference system fixed in the universe, defined by faint, distant galaxies. He had conceived this plan around 1919, when his Lick Observatory colleague Heber D. Curtis was proving that the "spiral nebulae" actually are distant "island universes," but he could not carry it out until after his friend Frank E. Ross had invented the wide-field camera that made it possible. Wright got the twenty-inch astrograph, designed to take the photographic plates for this program, into operation in the 1940s, just before his retirement. His successors carried out the program after he had left Mount Hamilton, and it began to bear fruit in the 1980s. He died in San Jose.

• A large number of Wright's letters are in the Mary Lea Shane Archives of the Lick Observatory, in the McHenry Library, University of California, Santa Cruz. Among Wright's most important papers are "Observations of the Spectrum of Nova Persei," with W. W. Campbell, *Astrophysical Journal* 14 (1901): 269–92; "Description of the Instruments and Methods of the D. O. Mills Expedition," *Publications of the Lick Observatory* 9 (1907): 25–70; "The Wave-lengths of the Nebular Lines and General Observations of the Spectra of the Gaseous Nebulae," *Publications of the Lick Observatory* 13 (1918): 193–268; "On Photography of the Brighter Planets by Light of Different Colours," *Monthly Notices of the Royal Astronomical Society* 88 (1928): 709–18; and "On a Proposal to Use the Extragalactic Nebulae in Measuring the Proper Motions of Stars, and in Evaluating the Precessional Constant," *Proceedings of the American Philosophical Society* 94 (1950): 1–12. Two memorial biographies are Paul W. Merrill, "William Hammond Wright: 1871–1959," *Publications of the Astronomical Society of the Pacific* (1959): 305–6, and C. D. Shane, "William H. Wright," National Academy of Sciences, *Biographical Memoirs* 50 (1979): 377–96. The latter contains a complete bibliography of Wright's published scientific papers. See also Donald E. Osterbrock et al., *Eye on the Sky: Lick Observatory's First Century* (1988).

DONALD E. OSTERBROCK

WRIGLEY, Philip Knight (5 Dec. 1894–12 Apr. 1977), chewing gum magnate and baseball team owner, was born in Chicago, Illinois, the son of William Wrigley, Jr., the creator of Wrigley chewing gum, and Ada Foote. As the son of a millionaire, Philip had a prosperous and comfortable childhood. He received his early education at the Chicago Latin School, a private boys school, and attended high school at Phillips Academy in Andover, Massachusetts. Because his father had taken him out of school so often for vacations and travel, he graduated from high school in 1914, about two years behind other boys his age. Admitted to Yale and Stanford, Wrigley decided to forego college in favor of entering the family business, and he persuaded his father to allow him to supervise the establishment of a new Wrigley chewing gum factory in

Australia. Wrigley and two other men established the entire Australia factory themselves, buying a garage, painting it, and installing machinery. When World War I began at the end of his first year in Australia, Wrigley returned to the United States with plans to enlist. Back in Chicago, he attended chemistry classes at the University of Chicago, set up a lab in his father's house, and waited for the opportunity to join the war.

When the United States entered the war in the spring of 1917, Wrigley applied for officer's training camp; upon being rejected, he enlisted for four years as a fireman third class in the U.S. Naval Reserve in June 1917. Based at the Great Lakes Naval Training Station, his unit began operations as a training school for naval aviators. Within six months, Wrigley was promoted to ensign and became the superintendent of a military training school for aviation mechanics. In the spring of the following year, he married Helen Blanche Atwater, whom he had met on many family vacations spent in Lake Geneva, Wisconsin. They would have two daughters and a son. Just a few days after his marriage, Wrigley received orders to go overseas; but, having determined that his services were needed more urgently by the training school, the navy canceled them. Wrigley was not assigned to active duty until February 1919; soon thereafter he was discharged with the rank of lieutenant junior grade.

Later in 1919 Wrigley rejoined a Wrigley Company that had grown tremendously during the war years. While the elder Wrigley had held the price at a nickel and advertised his gum through patriotic advertisements and war propaganda, American soldiers had taught Europeans to chew gum. The results were impressive. Between 1917 and 1919 sales of Wrigley's gum had risen from $15,402,000 to $27,000,000. In order to gain experience in every department of the massive Wrigley chewing gum empire, Philip Wrigley spent time in the company's Toronto and New York offices before moving to the home office in Chicago. In 1925 he was elected president of the company, replacing his father who became chairman of the board. As president, Wrigley advanced several corporate welfare programs such as life insurance and the five-day work week for Wrigley workers. When William Wrigley died in January 1932, Philip, or "P. K." as he was often called, took full responsibility for the company.

Agreeing with his father that "anyone could make chewing gum, the trick was to sell it" (Angle, p. 31), Philip Wrigley pioneered in using advertising both to promote his gum and to shape the public perception of his company. In the 1920s Wrigley experimented with radio advertising and print ads in women's magazines to increase the market for his gum. In 1927 the company sponsored the "Wrigley review," which was one of the first network radio programs to air nationally, and the following year established a company-sponsored show by Guy Lombardo and His Royal Canadians. Wrigley maintained a heavy advertising budget even during the Great Depression. When World War II began and most of the nation's manufacturing capacity turned to war-related production, Wrigley advertising took pains to justify the continued production of gum and redoubled earlier efforts to link Wrigley gum to patriotism. Wrigley personally donated his own ninety-eight foot yacht to the navy. Well-publicized Wrigley-supported surveys of defense workers asserted that gum-chewing workers were more accurate, experienced less fatigue or boredom, and made fewer trips to smoke or snack. Incorporating such themes, Wrigley ads kept the company name before the public long after diminishing supplies of sugar and chicle, an essential ingredient of gum, made it impossible to meet retail demand. When war shortages drastically cut into production, the company reserved all its supplies to produce gum for soldiers, who received packets of Wrigley gum in military rations. Although the company did invent a synthetic substitute for chicle, Wrigley insisted that this inferior product not bear the Wrigley trademark names of Spearmint, Juicy Fruit or Doublemint. The company continued to advertise Spearmint with the slogan, "Remember this wrapper," but stopped selling its major brands. Although it was a controversial strategy, ever-rising demand for Wrigley gum in the postwar years seemed to vindicate Wrigley's decision. Wrigley was also instrumental in the Wrigley Company's postwar policy of holding the price of Wrigley gum steady in spite of inflation. Long after competitors began selling their gum for a dime a pack, Wrigley gum sold for a nickel.

Following the lead of his father and his own personal interests, Wrigley pursued a wide range of other business ventures from the 1920s to the 1960s. He made several short-term experimental forays into new businesses such as commercial airlines, banking, horse ranching, and boat manufacture. In 1926 Wrigley helped form one of the first commercial airlines, American Airways, which later became part of United Airlines. He also established the first of several airlines serving Catalina Island, a small island off the coast of southern California purchased by his father in 1919. In the 1920s Wrigley built a furniture, brickyard, and tile plant on the island to furnish a Catalina resort constructed by his father. After his father's death, Philip Wrigley became president of the Santa Catalina Island Company, and in this capacity he supervised the restoration of the island, including the creation of a sandy beach, the planting of fifty-year-old palm and olive trees and the provision of water and electricity plants. The island also served as a Chicago Cubs training camp for many years. Although Wrigley never gave up an interest in Catalina Island, he gave the beach front and the utilities to local government and began to sell many of the island's concessions and operations after World War II. Citing "labor trouble," Wrigley spun off many of Catalina's operations after the Maritime Union began to make inroads among the island's employees. Though Wrigley confessed to once voting for Franklin D. Roosevelt, he was a business-minded conservative who was intolerant of unions and strikes. Criticism of his control of Catalina Island, most notably a 1970 exposé in *Forbes* magazine that portrayed Catalina as a company town, undoubtedly also contributed to his decision to increasingly pull out of the island's affairs.

Wrigley was perhaps most famous, or infamous, for his ownership and management of the Chicago Cubs from the 1920s until the 1960s. Already a Cubs stock owner, Philip inherited a controlling interest in the team from his father and became president of the Cubs in 1933. As president, he played an active role in all aspects of the team's management and supervised a number of innovations at the park to bring out the fans. Explaining his interest in baseball many years later, Wrigley said that baseball appealed to him because "the customers of the Cubs were exactly the same people that we sold our chewing gum to" (quoted in Angle, p. 57). Wrigley adapted a number of his advertising techniques to selling the baseball experience, adding such gimmicks as the first organ in a major league ball park. During World War II, when Wrigley began losing players to the military, he created the first professional women's baseball league, the All-American Girls Professional Baseball League. Although he managed to keep attendance high in Wrigley Field, the Cubs were much less successful. After winning three pennants in the first decade of Wrigley's management (1932, 1935, and 1938), the team entered a twenty-year slump that persisted in spite of many Wrigley-inspired player trades, management changes, and training tactics. Expressing his frustration, Wrigley explained, "In spite of everything we could think of to try and do . . . we were still in the also-rans" (Angle, p. 169). In addition to the Cubs, Wrigley owned the Los Angeles Angels of the Class AAA Pacific Coast League; the Angels' home ball park was also called Wrigley Field.

Though his son William permanently took over the presidency of the Wrigley Company in the 1960s, Wrigley maintained an interest in the Cubs, Catalina Island, and the company, particularly advertising, until his death. Ever the Cubs fan, Wrigley died while watching the team that had so preoccupied his adult life on television in Elkhorn, Wisconsin.

• The most complete, though fairly uncritical, source on Wrigley's life is Paul M. Angle's biography, *Philip K. Wrigley* (1975), which was written with access to Wrigley and some of his personal papers. A useful biographical sketch is Robert Boyle, "A Shy Man at a Picnic," *Sports Illustrated*, 14 Apr. 1958. Though Wrigley claimed it distorted and defaming, "The Island Kingdom of P. K. Wrigley," *Forbes*, 1 Nov. 1970, provides a critical perspective on the Wrigley family's involvement in Catalina Island. See also Bill Veeck with Ed Linn, *Veeck—As in Wreck* (1962); Seth King, "Wrigley: a 7-cent Bonanza," *New York Times*, 9 May 1971. On women and professional baseball, see Lois Brown, *Girls of Summer: In Their Own League* (1992), and Gai Ingham, *Women in Baseball: The Forgotten History* (1994). An obituary is in the *New York Times*, 13 Apr. 1977.

MICHELLE BRATTAIN

WRINCH, Dorothy Maud (12 Sept. 1894–11 Feb. 1976), mathematician and biochemical theorist, was born in Rosario, Argentina, the daughter of Hugh Edward Hart Wrinch, an engineer, and Ada Souter. Her parents were British subjects who returned to London, England, during her adolescence.

In 1913 Dorothy Wrinch entered Cambridge University's Girton College, where she excelled in mathematics and philosophy. While at Girton she met and became friendly with the philosopher Bertrand Russell, whose work in mathematical logic had a profound effect on her career. After receiving her B.A. in 1917, she remained at Girton as a research scholar for a year. From 1918 to 1920 she taught mathematics at the University of London's University College, where she also studied and earned her M.Sc. and D.Sc. in mathematics in 1920 and 1921, respectively. She returned to Girton in 1920 to accept a research fellowship. In 1922 she married John William Nicholson, the newly appointed director of studies in mathematics and physics at Oxford University's Balliol College, and the next year she became affiliated with Oxford as both a teacher and student. For four years she taught mathematics on a per-term basis at its five women's colleges, and in 1927 she was made a lecturer at Lady Margaret Hall, Oxford. She continued her studies in mathematics and received another M.Sc. in 1924, and in 1929, the first D.Sc. ever awarded by Oxford to a woman.

In 1930 Wrinch separated from Nicholson, who had become an alcoholic, and took their one child with her. After the separation (the marriage was dissolved in 1938), she decided to leave Oxford and pursue a new career devoted primarily to theoretical science. Although technically an applied mathematician, Wrinch had always been more interested in studying the philosophy of science in general and the nature of scientific thought and inquiry in particular, and about half of the work she had published before the separation dealt with this interest. She was convinced that further scientific developments depended on the ability of mathematicians and philosophers to work together to create new paradigms; she was particularly impressed by Russell's wedding of mathematics and logic in *Principia Mathematica*, which he coauthored with Alfred North Whitehead, as well as by the physicist Albert Einstein's incorporation of geometry and logic into his theory of general relativity. Consequently, in 1932 she became a cofounder of the Biotheoretical Gathering, a group that sought to explain "the secret of life" by discovering how proteins can perform so many different and complex roles in the structure and function of so many different living organisms, even though the vast majority of proteins are composed of only about two dozen different amino acids, most of which consist entirely of carbon, oxygen, hydrogen, and nitrogen.

Wrinch found this challenge enormously appealing. From 1931 to 1934 she used a number of fellowships and a leave of absence from Oxford to study physics, chemistry, and biology at the Universities of Vienna, Paris, Prague, and Leiden. In 1934 she investigated ways to apply the potential theory of mathematical physics (normally used to solve problems related to the distribution of electric capacity over a given mass) to chromosome mechanics. Between 1934 and 1936 she published five articles on the nature and behavior of chromosomes, and in 1936 the first of many papers on the cyclol theory of protein structure. Whereas conventional wisdom held that protein linkages were linear, Wrinch suggested that proteins formed into hollow, hexagonal, fabriclike structures rather than simple chains. Supported largely by a Rockefeller Foundation research fellowship from 1935 to 1940, she promoted her hypothesis in speaking engagements, including a tour of universities in the United States, where she was warmly received and hailed by the press as the "woman Einstein."

Although Wrinch gained support for her theory from Irving Langmuir, winner of the Nobel Prize for chemistry in 1932, she also aroused a great deal of animosity in other scientists, especially protein researchers, many of whom argued that cyclols did not exist in nature and could not be synthesized in the laboratory. Others, including John Desmond Bernal, a lecturer in structural crystallography at Cambridge University and a member of the Gathering, charged that she had published data compiled by her colleagues and their collaborators before they could do so. She became embroiled in a particularly nasty ongoing confrontation with Linus Pauling, winner of the Nobel Prize for chemistry in 1954, who led the charge against the cyclol theory on the grounds that it was thermodynamically unstable. Wrinch, whose standing as a professional academic was always marginal, was further handicapped because her training in the biological sciences was too superficial to allow her to conduct her own experiments, and so she was forced to rely on the work of others for support. When proof failed to materialize, both her theory and her reputation in England were ruined. Ironically, in the 1950s the cyclol structure was discovered in nature and reproduced in the laboratory, but by then the secret of life was being sought in the double helix of deoxyribonucleic acid (DNA), and the discovery of cyclols was dismissed as irrelevant.

In 1939, when her offer to aid the British war effort was turned down, Wrinch immigrated to the United States and obtained a position as lecturer in chemistry at Johns Hopkins University. In 1941, through the efforts of Amherst College's vice president Otto Charles Glaser, she moved to Massachusetts to become a visiting professor at Amherst, Smith, and Mount Holyoke Colleges. That same year she and Glaser were married; they had no children. In 1943 Smith College made her a special research professor of physics and in 1965 awarded her a Sophia Smith Fellowship, which she held until 1971. She spent her retirement in Woods Hole, Massachusetts, and died in Falmouth, Massachusetts.

Despite its ultimate failure to be accepted by the scientific community, the cyclol theory was Wrinch's main contribution to science. By advancing a theory of protein structure that reached beyond the boundaries of classical biology to encompass chemistry, physics, mathematics, and philosophy, she contributed to the development of molecular biology by inspiring other scientists to take a multidisciplinary approach to the study of life.

• Wrinch's papers are in the Dorothy Wrinch Collection at Smith College, Northampton, Mass. A good biography, with notes, is Pnina G. Abir-Am, "Synergy or Clash: Disciplinary and Marital Strategies in the Career of Mathematical Biologist Dorothy Wrinch," in *Uneasy Careers and Intimate Lives: Women in Science, 1789–1979*, ed. Pnina G. Abir-Am and Dorinda Outram (1987). A complete bibliography of her work is in Marjorie Senechal, ed., *Structures of Matter and Patterns in Science* (1980). Her obituary is in the *New York Times*, 15 Feb. 1976.

CHARLES W. CAREY, JR.

WRISTON, Henry Merritt (4 July 1889–7 Mar. 1978), educator, was born in Laramie, Wyoming, the son of Henry Lincoln Wriston, a minister, and Jennie Amelia Atcheson. He earned his bachelor's degree in English literature at Wesleyan College (Conn.), graduating in 1911. Wriston began an administrative career in higher education during his junior year at Wesleyan. Hired as the college publicist, he quickly came to know the president, the dean, and the librarian. His most important acquaintance was the one secretary at the college, whose efficiency and understanding of the necessity of tact provided Wriston with a lesson of lifelong value. His interest in the college presidency began with the inauguration of a new president and the academic procession, which he covered as the college publicist. The dignitaries present and the excitement of the ceremony were enough to convince Wriston to become a college president. He recognized the importance of the doctorate for that position and applied himself with new vigor to his undergraduate work (achieving election to Phi Beta Kappa) and later to his graduate studies.

In 1914, upon completing his doctoral coursework in history at Harvard University, Wriston returned to Wesleyan as a history instructor. That year he married Ruth Colton; they had two children. His service as the reference librarian in addition to his first teaching position taught him, as he declared in his autobiography, *Academic Procession* (1959), "the time and effort wasted by crude procedures." Applying that realization to his pedagogy, he learned to emphasize the best ways for students to write and to appreciate the importance of the many operations of a library. Wriston completed his dissertation for his Ph.D. in 1922.

While Wriston was a junior professor, the college embarked upon a large fundraising campaign, and because of his experience in writing a pamphlet on fundraising for World War I needs, the institution hired him to organize the drive. During the fundraising campaign at Wesleyan, the chair of the trustees met with Wriston to explain that the trustees wanted the president out, and they therefore expected that Wriston would make the campaign fail. Refusing to be a pawn, Wriston in fact worked to make it succeed. After the campaign's end, he returned to scholarship and teaching. Aware that the trustees continued to resent

him for failing to comply with their wishes and warned that some wanted him out of Wesleyan, he began to respond to inquiries about his former interest in presidencies.

In 1925 Lawrence College finally succeeded in attracting him. His inclination was to refuse the offer, but he accepted it following his wife's admonition to think carefully about the consequences of a quick decision. At Lawrence he founded the Institute for Paper Chemistry, which flourished despite its inauspicious beginning two weeks before the stock market crash of 1929. From its inception the institute offered a unique relationship between higher education and the paper and pulp industry. Renamed the Institute of Paper Science and Technology, it moved to Atlanta, Georgia, and continued its connections with higher education through cooperative efforts with the Georgia Institute of Technology.

In 1937 Wriston left Lawrence College to become president of Brown University in Rhode Island, where he remained until 1955. While at Brown, following his first wife's death, he married Marguerite Woodworth in 1947.

Wriston was the first president of Brown who was neither a Baptist nor a Brown alumnus. The Brown trustees recognized that he would probably try to change the institution, and he did. He increased the admission standards and reinvigorated the residential nature of the university. He also instituted curricular changes, increasing the elective choices for students in a system that stayed in place until 1969. He was personally involved in the appointment of new faculty members, seeking professors who would pursue scholarship and elevate Brown to top status. He also created two departments, the history of mathematics and Egyptology. Nevertheless, he was primarily interested in sustaining Brown's reputation as an undergraduate institution, refusing to allow the creation of a separate graduate faculty.

Wriston changed the composition of Brown's student body, merging the classes for the all-male Brown students and the all-female Pembroke College students. He also welcomed the GI students following World War II. His efforts in student life, curriculum, and faculty affairs fundamentally changed Brown University.

While at Brown, Wriston also coauthored the 1953 statement on academic freedom issued by the American Association of Universities (AAU). The statement, while recognizing the restrictions on freedom presented by requirements such as loyalty oaths, also explicitly affirmed the prerogative of colleges and universities to dismiss professors who were Communist party members.

At the end of his presidency at Brown, Wriston helped to reorganize the U.S. Foreign Service at the request of President Dwight Eisenhower. Following that six-month appointment, Wriston finished his educational career with the American Assembly, serving first as executive director (1955–1958), then president (1958–1962), and finally as chairman (1962–1965). He was a member of several commissions and committees in education and government, including the National War Fund during World War II, and served as the president of the Council on Foreign Relations from 1953 to 1964. He was a member of the editorial advisory board of *Foreign Affairs* from 1943 to 1967. Wriston died in New York City.

In his autobiography Wriston gave a great deal of credit to serendipity. A careful reading of his descriptions of his life suggests, however, that he learned a great deal from his experiences and used that education throughout his lifetime. Whether he was dealing with trustees, professors, administrators, or students, he sustained a sense of humor, an investigatory posture, and an enduring commitment to higher education.

Wriston was president of Lawrence and Brown at a time, particularly in his early years, when the axiom was that good teaching and good research did not go together. He thought that the opposite was true, and his lasting commitment to scholarship is evident in his many publications, for example, *Executive Agents in American Foreign Relations* (1929), *Challenge to Freedom* (1943), *Diplomacy in a Democracy* (1956), and *Perspectives on Policy* (1963). His leadership at Lawrence and at Brown was an important step for each institution in its continuing development, and his effect on Brown proved to be lasting.

• Wriston's published speeches, *Wriston Speaking* (1957), provide information about his perspectives on life. Ellen Schrecker, *No Ivory Tower: McCarthyism and the Universities* (1986), briefly discusses Wriston's role in the development of the 1953 AAU statement on academic freedom. An extensive description of Wriston's presidency at Brown is at http://www.brown.edu; and information on the Institute of Paper Science and Technology is available at http://www.ipst.edu.

PHILO A. HUTCHESON

WROTH, Lawrence Counselman (14 Jan. 1884–25 Dec. 1970), book historian and librarian, was born in Baltimore, Maryland, the son of the Reverend Peregrine Wroth, an Episcopal clergyman active in diocesan affairs, and Mary Augusta Counselman. In 1902 Lawrence Wroth entered the Johns Hopkins University, where he took the historical-political course and graduated with an A.B. in 1905. He hoped to be a writer and unexpectedly found the way to his subject and his career in the fall of 1905. When the position of librarian of the Episcopal Diocese of Maryland suddenly became vacant, Wroth was appointed to it. The diocesan library had an important collection of source materials ranging from the colonial period to the nineteenth century, and as Wroth became familiar with it, he began to write articles on Maryland history for scholarly publications. In 1911 he published his first book, a life of Parson Weems, George Washington's early biographer. He also edited the diocesan newspaper, the *Maryland Churchman*.

Wroth left the diocesan library in 1912 to become assistant librarian of the Enoch Pratt Free Library,

Baltimore's public library system. At the same time he served as managing editor of the new *Johns Hopkins Alumni Magazine*. Throughout his career, all Wroth's employers encouraged his literary work. From 1917 to 1919 he was on leave from the Pratt Library for military service, part of the time in France. After his discharge as a first lieutenant, Wroth returned to librarianship and writing. From this time on he made bibliographic history his specialty.

Wroth discovered in the Maryland state archives that printing in the colony began in 1686, forty years earlier than the standard history of American printing had indicated. He published his findings, with an account of all Maryland printers up to the Revolution, in *A History of Printing in Colonial Maryland, 1686–1776* (1922). Wroth found that the political and social history of the colony was reflected in the printing done there. The printers were dependent on the government for permission to work, and public documents were the chief output of their presses. Whenever the records made this possible, Wroth also described the printers' individual personalities. He was breaking new ground, for little had been written on printing in North America since the early nineteenth century, and there had never been a separate study of the trade in Maryland.

The book brought Wroth to the attention of the Committee of Management of the John Carter Brown Library. The library, affiliated with Brown University in Providence, Rhode Island, specialized in the history and exploration of the Western Hemisphere up to 1801 and had no librarian at that time. The position was offered to Wroth. In 1923 Wroth accepted the post, and for the rest of his life his home was in Providence. He married Barbara Pease, a teacher, in 1930, and they had three sons.

At the John Carter Brown Library, Wroth developed his knowledge of the Americas far beyond his Maryland expertise and built his career as a writer and bibliophile. From 1924 he wrote the library's *Annual Reports*, essays on the history revealed in its collections. He communicated the excitement of acquisitions, as he showed how individual books enlarged the picture of the Western Hemisphere that the library could present. He also became a steady contributor of reviews and articles to scholarly journals, edited a collection of essays in honor of the bibliographer Wilberforce Eames, and in 1926 published a short book on Abel Buell of Connecticut, the artisan who cast the first font of type in North America.

Wroth's second major work, *The Colonial Printer* (1931), describes the making of a typical hand-printed book in the North American colonies. It examines the equipment of the craft from type and presses to paper and ink; the working and economic conditions of the master printer and his assistants; the technical quality of their work; and finally, the many different things, from books to ephemera, that they printed. Wroth returned to the substance of the printers' work in *An American Bookshelf, 1755* (1934), which is concerned with the real books a fictitious Philadelphia merchant, well up on the affairs of his time, could have collected. As an author of books and an essayist, Wroth emphasized that bibliography did not stand alone and that any period could be understood better with a knowledge of its publications.

Wroth's literary style was formal but relaxed. He entertained while he informed and had a dry humor. In his monograph on Abel Buell he relates the story of how Buell, a jeweler by trade, gave a ring to the attorney general of Connecticut in hopes of influencing the state assembly to consider a petition. Then he comments wryly, "change New London to Bagdad and attorney general to wazir and we should have romance creeping into our matter-of-fact narrative."

Although he could be amusing as a writer and with his close friends, Wroth was rather shy and reserved. However, he was active and well known in the affairs of the book world of his time. He was the president of the Bibliographical Society of America from 1931 to 1933 and the American representative of the Bibliographical Society of London from 1925 to 1935.

His work as a librarian gave Wroth the subject of his historical work, the opportunity to pursue it, and his livelihood. His writing, which appeared mostly in journals or in small editions, could not have supported him and his family, and he referred to himself as a librarian by profession. He built the collections of the John Carter Brown Library by more than 5,000 volumes, increased its use by readers, and was a consultant to the Pierpont Morgan Library and to the Rare Book Division of the Library of Congress. When Yale University gave him an honorary degree in 1946, the citation described him as the "link between the mad collector and the sane librarian" for his understanding of the book in all its aspects.

In 1957 Wroth retired from the John Carter Brown Library. His last book, an account of the sixteenth-century explorer Giovanni da Verrazano along with the sources for his life and voyages, was published in 1970, ten weeks before his death in Providence, Rhode Island. With his research and presentation of his findings on the history of early American printers and their books, Wroth did much to define the field and support further study. His works on Maryland printing and colonial printers in general are regularly cited by scholars as standard resources for this fundamental part of American history.

• Wroth's papers are in the John Carter Brown Library, Providence, Rhode Island. Wroth had more than 500 publications to his credit, from newspaper articles to books, and a nearly complete bibliography of his work through 1950 is in *Essays Honoring Lawrence C. Wroth* (1951). Although he continued to publish after 1950, the bulk of his work appeared earlier. Particularly noteworthy are *The Way of a Ship: An Essay on the Literature of Navigation Science* (1937); "The Early Cartography of the Pacific," *Papers of the Bibliographical Society of America* 38 (1944): 83–268; and "The Chief End of Book Madness," *Library of Congress Quarterly Journal of Current Acquisitions* 3 (1945): 69–77. From 1937 through 1947 Wroth conducted the biweekly column "Notes for Bibliophiles" in the *Books* section of the *New York Herald Tribune*, writing most of the articles himself. Frederick R. Goff, "Wroth of the JCB," *Brown Alumni Monthly* 66 (May 1957): 8–9, is an appraisal of Wroth's accomplishments on the occasion of his retirement, while Thomas R. Adams, "In Memoriam: Lawrence C. Wroth, 1884–1970," *Papers of the Bibliographical Society of America* 65 (1971): 103–7, and Bradford F. Swan, "Lawrence Counselman Wroth," *Proceedings of the American Antiquarian Society* 81 (1971): 37–39, give an overview of his career and suggest his personality.

CAROLYN SMITH

WURTZ, Henry (5 June 1828–8 Nov. 1910), chemist and editor, was born in Easton, Pennsylvania, the son of John J. Wurts and Ann Novus. The family name, originally Swiss, had many variant spellings (e.g., Wirtz, Wirts); it is likely that Wurtz chose the name he liked best. He received his A.B. in 1848 from the College of New Jersey (now Princeton University), where he studied with the physicist Joseph Henry and the botanist-chemist John Torrey. After taking his degree, he moved on to the Lawrence Scientific School at Harvard, where he confirmed his interest in chemistry through the instruction of Eben Norton Horsford. In 1850 he worked in Oliver Wolcott Gibbs's laboratory in New York City, where he published his first papers (*American Journal of Science*, July and Nov. 1850), on mineral analyses and on the availability of New Jersey greensand (silica sand admixed with the clay mineral glauconite) as a source of potash.

From 1851 to 1854 Wurtz joined the group of young chemists who formed Benjamin Silliman, Jr.'s "Philosophy and the Arts" school of science at Yale, assisting in various researches. When the elder Silliman retired in 1853 and Silliman, Jr., took on a heavy teaching schedule in his place, Wurtz stayed for another year but accepted a position in 1854 as chemist and mineralogist to the New Jersey State Geological Survey. Here he published analyses of the waters of the Delaware River. In 1857 he studied the geology of North Carolina, publishing his findings of cobalt and nickel ores in Gaston and Lincoln Counties. His brief years as a formal academician followed. From 1857 to 1858 he served as a lecturer in chemistry at the medical college in Kingston, Ontario, Canada; then from 1858 to 1861 he worked as professor of chemistry and pharmacy at the National Medical College in Washington, D.C. (now a part of George Washington University). During these years he served as a chemical examiner in the U.S. Patent Office and published a valuable paper on the use of the blowpipe to identify positive and negative ions in minerals.

In 1861 Wurtz moved back to New York and opened a consulting laboratory. He found time in this enterprise to continue with his own work, developing a method for recovering precious metals from ores by amalgamating them with sodium metal, a process he patented in 1865 and published in the *American Journal of Science* the year after. (Such metals became more commonly recovered by mercury amalgamation or cyanide complexation.) He also published his investigation of an albertite-like mineral (a hardened, almost infusible bitumen) from Virginia, for which he proposed the name "grahamite" and gave suggestions for its use.

From 1868 to 1871 Wurtz was editor of the *American Gas Light Journal*, which led him to begin a series of studies on gas, coal, petroleum, and other fuels. During this time he moved his consulting laboratory to Hoboken, New Jersey. Here in 1869 he patented a new process for producing fuel gas from low-grade coal by treating it with alternate blasts of steam and heated air. He also published sanitary and chemical analyses on the water of the Passaic River, and on the water supplies of Newark and Jersey City (*American Chemist*, 1873 and 1874). In the following year he published "New Processes in Proximate Gas Analysis" in the same journal.

In 1876 Wurtz was appointed a judge of exhibits and special examiner of ceramics for the Philadelphia Centennial Exhibition. This led him into a study of Chinese and Japanese porcelains and porcelain rock, which he concluded was a silica made by high-temperature firing of kaolin and other clays and was not native jade; for this he received a special medal from the Centennial Commission. In an unexpected excursion into purely theoretical chemistry, he published in 1876 a long paper on geometrical chemistry, a topic that was just coming into full flower in Europe in the work of August Kekule, J. H. van't Hoff, and others. In the remaining years of the century Wurtz carried on his private consulting practice and turned out a spate of journal publications and patents, primarily concerned with improving the yield and purity of paraffin fuels obtained by distillation of coal or petroleum.

Wurtz is best characterized as a highly productive working chemist rather than a great discoverer or major theorist. His name is preserved in that of the bitumen-type mineral that he found and described, wurtzilite. He also named the silver-bearing minerals huntilite and animikite. Wurtz was a member of the American Association for the Advancement of Science. He died at his home in Brooklyn, New York, survived by his five children.

• A bibliography of Wurtz's publications to 1874 can be found in *American Chemist* 4 (Aug.–Sept. 1874): 109–10. Obituaries are in the *Brooklyn Daily Eagle*, 10 Nov. 1910, and the *New York Times*, 11 Dec. 1910.

ROBERT M. HAWTHORNE JR.

WYANT, Alexander Helwig (11 Jan. 1836–29 Nov. 1892), painter, was born in Evans Creek, Tuscarawas County, Ohio, the son of Daniel Wyant, an itinerant farmer and occasional carpenter, and Hannah Shanks. Between 1836 and 1838 the family moved to Defiance, Ohio, where he attended the village school and was apprenticed to a harness maker. Wyant apparently showed an early aptitude for art and sketched in charcoal. However, like many other painters of his time, he began his training as an artisan; in his teens he worked as a sign painter in Port Washington, Ohio. After making the decision to become a professional artist, Wyant visited Cincinnati, where he saw oil

paintings by George Inness on exhibition. Wyant was greatly impressed with them, even though Inness was just then beginning his career.

In 1858 Wyant went to New York to meet Inness, who had just returned from a trip to Europe. The details of the meeting are not known, but with Inness's help, Wyant secured the support of noted Cincinnati art patron and collector Nicholas Longworth. In 1860 Longworth paid for Wyant to study art in New York for one year. From 1861 to 1863 Wyant studied in Cincinnati and sold works through his connection with Longworth. Wyant moved once again to New York in 1863.

Wyant's early work was directly tied to the landscapes of the Hudson River School, a group of American painters who, under the influence of Thomas Cole, painted views of the Hudson River Valley, the Catskills, the Adirondacks, the White and Green Mountains, and the New England coastline. Elements of the Hudson River School style include a fidelity to nature, detailed foregrounds, dramatic use of sunlight, and panoramic vistas. By the 1850s a second generation of landscape painters, including Albert Bierstadt and Frederick Church, took elements of the Hudson River School to create more dramatic canvases of the American West and South America, respectively.

The Hudson River School influence is clearly seen in Wyant's *Falls of the Ohio and Louisville* (1863, J. B. Speed Art Museum, Louisville, Ky.), with its panoramic view, wide vista, and detailed foreground containing carefully drawn human figures. In New York in 1863 Wyant was impressed by the work of Hans Friedrich Gude. Wyant's interest in the Hudson River School also explains his desire to study with Gude, a Norwegian member of the Düsseldorf School, as the Düsseldorf landscapists shared many qualities with the Hudson River School. Although the Düsseldorf School is associated with a wide range of styles, its art in general was characterized by detail, accurate drawing, and non-esoteric subject matter, including genre and landscape. In 1864 Wyant exhibited at the National Academy of Design for the first time.

It must be kept in mind that Wyant, even at the beginning of his career, was also interested in the alternative landscape style represented by George Inness. This style, which has been termed "tonalist," is characterized by a smaller, more intimate scale, soft shadows, rounded contours, heavy impasto, and a more poetic rendering of nature. Many elements of the tonalist style can be traced to the French Barbizon school of landscape painting.

It is difficult to exactly pinpoint when Wyant changed from the Hudson River style to tonalism. It is best to consider it as a gradual development. *The Mohawk Valley* (1866, Metropolitan Museum of Art) stands as the best example of Wyant's mature Hudson River landscape style. After that date, however, his work shows a looser painting style along with more concern for atmosphere, as in his *Recollections of Eve-*

ning (1868, Baltimore Museum of Art) and *Sunset in the Hills, New York* (1869, Detroit Institute of Arts).

Like many other American artists of his time, Wyant went to Europe to study, probably on the advice of Inness. Inness continued to be a mentor to Wyant throughout his career. Wyant sought out Gude in 1865–1866, but he stayed with him only a short time as he found Gude to be an overbearing teacher. On his way home, he made short stops in England and Ireland. In England, he saw works by John Constable that later influenced his own style; similarly, Wyant's knowledge of the Irish landscape would also be found in his later work.

By 1866–1867 Wyant had settled in New York, and he had entered into a very productive period, exhibiting widely in Brooklyn, New York, and Philadelphia. In 1867 he joined the American Society of Painters in Water Color, and this medium remained an important part of his oeuvre throughout his career. The inherent properties of that medium may have affected his work in oil. Wyant was elected a full member of the National Academy of Design for his painting *The Upper Susquehanna.*

In 1873, motivated both by a desire to improve his failing health and to gather new material, Wyant joined a U.S. Geological Survey expedition to New Mexico and Arizona. Ironically, the primitive nature of the travel made Wyant more ill, and he suffered a paralytic stroke of the right side that was followed by a long recuperation in New York.

From 1874 until 1880 Wyant re-learned painting using his left hand, and he was remarkably successful. He maintained a studio in the YMCA Building on Twenty-third Street and summered in a rugged artists' colony in the Keene Valley in the Adirondacks. His switch to tonalism became complete after his stroke, but this change was probably not solely caused by his physical deterioration. This new style can be seen in *View in County Kerry, Ireland* (c. 1875, Metropolitan Museum of Art), which was inspired by Wyant's memories of his 1866 trip to Ireland. Wyant also produced a similar landscape of this Irish scene, *Blue Hills* (undated, Scripps College, Claremont, Calif.), in watercolor. Both *View in County Kerry, Ireland* and *Blue Hills* show an increasing use of gray, less detail, and concern with atmosphere, and demonstrate the interconnection between oil painting and watercolor in Wyant's oeuvre.

Wyant married Arabella Locke, one of his art students, in 1880. They spent more time away from New York in the Keene Valley after their marriage. Wyant's paintings in the 1880s show increasing interest in Barbizon painting, a combination of his own personal interests as well as an indication of his continuing association with Inness, whose art was also turning in this direction. Subdued color and lack of a broad, open, vista are seen in *An Old Clearing* (1881, Metropolitan Museum of Art). And the lowered viewpoint, spare use of pigment, haze, and subtle shadows of *A Gray Day, Arkville* (c. 1890, private collection), inspired Robert Olpin's assessment of Wyant that "In a certain

uniquely intimate way, Wyant surpasses everyone in this kind of quiet rest on a forest trek."

In 1889 Wyant and his wife purchased a house in Arkville, an artists' colony known as a center for Barbizon-style painting in the southern Catskills, as the artist's health had deteriorated to the point that he needed to be closer to his doctors in New York. Wyant's house had a front porch overlooking the Delaware River, on which Wyant could paint. His paralysis worsened and his mobility became limited. His last works are characterized by a pronounced lack of detail, more light and air than solid objects, and a sense of melancholy. After 1890, as he became more ill, Wyant made only occasional visits to New York, where he died.

When Wyant died he was a popular and well-known artist, and that fame continued for a time after his death. In the 1890s and during the first two decades of the twentieth century, he was given major exhibitions, often shown with his mentor Inness, though according to Olpin, Wyant "represents a different mood than that of Inness, and in a delicate and intimate view of nature is seldom excelled." From the 1920s, with the growing presence of modernism and social realism, Wyant's reputation began to decline, reaching its lowest point in the 1950s and 1960s. In the late 1960s and early 1970s, a revival of interest in nineteenth-century American painting caused Wyant to be seriously considered once again. In 1968 a major Wyant retrospective was organized at the Utah Museum of Fine Arts, University of Utah, and the artist has been included in major survey exhibitions of nineteenth-century American art since then.

• American museums with the largest collections of Wyant's work are the Metropolitan Museum of Art, the Rhode Island School of Design, Huntington Galleries, Huntington, W.Va., the Brooklyn Museum, and Brigham Young University. The major monographs on Wyant were written by the critic Eliot C. Clark: *Alexander Wyant* (1916), and *Sixty Paintings by Alexander H. Wyant* (1920). A modern assessment is Robert S. Olpin, *Alexander Helwig Wyant 1836–1892*, a catalog for the exhibition of the same name at the Utah Museum of Fine Arts, University of Utah (1968). Olpin's catalog contains a complete bibliography, including general references.

KAY KOENINGER

WYATT, Sir Francis (1588–Aug. 1644), colonial governor of Virginia, was born at Boxley Abbey, in Kent, England, the son of George Wyatt and Jane Finch, the daughter of Sir Thomas Finch of Eastwell. The Wyatts, an old gentry family, had settled in Kent in 1492 when their ancestor, Sir Henry Wyatt, a courtier of Henry VII, had acquired Allington Castle. The governor's great grandfather, Sir Thomas Wyatt, a poet and a courtier of Henry VIII, was granted Boxley Abbey in 1540 at the dissolution of the monasteries. Although the Wyatts lost the abbey for a time after Sir Thomas Wyatt the Younger's execution for leading a rebellion in 1554 against Queen Mary on the occasion of her marriage to Philip II of Spain, the family later recovered it. The Wyatts, however, never regained their leadership in Kent, though George Wyatt, the governor's father, was a scholarly country gentleman whose service as a soldier in the Low Countries and as a justice of the peace in Kent enabled him to aid his son's career.

Francis Wyatt was admitted to St. Mary Hall at Oxford in 1603 but left in 1604 without taking a degree to enter Gray's Inn to study law. He apparently did not follow the law as a career, though he may have rendered some service to the royal court, since he was knighted by James I in 1618. Little is known of his early life, but it is evident from his surviving letters and fugitive poems that he was a man of wit and polish with an analytical mind capable of appreciating theories as well as the practical problems of government. In 1618 Wyatt married Margaret Sandys, granddaughter of Edwin Sandys, archbishop of York. They had five sons and one daughter.

By his marriage Wyatt became connected with the faction in the Virginia Company of London headed by his wife's uncle, Sir Edwin Sandys. In 1620 Wyatt became a shareholder in the company, and the next year the earl of Southampton proposed him for the governorship of the Virginia Colony. Wyatt's subsequent election pleased the Virginians, who had wanted a governor with a more aristocratic background than their recent leaders.

Wyatt reached Virginia in October 1621, accompanied by his brother, the Reverend Hawte Wyatt, who later became the rector at Jamestown, and George Sandys, his wife's uncle and treasurer of the colony. The new governor's instructions included duplicates of those given his predecessor, Sir George Yeardley, which provided for an elected House of Burgesses. During his tenure as governor, Wyatt staunchly upheld the liberty given the Virginians to elect delegates to their general assembly. His first year in Virginia was especially difficult because of the arrival of 1,300 new settlers without adequate provision by the company for their supply and shelter. More tragic was the American Indian uprising of March 1622, when more than 300 settlers were massacred. Adding to the difficulties were famine and an outbreak of the plague. Despite inexperience, Wyatt exercised strong and resourceful leadership in both civil and military matters. He won the approval and respect of the Virginians generally, though a few thought he was too mild and cautious in his leadership. As his three-year appointment neared an end in 1624, he indicated that he was ready to relinquish the burden of office. The company in London prevailed on him to remain in Virginia and praised him for "his justice and aequanimitie towards all men who generally professed his Noble carriage" (Kingsbury, vol. 2, pp. 536–37). The Virginia Company, however, was dissolved in June 1624. Confidence in Wyatt and approval of his record in Virginia were evidenced by his continuation as governor under the royal commissions of James I in August 1624 and Charles I in 1625. Although Wyatt was granted permission in September 1624 to return to England be-

cause of his father's death, conditions did not allow him to leave. He remained at his post until May 1626. Even as the first royal governor of Virginia, he did not hesitate to call "convention assembly" in April 1625 without authorization from the Crown.

After returning to England, Wyatt established his residence at Boxley Abbey, which he had inherited. He did not lose interest in the Virginia enterprise, however, and in 1631 he was among those who petitioned unsuccessfully for a renewal of the Virginia Company's charter. The King's government did not overlook Wyatt's experience as a colonial administrator, for he served as a member of the Privy Council's subcommittee on plantations, dealing with colonial affairs from 1634 to 1639. In the latter year he was again sent to Virginia as royal governor to restore order in the troubled colony after the controversial Sir John Harvey had been removed as governor. Wyatt as well as the Virginians were pleased with his instructions that finally placed the elected House of Burgesses on a firm and permanent footing. This second period of office in Virginia was generally uneventful for Wyatt, who gave most of his attention to regulation of the tobacco trade. Sir William Berkeley succeeded him in February 1642, but Wyatt remained in Virginia until 1643 as a member of the council to aid the new governor.

On returning to England, Wyatt resumed the quiet life of a country gentleman at Boxley Abbey. He took no part in the civil war against Charles I, though Henry Wyatt, his eldest son, may have supported the Parliamentarians. Wyatt died at Boxley Abbey.

When he was first proposed as a governor for Virginia in 1621, Wyatt was described as "a gentleman recommended . . . for his many good parts . . . in respect of his parentage, good education, integritie of life, and faire fortunes" (Kingsbury, vol. 1, p. 436). Both as governor under the Virginia Company and as a royal governor, he measured up to this recommendation. Wyatt's tenures as governor won the approval of his employers in England as well as that of the colonials in Virginia, who remembered especially his support of representative government.

• Some of Wyatt's papers are in a collection of Wyatt family manuscripts, which are accessioned as Add. MSS 62135-6218, Department of Manuscripts, British Library, London. John Cave-Browne, *The History of Boxley Parish* (1892); J. Frederick Fausz and Jon Kukla, eds., "A Letter of Advice to the Governor of Virginia, 1624," *William and Mary Quarterly*, 3d ser., 34 (1977): 104–29; *The Papers of George Wyatt, Esq. of Boxley Abbey in the County of Kent*, ed. David M. Loades, Royal Historical Society, Camden, 4th ser., 5 (1968); and Stanley Charles Wyatt, *Cheneys and Wyatts* (1959), contain information pertaining to Wyatt's family background and early life. Accounts of Wyatt's governorship in Va. are in Alexander Brown, *The First Republic in America* (1898); Wesley Frank Craven, *Dissolution of the Virginia Company* (1932) and *The Southern Colonies in the Seventeenth Century* (1949); Richard Beale Davis, *George Sandys, Poet Adventurer* (1955); Susan Myra Kingsbury, ed., *The Records of the Virginia Company of London* (4 vols., 1906–1935); Richard L. Morton, *Colonial Virginia*, vol. 1 (1960); and Thomas J. Wertenbaker, *Virginia under the Stuarts* (1914).

MALCOLM LESTER

WYETH, Nathaniel Jarvis (29 Jan. 1802–31 Aug. 1856), New England ice merchant and western explorer, was born near Cambridge, Massachusetts, the son of Jacob Wyeth, the operator of the Fresh Pond Hotel, and Elizabeth Jarvis. He joined his father in the management of the hotel and in 1824 married his cousin Elizabeth Jarvis Stone. During the slack season, he harvested ice from Fresh Pond, first for the hotel's use and then for Frederic Tudor's ice company, which shipped ice to southern ports and to the West Indies. Wyeth's new invention of a horse-drawn ice cutter reduced the costs of harvesting ice from thirty cents to ten cents a ton. This enabled retailers to sell ice by weight instead of by measure, and it became a staple in the whole export trade of Boston, including the trade to the Far East.

Wyeth found his business arrangements with Tudor limiting, but rather than break with him, he sold his ice-cutting patent to Tudor for $2,500 and invested it and other money in an Oregon expedition through which he hoped to capitalize on the fur and salmon industries. Originally he had planned to join Hall Jackson Kelley's proposed colonizing expedition to the Northwest, but Hall's erraticism and delays convinced Wyeth to recruit his own "Band of Oregon Adventurers," which included his brother Jacob and his cousin John Wyeth. Furthermore, he was more interested in trade than in settlement. Arranging to be supplied from the cargo of a vessel scheduled to sail to the Northwest coast, he and his small group of twenty-four greenhorns traveled to Independence, Missouri, where they were able to join William Sublette and Robert Campbell, who were taking a supply caravan to the fur trade rendezvous at Pierre's Hole in present-day Wyoming. The caravan started out on 12 May 1832. After Pierre's Hole, where there was a battle with the Gros Ventre Indians, Wyeth attached his party, now reduced to eleven, to Milton Sublette and Henry Fraeb's trapping brigade as far as the juncture of the Snake and Owyhee rivers in southwestern Idaho. When he finally arrived at Fort Vancouver late in October 1832, he learned that the supply ship had been wrecked in the Pacific. That winter he explored the Lower Columbia and the Willamette Valley for potential farming and salmon-packing opportunities.

In early spring of 1833 Wyeth joined a Hudson's Bay Company fur brigade and went to the Flathead country in Montana, intending at some point to retrieve the furs that had been cached the previous summer. This he was unable to accomplish, but while camped along the Big Horn River he entered into an agreement with Milton Sublette and Thomas Fitzpatrick to supply the Rocky Mountain Fur Company with goods at the 1834 rendezvous. When he arrived in Boston in November with this contract, he found that his cousin John, who had withdrawn from the outbound expedition at Pierre's Hole, had criticized his leadership and abilities in *Oregon; or, A Short History of a Long Journey*. Referring to the book as "one of *little lies* told for gain," he organized the Columbia River Fishing and Trading Company with the backing of Henry Hall and the firm of Messrs. Tucker and Williams. The plan was for him to go overland again and meet Fitzpatrick and also to send the *May Dacre* with trade goods to the mouth of the Columbia, whence it and subsequent ships would return to the Boston market with furs and salmon. The ship, damaged by lightning, had to put in at Valparaiso, Chile, for repairs, and arrived in Oregon too late for the salmon run. Going west with Wyeth were the naturalists Thomas Nuttall and John K. Townsend, as well as Jason Lee and his Methodist missionaries.

When Wyeth reached the rendezvous with his trade goods, Fitzpatrick refused to buy them. Furious at his treatment, Wyeth decided to erect a post—Fort Hall—near the juncture of the Snake and Portneuf and from there conduct a rival fur trade. He made arrangements with John McLoughlin for supplies; sent the *May Dacre* with timber to the Hawaiian Islands; erected Fort William on present Sauvies Island; established a farm at French Prairie, forty miles up the Willamette from Fort William; spent the winter of 1834–1835 trapping in the area south of the Columbia; and when the *May Dacre* returned from Hawaii, packed the ship with 300 barrels of salmon for the Boston market, only half a cargo. Hall Jackson Kelley finally arrived at Fort Vancouver, where he and Wyeth had an unfriendly meeting.

His capital exhausted and unable to see a profit in the future in spite of herculean efforts, Wyeth accepted the fact that his more than $20,000 investment in a venture to open Oregon to American business had failed. He returned to Boston in 1836 and the next year sold Fort Hall to the Hudson's Bay Company, which had already established Fort Boise farther west on the Snake River. He resumed work for the Frederic Tudor ice company until 1840, when he established an ice business of his own, including the shipping of refrigerated vegetables and fruit. All the while he continued to improve or invent methods and implements needed in the ice and provision trade until his death at his Cambridge home.

The West remained important to Wyeth, and he wrote letters to Henry R. Schoolcraft giving his observations on the Flathead, Nez Perce, and Blackfoot Indians and in 1839 produced a long memoir on Oregon for the House Committee on Foreign Affairs. He was one of several who not only made it easier for Congress to support American interests in Oregon but also publicized the route of the Oregon Trail across South Pass.

• The best source on Wyeth is F[rederick] G. Young, ed., *The Correspondence and Journals of Captain Nathaniel J. Wyeth* (1899; repr. 1973). Reuben Gold Thwaites, *Early Western Travels*, vol. 21 (1905), contains the accounts of John B. Wyeth and John K. Townsend. An excellent biographical sketch is William R. Sampson's "Nathaniel Jarvis Wyeth" in *The Mountain Men and the Fur Trade of the Far West*, ed. Le Roy R. Hafen, vol. 5 (1968). Helpful also is Richard G. Beidleman, "Nathaniel Wyeth's Fort Hall," *Oregon Historical Quarterly* 59 (1957): 197–250. For the origins and growth of the ice industry, see Wyeth's "Ice Trade in the United States," *Bankers' Magazine*, Jan. 1849, p. 406. The odyssey of Wyeth has been captured by Christian McCord (pen name) in *Across the Shining Mountains* (1986), a novel in the Frontier Library.

MARY LEE SPENCE

WYETH, N. C. (22 Oct. 1882–19 Oct. 1945), artist, was born Newell Convers Wyeth in Needham, Massachusetts, the son of Andrew Newell Wyeth, a grain merchant, and Henriette Zirngiebel. As a boy growing up on his parents' small farm, he sketched local scenes and animals, developing a lifelong appreciation of nature. Despite paternal opposition, Wyeth's mother fostered his interest in art, enabling him to enroll successively in Boston's Mechanic Arts High School (graduated in 1899), Massachusetts Normal Arts School, and then in classes with illustrators Eric Pape (1901) and Charles W. Reed (1902).

At the urging of friend and fellow student Clifford Ashley, Wyeth journeyed to Wilmington, Delaware, in October 1902 to enter the Howard Pyle School, directed by the period's most well-known illustrator of books and journals. The rigorous course of study and the commanding presence of Pyle exerted a lasting influence on Wyeth. He wrote to his mother after the first week that "the composition lecture lasted 2 hours and it opened my eyes more than any talk I ever heard" (*Letters*, p. 21). Pyle advocated realism and authenticity, combined with an intense dramatic element. His students drew from plaster casts and models and in the summer painted outdoors in the countryside. Wyeth worked diligently and progressed rapidly under Pyle's instruction. In February 1903 he saw the publication of his first magazine cover, a spirited bucking bronco, for the *Saturday Evening Post*. By the time he left Pyle's classes in August 1904, commissions for magazine illustrations enabled the young artist to support himself.

Wyeth's early letters document a boundless enthusiasm for his work that translated into paintings of great action and vitality. He decided to concentrate on western scenes, and Pyle, who recommended direct knowledge of one's subject, urged him to travel west. Between 1904 and 1906 Wyeth made three trips to the western United States, where he absorbed the region through a variety of adventures and collected western gear that served as props for future paintings. During this period his commissions multiplied rapidly; his pictures appeared in many magazines, including *Century*, *Harper's*, *Outing*, *Saturday Evening Post*, and *Scribner's*. Among the best of his early western pictures are seven illustrations that accompanied "A Day with the Round-Up," an article Wyeth wrote for *Scribner's* (Mar. 1906) describing his own experiences on the range.

In 1907 *Outing* published four of Wyeth's pictures to illustrate an article titled "How They Opened the Snow Road" (Jan. 1907). Unusual compositions and masterful interpretations of snow and light create highly dramatic effects in these paintings. He excelled in action pictures, but his reputation also rested on subtle and sensitive depictions of Native Americans, including those of the eastern woodlands. In 1907 *Outing* offered its readers "The Indian in His Solitude," a portfolio of prints comprising five of Wyeth's paintings. To advertise these images of solitary men communing with nature, *Outing* described Wyeth as "one of our greatest, if not our *greatest* painter of American outdoor life." He was now firmly established with publishers in Philadelphia and New York.

Wyeth married Carolyn Brenneman Bockius of Wilmington in 1906, withdrew from Pyle's immediate circle, and settled in rural Chadds Ford, Pennsylvania. By 1908 his ardor for western subjects had begun to diminish, and he turned his attention to the land and people of the Brandywine River valley. The Chadds Ford area would remain his home for the next four decades and its hilly farmland and woods the inspiration for much of his painting. The Wyeths would have six children, one of whom died soon after birth.

In 1911, at the suggestion of Edwin Austin Abbey, Charles Scribner's Sons commissioned Wyeth to illustrate Robert Louis Stevenson's *Treasure Island*. The seventeen canvases he produced for that edition remain masterpieces of American illustrative painting. Exceptional for their design, color, and scale, these paintings even in reproduction enrich the drama of the narrative. Through masterful use of intense light, deep shadow, and subtle coloration, Wyeth constructed each picture to heighten the tensions between major characters in the story. He wrote prophetically to his mother, "I've turned out a set of pictures without doubt far better in every quality than anything I ever did" (*Letters*, p. 386). The critics agreed. His images for Stevenson's classic tale have themselves become classics, and his depictions of Old Pew, Billy Bones, and Long John Silver have influenced producers and actors of subsequent stage and film versions of the story.

With the *Treasure Island* commission, Wyeth established working methods that changed little throughout his career. He carefully read the story to select episodes that spoke to him of something within his own range of experience. Power and conviction in dramatic expression, he felt, rested fundamentally in autobiography. Detailed research on the various historical periods and figures followed; eventually he amassed a comprehensive reference library of more than 600 volumes. When possible, Wyeth would correspond with authors to seek clarification of a dramatic intention. For some commissions he would visit the site of the narrative, but because he firmly believed in the universality of nature he never felt the need to travel abroad. He began his artwork with a number of charcoal drawings, sometimes using family members or friends as models. For his illustrations he preferred to work in oil paint on large canvases, even though the images would be greatly reduced in reproduction.

The publication of *Treasure Island* firmly cemented what would become a long relationship between Wyeth and Charles Scribner's Sons, guided by Scribner's editor Joseph Chapin. Major titles illustrated by Wyeth in Scribner's Christmas gift-book series included *Kidnapped* (1913), *The Black Arrow* (1916), *The Boy's King Arthur* (1917), *The Last of the Mohicans* (1919), *Westward Ho!* (1920), *David Balfour* (1924), *The Deerslayer* (1925), and *The Yearling* (1939), among many others. First editions of these Wyeth-illustrated classics have become collectors' items, and beginning in 1981 Scribner's embarked on a project to reprint many of these books with new reproductions made from Wyeth's original paintings.

Wyeth did not work exclusively for Scribner's, however, and in the decade between 1911 and 1921 he produced more than 450 illustrations for books and magazines. Publishers such as Cosmopolitan, David McKay, Harper & Brothers, and Houghton Mifflin commissioned sets of illustrations for hardbound books. His pictures illustrated stories and articles in publications such as *Collier's Weekly*, *Harper's Monthly Magazine*, *Ladies' Home Journal*, *McCall's*, and *Saturday Evening Post*. He was a master of his craft; no one style characterized all of this work. Wyeth's great and varied technical abilities allowed him to match appropriate styles and techniques to the requirements of each text. His abiding respect for history and his profound love of nature permeated every picture, but he never became a slave to detail. Publishers, critics, and the public recognized his innate ability to select from a narrative the passages that would be best served by illustration. The critic John Black, writing in *Book Review* (Nov. 1921), affirmed that "Illustrated by N. C. Wyeth" on the cover of a book attracted as much attention as the name of a bestselling author. Although magazine and book illustration played a less important part in the second half of his career, Wyeth's place in American art rests mainly with his illustrative work.

Despite this success, throughout his life Wyeth wrestled with the pejorative connotations of the word "illustrator." His published letters reveal a lifelong struggle to devote himself to pure painting and to escape the rigid confines of text and technology that bound an illustrator. As early as 1907, Wyeth wrote to his mother, "I want to be *able* to *paint* a *picture* and that is as far from the realms of illustration as black is from white" (*Letters*, p. 202). His large family imposed financial obligations that necessitated the lucrative illustrative work, but Wyeth found time for personal painting as well. Recent scholarship has focused attention on his many still lifes, landscapes, portraits, and other personal paintings. His early letters document a strong interest in landscape painting, which only increased after he settled in the Brandywine valley. In the decade between 1910 and 1920 he painted a large number of landscapes and still lifes in various impressionistic styles, concentrating on light, atmospheric effects, and color. His letters credit the work of Daniel Garber,

Gari Melchers, and the Italian painter Giovanni Segantini as inspiration.

From about 1925 until the late 1930s Wyeth incorporated some modernistic elements into much of his private work, probably due to the influence of the art critic Christian Brinton, who lived in nearby West Chester, Pennsylvania. Brinton championed Russian émigré and Soviet art; his emphasis on fantasy, color, and the folk aesthetic as aspects of expressionism seemed to appeal to Wyeth. During this period Wyeth painted a group of enigmatic, highly personal canvases, such as *The Harbor at Herring Gut* (1925), *My Mother* (1929), and *Walden Pond Revisited* (1932), in a variety of styles and techniques, but his predilection for narrative kept him within the realist school. In 1939 he began to experiment with the tempera medium, producing a group of paintings in tempera or tempera and oil that depict the farmers of Chadds Ford and the fishermen of his summer home in Port Clyde, Maine. This late work shows similarities with paintings of the American Regionalist school, but Wyeth had actually always been a regionalist in his respect for the land and people around him. Exhibition records indicate that he sent work on a fairly frequent basis throughout his career to showings of contemporary American art, and he became a member of the National Academy of Design in 1940. To the general public, however, he remained first and foremost an illustrator.

Wyeth's mural commissions are another aspect of his work. In 1911 he completed a decorative scheme for the grillroom of the Hotel Utica in Utica, New York, based on several of his pictures of Native Americans that had appeared in *Scribner's*. In 1915 he designed a fanciful marine theme for the Hotel Traymore in Atlantic City, New Jersey. These two early commissions were subsequently destroyed, and only archival photographs document the images. In 1920 Wyeth was selected to contribute two murals to the decoration of the Missouri State Capitol (Jefferson City), each depicting a Civil War battle that had been fought in the state. Other commissions followed in rapid succession during the 1920s and 1930s, among them the Federal Reserve Bank Building, Boston; Westtown School, Westtown, Pennsylvania; First National Bank of Boston; Hotel Roosevelt and Franklin Savings Bank, both in New York City; Hubbard Hall, National Geographic Society, Washington, D.C.; First Mechanics National Bank, Trenton, New Jersey; and Wilmington Savings Fund Society, Wilmington, Delaware. Many of these murals depicted historical events; others, such as *The Giant* for Westtown School and *The Apotheosis of the Family* for the Wilmington Savings Fund Society, had allegorical themes. In 1940 Wyeth accepted a commission to decorate areas of the new Metropolitan Life Insurance Company building in New York City; he completed the first phase of this ambitious scheme illustrating the life of the Pilgrims in two years. The second phase, incomplete at his death, was finished by his son Andrew and son-in-law John McCoy. Most of Wyeth's murals have survived, but many are not at their original sites.

Throughout his career, Wyeth produced many images for advertising. In 1906 and 1907 he painted a series of pictures for the Cream of Wheat Company that rank along with his best western work. His pictures advertised the products of the American Tobacco Company, Aunt Jemima, Coca-Cola, General Electric, and Steinway and Sons, among many others. His later commercial work, done through a New York agency, however, is considered less inspired than earlier efforts. During both world wars, Wyeth contributed images for patriotic posters to the government and to agencies such as the American Red Cross.

Wyeth and a grandson died at a railroad crossing near his Chadds Ford home when a train struck his car. Although he left no formal school of students, Wyeth did leave five talented children, several of whom began their own careers in their father's studio. Henriette Wyeth Hurd, Carolyn Wyeth, and Andrew Wyeth forged highly individual artistic personalities, yet each acknowledged the tremendous debt owed to their father.

After his death Wyeth's reputation waned until 1965, when the Pennsylvania Historical and Museum Commission organized a major exhibition of his work, prompting a reevaluation of his place in American art history. Subsequent exhibitions have focused on various aspects of his career, such as his western work (Buffalo Bill Historical Center, 1980; Brandywine River Museum, 1990), and his personal paintings (Brandywine River Museum, 1982). The major exhibition, "An American Vision, Three Generations of Wyeth Art" (Brandywine River Museum, 1987), placed him at the head of a family of esteemed artists.

• The Brandywine River Museum, Chadds Ford, Pa., holds the largest collection of Wyeth's work, administers his Pennsylvania studio and house, and maintains an archive and catalogue raisonné. Significant collections of his illustrative work can be seen at the Wilmington (Del.) Public Library, the Philadelphia Free Library, and the New York Public Library. Wyeth expressed criticism of American illustration and included proposals for invigorating the field in "For Better Illustration," *Scribner's*, Nov. 1919, pp. 638–42. Ernest W. Watson published a wide-ranging interview with the artist in *American Artist*, Jan. 1945, pp. 16–22, 28. Wyeth's daughter-in-law, Betsy James Wyeth, edited a volume of his correspondence that chronicles his career and passions, *The Wyeths: The Letters of N. C. Wyeth, 1901–1945* (1971). Douglas Allen and Douglas Allen, Jr., *N. C. Wyeth: The Collected Paintings, Illustrations and Murals* (1972), contains a compilation of published images. Obituaries are in the Wilmington (Del.) *Morning News* and the *New York Times*, both 20 Oct. 1945.

CHRISTINE B. PODMANICZKY

WYETH, N. C. (24 Oct. 1911–4 July 1990), engineer and inventor, was born Newell Convers Wyeth in Chadds Ford, Pennsylvania, the son of Newell Convers "N. C." Wyeth, an acclaimed illustrator, and Carolyn Brenneman Bockius. Wyeth's childhood in Chadds Ford, with extended summer vacations in Port Clyde, Maine, was filled with creativity and exploration. While three of his four siblings were drawn immediately to studying art with their father, Wyeth showed an early interest and ability in engineering. When he was only three or four, his parents observed him rolling his buggy back and forth across the veranda, explaining his greasy hands after what was supposed to be a nap. This prompted his father to change Wyeth's name from Newell to Nathaniel, after his uncle, an engineer. Such an early disposition for physical manipulation occupied much of his youth. He frequently would dismantle clocks and use their parts to power model speedboats, and he spent a great deal of time fashioning scale models of furniture. One of the most influential lessons taught by Wyeth's father was the benefits of work done well. During Wyeth's first attempt at building a scale wooden ladder-backed chair, his father, while supporting his attempt, pointed out in what ways the chair could have been better. This quiet lesson and others like it were not lost on Wyeth, as he knew that the well-planned, carefully completed route to finishing any project would provide the best products. This patience, combined with skill, led him to become a talented and prolific inventor.

Already convinced of Wyeth's desire to attend school for engineering, his uncle Nathaniel compared programs and selected the University of Pennsylvania for young Wyeth. Prior to entering college Wyeth designed and built a small hydroplane for his family's power boat in Maine. The small craft worked fabulously, and it was so fast that the family called it "Ex-Lax." While at Penn Wyeth expanded on the idea of his small hydroplane, and beginning at about age eighteen he built a twenty-foot hydroplane out of white pine and ash, powered by a Ford V-8 engine. The boat, called the "Silver Foil" and traveling as much as forty-five to fifty miles per hour, was quite a sight and attracted a great deal of attention in Maine, almost garnering a spot in *Pathe News* in Boston. Wyeth believed strongly in the necessity for academic learning to provide the foundations for a career as an engineer and a life as an inventor. His own explorations into how things are made and designed, from wooden and metal model furniture to model speedboats and full-scale hydroplaning boats, was supplemented by the training he received at Penn. The basics of what could and could not work due to the laws of physics were learned in the classroom, but his creativity taught him how to use those laws to accomplish new tasks and to solve problems. He said, "The brain has a phenomenal ability to come up with new ways of doing things" (Brown, p. 368).

Wyeth's first job after completing his bachelor's degree in mechanical engineering was at the Delco Company plant, part of General Motors, in Dayton, Ohio. In 1936 Wyeth went to work at Du Pont, and the next year he married Caroline Pyle, with whom he had five children. Although he had wanted to be placed in the mechanical development laboratory, his initial position was in a routine engineering production laboratory as a field engineer and later as an assistant laboratory director. Shortly after demonstrating his ingenuity by redesigning a valve, he was offered an opportunity to transfer to the development laboratory. In the creative environment of Du Pont, Wyeth excelled. His first major project was developing an automatic method to form dynamite cartridges. His detailed isometric drawings—certainly an indication of the artistic nature of his family in addition to his own skill—illustrated the complete idea of a machine, clarifying requirements for carpenters and other workers. Another invention that was widely used is Typar, a nonwoven fabric of polypropylene thread used as carpet backing and in construction. The majority of Wyeth's contributions to Du Pont was in the form of improvements in machine efficiency, speed, and operation cost. The most universal of Wyeth's inventions while at Du Pont came in 1973, the same year of his wife's death. Until his development of a polyethylene-terephthalate (PET) bottle, the culmination of a project started in 1967, carbonated beverages could not be bottled in plastic. The ubiquitous soda pop bottle, patented by Wyeth and Ronald Newman Roseveare in 1973, revolutionized the beverage industry by providing a strong, clear, lightweight bottle to replace glass. The premise behind the PET soda pop bottle was that the plastic had to be stronger than the currently available plastic bottles; in order to contain the carbonation, the bottle had to be strengthened in two directions, both axially and transaxially, leading to the term biaxial oriented plastic.

Wyeth held at least twenty-three patents for inventions or process improvements during his forty-year career at Du Pont. In 1963 he was named the company's first engineering fellow, and in 1975 he was the first to be promoted to senior engineering fellow, the highest technical position available. He was a member of the American Society of Mechanical Engineers, which bestowed upon him fellow status in 1986. The Society of Plastics Engineers honored him with the International Award for Outstanding Achievement in Plastics Engineering and Technology in 1981. In 1986 he was elected to the Hall of Fame of the Society of the Plastics Industry. In addition to these awards he was granted a number of honorary doctorates. In 1984 he married Jean Grady. Wyeth's devotion to creativity is evidenced by his comment, "Saying everything's already been invented is like saying you've breathed all the air there is" (Brown, p. 377). Wyeth died in Glen Cove, Maine.

• The most useful resource for Wyeth's personal insights and beliefs is Kenneth A. Brown's *Inventors at Work* (1986), a series of interviews with prominent inventors; the section dealing with Wyeth, pp. 353–80, provides details about his youth and his most prominent discoveries. A lengthy obituary is in the *New York Times*, 7 July 1990.

JOANNA B. DOWNER

WYLER, William (1 July 1902–27 July 1981), American film director and producer, was born in Mülhausen, Alsace-Lorraine, the son of Leopold Wyler, haberdasher, and Melanie Auerbach. Preparing, without enthusiasm, to join the family business, Wyler briefly attended a commercial school in Lausanne, Switzerland, but changed his plans when his mother's cousin Carl Laemmle, founder and head of the Universal Film Manufacturing Company, visited from the United States. Laemmle offered Wyler a job and brought him to New York City in 1920. Starting as an office boy and occasional translator (into French and German) of publicity materials in Universal's New York headquarters, Wyler moved on to Universal City, Laemmle's 230-acre California studio, where he performed a series of odd jobs. He then worked his way up through the assistant director ranks to director of low-budget western shorts and features (1925–1928). Although highly formulaic and quickly and cheaply made, these films gave Wyler a thorough apprenticeship.

At the end of the twenties, when Hollywood was in the process of converting to sound technology, Wyler was promoted out of "B" westerns. Of the films he directed in this period, only *The Love Trap* (1929) and *Hell's Heroes* (1930) are extant. Released both as a silent and in a part-talkie version, *The Love Trap*, a bedroom farce, reveals early signs of what would become Wyler's strengths as a filmmaker: the careful staging of scenes in a dynamic, three-dimensional space and an interest in his actors as well as an ability to showcase their performances. *Hell's Heroes*, Wyler's first "all-talking" film, was a gritty, realistic return (on a class "A" budget) to the western genre. *A House Divided* (1931), the first of Wyler's sound films still available in its original form, was essentially a melodrama, but Wyler underplayed the emotions, concentrating on mise-en-scène—the orchestration of dramatic space through the purposeful positioning and movement of the actors, the objects around them, and the camera itself.

Wyler's mastery of mise-en-scène came to the fore in *Counsellor at Law* (1933), based on the play by Elmer Rice and starring John Barrymore. Although the play was set entirely in a suite of offices, Wyler, through staging, editing, and camera movement, dynamized a theatrical space into a specifically cinematic one. His success with this film, and his rapport with Barrymore, who gave a larger-than-life performance, enhanced Wyler's reputation in Hollywood. He directed several more films at Universal, including *The Good Fairy* (1935), which starred Margaret Sullavan. Wyler and Sullavan were married in 1934, while *The Good Fairy* was still in production. (They divorced in 1936.) Following a brief period of freelancing, Wyler signed a contract with the independent producer Samuel Goldwyn.

The first films Wyler made for Goldwyn—*These Three*, *Dodsworth* (both 1936), and *Dead End* (1937)—were drawn from plays, and each gave Wyler the opportunity to display his strengths as a director. In particular, he and his cinematographers experimented with composing scenes in depth as well as on the lateral plane. Wyler at the same time acquired a reputation as an "adult" filmmaker. *These Three* was based on Lillian Hellman's controversial play, *The Children's Hour*, which focuses on lesbian desire. *Dodsworth*, which treats a dissolving marriage in a nonjudgmental way, also was perceived as "mature" fare. And *Dead End* arrived in Hollywood with a reputation for strong social comment and salty language. Although the industry's Production Code restrictions considerably undercut some of the force in each work (the lesbianism was eliminated from *The Children's Hour*; Wyler remade the film, this time with the lesbian theme and under the play's original title, in 1961), Wyler was praised for his careful handling of potentially incendiary themes and characters.

By the end of 1937 he had reached a significant plateau in his career. He had been nominated for an Academy Award as best director for *Dodsworth*, and Warner Bros. had borrowed him from Goldwyn to direct its leading female star, Bette Davis, in *Jezebel* (1938). In this film Wyler effectively channeled Davis's talents, toning down her sometimes affected mannerisms while displaying her forceful personality to full effect. Davis won her first Academy Award as best actress for *Jezebel*, an honor that was thought to reflect on Wyler. The rapport between director and star led to two more films, one at Warner Bros., *The Letter* (1940), and one with Goldwyn, *The Little Foxes* (1941). *The Letter*, in particular, skillfully balances Davis's histrionic force with Wyler's restrained and calculated orchestration of space and movement. *The Little Foxes*, although not as harmonious an experience for director and star, permitted Wyler, working with cinematographer Gregg Toland, fresh from his experiments with deep focus on Orson Welles's *Citizen Kane* (1941), to refine his use of long takes and composition in depth.

In between *Jezebel* and *The Letter*, Wyler married Margaret Tallichet in 1938; they had five children. Soon after his marriage, Wyler directed, for Goldwyn, one of his best-remembered films, *Wuthering Heights* (1939). *Wuthering Heights* was a popular and critical success, and Wyler won the New York Film Critics director's award and was once again nominated for an Oscar. In early autumn 1941 he was invited to direct *Mrs. Miniver* for Metro-Goldwyn-Mayer. The story of an "average" British family during war, *Mrs. Miniver* was designed to arouse sympathy for England and to prepare Americans for their inevitable participation in the conflict. Released some months after Pearl Harbor, this enormously popular film won Wyler his first Oscar for direction and was voted best film of 1942 by the Academy. Although Wyler's directorial personality was partly submerged by MGM's conventional, unimaginative production style, he once again demonstrated his skill at providing force and conviction to highly sentimental material.

With the United States at war, Wyler volunteered to make films for the armed forces. As an army major (later, lieutenant colonel), he produced two 16mm color films under combat conditions, serving as one of his own cinematographers (he ended the war permanently deaf in one ear as a result). The more notable of the two, *Memphis Belle*, documented a B-17 bomber's twenty-fifth and final mission over Germany. Combining a realistic texture with a lyrical handling of editing, music, and narration, *Memphis Belle* remains one of the most impressive and least dated World War II propaganda films.

On his return to Hollywood, Wyler, together with directors Frank Capra, John Huston, and George Stevens, formed an independent production company, Liberty Films. However, he had one film remaining on his Goldwyn contract. Drawing in part on his own war experiences and emotions, he made what is generally considered his masterpiece, *The Best Years of Our Lives* (1946). A powerful, moving, and complex view of the plight of returning veterans, *Best Years* exhibits Wyler's style at its clearest. Working with Gregg Toland, he combines forceful compositions with staging in depth and deep-focus photography, highlighting the contrasting styles of his cast (including, notably, the performance of the handless veteran and first-time actor, Harold Russell) to tell the intertwined stories of three men who struggle in different ways to fit into an alien and alienating postwar world. If not as hard-hitting as some critics would have liked, *Best Years* nevertheless merges social commentary and personal drama with an honesty and compassion not often equaled in American cinema.

The Best Years of Our Lives, which won Wyler his second Oscar for best director (and also won for best picture, actor, supporting actor, screenplay, editing, and musical score), was released in a year that can be said to mark the highest point, as well as the beginning of the end, for Hollywood's "Golden Age." American society, and Hollywood's place in it, was changing dramatically. In response to the witch-hunt atmosphere brought to Hollywood by the House Committee on Un-American Activities, Wyler helped to form, in 1947, the Committee for the First Amendment, an organization long on good intentions but not notably effective. At the same time, the economics of independent production were proving such that, by the time Wyler was free of his Goldwyn contract, Liberty Films was no longer viable; Wyler, along with his partners, became a producer-director at Paramount, which had absorbed Liberty Films. He made five films for Paramount, of which *The Heiress* (1949) and *Roman Holiday* (1953) were the most critically successful. *The Heiress*, adapted (by means of a Broadway play) from a novel by Henry James (1843–1916), *Washington Square*, once again gave Wyler the opportunity to orchestrate distinct performance styles within a limited domestic space. *Roman Holiday*, filmed mostly on location in Italy, is primarily a pleasing showcase for Audrey Hepburn in her first important role. Two other Paramount films, *Detective Story* (1951) and *Carrie* (1952), were compromised by the censors and by the increasingly oppressive political and moralistic atmosphere of the early 1950s. Wyler completed his Paramount contract with a psychological crime drama, *The Desperate Hours* (1955).

For the remainder of his career, Wyler worked for a number of studios as a freelance director-producer. Without the structural base provided by the studio system, his projects were necessarily varied and uneven in quality. His later films included a pacifist fable (*Friendly Persuasion*, 1956), a large-scale western (*The Big Country*, 1958), a biblical epic (*Ben-Hur*, 1959), a light comedy (*How to Steal a Million*, 1966), a musical (*Funny Girl*, 1968), and a study of race relations (*The Liberation of L. B. Jones*, 1970). Although (or, perhaps, because) a number of these films were highly successful financially (*Ben-Hur* did much to save MGM from bankruptcy), Wyler's critical reputation declined significantly during this period; only *The Collector* (1965), essentially a two-character drama set in a confined location, was regarded as of a piece with Wyler's earlier films. Even in epics like *The Big Country* and *Ben-Hur*, however, Wyler continued to exhibit a sympathetic approach to performance and an ability to create focused, dramatic moments. His interest in and commitment to filmmaking clearly was waning, however, and in 1971 he retired. He lived to see a revival of interest in his work through the publication of a biography, several critical studies, and retrospectives of his films. In 1976 he received a Life Achievement Award from the American Film Institute.

• Letters, memos, and other working papers to and from Wyler are in the Ruth and Augustus Goetz collections in the New York Public Library and the Wisconsin Center for Film and Theatre Research in Madison. Other materials (scripts, clipping files, etc.) are in the UCLA Special Collections, the Academy of Motion Picture Arts and Sciences Library, and the American Film Institute Library, all in Los Angeles. The only biography is Axel Madsen, *William Wyler* (1973). A critical study of his films is Michael Anderegg, *William Wyler* (1979). See also Karel Reisz, *William Wyler: An Index* (1958); John Tuska, *Close-up: The Hollywood Director* (1978); Louis Gianetti, *Masters of the American Cinema* (1981); and Sharon Kern, *William Wyler: A Guide to References and Resources* (1984). An obituary is in the *New York Times*, 29 July 1981.
MICHAEL ANDEREGG

WYLIE, Andrew (12 Apr. 1789–11 Nov. 1851), college president and pastor, was born in Washington, Pennsylvania, the son of Adam Wylie, an immigrant from county Antrim, Ireland, and a farmer in Fayette County in western Pennsylvania (his mother's name is not known). A studious child, Wylie was educated at home and in local schools. At age fifteen he entered Jefferson College (Cannonsburg, Pa.), supporting himself in part by teaching in nearby schools. He graduated with honors in 1810 and was appointed tutor at the college. Two years later he became its president. He was licensed to preach in 1812 and ordained in the Presbyterian ministry in 1813. That year he married Margaret Ritchie; they had twelve children.

As president of Jefferson Wylie led a controversial effort to merge the college with nearby Washington College. When that effort failed he left Jefferson in 1816 and became the president of Washington College and a pastor in the Presbyterian church. After involving himself in theological disputes among local Presbyterian groups, he was forced to resign the presidency of Washington in 1828 but retained his pastorate. In October 1828 the trustees of Indiana College voted to offer its presidency to Wylie. After much deliberation Wylie accepted the position and began his duties in October 1829. Indiana College had been established in 1820 as Indiana Seminary, one of two state colleges in Indiana supported by land grants. Located in the south central Indiana town of Bloomington, it became Indiana College in 1828 and Indiana University in 1838.

Wylie brought to Indiana a firm commitment to traditional classical education and a somewhat formal, austere bearing that made it difficult for him to interact smoothly with the frontier society that surrounded the new college. He became the chief teacher of a small faculty and offered courses in moral sciences, mental philosophy, rhetoric, evidences of Christianity, belles lettres, and the Constitution of the United States. Under his leadership, Indiana College maintained a preparatory department and added a law department in addition to the traditional college courses. Enrollment in the college courses grew from 40 to 74 during his tenure. During his last year an additional 58 students were in the preparatory department and 28 in the law courses. Although he built a modest endowment, Wylie was not notably successful in expanding the budget; income during his tenure grew from $5,000 per year to $6,770, and the faculty expanded from three members to five. Although Wylie is credited with the college's survival in difficult circumstances, he was never able to win substantial state support or to keep pace with the curricular innovations of other midwestern state universities. Because of his scholarly activities and heavy teaching schedule, Wylie had little time for strictly administrative responsibilities such as academic planning or public relations work with Indiana citizens or state officials.

Wylie was Indiana University's first publishing scholar. Among his works were *English Grammar* (1822), *The Uses of History* (1831), *Eulogy of General Lafayette* (1834), *Latin and Roman Classics* (1838), and *Sectarianism Is Heresy* (1840). He was also a prolific speaker, who most often addressed scholarly and student groups.

Throughout his educational career, Wylie was an active churchman. Often at odds with other Presbyterians over Calvinist theology, he left that church to become in 1841 an ordained deacon in the Protestant Episcopal church and then in 1842 an ordained priest. Although Wylie was never entirely comfortable in frontier Indiana, he continued as president of Indiana University until his death of pneumonia in Bloomington.

• Many of Wylie's letters and publications are housed in the Indiana University Archives. The best treatment of Wylie's career is Thomas D. Clark, *Indiana University, Midwestern Pioneer*, vol. 1: *The Early Years* (1970). See also Theophilus A. Wylie, ed., *Indiana University, Its History from 1820,*

When Founded, to 1890 (1890); James A. Woodburn, *History of Indiana University, 1820–1902* (1940); and Theophilus A. Wylie, "Andrew Wylie, D.D., First President of Indiana University," *Indiana School Journal* 13 (May 1868): 175–86.

B. EDWARD MCCLELLAN

WYLIE, Elinor (7 Sept. 1885–16 Dec. 1928), poet and novelist, was born Elinor Morton Hoyt in Somerville, New Jersey, the daughter of Henry Martyn Hoyt, later solicitor general of the United States, and Anne McMichael. In 1887 the family moved to a Philadelphia suburb, where they enjoyed many comfortable years as members of the best society. Elinor attended Miss Baldwin's private school at Bryn Mawr until she was twelve. In 1897 her father became assistant attorney general of the United States, and the family relocated to Washington, D.C.

In 1905 Elinor married Philip Hichborn, the son of a prominent admiral, and had a son. Five years later, she left them both and ran off to Europe with Horace Wylie, a married lawyer seventeen years older than she. His wife would not divorce him until 1915, and Elinor and Horace lived together in spite of the ensuing scandal. They married in 1916 and returned to Washington in 1919. (Philip Hichborn committed suicide in 1912, and Wylie's son was raised by the Hichborn family.)

Wylie wrote poetry from an early age. Her first collection of poems appeared anonymously in England in 1912. Called *Incidental Numbers*, the book was printed privately by Wylie's mother. Her next collection, *Nets to Catch the Wind*, appeared in 1921 after she and Horace Wylie had returned to the United States. These poems were highly polished and clearly influenced by the metaphysical poets. *Black Armour* appeared in 1923 and contained similar verses.

Wylie also wrote four novels in a mannered, formal style that included verse-like fantasy. They were *Jennifer Lorn* (1923), which one critic described as "a humorous Gothic romance in the nineteenth-century tradition," *The Venetian Glass Nephew* (1925), *The Orphan Angel* (1926), and *Mr. Hodge and Mr. Hazard* (1928). The best known of these is probably *The Orphan Angel*, which hypothesized the fate of poet Percy Bysshe Shelley if he had been picked up by a Yankee ship rather than drowning. In the novel, Shelley lands in America where his character is contrasted with the pioneer environment. This popular book was a selection of the Book-of-the-Month Club.

During these productive years Wylie received support and encouragement from novelist Sinclair Lewis and William Rose Benét, poet and editor of the prestigious *Saturday Review of Literature*. In 1923 she divorced Horace Wylie and married Benét. Benét had children from a previous marriage but none with Wylie. In fact, she continued to be known as Elinor Wylie and seldom lived with Benét, keeping her own apartment and traveling frequently to Europe on her own. Always frail, high-strung, and plagued by high blood pressure, Wylie suffered the first of two strokes and accompanying facial paralysis in 1928, but she contin-

ued to write. *One Person*, her "passionately intense sonnet sequence," appeared in 1928 as did the collection called *Trivial Breath*. *Collected Poems* (edited by Benét) was published posthumously in 1932 and *Last Poems* in 1943.

Wylie's attitudes as expressed in her work were influenced by her unconventional lifestyle and public reaction to it. She lived passionately, modeling herself after Shelley, but her passion "estranged her from conventional people." Criticism made her satirical, if not cynical. Her work expressed the dichotomies in her life; she came from a genteel family but behaved like a bohemian and wrote in a controlled style about unwieldy passions.

Wylie's work is now considered erratic, ranging from very good—"delicate, subtle, highly unique"—to insincere and contrived. Because she moved in good society, however, and because she was well acquainted with and frequently entertained members of the highest literary echelon, her work was published and always acclaimed. In his biography *Elinor Wylie* (1969), Thomas Gray claims that Wylie often displayed "hysterical responses to criticism." She had "a strange and unforgettable beauty" and knew all the right people but was known to make scenes when adversely criticized; this behavior resulted in little public censure during her lifetime.

The best of Wylie's poems express sincere emotion and a critical edge. Her pessimism can also be seen in poems from *Angels and Earthly Creatures* (published posthumously in 1929). In "Let No Charitable Hope" (from *Nets to Catch the Wind*), Wylie writes:

> I was, being human, born alone;
> I am, being woman, hard beset;
> I live by squeezing from a stone
> The little nourishment I get.

She writes in "Full Moon" (from *Black Armour*):

> There I walked, and there I raged;
> The spiritual savage caged
> Within my skeleton, raged afresh
> To feel, behind a carnal mesh,
> The clean bones crying in the flesh.

Wylie served as patron to a number of young writers, including Edna St. Vincent Millay who wrote a series of elegies upon Wylie's death. She also inspired a number of biographies and memoirs, including William Rose Benét's *The Prose and Poetry of Elinor Wylie* (1934); *Elinor Wylie: The Portrait of an Unknown Lady* (1935) by the author's sister, Nancy Hoyt; *Three Worlds* (1936) by Carl Van Doren; *Life and the Dream* (1947) by Mary Colum; and essays in Edmund Wilson's *The Shores of Light* (1952). In 1979 Stanley Olson published his full-length biography, *Elinor Wylie: A Life Apart*.

Wylie died of a stroke in New York City on the day she finished correcting proofs for *Angels and Earthly Creatures*. Her life attested to her belief in "this poor armour, patched from desperate fears"; her work reflected her love for "words opalescent, cool, and pearly."

• Wylie's papers are in the Elinor Wylie Archive in the Beinecke Library at Yale University. The Berg collection at the New York Public Library has a group of her letters. Useful secondary sources not mentioned in the text are Elizabeth Shepley Sargeant, *Fire under the Andes: A Group of North American Portraits* (1927), and Judith Farr, *The Life and Art of Elinor Wylie* (1983). See also Sandra Gilbert and Susan Gubar, eds., *The Norton Anthology of Literature by Women* (1985); and Hyatt H. Waggoner, *American Poets: From the Puritans to the Present*, rev. ed. (1968). An obituary appears in the *New York Times*, 17 Dec. 1928.

ELAINE FREDERICKSEN

WYLIE, Philip Gordon (12 May 1902–25 Oct. 1971), writer, was born in North Beverly, Massachusetts, the son of Edmund Melville Wylie, a Presbyterian minister, and Edna Edwards, a novelist. His childhood was marked by experiences of lasting consequence: the death of his mother when he was five; his escape from his grief and loneliness into the imaginary world of books; a growing alienation from his father after he remarried in 1911; and a nearly fatal illness in 1912 caused by a burst appendix. Growing up as the eldest child in a minister's household in small towns (Delaware, Ohio, and Montclair, New Jersey), Wylie soon began to rebel against the "official piety" and middle class "propriety" that were forced on him by persons, like his father, whom he regarded as hypocrites and self-appointed authority figures. Even as a young adolescent, Wylie refused to recognize the jurisdiction of anybody or any doctrine or dogma over his freedom to think for himself and to seek out truth on his own.

Living in Montclair did, however, offer new educational opportunities for Wylie: proximity to the theaters and artists of New York City; unstructured experimental classes for gifted students; and a teacher who encouraged him to pursue writing. Later, Wylie's four semesters at Princeton introduced him to geology and Darwinism, to the use of the scientific method, and to satirical writers such as Jonathan Swift and Laurence Sterne. Unfortunately, his "genteel poverty" severely lowered his social status among his peers. His writings impressed no one, and he was dismissed early in 1923 for low grades and a "bad attitude" toward traditional courses of study and professorial authority. These humiliations strengthened Wylie's resolve to become a respected author—and a rich one.

Wylie immediately found financial success by composing public-relations copy and by running his own advertising agency—until that career was ruined by a well-publicized, though spurious paternity suit filed in late 1924. Dropped by his business clients and banished from Montclair because of the scandal, Wylie lost the case despite irrefutable evidence that someone else was the father. He thus learned firsthand the validity of an idea that he had already encountered in Sigmund Freud: Victorian suppression of all information about human sexuality has created in people intense feelings of guilt over even normal behavior—a

form of self-hatred that is projected onto any other person accused of sexual misconduct. Wylie had found a new mission in life: to end that conspiracy of silence.

In order to earn a living, Wylie turned to freelance writing. With the help and advice of Harold Ober, a knowledgeable literary agent, and Edwin Balmer, the editor of *Redbook*, Wylie quickly mastered the necessary skills. Over the next thirty-five years he became one of the profession's best paid (earning $40,000 per year during the worst years of the Great Depression), most prolific (sixteen million words, including nearly a hundred novels as well as many hundreds of short stories, essays, and syndicated columns), and most famous (his reputation as the author of the Crunch and Des deep-sea fishing stories in the *Saturday Evening Post* in the early 1940s lasted well past his lifetime). Wylie wrote in nearly every genre of popular fiction—romantic love stories, murder mysteries, fantasy, and science fiction—and he had few equals in constructing fast-moving plots and in setting clearly defined characters against carefully detailed, realistic backgrounds.

Despite the time and effort he devoted to freelancing, Wylie also produced a sizable body of writing on much weightier subjects. Drawing on some of his most unpleasant experiences of physical and emotional suffering, his novels project pictures of flawed human nature and of the frightening insecurity of mankind's existence that are quite unlike those in most magazine fare. *Heavy Laden* (1928) is a devastating portrait of a Presbyterian minister whose intellectual dishonesty drives his daughter into self-destructive rebellion. *Babes and Sucklings* (1929) is a frank account of the early years of Wylie's troubled relationship with his first wife, Sally Ondeck, whom he married in 1928 (they had one child and divorced in 1937). Two science-fantasy novels, *Gladiator* (1930) and *The Murderer Invisible* (1931), dramatize Wylie's conviction that truly superior persons cannot find acceptance or happiness in a world dominated by tradition-bound mediocrity. The most powerful—and enduring—of these partially autobiographical novels is *Finnley Wren* (1934), in which a fictional narrator named Philip Wylie probes into the tormented past of the title character, who, like the author, rebelled against his father, was damaged by a paternity suit, and was almost driven mad by an unfaithful "liberated" wife. This novel, justly praised for its indelible characterization (especially of its women), its flamboyant style, and its Sterne-like violation of the "rules" of the genre, is also important as the first work in which Wylie speaks his mind without restraint on a number of matters that infuriated him. Using Wren as spokesman, Wylie assaults the American educational system for teaching lies and not offering modern science or fostering independent, creative thinking. He also criticizes the lack of ethics in self-styled Christians, the willful ignorance of the "average" voter, the lurid sensationalism of newspapers, the self-centeredness and materialism of the "typical" woman, the anti-male doctrines of radical feminists, and the universal lack of scientific knowledge about sexual behavior and psychological processes.

During the next decade Wylie found additional targets: for example, he attacked left-wingers' infatuation with Soviet Communism in *Smoke across the Moon* (1937) and right-wing isolationists' refusal to see the menace of Adolf Hitler's Germany in *The Other Horseman* (1942). Composed at the suggestion of his second wife, Frederica Ballard (whom he had married in 1938 and with whom he had no children), his most influential work, *Generation of Vipers* (1943), is a connected series of essays denouncing at length every American institution, belief, and character type that Wylie despised. The book is still remembered but mostly for the section "Common Women," which portrayed "Mom" as the "Great Emasculator" and introduced the term "Momism" to the language. In demand as a "controversial" writer, Wylie had finally found a large audience for serious subjects. He set forth Jungian ideas in *An Essay on Morals* (1947), denounced feminist dogma on "equality" of the sexes in *The Disappearance* (1951), crusaded for civil defense programs against the Soviet atomic bomb threat in *Tomorrow!* (1954), and preached against the notion of a "win-able" thermonuclear war in *Triumph* (1963).

The best of Wylie's novels after *Finnley Wren* is the somber and compelling *Opus 21* (1949), in which a semifictional narrator named Wylie confronts his own fear of death while waiting for a biopsy report. Simultaneously, he discusses with the other characters his views on intellectual honesty and self-knowledge as they apply to contemporary events and issues. The best-received piece of this period—and his last popular success—was *The Answer* (1956), an ironic solution to the threat of thermonuclear war.

After 1957 Wylie's career as a freelance writer steadily worsened. The popular magazines that had for decades provided the bulk of his income succumbed to the competition of television. To a new generation of editors and publishers Wylie seemed a liability—an ex-celebrity whose ideas were overly familiar to the public—and they rejected his new books or did little to promote their sales. In a very short time Wylie used up all his savings, sold his home to pay his debts, and was struggling against chronic depression, emotional and physical exhaustion, and alcohol and amphetamine addiction. Nevertheless he managed to complete four more impressive books. *The Magic Animal* (1968) is a philosophical and scientific treatise influenced by pioneering environmentalists such as Konrad Lorenz. *The Spy Who Spoke Porpoise* (1969) is a spy thriller whose aging hero personifies Wylie's own fight to outlast the unbeatable forces of change. *The Sons and Daughters of Mom* (1971) condemns the leftist liberals and permissive parents who had seduced a whole generation into mindless rebellion. Finally, the posthumous novel, *The End of the Dream* (1972), predicts the end of mankind in a series of environmental disasters brought on by heedless use of technological developments, ignorance of science, and insatiable greed. Thus, even at the end of his career, Wylie was still

dedicated to the salvation of mankind through knowledge. In his lifetime he had, in fact, already freed the minds of many, especially his younger contemporaries, even as his name faded from the public's consciousness. He died in Miami, Florida.

• Some of Wylie's letters, manuscripts, and documents, along with his letters to his younger brother, Max Wylie, are stored in the Princeton University Library. His letters to Truman Frederick Keefer and interview tapes are in Keefer's possession. The definitive and only critical biography, based on extensive personal interviews, is Keefer, *Philip Wylie* (1977); it contains a selective bibliography, which includes published interviews, critical essays, and sources of biographical information as well as a reading list of Wylie's best work.

TRUMAN FREDERICK KEEFER

WYLIE, Robert (1839–12 Feb. 1877), genre and landscape painter, was born at Douglas, Isle of Man, an island between England and Ireland. He was orphaned, and at the age of ten he settled in Philadelphia with his uncle, a Presbyterian clergyman. Between 1859 and 1863 he studied at the Pennsylvania Academy of the Fine Arts. He also served as a curator for the academy, a job that was a "combination of janitor, superintendent, preparator and monitor" (Sellin, p. 11). Wylie also worked as an ivory carver and sculptor of clay pieces and was one of the founders of the Philadelphia Sketch Club.

In December of 1863, after first paying a visit to his native Isle of Man, Wylie went to France on a scholarship from the Pennsylvania Academy. He had planned to study sculpture at the École des Beaux-Arts, but he was unable to enroll because he was twenty-five, past the age of admission. Wylie did, however, study with Antoine-Louis Barye, a prominent animal sculptor, and he often posed during the zoological lectures. Without formal instruction, he also drew at the Académie Suisse. In 1864 he exhibited his *Death of Secession* at the Great Central Fair in Philadelphia; it was a work composed prior to his departure for Europe. He traveled the same year to Pont-Aven and established a permanent residence there in 1866. Pontaven-Finistere was "a little picturesque town in Brittany about three miles from the sea" ("Art Talks from Paris," p. 354). Wylie resided in this small fishing village until his death.

Gaining the admiration of Pont-Aven peasants and respect of American and French painters, Wylie became the guiding force behind a thriving colony of American artists; two of his better-known American colleagues were Frederick A. Bridgman and Thomas Hovenden. Wylie's paintings explored peasant customs and types, and he portrayed their costumes and traditions. He "adopted the dress and modes of living of the peasants . . . and was literally not only among them but of them" (A. V. Butler, "Robert Wylie," *The Aldine* 9, no. 4: 77–78). His work depicted a "multivalent view of peasantry" that was present in literary imagery but ignored in the works of American and French artists.

Wylie's first exhibit in Europe was at the Salon of 1870. His entry was *Baz-Walen demandeur en mariage dans la Basase-Bretagne* (*Reading the Letters from the Bridegroom*). The work explored the customs, the character types, and the strong family ties of the Breton families. In 1872 his *Soriere Breton* (*The Brittany Sorceress*) won him a second-class medal. He had been the fourth American to win this award at the Paris Salon and the second to win a second-class award. After the 1872 exhibition, the pinnacle of his career, Goupil and Company contracted to purchase all of his work. His work "sold immediately and as many could be placed as the painter could produce" ("Art Talks from Paris," p. 354). The painting explored the darker side of the oral tradition of fortune telling and superstitions associated with village life.

Wylie continued to exhibit his works in Paris Salons. In 1873 appeared his *L'Accueil de l'Orphelin, Bretagne* (*The Welcome of the Orphan Brittany*), which focused on the theme of a Breton family taking in a young orphan. Some of his other important works were *The Postman* (c. 1868), *Fortune Teller of Brittany* (c. 1873, Corcoran Gallery of Art), *Breton Neighbors Reading Hugo's 93* (c. 1873, unlocated), *Breton Audience* (c. 1873, unlocated), *The Card Players* (c. 1873, unlocated), *Colportoreur* (*Peddler*) (c. 1875, unlocated), *Mendicants in Brittany* (c. 1875, unlocated), *Le Conteur de Legendes* (*The Story Teller: Breton Interior*) (c. 1878, unlocated), *Brittany Peasant Girl* (c. 1878, unlocated), and *The Death of Vendean Chief* (c. 1878, Metropolitan Museum of Art). This last was Wylie's final major work, dealing with the Breton region's participation in the War of the Vendee.

Wylie died of a "hemmorage of the lungs." "Prior to his death he had been working very steadily for some two months past on a large picture and could have finished it for the Salon" (Hovenden, "The Death of Robert Wylie, 1877"). He was buried in Pont-Aven, having never married.

Wylie's paintings represented a modern interpretation of rural life. He was one of the few painters of peasant life who knew them and the only American artist known to have learned the Breton language. Peasants had become a symbol of oppressed people, a radical subject that oftentimes provoked social and political controversy. He influenced American artists, who after returning to the United States began painting genre scenes of rural country life idealized and grounded in close observations of nature. Douglas Volk's *Puritan Maiden* (c. 1880–1881) and Thomas Hovenden's *Breaking Home Ties* (1888) exemplify the Wylie-Breton style influence.

While much of his work was not exhibited in the United States, after the Civil War Americans looked to images of the French peasants as a means of identifying values feared in danger of being lost due to urbanization. Robert Wylie, expatriate and painter, influenced American artists in Europe, who, upon returning to the United States, developed a genre style that explored the customs of rural American life.

• William Young, ed. *A Dictionary of American Artists, Sculptors and Engravers* (1968), is a good source. A list of Wylie's earliest works is in James Yarnall and William Gerdts, comps., *The National Museum of American Art's Index to American Art Exhibition Catalogues* (1986). Wylie's career in Pont-Aven and his influence on Thomas Hovenden are discussed in Lee M. Edwards, "Noble Domesticity: The Paintings of Thomas Hovenden," *American Art Journal* 19, no. 1 (1987): 4–38. Julia R. Myers discusses Wylie's *Breton Sorceress* in "New Discoveries in American Art," *American Art Journal* 23, no. 2 (1991): 109–12. See also Albert Boime, *The Academy and French Painting in the Nineteenth Century* (1971); Boime, *Thomas Couture and the Eclectic Vision* (1980); David Sellin, *Americans in Brittany and Normandy 1860–1910* (1982); and Michael Quick, *American Expatriate Painters of the Late Nineteenth Century* (1976). A complete discussion of Robert Wylie in the context of other painters of the French peasantry is in Julia Rowland Myers, "The American Expatriate Painters of the French Peasantry 1863–1893" (Ph.D. diss., Univ. of Maryland at College Park, 1989). See also Michael Jacobs, *The Good and Simple Life: Artists Colonies in Europe and America* (1985). An obituary is in a letter from Thomas Hovenden to Goupil and Company on the day of Wylie's death titled "The Death of Robert Wylie, 1877," reprinted in the *New York Evening Post*, Mar. 1877. Another obituary is in "Art Talks from Paris," *The Aldine: The Art Journal of America* 8 (1876–1877): 354.

DEBI HAMLIN

WYMAN, Jeffries (11 Aug. 1814–4 Sept. 1874), comparative anatomist, naturalist, and anthropologist, was born in Chelmsford, Massachusetts, the son of Rufus Wyman, a physician, and Ann Morrill. He was named after the Boston physician James Jeffries, preceptor in medicine to Wyman's father. Wyman's family moved to Somerville, Massachusetts, when his father, a graduate of Harvard College and Harvard Medical School, was appointed physician of the McLean Asylum for the Insane. Wyman exhibited a childhood interest in dissection and sketching, two skills in which he later excelled.

After graduating from Harvard College in 1833, Wyman entered Harvard Medical School, at the same time studying medicine under preceptor John Call Dalton, Sr., father of the physiologist of the same name. Upon receiving his M.D. in 1837, Wyman appears to have attempted briefly to set up a medical practice. For the remainder of his career he did not practice medicine, although he taught in medical schools and maintained close ties to the medical community.

In 1837 Wyman became demonstrator to John Collins Warren, a professor of anatomy at Harvard Medical School and surgeon at Massachusetts General Hospital. Warren encouraged Wyman's interest in comparative anatomy, a subject that Warren taught at Harvard College. Wyman also began a lifelong association with the Boston Society of Natural History in 1837; he soon became an officer and a curator. From 1839 to 1842 Wyman served as paid curator of the newly founded Lowell Institute, which sponsored public lecture series by prominent men. In 1840 John Amory Lowell, the sole trustee, provided the neophyte Wyman with the opportunity to present his own course of Lowell Lectures, the munificent fee for which enabled him to spend a year and a half obtaining advanced training in science and medicine in Europe. Wyman attended lectures in comparative anatomy and natural history at the Muséum National d'Histoire Naturelle in Paris in 1841–1842, as well as lectures at the Faculté de Médecine and hospital clinics. Most significant for his later career were the several months in 1842 that he spent with the comparative anatomist Richard Owen at the Hunterian Museum in London. Based on the similarity of their theoretical views, Wyman may be regarded as an American disciple of Owen.

Wyman hoped that his training abroad would prepare him for a position at Harvard College. Disappointed when the new professorship of natural history went to Asa Gray in 1842, Wyman accepted a professorship of anatomy and physiology in the Medical Department of Hampden-Sydney College in Richmond, Virginia, which he held from 1843 to 1848. Unhappy in what he regarded as a southern cultural backwater, he longed to return to the Boston area.

During the 1840s Wyman acquired a reputation as an excellent comparative anatomist. He published on a wide variety of topics, including comparative anatomy, paleontology, parasitology, and ichthyology, and achieved some notoriety by exposing as a fake the skeleton of a supposed sea monster that was being exhibited to the public. His most memorable paper, "Notice of the External Characters and Habits of Troglodytes Gorilla, a New Species of Ourang from the Gaboon River. Osteology of the Same" (*Boston Journal of Natural History* 5[1847]: 417–43), named and described the gorilla based on bones sent from Africa by missionary Thomas Savage.

With the aid of Wyman's brother, Morrill, and friends David Humphreys Storer and John A. Gould, on the retirement of Warren in 1847, Warren's professorship was divided between the medical school and Harvard College, and a modest position was established for Wyman. Wyman was named Hersey Professor of Anatomy at Harvard College. Louis Agassiz was named a professor at Harvard a few months later. Soon after its founding in 1847 under Agassiz's leadership, Wyman became a member of the faculty of the Lawrence Scientific School of Harvard and shared in the training of Agassiz's advanced students. Wyman's career at Harvard paralleled that of the more famous Agassiz. Their expertise was remarkably similar, but their personalities were widely different. Unlike Agassiz and many other of his contemporaries, Wyman avoided entrepreneurial activities and public controversy and was at his best interacting with individuals in a local setting. Throughout his career he was assisted by the personal patronage of wealthy Bostonians.

At Harvard, Wyman taught anatomy and physiology, embryology, and zoology. He began the extensive Museum of Comparative Anatomy consisting of his private collection. His museum was moved in 1858 to the new Boylston Hall at Harvard, built with the aid of local donations to accommodate his collections as well as the chemistry laboratory of his colleague and friend Josiah P. Cooke.

A sufferer from tuberculosis, Wyman traveled frequently for his health and to increase his collections. He went to Labrador in 1849; to Paramaribo, Surinam, in 1857; to La Plata, Argentina, in 1858; and to Florida eight times in the period 1852–1874, mostly to the area around the St. Johns River. He visited Europe and toured museums in 1853 and 1870. It was during one of his annual late summer trips to northern New Hampshire for his health in 1874 that Wyman died suddenly from a hemorrhage in Bethlehem, New Hampshire.

From 1854 to 1870 Wyman served as president of the Boston Society of Natural History. During this period the society began a new series of memoirs and moved into a new museum building in Back Bay. He presided over meetings in 1860 at which the issue of evolution was heatedly debated. Wyman was offered but declined the directorship of the society's new museum; in part because he was seriously considering this offer he switched his affiliation from Harvard College to Harvard Medical School (which was in Boston) in 1866. In that year, Wyman became the first curator of the Peabody Museum of Archaeology and Ethnology at Harvard, in which position he wrote on craniology and the archaeology of shell mounds and made major purchases of collections.

Wyman's published works consist of approximately 200 mostly short and tersely written papers on comparative anatomy, embryology, parasitology, curious habits of animals, paleontology, bacteriology, anthropology, and archaeology. They appeared mainly in the *American Journal of Sciences*, the publications of the Boston Society of Natural History, and the *American Naturalist*. In keeping with his French training and work with Owen, Wyman took a morphological view of nature and, along with Agassiz, introduced "philosophical" (transcendental) anatomy to America. He became known for his thoroughness in research and care in writing, but also for his philosophical approach. Many of his papers established homologies of organs that suggested that animals were built according to an ideal plan or plans; some organs may exist in particular animals not because they have any practical function but to attest to the Creator's plan.

Wyman was sympathetic to Darwin's theories but tended to believe in a theistic, morphological form of evolution rather than natural selection. His major papers, besides that describing the discovery of the gorilla, included an examination of the blind fish of Mammoth Cave in Kentucky (1843 and 1854); the anatomy of Rana pipiens (1853); his review of Owen's monograph on the Aye-aye in which he discussed evolution (1863); homologies of limbs in vertebrates and the suggestion that animals exhibit a fore-and-hind symmetry (1868); experiments on spontaneous; generation in response to Pasteur, in which Wyman demonstrated his sympathy toward spontaneous generation, which he saw as necessitated by evolution (1862 and

1867); a demonstration that the cells of the bee were not perfectly designed, and, by implication, that the cells might have been perfected through evolution (1868); physical anthropology of human crania (1868); the discovery that the crocodile's range extended to Florida (1870); and the discovery of Indian shell mounds in Florida and evidence that they were made by pre-Columbian peoples (1875).

Wyman played a significant role as a teacher of many leaders of the next generation of naturalists including Frederic W. Putnam, Edward S. Morse, Nathaniel S. Shaler, Alpheus Hyatt, Burt G. Wilder, Alpheus S. Packard, and Addison E. Verrill. He acted as a balance to the often domineering and conservative Agassiz and helped their joint students make the transition to evolution. By promoting the careers of Henry Pickering Bowditch and S. Weir Mitchell, Wyman also encouraged the new discipline of experimental physiology in America.

A theist, Wyman attended the Unitarian Church at Harvard. He was twice married, in 1850 to Adeline Wheelright, who died in 1855, and in 1861 to Annie Williams Whitney, who died in 1864. He had two daughters, Mary and Susan, with his first wife and a son, Jeffries, father of the biophysicist Jeffries Wyman, Jr., with his second wife.

Wyman was widely admired for his modesty, integrity, care in methodology, and willingness to help others. He appeared to contemporaries as an exemplar of "the scientific life." William James, one of his students, wrote of him: "His extraordinary personal effect on all who knew him is to be accounted for by the one word, Character" (*Harvard Advocate*, 1874).

• The main collection of Wyman papers, which includes family correspondence and letters received by Wyman, is located at the Countway Library at Harvard University. Several of Wyman's letters have been published by George E. Gifford, Jr., including "An American in Paris, 1841–1842: Four Letters from Jefffries Wyman," *Journal of the History of Medicine and Allied Sciences* 22 (1967): 274–85; "Twelve Letters from Jeffries Wyman, M.D., Hampden-Sydney Medical College, Richmond, Virginia, 1843–1848," *Journal of the History of Medicine and Allied Sciences* 20 (1965): 309–33; and *Dear Jeffie: Being the Letters from Jeffries Wyman, First Director of the Peabody Museum, to His Son, Jeffries Wyman, Jr.* (1978). See also A. Hunter Dupree, "Some Letters from Charles Darwin to Jeffries Wyman," *Isis* 42 (1951): 104–10. Other recent articles on Wyman include R. N. Doetsch, "Early American Experiments on Spontaneous Generation by Jeffries Wyman (1814–1874)," *Journal of the History of Medicine and Allied Sciences* 17 (1962): 326–32; Toby A. Appel, "Jeffries Wyman, Philosophical Anatomy and the Scientific Reception of Darwin in America," *Journal of the History of Biology* 21 (1988): 69–94; Robert E. Murrowchick, "A Curious Sort of Yankee: Personal and Professional Notes on Jeffries Wyman (1814–1874)," *Southeastern Archaeology* 9 (1990): 55–66; and Toby A. Appel, "A Scientific Career in the Age of Character: Jeffries Wyman and Natural History at Harvard," in *Science at Harvard University: Historical Perspectives*, ed. Clarke A. Elliott and Margaret W. Rossiter (1992). Alpheus S. Packard's obituary in National Academy of Sciences, *Biographical Memoirs* 2 (1886), contains a bibliography of Wyman's publications.

TOBY A. APPEL

WYMAN, Seth (4 Mar. 1784–2 Apr. 1843), thief and author, was born in Goffstown, New Hampshire, the son of Seth Wyman and Sarah Atwood, farmers. Wyman documented his life and career in his posthumously published autobiography, *The Life and Adventures of Seth Wyman, Embodying the Principal Events of a Life Spent in Robbery, Theft, Gambling, Passing Counterfeit Money . . .* (1843). His earliest attempts at what he would later term "roguery" began at a very early age, when he stole a silver dollar from a neighbor's house, explaining to his mother that he had found it in the street. Although Wyman later praised both of his parents in print as honest and upright individuals, he soon graduated to more serious crimes, gaining a sense of satisfaction and accomplishment with each theft. He also displayed a streak of misanthropy, killing a neighbor's trees by girdling them for no apparent gain other than the neighbor's distress.

Wyman's father, a wealthy and successful farmer, tried to set up his son in farming on a large tract on the Penobscot River in what is now Maine, but honest labor (at which Wyman would make occasional efforts, including stints at farming, shipbuilding, and sledmaking—usually with stolen tools) never held his attention for long. Early in his career Wyman specialized in shoplifting, at which he became quite adept. His normal modus operandi was to enter a store and engage the clerk or shopkeeper in idle conversation. When another customer entered the establishment or the clerk was otherwise sufficiently distracted, Wyman would quickly stuff some item(s) of value under a large cloak that he wore during his escapades. Watches and bolts of cloth held particular appeal for Wyman, but he did not disdain stealing any item of value. He usually worked alone but would occasionally use one or more assistants. Careful always to stash his booty in a meticulously selected hiding place, Wyman thus avoided detection when the inevitable suspicion generated by his activities led to searches of his dwelling place. According to his autobiography, Wyman enjoyed a long string of uninterrupted successful thefts.

Usually moving from place to place in order to avoid the detection of his crimes, Wyman generally indulged in life's pleasures. He was no stranger to hard liquor, often fortifying himself for his more daring crimes with brandy. Enjoying fine dining and card playing, he also paid consistent attention to women, often promising various potential mates the moon and the stars regarding his intentions, on which he seldom if ever delivered. A relationship with an unhappily married woman, Welthy Loomis Chandler, eventually culminated in marriage in Boston in 1808. The couple, who had already had a long-standing common-law relationship—Wyman's first stint in jail was on a charge of adultery, not theft—eventually had six children. While Wyman seems to have genuinely cared for his wife (and his parents), he seems to have formed no other lasting relationship with any other person.

During his years of activity, Wyman shuttled between Massachusetts, New Hampshire, and what is now Maine. He was incarcerated on several occasions, during which he attempted (several times successfully) to escape. His *Autobiography* is replete with tales of fistfights with other men (in which Wyman was inevitably triumphant) and woeful descriptions of the harsh conditions under which he was forced to live during his periods of imprisonment. Late in his career, Wyman took up the passing of counterfeit money (manufactured in Canada and drawn from a variety of banks), at which he seems to have been successful.

Wyman relocated to Maine about 1815, having finally worn out his welcome in Goffstown. Although he attempted farming one last time, his old habits proved difficult to leave behind. He was convicted of larceny in June 1817 in Augusta, Maine, and received a three-year sentence to the state prison in Charlestown, Massachusetts. Pardoned after a year (which he spent composing verse), Wyman returned to New Hampshire. While the burden of supporting his wife and children (who had been living in a Boston almshouse) was lifted from the commonwealth of Massachusetts (a factor that helped him gain his early release), Wyman proved no more adept at remaining honest in his old surroundings. After once again stealing cloth (and again being caught), he was sent to the New Hampshire State Prison on 20 April 1820, where he served a full three-year sentence. Returning yet again to Goffstown following his release, he managed to live in relative peace (slowed by the effects of years of hard living as well as a serious injury to his back that he received from a fall from the third story of a factory while assisting in its construction). Plagued by poor health in his later years, he died in Goffstown after having apparently undergone an eleventh-hour conversion to religion.

While his lifestyle was hardly worthy of emulation, Seth Wyman's autobiography (published as a cautionary tale) provides a fascinating look at the social mores of the criminal element in early nineteenth-century American society.

• No organized collection of Wyman papers is known to exist. His life and career have received little attention; the best sources remain his *Autobiography* and G. P. Hadley, *History of the Town of Goffstown, 1733–1920* (2 vols., 1922). His incarceration records are held at the Massachusetts and New Hampshire state prisons.

EDWARD L. LACH, JR.

WYNEKEN, Friedrich Conrad Dietrich (13 May 1810–4 May 1876), Lutheran missionary and church leader, was born in Verden in the Kingdom of Hannover, Germany, the son of Heinrich Christoph Wyneken, a clergyman, and Louise Meyer. He attended universities at Göttingen (1827) and Halle (1828–1830). At Halle, he was influenced by Friedrich Tholuck, a leading representative of the nineteenth-century German Awakening. He served as a private tutor in Germany for several years and for a time was the rector of a Latin school.

In 1837 Wyneken was ordained a Lutheran pastor. Moved by mission accounts of scattered Germans on the American frontier who were without spiritual care, he came to the United States in 1838. After a brief stay in Baltimore, he established himself in Fort Wayne, Indiana, which became his base for extensive missionary trips throughout the surrounding frontier. Wyneken married Maria Sophie Buuck in 1841; they had thirteen children, eleven of whom survived infancy.

In the course of his missionary travels, Wyneken became a convinced proponent of a strict confessional Lutheranism. He relocated to Baltimore in 1845, then to St. Louis in 1850, and finally to Cleveland, Ohio, in 1864. He served as president of the theologically conservative Lutheran Missouri Synod during a period of significant development and growth (1850–1864).

Wyneken is best known for his *Distress of the German Lutherans in North America*, published in Germany in 1843. This document and earlier appeals with similar content give graphic descriptions of the spiritual conditions of Germans neglected by their church and drifting into heathenism or falling prey to other religions and the "vagabond" preachers so prevalent on the American frontier. It urges the Lutherans in Germany to take immediate steps to provide spiritually for their coreligionist countrymen in America. To increase the force of his arguments, Wyneken returned to Germany, where he spent over a year making personal contact with Lutheran leaders and giving lectures with a similar message throughout Germany. The effect of Wyneken's efforts was a general mobilization of energies among German Lutheran leaders to recruit and prepare ministers and teachers for the American frontier. One of the results was the venture of Wilhelm Löhe in Neuendettelsau, Bavaria, to take tradesmen, provide them with a rudimentary theological education, and send them to America. These "emergency" ministers and their frontier congregations constituted a major component of the Missouri Synod, formed in 1847, of which Wyneken was later to become president.

Wyneken is also credited with being one of the founders of Concordia Theological Seminary in Fort Wayne. Before its establishment in 1846 by Löhe and other Lutheran leaders in Germany as an American missionary seminary, Wyneken tutored students in Fort Wayne in preparation for service as ministers on the frontier. Although Wyneken was university trained, he recognized that frontier conditions in America called for greater emphasis on practical church work and less attention to the classical theological education provided in German universities. He was theologically conservative, but his main strength lay in his ability to motivate others to action. At heart he remained a missionary.

In dealing with other people, Wyneken could be very blunt. Yet he was also very caring, especially about the spiritual needs of others. In an obituary written by his friend C. F. W. Walther, he is described as "a man without deception whose entire being bore the mark of honesty, an opponent of all lies and hypocrisy." He was unpretentious, shaped by his missionary experiences on the frontier, "a faithful servant of the Lord who recognized in humility only his weakness, not his strength." However, he was a visionary when it came to the Lutheran "home mission" effort in America.

Wyneken was also an effective church leader. Under his presidency, the Missouri Synod divided into regional units or districts in 1854. The Civil War occurred during his presidency and, while a significant part of his constituency had sympathies for the Confederacy, his church remained united.

A man of action, Wyneken was not a prolific writer. For this reason his role in the development of the Lutheran Church in America has remained somewhat unrecognized in historical circles. To assess him, historians have to center their attention primarily on the effect that Wyneken's writings, especially his *Distress of the German Lutherans in North America*, had on the Lutheran mission effort in America. Without his propagandizing for this effort in Germany, it is likely that much of German Lutheranism in America would have disappeared. It is also doubtful that the Missouri Synod would have come into being or that it would have had the zeal for outreach to German Lutherans that marked its early history. Among the groups in America that Wyneken especially opposed were the Methodists, whose theology and approach to Christian piety were influencing many Lutherans in America at the time. Without the efforts of Wyneken, many of the Lutherans would probably have given up their faith entirely or would have become Methodists. Wyneken died in San Francisco.

• Information about Wyneken is in Johann Christoph William Lindemann, *A Biographical Sketch of the Honorable American Evangelist Friedrich Conrad Dietrich Wyneken to the Lutheran People of America in Grateful Love*, trans. James P. Lanning, ed. Robert E. Smith (1995); Norman J. Threinen, "F. C. D. Wyneken, 'Motivator for the Mission,'" *Concordia Theological Quarterly* 60 (Jan.–Apr. 1996): 19–45; Walter A. Baepler, *A Century of Grace* (1947); W. H. T. Dau, ed., *Ebenezer* (1922); Carl S. Meyer, ed., *Moving Frontiers* (1964); and Edward John Saleska, "Friedrich Conrad Dietrich Wyneken" (S.T.M. thesis, St. Louis Univ., 1946). The obituary by Walther is in *Der Lutheraner*, 15 May 1876.

NORMAN J. THREINEN

WYNN, Ed (9 Nov. 1886–19 June 1966), actor and comedian, was born Isaiah Edwin Leopold in Philadelphia, Pennsylvania, the son of Joseph Leopold, a hat manufacturer who had emigrated from Prague, and Minnie (maiden name unknown). Educated in Philadelphia public schools, Wynn ran away from his father's profitable business in 1901, briefly acting in a repertory company before returning to earn enough money to support himself.

Later commenting that he had never wanted to do anything but make people laugh, Wynn turned his middle name into a stage name in 1904, teaming with Jack Lewis in a vaudeville act called *Win and Lose*. In the skit "The Freshman and the Sophomore" ("Rah, Rah, Rah! Who pays the bills? Ma and Pa!") Wynn came onstage in the first of a career's worth of funny hats, carrying a bulldog. Wynn called the act sophisticated for its slapstick era: "We stood still and cut out the swatting."

Further developing his character, Wynn, sporting flapping, oversized shoes, earned his first important musical comedy role in 1910, twisting his hat into twenty-seven different shapes as Jupiter Slick in *The Deacon and the Lady*. In 1913 he caught Florenz Ziegfeld's attention as a nervous jester in a vaudeville sketch. Wynn's jester was in danger of death until he whispered one last story to the morose king. The king roared, and in a twittery lisp Wynn remarked, "Why didn't you say you wanted *that* kind of story?"

In his first Ziegfeld *Follies* (1914) the lisping Wynn was Joe King the Joke King. In the same year he married Hilda Keenan; they had one child (the actor Keenan Wynn, whose 1959 autobiography deals at length with Wynn). Wynn and Hilda were divorced in 1937. In the 1915 *Follies* Wynn added another trick: sitting in the audience, he tittered and commented upon other performers. He modified this after co-star W. C. Fields nearly kayoed him with a pool cue after discovering him stealing laughs from under the pool table.

In the 1916–1917 Jake and Lee Shubert show, *The Passing Show*, Wynn introduced a precursor of his typical nutty inventions: as a garage mechanic, he pleased gasoline-short motorists by blowing an electric fan in their faces to imitate wind sweeping back over a hood. (Later he created an eleven-foot pole for people you wouldn't touch with a ten-foot pole.) After performing in *Doing Our Bit* and *Over the Top*, Wynn's first solo billing came in the musical comedy *Sometime* (1918). Wynn never again co-starred, and he eventually co-wrote eleven shows.

By 1919 Wynn was a top headliner, making $1,750 weekly. Yet he supported the Actors' Equity Strike that began during his performances in *Gaieties of 1919*; Wynn was subsequently blackballed by managers. From then on he was his own producer, teaming with B. C. Whitney for *Wynn's Carnival* (1920)—a show in which he made his entrance juggling, paused, and asked the orchestra for something in a "jugular vein."

Ex-vaudeville comedians like Wynn were usually the main attractions in the revues and musical comedies of the 1920s; these loosely structured forms enabled them to exploit their "character," and the absence of radio or television meant that they would not run short of material. *The Perfect Fool* (1921), which ran a year on Broadway (an entire performance was also broadcast on radio) and two years on the road, brought Wynn's comic persona to definition as a bewildered overgrown baby with a pale, bulb-nosed face. Wynn bustled his way through the show, often dashing to the lobby afterward to kibitz with the audience.

There followed Wynn's long-running "entertainment" (he never used the word "revue") *The Grab Bag* (1924) and the musical comedy *Manhattan Mary* (1927). In the latter, playing a waiter told by a hungry customer that he "could eat a horse," returned with one, asking in a matter-of-fact tone, "Ketchup or mustard?"

Wynn played a hand-fluttering amateur detective in his first film, *Rubber Heels* (1927). *Manhattan Mary* became a 1930 Wynn film called *Follow the Leader.* Neither was successful; Wynn's popularity also survived the brief run of the musical comedy *Simple Simon* (1930). The show included a new Wynn trademark: Wynn pedaled around the stage on a tricycle, to which was fastened an upright piano with a girl sitting on it singing the sultry "Ten Cents a Dance." Its composer, Richard Rodgers, recalled Wynn's "stopping the show" by coming onstage, admiring the sylvan setting, and throwing his arms apart and shouting "I love the woodth! I love the woodth!"

During the 1930s the importance of comedians in musical comedy gradually waned, but Wynn proved an adaptable performer. After working on *The Laugh Parade* (1931) he turned to radio in 1932, performing as the Fire Chief, a title taken from his sponsor, Texaco. Wynn, ad-libbing and mangling advertisements, seemed to have no fear of the new medium's intimacy. The program was so popular that Wynn was allowed Tuesdays off from *The Laugh Parade* to do it. In 1933, his popularity and earning power at their peak, Wynn even tried to form a radio network, losing $250,000 but having a New York radio station (WNEW) named for him. In the same year he took his radio persona into the failed film *The Chief,* "a three-act radio opera," and he was parodied by Walter Catlett as "Ned Flynn" in the film *Arizona to Broadway.*

Wynn's radio fame increased for several years, through *Gulliver* (1935) and then through *The Perfect Fool* (1937). After the unremarkable play *Alice Takat* (1936), Wynn played his last memorable stage role as an inventor whose laughing gas eventually erases war from the earth through humor in the musical political satire *Hooray for What!* (1937). In that year Wynn married Frieda Mierse; the childless marriage ended in 1939, when a combination of personal problems and income tax difficulties led to Wynn's nervous breakdown and a temporary withdrawal from show business.

Wynn returned to Broadway for *Boys and Girls Together* (1940) and the wartime vaudeville show *Laugh, Town, Laugh* (1942). He moved from Long Island to California, where *Big Time* (1943) and *Ed Wynn's Laugh Carnival* (1948) were born, only to die later on the road. Brief wartime film and radio appearances preceded a nightclub act and another withdrawal from show business. In 1946 he married Dorothy Elizabeth Nesbitt; they had no children and were divorced in 1955.

In 1949 Wynn brought his entire comic paraphernalia to television, starring in "The Ed Wynn Show," the first regular program to originate from Hollywood and be viewed by the rest of the nation. In 1949 "The Ed Wynn Show" won an Emmy Award for best live show, while Wynn won an Emmy for most outstanding live personality. His career reborn, he giggled again in 1951 as the voice of the Mad Hatter for the Disney film *Alice in Wonderland.*

This revival also ran its course, and Wynn, in life a rather morose personality ("I never wanted to be a real person. . . . I think maybe I used up all my happiness on the stage"), was advised by television producers that comedy was "out"; it was the age of "serious drama." With his son's help, Wynn landed straight acting parts. In 1956 he won another Emmy as a watery-eyed handler of a prizefighter in the drama *Requiem for a Heavyweight.* As a cowardly Dutch dentist hiding from the Nazis, Wynn was nominated for a best supporting actor Academy Award in the film version of *The Diary of Anne Frank* (1959).

In his mid-seventies Wynn once more took up the role of perfect fool, often for Walt Disney films such as *Babes in Toyland* (1961). He continued to make guest appearances on television variety programs. In 1964, as the giddy Uncle Albert in Disney's *Mary Poppins,* he zoomed to the ceiling on waves of laughter, his childlike innocence and irresistible absurdity intact. Wynn died in Beverly Hills.

• An Ed Wynn manuscript collection is at the University of California, Los Angeles. Keenan Wynn's autobiography, *Ed Wynn's Son,* written with James Brough (1959), provides insight into Ed Wynn's private life. The best treatment of Wynn's particular onstage magic is Stanley Green, *The Great Clowns of Broadway* (1984). Frank Buxton and Bill Owen, *The Big Broadcast* (1966), is the best source for Wynn's radio career. Gerald Bordman's various books, particularly *American Musical Revue* (1985), are also helpful. An entertaining obituary by Bob Jackson is in the *Los Angeles Times,* 20 June 1966.

JAMES ROSS MOORE

WYTHE, George (1726?–8 June 1806), jurist and signer of the Declaration of Independence, was born probably at "Chesterville," the family plantation on Back River, Elizabeth City County, Virginia, the son of Thomas Wythe and Margaret Walker, planters. His father died in 1729, and his mother, reputedly a remarkably literate woman, is given credit for George's early education and for inspiring his lifelong pursuit of learning. It seems that he was largely self-educated; there is no evidence for nineteenth-century assertions that he received some formal schooling at the College of William and Mary or the Eaton-Symmes Free School in Hampton. In his midteens he entered a clerkship to study law with Stephen Dewey, his uncle by marriage. In 1746 he was admitted to practice in county courts, the bottom rung of the profession. Perhaps through another family connection he began practice with Zachary and John Lewis of Spotsylvania County. In December 1747 he married Zachary Lewis's daughter Anne Lewis, who died the following August.

Soon after her death Wythe left county court practice to enter the small General Court bar in Williamsburg under the patronage of Benjamin Waller, Anne's uncle. Waller probably arranged Wythe's appointment to the clerkships of two committees of the House of Burgesses. At the General Court bar Wythe quickly rose to prominence "among men of great ability." When the burgesses sent Attorney General Peyton Randolph to London in 1753 to represent the colony in a controversy with Governor Robert Dinwiddie, Wythe was appointed to fill the office, the third most powerful in Virginia government, until Randolph's return.

Wythe's older brother Thomas Wythe died childless in 1755, and George succeeded to the family property, which gave him a modest financial independence. About the same time he married Elizabeth Taliaferro, the daughter of Williamsburg planter and architect Richard Taliaferro; they had one child, who died in early infancy. As a wedding present the couple were given the gracious home on Palace Green, designed, it is said, by her father.

In 1754 Wythe was elected to the House of Burgesses for Williamsburg to fill the unexpired term of a deceased delegate. In 1756 he stood for a seat in the House from Elizabeth City County, where his inheritance had given him an immediate local importance, but received only one vote. After a second loss in 1758 he was chosen to fill the vacated William and Mary College seat. In 1761 he was at last elected from Elizabeth City County and reelected in 1766. During the second term he was appointed clerk of the House of Burgesses, a permanent position that required him to resign his seat but not his law practice.

Wythe was never reckoned an effective orator or a quick debater. His strength as a lawyer lay in his painstaking preparation and skill in explaining the law and its application to his client's case. War and his habit of burning the files he no longer needed combined to leave little but anecdotal evidence of the ways he understood and practiced law. But a Wythe letter and a case reported by Thomas Jefferson show that already in 1766 he was relying on one of the arguments against British rule later extended by other colonists: that North American colonial governments were empowered, implicitly if not expressly, to afford British settlers all the legal remedies that would be available to them in England.

Wythe's close, lifelong friendship with Jefferson, to whom he was very nearly a surrogate father, dates from this period. Jefferson enrolled in William and Mary in 1760 and was soon drawn into the familiar company of Wythe; his teacher, William Small; and Lieutenant Governor Francis Fauquier, the capital's most scholarly men. After college, from 1762 to 1767, Jefferson read law under Wythe.

Besides guiding the studies of aspiring lawyers, during most of his adult life Wythe also taught Greek and Latin classics, mathematics, and "approved English poets and prose writers" to an older boy or two of promise; he firmly declined compensation for such instruction.

In 1774 Wythe was one of the Williamsburg committee formed to enforce nonimportation, and in August 1775 he was elected a delegate to the Continental Congress. There John Adams counted him among the "independence men." Convinced that the king alone, not Parliament, was the link between the colonies and Great Britain, Wythe resolutely pursued the consequences of this conviction. He concluded that the king had defaulted on his obligations to the point of severing the political ties that bound the colonies to Great Britain. Though he did not figure large in public deliberations, Wythe's powers of persuasion were effective in personal contact and committee work.

Knowing that the state's delegation was safely committed to independence, Wythe had returned to Virginia, where the fifth revolutionary convention was preparing a constitution, when the Declaration of Independence was approved and signed in Philadelphia. It is unlikely that he personally signed it on his return in the fall, as some delegates did; he had probably authorized a clerk to do so for him when the document was engrossed.

Soon after, the first Virginia Assembly meeting under the new constitution appointed a committee, including Jefferson and Wythe, to revise the laws. In effect, Jefferson and Wythe produced the revision by themselves. It was radical, proposing 126 chapters to replace all previous statutory law. Repudiating the common law of England as at best ill adapted to revolutionary changes and American circumstances, the two men intended it to be the beginning of distinctive Virginian law. The legislature never approved the grand vision embodied in the whole, though ultimately it enacted many individual bills.

In 1778 Wythe was elected one of three judges of the newly established High Court of Chancery and as such also sat on the state's Supreme Court of Appeals. In later court restructurings he became sole chancellor with statewide appellate jurisdiction in equity, which no longer entailed a seat on the supreme court, and finally sole chancellor in the Richmond district, one of three into which the state was divided. He held this position to the end of his life.

In 1779, under Jefferson's impetus, the first professorship of law in America was established at William and Mary, and Wythe was appointed to the chair. Among the students prominent in later years was John Marshall. Wythe resigned in 1790.

Elected a Virginia delegate to the Constitutional Convention in 1787, Wythe was soon called home by the final illness of his wife and resigned. Though he was not a candidate, the people of York County elected him by acclaim to the ratifying convention a year later. Much of the credit for the thin margin by which Virginia ratified the Constitution is attributed to his great influence with many delegates who had been his pupils.

Immediately upon his wife's death, Wythe emancipated a number of slaves who may have been part of her estate. Later, his dicta in a now-lost Chancery decree evoked outrage for seeming to argue that slavery was inconsistent with the Virginia bill of rights.

In 1791 Wythe moved to Richmond. There he died, apparently poisoned by a grandnephew, George Wythe Sweeney, who lived with him and was to have been his principal heir. Sweeney had also forged checks on Wythe's account. Through a technicality he was never tried for the forgeries and escaped trial on the murder charge because the prosecution rested on the testimony of a freedwoman, which was inadmissible because she was black.

It is impossible today to form a coherent, detailed view of Wythe's legal thought because only fragmentary sources remain. However, some salient principles clearly emerge from a series of reports and comments Wythe published in the 1790s. These reports severely criticized the decisions of Edmund Pendleton, the presiding judge who dominated the Virginia Supreme Court of Appeals. Though personality must be taken into account in assessing the reports, they reflect fundamental differences in jurisprudence.

Wythe believed that Pendleton crafted decisions by drawing freely on revolutionary and colonial statutes, on English common law and treatises, on British and Virginian precedents, and on legislative history. Wythe agreed that the law inherited from a colonial past needed revision but thought that in a democracy such revision was the responsibility of a popularly elected legislature, not of judges. The thinking of a few men with life tenure, not popularly elected, could easily be skewed, believed Wythe, by considerations of interest and class.

Wythe was not tolerant of judicial lawmaking, in which judges distorted the plain sense of a statute to arrive at a result a court thought the legislature should have enacted. He understood that a mature system of justice would provide a remedy for the exceptional case if it was to produce the just results envisioned by the legislature without upsetting the regular course of settled law. This was the function of equity, and so he and Jefferson included a court of equity, the Chancery, in the judicial system they designed for Virginia.

It is further clear from Wythe's surviving judgments that he believed British common law, statute, and precedent (at least since the first settlement of the colony) could be adduced in support of a brief. But because they had been made for a different country and for different circumstances, Wythe considered them no more binding on Virginia courts than Roman law, for example, unless they could be shown to apply to distinctively American premises and conditions.

In 1782 in *Commonwealth v. Caton*, a celebrated case that came before the state Supreme Court of Appeals while he still sat on that bench, Wythe's opinion explicitly stated and endorsed the rationale of judicial review for statutory consonance with a constitution. And after ratification of the federal Constitution, he accepted it as the "supreme law of the land," resting a decree on the "full faith and credit" clause even though Congress had not yet passed enabling legislation.

Normally mild, urbane, even reticent, Wythe waxed vigorously indignant at violations of the ethical standards expected of judges and lawyers. "He lived in the world," said John Randolph of Roanoke, "without being of the world, and . . . was a mere incarnation of justice."

• No significant body of Wythe papers is known to exist. Of about 100 letters and documents, the greatest number, including those most important for a biography, are in the Jefferson papers in the National Archives, Washington, D.C. Wythe published fifty-three reports from his court, with notes illuminating his legal thought; forty-five appeared in one volume, *Decisions of Cases in Virginia, by the High Court of Chancery* (1795), and eight separately; all but one were reprinted under the same title in 1852, with a memoir and annotations by B. B. Minor. The most thorough study of Wythe's life and thought available so far is Robert Kirtland, *George Wythe: Lawyer, Revolutionary, Judge* (1986). Joyce Blackburn's *George Wythe of Williamsburg* (1975) is a popular biography, as is Alonzo Thomas Dill's carefully documented *George Wythe, Teacher of Liberty* (1979). Among brief sketches from the early nineteenth century, the most valuable are Thomas Jefferson's "Notes for the Biography of George Wythe," in *The Writings of Thomas Jefferson*, vol. 1, ed. A. A. Lipscomb and A. L. Bergh (1903), pp. 166–70; this is the main source of William R. Smith's entry, "George Wythe," in *Biography of the Signers to the Declaration of Independence*, ed. John Sanderson (1823).

ROBERT KIRTLAND

WYZANSKI, Charles Edward, Jr. (27 May 1906–3 Sept. 1986), attorney and federal district court judge, was born in Boston, Massachusetts, the son of Charles Edward Wyzanski, Sr., a real estate developer, and Maude Joseph. He was raised in the Boston suburb of Brookline in a comfortable upper-middle-class family that enjoyed sufficient wealth to send him to Phillips Exeter Academy and later to Harvard College, where he graduated magna cum laude and Phi Beta Kappa in 1927.

After graduating in 1930 from Harvard Law School, where his teachers included James Landis, Zechariah Chafee, and the redoubtable Felix Frankfurter, Wyzanski was sent off to New York to clerk successively for Judges Augustus Hand and Learned Hand on the United States Court of Appeals for the Second Circuit. He returned briefly to Boston in 1932 and joined the venerable law firm of Ropes & Gray, where one of his first assignments was to prepare a brief against the state's recently adopted anti-injunction law, which was patterned after the federal Norris-La-Guardia Act, a statute prohibiting federal judges from issuing injunctions in labor-management disputes. Believing the statute both desirable and constitutional, Wyzanski declined the task and received support from two of the firm's senior partners. That decision, along with Frankfurter's endorsement, landed Wyzanski the position of solicitor in Franklin D. Roosevelt's Department of Labor under Frances Perkins in 1933.

As Secretary Perkins's top lawyer Wyzanski, then only twenty-seven, played an important role in drafting the public works provisions and labor sections of the National Recovery Act, as well as the charter of the International Labor Organization. Behind the scenes, he worked to liberalize administration of the nation's draconian immigration laws, then also under the jurisdiction of the labor department.

Wyzanski's most celebrated role as a litigator came between 1935 and 1937, when Perkins loaned him to the Department of Justice as a special assistant in the legal defense of key New Deal programs, principally the National Labor Relations Act and the Social Security Act, both under constitutional challenge in the federal courts. Even among a group of brilliant contemporaries, including Benjamin V. Cohen, Thomas "Tommy the Cork" Corcoran, Paul Freund, Charles Fahy, and Joseph L. Rauh, Jr., Wyzanski's skills in brief writing and oral argument before the Supreme Court garnered unusual recognition.

In 1937 Wyzanski's presentations in five cases testing the scope of the National Labor Relations Act helped make constitutional history when a majority of the justices sustained the collective bargaining law and rejected a narrow interpretation of the federal commerce power articulated only a year before. A year later Wyzanski gained an equally important victory when the justices sustained the Social Security Act in an opinion based largely on his arguments concerning the scope of the general welfare and spending powers of the national government.

Wyzanski always attributed his triumphs in 1937–1938 to the political pressures on the Supreme Court generated by Roosevelt's overwhelming reelection victory in 1936 and by the president's later legislative threat to add additional justices to the Court. "The cases were won not by Mr. Wyzanski," he once quipped, "but by Mr. Zeitgeist." Those who watched Wyzanski before the Court, however, had a different opinion. John W. Davis, one of Wyzanski's opponents in the social security litigation, remarked to Perkins at the time, "Never in my palmiest days could I have matched that [Wyzanski's] argument."

More conservative than many of his allies in the New Deal, Wyzanski thought FDR's court-packing scheme dangerous, but he kept silent on the issue and returned to private practice at Ropes & Gray in 1938. Three years later, on the eve of World War II, Roosevelt named him to the federal district court at the age of thirty-five, despite the complaint of some critics that he was too young for such an august position. In 1943, offered a position on the federal court of appeals, Wyzanski declined the honor, noting that he preferred the trial level, where most citizens had their only contact with the institutions of the law. Friends believed he also prized the freedom of running his own courtroom. Also in 1943 Wyzanski married Gisela Warburg; they had two children.

Schooled in the public-service tradition of Louis D. Brandeis and Frankfurter, Wyzanski deplored the profit orientation and crass materialism of the profession. "At the end of the twentieth century in the United States," he wrote in 1975, "the lawyer is or ought to be the moral educator of the society. What he does in family advice, in handling business transactions, in drafting legislation, in standing before the public to express his or his client's views represents phases of moral opportunity."

Although a master of his profession, bench and bar never dominated Wyzanski's life. His intellectual range was wide and deep, spanning literature, philoso-phy, history, and the arts, and encompassing Marcus Aurelius, Montaigne, Lord Acton, and Mallarmé. His favorite haunts remained the used-book stores of Boston, New York, London, and Paris, where he often could be found in his signature black fedora and flowing bow tie.

On and off the bench, Wyzanski's independence, openmindedness, and creativity became legendary. At the time of the Nuremberg war-crimes trials, he wrote an article for the *Atlantic Monthly* criticizing them on both legal and moral grounds. He later penned another article that demolished his own arguments. Invited to write a new introduction to Learned Hand's famous Holmes Lectures, titled *The Bill of Rights*, in 1974, Wyzanski began with effusive praise for that jurist's "Shakespearean understanding of the range of the human spirit" and then proceeded to take apart Hand's essential thesis that judicial review constituted usurpation and tyranny. To curb judicial review, Wyzanski concluded, would "increase the possibilities of executive, legislative, or military tyranny, and could hardly promote the kind of democracy in which the Founding Fathers and Judge Hand were interested."

As his critique of Hand's position indicated, Wyzanski remained a judicial activist and did not shy away from innovations in his role as a district judge. His use of experts, including the hiring of economist Carl Kaysen as a law clerk for the case of *United States v. United Shoe Machinery Corp.* (1953), set a new standard for antitrust proceedings. During the Vietnam War he took a broader view of the scope of conscientious objection under the draft laws than the Supreme Court. He once sentenced a young draft resister to probation on the condition that he continue his musical studies and give recitals at public institutions. In 1969 he blocked efforts by high school officials to suspend students solely for wearing long hair. Four years later, he astounded all fourteen of the assistant U.S. attorneys in Boston by ordering them to file sworn statements about their own use of marijuana. Wyzanski noted that "hypocrisy begins at home" and criticized the federal attorneys for devoting too much time and effort to minor drug offenses that clogged the federal court.

In perhaps his most controversial decision, *United States v. Worcester* (1960), Wyzanski suspended an eighteen-month jail sentence imposed for income tax evasion on the condition that the defendant, an architect, cooperate in exposing an extensive network of illegal kickbacks on other state contracts. Wyzanski's tactic helped uncover wrongdoing at high levels of government, but civil libertarians condemned his sentencing practice as coercive. He shared some of these doubts, too, until Judge John Sirica broke open the Watergate scandal in the early 1970s with similar sentencing conditions. Wyzanski died in Boston.

Wyzanski excelled in many roles: as a litigator who successfully defended major programs of the New Deal in the 1930s; as a leading federal district judge whose opinions helped shape the law from 1941 until his death; and as a tireless servant of Harvard University, the Ford Foundation, the American Academy of Arts and Sciences, and the American Law Institute. In the opinion of many, he shared with one of his mentors, Learned Hand, the distinction of being among the ablest of American jurists who never sat on the U.S. Supreme Court.

• Wyzanski gave his personal and legal papers to the Harvard Law School Library. In addition to numerous articles in law journals and periodicals, he wrote four books: *A Trial Judge's Freedom and Responsibility* (1952), *Whereas—A Judge's Premises* (1965), *The Meaning of Justice* (1965), and *The Law of Change* (1968). His career in the New Deal period is covered by Peter Irons, *The New Deal Lawyers* (1982). Wyzanski's friends and colleagues paid tribute to his achievements in the *Harvard Law Review* 100 (Feb. 1987): 705–27.

MICHAEL E. PARRISH

X

XÁNTUS, John (5 Oct. 1825–13 Dec. 1894), natural history collector, was born in Csokonya, Hungary, the son of Ignác Xántus, a land agent, solicitor, and steward for a wealthy family, and Terézia Vandertich. He studied at the Benedictine Gymnasium at Györ, following a basic curriculum with good founding in natural history, and read law there, passing the bar in Pest in 1847. He signed on as sergeant in the Hungarian National Guard when Austria invaded Hungary in 1848 and was later promoted to lieutenant. Austrians captured and imprisoned him in February 1849; they pressed him into service as an enlisted man in the Austrian army. His mother bought his release, whereupon he joined Hungarian rebels, then was re-arrested and returned to the same regiment. He escaped to the United States in May 1851. (Ignoring facts, he later wrote that he was an officer in the Austrian Royal Artillery, executed "important missions" for the Hungarian secretary of war, was accused of desertion, and "found myself homeless & penniless and trown [*sic*] out to Asia." He also fabricated an extensive collecting trip with leading European naturalists in the United States. Unable to find work in the United States, he joined the Hungarian colony in New Buda, Iowa, which he left a year later with mutual disaffection. In 1855, without job prospects, he became naturalized in order to enlist in the U.S. Army, something he found so demeaning that he assumed a new name until discharged, Louis de Vésey.

Xántus's first post was Fort Riley in Kansas Territory. Assigned hospital duty, he served under Dr. William A. Hammond, close friend of Spencer F. Baird, assistant secretary for the new Smithsonian Institution. Hammond introduced Xántus to Baird by mail, suggesting that Xántus might be a good collector. Thus began a seven-year correspondence between Baird and Xántus. Hammond taught Xántus how to prepare mammal and bird skins, and Xántus shipped specimens to both the National Museum of Natural History at the Smithsonian and the Philadelphia Academy of Natural Sciences, which elected him to membership in 1856. The Academy published his "Descriptions of Two New Species of Birds from the Vicinity of Fort Tejon, California" (1858) and "Catalogue of Birds Collected in the Vicinity of Fort Tejon, California, with a Description of New Species of *Syrnium*" (1859). Baird arranged a transfer for Xántus to Fort Tejon, California, so that he could obtain natural history specimens. Xántus would report biweekly and would prepare and send all specimens to the Smithsonian; Baird would furnish collecting materials.

At Fort Tejon, Xántus's relations with officers and fellow enlisted men were unhappy. His letters to Baird were a litany of complaints, but they also provide in-

sights into the natural history of the region; many include charming, accurate watercolors of birds. By contrast, his letters home were full of grandiose achievements. His family published some of these letters in 1858 as *Xántos János Levelei Éjszakamerikából* (*Letters from North America*), which was well received in Hungary. In shipments from Fort Tejon, Xántus included a new hummingbird, *Hylocharis xantii*, and the Mojave Desert night lizard, *Xantusia vigilis*), plus nests and eggs, insects, bales of pressed plants, and minerals. After two years Baird arranged Xántus's discharge and persuaded the head of the U.S. Coast Survey, Alexander Bache, to station Xántus at Cabo San Lucas, at the southern end of Baja, California, as tide observer.

Xántus arrived April 1859 and remained twenty-eight months. He collected and prepared, all under considerable hardship, over 6,000 specimens of birds, of which 18 were new, 48 new crustacea, 57 new mollusks, 66 new fish, and 23 new reptiles and amphibians from the area. Nearly 40 of these (a gecko, *Phyllodactylus xantii*; 2 land snails and 4 marine mollusks; 3 birds; 5 fish; 10 plants; 14 crustacea) came to bear his name. He successfully preserved specimens, a tremendous feat since they were transported to Washington via occasional whalers that stopped at the cape. Almost without exception they arrived in excellent shape. Again his collecting took precedence over the Coast Survey's work (Bache judged him "the most unreliable man ever in the Coast Survey"), and the tide gauge records were useless. The Survey insisted he remain until he achieved accurate records.

In August 1861 they closed the station, and Xántus returned to the United States. With Baird's financial help he left for Hungary, where his family had published his second book of letters in 1860, *Utazás Kalifornia Déli Részeiben* (*Travels in Southern California*). Only about forty pages were original; the rest was freely cribbed, mainly from U.S. government surveys. In Hungary he became a corresponding member of the Hungarian Academy of Sciences. He returned briefly to the United States, where Baird managed an appointment for him as consul in Colima, Mexico (1863). Xántus committed a diplomatic faux pas, however, by involving himself, without authority, in a kidnapping and was quickly released by the State Department. Baird again advanced money for Xántus to return to the United States in exchange for his Colima collection.

Xántus returned to Hungary in 1864 and was elected director of the new zoological garden in 1866. Two years later he was invited to join the Austro-Hungarian East Asiatic Expedition. Overbearing, inconsiderate, rude, and insulting, he irritated everyone and departed the expedition in October 1869, continuing his travels alone and collecting in Borneo, Java, and Sumatra. On returning to Pest, Hungary, he was appointed keeper of the ethnographical section of the National Museum (1872); he then became director in 1873. That year he married Gabriella Doleschall, an actress; they had one child. After a divorce he married Ilona Steden. He guided the museum until his mental and physical health deteriorated in the mid-1880s. He died at home in Pest.

Xántus's scientific writings are undistinguished and minimal, and his letters home are full of fabrication and plagiarism. But under the sponsorship of Spencer Baird, Xántus became a skilled and independent collector, contributing nearly 300 new species to science. In his lively letters to Baird, concerned with the business of natural history collecting and surviving in an unfriendly world, there are flashes of originality and humor, vigor, and honesty. These letters illuminate not only the personality of the writer, but an important period of natural history exploration during which he greatly expanded knowledge of the little-known flora and fauna of mid-nineteenth-century North America.

• For his complete annotated letters to Spencer F. Baird, see Ann H. Zwinger, ed. *John Xántus: The Fort Tejon Letters,* *1857–1859* (1985) and *Xántus: The Letters of John Xántus to Spencer Fullerton Baird from San Francisco and Cabo San Lucas, 1859–61* (1986). The most thorough and reputable biography of Xántus is that of Henry Miller Madden, *Xántus, Hungarian Naturalist in the Pioneer West* (1949). Madden's translation of Xántus's Hungarian letters, "California for Hungarian Readers, Letters of Janos Xántus, 1857 and 1859," *California Historical Society Quarterly* 28 (1949): 125–42, is also useful. See also Edgar E. Hume, *Ornithologists of the United States Army Medical Corps: Thirty-six Biographies* (1942). Records of Xántus's work appear in various reports such as Spencer F. Baird, "Report of the Assistant Secretary," *Annual Report of the Board of Regents of the Smithsonian Institution* (1859, 1860, 1861, 1862); and in Baird, "Review of American Birds in the Museum of the Smithsonian Institution," *Smithsonian Miscellaneous Collections* 12 (1866). Individual collections were written up by authorities in the field: A. C. Davis, "A List of the *Coleoptera* of Fort Tejon, California," *Bulletin of the Southern California Academy* 31 (1932): 75–87; Asa A. Gray, "List of a Collection of Dried Plants made by L. J. Xántus, at Fort Tejon, and Vicinity, California, Near Lat. 35°, and Long. 119°, 1857–8," *Proceedings of the Boston Society of Natural History* 7 (1859–1861): 145–49; and John L. Le Conte, "Catalogue of the Coleoptera of Fort Tejon, California," *Proceedings of the Academy of Natural Sciences of Philadelphia* 13 (1859): 338–59.

ANN H. ZWINGER

Y

YALE, Elihu (5 Apr. 1649–8 July 1721), governor of Fort St. George (Madras) for the East India Company and benefactor-namesake of Yale College, was born in Boston, Massachusetts, the son of David Yale, a merchant, and Ursula Lloyd. His father's mother, Anne Lloyd Yale, widow of Thomas Yale of Wrexham, Denbighshire, Wales, and stepfather, Theophilus Eaton, a merchant and founder of New Haven colony (1638), had moved to New England in 1637. David Yale moved from New Haven to Boston in 1641, was a signer of Child's Remonstrance and Petition (1646), a plea for greater toleration of and rights for non-Puritans, for which he was fined £30, and returned to England in 1651, followed the next year by his wife, and his sons, David and Elihu. In the fall of 1662, Elihu briefly attended William Dugard's private grammar school in London. Appointed a "writer" or clerk in the East India Company in 1670 with a yearly salary of £10, Yale was soon posted to Fort St. George in Madras (1672).

During the next fifteen years, Yale advanced in the company's service while developing his own personal trading interests, particularly in precious stones such as diamonds. His business ventures were aided by the inheritance of Catherine Elford, widow of councilor Joseph Hynmers, whom Yale married in 1680. By 1681, he was appointed to the governor's council as mintmaster, the fifth-ranking position on the council. Later in the same year he completed a successful mission to Maratha country to establish a trading post during which he kept a detailed journal (India Office, London). In 1682 he became collector of customs (fourth position on the council), the next year warehousekeeper (third), and in 1684, bookkeeper (second). For a time in 1684–1685, while Governor William Gyfford made a tour of other East India Company factories, Yale served as acting governor, and was enthusiastic and efficient both in his promotion of trade and in the execution of justice in Fort St. George. On 23 July 1687, Yale became president and governor of this English trading outpost.

During his first year as governor, Yale dealt successfully with a famine and with the conquests of the Mughal emperor, Aurangzeb, who had captured Golconda, a nearby kingdom, and proceeded to menace English allies in the Gingee country and to threaten Madras, a situation complicated further by rival Dutch and French involvement in the area. Yale formally acknowledged Aurangzeb's authority and purchased new concessions from him. By 1689, rancor was visible on the council, as a majority were disaffected by Yale's alleged increasing arbitrariness and his private business dealings, which were characterized as taking precedence over company affairs, causing ne-

glect of duty. In September 1690, soon after a successful defense of the Fort from a French naval attack, these charges were formally drawn up by the council against Yale, adding to the previous allegations new charges against his brother Thomas, a merchant involved in company trade with China. Most of these and subsequent charges of a similar nature against Governor Yale were never proven. Like other company officials, Yale had in fact parlayed his initial annual salary (£10) into a personal fortune, an admitted sum in 1691 of 500,000 pagodas (c. £175,000). His efforts and expenditures on behalf of the East India Company seem in fact to have been mostly honorable and necessary if not always appreciated by distant London officials interested only in profit. His biographer claims that the death of his only legitimate son, David, in 1687, and the departure of his wife and three daughters for England in early 1689, affected him very badly: he became thereafter "domineering, opinionated, aggressive and unable to hold the confidence or the respect of the other members of the Council" (Bingham, p. 273). After he was replaced as governor in late 1692, and imprisoned at Fort St. George, an investigation and subsequent trial resulted in total fines for misuse of company money and repayments to the company of 10,032 pagodas. By early 1695, Thomas Yale had appeared on his brother's behalf before the English Privy Council, which consequently directed that Elihu be allowed to return to England to confront all company charges against him. He did not immediately return to England; instead, by 1696 he was allowed once again to trade for several years.

In August 1699, Yale arrived back in England, settling in London while maintaining the old family estate, "Plas-Grono," in Denbighshire, near Wrexham, in Wales. Active as an art collector, diamond merchant, and philanthropist, he eventually caught the attention of Jeremiah Dummer, colonial agent for Massachusetts, and soon for Connecticut, who suggested in a 1711 response to the Reverend James Pierpont, a New Haven minister, the possibility of the heirless Yale's patronage of the ten-year-old Collegiate School. In the spring of 1713, Yale was one of a group of 181 book donors brought together by Dummer, who contributed over 800 volumes to the struggling Connecticut college, adding his own approximately forty volumes to those offered by such as Sir Isaac Newton, Sir Richard Steele, and Sir Edmund Andros. Despite his own High Church Anglicanism, and active membership in the Society for the Propagation of the Gospel in Foreign Parts, Yale continued to be interested in the dissenters' Connecticut school. He responded to a January 1718 letter on its behalf from Cotton Mather of Boston, and to the ongoing efforts of Dummer and former colonial governor, Francis Nicholson, by forwarding several trunks of textile goods to Boston to be sold for the college's benefit. The total value of Yale's gifts, including some four hundred books, eventually amounted to over £800; the largest contribution to the college in its first century, Yale's support came at a particularly difficult moment for the school. In response, the trustees followed up on Mather's suggestion to Yale that the school might be named after him: "and your munificence might easily obtain for you such a commemoration and perpetuation of your valuable name, as would indeed be much better than an Egyptian pyramid" (Warch, p. 85). They did so in September 1718, saying, "We the Trustees in the Large & Splendid Hall of our Building, Have done our School the Honour of naming it with your Illustrious Name & have called it Yale-Colledge" (Bingham, pp. 329–30). Yale, however, died in London before he could make any further contributions to the school.

While he was an able if controversial servant of an East India Company, which was one of the vanguards of the first British Empire, Elihu Yale's principal claims to fame in American history are his benefactions to a college in another English colonial outpost in which he probably never set foot. His gifts did encourage the college enterprise in Connecticut at a sensitive moment, however, allowing it to remain in New Haven, and they did suggest that imperial resources such as Yale's could be lent to purposes useful to the American colonists. Yale indicated as much in his own epitaph (Bingham, p. 337):

Born in America, in Europe bred,
In Afric travell'd, and in Asia wed,
Where long he liv'd, and thriv'd; at London dead.
Much good, some ill, he did; so hope all's even,
And that his soul, through mercy's gone to heaven.
You that survive, and read, take care
For this most certain exit to prepare:
For only the actions of the just
Smell sweet and blossom in the dust.

• The principal source for Elihu Yale is Hiram Bingham's *Elihu Yale: the American Nabob of Queen Square* (1939). Of particular note is his bibliography, which documents extensive Yale primary source materials available in British depositories as well as numerous works concerning the East India Company during Yale's employment. Bernard S. Cohn, *The Development and Impact of British Administration in India* (1961), is a more up-to-date bibliographic essay on the subject. Bingham also has a brief chapter on Yale in Charles Edward Perry, ed., *Founders and Leaders of Connecticut, 1633–1783* (1934). An older, but useful discussion of "Governor Elihu Yale" by Franklin B. Dexter appears in the *Papers of the New Haven Colony Historical Society*, vol. 3 (1882). Very helpful regarding Yale's assistance to Connecticut higher education is Richard Warch, *School of the Prophets: Yale College, 1701–1740* (1973).

THOMAS W. JODZIEWICZ

YALE, Linus, Jr. (4 Apr. 1821–25 Dec. 1868), inventor and locksmith, was born in Salisbury, Herkimer County, New York, the son of Linus Yale, Sr., a locksmith, general mechanic, and inventor, and Chlotilda Hopson. His education was influenced by his father's Newport, New York, metalworking and lockmaking shop. His early inclination, though, was artistic rather than mechanical as indicated by his efforts as a portrait painter. He married Catherine Brooks from a nearby town in 1844. They had three children.

As an itinerant painter, Yale also had opportunities to observe and participate with his father in developing improved burglarproof bank locks. In 1851, at London's Crystal Palace Exhibition, there were well-publicized attempts to pick locks to test new designs. An American, Alfred G. Hobbs, picked the best English locks and countered with a superior American "Parautoptic" lock. This lock was subsequently evaluated and picked by the Yales. These efforts coincided with Yale's 1851 patent for a more unpickable bank lock.

Period bank locks were operated by keys with separate bit components to position the pin tumblers to activate the mechanism. Yale's radical concept was to transfer the key's bits away from that component of the key used as a carrier to a less accessible interior portion of the lock. This movement was accomplished by a single operator's wrench. The lock was patented in 1855 as the "Infallible." To exploit this and other developments, Yale moved to Philadelphia from New York State in 1855–1856. A separate sales office was established in New York City. Philadelphia was then a center for the manufacture of complex iron items that required significant mechanical precision. There Yale designed a series of locks culminating in a combination lock that eliminated the need for an external key. This lock, the Monitor, was probably introduced in 1862 during the Civil War.

While in Philadelphia, Yale became acquainted with William Sellers, one of the leaders of improved metalworking in the United States. This association would later have a crucial influence. Halbert Greenleaf of Shelburne Falls, Massachusetts, joined Yale in Philadelphia in 1859. He probably influenced Yale to move in 1861 to Shelburne Falls, where Yale and Greenleaf formed a partnership with Greenleaf as business manager. In 1863 Greenleaf left to join the Union army and did not return to the partnership after the war. James Sargent worked for Yale in Shelburne Falls as a salesman until they had a disagreement. Sargent joined Greenleaf in 1865 to manufacture locks in Rochester, New York. Yale remained in Shelburne Falls and eventually had about thirty employees producing bank locks. During this period he traveled considerably to consult on security issues.

The market for bank locks was relatively small, so Yale expanded to develop small key locks for general purposes. In 1861 and 1865 Yale patented the "cylinder lock," a pin-tumbler lock that became widely known as the "Yale lock." This lock, developed for a broader general market, was beyond the production capacity of the Shelburne Falls facilities. In July 1868 Yale went to Philadelphia to locate an associate to organize and manage the manufacturing operations and to obtain additional capital. Through William Sellers, Yale met Henry R. Towne, a young but highly trained mechanical engineer and experienced operations manager. Towne's wealthy father, also in the metalworking field, advanced 60 percent of the capital for his son's partnership with Yale, who contributed the existing business, patents, and inventive skill. This became the Yale Lock Manufacturing Company.

Statements in the later catalogs of the Yale Lock and Manufacturing Company suggest that the proximity of Stamford, Connecticut, to New York City led to its selection as the new location for the facility over Shelburne Falls; New York was a growing bank lock market as well as a large market for general sales. The new facility was intended to produce bank locks, general-use Yale locks, and special locks for post office boxes. Construction of the factory building started in October 1868, and Yale continued to operate the Shelburne Falls plant and perform consulting work. While on a consulting trip, Yale suddenly died in New York City. Towne later took charge of the new facility, which became operational in March 1869. The firm's name was changed to the Yale & Towne Manufacturing Company in 1883.

Yale is remembered for the innovative locks he designed. He was typical of the American inventor of the nineteenth century, of Yankee stock, raised in a rural community, trained with a keen perception of the fundamental principles involved in the devices he worked on, and resourceful enough to overcome the technical difficulties. Moreover, he worked with or was in contact with several individuals who provided American technical leadership. The Yale lock, tumblers aligned one behind another in a row, simply and efficiently, remains unaltered long after his death.

• There is very little primary material relating to Yale. The Deerfield Historical Society Library, Deerfield, Massachusetts, has his firm's letter book starting in 1868, but it contains no information about the decision to join in partnership with Henry R. Towne or the reasons for relocating to Stamford, Connecticut. The Stamford, Connecticut, Historical Society has secondary materials from nineteenth-century Yale & Towne Company publications. Though some of the materials relate to Yale, they are not consistent. A moderately full treatment is "The Mechanization of a Complicated Craft," a chapter in Siegfried Giedion, *Mechanization Takes Command* (1948). The Lock Museum of America in Terryville, Connecticut, has a collection of the technical details of the various locks patented by Yale. A brief obituary appears in the *New York Tribune*, 28 Dec. 1868.

JULIAN REITMAN

YAMAOKA, George (26 Jan. 1903–19 Nov. 1981), lawyer, was born in Seattle, Washington, the son of Ototaka Yamaoka and Jhoko Watanabe. From 1920 to 1923 he was a student at the University of Washington. Yamaoka received his J.D. from Georgetown University, Washington, D.C., in 1928. He was admitted to the New York bar in 1931 and the Japanese bar in 1949.

Always active in promoting U.S.–Japanese relations, Yamaoka served on the Japanese government commission for the Philadelphia Sesquicentennial Exposition of 1926. He was an adviser to the Japanese consulate general in the United States from 1928 to 1929. At the London Naval Conference of 1929–1930 he was an adviser to the Japanese delegation.

Yamaoka began private law practice in New York in 1931, first as an associate with Hunt, Hill & Betts. In 1933 he married Henriette d'Auriac; they had one daughter. In 1940 he moved from associate to partner with the same firm. He became a senior partner in 1956 with the New York firm and also with the Tokyo firm of Hill, Betts, Yamaoka & Logan. The New York firm was renamed Hill, Betts, Yamaoka, Freehill & Longcope, with Yamaoka functioning as senior partner from 1960 to 1970. After 1970 he continued in the same role with Hill, Betts & Nash.

Yamaoka's most internationally recognized role came immediately after World War II. He was appointed by U.S. general Douglas MacArthur to the Allied Powers International Military Tribunal for the Far East, on which he served from 1946 to 1949. The primary purpose of the tribunal was to try the cases of Japanese military and civilian leaders who had been charged with war crimes by the Allied powers. Yamaoka was given the position of counsel general for the accused. In particular, he advised former prime minister Koki Hirota, who was found guilty. The result was appealed to the U.S. Supreme Court. Yamaoka argued the case before the court, which decided on a 6–1 vote that it lacked jurisdiction and refused to intervene. Hirota was later executed.

In another government-related aspect of his practice, Yamaoka served as a member of the advisory panel on international law of the U.S. Department of State from 1972 to 1974. However, most of his work was in civil law. Yamaoka's practice involved him with major companies in the United States and Japan, on some of whose boards of directors he served. He was chair of the board of Yasuda Fire & Marine Insurance Company and director of Ehrenreich Photo Optical Industries, Inc.; the Bank of Tokyo Trust Company (N.Y.); Okura & Company; Jiji Press (N.Y.) Ltd.; and 24 Gramercy Park, Inc. Yamaoka was also a director of the Japanese Chamber of Commerce and honorary director of the Japan Society of New York. He was named honorary president of the Japanese-American Association of New York.

Yamaoka was a member of the American Bar Association, as well as the federal, New York, and First (Tokyo) bar associations. He belonged to the Consular Law Society, American Foreign Law Association, International Law Association, Maritime Law Association, and Downtown Athletic Club. In 1968 Yamaoka received the honor of the Third Order of the Sacred Treasure from the government of Japan. He died in New York City and was posthumously awarded the Second Order in 1981.

• The case Yamaoka argued before the Supreme Court is *Hirota v. MacArthur*, 338 U.S. 197 (1948). An obituary is in the *New York Times*, 22 Nov. 1981, and on the Jiji Press ticker service, 21 Nov. 1981.

BARRY RYAN

YAMASAKI, Minoru (1 Dec. 1912–6 Feb. 1986), architect, was born in Seattle, Washington, the son of Japanese immigrants John Tsunejiro Yamasaki, a janitor and stockroom clerk, and Hana Ito, a pianist. As a child, he lived with his family in the small Japanese-American community on Yesler Hill, near Seattle's waterfront. In 1926 his uncle Koken Ito, an architect practicing in Tokyo, visited the family and inspired Yamasaki to become an architect.

Yamasaki's academic training at the University of Washington was in the Beaux-Arts tradition. He financed his education by toiling for five summers in salmon canneries in Alaska. The harsh and dehumanizing conditions of this experience, recounted in his autobiography, *A Life in Architecture* (1979), motivated him as a student and intensified his resolve to become an architect.

After graduating in 1934, Yamasaki moved to New York City to distance himself from anti-Japanese sentiment in the Pacific Northwest and to seek work in architecture. In 1935 he volunteered to assist the firm of Githens and Keally with drawings submitted in a competition for the Oregon State Capitol. After Githens and Keally won the competition, Yamasaki received his first professional job as a designer and draftsman. In 1935–1936 he also attended graduate courses and taught painting at New York University.

In 1937 Yamasaki joined the firm of Shreve, Lamb & Harmon as a draftsman, designer, and job captain. He retained this position until 1943. In late 1941 and early 1942, during a harrowing time for the Nisei following the entry of the United States into the Second World War, Richmond Shreve took a personal interest in his welfare and even assigned him to supervise his firm's projects for the navy. In 1941 Yamasaki married Teruko Hirashiki, a pianist from California; they had three children.

Between 1943 and 1945 Yamasaki taught architectural design at Columbia University. He simultaneously worked as a designer for the prominent firms of Harrison, Fouilhoux, and Abramovitz and Raymond Loewy Associates. His first published work, a design for a "postwar converted apartment" in New York City, appeared in *Architectural Forum* in November 1944. The following year he moved to Detroit, Michigan, to join the firm of Smith, Hinchman, & Grylls as chief architectural designer. Two of his projects with this firm were International Style office buildings, the Michigan State Office Center (Lansing, 1947) and the Federal Reserve Bank annex (Detroit, 1950).

In 1949 Yamasaki entered into a partnership with two colleagues from Smith, Hinchman, & Grylls, Joseph Leinweber and George Hellmuth. He was the lead designer for two nationally recognized projects in Missouri, the Pruitt-Igoe Housing Project for the St. Louis Housing Authority (1952, demolished 1972) and the Lambert Field–St. Louis Airport Terminal Building (1956). The housing project, a milestone in the annals of postwar urban renewal and social engineering, was originally designed to assemble 26 twelve-story buildings on a 96-acre site. Although in the early 1950s the project generated widespread acclaim within planning and architectural circles, Yamasaki freely criticized changes during construction to his design and site plan. He later expressed regret about the quixotic notion of using "nice buildings" to cure social ills. The terminal building, an imaginative composition of concrete shells and intersecting barrel vaults, began an international tradition of placing architect-designed landmark buildings in major airports. Praised for its originality, the terminal building received a first honor award in 1956 from the American Institute of Architects. With the housing project, it established Yamasaki's reputation as an accomplished designer of large-scale projects.

In 1955, after a long bout with bleeding ulcers, Yamasaki reorganized his firm into a two-person partnership with Joseph Leinweber. He also traveled throughout Japan, India, the Middle East, and Europe. Impressed during his travels by the "ancient tools of sunlight, surface, and surprise," he returned to his profession with a new perspective on design and a commitment to infuse his work with eye-catching surfaces and shapes.

His first work in a search for a contemporary ornamental style was the American consulate in Kobe, Japan, a simple rectangular pavilion wrapped in a delicate bronze trellis (1956). With the McGregor Memorial Community Center at Wayne State University (Detroit, 1958) and the Reynolds Metals Company Building (Southfield, Mich., 1959), he briefly achieved a highly personalized idiom expressed in brilliant white surfaces, gold anodized metal screens, luminous interior atriums, and reflecting pools. While drawing criticism from proponents of austere modernism, these buildings found favor among many architects and the public at large.

After the McGregor and Reynolds buildings received first honor awards (1959, 1960) from the American Institute of Architects, Yamasaki emerged in the forefront of a national controversy in architectural spheres about the future directions of the profession. He became a leading advocate of "enjoyment" and "visual delight" in architecture, contributing articles to professional journals, speaking on panels, and promoting his ideas in interviews with major newspapers and magazines.

In 1959 Yamasaki formed his own firm, Minoru Yamasaki & Associates, in suburban Detroit. The following year he was elevated to a fellow of the American Institute of Architects. In the early 1960s he continued to explore ornament by festooning buildings with Gothic-like tracery, as in the Federal Science Center at the Century 21 Exposition in Seattle in 1962. With the Michigan Consolidated Gas Company building (Detroit, 1963), he first exhibited the architectural palette that typified his neoformalist work through the 1960s and 1970s: an emphasis on "aesthetic thinness" and verticality, centering on angled window headers and sills set between narrowly spaced mullions; white exterior cladding; pools and fountains; and spacious lobbies with abstract sculpture. Having been divorced from his first wife in 1961, he married Peggy Watty in 1963. After their marriage ended, he married a Japanese woman (name and date of marriage unknown). And in 1969 he remarried his first wife, Teruko Hirashiki.

Among his most notable neoformalist designs were the Northwest National Life Insurance Company building (Minneapolis, 1964) and the Eastern Airlines Terminal (Logan Airport, Boston, 1969, with Desmond & Lord). Toward the end of his career he, along with Helmut Jahn, Emery Roth, Edward Durell Stone, I. M. Pei, Gordon Bunshaft, and Hugh Stubbins, became increasingly identified as a master architect of high-rise office towers. His major commissions included the Montgomery Ward headquarters (Chicago, 1975), the Century Plaza Towers (Los Angeles, 1975), the Rainier Tower (Seattle, 1977), and the Bank of Oklahoma (Tulsa, 1977). His largest and most famous commission was the World Trade Center in New York City (1972–1973). He dismissed critics of the Cyclopean 110-story buildings as anti-urbanists and claimed that the silver-colored, aluminum-clad towers would be revered in the future as emblems of the Manhattan skyline.

Described as serene, modest, and talented, with a proclivity for "gently explosive humor," Yamasaki dedicated much of his time outside of architecture to advancing the status of Japanese Americans. He died in Detroit.

Associated with more than eighty-five major commissions in the United States, Japan, and Saudi Arabia, Yamasaki was the first Japanese-American architect to preside over an internationally active and influential firm. He acquired much of his early fame by joining a "counterrevolution" against the conventions of International Style modernism and by popularizing machine-made ornamentation on buildings. His most enduring contributions, though, were to the development of corporate skyscrapers across the American urban landscape of the 1960s and 1970s.

• Many of Yamasaki's drawings from his fifty-year career as an architect no longer exist. His firm, Minoru Yamasaki & Associates of Rochester Hills, Mich., maintains a collection of drawings and other archival materials. Among his writings are his short autobiography, "Humanist Architecture for America and Its Relation to the Traditional Architecture of Japan," *Journal of the Royal Institute of British Architects* 68 (Jan. 1961), and "Toward an Architecture for Enjoyment," *Architectural Record* 118 (Aug. 1955): 142–49. The most comprehensive list of interviews and articles on him is in Muriel Emanuel, ed., *Contemporary Architects*, 3d ed. (1994). See also "The Road to Xanadu," *Time*, 18 Jan. 1963, pp. 54–64; "A Conversation with Minoru Yamasaki," *Architectural Forum* 110 (July 1959): 110–18; and Russell Bourne, "American Architect, Yamasaki," *Architectural Forum* 109 (Aug. 1958):

85, 166, 168. Nearly all commentaries on his work focus on his explorations of exoticism and ornament in the late 1950s and early 1960s. See, for example, Ada Louise Huxtable, "Pools, Domes, Yamasaki—Debate," *New York Times Magazine*, 25 Nov. 1962; Robin Byrd, *The Puzzle of Architecture* (1965); and Thomas Hine, *Populuxe* (1986). Apart from numerous articles on the World Trade Center, the literature assessing his greater role as an architect of urban high-rise towers is incomplete. An obituary is in the *New York Times*, 9 Feb. 1986.

JEFFREY CRONIN

YANCEY, Mama (1 Jan. 1896–4 May 1986), blues singer, was born Estella Harris in Cairo, Illinois. Her parents' names are unknown. She moved to Chicago at six months of age and was raised there. Her interest in music was developed early; she frequently sang in the local church choir as a child and learned guitar as a youth, perhaps from her mother who was a singing guitarist. Her mother died when Mama was thirteen, after which she was raised by her father. In 1917 (some sources cite 1919) she married Jimmy Yancey, a boy she had grown up with in Chicago. They probably had at least one child, but details are unavailable. At the time, Jimmy was a singer and dancer, but according to an interview with Mama by Bob Rusch, he became interested in blues piano in 1919, after which he began traveling around playing for house "rent" parties, where the occupants charged guests a fee to help them pay their rent. Jimmy Yancey subsequently developed a unique blues piano style that contained certain basic principles of the boogie style and is said to have influenced a host of pianists, including Meade "Lux" Lewis and Albert Ammons.

Mama Yancey's father discouraged his daughter from singing on stage, and in the beginning, she and her young husband tried settling down to a steady home life. As she later said, "I had a very strict father and my father is the one that held me back. See, he never wanted me to go on the stage no kind of way, shape, or fashion. Then after he died I was thirty-two, then I just had my own way after he died" (Rusch, p. 3). Jimmy worked steadily for thirty-three years as a Chicago White Sox groundskeeper. However, in addition to rent parties he also frequently played at other local private parties and various music clubs. Mama Yancey sometimes joined her husband, performing for gatherings at their home or at parties on Chicago's South Side, but she sang primarily only for her husband. Influences on her life included Lottie Grady (a friend of her father's), Memphis Minnie, and Bessie Smith. Singing on stage taught Yancey that it was no place for a married woman because "when you're on the road, you're here tonight, you may be having an engagement in London, England, tomorrow. Look at the hopping around that you gotta do, and you're changing beds from night to night."

Yancey's musical development was different from other "classic" blues singers of her generation. She did not sing in theaters, cabarets, or vaudeville and tent shows. In fact, she rarely broke out of the boundaries of her own home; therefore, she was not forced to maintain the large musical repertoire characteristic of other working blues singers. Instead she chose to sing a small number of songs over and over again—songs that were important primarily to her. Since she rarely sought employment as a singer, her talent became an outlet for self-expression. She actually deplored the commercialization of blues music, stating that "blues is what comes from your heart."

To Mama Yancey, her marriage, her occasional work as a Democratic precinct captain (which began in 1945 and continued through the 1960s), and her friends and family came first. Her home became a gathering spot for students from around the Chicago area. Mama boasted that her house was the place to be on Saturday nights, adding that it was "crowded like a dance parlor and people had to wedge in with a shoe-horn."

Her first documented performance was with her husband, four songs recorded by Phil Featheringill for the Session label in December 1943. In 1945 she sang with Richard Jones at the Art Institute in Chicago, and with Jimmy Yancey and Kid Ory, among others, at Carnegie Hall in New York City. In 1948 she sang with her husband at Chicago's Orchestra Hall and, from 1948 to 1950 occasionally sang with him on his weekend gigs at Chicago's Bee Hive Club. Mama and Jimmy recorded again, this time in 1951 for Atlantic Records. "When we cut that session," Mama later recalled, "all the time [Jimmy] was playing I was bathing his face in cold water with a washcloth. Jimmy was diabetic. It wasn't two weeks after that session that he went into a coma and passed away."

During the next twenty-five years, Yancey returned to her more private life, interspersed with a few performances and recordings. In 1952 she recorded with Don Ewell for the Windin' Ball label, Chicago; worked Sugar Hill Club, San Francisco, 1961; recorded with Little Brother Montgomery, Riverside label, Chicago, 1961; worked Chicago's Limelight and Red Lion clubs in 1962 and the Touch of Olde Club in 1964; recorded with Art Hodes, Verve-Folkways label, Chicago, 1965; and appeared with Hodes on "Jazz Alley," PBS-TV in 1969.

When Yancey turned eighty in 1976, she returned to performing in earnest. During the next eight years she appeared with pianist Erwin Helfer at numerous events, including the University of Chicago folk festival; together they released the recording *Maybe I'll Cry* in 1983. She also performed during those years with Earl Hines at Northwestern University in 1977, and sang with German pianist Axel Zwingenberger in 1982–1983, although their recordings were not released until 1988.

Mama Yancey's recorded repertoire includes approximately twenty-four songs, several of which she wrote the lyrics for, including "Mama Yancey's Blues," "Death Letter Blues," "Maybe I'll Cry," and "Four O'clock Blues." In live performances she is known to have sung another dozen songs that she improvised onstage. Of the twenty-four recorded songs,

eight were recorded more than once, and seven constituted her central repertoire. Her favorite songs, "Make Me a Pallet on Your Floor" and "How Long Blues," were both recorded six times and were sung at nearly every one of her performances that can be documented. She died in Chicago.

Since she mostly stayed away from the commercial jazz scene, Mama Yancey was able to develop her own style according to her own needs and desires. Her music, therefore, contains personal insights often missing from the repertory of other blues singers. She sang with urgency in a "dry, salty voice, full of feeling, and full of the blues" (Stewart-Baxter, p. 3). Rudi Blesh, author of *Shining Trumpets* (1946), considers Mama Yancey to be the greatest blues singer.

Mama sang with unusual wisdom. As she explained it, "The world is like a piano, and everybody's playing their own song."

• There is an Estella Yancey file at the Chicago Public Library. For additional information see Jane Bowers, "The Meanings of the Blues of Estella 'Mama' Yancey," *American Music* 11 (Spring 1993): 28–53, and "Mama Yancey and the Revival Blues Tradition," *Black Music Research Journal* 12 (Fall 1992): 171–99; Walter Bruyninckx, *Sixty Years of Recorded Jazz, 1917–1977* (1980); Sheldon Harris, *Blues Who's Who: A Biographical Dictionary of Blues Singers* (1979), pp. 591–92; Howard Mandel, "No Blues Now for Mama Yancey," *Chicago Tribune*, 20 Jan. 1977; Bob Rusch, "Mama Yancey: Interview," *Cadence* 4 (Fall 1978): 3–5; and Derrick Stewart-Baxter, "Mama and Jimmy Yancey," *Jazz Journal* 8 (Oct. 1954): 3–4.

NANETTE DE JONG

YANCEY, William Lowndes (10 Aug. 1814–27 July 1863), U.S. congressman, secessionist, and Confederate senator, was born at the shoals of the Ogeechee River, on the boundary between Warren and Hancock counties, Georgia, the son of Benjamin Cudworth Yancey, an attorney and South Carolina state legislator, and Caroline Bird. Benjamin Yancey died in 1817, and in 1821 Caroline married Nathan S. S. Beman, a Presbyterian minister. In 1823 Beman moved his new family to Troy, New York, where William Yancey grew up. Beman was a major figure in the New Light movement among the Presbyterians, and Yancey's youthful environment was marked by intense evangelical fervor. The boy's home also was riven by constant, bitter arguments between his mother and stepfather. Beman engaged in the psychological, and perhaps physical, brutalization of his wife, and young William, siding with his mother, came increasingly to regard northerners as cruel and hypocritical fanatics.

Yancey entered Williams College in 1830 but left at the end of his junior year, in 1833, and went to reside with his mother's sister and her husband, the wealthy planter Robert Cunningham, in the Upcountry of South Carolina. At this time Cunningham was a leader of the Unionist forces fighting nullification, and Yancey at once joined his uncle as a spokesman for this cause. He began reading law in Greenville, South Carolina, under another Unionist leader, Benjamin F.

Perry, and became the editor of the Greenville *Mountaineer*, a Unionist organ. In 1835 he married Sarah Caroline Earle. The couple would have ten children.

Yancey's wife was the owner of thirty-five slaves. In 1836 Yancey purchased a plantation near Cahaba, Alabama, adjoining that of another of his mother's sisters. Just before Yancey was to move permanently to Cahaba, he became involved in an argument with his wife's uncle Robinson Earle. A fight between the unarmed Earle and Yancey, armed with a pistol, a knife, and a sword, resulted in Earle's death on 7 September 1838. Convicted of manslaughter, Yancey was sentenced to a year in prison and fined $1,500, but Governor Patrick Noble commuted the sentence to three months and a fine of $500. Yancey was released from prison at the end of January 1839 and moved at once to Cahaba. The next year he purchased the Wetumpka *Argus* and settled permanently in Wetumpka. In that year the census recorded him as owning six slaves.

In the meantime, in 1835 Beman had become an active abolitionist and began to find his southern wife an increasing source of shame. In 1837 he forbade her to have contact with their children, and seizing all her assets, he sent her to live with her sons by her first marriage. There she discovered that she had contracted tuberculosis while nursing one of Beman's sons from his first marriage; from this disease she eventually died. The acrimonious separation of his mother and stepfather produced the beginnings of Yancey's political transformation. From the ardent Unionist of the early 1830s, Yancey turned more and more toward a furious fixation on what he conceived to be the threat posed to the gentle and maternal South by malignant abolitionist zealots. At the same time, Yancey retained from his youth with Beman a fervid evangelical belief in the righteousness of his convictions and in the evil of all compromise. With these attitudes Yancey began his political career, telling voters that he sought office not as a politician but as a political moralist.

In 1841 Yancey was elected to represent Coosa County in the Alabama House of Representatives, where he was an outspoken advocate of Democratic party dogma. In 1843 he ran for the state senate and was elected by a narrow margin in a canvass that focused primarily on Yancey's approval of the Democratic plan to apportion congressional districts on the basis of white population alone, without counting three-fifths of the slaves. In the senate this champion of southern rights supported other egalitarian measures. Sensitive to his mother's plight, he strongly favored guaranteeing married women their separate estates. As an ex-convict, he sought to forbid the whipping of prisoners, and he fought to limit the power of railroads and banks.

In 1844 Yancey ran for Congress and was elected over Whig Daniel Watrous after a close contest. In his maiden speech, he argued that Great Britain did not favor the abolition of slavery out of humanitarian motives. Rather, after emancipating the slaves in its West Indian colonies, Britain, according to Yancey, had come to realize the superiority of slave over free labor in tropical and semitropical climates and now sought to eliminate the comparative advantage of slaveholding areas. In this same speech, Yancey used such extraordinarily insulting language toward Representative Thomas L. Clingman of North Carolina that a duel resulted, but the police broke it up before either man could be injured. As a freshman congressman, Yancey opposed repeal of the gag rule, favored the annexation of Texas, and voted against an amendment prohibiting slavery in the Oregon Territory, though he later voted for the final passage of the bill despite the amendment.

At the beginning of his second congressional session, Yancey broke with the James K. Polk administration over the new president's proposal to terminate the Oregon joint occupancy agreement with Britain. Yancey argued that war with Britain would result at best in a bloody stalemate and would produce a vast national debt, an expanded paper currency, and an irreversible centralization of the government. In contrast, he strongly supported the war with Mexico and expected Mexico to cede substantial territory. Congressman Yancey also vigorously fought for the Jacksonian economic agenda: a low tariff, no federal internal improvements, reduction of public land prices, and the establishment of the independent subtreasury system.

On 1 September 1846 Yancey resigned from Congress to establish a law partnership with John Archer Elmore in the new state capital of Montgomery, located in another congressional district. Yet his two years in Congress represented a turning point in his political life. In the course of battling for the Jacksonian program, he became convinced that most northern Democrats were not members of the party out of principle but were simply office-hungry politicians. In his final congressional speech, he warned that, if the Democratic National Convention of 1848 failed to adopt a platform explicitly committing the party to strict constructionist principles, he would dissolve his connection with it.

On his return to Alabama, he at once began seeking to arrange this test. At the Democratic state convention of February 1848, Yancey and his allies offered the resolutions that became known as the Alabama Platform, demanding that the American government protect the property rights of any U.S. citizen who settled in a territory, including the ownership of slaves, and instructing Alabama's delegates to withdraw from the convention unless that position was secured. The Alabama Democracy adopted the platform, and Yancey was chosen a member of the national convention delegation. At the national convention in Baltimore in May, Yancey offered a milder version of the Alabama Platform, and when it was rejected, he walked out. The remainder of Alabama's delegates stayed and endorsed the nomination of Lewis Cass.

Yancey remained neutral during the presidential campaign of 1848, and in 1849, in the midst of the crisis over the admission of California to the Union, he began trying to create a southern rights organization independent of either party. Calling the Compromise of 1850 a surrender to abolitionism, he urged Alabamians to affirm the right of a state to secede and to commence planning for the possibility of that action. In the presidential election of 1852, he voted, though with some misgivings, for George M. Troup, whom the state's extreme southern rights faction ran against the two regular party nominees.

The rise of the Know Nothings, whose program Yancey condemned, and his general approval of the policies of the Franklin Pierce administration led Yancey to a hesitant return to the Democratic fold in the middle 1850s. He went as a delegate to the party's national convention in Cincinnati in 1856 and managed to convince himself that the platform adopted there represented an endorsement of the positive protection position that had been rejected by the party in 1848. He therefore accepted a position as an at-large member of the state's Democratic electoral ticket and campaigned actively for James Buchanan. In 1857 a number of southern rights Democrats urged Buchanan to appoint Yancey to his cabinet. Buchanan instead appointed Yancey's younger brother Benjamin Yancey minister to Argentina.

An enthusiastic group of younger Alabama Democrats, admiring his unswerving devotion to principle and hostility toward politicians, raised Yancey to the head of an increasingly powerful faction of the state's party. His economic situation had likewise substantially improved; his holding of eleven slaves in 1850 had grown to thirty-five by 1860. His supporters ran him for the U.S. Senate in 1859 against the incumbent Benjamin Fitzpatrick, but after considerable maneuvering, the legislature voted to postpone the election to 1861.

The prospective nomination of Stephen A. Douglas for president on a platform accepting squatter sovereignty in the territories, however, threatened to subvert Yancey's recent rapprochement with the Democracy. At the state convention in January 1860, Yancey obtained the adoption of resolutions instructing Alabama's delegates to walk out of the national convention if it refused to adopt a platform endorsing positive federal protection of all private property in the territories, including slaves. Yancey was chosen a member of the Alabama delegation, and when the national convention in Charleston rejected positive protection, he withdrew. Unlike 1848, however, he was accompanied this time by his entire delegation and those of several other southern states.

Yancey seems sincerely to have believed that, if northern Democrats were anything more than mere spoilsmen, this united action on principle would cause them to yield on the positive protection question. He and his colleagues presented themselves at the Baltimore adjournment of the Charleston convention in June with the offer to resume their seats if the platform were now amended to their liking. When the convention seated a rival Douglasite delegation instead, Yancey supported the nomination of John C. Breckinridge as a Democratic alternative to Douglas and campaigned for Breckinridge throughout the country.

The election of Abraham Lincoln in November convinced Yancey that the time had arrived for immediate secession. He was elected to represent Montgomery County in the secession convention and was appointed chair of the committee that drafted the ordinance of secession. When the Confederacy was organized in February 1861, President Jefferson Davis nominated him together with Pierre A. Rost and A. Dudley Mann as a delegation to present the South's case to the European powers. Yancey arrived in London on 29 April and spent the next year vainly seeking diplomatic recognition for the new government. In November 1861 the Alabama legislature unanimously elected Yancey to the Confederate Senate. He then resigned his diplomatic mission and managed to return to the Confederacy via Havana and New Orleans. He took his senate seat on 27 March 1862.

Yancey soon became a leading states' rights opponent of the nationalistic Davis administration. He sought extensive exemptions from the Conscription Act and proposed the highly unpopular exemption of an overseer on every plantation with twenty or more slaves whose owner was absent. He fought to restrict the army's impressment of goods, and he strongly opposed allowing the Confederate Supreme Court to hear appeals from state supreme courts. During the debate on the bill to create the Supreme Court, in February 1863, he became involved in a violent encounter with Senator Benjamin Hill of Georgia on the senate floor and suffered injuries that forced him to absent himself for several days.

In the summer of 1863 this unyielding man of principle developed a urinary tract infection, and he died of it at his plantation near Montgomery. His fits of blind anger, his conviction of both personal and regional persecution, and the absolute confidence in his own superior righteousness and devotion to principle that sustained him throughout his life all seem to have been scars left by his unusually unfortunate childhood.

• Few of Yancey's personal papers have survived, though the Alabama Department of Archives and History, Montgomery, holds a small collection, chiefly of speeches and clippings. The papers of Yancey's brother, Benjamin Yancey, at the Southern Historical Collection, University of North Carolina at Chapel Hill, contain a substantial number of letters from Yancey and much material about the family. Ralph B. Draughon, Jr., "William Lowndes Yancey: From Unionist to Secessionist, 1814–1852" (Ph.D. diss., Univ. of North Carolina, Chapel Hill, 1968), is an excellent monograph that has superseded all other accounts for the years covered. For the last decade of Yancey's life, we are left with John W. Dubose, *The Life and Times of William Lowndes Yancey* (1892), an official biography approved by Yancey's brother. J. Mills Thornton III, *Politics and Power in a Slave Society: Alabama, 1800–1860* (1978), offers an interpretation of Yancey's public actions in the final antebellum years.

J. MILLS THORNTON III

YANDELL, David Wendel (4 Sept. 1826–2 May 1898), surgeon, was born at "Craggy Bluff" near Murfreesboro, Tennessee, the son of Lunsford Pitts Yandell, a physician, and Susan Wendel. He grew to maturity in Lexington and Louisville, Kentucky, where his father taught chemistry in the medical department of Transylvania University and at the Louisville Medical Institute. Despite his lack of diligence as a student—a faculty member accused him of being a "damned unpromising specimen"—he graduated from the Louisville Medical Institute in 1846. Shortly thereafter he sailed for Europe and two years of postgraduate studies in French and British hospitals. His witty letters to his family, filled with observations about teaching and treatment techniques, were published in the *Louisville Journal* and the *Western Journal of Medicine and Surgery*. Consequently, on his return to Louisville in 1848 he had already acquired a reputation for excellence and quickly attracted a large clientele of patients and apprentices. In 1851 he married Frances Jane Crutcher of Nashville; two of their four children survived to adulthood. In 1859 Yandell joined the medical faculty of the University of Louisville, but he resigned in September 1861 to enlist in the Confederate Medical Department. A month later he transferred to Albert Sidney Johnston's command and became medical director of the Army of the West.

Encamped across southern Kentucky, from Cumberland Gap to the Mississippi River, and headquartered at Bowling Green (a town of about 2,000), the army eventually consisted of about 48,000 poorly provisioned men. To care for illnesses and anticipated battle wounds, Yandell created hospitals in tents, commandeered buildings in Bowling Green and other area towns, set up convalescent facilities in Nashville, sought provisions for these facilities from area residents, hired civilian nurses, and created a medical examiner board to screen applicants who wished to serve as military physicians. Despite his efforts, thousand of soldiers sickened from measles, typhoid, scurvy, dysentery, influenza, pneumonia, "camp fever," and other life-threatening maladies. More than one-tenth of the army died during its five-month stay in southern Kentucky; many more required medical attention or died following the army's mid-February withdrawal from south central Kentucky to the Nashville area during a snowstorm. Improving weather facilitated Yandell's task as the army moved on to northern Mississippi, but the nightmare began again with the battle of Shiloh on 6–7 April 1862.

In addition to creating, provisioning, and staffing hospitals and caring for the sick and wounded, Yandell served as personal physician to his commanders. On the first morning of the battle of Shiloh, Yandell accompanied Johnston to watch the Confederates' progress. Coming upon a group of wounded Union soldiers, Johnston insisted that the physician care for the unattended men and then rode on to his death when a minié ball struck him below the knee, tearing the popliteal artery. Had Yandell been with Johnston, the surgeon might have prevented the general from bleeding to death.

General P. G. T. Beauregard replaced Johnston and elevated his own personal physician to medical director. Having lost his coveted position, Yandell accepted an appointment as medical director to William J. Hardee's corps and was with him at the battles of Munfordville and Perryville. In May 1863 he was sent to watch over the health of General Joseph E. Johnston. Following the fall of Vicksburg, Yandell wrote to a friend, blaming President Jefferson Davis and Confederate officials at Richmond for the loss of Vicksburg because they did not provide Johnston with sufficient support. The letter appeared in a number of southern newspapers, and in November 1863 the irate Davis ordered Yandell banished to an area where he would have little influence. Yandell spent the remainder of the war serving as medical director for General Edmund Kirby Smith and the Army of the Trans Mississippi.

Personable as well as professionally competent, Yandell won friends and admirers in both Confederate and Union camps and made contacts that proved important during his postwar career. Yandell called the army a "great though terrible school," where he treated an infinite variety of medical and surgical problems seldom seen in civilian life. Army experiences also sharpened Yandell's awareness of the nation's large number of poorly trained doctors; he dedicated the remainder of his career to the correction of this inadequacy.

Returning to Louisville at the war's end, Yandell reestablished his medical practice and opened a small dispensary where medical apprentices gained practical experience and indigents received free treatment. In 1867 he rejoined the University of Louisville medical faculty as professor of clinical medicine; two years later he became professor of clinical surgery and in 1871 professor of surgery. Yandell flavored his lectures and classroom demonstrations with witty advice and bits of medical history and enjoyed a reputation among his students as a superb teacher and deft surgeon. But his colleagues often found him egotistical and overbearing, for he badgered them to establish teaching clinics, create an internship program, and upgrade admission and curriculum standards. When they pleaded that these improvements would force tuition increases and result in declining enrollment, Yandell threatened to resign. Because he was the school's most prestigious faculty member, his colleagues eventually conceded to his demands, and the expanded offerings and requirements were put in place.

Yandell also stressed the need for continuing education. To reach those already practicing medicine, Yandell and Theophilus Parvin founded in 1870 the monthly journal *American Practitioner* (which in 1886 merged with the *Louisville Medical News*, becoming the biweekly *American Practitioner and News*). For more than twenty years Yandell served as editor of the 65–70 page journal, which carried articles about scientific theories and findings, medications and new techniques, reviews of professional publications, news and minutes of medical society activities, and articles, addresses, and editorials concerning medical history, organizations, and procedures written by Yandell.

A proponent and active member of state and national medical societies, Yandell was elected president of the American Medical Association in 1871 and president of the American Surgical Association in 1889, served as chair of the surgery section of the 1881 International Medical Congress in London, was named honorary fellow in the Medical Society of London in 1883, was elected to honorary membership in the College of Physicians and Surgeons of Philadelphia in 1887, and founded the Louisville Surgical Society in 1890. Famous for his charm and wit, Yandell helped Louisville officials entertain postwar visitors, including Grand Duke Alexis of Russia, emperor of Brazil Dom Pedro, and Presidents Ulysses S. Grant, Rutherford B. Hayes, and Chester A. Arthur. He also served as a member of the Louisville school board; belonged to the Pendennis Club (a men's social club), the Salmagundi Club (a literary group), and the Filson Club (an organization that collected, preserved, and studied materials about Kentucky's past); and in 1894 founded the Louisville Kennel Club. Yandell's twentieth-century successors at the University of Louisville honor his memory with an annual guest lectureship. Yandell died in Louisville following several years of poor health.

• The Yandell Family Papers, at the Filson Club, Louisville, Ky., contain newspaper clippings and correspondence by and to Yandell. For a full biography see Nancy Disher Baird, *David Wendel Yandell: Physician of Old Louisville* (1978). Obituaries are in the *Louisville Courier-Journal*, 3 and 5 May 1898.

NANCY DISHER BAIRD

YANDELL, Enid (6 Oct. 1869–12 June 1934), sculptor, was born in Louisville, Kentucky, the daughter of Lunsford Pitts Yandell, Jr., a physician and medical professor, and Louise Elliston. She attended private schools in Louisville and graduated in 1889 from the Cincinnati Academy of Art. Early in life Yandell developed an interest in wood carving and clay modeling. Appreciating her talent, Yandell's mother encouraged her to study art and pursue a career; her uncle David Yandell, who probably financed her education following the 1885 death of her father, once announced that Enid's independence was a "family disgrace," for she was the "first woman of the name who ever earned a dollar for herself." Yandell made few public comments about the difficulties of succeeding in a man's field. To a New York reporter she proclaimed that sculpture was a "lovely occupation for women," but she also advised a group of Louisville women to "get married. Success in other lines is hard won." She herself never married.

Yandell's career began when Bertha Palmer, president of the Board of Lady Managers, hired her to work under the supervision of Lorado Taft and Philip Mar-

tiny to help prepare sculpture for the 1893 World's Columbian Exposition. In addition, she designed the caryatids for the roof garden of the fair's Women's Building, for which she won a gold Designer's Medal. She also modeled a seven-foot statue of the Midwest pioneer Daniel Boone at the request of the Filson Club, a Louisville group dedicated to collecting and preserving area history. The plaster frontiersman stood at the Chicago fairgrounds and later graced the 1897 Tennessee Centennial Exposition; in 1906 the statue was cast in bronze and placed in Louisville's Cherokee Park. It is probably the best known and most realistic of all the replicas of Boone.

In 1892 Yandell and her roommate Laura Hayes published a charming book about their Chicago experiences. Entitled *Three Girls in a Flat*, the volume includes an account of Yandell's visit to the Palmer home, where she met the widow of Ulysses S. Grant, Julia Dent Grant. When the latter expressed disapproval of Yandell's career and insisted that a woman's role was to care for a husband and children, Yandell assured the former first lady that sculpture would prepare her for domestic life; she was "developing muscle with which to beat biscuit."

After her Chicago successes, Yandell served as Karl Bitter's assistant on decorations for the Astor and Vanderbilt homes in New York and the facade of Philadelphia's Pennsylvania Railroad Station. In the winter of 1894 she journeyed to Paris for further art studies, remaining there for three years. At her Left Bank studio she created a 25-foot plaster copy of the Louvre's *Pallas de Velletri Athena*, which became the focal point for Tennessee's centennial celebration. A decade later she filled a commission for a statue of John Thomas, who had served as president of the centennial's board of directors. Weather destroyed the plaster Athena, but the twelve-foot bronze of Thomas still stands in Nashville's Centennial Park.

In 1899 Yandell designed the Carrie Brown Memorial Fountain for Providence, Rhode Island. Modeled in her Paris studio, the fountain was cast at the Gorham Foundry in Providence and placed near the city's new railroad station. Because she won the commission over seventeen male contestants, the bronze fountain generated considerable publicity and undoubtedly won for Yandell numerous other contracts, including one for a fountain for Louisville's Cherokee Park. Unveiled in 1905, the Hogan Fountain (named for its donor) features the mythological Pan dancing and playing his flute for four terrapins.

Between 1900 and World War I, Yandell collaborated briefly with George Grey Barnard in preparing sculpture for the facade of New York City's Amsterdam Theatre; modeled hundreds of miniature portrait figurines, busts, and bas-reliefs in her New York City studio; and periodically visited France "for inspiration." During a 1913 visit to Paris she created her last piece of public statuary, the kneeling figure of an American Indian. Today, her imposing figure of "Chief Ninigret" gazes across the harbor at Watch Hill, Rhode Island.

The outbreak of World War I caught Yandell in France. To aid members of the art community impoverished by the war, Yandell helped found L'Appui aux Artistes and joined the Red Cross to care for orphaned and abandoned children. After her return to the United States, she raised thousands of dollars for the children of France and worked for several years for the American Red Cross. She also operated an art school at Martha's Vineyard, campaigned for the U.S. senator from Massachusetts William Butler and for President Calvin Coolidge, and actively supported the woman suffrage movement. But she created few pieces of statuary during the postwar years. Yandell died in Boston, Massachusetts.

A member of the National Sculpture Society, the French Academy, the National Art Society, the National Arts and Crafts Society, and the Women's Cosmopolitan Club, Yandell exhibited her work in at least twenty-seven major shows, including international expositions at Chicago (1893), Buffalo (1901), and St. Louis (1904). Yandell's best-known works—the Boone, Thomas, and Chief Ninigret statues and Hogan and Brown fountains—stand in public parks. Although much of her smaller sculpture remains in private hands, a variety of fine pieces belongs to public repositories, including busts of John B. Castleman (owned by the Louisville Free Public Library), Reuben T. Durrett and Alfred DuPont (Filson Club), William Goebel (Kentucky Historical Society); bas-relief of Mary Crosby Hunt (Hartford, Conn., Medical Society Museum); figurines of Frank Worthing (Edgartown, Mass., Public Library), Charles Cross Goodrich, (B. F. Goodrich Company, Akron); and the *Kiss* tankard (Rhode Island School of Design, Providence). The J. B. Speed Museum in Louisville owns fifteen plaster artworks, numerous awards and medals, and a scrapbook of newspaper clippings.

• Yandell's papers are deposited at the Filson Club, Louisville, Ky. Letters written to Yandell by her mother and photographs of her sculptures compose the bulk of the collection. Filled with Louisville news and gossip, the correspondence also contains comments on the artist's educational and professional activities. Yandell's years in Chicago are described in the volume she coauthored with Laura Hayes, *Three Girls in a Flat* (1892). A useful secondary source is Nancy D. Baird, "Enid Yandell: Kentucky Sculptor," *Filson Club History Quarterly* 62 (1988): 5–31.

NANCY DISHER BAIRD

YANDELL, Lunsford Pitts, Sr. (4 July 1805–4 Feb. 1878), physician and minister, was born in Sumner County, Tennessee, the son of Wilson Yandell, a physician, and Elizabeth Pitts. Yandell attended Bradley Academy in Murfreesboro, Tennessee, and the medical department of Transylvania University in Lexington, Kentucky. Earning a medical degree from the University of Maryland in 1825, he practiced medicine in Murfreesboro and Nashville and in 1831 joined the faculty of Transylvania University as professor of chemistry. Although he had limited training in the field, he apparently elevated chemistry at Transylvania to the "dignity of a science," and students lauded his "fine style" of teaching. In 1837 he and several colleagues founded the Louisville Medical Institute (forerunner of the University of Louisville School of Medicine), where Yandell taught chemistry, materia medica, and physiology. Proud of the institution he helped create, Yandell once wrote that when he felt "low spirited," he found "confidence and hope" by surveying the "grand dimensions [and] splendid and graceful proportions" of the magnificent structure that housed the school. He married Susan Juliet Wendel in 1825; four of their thirteen children survived to adulthood.

In April 1859 Yandell and his second son, Lunsford, Jr., accepted positions at the Memphis Medical College, whose faculty hoped that Yandell's "influence and . . . pen" would rescue the financially failing school. Yandell spent that fall and spring reorganizing the institution, hiring faculty, and trying to "write the professors into famous reputations and the school into prosperity." The institute opened for classes in November 1860, but the outbreak of war that spring forced the school's demise at the end of the session. In 1861, a year after his wife's death, Yandell married Eliza Bland; they had no children.

In November 1861 Yandell's oldest son, David, who served as medical director of the Army of the West, appointed him to supervise a military hospital in Memphis, and shortly thereafter Yandell assumed additional responsibilities when he was licensed to preach at the Dancyville Presbyterian Church; he was ordained in 1864. After Memphis fell to Federal forces in the summer of 1862, Yandell moved to his wife's family plantation near Dancyville and for the remainder of the conflict farmed and provided medical and ministerial care for area residents. Pro-Confederate, Yandell nevertheless performed nonpartisan missions of mercy. He worked for the release of two Union surgeons imprisoned by the Confederates, rescued two southern sympathizers at Memphis who were under sentence to be executed as spies, and visited a military prison near Louisville to aid an amputee's journey back to Memphis.

Returning to Louisville in 1867, Yandell resumed his medical practice, and although he expressed interest in the school, he refused to rejoin the University of Louisville faculty, pleading disgust with the faculty's constant feuding. The remainder of his life he spent actively engaged in the practice of medicine, in occasional preaching at Louisville's churches, and in writing treatises relating to medicine and natural science. In 1872 he was elected president of the Louisville College of Physicians and Surgeons and in 1878 became president of the State Medical Society (later Kentucky Medical Association), an organization he had helped found twenty-six years earlier. He also belonged to Boston's Academy of Sciences and the Philadelphia Academy of Natural Sciences.

Because Yandell's scientific interests extended to geology and paleontology, he spent much of his time exploring the fossil-rich coral reefs and limestone out-croppings of the Falls of the Ohio and the fossiliferous beds of Louisville's Beargrass Creek. Believing the area "unequaled, perhaps, in richness and extent by any bed of ancient corals known in the world," Yandell amassed an extensive collection of fossils and wrote a number of articles about his findings. In 1847 he published with Dr. Benjamin F. Shumard, *Contributions to the Geology of Kentucky*. The following year the Geological Society of France printed an article, unsigned but credited to Yandell, on the discovery of calcareous arms in Pentremites Florealis. His articles on the Crinoidea appeared in the *Proceedings of the American Association for the Advancement of Science* (1851) and the *American Journal of Science and Arts* (Nov. 1855). In the 1870s he contributed several articles on imprints in stone of prehistoric life to a Louisville journal, *Home and School*. Paleontologists have saluted Yandell's contributions by naming six fossils for him.

A prolific writer, Yandell edited the *Transylvania Journal of Medicine* (1832–1836), coedited the *Western Journal of Medicine and Science* (1840–1855), and wrote more than a hundred treatises, many of which appeared in these and other periodicals. His works encompassed a wide variety of topics: cholera in Lexington; Kentucky's mineral springs and their medicinal value; old age; medical literature; biographical sketches of medical colleagues; histories of the medical department of the University of Louisville and of the dissolution of the medical faculty of Transylvania University; and Kentucky's geology. Yandell died in Louisville.

• The Yandell Family Papers, in the Filson Club, Louisville, contain several diaries as well as hundreds of letters written by Lunsford, Sr., and other members of the family. See also Theodore S. Bell, "Memorial Address on the Life and Services of Lunsford P. Yandell," *American Practitioner* (1878), appendix; V. F. Payne, "Lunsford Pitts Yandell (1805–1878)," *Filson Club History Quarterly* 30 (July 1956): 232–39; and Robert Peter, "Doctor Lunsford P. Yandell, Sr.," in *Some of the Medical Pioneers of Kentucky*, ed. Joseph Nathaniel McCormack (1918), pp. 74–76. An obituary is in the Louisville *Courier-Journal*, 5 Feb. 1878.

NANCY DISHER BAIRD

YARROS, Rachelle (18 May 1869–17 Mar. 1946), physician and reformer, was born Rachelle Slobodinsky at Berdechev near Kiev, Russia, the daughter of Joachim Slobodinsky and Bernice (maiden name unknown). Educated in primary schools, as a teenager she joined a radical revolutionary group, a move her wealthy family opposed. Eventually she realized that she might be sent to jail or Siberia, and she accepted enough money from her parents for passage to the United States. She arrived in New York in the late 1880s.

Rachelle took a job at a sweatshop in Rahway, New Jersey. She went to live among the poor working classes to better understand their environment. At the factory she led a strike but was devastated when her attempt ended in failure. In 1890 Russian friends convinced her to seek a medical degree and gave her financial help. That year she enrolled in the College of Physicians and Surgeons of Boston, the first woman admitted. In her spare hours she nursed the sick at the Tewksbury State Institution. The following year she moved to Philadelphia where she was admitted to the Women's Medical College of Pennsylvania. After receiving her M.D. there in 1893 she interned at the New England Hospital for Women and Children. She continued with postdoctoral studies in pediatrics at the New York Infirmary for Women and Children.

One friend who had encouraged her to become a doctor was Victor S. Yarros, a political exile from the Ukraine and a journalist. The two married in 1894, then settled in Chicago, Illinois, and adopted a daughter. After completing her medical residency and postdoctoral studies at Michael Reese Hospital in Chicago, Yarros started an obstetrical and gynecological practice and dispensary on the Near West Side in 1895.

Two years later Yarros took an unsalaried part-time teaching position at the College of Physicians and Surgeons, an extension of the University of Illinois. She thought students should have hands-on instruction by assisting her with home deliveries at the dispensary, and within the year she had convinced the dean to permit the program. Called by students the "Department of Obstetrics in the Ghetto," this medical training enabled babies to be delivered under the safest and most sanitary conditions. The program ran for twelve years. In addition to becoming an associate professor at the university in 1902, a post she held until 1926, she was an associate director of the Chicago Lying-In Hospital.

In 1907 Yarros and her husband became residents of Jane Addams's Hull-House and remained there for the next twenty years. In 1908 Yarros was appointed director of an obstetrical dispensary. Working with the immigrant poor in the neighborhoods surrounding the social settlement house, she saw the problems of women who had too many children and too little education yet desired to improve their lives. Sympathetic to their needs, she saw them as "victims of exploitation and industrial autocracy" and thus became an activist seeking to change the ills of society.

Education of the poor to eliminate prostitution and resultant venereal disease was of primary concern to Yarros. She recalled her volunteer work at the asylum in Massachusetts where patients had suffered horribly from syphilis. This awareness prompted her to help found the American Social Hygiene Association in 1914. A year later she accepted the vice presidency of the Illinois Social Hygiene League at which she established the first premarital and marital consultation service. She also supervised some of the activities of the Chicago Health Department and the Illinois Board of Health.

When Yarros enlisted the aid of clubwomen, she received criticism from many male physicians who thought that clubwomen would be of little help. In a few years the physicians' attitudes changed when they realized that these women, sensing the need for social justice, worked aggressively to improve health legislation or health education. The General Federation of

Women's Clubs put Yarros in charge of the Social Hygiene Committee to set up a birth control committee. In 1915 the Illinois Birth Control League was formed, and Yarros became its general medical director.

During World War I Yarros was a special consultant to the venereal disease division of the public health service. In the 1920s she continued to educate the public through lectures. Her service earned her an appointment to a professorship in social hygiene on the University of Illinois Medical School's clinical staff in 1926. She held this position until 1939.

Yarros fully supported disseminating contraceptive information to working-class women to ensure a healthier way of life. She had witnessed the effects on immigrant women who had undergone abortions, often self-induced. Some women had suffered serious problems requiring surgery, others had chronic inflammations. Inspired by hearing Margaret Sanger speak and aided by the Illinois Birth Control League, she opened the second birth control clinic in the United States in 1923. She defied opposition from the Roman Catholic clergy and health officials by opening a medical center and clinic that distributed contraceptive literature in the business district in 1924. Encouraged by the strong response she received, Yarros opened additional centers in ethnic and minority neighborhoods. By 1930 Chicago had eight birth control clinics, more than any other American city.

In addition to numerous articles, Yarros published *Modern Woman and Sex* (1933). In 1938 she requested a reissue of the book in a less costly edition. The new edition was titled *Sex Problems in Modern Society*; it discusses her theories on contraception, hygiene, and marriage and divorce but also looks toward a more equitable reevaluation of woman's place in society, in the home, and in her role as a sexual being. Yarros and her husband traveled extensively to study health and welfare conditions in other countries. She found Russia's health facilities to be superior. An agnostic politically affiliated with socialism, she retired in 1939 and died in San Diego, California.

Yarros encouraged women physicians to make their own opportunities. A valiant reformer of women's health issues, she carried her message to social agencies, settlements, hospitals, teachers, and clubs in an effort to educate the public about social disease, hygiene, and the methods of birth control.

• Some manuscript materials by Yarros are in the Special Collections, University of Illinois Library, Chicago. Her informative articles include "Birth Control and Its Relation to Health and Welfare," *Medical Woman's Journal* 32 (Oct. 1925): 268–72, and "Women Physicians and the Problems of Women," *Medical Woman's Journal* 50 (Jan. 1943): 28–30. Biographical sketches appear in the *Journal of Social Medicine* 27 (Mar. 1941): 132–33, and in the Council of the Chicago Medical Society, *History of Medicine and Surgery and Physicians and Surgeons of Chicago* (1922). Other sources are Caroline Hadley Robinson, *Seventy Birth Control Clinics: A Survey and Analysis Including the General Effects of Control on Size and Quality of Population* (1930); Alice Hamilton, *Exploring the Dangerous Trades: The Autobiography of Alice Hamilton, M.D.* (1943); Allen F. Davis and Mary Lynn McCree, eds., *Eighty Years at Hull-House* (1969); Cecyle S. Neidle, *America's Immigrant Women* (1975); Adade Mitchell Wheeler and Marlene Stein Wortman, *The Roads They Made: Women in Illinois History* (1977); James Reed, *From Private Vice to Public Virtue: The Birth Control Movement and American Society since 1830* (1978); Barbara Sicherman, *Alice Hamilton: A Life in Letters* (1984); Regina Markell Morantz-Sanchez, *Sympathy and Science: Women Physicians in American Medicine* (1985); and Ellen Chesler, *Woman of Valor: Margaret Sanger and the Birth Control Movement in America* (1992). An obituary is in the *Journal of Social Medicine* 32 (Oct. 1946): 184.

MARILYN ELIZABETH PERRY

YATES, Abraham, Jr. (Aug. 1724–30 June 1796), public servant and political writer, was born in Albany, New York, the son of Christoffel Yates, blacksmith, and Catharina Winne. He grew up in a multicultural community where his mother and grandmother represented the Flemish and French ancestry roots of New Netherland. Initially apprenticed as a cobbler, by the 1750s Yates had climbed out of the working class to clerk in the Albany law office of Peter Silvester. There he read for the bar and discovered doctrines of the "Rights of Man" as espoused by the radical writers of the English Enlightenment. In 1746 he had married Anna De Ridder, the daughter of a landed Saratoga farmer; they had at least five children, and the marriage provided him with access to several regional networks. The couple settled in Albany, where Yates eventually prospered, supported by what became an extensive legal practice, management of the De Ridder lands, and some importing.

With the agency of Robert Livingston, Jr., Yates was appointed sheriff of Albany County in 1754. This royal office brought him into contact with New England titleholders squatting on Livingston and Van Rensselaer manors, as well as with those who faced imprisonment for nonpayment of debts and other noncriminal offenses. His tenure as sheriff during the French and Indian War (1754–1759) was marked by firsthand experience with the place of civil rights in the face of British military imperatives, as he became a local advocate in direct opposition to British commanders and provincial leaders such as William Shirley and William Johnson. Those experiences caused him to question the inequity of access to wealth in America and, more fundamentally, the place of American colonists in the imperial scheme of things. They also shaped his personal life, as he was captured and imprisoned by angry New Englanders, assailed by British officers, censured by provincial officials, and suffered the deaths of several of his children.

Entering local politics, Yates drew on popular support to be elected annually to the Albany common council from 1753 to 1773. This accession of a blacksmith's son to the council was unprecedented as Albany's aldermen mostly had represented the city's commercial elite. A lawyer among merchants, Yates was called on to provide legal services for the city corporation. In so doing he showed himself to be a proponent of liberty and opportunity over property and privilege, and thus he alienated much of the community's traditional political establishment. His bid for the provincial assembly in 1761 was thwarted by both landed and court interests who had identified Yates as a dangerous leveler. Embittered by defeat, Yates turned away from conventional politics and began to articulate his reservations about the provincial establishment. He soon had an opportunity to stand for American rights in opposition to the Stamp Act and then the Intolerable Acts. During that time he began to build a local action network that included several nephews and other ambitious but not well-born young men.

Ousted from the Albany council following a staged election dispute in 1773, Yates resurfaced in 1775 as the first chairman of the Albany Committee of Correspondence, Safety, and Protection. Beginning in 1775 he was elected to represent Albany in each of the four New York provincial congresses. Commuting between Albany and New York City, Yates attended the congress as it fled before the British in 1776, served as its temporary president, and chaired the committee that produced the first New York state constitution. Despite disabling illness during the winter of 1776–1777, Yates participated in the drafting of the constitution and led a mostly unsuccessful floor campaign to have some of the egalitarian features of earlier drafts restored to the final document that was adopted and proclaimed by the New York State Convention in April 1777.

Firmly established as a revolutionary stalwart in New York State, Yates became closely identified with the insurgent politics of new governor George Clinton and spearheaded Clinton's program in the state legislature. He continued to shape the political revolution as a member of the transitional Council of Safety (1777–1778), state senator and member of the Council of Appointment (1777–1790), Albany city recorder (1778–1779), state loan officer (1779–1783), and then as a delegate to the Continental Congress (1787–1788).

During the 1780s Yates became increasingly troubled by what he suspected was a conscious effort to subvert the fruits of the Revolution to the ambitions of a privileged few in order to establish a more powerful central government. Now in his sixties, Yates began to express in writing his opposition to the emerging forces of nationalism. In 1786 he published a polemical monograph entitled *Political Papers Addressed to the Advocates of a Congressional Revenue in the State of New York*. He also wrote a series of essays in opposition to a stronger central government under the pseudonyms "Cato," "Sydney," and "A Rough Hewer." Published over a period from 1783 to 1792, these newspaper articles were perhaps the most widely read expositions of the antifederalist point of view. During that time Yates resurrected and revised his earlier histories of Albany, Rensselaerswyck, and colonial New York, underscoring and intensifying his claims of a historical conspiracy to deprive ordinary people of their essential human rights. These histories served as background for a major polemical tract that Yates wrote in 1789 on the movement for the U.S. Constitu-

tion and that explained his charges in the events of the past decade. With the adoption of the Bill of Rights, Yates ended his writing efforts, and these essays remained unpublished.

In 1790 Yates was appointed mayor of Albany, and he served in this position until his death. His final years were marked by the emergence of his native city as a major American entrepot and as the capital of New York State. He died in Albany. Throughout his career Yates maintained his faith in the worth and virtue of the common man and also his distrust of aristocracy and special interests. Although Yates did not live to see the democratic triumph in the election of Thomas Jefferson in 1800, he had been one of its grass roots architects since the 1750s.

• The core of Yates's personal papers and essays are in the New York Public Library. Because he was primarily an officeholder, government and legislative records represent an important supplemental resource. Copies of all extant materials relating to Yates are at the Colonial Albany Social History Project in Albany, N.Y. See Stefan Bielinski, *Abraham Yates, Jr. and the New Political Order in Revolutionary New York* (1975); Stephen Wolf, "Abraham Yates, Jr., Der vergessene Grundvater der amerikanischen Republik" (Ph.D. diss., Heidelberg Univ., 1996); Theophilus Parsons, Jr., "The Old Convictions versus the New Realities: New York Antifederalist Leaders and the Radical Whig Tradition" (Ph.D. diss., Columbia Univ., 1974); Carol M. Spiegelberg, "Abraham Yates: An Eighteenth Century Public Servant" (M.A. thesis, Columbia Univ., 1960); and Staughton Lynd, "Abraham Yates's History of the Movement for the United States Constitution," *William and Mary Quarterly* 20, no. 2 (1963): 223–45.

STEFAN BIELINSKI

YATES, Herbert John (24 Aug. 1880–3 Feb. 1966), motion picture executive, was born in Brooklyn, New York, the son of Charles Henry Yates, a salesman, and Emma Worthington. After an education in the New York City public schools, Yates attended Columbia University at night but withdrew at nineteen to become a full-time salesman for the Virgin Leaf Tobacco Company. He took to the tobacco business and eight years later was appointed assistant to the vice president of sales at another leading company, Liggett & Myers. Yates was known in the business as the man who made the success of Fatima cigarettes.

Yates soon was rich. With his new wealth he turned to the movies after 1910, financing several Roscoe "Fatty" Arbuckle productions. But he thought an avenue for making even more money was in film processing. Between 1910 and 1920 Yates set up a film processing laboratory and took over several others. By the early 1920s, Yates's Consolidated Film Laboratories reigned as a major processor of Hollywood's films.

The Great Depression changed the direction of Yates's career. During those lean years independent theater owners in rural America desperately looked for new ways to win customers away from theaters owned and operated by the giant major Hollywood studios. Borrowing a technique from the dime store down the street, small neighborhood houses began to regularly offer two films for the price of one—the double feature. By 1935 they were looking out for new supplies of motion pictures. In stepped Yates, entering Hollywood production through the back door. As the depression drove under many small producers who owed Consolidated thousands of dollars in film processing bills, Yates took their company stock as payment. Soon he controlled a half dozen small producers, and in 1935 he merged them to create Republic Pictures.

Republic supplied cheap productions (so-called "B" movies) and weekly editions of action serials to some 10,000 U.S. theaters. Singing cowboys Gene Autry and Roy Rogers were Republic's biggest stars, but this tiny operation also featured films with Johnny Mack Brown, Judy Canova, Ray "Crash" Corrigan, "Wild Bill" Elliott, Allan "Rocky" Lane, Joan Leslie, Bob Steele, John Wayne, and the figure skater who became his second wife, Vera Hruba Ralston. At the height of the studio era, filmmakers at such major studios as Paramount or MGM looked down on the lowbrow Republic fare, but movie fans in rural America loved the action, adventure, and quick pace of whatever came from the Yates production machine. Republic did so well during World War II that profits soared beyond $1 million a year, a figure unheard of outside Paramount, MGM, Warner Bros., or Twentieth Century-Fox. After the war Yates set out to become "respectable" and produced a score of prestigious pictures including Orson Welles's *Macbeth* (1948), Frank Borzage's *Moonrise* (1948), John Ford's *Rio Grande* (1950), Fritz Lang's *The House by the River* (1950), and Nicholas Ray's *Johnny Guitar* (1954). Only a handful, however, in particular Ford's *The Quiet Man* (1952), made money or earned an Oscar.

The postwar period also was a turning point in Yates's private life. Early in his career he had married Petra Antonsen. Although he kept the details secret, it is known that they had four children. But by the late 1930s Yates was infatuated with Vera Hruba Ralston, runner-up to Sonja Henie in the 1936 Olympic ice skating championships. Yates first made Ralston a Republic star, although the movie-going public never took to her films. In 1952, after a secret divorce, Yates married Ralston.

Having had little success with big-budget films, by the mid-1950s the Republic Pictures movie-making empire was crumbling. Changes in American society, suburbanization in particular, and television's lure signaled the beginning of the end. The need for Republic low-budget fare disappeared. For a time Yates kept Republic Pictures in business by selling old films to be shown on television.

In 1959 Yates sold his film-making and processing properties and retired a rich man. He died in Sherman Oaks, California.

• No Yates papers are known to exist. The most comprehensive guide to Republic Pictures is Richard Maurice Hurst, *Republic Studios* (1979). See also Gene Fernett, *Poverty Row* (1973), and Todd McCarthy and Charles Flynn, *Kings of the Bs* (1975). For an understanding of how Republic Pictures fit into movie economics, see Douglas Gomery, *The Hollywood Studio System* (1986). An obituary is in the *New York Times*, 4 Feb. 1966.

DOUGLAS GOMERY

YATES, Joseph C. (9 Nov. 1768–19 Mar. 1837), politician and judge, was born in Schenectady, New York, the son of Christopher Yates, a merchant and veteran of the French and Indian and revolutionary wars, and Jane Bradt. He was educated by a number of tutors and ad hoc schools that basically served as the equivalent of a college education. It was sufficient to allow him to undertake the required three-year legal clerkship with a cousin of his father, Albany attorney Peter W. Yates. Admitted to the bar in 1791, he returned to practice in Schenectady, and his excellent family connections helped him to prosper. Active in civic affairs, he helped found Union College, for which he was one of the first trustees. He was married three times: to Ann Ellice, with whom he had no children; to Maria Kane, with whom he had one daughter; and to Ann Elizabeth Delancy, with whom he had two daughters.

When Schenectady was incorporated as a city in March 1798, Yates was selected as its first mayor, and he remained in the position for ten years. His mayoral duties were not onerous and allowed him to continue his prosperous law practice. In 1805 he won election to the state senate and was reelected to single-year terms in 1806 and 1807. The Yates clan had been strong supporters of Governor George Clinton and had joined him first in opposing approval of the federal constitution and after its adoption in the creation of the Jeffersonian Republican party. Yates ran as a Republican for the state senate, but in his first election, the composition of the district was such that his main opponent was also a Republican, and Yates required Federalist support to win. This Federalist support is indicative both of Yates's popularity and his conciliatory nature. With Justice Daniel D. Tompkins's election as governor in 1807, Yates, supported by DeWitt Clinton, was selected by the council of appointment to fill Tompkins's place on the state supreme court in February 1808. The appointment, like Tompkins's election, reflected the triumph of the Clintonian faction of the Republican party.

Indicative of the ceremonially prestigious position of supreme court justices, Yates headed the winning New York Electoral College slate for DeWitt Clinton in 1812, although the latter lost to James Madison. Yates remained friendly toward Clinton, despite the latter's ostracization by the Republican party in 1812, in part for his challenge to Madison, and declined to run against Clinton in 1817 for the vacant governorship, created by Tompkins's becoming vice president. But the two became estranged when Clinton, who had ridden the wave of canal mania to the governorship, dragged his feet over calling a constitutional convention, which Yates favored. Both men were in position to affect the convention call as members of the council of revision. Consisting of the governor, justices of the supreme court, and the chancellor, the council was

New York's 1777 constitution's version of the veto. Unlike a number of his judicial colleagues, most of whom were Federalists, Yates did not incur the wrath of legislators who felt that these judges were acting as a superlegislature. He did, however, receive the reprobation of Federalists. One-time colleague James Kent observed that "there was never a more dull & ignorant man advanced to that high office. His opinions . . . were below contempt." A reading of Yates's opinions does not significantly alter Kent's harsh judgment.

The 1821 constitutional convention meant not only a new basic document for the state but also the triumph of Martin Van Buren's "Bucktail" faction as the major political force in the state. Correspondingly, it signaled the temporary decline of DeWitt Clinton, who chose not to seek reelection in 1822 under the new constitution. Yates moved into the void as he became the Bucktail, or Albany Regency's candidate (reflecting Senator Martin Van Buren's absence in Washington, D.C.), in preference to the more radical and less manageable Samuel Young. The Bucktail nomination was tantamount to election, and Yates drubbed the erratic Solomon Southwick, 128,493 to 2,910.

In addition to broadening the suffrage by lowering property requirements (despite the fact that Yates ran with minimal opposition, the 1822 election attracted almost 40,000 more voters than the hotly contested race of 1820), the new constitution, by eliminating the councils of appointment and revision, gave the governor more patronage power as well as the veto. The term of office was, however, shortened to two years. Yates quickly became a likely one-term governor. Both the Young and Clinton camps were anxious to pounce on any mistakes that Yates would make, and he obliged by following his conservative instincts and nominating his three former supreme court colleagues to the new court, despite the fact that the actions of two of them, Chief Justice Ambrose Spencer and Jonas Platt, had been the reason for the old court's abolition; the nominations were rejected.

Further complicating the political scene was the question of selection of presidential electors. The democratization that occurred in the 1821 constitution did not include presidential electors selection, which was still done by the legislature. In 1823 the Regency's opponents formed the People's party, favoring popular election of electors. In his annual message in January 1824 Yates, with customary opaqueness of language, seemed to imply that congress should designate that the voters select the electors. The Regency wanted no change and in April 1824 nominated Young to succeed Yates, who was not regarded as a team player. Presumably to curry favor for the People's party nomination, Yates convened the legislature in June 1824 to solve the presidential electors question, but it did nothing. The People's party nominated Clinton, who defeated Young, and Yates was sent into retirement. Ironically, the Regency found use for Yates in 1828, as he won his district as a presidential elector for Andrew Jackson. He died in Schenectady.

• For more information on Yates see John S. Jenkins, *Lives of the Governors of the State of New York* (1851). James Kent's sketch of Yates is found in Donald M. Roper, "The Elite of the New York Bar as Seen from the Bench: James Kent's Necrologies," *New-York Historical Society Quarterly* 56 (July 1972): 199–237. Yates's political career can be traced in Jabez D. Hammond, *The History of Political Parties in the State of New York from the Ratification of the Federal Constitution to December, 1840* (2 vols., 1842). His court opinions are found in *Johnson's Reports*, vols. 3–20 (1808–1823), and his messages as governor in vol. 3 of Charles Z. Lincoln, ed., *Messages from the Governor* (1909).

DONALD M. ROPER

YATES, Josephine A. (15 Nov. 1859–3 Sept. 1912), educator, was born in Mattituck, Suffolk County, New York, the daughter of Alexander Silone and Parthemia Reeve. She attended schools in New York until she was eleven, at which time she went to live with an uncle in Philadelphia, Pennsylvania. There she enrolled in the Institute for Colored Youth. Later Josephine moved to Newport, Rhode Island, and attended Rogers High School in that city. The only African-American student in her class, she graduated as valedictorian in 1877. She earned a teaching certificate enabling her to teach in public schools in Newport, the first African American to do so in that city. Yates then attended and graduated from the Rhode Island State Normal School in Providence in 1879, also the only African-American graduate that year. She later received an M.A. from National University in Illinois.

In 1879 Yates began her teaching career at Lincoln Institute (now Lincoln University) in Jefferson City, Missouri. Employed as the chairperson of the Department of Natural Science, Yates held the distinction of being the first woman elected to a professorship at the school. For the next ten years she devoted her life to teaching and educating the students at Lincoln Institute. In 1889 she left the school to marry William Ward Yates, the principal of the Wendell Phillips School in Kansas City, Missouri. The couple had two children. Not without an opportunity to influence public education, Josephine Yates, while in Kansas City, conducted a private school for domestics and others who had not had the opportunity to attend school previously.

In addition to her experience and devotion to the field of education, Yates also became involved in the activities of numerous women's clubs. She assisted in organizing the Kansas City League and served as its first president in 1893. On the national level, Yates served as vice president of the National Association of Colored Women from 1897 to 1899, as treasurer from 1899 to 1900, and as president from 1900 to 1904. During her tenure as president, Yates used her leadership to incorporate the National Association of Colored Women, as well as to affiliate the organization with the National Council of Women. Following her term as the national president, Yates also served as state president of the Missouri Association of Colored Women from 1907 to 1911.

During this time, however, Yates had not lost her desire to teach, and in 1902 the Lincoln Institute's new president, Benjamin Franklin Allen, had convinced her to return to the school. In her new position, Yates served as the chairperson of the departments of English and history. In 1908, when she attempted to resign from the institution for a second time, the school's Board of Regents refused her resignation and convinced her to stay. At that time Yates's duties at Lincoln Institute increased, and in addition to teaching, she also began to advise students. Along with her roles as both teacher and adviser, Yates also continued to work with numerous women's clubs and traveled the country giving lectures. She gained considerable reputation as a speaker to African-American men and women, especially in locations such as Chicago, Kansas, and New York. During her public appearances she discussed the benefits of the work accomplished by the National Association of Colored Women and the importance of that organization to African-American women. She called the group a "non-sectarian body organized for the definite and avowed purpose of race elevation." Those African-American women who belonged to the National Association of Colored Women were, in most cases, not women of leisure but women who worked hard to elevate themselves and their families. Yates emulated such self-determination in both her career and personal life.

After her husband died in 1910, Yates left Lincoln Institute to take over the care of her family and home in Kansas City. For the next two years she worked for the Kansas City Board of Education, teaching young people until her death in that city.

In addition to her success as an educator, Yates also earned fame as a writer, contributing many articles to magazines and newspapers during her career. She served as editor of the *Negro Educational Review* in 1904 and wrote articles for inclusion in the *Boston Herald*, the *Transcript*, the *Los Angeles Herald*, and the *Pacific*. Under the pseudonym "R. K. Potter," Yates also wrote "The Isles of Peace," as well as other poems and works. In *Twentieth Century Negro Literature*, Yates wrote concerning the status of African Americans in society. She addressed her concerns to advancements made in the nineteenth century and how those advancements, or lack thereof, affected African Americans in the twentieth century. Of particular interest were achievements in education, morality, and wealth, as well as any opportunities available to black individuals. In discussing the advancements made, Yates wrote, "The measure of the success of a race is the depths from which it has come . . . we conclude that educationally, morally, financially, the Negro has accomplished by means of the opportunities at his command about all that could be expected of him or any other race under similar conditions." However, Yates also spoke of the success of women in society, of which she said, "The women of a race forms, perhaps, the surest index of its real advancement." Emphasizing the importance of teaching, she concluded that "future success . . . is ours, if we hew to the line in teaching our sons and daughters to love virtue and that a good name is rather to be chosen than great riches."

• The Ethnic Studies Center, Inman E. Page Library, Lincoln University, contains the papers of Yates. In addition to portraits and photographs of her, the center has documents gathered in connection with the dedication of a historical marker designating the place that Yates Hall once stood on the Lincoln University campus. The Friends of Lincoln University and Missouri Association of Colored Women's Clubs, Inc., worked to erect this honor. The clippings and short biographical sketches that comprise the collection of papers provide a look at Yates's life during her tenure at Lincoln Institute, as well as her childhood and time spent away from the school. These biographical sketches are based on several published sources, including Robert T. Kerlin, *The Voice of the Negro* (1920; repr. 1968); Sylvia G. L. Dannett and the Negro Heritage Library, *Profiles of Negro Womanhood*, vol. 1 (1964–1966); and Elizabeth Carter-Brooks, "Josephine Silone Yates, Second President of the N.A.C.W.," in *Lifting as They Climb*, ed. Elizabeth L. Davis (1933), which also includes a reprint of "The Isles of Peace." Also useful are Daniel W. Culp, *Twentieth Century Negro Literature* (1902); Fannie B. Williams, "The Club Movement among Colored Women of America," in *A New Negro for a New Century*, ed. Booker T. Washington et al. (1900; repr. 1969); Jessie Carney Smith, ed., *Notable Black American Women* (1992); Dorothy C. Salem, ed., *African American Women: A Biographical Dictionary* (1993); and Darlene Clark Hine, ed., *Black Women in America: An Historical Encyclopedia* (1993).

STEPHANIE A. CARPENTER

YATES, Richard (18 Jan. 1815–27 Nov. 1873), governor and senator, was born in Warsaw, Gallatin County, Kentucky, the son of Henry Yates, a farmer, and Millicent Yates, granddaughter of Michael Yates of Virginia. The youth attended local schools and worked on the farm until the family moved to Sangamon County, Illinois, in 1831. He attended Miami University in Ohio and Georgetown College in Kentucky before graduating from Illinois College in Jacksonville in 1835. After studying law in the office of John J. Hardin in Jacksonville and at Transylvania University in Lexington, Kentucky, Yates was admitted to the bar in 1837, practicing in Jacksonville, Illinois, his permanent residence. In 1839 he married Catharine Geers; they had five children, one of whom, Richard Yates, served as governor of Illinois from 1901 to 1905.

While developing his growing law practice, Yates pursued his interests in politics. Opposed to the Democratic philosophy of Presidents Andrew Jackson and Martin Van Buren, Yates joined the Whig party, favoring protective tariffs, federally sponsored internal improvements, and Senator Henry Clay's American System. Yates canvassed Illinois in 1840 for William Henry Harrison, the successful Whig presidential standard-bearer. Yates then served three terms (1842–1846, 1848–1850) in the state legislature. In 1850 he was elected to the U.S. House of Representatives, where he served from 1851 to 1855, failing to secure reelection in 1854 because of Democratic redistricting of the state. He was the youngest member of the Thirty-second Congress and the only Whig from Illinois in one of his congressional terms. He served on the Committee on Revolutionary Claims and the Committee on Territories among others. During his congressional years, Yates urged the establishment of federal land-grant colleges, favored the development of the Pacific railroad, opposed the repeal of the Missouri Compromise of 1820, denounced slavery, and supported homestead laws to attract settlers to the West. His speech to the House on 28 February 1854 underscored his unwavering position on homesteading.

With the demise of the Whig party, Yates joined the newly created Republican party. He participated in the Republican State Convention in 1854 and stumped the state in 1856 for John C. Frémont's presidential candidacy. He campaigned for Abraham Lincoln in his 1858 senatorial race against Democratic senator Stephen A. Douglas. Although opposed to slavery, Yates, like Lincoln, was no extreme abolitionist. Having long been friends and political allies with Lincoln, Yates endorsed him for the presidency and attended the 1860 Republican National Convention in Chicago, which nominated Lincoln for the nation's highest office. During these years, Yates continued to practice law while also maintaining his interest in the Tonica and Petersburg Railroad Company (later the Chicago and Alton).

Yates's popularity and valuable political contacts strengthened his position among Illinois Republicans. In 1860 he was chosen as the party's gubernatorial candidate, defeating his Democratic opponent, James C. Allen, by some 13,000 votes. A firm chief executive, Yates was a political partisan who equated patriotism with support of the Republican national and state administrations. After the destruction of the American flag at a recruiting station in Illinois in 1861, he ordered that if anyone tried to prevent the raising of the U.S. flag on Illinois soil, the assailant would be shot. If a jury ever convicted a person of obeying this order and shooting the traitor, Yates announced that he would pardon him. The governor convened the state legislature into extra session on 12 April 1861 and took military possession of Cairo, located at the southern tip of the state.

Yates stood against any concessions or compromise with the Confederacy. The governor proposed emergency measures, visited hospitals, rallied the troops, delivered highly partisan speeches, scoffed at his detractors, and praised Lincoln. He used the war's emotional fervor to advance his causes and shrewdly gain the upper hand in his conflict in the legislature with opponents of the war known as Copperheads. Yates's actions enhanced his popularity with the people and strengthened his position as wartime leader of Lincoln's home state.

Asking the legislature to appropriate additional funds for soldiers, Yates vigorously recruited troops for the Union. Illinois contributed more than 250,000 enlistments to the cause. The governor busied himself with reviewing the troops, creating army units, raising bounties, discussing the conduct of the war with Lincoln and other officials, and supporting the enlistment of loyal African Americans in the Union army. He also appointed Ulysses S. Grant as mustering officer for the state and later as colonel of the Twenty-first Regiment of Illinois Volunteers, thereby placing Grant in the military arena from which he emerged successfully as the general in 1865 who accepted Robert E. Lee's surrender in Virginia.

Although Yates endorsed Lincoln's policies during the Civil War and supported the Emancipation Proclamation, he was more controversial and radical than Lincoln. Yates often could not understand the delays in conquering the South, and he exhibited no talent for compromise. He never hesitated to voice his disapproval of Lincoln's war leadership, contending the president was too slow in calling out men and too slow in issuing the Emancipation Proclamation. But later Yates, who inclined to be hysterical, admitted that Lincoln's timing was right.

Yates vehemently castigated what he perceived to be treason on the part of Illinois Democrats, who after the death of Douglas were left without strong leadership. As the fighting dragged on, many who lacked Yates's fervor and determination became discouraged with the course of the conflict, resulting in spreading acrimony across Illinois during a bitterly partisan period in the state's history. The Illinois House of Representatives, controlled by a Democratic majority desirous of embarrassing the governor, passed a resolution in 1863 to compromise with the seceded states by means of an armistice or convention of delegates to achieve peace. Yates retaliated by using his constitutional prerogative in case of a disagreement over adjournment to prorogue the legislature, which endured for a year until a solid Republican majority returned to power. Yates tolerated no nonsense and exhibited no kind feelings toward those who advocated secession or disunion or who demonstrated an absence of loyalty to the United States or Illinois. He served notice on his opponents that war would continue until victory was won by the South's unconditional surrender. Yates strongly believed that the entire force of the government in its moral, political, and physical dimensions had to be utilized to defend the Constitution.

Upon the conclusion of the Civil War and his gubernatorial term in 1865, Yates served one term in the U.S. Senate, from 1865 to 1871. During this time, he supported a harsh Reconstruction policy toward the South. In a Senate speech on 8 June 1866, Yates addressed the matter of impartial suffrage, which he contended was a remedy for American evils. He advocated justice for loyal African Americans and continued his fight against southern sympathizers. In 1870 he spoke on the topic of national sovereignty over states' rights. He also voted in 1868 to convict President Andrew Johnson in the impeachment trial. Yates was not a candidate for reelection to the Senate.

At the close of his senatorial service in 1871, Yates returned to his law practice and home in Jacksonville. He held the position of U.S. commissioner to inspect land subsidy railroads, an appointment tendered him by President Grant. While returning from Arkansas, where he had been examining a railroad, Yates died of a heart attack in St. Louis, Missouri.

Serving as the wartime governor of Illinois, Yates gained a reputation as a strong chief executive. Had he been in office during a time of peace, his reputation might not have been as well remembered. A leader possessed with oratorical powers, intelligence, personal integrity, and perseverance, Yates, despite his occasional overindulgence with liquor, was a dedicated public servant who carefully guarded his state's interests. He is recognized as one of the strongest governors of Illinois.

• Yates's papers are at the Illinois State Historical Library in Springfield. The Illinois State Archives in Springfield holds the governor's correspondence from 1861 to 1865. His speeches are in the *Congressional Globe* from 1851 to 1855 and from 1865 to 1871. See also Logan U. Reavis, *The Life and Public Services of Richard Yates* (1881); Richard Yates and Catharine Yates Pickering, *Richard Yates: Civil War Governor*, ed. John H. Krenkel (1966); E. L. Kimball, "Richard Yates: His Record as Civil War Governor of Illinois," *Journal of the Illinois State Historical Society* 23 (1930): 1–83; and Richard Yates, Jr., "Richard Yates, War Governor of Illinois," *Transactions of the Illinois State Historical Society* (1923): 171–205, written by his son and namesake. Helpful works by Jack Junior Nortrup are, "Richard Yates, Civil War Governor of Illinois" (Ph.D. diss., Univ. of Illinois at Urbana-Champaign, 1960), "Richard Yates: A Personal Glimpse of the Illinois Soldiers' Friend," *Journal of the Illinois State Historical Society* 56 (1963): 121–33, "Governor Yates and President Lincoln," *Lincoln Herald* 70 (1968): 193–206, "Yates, the Prorogued Legislature, and the Constitutional Convention," *Journal of the Illinois State Historical Society* 62 (1969): 5–34, and "A Western Whig in Washington," *Journal of the Illinois State Historical Society* 64 (1971): 419–41. Additional information is in *Reports of the General Assembly of Illinois* (1861–1865); *Report of the Adjutant General of the State of Illinois* (1861–1865); William B. Hesseltine, *Lincoln and the War Governors* (1955); Victor Hicken, *Illinois in the Civil War* (1966); and Frank L. Klement, *The Copperheads in the Middle West* (1960). Obituaries are in the *New York Times*, 28 Nov. 1873, the *Chicago Tribune*, 28, 29 Nov. 1873, and the *Jacksonville Daily Journal*, 29 Nov. 1873.

LEONARD SCHLUP

YATES, Robert (27 Jan. 1738–9 Sept. 1801), statesman and jurist, was born in Schenectady, New York, the son of Joseph Yates and Maria Dunbar. His great-grandfather had immigrated to Albany, New York, c. 1700, and Robert Yates was associated with that city throughout his life. Yates's family provided him a decent upbringing and a good education, but the family was of the middling gentry. Even at the height of his career, Yates was not among the Empire State's social elite. He had a classical education in New York, then read law in the office of William Livingston, who would rise to the post of governor of New Jersey. Admitted to the bar on 9 May 1760, Yates made his living at the law. In 1765 he married Jannetje Van Ness; they had six children.

Yates was an alderman in Albany from 1771 to 1775, a member of the Committee of Public Safety in 1775, and a member of the provincial congresses and convention during the period 1775–1777. His career in the New York Congresses included service on the thirteen-man committee that drew up New York's first constitution, among other important assignments. Appointed a justice of the New York Supreme Court on 8 May 1777, he served from 1790 to the end of his tenure in 1798 as the chief justice of that court. Alexander Hamilton, a political foe at a later time, commented, "Judge Yates is upright and respectable in his profession" (Young, p. 43). As a supreme court justice, Yates was a member of the Council of Revision, but few examples of veto messages are extant in his prose. As a councilman, he was involved in resolving New York's boundary disputes with Vermont and Massachusetts. A friend of Governor George Clinton, he opposed requests from the Confederation Congress in the 1780s for more power, particularly the power to levy an impost. Yates was only loosely identified with any particular political faction in New York.

Yates is best known for the role he played in the Philadelphia federal convention in the summer of 1787 and for his opposition to the convention's proceedings during and after the convention. He was one of three members of the New York delegation. One of the others, John Lansing, sided with Yates in most instances, thereby depriving the third, Hamilton, of the opportunity to promote his nationalist program with his delegation's vote. One familiar with Yates's positions in the 1780s could have predicted his posture in Philadelphia. He left Philadelphia before the conclave's end to rouse opposition to his fellow delegates' product, and he was the floor leader of the New York opponents of the proposed federal Constitution in the New York ratification convention, which convened in Poughkeepsie on 17 June 1788.

In the interim between Yates's departure from Philadelphia and the Poughkeepsie convention, he and Lansing sent Governor Clinton an epistle in which they rested their antifederalism on the usurpation of the Philadelphia convention delegates, who had exceeded their mandate to propose constructive amendments to the Articles of Confederation. They also opined that the continued primacy of the states, and not a consolidation in the center, was the best guarantor of the people's liberty.

Herbert J. Storing has supported the suggestion that Yates was the author of the "Brutus" letters, a series of Antifederalist letters that appeared in the *New York Journal* between October 1787 and April 1788. Storing also points to the discrepancy in quality between the "Brutus" essays and those of "Sydney" as evidence that the author of the former cannot have been the author of the latter. Strangely, although he had given serious thought to the question of the proper form of a republican government, Yates made a weak showing as the Antifederalist leader in Poughkeepsie, speaking only once and failing to offer a persuasive set of amendments. When New York ratified the Constitution by a narrow margin, Yates found no trouble in shifting to the Federalist party at the next election, a turn of events highlighting the degree to which New York politics were more personal than ideological.

Yates ran for governor in 1789 as a Federalist, opposing Clinton and supported by Hamilton. He lost by a vote of 6,391 to 5,962. In 1795, after Clinton's retirement, he tried again as an Antifederalist, only to be bested by John Jay. Unlike many of his New York fellows, Yates refused to profit via speculation in confiscated estates during and after the Revolution. "No I will sooner die a beggar than own a foot of land acquired by such means," he reportedly said (Young, p. 43). His poverty at the end of his life was thus a sort of badge of principle.

• Yates's work as a member of the N.Y. Supreme Court is contained in the New York reports. The notes Yates took in the Philadelphia convention are in the notes of the convention, originally published as *Secret Proceedings and Debates of the Convention Assembled . . . for the Purpose of Forming the Constitution of the United States* (1821). The "Brutus" essays are in Herbert J. Storing, ed., *The Complete Anti-Federalist*, vol. 2 (repr. 1981). Yates's role in Philadelphia is also charted in James Madison's notes, which are available in myriad editions; one such edition is *Notes of Debates in the Federal Convention of 1787 Reported by James Madison*, ed. Adrienne Koch (1966). Biographical information concerning Yates is in M. E. Bradford, *Founding Fathers: Brief Lives of the Framers of the United States Constitution* (1994). The ratification contest in N.Y. is the subject of Linda De Pauw, *The Eleventh Pillar: New York State and the Federal Constitution* (1966), and several essays in Stephen Schecter, ed., *The Reluctant Pillar: New York and the Adoption of the Federal Constitution* (1985). The rise of Thomas Jefferson's party in N.Y. is the subject of Alfred F. Young, *The Democratic Republicans of New York* (1967).

K. R. CONSTANTINE GUTZMAN

YAWKEY, Tom (21 Feb. 1903–9 July 1976), baseball owner and philanthropist, was born Thomas Yawkey Austin in Detroit, Michigan, the son of Thomas J. Austin, a businessman, and Augusta Lydia Yawkey. His father died when Yawkey was seven months old, and he was raised by his mother's brother, William H. Yawkey, and his wife, Margaret Williams Draper. When his mother died in 1918, his aunt and uncle adopted Yawkey, and he legally interchanged his middle and last names.

Yawkey grew up in Sandwich, Ontario, Canada, and New York City. His uncle controlled the family's investments in forest land, mines, oil fields, and related businesses. The owner of the Detroit Tigers baseball team from 1904 until 1907, his uncle maintained a partnership in the club until his death in 1919. As a result, Yawkey met many of the Tigers players and developed a lifelong passion for the sport.

Yawkey attended the Irving School in Tarrytown, New York, and Yale University's Sheffield Scientific School, where he studied chemistry, mining, and metallurgy. He earned his B.S. in 1925. That same year he married Dora Elise Sparrow, a union that ended in divorce in 1944. They adopted one child. Yawkey married Jean Hollander Hiller, a New York City fashion model, in 1944. They had no children.

After college Yawkey returned to New York City, where he ran the family businesses and amassed by 1933 a personal fortune of an estimated $20 million. With the encouragement of former Tigers star Ty Cobb and fellow Irving School alumnus Eddie Collins, another retired major league great, Yawkey decided to buy a major league baseball team. After making an unsuccessful bid for the New York Giants and declining an opportunity to buy a share of the Brooklyn Dodgers, he purchased the hapless Boston Red Sox for $1.2 million in February 1933.

The Red Sox at the time of Yawkey's purchase had spent eight of the previous ten seasons in last place in the American League, winning just 43 of 154 games in 1932 while drawing an average crowd of barely 2,200 fans a game. The team had a history of mismanagement, symbolized by former owner Harry Frazee's decision to sell Babe Ruth to the rival New York Yankees in 1919 for $100,000 in cash and a $300,000 mortgage on Fenway Park. Yawkey immediately paid off the team's debts, spent $750,000 to refurbish the ballpark, hired Collins as general manager, and set about rebuilding the team.

Yawkey spent lavishly to restore respectability to the Red Sox. He first bought established veterans such as pitcher Lefty Grove, slugging infielder Jimmy Foxx, and shortstop Joe Cronin. By the end of the 1930s younger prospects such as Dom DiMaggio, Bobby Doerr, and Ted Williams, perhaps the greatest batter of his time, joined the team. Game attendance at Fenway Park increased, and the Red Sox rose to second place in the American League, behind only the Yankees.

The Red Sox finally captured the league championship in 1946 but lost to the St. Louis Cardinals in the World Series. The team lost the pennant in a playoff to the Cleveland Indians in 1948, and its fortunes sagged badly in the 1950s. Critics charged that Yawkey overpaid and pampered his players, and that was no doubt true. Yawkey looked after his stars, especially Williams and later outfielder Carl Yastrzemski, inviting many to accompany him on hunting and fishing trips to the vast Yawkey family game preserve in South Carolina. Until 1948, when he hired former Yankee manager Joe McCarthy to run the team, he was a constant presence in the Red Sox locker room. When a friend informed him that McCarthy believed his visits were a distraction, Yawkey refrained and did not set foot in the locker room until the Red Sox won their next pennant in 1967. The team returned to the World Series once more during Yawkey's tenure, 1975, but never won the world championship.

Yawkey was often criticized for failing to sign African-American players. In 1946 the Red Sox conducted a tryout for several Negro League stars, including Jackie Robinson, who would become the first black major leaguer of modern times with the Dodgers in 1947, and Sam Jethroe, who would star for the rival Boston Braves. Robinson claimed he heard Yawkey say "get those niggers off the field" (Shaughnessy, p. 56) and publicly branded the Red Sox owner a racist.

Yawkey always denied the story, and others who were on hand were uncertain who uttered the remark, but the Red Sox were the last major league team to field a black player, finally breaking the color line in 1959.

Yawkey spared no expense in supporting his Red Sox and estimated in 1974 that owning the team had cost him over the years $10 million. He gave millions more to charities in New England and South Carolina. Yawkey helped organize and support the Jimmy Fund, which supported research into children's cancer at the Dana-Farber Institute in Boston. He was also the major supporter of Tara Hall, a home for troubled boys in South Carolina, and donated a wing to Georgetown (S.C.) Memorial Hospital. An avid conservationist, hunter, and angler, he actively supported a variety of environmental and wildlife management organizations. He died in Boston and willed 15,000 acres of his family's land to the state of South Carolina as a wildlife preserve along with a $10 million trust fund for its maintenance. In 1980 he was honored posthumously through his induction into the National Baseball Hall of Fame.

In 1978 Jean Yawkey and a syndicate including Red Sox general manager Haywood Sullivan and former team trainer Edward "Buddy" LeRoux purchased the team. While Yawkey sought to continue her late husband's policy of spending lavishly on players, LeRoux wanted to increase the investors' return. In 1983 LeRoux and several minority partners tried to seize control of the Red Sox. Yawkey and Sullivan took LeRoux to court and, after several years of legal wrangling, bought him out in 1987.

Tom Yawkey was among the last of the professional sports franchise owners who were sportsmen first and foremost; he was autocratic and paternalistic, yet utterly devoted both to the game and to his team. He enjoyed mingling with players and, in his younger days, taking batting practice at the ballpark. Yawkey also understood, however, the special place the Red Sox occupied in the life of New England. After Yawkey's death, Bill Veeck, president of the Chicago White Sox, told the *Boston Globe* that Yawkey was "the only true sportsman I ever met in sports. He thought baseball . . . was bigger than the deeds of individual teams. . . . He was the least selfish of all ball club operators."

• The National Baseball Library, Cooperstown, N.Y., holds extensive files of correspondence and news clippings related to Yawkey's career. Among the many popular histories of the Red Sox, Dan Shaughnessy, *The Curse of the Bambino* (1990), and Peter Golenbock, *Fenway* (1992), offer somewhat caustic views, while Frederick G. Lieb, *The Boston Red Sox* (1947), is a straightforward account of the early years of Yawkey's ownership. An obituary and several related articles are in the *Boston Globe*, 10 July 1976. The *Globe* provided the most perceptive coverage of Yawkey and the Red Sox over the years.

TIM ASHWELL

YEAMAN, William Pope (28 May 1832–19 Feb. 1904), Baptist minister and denominational leader, was born in Hardin County, Kentucky, the son of Stephen Minor, a lawyer, and Lucretia Helm, the daughter of Kentucky governor John Larue Helm. Yeaman studied law with his uncle, John Z. Helm, was admitted to the bar at age nineteen, and then practiced law in Kentucky. In his memoirs Yeaman recalled that his first case was tried in Hardin County, Kentucky, while he was still a minor. He won the case and soon developed an extensive legal practice, which he maintained for nine years.

In his late twenties, Yeaman believed he had received a divine call to the ministry and was ordained, becoming pastor of a Baptist church in Nicholasville, Kentucky. In 1862 he was called as pastor of the First Baptist Church of Covington, Kentucky, a town located on the Ohio River near Cincinnati. In Covington, Yeaman joined another minister, George Varden, in editing the *Baptist Monthly*, an endeavor that lasted for about a year. The magazine published articles on a variety of theological, political, and ecclesiastical issues. Yeaman's decision to leave Covington in 1868 to become pastor of Central Baptist Church in New York City led to the suspension of the periodical.

Yeaman had only a brief tenure in New York. He left the city in 1870 to accept the pastorate of Third Baptist Church in St. Louis, Missouri. He spent the next thirty years of his career in service to Missouri churches and educational institutions. In 1876 he resigned from the Third Baptist Church and joined with a group of members from that congregation to found the Garrison Avenue Baptist Church—later called the Delmar Avenue Baptist Church—in St. Louis. He remained in that parish for two years.

Yeaman's work in religious journalism continued when, in 1872, he became co-owner and coeditor of the state Baptist newspaper, the *Central Baptist*, then in serious financial straits. The paper prospered under his leadership, and he sold his interest in the periodical after about a year. In 1875 the journal experienced another financial crisis, and Yeaman again stepped in to provide monetary and editorial assistance. Once again he helped restore the publication, which provided news and information for churches in the Missouri Baptist Convention.

In addition to his work as pastor and editor, Yeaman was active in service to numerous Missouri Baptist agencies, particularly educational institutions. He served as chancellor of William Jewell College in Liberty, Missouri, from 1875 to 1877 and was a member of the college's board of trustees from 1871 until his death. He was president of Grand River College in Gallatin, Missouri, from 1893 to 1897 and was a member of the board of trustees of Stephens College, a woman's college in Columbia, Missouri.

A leader among Baptists in Missouri, Yeaman served on several denominational boards and agencies. From 1884 to 1886 he was secretary-president of the Board of State Missions, and for twenty years (1877–1897) he was moderator (presiding officer) of the Missouri Baptist General Association. His book, *A History of the Missouri Baptist General Association* (1899), written at the request of Missouri Baptists, chronicles the history of the state Baptist convention from 1844 to

1894. Also active in the affairs of the national denomination, Yeaman was a trustee of the Foreign Mission Board of the Southern Baptist Convention and in 1880 was elected to one term as vice president of the Southern Baptist Convention.

In 1886, at the urging of friends, Yeaman agreed to seek the Democratic party's nomination for the U.S. Congress. He did not secure the nomination, however, and later used the experience as evidence that ministers should not seek elective office. He came to believe that political service was inappropriate for ministers because it required them to be partisan, it led persons to suspect their devotion to God, and because the political world was exceedingly immoral. He became convinced that the forces of corruption were so powerful that it was difficult if not impossible for politicians to remain untainted.

In 1897 Yeaman retired to a farm near Columbia, Missouri, and accepted the pastorate of the Walnut Grove Baptist Church, a rural congregation near his home. He remained in that position until a few months before his death at his farm.

For more than fifty years Yeaman was married to Eliza Shackleford, like her husband a native of Hardin County, Kentucky. The couple had eight children, all of whom lived to adulthood. Eliza Yeaman preceded her husband in death by only three weeks.

Yeaman was primarily a preacher/pastor known for his oratory and doctrinal conservatism. His only other published work was a treatise, not completed, entitled "The God-Man." It is included as a chapter in J. C. Maple's biography of Yeaman. The article deals with the question of christology and represents Yeaman's effort to reassert traditional Christian orthodoxy in response to developments in theological and philosophical liberalism. One of his last addresses, "Baptists a World Power," was given to the Missouri Baptist Historical Society in 1900. In it he asserted that Baptists, long persecuted and caricatured by other Christian groups, had come of age in the modern world. As Yeaman saw it, Baptist ideals regarding freedom of conscience, religious liberty, and democratic government had at last found acceptance in modern society. For him, Baptists were in the vanguard of the new era of democracy and progress, which was evident at the beginning of the twentieth century.

• Biographical details of Yeaman's life are sketchy. The most extensive biographical material is found in Joseph Cowgill Maple, *Life and Writings of Rev. William Pope Yeaman, S.T.D.* (1906); this volume also contains a small collection of his sermons and treatises, including "The God-Man," his most elaborate theological work. Useful biographical sketches are in *Encyclopedia of Southern Baptists*, vol. 2 (1951); Robert Samuel Duncan, *History of the Baptists in Missouri* (1882); and Maple and R. P. Rider, *Baptist Biography*, vol. 1 (1914).

BILL J. LEONARD

YEAMANS, Sir John (1611–Aug. 1674), member of the Council of Barbados and a governor of Carolina, was born in Bristol, England, the son of John Yeamans, a brewer. (His mother's name is not known.) Yeamans fought on the Royalist side in the English Civil War, rising to the rank of colonel. Like many other Royalists in the wake of the parliamentary victory and the execution of Charles I, in 1650 Yeamans emigrated to Barbados. His motives, however, were perhaps as much economic as political, for as a younger son Yeamans inherited only forty pounds from his father. In the West Indies Yeamans became a man of wealth, status, and power. He was one of the largest landowners on Barbados and served as a judge of the Court of Common Pleas for the parishes of St. Peter's, All Saints', and St. Lucy's. By 1660 he had become a member of the Council of Barbados.

In the 1660s, as a result of a series of policy decisions by the British government, the opening of other English Caribbean colonies to sugar cultivation, and the exhaustion of the soil on their own island, Barbados planters faced lower sugar prices, higher labor costs, and more expensive imported goods. Seeking greater profits they turned to other islands and the North American mainland for economic opportunities. It was against this background that in 1663 Yeaman's son William negotiated with the proprietors of Carolina on behalf of both his father and more than eighty other Barbadians a series of articles of agreement under which they proposed to establish a settlement in Carolina. (William Yeamans was one of three children borne by John Yeamans's second wife, Margaret Foster. His first wife, who presumably predeceased him, was the daughter of a Mr. Limp.) The proprietors appointed John Yeamans governor of the intended colony and, in anticipation of his future services, persuaded the king to make Yeamans a baronet. Led by Yeamans, the settlers arrived at Cape Fear in late 1665 to found a short-lived colony, but Yeamans soon returned to Barbados. The other settlers struggled to establish a viable colony until mid-1667 before dispersing to other mainland settlements. The failure of the Cape Fear colony resulted in part from the hardship caused by the onerous conditions of settlement imposed by the articles of agreement. More important perhaps was that the venture coincided with the Second Dutch War. Preoccupied with their own defense, the Barbados authorities had neither the time nor the resources to aid the infant colony.

In 1669 a fleet bound for what was to become Charles Town arrived in Barbados from England under the command of Joseph West. The proprietors of Carolina had sent an accompanying blank commission for the position of governor with instructions for Yeamans to fill in his own name or that of his choice. Accordingly, Yeamans assumed command of the expedition. After the ships left Barbados, however, a severe storm separated them, blowing the *Carolina*, with Yeamans aboard, to Bermuda. There Yeamans resolved to return to Barbados, justifying his decision on the grounds that he was required to participate in discussions with the French over their expulsion of English settlers from St. Christopher's. In his place he nominated as governor William Sayle, "a man of noe great sufficiency yett the ablest I could then meete with" (quoted in McCrady, p. 124).

In April 1671 the proprietors appointed Yeamans a landgrave, and when he finally arrived in Carolina several months later he claimed the governorship from Joseph West, who had assumed the position after Sayle's death. West, however, supported by the Grand Council (the local governing body), refused to surrender the post until he received instructions from the proprietors. West called a parliament, of which Yeamans was chosen Speaker. Yeamans apparently used this office solely to challenge the legality of West's position, with the result that the assembly soon became unworkable, prompting West to dissolve it.

In August 1671 Yeamans achieved his ambition when the proprietors commissioned him as governor; they were soon disillusioned with their choice. With the colony's food supply low, Yeamans imported provisions on the proprietors' account and sold them at exorbitant prices to the settlers, keeping the profits for himself. At the same time, the proprietors learned that Yeamans's "forward Grasping at the Government when [he] first came thither" had contributed to the emergence of political factions and instability in the colony. In April 1674 they decided to replace him as governor, but Yeamans died (probably in Charles Town) before their instructions reached Carolina.

Almost half of the settlers arriving in the first decade of Carolina's settlement were Barbadian, and Yeamans shared the motives of these early settlers. Spurred by the declining opportunities in Barbados, he was determined to make his fortune in Carolina. His use of political office to advance his own economic interests set an example that was to characterize Carolina's politics until the end of the proprietary period. He was one of the first Englishmen to import slaves in significant numbers, although the absence of a lucrative commercial crop in early Carolina prevented him from profiting from plantation slavery.

• Yeamans's father's will is in the Public Record Office, London. Yeamans's political career in Barbados may also be traced there in the Minutes of the Council of Barbados, 1654–1658. Papers relating to the settlement at Cape Fear are in Langdon Cheves, ed., *The Shaftesbury Papers, Collections of the South Carolina Historical Society*, vol. 5 (1897), and William L. Saunders, ed., *The Colonial Records of North Carolina* (10 vols., 1886–1890); the former also contains letters between Yeamans and the Carolina proprietors during his governorship from 1671 to 1674. For studies relating to the background of the settlement of Carolina and the colony's early history, see M. Eugene Sirmans, *Colonial South Carolina: A Political History, 1663–1763* (1966); Richard Waterhouse, *A New World Gentry: The Making of a Merchant and Planter Class in South Carolina, 1670–1770* (1989); Robert M. Weir, *Colonial South Carolina: A History* (1983); and Edward McCrady, *The History of South Carolina under the Proprietary Government, 1670–1719* (1901).

RICHARD WATERHOUSE

YEARDLEY, Sir George (July 1587–12 Nov. 1627), Virginia planter and governor, was born in the Southwark borough of London, England, the son of Ralph Yeardley, a member of the Merchant Taylors Guild, and Rhoda Marston. Apparently he was christened on 6 August. When his parents died in the plague of 1601, George became the ward of his godfather Sir Henry Peyton, a ship captain and one of the subscribers to the fund for colonizing Virginia. John Saris, his other godfather as well as a merchant and ship captain, established trade with Japan as an employee of the East India Company. Both were influential in Yeardley's life.

At about the age of fourteen Yeardley was sent to the Netherlands to serve a military apprenticeship under Captain Thomas Gates, a friend of Peyton's. In 1609 Yeardley sailed for Virginia as a captain with Gates, newly designated governor of the colony. They were shipwrecked in the Bermuda Islands in June and did not reach Virginia until the next May. This wreck is said to have been the inspiration for Shakespeare's *The Tempest*. In a military capacity, Yeardley served well in the colony under various leaders who were governors, presidents of the Council, or deputy governors. Finally, in April 1616 Yeardley became deputy governor himself, acting for the designated governor, Thomas West, Baron De La Warr, who spent most of his time in England. Yeardley served until 15 May 1617, when Samuel Argall succeeded him. Like others in similar positions, Yeardley took advantage of his situation to identify desirable land and to secure the services of apprentices or indentured servants. His subsequent preferment suggests that as deputy governor he was satisfactory to his superiors. The position also gave him an opportunity to begin laying the foundations for an extensive fortune.

Yeardley returned to England on the same ship that delivered Argall. While in London he met and after a brief courtship married Temperance Flowerdieu in 1617; they had three children. Experienced in Virginia affairs, he attended meetings and conferred with officers of the Virginia Company, which controlled the colony. Plans were laid for major reforms in Virginia to encourage more rapid settlement: abandonment of the former military-style rule, creation of a civil government, and expansion of the policy adopted in 1616 to end the company's monopoly on landholding and to award estates to individuals.

On 18 November 1618 Yeardley was appointed governor in his own right for a three-year term. Fresh instructions for the new governor were drawn up to implement the reforms that had been decided upon. This document came to be called the "Great Charter." It provided for representatives to be elected to an assembly to enact laws for the colony, the first such legislative body in an English colony. On 22 November King James I knighted Yeardley. As his secretary the new governor chose his wife's cousin, John Pory, a professional newsletter writer and former member of Parliament. Sir George undertook to recruit new colonists and to secure supplies for tenants on land reserved for the benefit of investors in the Virginia Company as well as on land that he soon acquired for himself. These and other tasks delayed the fleet until 19 January 1619, and it was not until 18 April that Yeardley formally assumed office in Jamestown. He issued orders for the planting of corn and grain for food before planting tobacco for trade. He also directed that armed guards continue to protect the colony and supervised work on the company's plantation.

In accordance with Yeardley's instruction, the settled region of Virginia was divided into plantations, called boroughs, each of which elected two delegates to the assembly. Under Governor Yeardley's guidance, the assembly chose Secretary Pory as its Speaker. Relying on his experience as a member of Parliament, Pory organized and conducted the first representative legislature in America, which convened on 30 July 1619. In that year, too, a shipload of women arrived from England as potential brides, for although there were married women in Virginia, many men were still single. Also in that year a Dutch trading ship brought the first Africans. It is not known whether they became indentured servants or slaves, but in either case Yeardley acquired the services of some of them for himself and for the company's plantation.

Yeardley took the lead in representing to the Virginia assembly the company's concern that the colony produce a broad range of products. Besides taking steps to prevent the growing of tobacco to the neglect of food crops, he encouraged the production of wine, silk, hemp, and flax. On the other hand, the governor protested to the company that it was sending colonists without notifying him in time to ready accommodations for them. Governor Yeardley's term of office expired on 18 November 1621, when he must have reflected with satisfaction that he had implemented the great reforms of 1619, including establishment of the assembly and the apportionment of land to individual owners.

Succeeded by Sir Francis Wyatt, Yeardley managed his 80,000-acre estate, "Flowerdieu Hundred," which provided him a good income and was the source of a considerable fortune. His was one of the privately owned "particular plantations" by which colonists were dispersed into the countryside. The consequent poor defense of the open country contributed to the losses in the Indian massacre of 1622. Yeardley's plantation was spared and he was able to furnish corn to the survivors.

In 1624 the Crown revoked the company's charter, thereby making Virginia a royal colony, but King James kept Wyatt in the post. In 1625 Yeardley went to London to petition for the continuation of the general assembly under the royal governor and to explain the pressing needs of the colony. Although his proposals were received with favor, he did not live to see the assembly reinstated. Following Wyatt's retirement on 28 July 1626, Yeardley received the royal nod and remained in office until his death but was not privileged to call an assembly. He died in Virginia, probably in Jamestown, and was buried there.

George Yeardley, virtually penniless when he went to Virginia, at his death eighteen years later was one of the wealthiest men in the colony. Some felt that he had

been excessively devoted to his own welfare, yet he had served as captain of the militia, a councilor, deputy governor, and governor, had implemented the elected legislature, and had contributed to relief measures following the Indian massacre of 1622.

• Susan M. Kingsbury, ed., *Records of the Virginia Company of London* (4 vols., 1906–1935), is the leading collection of primary sources concerning the early government and settlement of Virginia. Philip L. Barbour, ed., *The Complete Works of Captain John Smith (1580–1631)* (3 vols., 1986), is the most recent edition of Smith's writings, which are the source of much that is known about Virginia during the period under consideration and contain a great deal about Yeardley. William S. Powell, *John Pory, 1572–1636, the Life and Letters of a Man of Many Parts* (1977), includes transcripts of contemporary newsletters with many references to Yeardley. Alexander Brown, *The Genesis of the United States* (2 vols., 1890), reproduces many documents of the period. Edmund S. Morgan, *American Slavery, American Freedom: The Ordeal of Colonial Virginia* (1975), contains a careful account of conditions in the colony in the seventeenth century. James P. C. Southall, "Concerning George Yardley and Temperance Flowerdew," *Virginia Magazine of History and Biography*, July 1947, pp. 259–66, raises a number of interesting but speculative questions about the Yeardleys. Eric Gethyn-Jones, *George Thorpe and the Berkeley Company, a Gloucestershire Enterprise in Virginia* (1982), presents new information from both English and American sources on events in Virginia during the years that Yeardley was active there. Wesley Frank Craven, *Dissolution of the Virginia Company* (1932), has long been the principal source for an understanding of the factions within the company. Richard Beale Davis, *George Sandys, Poet-Adventurer* (1955), contains information on both the personal life and the official duties of Yeardley. Although Nora Miller Turman's *George Yeardley, Governor of Virginia* (1959) is in part fictionalized, it contains information based on research in contemporary records as well as a transcription of Yeardley's will.

WILLIAM S. POWELL

YEATMAN, James Erwin (27 Aug. 1818–7 July 1901), banker and philanthropist, was born in Bedford County, Tennessee, the son of Thomas Yeatman, a well-to-do banker and foundry owner, and Jane Patton Erwin. Yeatman attended the New Haven Commercial School and made a tour of Europe. He first worked in his father's business in Cumberland, Tennessee, but in 1842 went to St. Louis as the representative of this business. Yeatman quickly became a leader in the St. Louis business community. In 1850 he was a founder of the Merchants' Bank. In 1860, when the bank was reorganized as the Merchants' National Bank, he became its president, a post he held for thirty-five years. On 12 March 1849 he became one of the nine organizers and directors of the Missouri Pacific Railroad. Deeply involved in civic projects, he was a founder and the first president of the St. Louis Mercantile Library, which was established in 1846.

Yeatman's most important public service occurred during the Civil War. After the death of his father, Yeatman's mother had married John Bell, the Union ticket candidate for president in 1860, and Yeatman supported him. Yeatman, though thoroughly southern and a resident of a slave state, recoiled from the prospect of a sundered union. On 10 May 1861 a violent clash took place at Camp Jackson in St. Louis between secessionists and unionists led by Captain Nathaniel Lyon, an antisouthern Connecticut Yankee. After defeating the secessionists, Lyon's troops and volunteer German-American regiments were jeered by St. Louis civilians. After one of Lyon's officers was shot, his men fired into the crowd, killing twenty-eight. Lyon said that he would see "every man, woman, and child in the State dead and buried . . . " rather than concede to secession. In an effort to preserve peace in Missouri after the Camp Jackson affair, Yeatman went to Washington with Union governor Hamilton R. Gamble to recommend to President Abraham Lincoln a policy of reconciliation and the transfer of Lyon out of Missouri. The president, though impressed, was persuaded by Francis P. Blair, a founder of the Republican party and an adviser to Lincoln, to retain Lyon and promote him to brigadier general. Nevertheless, Yeatman firmly adhered to the Union. In *The Crisis* (1905), which was set in St. Louis during the Civil War, Winston Churchill, the St. Louis novelist who married Yeatman's niece, Mable Hall, admittedly based his character "Calvin Brinsmade" on Yeatman. Although southern in outlook, Yeatman, like Brinsmade, remained faithful to the Union at the outbreak of the war, and his example was very helpful to the Union cause in Missouri.

Yeatman served as an adviser to President Lincoln. He was appointed president of the Western Sanitary Commission, set up by Major General John C. Frémont in St. Louis on 5 September 1861 to coordinate medical service and relief work. As president of the commission, Yeatman devoted himself effectively and tirelessly to setting up hospitals and medical service for the Union army, founding homes for orphans and disabled soldiers, and improving the sanitary conditions and diet in prisons. To soldiers he was known as "Old Sanitary." Under his administration the Western Sanitary Commission outfitted the first railroad hospital cars and in 1862 put the first Mississippi River hospital boat into service.

In 1863 Yeatman went down the river to inspect the conditions of freed slaves. Yeatman, a former slave owner, formulated a plan that became the basis for the Freedmen's Bureau. In his report he recommended the leasing of abandoned plantations to freed slaves. In 1864 he was summoned to Washington and so impressed Lincoln that the president asked him to head the Freedmen's Bureau. Yeatman, however, declined the offer.

Yeatman's exemplary public service continued after the war. He was president of the Soldiers' Orphans' Home; director of the Working Women's Home; trustee and director of the Blind Girls' Home, the Colored Orphans' Home, and a training school for nurses; and a trustee of the Home for the Friendless, the Home for Aged Men and the Home for Aged Men and Their Wives. He was also secretary and trustee of St. Louis Medical College, a trustee and benefactor of Washington University, and an original trustee of Henry Shaw's Missouri Botanical Garden.

Yeatman's kindness and benevolence were exceptional and characterized his private as well as public life. According to Churchill, he personally served as "banker" to hundreds of poor women, domestic servants, and female factory workers whose meager savings he held and safeguarded. He gratuitously provided this service and even supplemented the savings of his "clients" from his own pocket. For forty years he stuffed his pockets with candy to distribute to children as he returned to his home in the evening.

In 1838 Yeatman married Angelica Charlotte Thompson of Alexandria, Virginia. She died in 1849, and in 1851 he married Cynthia Ann Pope of Kaskaskia, Illinois. In 1854 his second wife died. He had five children. Yeatman died in St. Louis and was buried in Bellefontaine Cemetery, for which he had served as a trustee and president. He had given so much to charity that he left little other than his personal library. Churchill said that he "had spent two fortunes on charity in the public good, and he died a poor man" (*American Review of Reviews*, p. 187).

• Printed and limited archival material on Yeatman is housed at the Missouri Historical Society in St. Louis. Information on Yeatman's work on the Western Sanitary Commission is in his *Report to the Western Sanitary Commission* (1864) and *Report to the Western Sanitary Commission in Regard to Leasing Abandoned Plantations, with Rules and Regulations Governing the Same* (1864). Both are located in the Library of Congress; the latter is available on microform. Printed reports of the commission that were compiled under the administration of Yeatman also are located in the Library of Congress. See: *Report to the Western Sanitary Commission on the General Military Hospitals of St. Louis, Mo.* (1862), *Report of the Western Sanitary Commission for the Year Ending June 1st, 1863* (1863), and *Report of the Western Sanitary Commission, on the White Union Refugees of the South, Their Persecutions, Sufferings, Destitute Condition, and the Necessity of Giving Aid and Relief on Their Coming to Our Military Posts* (1864). Secondary information on the commission is in Jacob Gilbert Foreman, *The Western Sanitary Commission: A Sketch of Its Origin, History, Labors for the Sick and Wounded of the Western Armies, and Aid Given to Freedmen and Union Refugees, with Incidents of Hospital Life* (1864), and William Romaine Hodges, *The Western Sanitary Commission and What It Did for the Sick and Wounded of the Union Armies from 1861 to 1865* (1906). See also J. Thomas Scharf, *History of St. Louis City and County* (1883); James Cox, *Old and New St. Louis* (1894); Ernest Kirschten, *Catfish and Crystal* (1960); and William E. Parish, *Turbulent Partnership: Missouri and the Union, 1861–1865* (1963). Obituaries are in the *St. Louis Post-Dispatch*, 7, 8, 9 July 1901, and the *St. Louis Globe-Democrat*, 27 Dec. 1901; and "A Great Citizen—James E. Yeatman," which draws on the novelist Winston Churchill, appeared in *American Review of Reviews* 24 (Aug. 1901): 186–87.

BERNARD A. COOK

YEATMAN, Thomas (25 Dec. 1787–12 June 1833), merchant and banker, was born in Brownsville, Pennsylvania, the son of John Yeatman, a ship and boat builder on the Potomac and Monongahela rivers, and Lucy Patty. Very little is known of Yeatman's early life. He arrived in Nashville about 1807 and probably soon became a river trader. W. W. Clayton, in *History of Davidson County* (1880), records a Yeatman among Nashville's early merchants. By 1815–1817 Yeatman was sufficiently wealthy to buy land for warehouses and offices on the waterfront and in the public square.

Yeatman Woods, the partnership that Yeatman formed with Nashville merchants Joseph and Robert Woods in the early 1820s, dispatched cotton and tobacco southwards from Nashville down the Cumberland and imported all types of manufactures and provisions from New Orleans, Pittsburgh, and Philadelphia. This trade opened after 1815, and the first steamboat up to Nashville, the *General Jackson*, arrived in June 1819. The Woods owned the *Rifleman*, the second boat up to Nashville, that arrived in February 1820. Yeatman was agent for the *General Jackson*'s second voyage in 1820–1821, just before it sank on the Harpeth shoals below the city. At first the river trade was very profitable, despite the hazards, but profits fell rapidly as more vessels arrived. However, although Yeatman moved out of steamboats in the 1820s, his family and the Woods continued to have interests in steamboats until the mid-1840s. They would therefore have been able to assist the trading house when necessary.

Yeatman Woods, as commission merchants and steamboat operators, had excellent opportunities to speculate. The partners soon established good contacts in New Orleans and the eastern ports. They made their fortune, probably in 1825, when "Mr Yeatman happened to be in Philadelphia. News came from Europe of a heavy advance in cotton. Mr Yeatman, on horseback beat the mail and express to Nashville, and brought all the cotton there at twelve and a half cents. His brother, Preston Yeatman, living in Huntsville, bought all there. Cotton soon advanced to twenty five cents a pound. . . . They then sold out their warehouse and steamboats . . . and went to banking, and commenced building the Cumberland Iron works" (Clayton, p. 203). No records exist to confirm this account. However, Yeatman Woods had created a private bank in the early 1820s to take advantage of the general credit shortage in Tennessee, and this absorbed their energies in the late 1820s.

They succeeded so well that in the early 1830s they became the leading correspondents in the South of the Barings and the Browns, the two most powerful Anglo-American houses of the day. Thomas Yeatman requested credits from the Barings in 1830 in order to speculate against regular seasonal changes in the sterling dollar rates and to make advances to planters. The Barings' New Orleans correspondent reported that Yeatman knew all the planters in middle Tennessee and regularly advanced on 25,000 to 30,000 bales of cotton. The correspondent wrote that Yeatman "appears a very shrewd intelligent man, is unceasing in his application to his business . . . and apparently extremely economical." However, although the Barings did offer Yeatman large credits, Yeatman's business with them did not expand. Instead, in 1831–1833,

Yeatman regularly borrowed from Alexander Brown of Baltimore even larger sums, up to £50,000 to £60,000—or $250,000 to $300,000—against equivalent security. These credits were then distributed to factors and planters who paid commissions and consigned the cotton to Brown's Liverpool house. Alexander Brown commented to his partners in Liverpool that Yeatman Woods were very "prompt pleasant people to do business with."

Banks were a major issue in Tennessee politics in the 1820s. Chartered banks generally were blamed for the panic of 1819 and consequently were restricted in the 1820s. Yeatman Woods, being private, was relatively untouched, and before the Nashville branch of the Second Bank of the United States was established in 1827, it was sometimes the only effective bank. Yeatman met the new competition through his alliance with the Browns and by reportedly keeping "spies upon it, & in it, and upon its frds [friends], the leaders." He did not, however, escape unscathed. In 1825 the State Bank party, supported by Andrew Jackson, attempted to outlaw private banks. Yeatman was successfully defended by Governor William Carroll and the probank merchants' party led by Andrew Erwin, Yeatman's father-in-law. John P. Erwin, Andrew's son and later mayor of Nashville, reported to Henry Clay, his brother-in-law, that "A violent effort was made to put down Mr. Yeatman's bank—We think the Old Genl. wished it done, Mr Y being the son in law of a man he very much disliked." Yeatman in turn opposed Jackson. He was willing to support "anything that will serve that great and good man Henry Clay, or that will injure and perplex Jackson, or any of his wicked and rascally adherents." Yeatman's family was thus central in contemporary Tennessee politics, but he himself claimed to despise "the vain and giddy fashions of polished society."

Thomas Yeatman's other new business was the Cumberland Iron Works. Charcoal-fired iron had been smelted in Tennessee since 1790, especially in Stewart County on the Cumberland below Nashville. Yeatman had inquired about the markets for iron castings and the availability of iron managers in Philadelphia in 1824. Between 1828 and 1832 Yeatman Woods built two large furnaces and rolling mills at Dover and Bear Springs in Stewart County. The firm's immediate need for iron castings was to meet demand from the Nashville market for steamboat construction and to fulfill a city waterworks contract. By 1832 Yeatman Woods had acquired thousands of acres of forest and was shipping iron to Nashville, Memphis, Vicksburg, New Orleans, and even Pittsburgh. The firm spent more than $100,000 annually on labor and supplies. In 1834 the works were worth about $350,000 and in the middle 1830s owned or hired nearly 500 slaves and produced about 6,000 tons of iron annually.

When Thomas Yeatman died suddenly of cholera on the steamboat *Mount Vernon* on the Ohio, he was well advanced in creating a large diversified enterprise grouped around the Yeatman Woods bank. He had become one of the leading bankers and richest men in the South, and he left about $500,000. He was married twice, first in 1814 to Martha Beckwith, by whom he had one son before her death in 1815. In 1817 he married Jane Erwin, by whom he had three boys and two girls. Three years after his death Jane Yeatman married John Bell, who opposed Jackson's bank policy in Congress and who ran against Abraham Lincoln in 1860. Yeatman's assets were effectively divided in court and by agreement among his children, the Bells, and the Woods. The bank was destroyed by the financial crises of 1837–1839, but the families operated the furnaces until the 1870s.

• Few of Thomas Yeatman's personal or business papers survived his early death and the demise of the firm, but his career can be re-created from surrounding records. The Yeatman-Polk manuscripts in the Tennessee State Archives in Nashville provide family background. Early Nashville city, court, and tax records list Yeatman, the Woods, and the Erwins among Nashville's leading merchants, bankers, and property owners. Late nineteenth-century surveys such as John Woolridge's compendious *History of Nashville* (1890) and Clayton's *History of Davidson County* confirm their economic and political importance and recount local myths. Numerous middle Tennessee planters' papers demonstrate their role as factors. Accounts of the river trade, for instance Byrd Douglass, *Steamboatin' on the Cumberland* (1961), document their steamboat interests.

Baring Brothers records in London and Alexander Brown's letter-books in the Library of Congress describe their international financial operations. The published correspondence of Henry Clay, Andrew Jackson, and James K. Polk, and, for instance, C. G. Sellers, "Banking and Politics in Jackson's Tennessee, 1817–1827," *Mississippi Valley Historical Review* 41 (1954–1955): 61–84, reveal Yeatman's political and social relations. The partners' iron business is described in G. Troost, *Fifth Geological Report to the Twenty-third General Assembly of Tennessee* (1840), and in the family papers. Jane Erwin Yeatman's marriage to John Bell, the division of Yeatman's assets, and the later history of the Yeatman and Woods families are described in Joseph H. Parks, *John Bell of Tennessee* (1950), and in the family records.

J. R. KILLICK

YEHOASH (Mar. 1870–10 Jan. 1927), Yiddish poet, was born Solomon Bloomgarden in Lithuania, the son of Caleb Bloomgarden, a Talmudic scholar, and Dobre-Chave. Yehoash received a traditional education for a Russian Jew of his time, including intensive religious instruction and training in Hebrew lore, as well as unusually ample exposure to secular literature and philosophy. He attended the highly renowned Volozhin Yeshiva as a teenager and during that period also taught himself to read in English. He began reading world literature in the original, and at age eighteen he translated a group of poems by Byron into Yiddish. This translating exercise proved satisfactory to Yehoash and formative as well. Pleased with his work, he sent the translations to the famous Yiddish poet I. L. Peretz. Peretz praised his work and had the translations published in his anthology, *Yiddish Bibliotek*.

Perhaps still unsure about pursuing a career as a writer in Russia and fearing conscription in the Russian army, Yehoash left his hometown for New York City in 1890. There Yehoash took odd jobs, including a stint working in a glass factory and teaching Hebrew lessons. Life was difficult for new immigrants during this period. The changes were dizzying, and the young man wrote little.

In 1900 Yehoash contracted acute tuberculosis, a diagnosis that proved momentous to the poet. He was sent by doctors to a Jewish sanitarium in Denver and placed in the hands of Dr. Charles Spivak. In Denver Yehoash found inspiration and encouragement for his poetry. The sublime Rocky Mountains gave Yehoash cause to meditate on nature and man's place in it. Also, he found more time for solitude in the mountains than he had in New York, and his poetry grew more contemplative. In 1907 Yehoash published a volume of new and original verse in Yiddish, and in 1911, with Dr. Spivak as his collaborator, he published a dictionary of Hebrew and Aramaic terms in Yiddish.

Yehoash's early work stands out as unique among contemporaneous Yiddish poetry for its outstanding display of poetic form. Yehoash was especially prosodic when compared with the rest of the mostly autodidactic Yiddish poets of the age who knew little about the rigors of rhythm and meter. In contrast, Yehoash's early poetry is dexterous with iambs and trochees, imaginative with line lengths and stanza composition.

Concurrent with his poetic endeavors, Yehoash lived an active and social life in Denver. He recovered fairly well with Dr. Spivak's care and so was inspired to found the Jewish Consumptive Relief Society, providing help to many Jewish victims of tuberculosis in the 1900s. In 1903 Yehoash married Flora Smirnow, and they had one daughter, Evelyn.

In 1909 Yehoash's health was sufficiently restored for him to return to New York with his new family. Yehoash continued to write, mostly articles and poetry for Yiddish newspapers. In 1913 he collected his recent poems into one volume and published it under the title *Through the Mist and Sunshine*. In this collection Yehoash continues his dedication to poetic form while maintaining the sublime note present in his earlier verse. There are many lively lyrics that partake of the pastoral tradition, and a number of poems mourn for lost love.

Yehoash moved again in 1914, this time to Palestine to prepare for what is now considered his greatest literary achievement, the translation of the Hebrew Bible into Yiddish. The poet quickly immersed himself in the lore and language of the land. He wrote stories, translated sections of the Koran into Yiddish, and studied Biblical Hebrew intensively. The outbreak of World War I and its ensuing dangers forced Yehoash to return to New York in 1917 prior to completing his work.

Upon his return from Palestine Yehoash continued his translation project while producing a prodigious amount of poetry. He earned a living through publishing in Yiddish journals and was able to secure a contract with *Der Tog* to serialize a narrative of his travel experiences in Palestine. This was later published in

Yiddish in a two-volume text titled *To Rehovoth and Back*.

During the last decade of his life Yehoash wrote highly sensitive lyric poetry, as well as fables and nature poems. These were published in several volumes and were widely read by the Yiddish community, who saw Yehoash by then as a dean of contemporary Yiddish poetry. His most important endeavor at the end of his life was his intensive work on his translation of the Hebrew Bible. The poet worked feverishly, eventually dedicating all his time to his translations. His goal was not just to complete the translation but to capture every nuance of the original Hebrew, to communicate all the beauty and conundrums into Yiddish.

In the end the project became a group effort. With his failing health diminishing his capacity to work, Yehoash knew that he was in a race against time to finish his translation before he died. In 1923 he expressed the urgency of his effort: "Joy is no longer for me. I have only one interest, and that is to complete my work. Perhaps even more in the *completion* than in the work itself . . . I work, Flora works, and I have harnessed others" (Madison, p. 169). By the time Yehoash died in New York City, he had finished his translations and commentaries; Flora edited the text and published it shortly after.

In addition to leaving a legacy of fine and original poetry, Yehoash is responsible for fostering a florescence of Yiddish poetry in New York. He encouraged young poets to write and helped many publish their work. More significantly, Yehoash's translations of Longfellow, Byron, and the Hebrew Bible added greatly to the Yiddish language.

• Interested readers can find Yehoash's *To Rehovoth and Back* translated into English under the title *The Feet of the Messenger* (1923). Charles A. Madison, *Yiddish Literature: Its Scope and Major Writers* (1968), contains a useful overview of Yehoash's poetry, nicely contextualizing his place in the Yiddish canon. Sol Liptzin's treatment of Yehoash in *A History of Yiddish Literature* (1985) is more condensed, while treating the subject of Yiddish literature in general comprehensively. A. A. Roback credits Yehoash for the inspiration to write *The Story of Yiddish Literature* (1940), and the poet receives a careful review in that book.

DEAN JOSEPH FRANCO

YELL, Archibald (9 Aug. 1797?–23 Feb. 1847), attorney, was born in Jefferson County, Tennessee, the son of Moses Yell, a yeoman farmer, and Jane Curry. Archibald, named for his maternal grandfather, received a limited education and gained his first public distinction by enlisting in the U.S. Army during the War of 1812. He served in the Second Regiment of Tennessee Mounted Volunteer Gunmen, saw action first in Andrew Jackson's campaign against the Creek Indians, then at the battle of Pensacola, and finally at the battle of New Orleans. He was promoted to sergeant before the war was over. During the next two years he served in the Forty-seventh Tennessee Militia, earning the rank of captain, then reenlisted in the U.S. Army in 1818, as a lieutenant, to participate in the Seminole

War. After that war he returned to Shelbyville, studied law, and opened a practice with William Gilchrist, his former teacher. In 1821 he married Mary Scott, the daughter of a neighboring farmer, but fourteen months later she died while giving birth to twins. One of those children also died. In 1827 he married Ann "Nancy" Jordan Moore; they had four children.

In the 1820s Yell also became actively involved in the Freemasonry movement; state politics, supporting Jackson's gubernatorial and presidential campaigns; and developed a close friendship with future president James K. Polk. Through Polk, Yell kept Jackson informed as to friend and foe, identified which of the president's policies were popular or unpopular, and also sought political appointments for his own friends. In 1827 Yell was elected to the Tennessee legislature, where he remained for three years before his involvement in a much publicized public brawl forced him to retire. Jackson then appointed him, in December 1831, as receiver for the Little Rock branch of the U.S. Land Office. In less than a year, malaria forced him to resign that position and return to Tennessee.

In 1835 Jackson appointed Yell circuit judge of Arkansas's northern district. In this more healthful climate he quickly earned a reputation for fairness on the bench and involvement in civic activities. Although not an "insider" with the territory's political leaders, his personal charisma made him a formidable politician, and he resigned his judgeship to run for the congressional seat when Arkansas was admitted as a state in 1836. He won election, but his freshman year was undistinguished. Due to the timing of Arkansas's entrance into the Union, Yell had to stand for reelection in 1837. Opponents criticized him for being absent from the House during critical debates on issues involving slavery. Even so, he was easily reelected but did not seek a second full term in 1838. Instead, he actively promoted real estate sales in the newly organized town of Ozark in Franklin County and was a leading member of the newly chartered Masonic lodge in Fayetteville.

Yell also planned for the 1840 gubernatorial campaign. In that race he easily defeated the Whig candidate, David Walker, his former business associate in the Ozark real estate market. As governor, Yell frequently clashed with state legislators. A major fight developed over Yell's demand for an investigation of the state's banking practices, but he also angered legislators when he opposed their efforts to be paid in specie rather than Arkansas paper money. Perhaps in response to these controversies, the general assembly killed Yell's key campaign proposal, a free public school system, by refusing to appropriate funds for the program. Yell's third marriage, in 1840 to Maria Ficklin, a widow, followed Ann's death. They had no children, and Ficklin also died before Yell.

Rather than seeking a second term for governor in 1844, Yell decided to campaign for his old seat in Congress. That his close friend James Polk was running for the presidency that year may have influenced his decision. He was reelected, but his political career was again interrupted with the outbreak of the Mexican War. Yell resigned his position in the House and returned to Arkansas to enlist as a volunteer in a hastily organized militia regiment. He was elected colonel and accompanied the unit to northern Mexico to join General Zachary Taylor's command. A few weeks later Yell was killed at the battle of Buena Vista while leading a charge against a Mexican lancer unit.

• Extensive correspondence by Yell during his public career is in the presidential papers of James K. Polk. The standard biography on Yell is William W. Hughes, *Archibald Yell* (1988). Additional biographical material is in Timothy P. Donovan and Williard B. Gatewood, eds., *The Governors of Arkansas: Essays in Political Biography* (1981); John Hallum, *Biographical and Pictorial History of Arkansas*, vol. 1 (1887); Fay Hempstead, *A Pictorial History of Arkansas: From Earliest Time to the Year 1890* (1890); and Hempstead, *Historical Review of Arkansas* (1911).

C. FRED WILLIAMS

YELLIN, Samuel (2 Mar. 1885–3 Oct. 1940), metalsmith, was born in Mogilev, in the province of Galicia, Poland, the son of Zacharias Yellin, a lawyer, and Kate Weintraub. Apprenticed at around age twelve to a blacksmith, Yellin became a master by seventeen. From about 1901 to 1905 he traveled and worked in ornamental metal workshops in Germany, Belgium, and England. In 1906 Yellin immigrated to Philadelphia, where from 1907 to 1919 he taught a course in wrought iron at the Pennsylvania Museum School of Industrial Art. By 1909 he had established a small shop in Philadelphia and was showing examples of his ironwork designs to architects such as Cass Gilbert, Bertram Goodhue, and C. Frank LaFarge, who in 1911 commissioned Yellin to fabricate the gates for J. P. Morgan's estate on Long Island.

In 1913 Yellin married Leah Josephs, with whom he would have two children. The Yellins lived in Wynnewood, Pennsylvania. In 1924 Yellin became an American citizen, and in 1925 he was the recipient of the Philadelphia Civic Award established by Edward W. Bok.

In 1915 Yellin opened a large shop in Philadelphia, where he employed as many as 200 workers and executed many large-scale commissions in the form of grilles, gates, railings, lighting fixtures, and door hardware, as well as miscellaneous decorative accessories of every description. His commissions included the Federal Reserve Bank of New York (1923) and Philadelphia (1932); the National Cathedral, Washington, D.C. (1927–1934); the McKinlock Memorial gates, Northwestern University (1927); and architectural ironwork for Bryn Mawr College (1926), Yale (1927–1932), Princeton (1928), Harvard (1930–1931), and for the Universities of Pennsylvania (1927), Pittsburgh (1936), Michigan (1930–1932), and Virginia (1938)—a prodigious body of decorative ironwork that enriched a wide variety of architectural forms and won him the respect and admiration of architects and builders alike.

Yellin collaborated with prominent Beaux-Arts architects, who gave him free reign to improvise, incorporating new ideas within a framework of familiar European stylistic traditions in which he felt totally at ease. He believed and taught that blacksmiths should study these traditions and that they should be thoroughly grounded in all aspects of iron fabrication. His accomplishments in the sphere of ornamental ironwork constitute a virtual compendium of forms in the medium, resplendently a part of a myriad of structures: ecclesiastical buildings, universities, banks, libraries, museums, and private residences from coast to coast in forty-five states. Yellin both designed and executed his creations, and the craftsmen who worked with him were well versed in the techniques required to carry out his variations on traditional motifs. Yellin's innovative approach to design was revealed in his writings and lectures as well as his commissioned work. He enjoyed harmonious relations with architects and contractors primarily because he paid strict attention to the practical requirements of a commission, providing detailed measurements and full-scale working drawings in addition to models, what he called "sketches in iron."

Widely recognized for his artistic achievements, Yellin received the Art Institute of Chicago Award in 1918, the American Institute of Architects Award in 1920, and the Gold Medal Award from the Architectural League of New York in 1922. In 1930 he was given the Alumni Medal from the Pennsylvania Museum School of Industrial Art. In 1936 Yellin was appointed a visiting professor of design and craftsmanship at the University of Pennsylvania School of Fine Arts, and he also was an adviser to the Philadelphia Museum of Art. In 1927 the Metropolitan Museum of Art made two films of the blacksmith working at his forge. Yellin died of a heart attack in New York City.

During three decades of intensive work, Samuel Yellin achieved a rebirth of ornamental wrought ironwork parallel to, but independent of, contemporary developments of the craft in Europe. His work, imbued with qualities strongly his own, showed, in numerous important commissions, Yellin's complete grasp of the styles of earlier periods and his absolute technical mastery. No matter what the historical style he was working in, Yellin's broad range of technical expertise and visual knowledge allowed him to create forms of notable variety that depended specifically on the structure's requirements. His subtle decorative flourishes thus enriched every architectural ensemble of which his work was a part.

Yellin was by disposition inclined toward monumental effects and scale that expressed a sturdy, robust grandeur. However, if the commission so demanded, his creations could be understated, of lacy and intricate profile. Despite a pervasive sense of elaborate workmanship that is bound up in the medium itself, Yellin's works were not merely functional, not just surface ornament, but served a forceful, intentional role in rhythmically punctuating the architectural elements of the structure. In so doing, his iron stimulates our perceptions of the greater whole, of its space, scale, and atmosphere.

Samuel Yellin was a man of convictions, boundless energy, masterful organizational skill, and creative talent. His tangible legacy, today admired and studied by younger American blacksmiths, constitutes his most important contribution to the age-old traditions of blacksmithing, the living craft of which he was so decisively and proudly a part.

• Documentation and photographs of commissions, correspondence, and 4,000 drawings and sketches are on microfilm (12 reels, nos. 3595–601 and 3913–17) in the Archives of American Art, Smithsonian Institution. For Yellin's views on metalsmithing see his "Iron in Art," *Encyclopedia Britannica*, 14th ed., vol. 12 (1929), pp. 679–81. See also Myra Tolmach Davis, *Sketches in Iron: Samuel Yellin, American Master of Wrought Iron, 1885–1940* (1971), which includes a bibliography; Richard J. Wattenmaker, *Samuel Yellin in Context* (1985); Harvey Z. Yellin, "Samuel Yellin: 1885–1940," *Anvil's Ring* 13 (Fall 1985): 10–13; Edward S. Cooke, Jr., *The Art That Is Life: The Arts & Crafts Movement in America, 1875–1920*, catalog of the Museum of Fine Arts, Boston (1987), pp. 137–38; Vincent Scully, *Samuel Yellin: Metalwork at Yale* (1990); and Jack Andrews, *Samuel Yellin, Metalworker* (1992), which includes a list of commissions, 1912–1940. An obituary is in the *New York Times*, 4 Oct. 1940.

RICHARD J. WATTENMAKER

YELLOWLEY, Edward Clements (12 Aug. 1873–8 Feb. 1962), federal Prohibition and Internal Revenue administrator, was born on a plantation near Ridgeland, Mississippi, the son of James Brownlow Yellowley, a lawyer and planter, and Jessie Perkins. His parents belonged to the antebellum plantation aristocracy and were financially devastated by the Civil War. The family moved to a plantation near Greenville, North Carolina, during his childhood. Best known as E. C., Yellowley attended a military academy in 1888 and subsequently operated his father's plantation. He married Mary Helms about 1896; she died childless two years later.

Yellowley joined the Bureau of Internal Revenue in 1899 as a revenue collector in Mississippi. At that time the bureau's chief responsibility was the collection of alcohol taxes, and Yellowley apprehended moonshiners in Tennessee and pursued rumrunners in Florida. Other assignments took him by 1919 to San Antonio, Philadelphia, St. Paul, Atlanta, and San Francisco. Promotions accompanied transfers, first to collector in charge in 1907 and to agent in charge in 1910. His excellent administrative abilities earned him a transfer to Washington, D.C., in 1919 to create a field audit system for the bureau's income and estate tax units. The next year he was back in San Francisco as Internal Revenue's regional supervisor. In 1912 he married Callie H. Gibbons, who died in 1927. This marriage was also childless.

With the adoption of the Eighteenth Amendment in 1920, which banned the production and sale of alcoholic beverages, Congress created the Prohibition Bureau to assist local law enforcement, under the super-

vision of Internal Revenue. Yellowley served a brief stint as acting director of Prohibition in New York City in 1920 but returned to Washington, D.C., in 1921 to become chief of special Prohibition agents who were assigned to those areas where enforcement lagged. His first deployment was to New York City, which he promised to "dry up." Within months twenty-six local agents were dismissed. Hotels and restaurants suspected of selling liquor were closely watched, and violators were prosecuted. Liquor imported from abroad by ship or across the Canadian border was interdicted—the latter effort was aided once U.S. Customs began notifying Yellowley of duties assessed on incoming alcohol. His work more than doubled the price of illegal whiskey to $20 a quart.

From 1923 until 1925 Yellowley and his unit were headquartered in Washington, D.C., from which he traveled to almost every state. When a reorganization of the Prohibition Bureau in 1925 replaced Yellowley's national unit with twenty-four federal enforcement districts, he was assigned to the challenging Chicago office. There Yellowley's New York tactics confronted the power and political influence of Al Capone, who had built a $100-million-a-year bootlegging empire. Capone's combination of bribery and violence frustrated Yellowley. Through an aide, Yellowley secured the efforts of agent Eliot Ness to recruit special agents immune to blandishments. The resulting unit became popularized as the "Untouchables."

Yellowley left Prohibition enforcement in 1930 when the bureau was transferred from the Treasury to the Justice Department, but he remained in Chicago to become supervisor of liquor permits in the area. Four years later, after Prohibition's repeal, he became Chicago regional supervisor of the alcohol tax unit at Internal Revenue. By 1939 his district included more than 164 million gallons of liquor in Internal Revenue–bonded warehouses and nearly 37,000 retail outlets. Although attacks on bootleg alcohol remained a responsibility, his more permanent legacy was in designing a model system for the collection of federal liquor taxes. Some 300 agents were working under his direction when he retired in 1946. He continued to live in a downtown Chicago hotel until his death.

Yellowley was known as a superb administrator and an incorruptible agent. It was said he could judge an agent's honesty by looking him in the eye. Zealous in his enforcement of Prohibition, he disguised his agents to fit the situation. They posed as truck drivers and garment workers and even donned formal attire for New Year's celebrations in cabarets. Izzie Einstein and Moe Smith, legendary for their use of disguises, worked for Yellowley in New York City. His zeal earned him many enemies. Restaurant managers complained it was impossible to intercept flasks smuggled in by patrons. A Detroit attorney sued Yellowley in 1925 for false arrest in a cabaret raid.

Apprehending bootleggers and imbibers was not Yellowley's only concern. He was also responsible for ensuring that alcohol manufactured for legal purposes—medical, sacramental, and industrial—was not di-verted to illicit uses. Yellowley allegedly refused a $250,000 bribe from a Chicago alcohol plant operator to overlook irregularities. He also sought to close loopholes in the law by restricting physicians in New York from prescribing alcohol as a tonic and by arresting rabbis for allegedly selling wine illegally.

Yellowley's accomplishments can best be appreciated within the context of his working environment. The Prohibition Bureau was noted for the low caliber and frequent turnover of its personnel and for political influence from various quarters. Yellowley advised his state directors that job applicants "secure congressional endorsement, endorsement of the Anti-Saloon League, and other endorsements" (quoted in John Kobler, *Ardent Spirits: The Rise and Fall of Prohibition* [1974], p. 275). Yellowley's knowledge of a "sting" operation to purchase and transport Canadian liquor aroused the ire of New York congressman Fiorello La Guardia in 1927. When retired general Lincoln C. Andrews, the bureau's third director in five years, sought in 1925 to eliminate political influence (and Yellowley's position) as part of his reorganization of the agency, Congress forced his resignation within two years. Yellowley's survival and his support by some temperance groups to succeed Andrews in 1927 attest to his political acumen as well as to his considerable abilities. He remained steadfast in his faith in enforcement. "'Any law can be enforced,' he avow[ed] smilingly, 'if the administrators of enforcement of the legislation are 100 per cent behind it'" (*Wichita Beacon*, 28 Jan. 1940).

• In the National Archives, the Presidential Appointment Files in the General Records of the Treasury Department (RG 56) contain two files for Yellowley, including the pages of recommendations when he was being considered for promotion in 1926 and in 1940. Records of the Internal Revenue Service (RG 58) include General Correspondence of the Prohibition Unit, 1925–1930, and *may* contain information on Yellowley's career. There are no secondary works on Prohibition that discuss Yellowley's career at length. Information on Yellowley is in the *Chicago Tribune*, 30 Apr., 22 Aug., and 5 Sept. 1925, 24 Dec. 1926, and 11 Aug. 1960; the *Chicago Daily Journal*, 5 Apr. 1926; the *Chicago Daily News*, 22–23 Mar. and 31 Dec. 1927; and the *New York Times*, 17, 24 Feb., 9 Mar., and 15 July 1927, 2 and 11 Feb. 1930, and 31 July 1934. For a general background of federal problems in enforcing Prohibition, see Andrew Sinclair, *Era of Excess: A Social History of the Prohibition Movement* (1962). Obituaries are in the *Chicago Daily News* and the *Chicago American*, both 8 Feb. 1962, and in the *Chicago Sun-Times*, the *Chicago Tribune*, and the *New York Times*, all 9 Feb. 1962.

LLOYD L. SPONHOLTZ

YERGER, William (22 Nov. 1816–7 June 1872), lawyer and judge, was born in Lebanon, Tennessee, the son of Edwin Michael Yerger and Margaret Shall. Yerger graduated from the University of Nashville in 1833 and shortly thereafter was admitted to the bar. In 1837 he married Malvina Hogan Rucks; they had twelve children. In 1838 they moved to Jackson, Mississippi, where Yerger built one of the most lucrative legal practices in the state. He was, in fact, one of the leaders of the Mississippi bar until his death. His practice was eclectic: at the 1847 term of the state supreme court, for instance, he argued cases that involved both the validity of a contract for the sale of a slave (*Adams v. Rowan*) and the proper construction of a state charter of a railroad (*Donnaher v. State*). His legal eminence led him only once to the High Court of Errors and Appeals, in 1851, the year of the resignation of the court's chief justice, William Lewis Sharkey, a man with whom Yerger shared much in common.

Like Sharkey, Yerger abhorred repudiation by state banks. Repudiation of obligations, suspension of payments, and bankruptcies were all too common after the destruction of the Second Bank of the United States in the 1830s. Elected to the state supreme court in 1851, Yerger wrote a strong concurring opinion that upheld the liability of the state for bonds issued to the Mississippi Union Bank (*State v. Johnson* [1853]). Fully realizing the political implications, he wrote, "As judges, it is our duty to declare the law, not to make it. Reasons of State policy or political expediency should not influence our judgment." Despite his claim to disinterested judgment, the opinion cost him reelection to the court by the populace in 1853. Within the area of slave law, Yerger also mirrored a view of Sharkey's, which was that slaves ought to receive due process like any free defendant. In *Van Buren (a slave) v. State* (1852), for instance, Yerger overturned the conviction of a slave because the confession on which it was based was "obtained under the influence of fear, arising from . . . whipping." From 1853 to the secession crisis of 1860–1861 Yerger resumed his law practice and, on occasion, appeared in some crucial cases. In 1856, for instance, he successfully argued a significant political case, *Green v. Weller*, which involved the legislative abolition of superior courts of chancery. It was a hotly contested case, and Yerger presented the oral argument on behalf of abolishing the courts.

Politically, Yerger was a Whig. By the time of secession he, again in tandem with Sharkey, was a strong Unionist and opponent of the withdrawal of Mississippi. Later, like Sharkey, he worked to bring the state back into the Union as early as the fall of Vicksburg. He and Sharkey, however, differed in their relationship to the Confederate government. Yerger did not refuse to cooperate with the Confederacy as did Sharkey and, in fact, he served in the Mississippi Confederate legislature and was president of the senate of that body at the end of the war. He was closely associated with the "Peace party" that sought a restoration to the Union based on the Constitution.

During Reconstruction Yerger became even more prominent within Mississippi. He was chosen to go to Washington, along with Sharkey and Thomas Wharton, a secessionist Democrat (who declined the appointment), to confer with President Andrew Johnson about the terms for the readmission of the state. He was a member of the state constitutional convention of 1865, during which he vigorously argued for a conservative, conciliatory course for the state. One measure of that was his effort to divert a move to declare that slavery had ended in the state by action of the federal government. Those who favored such a declaration did so to provide a basis for a claim for compensation from the federal government under the Fifth Amendment for the loss of their slaves. While deploring the loss of the institution, Yerger recognized that slavery was gone and that any immovable position would be unproductive in negotiations with the North. There were things that could not be changed, and the loss of slavery was one of them. Yerger also noted, "Of all the industrial systems, that of slavery was probably the most costly." His plea was effective. The legislature, however, shunned his advice not to adopt a punitive black code. His position was to follow a prudent, pragmatic course, but he did not favor Republican Reconstruction and did not become part of the new government. In response to congressional Reconstruction Yerger pursued a course, along with other Democratic and former Mississippi Whigs, that was designed to cooperate with moderate Republicans in congress in order to turn aside the imposition of radical Republican rule in the state. The cooperationist movement failed. When it became obvious that black suffrage would be imposed in the state, he tried to persuade the freedmen to support the traditional white rulers of Mississippi. When the Loyal League tried to herd the freedmen to the polls to vote for the radical constitution of 1868, Yerger, in a widely circulated statement, warned that this amounted to a criminal conspiracy because it interfered with the free exercise of the right to vote. His legalistic argument was designed to assure traditional white rule in Mississippi.

While he generally advised against efforts to block congressional Reconstruction, Yerger actively opposed military rule in Mississippi. This was clear when he became involved in the defense of his hot-tempered nephew, Edward M. Yerger, who was brought before a military commission in Mississippi to stand trial for the murder of an army officer who was acting as the mayor of Jackson. Yerger argued that, as a civilian, Edward ought to be tried under Mississippi law rather than by military commission and given the advantages of the grand and petit juries. He lost before the military commission, but this case was carried to the U.S. Supreme Court, and in the landmark case of *Ex parte Yerger* (1869) the court held that Edward was entitled to the benefit of the federal writ of habeas corpus and thus to a civilian trial. This judgment amounted to an important qualification to *Ex parte McCardle* (1868), which Sharkey had argued unsuccessfully. In that case, the Supreme Court had accepted the validity of an act of congress that stripped it of a statutory habeas corpus jurisdiction. That jurisdiction involved hearing a case that challenged the constitutionality of congressional Reconstruction, an approach to Reconstruction that relied upon temporary military rule. In *Yerger* the court claimed that a general habeas corpus jurisdiction remained even after the precise statutory jurisdiction had been removed. Back in Mississippi, Edward walked away free in 1871 after a successful plea of double jeopardy. One year after his legal triumph, Yerger died in Jackson.

• There is no collection of Yerger's papers. His career is best followed in the volumes of the Mississippi reports and in occasional newspaper columns. There is no full-scale biographical study of Yerger. An uncritical sketch is in J. D. Lynch, *Bench and Bar of Mississippi* (1881). James W. Garner, *Reconstruction in Mississippi* (1901); William Harris, *The Day of the Carpetbagger: Republican Reconstruction in Mississippi* (1979); and Vernon Lane Wharton, *The Negro in Mississippi 1865–1890* (1947), all have valuable, if brief, references to Yerger. His involvement in Mississippi Reconstruction and in cases that reached the U.S. Supreme Court is covered in Charles Fairman, *History of the Supreme Court of the United States: Reconstruction and Reunion 1864–88*, pt. 1 (1971).

THOMAS D. MORRIS

YERKES, Charles Tyson (25 June 1837–29 Dec. 1905), investment banker and traction entrepreneur, was born in Philadelphia, Pennsylvania, the son of Charles Tyson Yerkes, a bank president, and Elizabeth Link Broom. Yerkes, of Quaker descent, graduated from Philadelphia Central High School and began his career as a clerk in a commission broking house, James P. Perot Brothers. In 1859 Yerkes married Susanna Gutteridge Gamble; they had six children. In 1862 Yerkes started his own investment bank. He specialized in high-risk deals, and in 1866 he gained a reputation as a financial wizard by selling a new issue of Philadelphia Municipal Bonds at par while the city's other debt was selling at 65 percent of issued value. In 1871 the Chicago Fire caused panic on the Philadelphia Stock Exchange. Yerkes was overcommitted and unable to pay to the city monies he had been paid for municipal bonds. He was indicted for embezzlement, tried, convicted, and received a jail sentence of two years and nine months, of which he served seven months before obtaining a pardon.

After his release from prison, Yerkes returned to financial gambling. In 1873, during the chaos surrounding the failure of Philadelphia's Jay Cooke & Co., Yerkes won back his fortune. But as Yerkes faced adultery charges that shocked his native city, he found Philadelphia an uncomfortable place in which to live. In 1881 he divorced his first wife and married Mary Adelaide Moore, and in 1882 he took his new bride to Chicago.

Yerkes's Chicago career proved controversial. He quickly established a brokerage firm, but his main interest turned to public utilities. Yerkes used his friendship with Philadelphia's street railway baron, Peter A. B. Widener, to borrow funds for his new ventures, the first of which included a horsecar line, the North Chicago Street Railway.

In entering the traction business, Yerkes placed his financial talents at the service of a capital-intensive, and necessary, public utility. Unfortunately, traction had a dirty side. Unlike Chicago's more conventional "honest" enterprises, such as department stores, slaughter houses, and steel mills, traction was at the mercy of politics. Streetcars operated largely on public streets and required city franchises. In Chicago franchises were approved by the City Council, which at that time was composed of over sixty poorly paid alderman who became adept at receiving bribes for permission to use streets. They rigorously restricted franchises to the shortest possible periods so that streets could be sold often. Yerkes recognized the crucial link between the private financiers who supplied the capital for utilities and the political bosses who built electoral machines by granting favors to voters in the form of jobs and donations of goods during times of need. He formed an alliance with Alderman John Powers from the Nineteenth Ward, which was dominated by Irish and Italian immigrants. Yerkes paid Powers handsomely for the franchises that gave him control over most of Chicago's vast horsecar network.

Yerkes was also a builder, however. He became a prime mover in the conversion of horsecar lines to cable traction, a process that had started immediately prior to his arrival. Chicago's transport system required vast amounts of capital. By 1899 Chicago's cable railways alone, most of which Yerkes controlled, represented an investment of more than $25 million, a staggering sum for the time. During their brief period of operation (1882–1906), cable cars moved large numbers of people more rapidly and reliably than horsecars. Yerkes's north Chicago and west Chicago lines reached the city's downtown through tunnels that bored underneath the Chicago River. This was an enormous advantage since during navigation season river drawbridges remained open nearly one-quarter of the time. Yerkes's lines looped around the central business district, and it was this cable loop that provided the district with its nickname, "The Loop." In the 1890s Yerkes's companies took the lead in building Chicago's elevated railway, which also circled the business district on a loop and has remained his lasting memorial.

By the turn of the century, Chicago street railroads, nearly all of which were Yerkes's companies, directly employed more than 7,400 wage earners. This figure did not include the elevated lines or any of the thousands of laborers involved in the construction of the expanding street railway and elevated network, nor did it include those employed in electric power stations that supplied current to streetcars and elevated trains. Most of the workers were unskilled motormen, conductors, track maintainers, car cleaners, and window washers. Yerkes allowed the political bosses to nominate candidates for vacant positions, and this policy, together with bribes, made Yerkes Chicago's unelected political king.

Yerkes's campaign to monopolize Chicago's transit system lasted nearly two decades. His alliance with the city's alleged chief corruptionist evoked the condemnation of the "better classes," but his confinement in a Pennsylvania prison had toughened him. Early in Yerkes's Chicago career, Joe Dunlap, who controlled a racy scandal sheet, the *Chicago Dispatch*, sent a reporter with a draft article detailing Yerkes's prison experience. Yerkes told him, "You're damn right it's true.

And you can tell that God-damned Dunlap that if he ever publishes a line or tells a soul I will kill him the first time I see him" (Wendt and Kogan, p. 37). Dunlap did not print the story.

Yerkes made many indiscreet remarks. While much of his financial support came from the public who bought his shares, one day he summarized his philosophy as "buy old junk, fix it up a little, unload it on the other fellow." When accused of not running enough streetcars and thus forcing passengers to stand, he commented, "It's the straphangers who pay the dividends." Such statements, which Yerkes intended as half humorous, did not become a conspicuous consumer who maintained a stable of purebred horses, owned a large mansion, possessed an art collection worth more than $750,000, and found the money in 1892 to donate a state-of-the-art astronomical observatory to the University of Chicago.

Despite his success with the Chicago machines, Yerkes's long-term goal was to extricate himself from dependence upon the political system by securing fifty-year franchises for his traction empire. In the beginning of the 1890s Yerkes changed his focus to the state level; through bribery he managed to control the state convention's nominations of candidates for the legislature. The Yerkes legislators passed a series of bills that renewed his Chicago franchises for 100 years with no payment to the city. Even when John Altgeld, Illinois's maverick Democratic governor, vetoed the legislation, the ever hopeful Yerkes tried again. The result was the Allen Bill, which the legislature passed; it was signed by Altgeld's Republican successor, John Tanner. This law allowed the Chicago City Council to issue fifty-year franchises (instead of the maximum of twenty under old legislation) and eliminated all fees paid to the city. The *Chicago Tribune* charged that the city would lose $150 million if the council issued franchises under the Allen Law. Chicago's "streetcar franchise war" of 1898 followed. As usual, Yerkes's forces were led by Alderman Powers, who thought he had enough votes on the council to give Yerkes a fifty-year franchise. Neither reckoned on the intensity of the opposition, which consisted of such disparate groups as the Chicago Reform Democrats under Mayor Carter Henry Harrison II, the city's middle class, and the wealthy aristocracy. Leading newspapers whipped up enormous popular opposition to Yerkes, and the City Council narrowly defeated his proposals. The state legislature then repealed the Allen Bill. For Yerkes, this was the end. In 1899 he sold out his Chicago interests for almost $20 million and moved to New York.

Chicago's experiences with Yerkes's transit enterprises, while better publicized, merely replicated similar struggles in such places as Philadelphia, San Francisco, New York, and Boston. On balance, Yerkes built a modern and effective public transport system that at the time of his departure included approximately 479 miles of streetcar lines (cable, horse, and electric powered) as well as forty miles of electric powered elevated railways. Despite Yerkes's own statements about buying junk, fixing it up, and passing it on to the next person, he built many new lines and employed cutting-edge technology. His North Chicago Street Railroad (a cable line) bought some of the largest cable cars ever operated. Some of the problems with the North Chicago Line were caused by Yerkes's selection of a cable grip designed for Philadelphia. Yerkes's motive was to avoid paying royalties required for the use of the original San Francisco cable grip mechanism (which proved to be more effective). Significantly, when Yerkes took over the city's west-side cable cars and rebuilt and improved them, he did not use a Philadelphia grip. Other problems that typified Yerkes's streetcar lines were cable breaks, which were problems on such systems the world over. Unfortunately, a broken cable would stall traffic over the entire line, often for several hours, causing widespread passenger inconvenience and annoyance.

Yerkes's biggest innovation occurred on the city's elevated lines. The first Chicago elevated railway opened in June 1892 and followed the New York City precedent where trains were pulled by steam locomotives. Chicago quickly embraced electricity, and the city's Metropolitan West Side Elevated Railroad became the first such operation in America to operate solely with electricity. This line opened in May 1895. It did not use locomotives but had powered passenger cars that dragged behind them several nonpowered trailers. This was a cumbersome practice that was characterized by slow starts and stops and comparatively low overall speed. In 1898 Chicago's south-side line, which connected into Yerkes's loop, abandoned its steam power in favor of multiple-unit electric car operation. This was the world's first multiple-unit operation; an invention of Frank Sprague, it was an enormous improvement. Each carriage had its own electric motors and therefore was fully powered; however, a single operator sitting in the lead car could simultaneously control all units as one. This allowed rapid acceleration and deceleration, which greatly speeded service. Multiple-unit electrification produced dramatic financial results for the south-side system with net earnings rising nearly four times from approximately $10,000 a month to $40,000 a month.

While Yerkes did much to build comprehensive city transportation systems, it remained for his successor, Samuel Insull, to achieve a truly unified Chicago traction system with a long-term franchise. In 1900 Yerkes moved to London, England, where, in opposition to J. P. Morgan, he won the rights to construct the London tube system. However, Yerkes's London venture did not go well, and at the end of his life in 1905 he was close to bankruptcy.

• Yerkes's Chicago career received much attention in Lloyd Wendt and Herman Kogan's *Lords of the Levee* (1943), reprinted in 1967 under the title *Bosses in Lusty Chicago: The Story of Bathouse John and Hinky Dink*. See also Sidney I. Roberts, "Portrait of a Robber Baron: Charles T. Yerkes," *Business History Review* 35, no. 3 (1961): 345–71. Chicago's cable railroads are featured in George W. Hilton's *Cable Railways of Chicago, Bulletin No. 10 of the Electric Railway Historical Society* (1954). The novelist Theodore Dreiser

wrote a trilogy based on Yerkes's life; it includes *The Financier* (1912), which describes Yerkes's Philadelphia career; *The Titan* (1914), detailing his Chicago exploits; and *The Stoic* (1947), an account of his London downfall. Also helpful are George Krambles and Art Peterson's *CTA at 45: A History of the First 45 Years of the Chicago Transit Authority* (1993), which contains a brief summary of the Yerkes days, and the anonymous, privately printed *A History of the Yerkes System of Street Railways* (1897). Obituaries are in the *New York Times*, 30 Dec. 1905, and the *Chicago Tribune*, 30 and 31 Dec. 1905.

STEPHEN SALSBURY

YERKES, Robert Mearns (26 May 1876–3 Feb. 1956), comparative psychologist, was born in Breadysville, Pennsylvania, the son of Silas Marshall Yerkes and Susanna Addis Carrell, farmers. Yerkes's childhood as a member of an extended farm family in Bucks County, the vegetable basket of Philadelphia, provided him with an intimate knowledge of nature, a comfortability with such living things as worms, snakes, and farm animals, and a facility for devising mechanical devices to help with his work. From his Presbyterian parents he acquired habits of hard work and moral commitment, as well as nativist pride in the accomplishments of old-stock Americans. Yerkes, who learned early on that he did not want to be a farmer, found a model of male authority in the family physician and escaped his father's supervision at age fifteen by attending the State Normal School at West Chester and Ursinus Academy and College, where he earned his way as a live-in servant for an uncle who was a medical doctor. Through science and philosophy courses, Yerkes became a convert to evolutionary naturalism and received an A.B. in 1897.

Inspired by an independent research project at Ursinus, Yerkes sought exposure to accomplished research scientists. In 1897 an anonymous relative's loan enabled him to attend Harvard University as a special student. He received a second A.B. in 1898 and an M.A. in 1899 in zoology and was admitted as a Ph.D. candidate. Charles B. Davenport and William Castle, prominent figures in genetics, became mentors for Yerkes, who devoted his career to charting the role of intelligence or effective response to environment in the evolutionary process. Under the direction of Harvard psychologist Hugo Münsterberg, Yerkes began to develop a methodology that would allow him to delineate the relationship between behavior and neurological capacity in a range of increasingly more complex animals. After receiving his Ph.D. in 1902 for a study of sensory reaction in jellyfish, Yerkes spent fifteen years at Harvard in junior faculty appointments. In 1905 he married Ada Watterson, a botanist; they had three children. She was to be his coauthor in the writing of *The Great Apes* (1929).

Yerkes became a leader among a new breed of comparative psychologists who worked with animal subjects in a laboratory setting. Convinced by evolutionary theory that simpler forms of life might be viewed as living fossils, Yerkes traced the development of intellectual capacity in studies of the behavior of jellyfish, frogs, crustaceans, worms, mice, crows, swine, and raccoons. His classic monograph *The Dancing Mouse* (1907) helped to establish small rodents as standard subjects for psychobiological research. In collaboration with Johns Hopkins behaviorist John Watson in 1911, he standardized methods for the study of vision in animals and edited the *Journal of Animal Behavior* (1911–1919). Yerkes also developed a multiple-choice method that allowed him to study learning in different kinds of animals despite differences in perceptual and motor abilities or level of activity. His commitment to evolutionary naturalism led him to argue for the similarity between animal and human mental processes, and he became convinced that observing the mental processes of apes would be of great value in understanding human behavior. Yerkes's original interest in medicine was transformed into a persistent effort to apply basic research to human problems. From 1913 to 1917 he worked with the psychiatrist Ernest E. Southard at the Boston Psychopathic Hospital, where he developed the point-scale intelligence test as a diagnostic tool. This pioneering attempt to improve Alfred Binet's scoring system by grading answers rather than simply counting them right or wrong anticipated later criticism of the Stanford revision of Binet's test.

At Harvard Yerkes proudly exchanged reprints with Ralph Barton Perry, E. B. Holt, Walter B. Cannon, Southard, and other distinguished junior faculty who would help to shape the emerging research-oriented university. Early in his career, his Protestant nativism mutated into a commitment to eugenics and social engineering, and he became a leader among progressive academics who claimed that their disciplines could provide answers to the disorders of modern society. Elected president of the American Psychological Association for 1916–1917, Yerkes recognized the opportunity provided by World War I to demonstrate that psychology possessed valuable technology for social management and convinced the Office of the Army Surgeon General to create a Division of Psychology with Yerkes at its helm. The division's psychologists tested more than 1.7 million recruits, and Yerkes edited a massive National Research Council monograph on the program, which helped convince educators of the value of intelligence tests.

Although he had accepted the chairmanship of psychology at the University of Minnesota in 1917, Yerkes resigned the position after World War I and remained in Washington, D.C., where he served the National Research Council in efforts to promote academic science in the service of the nation. As a protégé of the astronomer and NRC chairman George Ellery Hale, Yerkes came to believe that the future of science depended on capital-intensive and bureaucratically organized research, the high costs of which required coordination and cooperation among scientists. As director of the Research Information Service (1919–1924) and of Science Service (1921–1925), and chairman of two NRC grant-making committees—the Committee for Research in Problems of Sex (1921–1947) and the Committee on Scientific Problems of Human Migration (1922–1924)—Yerkes was one of the academic influentials who mediated between corporate philanthropists seeking scientific answers to social questions and university-based scientists needing funds to transform American colleges into modern universities. The work of the sex research committee proved to be among the most successful efforts in American history to promote scientific investigation. During Yerkes's tenure as chair the committee coordinated and funded work on the mammalian reproductive cycle that led to the identification of the hormones that serve as the body's internal regulatory system. Revolutionary changes in medicine followed as synthetic analogs of these molecules found clinical application. The committee also supported a wide range of behavioral studies that established sex research as a part of the academic canon, including Alfred Kinsey's documentation of vast and changing differences between traditional values and middle-class behavior in the United States.

In 1915 Yerkes had extended his comparative study of intelligence to the orangutan and had argued that his subject's learning curves demonstrated the ability to think rather than the simple reinforcement of correct responses. In 1923 he purchased two chimpanzees with his own funds and began the intensive work with primates that would be the focus of the rest of his career. These efforts found institutional support when he began work at Yale University, where he served as a member of the Institute of Psychology (1924–1929), professor of comparative psychobiology (1929–1944), and director of Yale Laboratories of Primate Biology (1929–1941). Yerkes's leadership as a research director and fundraiser led to the creation of the first large-scale primate laboratories in New Haven, Connecticut, and Orange Park, Florida, and to the acceptance of primates as subjects of choice in many areas of biomedical and behavioral science. Yerkes anticipated later debates over "sociobiology" when his popular account of his research, *Chimpanzees: A Laboratory Colony* (1943), suggested that male dominance and altruism were deeply rooted in primate biology, which evoked a rebuttal from feminist Ruth Hershberger in *Adam's Rib* (1948), a collection of critical essays on the anti-feminist bias of U.S. culture, including science and law.

During World War II, Yerkes again played a key role as promoter and coordinator of his discipline. He accepted the call of Karl M. Dallenbach, chairman of the NRC's Emergency Committee in Psychology, to lead a subcommittee on survey and planning to chart the future of the discipline, which was increasingly divided between competing associations for research and applied orientations. The deliberations of Yerkes's group laid the foundation for a rewriting of the bylaws of the American Psychological Association to provide a divisional structure that would represent the whole range of interests among psychologists. He remained active as an academic elder statesman until disabled by a stroke in 1954. He died in New Haven, Connecticut.

Yerkes was one of the architects of the academic research establishment in the United States and believed that his greatest contributions were as a promoter and administrator of research rather than in specific empirical discovery. Nevertheless, he made many original contributions to comparative psychology and was the key figure in the development of the use of primates as scientific models. His career was a case study in the emergence of the expert as a source of authority in a secular society, where evolutionary naturalism and the promise of technocracy strongly influenced social thought and public policy. Although shy in public relationships, Yerkes had an extraordinary network of professional intimates. His extensive correspondence with them provides a rich source for the history of psychology. A list of Yerkes's professional associates might include such primate subjects of his research as Julius the orangutan, Congo the gorilla, and many chimpanzees who were immortalized in Yerkes's publications. He regarded himself, like his subjects, as the servant of an instrumental science, a discipline dedicated to "the dignity and perfectibility of man as part of the natural order" (Yerkes, "Personal Creed," in "The Scientific Way").

• The Yerkes papers, including "The Scientific Way," his manuscript autobiography, are in the Sterling Library, Yale University. A substantial autobiographical essay is in *A History of Psychology in Autobiography*, vol. 2, ed. Carl Murchison (1932), pp. 381–407. Yerkes's important books not mentioned in the text are *Methods of Studying Vision in Animals*, with J. B. Watson (1911); *A Point Scale for Measuring Mental Ability*, with R. S. Hardwick and J. W. Bridges (1915); *The Mental Life of Monkeys and Apes* (1916); *Psychological Examining in the United States Army*, Memoirs of the National Academy of Sciences, vol. 15 (1921), a collaborative work that he edited; *Almost Human* (1925); *Chimpanzee Intelligence and Its Vocal Expressions*, with B. W. Learned (1925); *The Mind of a Gorilla* (3 vols., 1927–1928); *Modes of Behavioral Adaptation in Chimpanzee to Multiple-Choice Problems* (1934); and *Oestrus, Receptivity, and Mating in Chimpanzee* (1936). Ernest R. Hilgard provides a sympathetic assessment and complete bibliography in *Biographical Memoirs* (National Academy of Sciences) 38 (1965): 412–25. For critical interpretations of Yerkes's career in the context of the history and sociology of American science see Hamilton Cravens, *The Triumph of Evolution: American Scientists and the Heredity-Environment Controversy, 1900–1941* (1978); Robert Boakes, *From Darwin to Behaviourism: Psychology and the Minds of Animals* (1984); John M. O'Donnell, *The Origins of Behaviorism: American Psychology, 1870–1920* (1985); and Donna Haraway, *Primate Visions: Gender, Race, and Nature in the World of Modern Science* (1989). For analysis of the World War I army testing program and Yerkes's work in mental testing see Franz Samelson, "Putting Psychology on the Map: Ideology and Intelligence Testing," in *Psychology in Social Context*, ed. Allan Buss (1979), pp. 103–67; and James Reed, "Robert M. Yerkes and the Mental Testing Movement," in *Psychological Testing and American Society: 1890–1930*, ed. Michael Sokal (1987), pp. 75–94. An obituary is in the *New Haven Register*, 5 Feb. 1956.

JAMES W. REED

YEZIERSKA, Anzia (1880?–21 Nov. 1970), novelist and short-story writer also known as Hattie Mayer, was born in Plotsk on the Russian-Polish border, the daughter of Baruch Yezierska, a Talmudic scholar, and Pearl (maiden name unknown). During the great Jewish migration her family came to the Lower East Side of New York about 1890. Assigned the name Mayer by immigration officials, the family suffered from severe poverty, and as a young girl Yezierska was forced to work at many menial jobs. Determined to escape from poverty, she taught herself English, attended night school, and secured a scholarship to Columbia University, graduating as a domestic science teacher in 1904. Her desire for education, however, was far greater than to learn a way merely to earn money; it was one aspect of the spiritual hunger that informed her writings all her life. Interviews published during her lifetime omit many significant facts, among them her two marriages. The first, to Jacob Gordon in 1910, was annulled within a few months, and the second was to Arnold Levitas in 1911. The daughter born during her second marriage lived with Yezierska after she left her husband, but she relinquished custody to Levitas when the girl was four years old.

Yezierska's efforts to become a writer were evident at least as early as 1910 with the poems she sent to her husband, but her work received a major impetus when she forced a meeting with the eminent philosopher John Dewey. The aristocratic Puritan professor was apparently entranced by the "intense, hungry, driving will [of this] ardent rebel," as Yezierska's daughter later characterized her mother. The affair was short lived; nevertheless, it had great significance for both, leading Dewey to write a series of poems dedicated to Yezierska, which were discovered after his death. Dewey's encouragement helped Yezierska find the self-confidence to devote herself solely to her writing and guided her to the themes that would characterize her works—the difficulty faced by a woman, an immigrant, and an artist striving to partake of the American Dream.

Her first published story, "The Free Vacation House," appeared in 1915 in *Forum*. Her stories were replete with dialogue that captured the cadences and speech patterns of Yiddish, and she used the extravagant hyperbole and sharp bite of that language with extraordinary power. Her stories' lack of traditional form caused many publishers to reject her work, but when "The Fat of Land" was finally published, it was chosen by Edward J. O'Brien as the best short story of 1919 and became part of her first book, *Hungry Hearts* (1920). This collection of stories traced the sufferings and frustrated ambitions of the Jewish immigrant woman as well as the failure of material success to satisfy the spiritual hunger. One of the first Eastern European Jewish women authors writing in English, Yezierska created Sonya, a character who captured her problem, saying, "I am a Russian Jewess, a flame, a longing . . . a soul consumed with hunger for heights beyond reach. I am the ache of unvoiced dreams . . . the unlived lives of generations stifled in Siberian prisons" (*Salome of the Tenements*, p. 65). When these stories were bought by Samuel Goldwyn for the then extraordinary sum of $10,000, he offered Yezierska a contract as a screenwriter. With the help of the movie studio's publicity department, Yezierska achieved national fame as the "sweatshop Cinderella," leading many readers to assume that the stories were autobiographical, even though much of the information came from the lives of friends and relatives. Often readers believed that Yezierska herself was almost illiterate, even though there was ample evidence of well-crafted prose in the book.

The Hollywood experience proved to be disastrous. Although the movie appeared in 1922, Yezierska felt that her sense of artistic integrity had been compromised because a comic writer was hired to add humor to her tale of poverty and suffering. Abandoning the glamour and wealth, she returned to New York. Her next book, the novel *Salome of the Tenements* (1923), was based on the experiences of her friend Rose Pastor, a poor Jewish immigrant who had married James Phelps Graham Stokes, the scion of a prestigious White Anglo-Saxon Protestant family. As the title suggests, Yezierska's version stressed the young woman's fierce determination to use any means necessary to marry the man of her choice. The failure of the liaison reinforced Yezierska's awareness that Jewish values were not easily dismissed even when Americanized goals were achieved. Her next book, *Children of Loneliness* (1923), a series of short stories and essays, some of which had been written before the novel, explored the difficulty faced by Americanized children torn between their parents' Old World values and their own assimilation into the new culture, of the emerging middle class choosing between financial rewards and spiritual values.

During the 1920s Yezierska enjoyed a degree of fame and enough economic security to permit her to live in relative comfort. Her best novel, *Bread Givers* (1925), was a product of this newfound ease. Loosely based on her own childhood, it clearly presents the struggle of a Jewish girl to escape from a tradition that limited the woman's role and to achieve an independent and creative life for herself. The father, a Talmudic scholar exempted from work by the holiness of his study, tyrannizes his daughters, forcing them to support him and to marry the men he chooses for them. Only the youngest, Sara, refuses his domination and leaves home to secure the education that will permit her to live her own life. Father and daughter clash violently, but they achieve an uneasy reconciliation at the end, the young woman having a career as a teacher and finding love and marriage with the Americanized Jewish principal of her school. This novel was out of print for decades until it was discovered by Alice Kessler-Harris, who arranged for its reprinting in 1975. The book with her introduction became the first step toward the restoration of Yezierska's significance in American fiction.

As social and economic concerns of Americans changed in the latter part of the 1920s, interest in Yezierska's work steadily declined, and each new novel, repeating as it did the same sort of story, found fewer readers. Neither *Arrogant Beggar* (1927), which exposed the callousness of institutional charity, nor *All I Could Never Be* (1932), a story of the love between an older, American professor and a young passionate immigrant woman, achieved recognition or money. During the depression she joined the WPA (Works Progress Administration) Writers Project in New York, where she met Richard Wright. Although Yezierska continued to write, she remained unpublished until 1950, when *Red Ribbon on a White Horse* appeared with an introduction by W. H. Auden and was favorably reviewed. Billed as an autobiography, it was instead a highly fictionalized version of some of the events in her life. For a brief period she was once more a noted writer.

The need to write and the practice never ended, even though Yezierska found few publishing outlets. She wrote more than fifty book reviews for the *New York Times* in the 1950s. For her short stories she discovered new subjects, the plight of the elderly in a society that valued youth and the difficulties facing the Puerto Rican immigrants who were new to New York. Despite her physical decline and failing eyesight, she was able to create a few poignant stories, the best of which, "The Open Cage," became the title story for a collection of her tales published after her death. She died in a nursing home in Ontario, California.

Of the numerous writers on the immigrant Jewish experience, Yezierska holds a special place. Unlike Mary Antin, who also wrote of the Jewish immigrant woman's experience, Yezierska maintained an understanding of the cultural pull of Judaism. Although Abraham Cahan had preceded her in presenting the immigrant's story, her fiery prose captured the emotional quality of Jewish life and presented the special problems that immigrant women faced. Henry Roth's *Call It Sleep* is a more eloquent work that presents the beauties of educated Yiddish speech, but it lacks the gritty qualities of the less literate. Unlike Michael Gold in *Jews without Money*, Yezierska not only presented the poverty-stricken but also the rise of immigrants to middle-class status and its costs. No one has captured so well as she the struggle of the Jewish woman to find her own place in American life, of the immigrant to balance the needs of the past against the potential of the future, and of the artist to maintain a sense of integrity in a materialistic world.

• Yezierska's papers and manuscripts are in the library of Boston University or with her daughter, Louise Levitas Henriksen. Reprints, in addition to *Bread Givers* (1975, with Kessler-Harris's introduction), include *Red Ribbon on a White Horse* (1981, with an introduction by W. H. Auden); a collection of short works, *The Open Cage* (1979); all extant short pieces collected in *How I Found America* (1991, with an introduction by Vivian Gornick); and *Salome of the Tenements* (1995, introduced by Gay Wilentz). Louise Levitas Henriksen's biography, *Anzia Yezierska: A Writer's Life* (1988), provides a wealth of detail. Mary V. Dearborn, *Love in the Promised Land: The Story of Anzia Yezierska and John Dewey*

(1988), studies this relationship, first described by Jo Ann Boydston in her introduction to *The Poems of John Dewey* (1977) and fictionalized by Norma Rosen, *John and Anzia: An American Romance* (1989). Carol Schoen, *Anzia Yezierska* (1982), provides a critical analysis of the writings plus biographical information.

Articles in *Studies in American Jewish Literature* include Ellen Golub, "Eat Your Heart Out: The Fiction of Anzia Yezierska," vol. 3 (1983): 51–61; Rose Kamel, "Anzia Yezierska, Get Out of Your Own Way: Selfhood and Otherness in the Autobiographical Fiction of Anzia Yezierska," vol. 3 (1983): 40–50; Susan Hersh Sachs, "Anzia Yezierska: 'Her Words Dance with a Thousand Colors,'" vol. 3 (1983): 62–67; and Shelly Regenbaum, "Art, Gender and the Jewish Tradition in Yezierska's *Red Ribbon on a White Horse* and Potok's *My Name Is Asher Lev*," vol. 7 (1988): 55–66. Discussions of Yezierska's works appear in Cecyle S. Neidle, *American Immigrant Women* (1976); C. Davidson, *The Lost Tradition* (1980); Blanche H. Gelfant, *Women Writers and the City* (1984); Dearborn, *Pocahontas's Daughters* (1986); Louis Harap, *Creative Awakening* (1987); Ellen Serlan Uffen, *Strands of the Cable* (1992); Diane Lichtenstein, *Writing Their Nations* (1992); and Thomas J. Ferraro, *Ethnic Passages* (1993).

CAROL SCHOEN

YOGANANDA, Paramahansa (5 Jan. 1893–7 Mar. 1952), founder of the Self Realization Fellowship, was born Mukunda Lal Ghosh in Gorakhpur, a town near the Nepali border in northeastern India, the son of Bhagabati Charan Ghosh, a railway vice president, and Gurru (maiden name unknown).

His youth was spent in a well-to-do, religious family of Bengali origin. His parents became the disciples of Lahiri Mahasaya, a guru from Benares who initiated them into the meditative practice of kriya yoga, which has as its object direct union with God by means of discipline of body, breath, and mind. Guided in meditation by their masters, followers accelerate their natural "spiritual evolution," transcending the temporal, material world and moving closer to the eternal, personified in God. Yoga recognizes both great gurus and figures from various world religions, regardless of specific creed, as "saints," persons who have achieved harmony with the infinite. Union with God endows the devotee with perfect happiness and immense wisdom; personal messages from the Divine are often received through telepathic and supernatural experiences. Mukunda also experienced the power of Mahasaya's teaching, and he himself began to have mystical presentiments and visions, including a dream omen of his mother's impending death.

While still in high school, Mukunda met his own guru, Swami Sri Yukteswar Giri, and began serving him diligently in his ashram in Serampore, near Calcutta. While training with Swami Yukteswar, Mukunda rather reluctantly continued his academic studies, receiving his A.B. in 1914 from Calcutta University. A few weeks later, he was initiated by his guru into the Swami Order and given the name Yogananda, meaning "the bliss attained by the practice of yoga."

As his first act of service, in 1917 Yogananda founded a school for boys at Ranchi, in Bihar, India, and called it Yogoda Satsanga Brahmacharya Vidyālaya. The curriculum of the school included academic, vocational, and spiritual subjects.

With the encouragement of his guru and the financial support of his father, Yogananda accepted an invitation to be a delegate to the International Congress of Religious Liberals in Boston in 1920. For four years after the congress, Yogananda stayed in Boston, teaching, lecturing, and writing. After a lecture tour of North America, in 1925 he founded the Self Realization Fellowship, an organization to promote the teaching of kriya yoga in the United States, which was chartered in California in 1935 as a nonsectarian, nonprofit corporation. Between 1925 and 1936, having found his life's work, Yogananda taught his kriya yoga all over the United States, lecturing in dozens of American cities.

In 1935 Yogananda returned to India to see Swami Yukteswar and attend to his school in Ranchi. During that time, Swami Yukteswar, with clairvoyant anticipation of his own imminent death, bestowed on Yogananda the additional honorific title of Paramahansa (Great Swan).

After leaving India, Yogananda arrived in England in September 1936 to lecture students of yoga. He went back to the United States in October 1936 to find that his devotees had built a Self Realization Fellowship hermitage in Encinitas, California. Yogananda withdrew from nationwide public lecturing and concentrated on writing and teaching the system of kriya yoga in his own SRF temples. Centers in Hollywood, San Diego, and Long Beach were opened, and in 1949 an estate in Pacific Palisades, California, was anonymously donated for the creation of the idyllic Lake Shrine. Paramahansa Yogananda died of a heart ailment after a public lecture in Los Angeles in honor of the Indian ambassador, B. R. Sen.

• Of all Yogananda's writings, the most famous is his *Autobiography of a Yogi* (1946). Other spiritual, meditational, and devotional collections of Yogananda's writings were issued during his lifetime and afterward by his followers. They include *Whispers from Eternity* (1929), *Cosmic Chants* (1938), *The Science of Religion* (1953), *Man's Eternal Quest* (1975), *The Second Coming of Christ* (3 vols., 1982–1986), *The Divine Romance* (1986), and *The Essence of Self Realization*, comp. J. Donald Waters (1990). An obituary is in the *New York Times*, 9 Mar. 1952.

GAIL HINICH SUTHERLAND

YON, Pietro Alessandro (8 Aug. 1886–22 Nov. 1943), organist, composer, performer, and teacher, was born in Settimo Vittone, Italy, the son of Antonio Yon and Margherita Piazza. His father was a watchmaker, photographer and storekeeper in the small village where they lived. By the age of six, Yon had begun to study the organ with Angelo Burbatti, the cathedral organist in the nearby city of Ivrea. When he was twelve, Yon entered the Royal Conservatory in Milan, using prize winnings from a bicycle race to finance his first year of study. He received a scholarship at the end of his first year that enabled him to complete his studies. A second scholarship saw him through studies at St. Cecilia's Academy in Rome where he completed the normal eleven year course in only five years. At graduation in 1905, he was awarded every prize the academy offered. His first professional position was as assistant organist at St. Peter's Basilica in Rome.

Yon emigrated to the United States in 1907 at the invitation of the Reverend John B. Young who was the organist at St. Francis Xavier Church in New York City. Yon served there for twenty years, except for 1919–1921 when he was in Rome as assistant organist of the Cappella Giulia at St. Peter's. At St. Francis, Yon directed the boys choir Rev. Young had founded. During his tenure there he also established his American reputation as a virtuoso performer, introducing the paid-admission organ concert and the memorized program to New Yorkers. His reputation made Yon a much sought after teacher. He and his older brother, Constantino, who was the organist at the Church of St. Vincent Ferrer, opened a studio in Carnegie Hall. One of Yon's many students was Cole Porter.

Yon began concert tours in the United States shortly after opening his studio. During one of those tours in Kansas City he was abducted by the Ku Klux Klan, apparently because he was an Italian immigrant. He escaped and would have given his organ concert except for the fact that the KKK sabotaged the electricity in the concert hall. After calming the audience, Yon gave his concert anyway, in the dark.

In 1919 he married Francesca Pessagno, and they had one son. Yon became a U.S. citizen in 1921. The stock market collapse in 1929 wiped out most of the family's savings. That year his wife died. Yon returned to work almost immediately after her death, acting as a consultant to a committee that planned the tonal design of the Carnegie Hall organ, an instrument he later played at the dedication ceremony attended by Franklin D. Roosevelt. In 1930 he also played at the dedication of the St. Patrick's Cathedral grand gallery organ, an instrument he had designed himself.

After Yon's first concert performance in Carnegie Hall in 1927, Cardinal Hayes asked him to come from St. Francis Xavier to St. Patrick's Cathedral as organist. Two years later he was appointed music director there, the same year that King Victor Emmanuel III of Italy conferred knighthood on him at the Royal Palace in Rome. He remained at St. Patrick's until his death in Huntington, New York.

In his own day Yon was known as a consummate organist, a musician, and an accomplished composer. Historically he is best known for a single vocal composition, "Gesu, Bambino," based on a folk tune from his native Italy combined with a fragment of "O Come All Ye Faithful." This piece, with its wide popular appeal, became virtually the only one of Yon's compositions still performed. Particularly among organists, who consider his work to be too sentimental, Yon's works were dismissed, not least of all because they demand virtuosic performance. In the postmodern 1990s, Yon's unabashed romanticism, despite the technically demanding nature of his compositions was considered insufficiently intellectually challenging for many academically trained organists. The accessibility of "Gesu, Bambino," which made the piece so appealing to nonmusicians, colors organists perceptions of all Yon's compositions, particularly those written for organ. Despite his breadth of compositional technique and content, this single piece continued to be played on a regular basis, precisely because it is not an organ composition.

Yon composed more than thirty masses, more than 100 religious songs and carols, fifty ballads, one oratorio, and six orchestrated concertos or sonatas with choral arrangements—compositions considered at the time to be of the highest caliber. However, the bulk of his work is unknown and much of it is no longer in print. His instruction book *Organ Pedal Technic*, which was published posthumously in 1944, is also out of print.

• Very little information on Yon exists outside of newspaper articles, mostly from the *New York Times*, articles in the *American Organist* and *Diapason*, and some archive materials at St. Patrick's Cathedral in New York City. The primary source of information used here is personal communication from Thomas G. Young, archivist at St. Patrick's Cathedral, New York City. An interview with organist Bruce Oelschlager, Lansing, Mich., who performs some of Yon's pieces, provided insight into many organists' attitudes toward Yon's work. A biographical novel of Yon's life, *The Heavens Heard Him*, was published in 1963 but is no longer in print. An obituary is in the *New York Times*, 23 Nov. 1943.

M. RINI HUGHES

YORK, Alvin Cullum (13 Dec. 1887–2 Sept. 1964), World War I soldier, was born in Pall Mall, Tennessee, the son of William York and Mary Brooks, farmers. A skillful hunter and marksman, York worked as a farmer, a laborer, and a blacksmith before the war. He received approximately three years of formal schooling. His drinking and brawling earned him a reputation as a local rowdy, but an emotional religious experience in 1915 prompted him to join the Church of Christ in Christian Union, a deeply conservative congregation originally founded in reaction to the carnage of the Civil War period. Because church members rejected violence, York sought conscientious objector status when the United States entered World War I, but the Selective Service denied his appeal. Once York was drafted, his Eighty-second Infantry Division superiors persuaded him that America was fighting God's battle in the war, an argument that transformed the pacifist from the Tennessee mountains into a veritable soldier of the Lord.

On the smoke-shrouded morning of 8 October 1918, during the battle of the Argonne Forest, York and his patrol were isolated and under fire behind enemy lines near the French village of Châtel-Chéhéry. With half of his sixteen men dead or wounded, York out-shot an entire German machine gun battalion, silencing some thirty-five guns and killing approximately twenty of the enemy. In addition he captured 132 prisoners. Supreme Allied Commander Ferdinand Foch described his exploit as the "greatest thing accomplished by any private soldier of all the armies of Europe." Promoted to sergeant, he received the Medal of Honor and decorations from most of the Allied nations.

Initially York's exploit attracted little public attention, but on 26 April 1919, *Saturday Evening Post* correspondent George Pattullo published "The Second Elder Gives Battle," an account of the firefight that made York a national hero overnight. York's explanation that God had been with him during the fight meshed neatly with the popular attitude that American involvement in the war was truly a holy crusade, and he returned to the United States in the spring of 1919 amid a tumultuous public welcome and a flood of business offers from people eager to capitalize on the soldier's reputation.

These offers would have brought him in excess of $250,000, but York had religious scruples about capitalizing on his military service. Instead he returned to Pall Mall, where he devoted himself to public service, most notably securing a state-supported high school in Fentress County. He married neighbor Gracie Williams in 1919, and the couple had eight children. On the eve of World War II, he finally permitted a film biography after producer Jesse Lasky convinced him that such a portrait would be a patriotic service. With Gary Cooper in the title role, *Sergeant York* opened to popular and critical acclaim just a few months before the United States entered the war. Poor management of his income from the film created tax problems that plagued York's last years, but public donations settled his account with the Internal Revenue Service shortly before his death in Nashville.

York's Appalachian heritage was central to his popularity because the media portrayed him as the archetypical mountain man. At a time of domestic upheaval and international uncertainty, York's pioneerlike skill with a rifle, his homespun manner, and his fundamentalist piety endeared him to millions of Americans as a "contemporary ancestor" fresh from the backwoods of the southern mountains. As such, he seemed to affirm that the traditional virtues of the agrarian United States still had meaning in the new era. York represented not what Americans were but what they wanted to think they were. He lived in one of the most rural parts of the country when a majority of Americans lived in cities; he rejected riches when the tenor of the nation was crassly commercial; he was pious when secularism was on the rise. For millions of people, York was the incarnation of their romanticized understanding of the nation's past when men and women supposedly lived plainer, sterner, and more virtuous lives. Ironically, while York endured as a symbol of an older America, he spent most of his adult life working to bring roads, schools, and industrial development to the mountains, changes that were destroying the society he had come to represent.

• No significant collection of Alvin York papers exists. The most complete study of his life is David D. Lee, *Sergeant*

York: An American Hero (1985). Dated but valuable are Thomas Skeyhill, ed., *Sergeant York: His Own Life Story and War Diary* (1928); Skeyhill, *Sergeant York: Last of the Long Hunters* (1930); and Samuel Cowan, *Sergeant York and His People* (1922). Nat Brandt, "Sergeant York," *American Heritage* 35, no. 2 (1981), is a fine summary of York's exploit. An obituary is in the *New York Times*, 3 Sept. 1964.

DAVID D. LEE

YORKE, Peter Christopher (15 Aug. 1864–5 Apr. 1925), Catholic priest and social justice advocate, was born in Galway, Ireland, the son of Gregory Yorke, a fisherman, and Bridget Kelly. His father died when Yorke was six months old, and his mother remarried. Sometime in the 1870s or 1880s his mother and family immigrated to British Columbia and, after her second husband's death, moved to San Francisco. Yorke, however, stayed in Ireland where he received most of his early education in Galway and Tuam.

From 1882 to 1886 York studied for the priesthood at St. Patrick's College at Maynooth, Ireland. His family encouraged him to become a priest in San Francisco, and the archbishop of San Francisco, Patrick William Riordan, invited him to finish his education for the priesthood at St. Mary's Seminary in Baltimore and join the San Francisco diocese. At St. Mary's Seminary between 1886 and 1887, he studied under the French Sulpician Alphonse Magnien, a progressive theologian who worked to reconcile the church and the new age of science.

After his ordination in 1887, Yorke served as a curate at St. Mary's Cathedral in San Francisco. In 1889 Archbishop Riordan sent Yorke to the newly established Catholic University of America in Washington, D.C., to obtain a doctorate in theology. Yorke received a bachelor (S.T.B., 1890) and a licentiate (S.T.L., 1891) in theology but did not continue on for the doctorate because of a personal dislike for the program and pressing needs for clergy in the diocese of San Francisco.

Recalled to San Francisco in 1891, Yorke began a career as a forceful apologist for Catholicism, a journalist, a leader in Catholic education and liturgical reform, an activist for social justice for laborers, and a well-known Irish nationalist. He joined the archbishop's cathedral staff and was appointed editor of the diocesan newspaper, the *Monitor*, and chancellor of the diocese (1894–1899). As editor (1894–1899) he gained immediate public attention writing forceful responses to the San Francisco American Protective Association's (APA) polemical attacks on the Catholic church. He also championed the archbishop's attempts to have anti-Catholic textbooks removed from the public schools.

Yorke played a role in the municipal elections of 1896 when he supported the successful bid of James Phelan, of the reform Democratic ticket, for mayor against candidates supported by the APA. By 1898, however, Yorke turned against Phelan and other rising middle-class Irish Catholic progressive Democrats because he thought they had betrayed their Irish and

Catholic heritages and had capitulated to APA demands. Pressured by some of these politicians and angered by Yorke's less than temperate assault on them, Archbishop Riordan removed Yorke from editorship of the paper and as chancellor of the diocese.

After a year of travel in Europe in 1899, Yorke returned to San Francisco. In a succession of positions he became involved in labor issues: as assistant at St. Peter's in San Francisco (1899–1903), as pastor of St. Anthony's in Oakland (1903–1913), and as pastor of St. Peter's (1913–1925). In 1901 he supported the waterfront strike in San Francisco and obtained aid from the governor to assist the labor unions in their struggles with their employers. In 1902 he founded the *Leader*, a prolabor journal that promulgated the principles of social justice found in Pope Leo XIII's *Rerum Novarum* (1891), supporting in particular collective bargaining. As editor, he was a forceful, at times intemperate advocate for labor, and Riordan ordered him to withdraw as editor in 1909. Nonetheless, he continued to support labor, to write for the paper, and to oppose the bourgeois mentality of Progressive Era politicians whom he thought had little awareness of or sympathy for the needs of labor.

During his career as journalist and pastor, Yorke also became a national leader in Catholic education. In 1918 he was elected vice president of the newly established National Catholic Education Association and wrote numerous religious and educational textbooks. Yorke criticized educational reformers like Father Thomas Edward Shields who wanted to depart from the time-honored methods of memorization. The Catholic schools were for him the primary means of preserving Catholic identity, of uplifting immigrants socially, and of providing economic mobility for Catholic children. Within Catholicism, moreover, Yorke called for the renewal of the liturgy, in the spirit of Pope Pius X, as a fundamental source for spiritual regeneration and as a means for raising Catholic consciousness of communal identity and social responsibility to those in need.

From his early days in Tuam, Ireland, under the influence of Archbishop John McHale, Yorke had been an Irish nationalist. In San Francisco he became the vice president of the American Irish Sein Fein and the founder of Innesfael, a working-girls' residence. His support for Irish nationalism and the liberation of Ireland from British rule became a focal point of much of his work and his writings for the *Leader* after 1913. Repeatedly he mounted fund drives for Irish liberation, and at the end of World War I he called on President Woodrow Wilson to provide U.S. intervention to aid Irish emancipation from England. He became the California state president of the American Association for the Recognition of the Irish Republic in 1921 and thereafter lectured throughout California against the Irish Free State and in favor of the establishment of a sovereign Irish republic.

Yorke's strong advocacy of various national and local ecclesiastical causes, his involvement in politics and social justice issues, and his continuing pastoral responsibilities gradually affected his health. He died in his San Francisco parish of St. Peter.

• Yorke's letters and unpublished papers are located primarily in the archives of the Archdiocese of San Francisco, the Bancroft Library of the University of California, Berkeley, and the Gleeson Library of the University of San Francisco. Among Yorke's published works are *Fr. Yorke to Mr. Phelan* (1898), *Fr. Yorke to Mr. Maguire* (1898), *Roman Liturgy* (1903), *Altar and Priest* (1913), *The Ghosts of Bigotry* (1913), and a collection of his *Sermons* (2 vols., 1931). He also edited four volumes of *Textbooks of Religion for Parochial and Sunday Schools* and wrote numerous articles for the *Monitor* and the *Leader*. Two positive assessments of his career are found in Bernard C. Cronin, *Father Yorke and the Labor Movement in San Francisco, 1900–1910* (1943), and Joseph S. Brusher, *The Consecrated Thunderbolt: Father Yorke of San Francisco* (1973). More critical assessments can be found in Timothy Sarbaugh, "Father Yorke and the San Francisco Waterfront, 1901–1916," *Pacific Historian* 28 (1981): 28–35; James Walsh, "Regent Peter C. Yorke and the University of California, 1900–1912" (Ph.D. diss., Univ. of Calif., Berkeley, 1970); and Dominic P. Scibilia, "Edward McGlynn, Thomas McGrady, and Peter C. Yorke: Prophets of American Social Catholicism" (Ph.D. diss., Marquette Univ., 1990). Obituaries are in the *San Francisco Call*, 7 Apr. 1925, and the *San Francisco Examiner*, 10 Apr. 1925.

PATRICK W. CAREY

YOST, Don Merlin Lee (30 Oct. 1893–27 Mar. 1977), chemist, was born near Tedrow, Ohio, the son of William Nicholas Yost, a teacher and farmer, and Viola Lorena Lee, a midwife and music teacher. The family moved frequently, and Yost's early education was often interrupted. When he was nine, Yost's family moved to a ranch in southwestern Idaho near Boise, where he attended local schools, displaying an early fascination with languages, electricity, and mathematics. In his unpublished family history Yost later recalled his frontier schooling and his summer jobs, his radio club, and his father's working days. In high school Yost set his sights on going to either Berkeley or Harvard; having been told by "an ex-cowboy that Harvard was too old fashioned," he left Boise in August 1914 for the University of California.

Under the influence of his freshman chemistry professor, Joel Hildebrand, and his laboratory and recitation instructors, Gerald E. K. Branch and Richard Chace Tolman, Yost shifted his interest from engineering to chemistry. He minored in mathematics, a subject he pursued as an avocation for many years. In his second year of college, Yost met Susan Marguerite Sims, whom he married in March 1917; they had two children. Yost then dropped out of college, and when the United States entered World War I, he enlisted in the navy, where he served for two years. After receiving his honorable discharge in 1919, he moved to Salt Lake City, where his wife was living, and enrolled at the University of Utah for a semester.

Yost resumed his undergraduate studies at Berkeley in 1921. He attracted chemist William C. Bray's attention in class the following year and was promptly recruited to help Bray with his monumental research on rare elements. Yost's first book, *Systematic Inorganic Chemistry* (with H. Russell, Jr., 1944), was dedicated to Bray. After receiving his B.S. with honors in chemistry in 1923, he returned to the University of Utah on a graduate fellowship for one year, studying with Walter Bonner; he then transferred in 1924 to the new California Institute of Technology (Caltech) in Pasadena, to work under Arthur Amos Noyes.

Caltech dazzled Yost. He later wrote, "The faculty in mathematics and mathematical physics were outstanding, as well as the visiting professors. H. A. Lorentz, Albert Einstein, Schroedinger, Raman, and others lectured on their researches . . . during my early years there. For a country boy from rural Idaho to be involved actively in all this very modern and highbrow scientific endeavor struck me as almost unbelievable." He attended Robert Millikan's lectures on electron theory, Harry Bateman's on geometrical transformations and invariants, and Paul Epstein's on theory of electricity and magnetism, while doing research in physical inorganic chemistry. In 1926, with a research fellowship at Caltech assured, Yost submitted reprints of four papers as a thesis ("The Mechanisms and Rates of Certain Oxidation-Reduction Reactions in Aqueous Solution; The Existence of Trivalent Silver"), and obtained his Ph.D. in chemistry. He became an instructor the following year, taught freshman chemistry, and continued to do research.

In 1928 Yost received a National Research Council fellowship, which he used to go to Europe for a year. He worked first at the University of Uppsala with Manne Siegbahn on X-rays, and then at the University of Berlin with Peter Pringsheim on the newly-discovered Raman effect. While abroad, he was appointed assistant professor of chemistry at Caltech. Yost spent the rest of his career there, except for visiting professorships at Berkeley (1946), Harvard (1951), and the Massachusetts Institute of Technology (1953).

Yost's interests at Caltech covered a wide range in the fields of chemistry and physics. The author of more than two hundred scientific papers, he pioneered the application of Raman spectroscopy to chemical problems. In physical chemistry, he worked on chemical equilibria and cell potentials and studied the physical and thermodynamic properties of liquid metals; in inorganic chemistry, he studied the rate of reaction of ozone and nitrogen and the use of nuclear resonance phenomena. He published papers contributing to chemical kinetics, low-temperature thermodynamics, radioactivity and neutron physics, electrochemistry, microwave spectroscopy of gases, and carbon-14 dating. Long interested in the chemistry of the rare elements, Yost gained an international reputation for his experiments on the volatile fluorides. A former student, Edwin McMillan, remembered him as "one of those loner types that was always doing odd kinds of chemistry." McMillan added, "he was a very interesting guy and he was always working on something that was very poisonous or very explosive" (quoted in Waugh, 1996).

In the case of the rare earths, the challenge of deciphering their chemistry may well have appealed to Yost's frontier spirit. "Inorganic chemists," he once told an audience, "are not content to see the bottles and packages of elementary substances resting on the laboratory shelves." His own interest began when Noyes and Bray assigned him to find out why the solubility of scandium fluoride first decreased and then increased as the concentration of added fluoride ion was increased, and then to separate rare earths by oxidation-reduction and precipitation methods. Later Clifford Garner and Horace Russell, Jr., joined forces with him in an effort to collect and systematize information on these fifteen elements. By the end of the 1930s they had completed their studies, and in 1947 the three coauthored the landmark book *The Rare-Earth Elements and Their Compounds*. It remained a standard text (as did Yost's earlier volume with Russell) for many years.

During World War II Yost served as a section chairman of the Office of Scientific Research and Development and directed research groups at Northwestern University, Caltech, and Los Alamos; he had contacts with war-research groups in England as well. In 1944 he was elected to the National Academy of Sciences; in 1948, he received the Presidential Certificate of Merit for his wartime efforts.

Yost did not like regulations. An avid believer in individualism, he railed against government bureaucracy and government grants; and he disapproved of the style and shape of the scientific enterprise after the war. "For a working scientist," he wrote in 1950 to Kenneth Pitzer, "the cost of research contracts in self-respect and equanimity is great, but the incentive is uninspiring." He started phasing out the supervision of graduate students and turned his back on divisional matters at Caltech; he was critical of Linus Pauling's school of modern structural chemistry, and his relations with Pauling, then divisional chairman, deteriorated. After he retired in 1964, he took a keen interest once again in mathematics and kept up an active correspondence with other members of the Iron Nail Club, composed of former students, friends, and colleagues. He died of emphysema in Pasadena.

• Yost's scientific and personal papers are in the California Institute of Technology Archives. See also John S. Waugh, "Don Merlin Lee Yost," National Academy of Sciences, *Biographical Memoirs* 62 (1993): 467–83, which includes a complete bibliography and a portrait; Terry Cole, "Don M. Yost, 1893–1977," *Engineering and Science* 41 (1977): 28–29; and Edwin McMillan's interview by Charles Weiner, archived at the American Institute of Physics, College Park, Md.

JUDITH R. GOODSTEIN

YOST, Fielding Harris (30 Apr. 1871–20 Aug. 1946), college football coach and athletic director, was born in Fairview, West Virginia, the son of Permenus Wesley Yost, a farmer and general store owner, and Elzena Jane Ammons. As a teenager, Yost worked as a deputy marshal in Fairview. After graduating from high school in 1889, he attended Fairmont (West Virginia)

Normal School, quickly completing a brief program before teaching in Patterson Creek, West Virginia, during the 1889–1890 academic year for $30 per month. In 1890 Yost enrolled at Ohio Normal College (later Ohio Northern University) in Ada, where he was introduced to football and participated in organized sports for the first time as a first baseman on the school's baseball team.

Disenchanted with the prospects of a teaching career, Yost returned to Fairview and worked in the local oil fields. Enthralled with the petroleum business and evidently hoping to capitalize on its legal aspects, Yost in 1895 decided to study law at West Virginia University, where he played intercollegiate football as a 6-foot, 195-pound tackle. Taking advantage of lax eligibility rules, Yost also played several games with Lafayette College in 1896. The following year he received a bachelor's degree in law.

Rather than pursuing a full-time legal career, Yost accepted a position as head football coach at Ohio Wesleyan University in the fall of 1897. He led the school to a self-proclaimed state championship with seven wins, one loss, and one tie. Hoping to see as much of the country as he could, Yost left Ohio Wesleyan after one year, and in successive seasons he served at the University of Nebraska (7–4), the University of Kansas (10–0), and Stanford University (7–2–1). At each school he guided his team to a conference title. Seemingly inexhaustible, in 1900 Yost simultaneously coached the Stanford varsity and freshman squads as well as the football teams at San Jose Teachers College and the San Francisco area's Lowell High School and Ukiah High School.

In 1901 Yost accepted an offer from the University of Michigan to become head coach in Ann Arbor for $2,300. He remained at Michigan for the rest of his career, serving as football coach (1901–1923 and 1925–1927) and athletic director (1921–1941). He immediately established a national reputation for Michigan and himself by leading the legendary "point-a-minute" squads from 1901 to 1905. The 1901 season was capped with a convincing victory over Stanford, 49–0, in the first postseason Rose Bowl game. During those five seasons, which included 55 victories, only one loss, and one tie, the Wolverines averaged 49.8 points per game to their opponents' .7-point average. Yost suffered his first loss as the Michigan coach in 1905, his fifth year at the helm. He relied heavily on shrewd recruitment, as evidenced by the enlistment of All-America halfback Willie Heston, whom Yost took with him from San Jose Teachers College. Yost regarded Heston as "the fastest and greatest football player . . . in the history of the game."

Yost quickly earned the nickname "Hurry Up" from his players for his continual exhortations to move and execute with great speed. Yost emphasized field position with quick kicks and passing plays (although, ironically, he fought hard against the legalization of the pass in 1906) and capitalized on his opponents' miscues—a system he sometimes referred to as "punt, pass, and prayer." While some observers regarded his approach as less than exciting, Yost added up his victories and replied, "Let 'em holler about a punt, a pass, and a prayer. We generally have the last laugh."

In 1905 Yost wrote his only book, *Football for Player and Spectator*. The following year he married Eunice Josephine Fite; they had one child.

Through 1921 Yost worked at the university only during the football season, which afforded him time to pursue other interests and business activities. After 1901 Yost worked for the West Virginia Investment and Development Company, in Clarksburg, searching for potentially profitable natural resources. Yost engaged heavily in the oil business, developing companies and selling leases. He promoted and oversaw the construction of a hydroelectric project on the Caney Fork River in central Tennessee (1907–1914). He also served as a director of the Dixie Cement Company of Chattanooga, Tennessee (1908–1914), and the Cumberland Valley National Bank of Nashville, Tennessee (1912–1919). With these and other pursuits, Yost achieved financial security.

Yost became a year-round employee of the University of Michigan in 1921, when he accepted the position of director of intercollegiate athletics. Spurred by the provost marshal's 1917 report, which indicated that more than one-third of America's young men were unfit for military service in the First World War, Yost attempted to make sports accessible to as many students as possible. During his first decade as athletic director, he developed athletic curricula and oversaw the construction of Memorial Stadium (completed 1923; now Michigan Stadium), a field house bearing his name, a women's athletic building, an ice rink, a golf course, a gymnasium, and tennis courts.

Meanwhile, Yost still engaged in coaching, except in 1924 when his physician recommended rest. Apparently infuriated by Michigan's loss to Illinois that year, Yost returned to coaching for two more seasons. He regarded his 1925 squad, featuring the passing combination of Benny Friedman and Bennie Oosterban, as his greatest of all, even better than the point-a-minute teams. After 1926 Yost gave up coaching football and devoted all his energies to his athletic directorship. He retired in 1941, succeeded by Fritz Crisler. His efforts at Michigan resulted in 165 victories, 29 losses, and 10 ties. Eight of his Wolverine teams went undefeated and eight won or shared Western Conference championships. His career won-lost record was 196–36–12.

Taking advantage of his prominence, Yost often spoke inspirationally of "football's four cornerstones of success: brains, heart, courage, and character." Although he often chewed on an unlit cigar, Yost was a staunch opponent of smoking as well as drinking and swearing. He also served as a Boy Scout commissioner and developed an expertise in Civil War military history. He died in Ann Arbor.

Yost's achievements as a coach have made him a legendary football figure. Willie Heston remembered Yost with these words: "As a coach, in my judgment, he was the greatest that ever stepped on a gridiron" (Danzig, p. 155). Revered at the University of Michigan, Yost left the institution "a boundless energy, an admirable executive capacity, and a consuming desire for widespread athletic involvement" (Behee, p. 199). While some contemporaries questioned his recruitment tactics, Yost was nevertheless a prototype for the modern college football coach and athletic director. He consistently advanced his institution's athletic programs and brought great prominence to college sports in America.

• Yost's papers are located in the University of Michigan Library, as is the Fielding Harris Yost Photograph Series, a collection of photographs of family members and material related to Michigan football. In addition to his book, Yost wrote approximately fifty syndicated installments of his memoirs, "My 30 Years in Football," for a number of newspapers, including the *Chicago Herald and Examiner*, in 1925 and 1926. The most authoritative and lengthy study of Yost is John R. Behee's biography, *Fielding Yost's Legacy to the University of Michigan* (1971). Profiles of Yost and his years at Michigan appear in Tim Cohane, *Great College Football Coaches of the Twenties and Thirties* (1973); Allison Danzig, *The History of American Football* (1956); Edwin Pope, *Football's Greatest Coaches* (1955); Richard Whittingham, *Saturday Afternoon: College Football and the Men Who Made the Day* (1985); and Howard Roberts, *The Big Nine: The Story of Football in the Western Conference* (1948). See also W. B. Shaw, "Michigan and the Conference: A Ten-Year Argument over the University's Athletic Relations," *Michigan Alumnus* 54 (1947): 34–48, which elaborates on Yost's and Michigan's problems with the conference. An obituary is in the *New York Times*, 21 Aug. 1946.

MARC S. MALTBY

YOU, Dominique (c. 1770–14 Nov. 1830), buccaneer and artillerist, was born either at Port-au-Prince on the island of Santo Domingo, c. 1770, or at St. Jean d'Angély, France, c. 1772. Much of his life is shrouded in mystery, and little is known of his early life. Tradition has it that You was a sailor, possibly in the French navy, and that he served in the French army as an artillerist during the wars of the French Revolution and participated in General Charles Victor Emmanuel Leclerc's 1802 expedition to Haiti. There is general agreement that he was a skilled professional.

After a stint of unsuccessful privateering, sometime around 1810 You went to New Orleans and in the autumn of 1811 joined Jean and Pierre Lafitte at their private stronghold of Barataria. (One source claims that You was actually Alexander Lafitte, oldest brother of Jean.) You became a close friend of Jean Lafitte and was soon his chief lieutenant. Known as "Captain Dominique" and "Johnness," You was respected for his audacity and bravery. You was said to be of slight stature but broad-shouldered and physically strong.

Barataria was a community of slave runners, smugglers, and pirates that claimed legitimacy on the basis of letters of marque purchased from the "government" of Cartagena, Colombia, which had declared itself independent of Spain. Sailing under Cartagenian colors, You waged war on Spain and captured a number of its vessels in the Gulf of Mexico, including slavers from Africa. On occasion the Baratarian pirates also attacked ships of other nations, including the United States.

You's activities in the Lafittes' private operations led a New Orleans grand jury in 1814 to indict him for piracy, but he remained at large. In September 1814, however, Master Commandant Daniel Patterson led a successful U.S. Navy raid on the Baratarian stronghold at Grand Terre. All pirate vessels in the harbor were taken, but most of their crews escaped. You, described as being second in command, was among those captured.

When the English mounted a military assault on New Orleans, Jean Lafitte offered his services to General Andrew Jackson. The Americans released from imprisonment and armed the Baratarians they held, among them You, who was given command of one of two 24-pounder cannon manned by Baratarian gunners (the other was commanded by Renato Beluché) in Line Jackson. They took part in battles on 28 December and 1 and 8 January. These artillerists were the only Baratarians who saw action. Their services were so valued during the 8 January 1815 battle of New Orleans that Jackson's general order of 21 January specifically mentions "Captain Dominique" and Beluché, "lately commanding privateers of Barataria," in these words: "The general cannot avoid giving his warm approbation of the manner in which these gentlemen have uniformly conducted themselves while under his command and the gallantry with which they redeemed the pledge they gave at the opening of the campaign to defend the country." In recognition of his role in the American victory, all proceedings against You were dropped, and in February 1815 President James Madison pardoned him and other Baratarians.

After the war Jean Lafitte repurchased his vessels that Patterson had captured and sold as prizes. The Lafittes, You, and many other Baratarians sailed to Port-au-Prince, where they expected to be welcomed and hoped to set up operations. Allowed only to take on supplies, they were turned away at Port-au-Prince. The Lafittes then sailed to Galveston, but You parted company with them and returned to New Orleans.

In 1817 You settled permanently in New Orleans, where he became quite popular. An avid supporter of General Jackson, You's example was important in helping rally the lawless elements of the population to the United States.

In 1820 You was involved with Nicholas Girod, millionaire former mayor of New Orleans, in a plot to bring Napoleon Bonaparte to New Orleans from Saint Helena. You was to have carried out the rescue of the former French emperor from the island. Three days before You was to sail in the schooner *Serpentine* for Saint Helena, word was received in New Orleans of Napoleon's death.

You died in poverty in New Orleans. Given a military funeral at state expense, he is buried at St. Louis Cathedral in the French Quarter. His tombstone proclaims him "the intrepid warrior of a hundred battles on land and sea."

• A full-length biography of You has yet to be published. On his career as a pirate, see Lyle Saxon, *Lafitte the Pirate* (1930). For information on his role in the War of 1812, see Wilburt S. Brown, *The Amphibious Campaign for West Florida and Louisiana, 1814–1815* (1969). Also see James Grant Wilson and John Fiske, eds., *Appleton's Cyclopedia of American Biography* (6 vols., 1888–1889; repr. 1968), vol. 6, p. 642.

SPENCER C. TUCKER

YOUMANS, Edward Livingston (3 June 1821–18 Jan. 1887), scientific popularizer and editor, was born in Coeymans, New York, the son of Vincent Youmans, a farmer and mechanic, and Catherine Scofield, a teacher. A voracious reader raised in a home where books and ideas were valued, Youmans early developed an interest in science and largely educated himself after completing common-school studies. An attack of ophthalmia in 1835 damaged his eyesight and prompted his move to New York City for treatment in 1839. There he met Horace Greeley and Walt Whitman and formed a lasting professional connection with publisher William Henry Appleton.

While undergoing treatment for his eyes, Youmans studied chemistry and physics with the help of his sister Eliza, who read to him and conducted his experiments. He invented a device that enabled him to write, and his eyesight so improved that he completed a medical degree through the University of Vermont (c. 1852). He never practiced medicine, however, and instead embarked on a career as a writer and lecturer on scientific topics. Youmans produced a stream of books, including *A Class-book of Chemistry* (1851), a popular textbook that went through three editions; *Alcohol and the Constitution of Man* (1853), a study of the effects of alcohol on the human body (the product of a passing enthusiasm for state prohibition); *The Handbook of Household Science* (1857), on the application of science to domestic heating, ventilation, food preparation, and cleaning; and two edited collections of essays on the implications of recent scientific developments for education and modern culture.

Youmans lectured extensively on the lyceum circuit from 1851 to 1868, when health problems, including rheumatism, drove him from the rostrum. As a speaker he was given to "excited gyrations," expressive of his "explosive animal spirits" (Fiske, p. 79). Youmans drew large crowds to lectures on topics such as "Ancient Philosophy and Modern Science" and "The Chemistry of the Sunbeam." He also advised the Appleton company on scientific publications and translations, and in 1871 he founded their International Scientific Series, a line of popularized monographs by thinkers including Charles Darwin, Walter Bagehot, and E. B. Tylor, which eventually ran to more than seventy volumes. Above all, Youmans advanced the cause of scientific popularization through the *Popular Science Monthly*, which he founded in 1872 and edited with the aid of his brother William until Edward's death. Oliver Wendell Holmes, Sr., recognized the magazine's role in disseminating scientific thought

when he praised it for sustaining him "like the air they send down to the people in a diving bell" (Fiske, p. 315).

John Fiske dubbed Youmans America's "apostle of evolution," and historians have especially recognized his crucial role in building an American audience for the ideas of the British evolutionary philosopher Herbert Spencer. On encountering a prospectus in 1860 for Spencer's *Synthetic Philosophy*, a series of works that would apply the principle of evolution to every branch of human inquiry, Youmans eagerly wrote to the author offering to do "anything in my power to forward the enterprise" (Fiske, p. 107). This he did most energetically over the ensuing years, soliciting subscriptions and contributions to support Spencer's work, reviewing and promoting the books in magazines and newspapers, and arranging for their U.S. publication. Youmans thought the progressive, optimistic Spencer an especially appropriate sage for Americans and trumpeted the promise that Spencer's "large, organizing ideas" (Fiske, p. 169) would lay the foundation for a coherent, modern, scientific culture. In Youmans's preface to the American edition of *First Principles* (1865), he praised the author as "bold," "earnest," and "practical," a thinker "eminently suited to the genius of our people" (pp. xi–xii). Indeed, Youmans founded the *Popular Science Monthly* initially to serve as a U.S. outlet for the series of Spencer's articles that became *The Study of Sociology* (1873), and Spencer ultimately published ninety-one articles in Youmans's magazine. It was Youmans who organized the Delmonico's banquet in New York City that capped Spencer's U.S. tour in 1882, and which historians have seen as representing the apex of Spencer's American influence.

Youmans had married the widow Catherine E. Newton Lee in 1861, and she became a valued coworker; they had no children. He died at his home in New York City. The *New York Times*'s obituary counted him "a most earnest worker for the advancement of science," and it is especially in this light that he should be recalled. Youmans's lasting importance may be said to lie less in his popularization of the now-defunct ideas of Herbert Spencer than in his broader role as an apostle of scientific thinking and education, and especially as an evangelist of that generalized late nineteenth-century faith that a properly scientific stance would illuminate every realm of inquiry and culture—a faith for which Spencerianism served as a powerful if transient vehicle. Youmans possessed a genuine talent for rendering vast amounts of scientific material into clear, understandable prose and for connecting the contributions of various thinkers into a single narrative that offered the reader not only comprehension but a sense of mastery over both the past and the present of science. In *The Culture Demanded by Modern Life* (1867), Youmans forcefully linked the Emersonian project of American cultural independence and advancing social improvement with the progress of science and with his own vocation of popular scientific education. A Victorian thinker determined to contain the surging forces of modernity, he insisted in *The Correlation and Conservation of Forces* (1864) that science was not grossly materialistic but led to an ever higher plane of knowledge and experience, "to a truth of the spiritual world" (p. xii). In Youmans's (as in Spencer's) view, science would ultimately promote stability, order, morality, and certainty, not anarchical, amoral liberation from past constraints. "The movement," he avowed, "is upward and onward toward greater good" (Bannister, p. 74). In this "earnest worker" one finds a fervent witness to Victorian hopes for an evolving, progressive, scientific culture.

• There is no known collection of Youmans papers. In addition to works cited above, Youmans's principal books include *Chemical Atlas* (1854), featuring colored diagrams as teaching aids, and *Herbert Spencer on the Americans, and the Americans on Herbert Spencer* (1883), which contains Youmans's report on his interview with Spencer, an account of the 1882 farewell banquet at Delmonico's, and the evening's speeches and related letters. Otherwise, the bulk of Youmans's output consists of editorials and reviews for the *Popular Science Monthly*. A selection of these that address various facets of the woman question are gathered in Louise Newman, ed., *Men's Ideas/Women's Realities: Popular Science, 1870–1915* (1985).

Most secondary accounts draw heavily on John Fiske, *Edward Livingston Youmans: Interpreter of Science for the People* (1894), which remains valuable as a source of information on Youmans's life from the perspective of an old friend, protégé, and professional colleague; Fiske reproduces many letters and several of Youmans's most important essays. Two articles are helpful on Youmans: Charles M. Haar, "E. L. Youmans: A Chapter in the Diffusion of Science in America," *Journal of the History of Ideas* 9 (1948): 193–213, sums up Youmans's career and main concerns; and William E. Leverette, Jr., "E. L. Youmans' Crusade for Scientific Autonomy and Respectability," *American Quarterly* 17 (1965): 12–32, addresses arguments in the magazine regarding the authority and status of science. In the monographic literature, Richard Hofstadter, *Social Darwinism in American Thought* (1944), discusses Youmans's role as a popularizer of Spencer and an apostle of social Darwinism, while Robert C. Bannister's *Social Darwinism: Science and Myth in Anglo-American Social Thought* (1979) challenges historians' portrayal of Youmans as a social Darwinist and offers a careful analysis of the political and scientific terms on which Youmans defended Spencer. Obituaries are in the *New York Times*, 19 Jan. 1887, and (by Youmans's sister Eliza) in the *Popular Science Monthly*, Mar. 1887.

MARK PITTENGER

YOUMANS, Vincent (27 Sept. 1898–5 Apr. 1946), popular composer, was born Vincent Millie Youmans in New York City, the son of Vincent Youmans, an owner of hat stores, and Lucy Millie. Educated at private schools in Mamaroneck and Rye, in 1916 Youmans left Yale University, where he was studying engineering, to make piano-roll recordings for the Aeolian Company.

After enlisting in the navy in 1917, Youmans began composing for the band at Great Lakes Naval Station. In 1919 he became a song plugger, playing the tunes of his music publisher employer (Remick's) in music stores and other locations where the songs' possible

purchasers—usually vaudevilleans—might be found. Remick's published Youmans's first song, "The Country Cousin," in 1920. His first Broadway song, "Maid to Order Maid," was interpolated into *Linger Longer Letty* (1920), while others found their way into *Piccadilly to Broadway* (1920). In 1921 Youmans became staff composer at Harms music publishers.

Never a prolific composer, with only ninety-three songs published during his entire career, Youmans still became the most popular American composer of the 1920s. Unlike early rivals like Jerome Kerns or later ones such as Richard Rodgers, Youmans never settled on a favored lyricist; unlike Irving Berlin and Cole Porter, he took no interest in writing his own lyrics. Youmans's first musical comedy score, for *Two Little Girls in Blue* (1921), was shared with Paul Lannin; several lyrics also came from Ira Gershwin, then writing as Arthur Francis. The selection "Oh Me! Oh My! Oh You!" demonstrated a trademark of Youmans's, an insistently repeated key phrase—in this instance a two-note drop—that gained freshness through harmonic variations. Such songs became popular so quickly that in her novel *Save Me the Waltz* (1934), Zelda Fitzgerald evoked the spirit of New York in the 1920s with them: "Vincent Youmans wrote the music for the twilights just after the war. . . . Youmans wrote a new tune. The old tunes floated through the hospital windows . . . and the new tunes went the rounds of lobbies and grills, palm-gardens and roofs." Though Youmans wrote only for the theater, his songs quickly made their way into the repertoires of dance bands, where they sat easily alongside standard Tin Pan Alley fare. Musicologist Alec Wilder noted that they were "of a swinging nature" long before swing bands existed.

While playing rehearsal piano for the operetta *Orange Blossoms* (1922), Youmans decided that his future lay in writing such shows. When Rudolf Friml withdrew from *Wildflower* (1923), producer Arthur Hammerstein hired Youmans. *Wildflower* enjoyed long runs in both New York and London, and its lurchingly repetitive "Bambalina" continued Youmans's success. For a time Youmans had three shows simultaneously in production, including *Mary Jane McKane* (1923) and *Lollipop* (1924).

No, No, Nanette became the most popular musical comedy of the 1920s. Having opened in Detroit in April 1923, it underwent change after change, moving around the nation and eventually overseas. By its New York opening in September 1925, *No, No, Nanette* had already achieved success earlier that year in Paris and London. Soon there were two English companies, another in Berlin, and three in America. Youmans's lyricists for *No, No, Nanette* were Otto Harbach and Irving Caesar. The show's most popular song, "Tea for Two," was as simplistic as a nursery rhyme with a lyric by Caesar originally meant as a stopgap until something better came along. Nearly as popular was "I Want to Be Happy," a melody that maintained its repetitions right through the release. When Sandy Wilson created his British pastiche of the 1920s (*The Boy*

Friend, 1954), he patterned most of his songs after Youmans's.

Although Youmans professed to hate all jazz or swing versions of his music, his short-lived adaptation of the Franco-British *A Night Out* (1925), which actually opened in New York before *No, No, Nanette*, included "Sometimes I'm Happy," which became a favorite basis for jazz improvisation within what Wilder called "one of the narrowest ranges I have come across, a half tone less than an octave." Then in 1926 comedienne Beatrice Lillie introduced the rousing, wonderfully harmonic "I Know That You Know" in Youmans's *Oh, Please!* In 1927 Youmans married Anne Varley; they had two children before they divorced in 1933. Youmans married Mildred Boots in 1935; they had no children and were divorced in 1946.

From another hit show, *Hit the Deck!* (1927), came "Halleleujah!" a buoyantly upbeat jazz spiritual. By then Youmans was so dominant that Cole Porter wrote him into the lyrics of his song "You're the Top." *Hit the Deck!* was Youmans's debut as his own producer and the last of his hit shows. In 1928 he set up his own publishing company, the Vincent Youmans Publishing Company; it was reasonably successful.

Rainbow (1928), an ambitious American operetta about the California gold rush, closed within a month. Youmans then acquired a theater and produced the sprawling *Great Day* (1929). Dealing with race relations and riverboat gambling, it also failed despite three outstanding compositions: the "Halleleujah!"-like title song and two that displayed a new complexity, the graceful "Without a Song," a favorite within the concert repertoire, and the haunting "More Than You Know," which with its long melodic line, became a particular favorite of jazz musicians. Youmans produced *Damn Your Honor* in 1929 and contributed songs to *Show Girl* that same year, but his all-star musical comedy for Florenz Ziegfeld, *Smiles* (1930), ran only a month; its British version, *The One Girl*, also failed. Its most important and popular song, the hypnotic "Time on My Hands," later became the ironic theme song of the prison orchestra at San Quentin, California.

His early attempts at writing for films, generally by recycling his show tunes, were unsuccessful. These included *Hit the Deck!* (1930); *Song of the West* (1930), which included most of the songs from *Rainbow*; and *The Prodigal* (1931), based partly on an abandoned film of *Great Day*. Youmans's first original film score was *What a Widow!* (1931), a Gloria Swanson venture produced by Joseph Kennedy.

In New York, *Through the Years* (1932), said to have been Youmans's personal favorite, closed after only twenty performances despite the title song and the booming "Drums in My Heart." His last Broadway show was the successful revue *Take a Chance* (1932), but most of its hits were written by other composers, with Youmans's only hit being the optimistic "Rise 'n' Shine."

In 1933 Youmans wrote the score (lyrics by Edward Eliscu and Gus Kahn) for *Flying Down to Rio*, a visually inventive RKO film, which along with Warner Bros.' *Forty-second Street*, is credited with reviving the film musical. Calling Youmans's score "jeweled," dance historian Arlene Croce particularly commended the Latin sounds of "Orchids in the Moonlight" and "The Carioca." The latter, which she called a "fast tango," became a favorite of dancing teachers; dance historian John Storm Roberts thought Youmans had created the harbinger of the samba. Alec Wilder called *Flying Down to Rio* Youmans's "most consistently theatrical score."

Despite the success of *Flying Down to Rio*, RKO rejected Youmans's demands to become his own producer, and, holding out for operettas, Youmans was passed over for the Fred Astaire–Ginger Rogers film that became *Swing Time*. In 1934 he was diagnosed with tuberculosis. He lost his music publishing company in that year, and in 1936, declaring bankruptcy, he sacrificed his theater.

Around 1936 Youmans told friends he was working on "serious" compositions, apparently influenced by Latin composers such as Carlos Chavez and Ernesto Lecuona. A 1940 film version of *No, No, Nanette* caused little stir, and the *Vincent Youmans Concert Revue*, subsequently renamed the *Vincent Youmans Ballet Revue*, closed on the road in 1944.

Youmans died in Denver, Colorado. His biographer, Gerald Bordman, was apparently unable to find evidence of the 150 manuscripts written in a "cryptic shorthand" that Youmans had allegedly left unpublished. A 1950 film version of *No, No, Nanette* was called *Tea for Two*, and a 1955 film of *Hit the Deck!* achieved critical acclaim. Likewise, a 1970 Broadway revival of *No, No, Nanette* with Ruby Keeler ran for nearly three years. In his 1972 *American Popular Song: The Great Innovators* Wilder remarked on Youmans's "search for new ways to make simple, direct statements," saying that Youmans's songs "never sounded in any respect like those of his contemporaries."

• Youmans's papers are still held by family members. A biography is Gerald Bordman, *Days to Be Happy, Years to Be Sad* (1982). Although in disagreement with Bordman on several issues, the best assessment of Youmans as songwriter is Alec Wilder, *American Popular Song: The Great Innovators* (1972). Arlene Croce, *The Fred Astaire and Ginger Rogers Book* (1972), clearly demonstrates Youmans's strengths as a composer for dancers. An obituary is in the *New York Times*, 6 Apr. 1946.

JAMES ROSS MOORE

YOUMANS, William Jay (14 Oct. 1838–10 Apr. 1901), science writer and editor, was born in Milton, Saratoga County, New York, the son of Vincent Youmans and Catherine Scofield, farmers. Life was hard at the Youmans homestead, but the parents instilled a love of literature and a social conscience in their children.

Still, accident did much to shape William Jay Youmans's future career choices. Older brother Edward Livingston Youmans, who was going blind and had failed to kindle enthusiasm for scientific subjects in one younger brother, settled instead on William as a future collaborator in projected literary and scientific undertakings. Edward prodded him to study at Columbia College and Yale's Sheffield Scientific School, after which William took a medical degree at the University of the City of New York (later New York University) in 1865.

Youmans's interest in physiology and chemistry led him in 1866 to London, England, where he studied under the important biologist Thomas Henry Huxley. Youmans married Celia Greene that same year; they had two sons and two daughters. Upon his return to the United States in 1867 and before he settled in Winona, Minnesota, to practice medicine, Youmans recast Huxley's *Lessons on Elementary Physiology* (1866) into a format more suitable for the American market. The *Elements of Physiology and Hygiene* (1868), containing the addition of seven chapters on hygiene written by Youmans, even won the praise of Huxley's son Leonard, who usually detested American publishers for pirating English works. In Youmans's view, the subject of hygiene could be treated only after the fundamental principles of physiology had been grasped.

In a second edition of Huxley's work, published in 1873, Youmans more fully reworked his mentor's text. Youmans explained that Huxley's compressed and concise writing style had made the *Elements* too difficult for the average reader, so he had simplified the prose, particularly its technical terms, and incorporated more illustrations. The revised edition had been called forth by a growing demand to treat the subject of hygiene within the context of general education.

Youmans found his life's work in 1872, when he moved to New York to assist his brother Edward in producing what became one of America's leading scientific magazines, *Popular Science Monthly*. Youmans's collaboration began with the first issue in May 1872; he became sole editor upon his brother's death in 1887 and continued in the position until his retirement in 1900.

According to an editorial preface, *Popular Science Monthly* aimed to further public education by allowing "scientific men" to explain their work to the nonscientific public in place of the "light articles and shreds of information" purveyed by the general press. In the view of the brothers Youmans, the diffusion of science was a noble undertaking, and *Popular Science Monthly* offered the most complete record of recent intellectual work.

Popular Science Monthly, published by D. Appleton and Co., soon attained a circulation of 11,000, a remarkable figure given its specialized and philosophical subject matter. Each month Youmans published a detailed biography of a leading naturalist, physician, or geologist, nearly all of which he wrote himself. Fifty of them were republished in 1896 under the title *Pioneers of Science in America*. He also supplied several articles in each issue on science education, the applications of science, and recent discoveries in the physical sciences under the heading "Editor's Table."

Youmans and his brother were enthusiastic followers of the evolutionary doctrines of the Englishman Herbert Spencer, leading them to recruit Spencer (as well as fellow evolutionist Huxley) as authors. The Youmans brothers saw evolution as a universal process in nature, and they were particularly concerned to show its bearings on human life and social development. *Popular Science Monthly* thereby became distinguished for its early advocacy and popularization of evolution in America. Apart from *Popular Science Monthly*, from 1880 to 1900 Youmans contributed four major articles a year—on topics as diverse as physiology, chemistry, metallurgy, and meteorology—to another undertaking of the Appletons' publishing firm, the *Annual Cyclopaedia*.

Youmans was a fellow of the American Association for the Advancement of Science and of the New York Academy of Sciences. He died in Mount Vernon, New York.

• Youmans is mentioned in John Spencer Clark, *Life and Letters of John Fiske* (1917), and in John Fiske, *Edward Livingston Youmans: Interpreter of Science for the People* (1894). Obituaries of Youmans are in *Appletons' Annual Cyclopaedia* (1901, with portrait) and in *Popular Science Monthly*, May 1901.

SUSAN SHEETS-PYENSON

YOUNG, Allyn Abbott (19 Sept. 1876–7 Mar. 1929), economist, educator, and government adviser, was born in Kenton, Ohio, the son of Sutton Erastus Young, a school superintendent, and Emma Matilda Stickney. After graduating with a Ph.B. from Hiram College in 1894 and working as a printer in Ohio and Minnesota, Young began his graduate education in economics at the University of Wisconsin in 1898. Young spent the academic year of 1899–1900 in Washington, D.C., working in the Section of Analysis and Research for the Twelfth Census. He returned to Wisconsin in 1900 and earned his Ph.D. in 1902. In 1904 Young married Jessie Bernice Westlake; they had one child.

Young spent his early teaching career at Western Reserve (1902–1903), Dartmouth (1904), and the University of Wisconsin (1905–1906). At Wisconsin he joined Thomas Adams and Max Lorenz in coauthoring a revision of Richard Ely's *Outlines of Economics*, then the leading U.S. economics textbook. Young coauthored subsequent editions between 1908 and 1930. In 1906 he accepted an invitation to chair Stanford University's economics department and arranged for University of Chicago economist Thorstein Veblen to join him. After four years filled with conflict over control of the department's academic program and personnel decisions, he used a year as visiting professor at Harvard University (1910–1911) to seek another position and accepted the chairmanship of economics at Washington University in St. Louis in the fall of 1911.

In "Some Limitations of the Value Concept" (*Quarterly Journal of Economics* 25 [May 1911]: 409–28) Young argued that we need to distinguish more carefully between price and value in order to avoid confusion in both equilibrium analysis and the theory of wealth. Consulted by the St. Louis Public Services commission in a rate case, he also argued in "Depreciation and Rate Control" (*Quarterly Journal of Economics* 28 [May 1914]: 630–63) that normal business activity and growth will ensure that replacement and additions will offset the decline in the value of older assets, thus opposing the common assumption that the value of assets should be scaled downward if the utility has not maintained a reserve for accumulated depreciation. Under the usual assumption, the revelation of utility assets for rate control purposes amounted to the taxation of past profits.

In 1913 Cornell University offered Young a professorship in economics and finance, his first opportunity to teach in a graduate program on a permanent basis. At Cornell, he supervised the thesis of his best-known student, Frank H. Knight, on the theory of profit; the work was later published as *Risk Uncertainty and Profit* (1913). Despite differences over increasing returns and cost theory, the two remained close associates until Young's death.

Also in 1913 Young wrote an influential critique of A. C. Pigou's *Wealth and Welfare* (London, 1912), a discussion of the taxation of increasing cost industry. Pigou argued that resources could be misallocated in competitive economies containing increasing or decreasing cost industries. Although society would benefit from further investment in decreasing cost industries, the private cost to the industry would be prohibitive. In increasing cost industries, where private cost was low, investment would occur despite a high social cost. Pigou thus proposed a tax on increasing cost industries coupled with a subsidy for decreasing cost industries. In his review, which appeared in the *Quarterly Journal of Economics* (27 [1913]: 672–86), Young argued that increasing cost industries were not amenable to the equilibrium analysis Pigou used, thereby laying the foundation for the theory of increasing returns and economic growth, which he developed fifteen years later.

Young's Cornell years were also marked by service to the wider academic community, first as secretary of the American Economic Association from 1914 to 1920 and then as president of the American Statistical Association in 1917. During the war Young moved into government service, taking a two-year leave of absence from Cornell (1917–1919). Serving first as the director of the Bureau of Research for the War Trade Board, Young then joined the group of scholars gathered by Colonel Edward M. House to formulate potential solutions to international problems in preparation for the peace settlement. Young accompanied the American Peace Commission to Paris in 1918–1919 as the chief of the Division of Economics and Statistics and was consulted in the negotiations, particularly on the problems of reparations and postwar international trade policies. When British economist John Maynard Keynes published his *Economic Consequences of the Peace* (1918), protesting the imposition of large reparations on Germany on the grounds that they could never be repaid, Young wrote a review cautioning

readers of the *New Republic* (21 [25 Feb. 1920]: 338–89) against accepting Keynes's argument. Where Keynes was frustrated when clear "economic right" did not prevail, Young accepted the fact that treaty negotiations had been mired in the tensions of competing public, political, and economic pressures and asked Americans to look beyond the treaty itself to the framework for post-treaty reparation discussions that had been established.

After his return to Cornell in 1919, Harvard University offered Young a professorship, which he began in 1920. Through his position at Harvard, Young exercised considerable influence on U.S. monetary theory, empirical study, and policy analysis. An adviser of Benjamin Strong, governor of the New York Federal Reserve Bank, Young also counted among his students Lauchlin Currie, who initiated reform of the Federal Reserve System in 1935. A compilation of Young's statistical work on banking, *An Analysis of Bank Statistics for the United States*, was published in 1928, and at the time of his death he was preparing a book on monetary economics. Young also supervised Edward Chamberlin's dissertation on the theory of monopolistic competition, launching another important mid-twentieth-century research program.

Young's participation in the peace negotiations had made him a spokesperson for international cooperation. He became an adviser to the Council of the League of Nations and assisted in working out a reconstruction plan for Hungary on behalf of the league in 1924–1925. The council asked Young to help plan a world economic conference to be held in Geneva in 1927. When he was elected president of the American Economic Association in 1925, Young used his presidential address, titled "Economics and War," to promote international economic cooperation.

Young's prominence within the economics profession was crowned in 1927 by his selection to fill a new chair in political economy at the London School of Economics. Young's selection was widely hailed as a mark of the maturity of American economics, because no American economist had ever been selected for a full professorship in England. The appointment was for a three-year term, at which time Young could either stay or return to his post at Harvard. Unfortunately, sickness and then death intervened. Eighteen months after his appointment, at the age of fifty-two, Young died suddenly in London of pneumonia after contracting a mild case of influenza.

In September 1928, shortly before his death, Young delivered the presidential address of Section F (Economics and Statistics) of the British Association for the Advancement of Science. As the first American selected as a BAAS president, Young used the opportunity to provide a conception of economic theory that stood in striking contrast to the static equilibrium analysis emerging as the standard form of contemporary Anglo-American economics. Beginning by rejecting perfect competition as the appropriate starting point for economic analysis, Young went on to sketch out a theory of economic growth that took increasing returns to be "natural phenomena, like the precession of the equinoxes." Drawing on Adam Smith's understanding of the relation between the division of labor and the size of the market, Young argued that economic progress was accomplished through the entrepreneurial search for new markets. The expansion of a market generated increasing returns, but it also created external economics in other markets, which entrepreneurs there would react to, allowing further market expansion. ("Increasing Returns and Economic Progress" was published in the *Economic Journal* 38 [1928]: 527–42.)

Young's argument provides an indication of the new direction his theoretical work had found and suggests possible themes for the book on economics he had been planning to write at the time of his death. Because this book remained unwritten, and the partial manuscript on monetary economics was lost in the hasty departure of his wife from London, no systematic treatment of Young's economic theory has survived. His legacy, therefore, is the tradition of creative thought he inspired in his students, who were stimulated by his superb teaching, the catholicity of his interests, and his unstinting willingness to serve.

• Collections of Young's papers are in the Hiram College archives and in the Harvard University Archive. His articles in the *Quarterly Journal of Economics* and his "Economics and War," *American Economic Review* 16 (Mar. 1926): 1–13, are reprinted in the volume *Economic Problems: New and Old* (1927), along with essays and memoranda from his years at Cornell and Harvard. See also, on the peace, "The United States and Reparations," *Foreign Affairs* 1 (1922): 35–47, and "The Economic Settlement," in *What Really Happened at Paris*, ed. Edward Mandell House and Charles Seymour (1921), pp. 291–318. His lecture notes, *Encyclopedia Britannica* entries, and a sample of his unsigned articles in the *Book of Popular Science* appear in the combined third and fourth number of the *Journal of Economic Studies* 17 (1990). Charles Blitch, *Allyn Young: The Peripatetic Economist* (1995), is a book-length treatment of Young's work. On Young's treatment of increasing returns and its contribution to the theory of economic growth, see Blitch, "Allyn Young on Increasing Returns," *Journal of Post Keynesian Economics* 5 (Spring 1983): 359–72, and Lauchlin Currie, "Allyn Young and the Development of Growth Theory," *Journal of Economic Studies* 8 (1981): 52–60. Obituaries are in June 1929 issues of the *Economic Journal* and the *American Economic Review*; see also Currie, "Recollection of Allyn Young," *Review of Economic Studies* 17 (1990): 10–13.

ROSS B. EMMETT

YOUNG, Ammi Burnham (19 June 1798–13 Mar. 1874), architect, was born in Lebanon, New Hampshire, the son of Captain Samuel Young, a builder, and Rebecca Burnham. Young trained as a carpenter and builder with his father. In 1822 he married Polly Hough; they had one child. Polly Young died in 1825. He later married Hannah G. Ticknor. She died in 1860.

Possibly through the influence of his brother Ira, a professor of astronomy at Dartmouth College, Young was commissioned to design buildings for the college:

Wentworth Hall and Thornton Hall (both 1827–1828) on either side of the existing Dartmouth Hall, which, together with Reed Hall (1839–1840), a more stylistically sophisticated neoclassical dormitory, became known as "Old Row." Wentworth, Thornton, and Reed halls were simple rectangular buildings with triangular gable ends to the roofs that could be read as pediments. The earlier Kimball Union Academy at Meriden, New Hampshire (1825), Young's first authenticated building, was similar in design. His work at Dartmouth concluded with the observatory in 1854.

Young's design for the Congregational church at Lebanon (1828) was very much in the tradition of New England meetinghouses as illustrated in the publications of Asher Benjamin, who in turn relied on the churches with elaborate towers by the English architect James Gibbs. Most of Young's designs were in the classical mode, but he did make excursions into the medieval idiom. St. Paul's Episcopal Church in Burlington, Vermont (1832, now destroyed) was Young's only structure in the Gothic revival style, although he unsuccessfully submitted a medieval entry in the competition for the Mount Auburn Cemetery Chapel, Cambridge, Massachusetts, in 1844.

Young's two most significant designs were in the Greek revival style, the Vermont State House at Montpelier (1833–1836) and the Boston Custom House (1837–1847). The state house portico was borrowed from the Theseion in Athens, while the dome was inspired by the Pantheon in Rome, even though there is no usable internal space below it. Although modified after a fire in 1857, it still functions as a legislative building. Similar in character but a much more mature design was the Boston Custom House. Greek Doric detailing and monolithic granite columns dominated the exterior, but in this building the dome actually covered a Pantheon-like internal great room well-lighted from its sides and an oculus at its apex. At a cost of well over $1 million, this structure, ten years in construction, was one of Young's finest works. The whole building later became the base for a 500-foot-high tower constructed by Peabody and Stearns in 1915.

Young moved from Lebanon to Boston in 1838. He designed the Broomfield Street Methodist Church (1848–1849) and courthouses at Worcester (1842–1845), and Lowell (1850), Massachusetts. During 1850 he submitted four different projects for extending the U.S. Capitol in Washington, D.C., none of which were accepted.

As a significant emerging architect, Young was a logical choice for the position of supervising architect of the Treasury Department's Bureau of Construction, a position equal to that of its engineer, Captain Alexander Hamilton Bowman of the Corps of Engineers. Over a ten-year period beginning in 1852, Young and Bowman collaborated on the design of about seventy federal buildings, including postal, customs, and court facilities; about fifteen marine hospitals also were built. Young used the Roman temple form for several buildings, such as the extant Custom House at

Norfolk, Virginia (1852–1859), but his predominant stylistic idiom was Italianate, derived from the English architect Sir Charles Barry. This style is best seen in the Custom House and Post Office at Windsor, Vermont (1856–1858), which remains in its original condition. Bowman and Young were concerned with fire protection in federal buildings and turned to cast iron for both structure and decorative detail; wrought iron was introduced for beams. Doors, window frames, and internal shutters were all of cast iron, as can be seen at the Custom House and Post Office in Galveston, Texas (1857–1861).

Young was dismissed from the supervising architect's position in 1862 because of extravagant costs in construction, notably on the continuation of Robert Mills's Treasury Building, where the monolithic columns were costing $5,000 apiece. During the last twelve years of his life, Young practiced architecture in Washington, employing Bartholomew Oertley from the Bureau of Construction, but nothing is known of his projects. Young died in Washington, D.C.

• Architectural drawings and engravings by Young are located in the Dartmouth College Archives, the Vermont Historical Society, the Society for the Preservation of New England Antiquities, the American Institute of Architects (Washington, D.C.), and the Boston Public Library. The National Archives (Record Group 121) has correspondence, drawings, and watercolors of seventy post office, custom house, and courtroom buildings and marine hospitals that were built. Those designs, plus many others that were projected but not built, were published as lithographs in *Plans of Public Buildings in Course of Construction under the Direction of the Secretary of the Treasury* (5 vols., 1855–1856) and another new series volume (1857). All projects are listed together with progress information in the annual *U.S. Treasury Report* (1853–1861). Other Young correspondence is in the Sheldon Museum Research Library, Middlebury, Vt. The only overview of Young's life and work is Lawrence Wodehouse, "Ammi Burnham Young: 1798–1874," *Journal of the Society of Architectural Historians* 25 (1966): 268–80, although there are a number of brief articles on specific buildings, attributions, buildings within a specific geographic area or of a specific architectural style. For Young's contribution to nineteenth-century public architecture, see Lois Craig, *The Federal Presence* (1978), and Bates Lowry, *Building a National Image* (1985).

LAWRENCE WODEHOUSE

YOUNG, Ann Eliza (13 Sept. 1844–?), antipolygamy crusader, was born Ann Eliza Webb in Nauvoo, Illinois, the daughter of Chauncey G. Webb, a Mormon and a wheelwright, and Eliza Churchill, a schoolteacher. In 1846, in keeping with what was then the practice of the Mormon church, Ann Eliza's father took a second wife. In 1848 the family moved to Salt Lake City (in what later became the state of Utah), where Chauncey Webb took three more wives.

In 1862 Brigham Young asked Ann Eliza to join the Deseret Dramatic Association. She spent four nights a week at "Lion House," the official residence of Brigham Young's wives and children.

In April 1863 Ann Eliza married James Leech Dee, a plasterer and amateur actor who had emigrated from England. Within a month Dee began courting other women. Ann Eliza experienced repeated physical abuse, including an attempt to strangle her. With the help of Brigham Young, she divorced Dee in 1865 and retained custody of their two sons. She then moved with her father and his wives to a farmhouse in the countryside. There Brigham Young courted her, and she became his polygamous wife in April 1868. He was sixty-six years old.

By the summer of 1872 the marriage had deteriorated. Ann Eliza felt that Brigham was not acting as a good stepfather to her sons (he had fifty-six children of his own). He built a home for her, which she turned into a boardinghouse. She suffered from various nervous ailments and became increasingly disillusioned with Brigham Young, her marriage, and the Mormon church. With the assistance of non-Mormon boarders, she filed for divorce in the summer of 1873.

In the divorce suit Ann Eliza asked for the exorbitant amount of $1,000 a month; an additional $200,000 for herself and her sons; and another $20,000 for attorney fees (soldiers at the time earned $13 a month; Brigham during their courtship had promised her $1,000 a year). Brigham offered her $15,000 and safe passage out of the Utah Territory to drop the suit. She was instantly surrounded by news reporters from all over the country who saw her action as a repudiation of polygamy.

The divorce case would drag on for four years, mostly because of the issue of whether a polygamous marriage was a lawful marriage with attendant alimony requirements. In the meantime, receiving various offers from the lecture circuit, Ann Eliza Young prepared three different lectures, "My Life in Bondage," "Polygamy as It Is," and "The Mormon Religion." Her manager was a former boarder and newspaper reporter, Major James Burton Pond.

Young's presentations began when lectures were an extremely popular form of American entertainment. Her lectures fed into the reform movements of the day, including growing interest in women's rights (she often compared the situation of Mormon wives to that of black slaves). Her lectures had the further appeal of presentable salaciousness: the public's interest in Mormon "harems" could be given respectability with moral indignation at the practice and with official sponsorship of the lectures by Protestant churchmen.

On the eve of Young's first appearance in Boston, Massachusetts, scandal erupted. The *Chicago Times* accused her and her manager of having sexual relations. The Young Men's Christian Association of Bloomington, Illinois, investigated the story and judged it to be unfounded.

Young's Boston appearance was successful. In New York City she told a reporter that Congress needed to legislate Mormonism out of existence. To that end, she traveled to Washington, D.C., went to the Ladies Reception Room of the House of Representatives, and passed out photographs of polygamous wives to show from their faces the effects of polygamy. President Ulysses S. Grant and his wife attended one of her lectures and personally congratulated her.

Not long afterward Congress passed the Poland Law, which took civil and criminal cases out of Mormon probate courts and gave them to the federal government and stated that jurors who believed in plural marriage or practiced it could not serve. The *Salt Lake Tribune*, an anti-Mormon newspaper, credited Young's influence for the enactment of the law.

Eight months after her departure from Salt Lake City, Young returned and lectured at the local Methodist church. She was excommunicated from the Mormon church in October 1874. Whether from need of church sponsorship or her own spiritual inclinations, she converted to the Methodist Episcopal faith in 1875.

In the meantime, Brigham Young filed an answer to her suit claiming his gross income of $6,000 per month would allow him reasonably to pay only $100 a month in alimony. He claimed he was lawfully married to Mary Ann Angell and that Ann Eliza was the legal and undivorced wife of James Dee. Judge James B. McKean ruled in 1875 that the marriage was legal and ordered Brigham to pay $500 a month in alimony, retroactively. Brigham paid $3,000 for Ann Eliza's legal fees but refused to pay the alimony. McKean sentenced him to a night in jail. McKean was soon removed by presidential dispatch. It took two more years and three more judges before the dispute was settled in April 1877. Brigham Young paid another $3,600 and all court costs.

Meanwhile, Ann Eliza Young supported herself by lecturing. In 1876 she published *Wife No. 19; or, A Life in Bondage . . . A Full Exposé of Mormonism.* Brigham Young died in August 1877, four months after the divorce was finally resolved. Ann Eliza wrote that he was "the great deceiver and false Prophet whose teachings brought such strange vicissitudes and misery upon us all." She continued her fight against polygamy, including writing letters to President Rutherford B. Hayes and his wife, Lucy. With her major antagonist dead, however, her popularity dwindled. Also contributing to her declining popularity was the 22 March 1882 signing of the Edmunds Act, which imposed fines and imprisonment on polygamists. In addition, the act barred polygamists from voting or holding federal office.

By 1882 Young had fallen in love with Moses R. Denning, a lumber and oil tycoon and bank director in Manistee, Michigan. Denning was already married with at least five grown children. His wife of more than twenty-five years divorced him in 1883, charging him with "severe acts of cruelty." Young gave her farewell lecture in Napoleon, Ohio, on 24 April 1883 and married Denning a month later.

Young's happiness, however, did not improve. She suffered from "nervous dyspepsia" and was not sexually compatible with her husband. She accused him of "caressing, handling and lewdly conversing" with servants. She buried her suffering in religion and con-

verted a third time, this time to Christian Science. She immersed herself in church work and efforts favoring woman suffrage.

As Denning continued his infidelities, Young refused him sex. In 1892 he left her and moved to Pennsylvania. Young divorced him in August 1893 and remained in their Manistee mansion for four years until she, out of financial necessity, was forced to sell it and move to Denver, Colorado, to be near her son. Constrained finances made her dispossess her son in 1899 and sell the Denver property. He died in 1902, and she moved to El Paso, Texas, to be near her brother Gilbert, who was working on the railroad in Chihuahua, Mexico.

In 1906 Young revised *Wife No. 19* and had it published by a vanity press. Few copies sold. After 1907 any record of her existence disappears. Varying stories place her in New York, Arizona, or California up through the 1920s, but none has been verified.

Young's lectures on her marriage and the Mormon religion entertained the American public for several years and helped influence legislation so that the Mormon church in 1890 issued a Manifesto advising church members to refrain from marriages forbidden by the law of the land. Her life, however, was a personally unhappy one; she failed in her attempts to destroy the church, and her end remains a mystery.

• The major source of information about Young's life is her autobiography, mentioned above. See also Irving Wallace, *The Twenty-seventh Wife* (1961). Further information can be found in the multivolume work published by the Daughters of the Utah Pioneers, Kate B. Carter, ed., *Our Pioneer Heritage*, vol. 1 (1958), vol. 11 (1968), vol. 19 (1976), and vol. 20 (1977). B. H. Roberts, *Comprehensive History of the Church*, vol. 5 (1930), pp. 442–47, covers the Youngs' divorce.

ANN W. ENGAR

YOUNG, Arthur Henry (14 Jan. 1866–29 Dec. 1943), cartoonist, known as Art, was born on a farm near Orangeville, Illinois, the son of Daniel Stephen Young and Amanda Wagner, farmers. The family moved when he was a year old to nearby Monroe, Wisconsin, where his father operated the general store. Passionate about drawing, the youth saw little value in a formal education and quit high school without graduating; and when he sold a cartoon to *Judge* magazine in 1883, his career preference was confirmed. That fall, he went to Chicago, where he enrolled in the Academy of Design (later merged with the Art Institute).

While attending classes, Young freelanced his humorous drawings to such publications as the *Nimble Nickel* (a weekly wholesale grocery house paper), *American Field* (a sportsman's magazine), and the *Evening Mail* (a daily paper). In fall 1886 Young was hired by the *Chicago Daily News*; he also worked for the *Chicago Tribune* briefly before going in 1888 to New York, where he enrolled in the Art Students' League. In fall 1889 he went to Paris to enter the Académie Julien. Six months later he was stricken by pleurisy, and to convalesce he returned to Monroe, where he stayed until 1892, when he joined the staff of the *Chicago Inter*

Ocean to produce a daily front-page political cartoon, the first such effort in the Midwest. In September of that year, Young participated in another inaugural event when he drew pictures for the *Inter Ocean*'s Sunday supplement, the nation's first newspaper Sunday supplement to be printed in color. Late that year, Young published his first book of drawings and text, *Hell Up to Date*, in which the cartoonist indulged his fascination with both Dante and Doré by depicting contemporary malefactors in torments appropriate to their sins.

Young married Elizabeth North, of Monroe, in January 1895, and soon after he went to work for the *Denver Times* in Colorado. While there, he heard lectures by Christian Socialist minister Myron Reed and British labor leader Keir Hardie and began to question the social justice of capitalism. In fall 1895 he went to New York, where he freelanced cartoons to the weekly humor magazines *Puck*, *Judge*, and *Life*; he also worked briefly as political cartoonist for William Randolph Hearst's *Evening Journal*, where he joined the chorus advocating war with Spain.

Almost from the day of his wedding, Young had felt keenly the loss of the freedom he had previously enjoyed to pursue his art without regard to the daily "routines and binding extractions . . . the duties and courtesies" (as he said) of married life, and his growing depression affected his work. After a couple of years of marriage, he separated from his wife in order to be able to work and earn enough to support her. They reconciled in 1900, and the first of their two sons was born that fall. In 1905 they purchased a farm in the country near Bethel, Connecticut, but they separated permanently later that year. Young wrote in his autobiography that "it had become impossible to combine domesticity and creative work" (*Art Young: His Life and Times*, p. 243). Never divorced, he continued to contribute to his family's support.

In 1902 Young returned to Wisconsin to lend his pen to Republican Progressive Robert La Follette's gubernatorial reelection campaign. But by 1905 Young had rejected the Republican politics of his heritage (including "all bourgeois institutions") and had resolved never again to draw a cartoon whose ideas he didn't believe in. In 1910 he realized that he belonged with the Socialists "in their fight to destroy capitalism"; late in the year, he joined others in launching the *Masses*, a radical magazine to which he regularly contributed (without pay) "pictorial shafts" against the symbols of the corrupt system—chiefly, financiers and politicians. In 1912 he accepted a remunerative assignment with another radical publication, *Metropolitan Magazine*, to produce in words and pictures a monthly review of governmental action in Washington, D.C., for which he made regular trips to the nation's capital for the next six years while continuing his other work in New York.

His mature drawing style was distinguished by its uncluttered simplicity at a time when most of his colleagues embellished their work with extensive crosshatching. Working in bold outline, Young created visual impact with solid black shapes contrasted against the open white areas of his pictures; sometimes, he shaded boldly with grease crayon. He crusaded against sweatshops, firetrap tenements, child labor, racial segregation, and discrimination against women as well as the traditional industrial and political foes of Socialism. One of his most reprinted cartoons depicts two slum urchins staring up at the night sky, one declaring: "Chee, Annie—look at the stars, thick as bedbugs." In another labeled "Capitalism," Young shows a bloated glutton at a dinner table strewn with the leftovers of a feast for one; drinking from a large urn, the man is tipping his chair backward, teetering on the brink of an abyss.

In 1913 Young and Max Eastman, editor of the *Masses*, were indicted for criminal libel by the Associated Press because the magazine contended that the AP had suppressed news in its reporting of a coal miners' strike in West Virginia. The indictment was dismissed a year later. Then in 1917 during World War I, the cartoonist and several *Masses* contributors were charged under the Espionage Act with "conspiracy to obstruct the [army's] recruiting and enlistment" by objecting to the war. One of Young's outspoken cartoons was called "Having Their Fling": it depicted an editor, capitalist, politician, and minister dancing with joyful abandon to the music played by an orchestra of cannons and other weapons under the direction of Satan. Called to the witness stand and asked why he drew antiwar cartoons, Young responded with simple eloquence, "For the public good." The trial ended in a hung jury, an outcome repeated at a second trial in September.

Young and several *Masses* alumni started the *Liberator* in 1918, and the next year Young helped found another magazine, *Good Morning*, a weekly with a radical sense of humor. Within five months of its debut, Young had become editor and publisher—and the chief contributor of both words and pictures—in which capacities he continued until the jovial little magazine expired in October 1921. Throughout the decade Young contributed to several other publications, including *Life*, the *New Yorker*, and the *Nation*; and his cartoons were fixtures in the pages of the *New Masses*, born in 1926. By the 1930s, plagued by the infirmities of old age, he was producing much less work, and he was occasionally supported financially by his friends.

At his death in New York City, the *New York Times* noted editorially that "he was a lovable soul in spite of his sometimes heterodox opinions" in the advocacy of which "he had sacrificed the chance to accumulate a fair share of this world's goods." That he was a kindly, thoughtful man, selfless and sincere, with simple but firmly held convictions is borne out by every page of his two autobiographies. He ran unsuccessfully as a Socialist candidate for public office twice—for the New York assembly in 1913 and for the state senate in 1918. Observing that "in his crusading, he was in deadly earnest," the *New York Times* called him "a good American" whose calm voice "will be missed."

• Collections of Young's original art are archived at the New York Public Library, Philadelphia Free Library, and the Argosy Gallery in New York City. Young's own selection of his work was published in *The Best of Art Young* (1936). His other books are *Hell Up to Date* (1892; a "deluxe edition" was published as *Hades Up to Date*), *Through Hell with Hiprah Hunt* (1901), *Trees at Night* (1927), and *Art Young's Inferno* (1934); works he illustrated include *Authors' Readings* (1897; for which he also assembled the text), Charles Erskine Scott Wood's *Heavenly Discourse* (1928), and Upton Sinclair's *The Goose-step* (1923) and *The Goslings* (1924). Young himself gives the most complete account of his life and work in *On My Way* (1928) and *Art Young: His Life and Times* (1939). Obituaries are in the *New York Herald Tribune* and the *New York Times*, which also published an editorial on the occasion, both 31 Dec. 1943.

ROBERT C. HARVEY

YOUNG, Brigham (1 June 1801–29 Aug. 1877), second president of the Church of Jesus Christ of Latter-day Saints (Mormons), first governor of Utah Territory, and colonizer, was born in Whitingham, Vermont, the son of John Young, a farmer and revolutionary war veteran, and Abigail Nabby Howe. Three years later the family moved to central New York State and in 1813 to Sherburne in South-central New York. As a typical frontier boy, Brigham fished; trapped animals; helped clear land, build sheds, and dig cellars; milked the cow; and assisted with the planting and harvest. He received only eleven days of formal schooling but learned to read and write from his mother, with whom he regularly read the Bible. He helped care for her when she became debilitated from tuberculosis. The Young family frequented revivals in that religiously active region, and most of them became active Methodists.

After his mother's death in 1815 and his father's remarriage to Hannah Brown, Brigham left home to learn the trades of carpenter, joiner, painter, and glazier. In nearby Auburn he helped build a theological seminary, a prison, a marketplace, and a home later occupied by William H. Seward, who subsequently became governor of New York and secretary of state for Abraham Lincoln. In 1824 Young married Miriam Works, joined the Methodist Reformed church, associated with a group of religious seekers, participated in a debating society, and established a shop and mill in Mendon, New York, where he made and repaired furniture, put in windowpanes and doorways, and did landscaping. Some chairs, desks, staircases, and mantelpieces Young made have survived. The Youngs had two daughters before Miriam's death from tuberculosis in 1832.

Young first read a copy of the Book of Mormon in 1830 when it was initially published. He thought highly of it and believed it answered many of his religious questions, but he cautiously wanted to make sure the Mormons were sincere and sensible in their faith. He listened to their traveling missionaries, visited a Mormon congregation in Pennsylvania, prayed with them, was persuaded of their biblical focus, and submitted to baptism in 1832. He and a friend immediately traveled to Kirtland, Ohio, to meet the Mormon leader, Joseph Smith, Jr. Young found the 26-year-old prophet to be intelligent, straightforward, well schooled in the Bible, and a genial person. Impressed with the Mormon gospel and its leader, Young, as with many early converts, abandoned his shop and began a series of preaching missions in New York, Pennsylvania, New England, and upper Canada. He returned to the Mormon headquarters in Ohio, where he alternated between preaching in nearby areas and working on the construction of the Mormon temple in Kirtland, which was dedicated in 1836.

In 1834 Young married Mary Ann Angell. That year he joined some two hundred other men in marching with Smith to Jackson County, Missouri, to wrest control of Mormon lands from the anti-Mormon mob that had driven the Mormons out. Although Zions Camp, as it was called, did not achieve its goals, Young learned valuable lessons in how to organize and manage a group of people on the march.

In 1835 Young was appointed "apostle," one of twelve central church leaders. He and his family followed the prophet to Missouri in 1838. When Smith was jailed and his followers were banished from Missouri in 1839, Young, as senior apostle, assumed direction of the removal of the 12,000 Latter-day Saints to Illinois. After a brief sojourn in Quincy and other communities, they settled along the Mississippi River at Commerce in western Illinois. They renamed the place Nauvoo, which they said was Hebrew for "the Beautiful."

In 1840 Young and other Latter-day Saint (LDS) apostles were sent to England to direct missionary work there. He published the first British edition of the Book of Mormon; *The Latter-day Saints Millenial Star*, a monthly periodical; and thousands of doctrinal pamphlets. The mission was remarkably successful and as many as 8,000 Britons were baptized. Impressed with the poverty of the working class in England, Young established a shipping agency and arranged for the transportation of thousands of converts to Nauvoo and later to the Salt Lake Valley.

After Young's return to Nauvoo on 1 July 1841, he served as Smith's special assistant in supervising missionary work, immigration, settlement of converts in western Illinois locations, and the collection of tithes and offerings. A successful, enterprising community expanded and developed as a result of his and others' religious leadership. Young continued to listen carefully to Smith's teachings. Young's wife, sisters, and sisters-in-law attended the Mormon Women's Relief Society, which elevated women in citizenship, spirituality, and compassionate service.

Despite the progress, individual and collective, the Mormon community had many problems. Smith introduced new doctrines and practices, such as "celestial marriage," thus initiating plural marriages, and under the Nauvoo City Charter the citizens controlled a legal system that their enemies thought was partial to Mormons. They had their own newspaper and militia and were constructing a temple where sacred ceremonies would be performed. The closely bound Mormons were becoming a political force in Illinois, and other settlers, fearful of losing political and economic control, were urged by agitators to drive them out. When the prophet was arrested in June 1844, a mob of old-line settlers and Illinois militiamen with blackened faces forced their way into the jail at Carthage and murdered Joseph Smith and his brother Hyrum Smith.

As president of the Twelve Apostles, Young became president of the church, an action ratified formally in 1847. A few dissidents followed James Strang into Wisconsin, Lyman Wight to Texas, and Sidney Rigdon to Pittsburgh, but the vast majority were content to follow Young and the Twelve Apostles. Threatened by hostile mobs, the Mormons were forced to leave Illinois in 1846, a year and a half after the prophet's death. Young directed the removal of approximately 16,000 members to Council Bluffs, Iowa, and Winter Quarters (now Florence), Nebraska, where they remained on American Indian lands during the winter of 1846–1847. At Young's insistence, the persons of means were asked to sign the Nauvoo Covenant, helping to ensure that those with property would assist those without. This mutual helpfulness continued throughout this and other Mormon migrations west. Young carefully planned the preparation of wagons, teams, and food for the trek. Also under his urging, in 1846 some five hundred Mormon men and seventy women, as cooks and laundresses, volunteered for national military duty during the Mexican War and marched to Santa Fe and San Diego. Their pay thus helped finance the Mormon trek west.

In 1847 approximately 2,000 persons traveled on the Mormon Trail to a Rocky Mountain haven in the valley of the Great Salt Lake. Young organized them into tens, fifties, hundreds, and outriders and appointed leaders over each. He personally directed the construction of bridges and ferries and helped blaze the trail.

Leading the advance company, Young entered the Salt Lake Valley on 24 July 1847, declaring, as it was said, "This is the Place." Young organized groups to explore, colonize, build a fort, plant seeds, commence irrigation, and initiate friendly meetings with groups of Native Americans. After a month, he returned to his family in Winter Quarters, along the way encountering the next company headed for the valley, and in the spring and summer of 1848 led a second large migration to the "Promised Valley." Substantial migrations followed in succeeding summers.

The gold rush of 1849, with many thousands headed for Eldorado by way of the Salt Lake Valley, presented both opportunities and challenges to the fledgling Mormon community. Overland travelers were happy to exchange goods and cash for fresh teams and produce, thus strengthening the local economy. At the same time many Latter-day Saints wanted to join the rush to the mines. Young counseled: "God has appointed this place for the gathering of His Saints, and you will do better right here than you will by going to the gold mines. . . . Here is the place God has appointed for his people. . . . Brethren, go to, now, and plant out your fruit seeds."

Young's pleas were heeded, but he established a colony at San Bernardino, in southern California, as a way station for those traveling to and from California. The colony was abandoned in 1858. Young also sent a few dozen young men to California to mine gold on behalf of the church. They returned with some gold that he used to mint coins and to back Mormon currency.

By 1852 the 16,000 Mormons in the Missouri River camps had migrated to Utah, and settlements had been established in northern, central, and southern Utah and in Carson Valley, Nevada, as well as in San Bernardino. By the time of Young's death, he had founded approximately 350 settlements in the Great Basin and other locations in the American West. They were inhabited by something like 100,000 Latter-day Saints, principally Americans, Britons, and Scandinavians, who were drawn to the region with the noted system of missionary work that Young supervised. In order to develop the region and increase self-sufficiency, he and his fellow Latter-day Saint leaders founded a wagon-express company; a ferryboat company; industries for the manufacture of beet sugar and cotton and woolen goods; mills for the processing of hides and lumber; iron, coal, and lead mines; a regional bank; and general stores in each settlement that received and disbursed tithings-in-kind that supported the church and its enterprises. By means of a church land office, each family was apportioned land for a home, garden, and farm that it owned and farmed individually. Most settlements had cooperative livestock herds. Larger enterprises—mills, shops requiring machinery, and of course public buildings—were supported by the local and general church. Many persons deeded their property over to the church in the 1850s, but since a federal land office was not established until 1869, the action of these settlers was simply a loyal gesture. Young admonished each settler to be a good steward and pay an honest tithe.

The Mormons applied for statehood in 1849, but in 1850 Congress created Utah Territory. President Millard Fillmore appointed Young governor and superintendent of Indian affairs but sent out federal judges and a territorial secretary who were hostile to Young, the Mormons, and the Mormon religion. Conflicts were inevitable. Federal appointees were opposed to theocratic politics, the practice of plural marriage, and the attempts at economic exclusivity. In 1857 President James Buchanan, unduly impressed by the letter of one judge and without any investigation, replaced Young as governor. Without notifying Young and the territory, Buchanan sent some 5,000 army troops, freighters, and suppliers to Utah on the mistaken assumption that this was necessary to ensure federal supremacy.

Learning on 24 July of the approach of the troops and supposing that they were intent on destroying the Mormons, Young declared martial law, organized the territorial militia to intercept the troops and "defend Zion," and instructed Utah settlers to husband their food and prepare for the worst. Tragically, a company of Arkansas migrants joined by Missourians came through the territory during these weeks. The latter cursed the Mormons for not selling food to them and boasted of their role in driving the Mormons out of Missouri. They allegedly poisoned a spring from which some Indians died, and the tribe vowed revenge. While the company was camped at Mountain Meadows in southern Utah, a strong force of Indians supported by Mormons attacked and killed all but the children, creating a blot on the Mormon escutcheon that has remained. When Young was alerted by a rider assigned to carry the information of the imminent Indian attack, he dispatched the rider immediately to leaders in southern Utah with a note counseling them that they should let the migrants pass, but this advice came to them too late. Young was not told of Mormon involvement in the massacre for several years, and when informed, he sought to minimize the effects on the image of the church and its members.

Mormon raiders under the command of Lot Smith succeeded in burning supply trains and capturing livestock intended to supply the federal troops, and Colonel Albert Sidney Johnston was forced to spend the winter at Fort Bridger, Wyoming. In the spring, when the troops were about to resume their march to the Salt Lake Valley, Young, fearful of an incident that might lead to fighting, ordered all residents in the Salt Lake Valley and northern Utah to abandon their homes and move to central and southern Utah. Some 35,000 made the move and placed straw in their homes to be lit if the army threatened occupation. The army passed peacefully through an abandoned Salt Lake City and established Camp Floyd forty miles southwest of the Mormon capital.

The Utah War ended in 1858 without the loss of life, but friction continued between Colonel Johnston, who distrusted Young and his associates, and the settlers, virtually all of whom were loyal to Young. With the outbreak of the Civil War, the army abandoned the territory, some to fight for the North and some for the South. Young contracted on behalf of the church to erect the hurriedly built transcontinental telegraph within Utah borders and then constructed a church-owned telegraph system to connect each settlement with Salt Lake City and the nation. Not entirely certain of Mormon loyalty to the Union, Lincoln sent a regiment of California volunteers to Utah. They established Camp Douglas in central Salt Lake City to prevent Indian raids and "watch over the Mormons." Their leader, Patrick Connor, was violently anti-Mormon and used his troops to prospect for minerals in Utah's mountains, hoping to induce a rush of miners to the territory to outnumber the Mormons. Minerals were found, but they could not be economically worked until the completion of the transcontinental railroad in May 1869.

Young was an enthusiastic supporter of the railroad. He took contracts on behalf of the church to build the roadbed and bridges in Utah and, upon its completion, supervised the building of connecting roads north from Ogden, Utah, to the Montana mines and south to Juab in central Utah. Because of the railroad, miners, freighters, merchants, and bankers were attracted to Utah, and the territory grew into a bifurcated economy, featuring the Mormon agricultural-craftsman base and a largely non-Mormon mining and commercial segment. Young adopted measures to protect the self-sufficient Mormon economy from the incursion of eastern freewheeling enterprisers interested in making a "quick buck" and then leaving. He organized a locally supported general "cooperative" store in each settlement, mills and factories in each region of the territory, and a church-owned bank and wholesale establishment to serve the whole territory and Mormon settlers in Arizona, Nevada, and Idaho.

Despite federally appointed governors, secretaries, and judges who were almost universally anti-Mormon, Young remained the dominant figure in Utah politics, business, and culture, and he retained the fervent support of most Latter-day Saints. He established the Salt Lake Theater, which invited leading national and international artists to perform; held dances, entertainments, and concerts in the Social Hall; founded the University of Deseret (later the University of Utah), Brigham Young Academy (now Brigham Young University), and Brigham Young College (later absorbed into Utah State University); presided over services in the Salt Lake Tabernacle; visited each Latter-day Saint settlement at least once a year; and supervised the publication of the *Deseret News* in Salt Lake City, the *Millenial Star* in England, and other church publications.

Near the end of his life, during the winter of 1873–1874, Young supervised the organization of each LDS community into what he called the United Order of Zion. The order was to be the means of preserving internal unity and harmony during the continued influx of "outside" miners, merchants, and bankers. Each Latter-day Saint was asked to contribute all of his or her economic or productive property (land, teams, implements) to the community United Order, in return for which he or she received capital stock. The person then made available his/her time to do assigned work—plow, irrigate, harvest, tend the cow herd, weave cloth, or manage the store. To accomplish spiritual as well as temporal union, each participant was baptized in a sacred ceremony in which he/she made a firm promise not to lie, backbite, loaf, or quarrel. All were to live as good Latter-day Saints ought. They were to pray daily, not use liquor or tobacco, obey their leaders, be frugal and industrious, and cultivate, in Young's words, "the simple grandeur of manners that belong to the pure in heart." All this had been expected of members from the time of their conversions, but Young was realistic enough to know that all were not living as they should. They were now offered a special incentive to live up to these and other Christian ideals.

Young and his associates organized approximately two hundred settlements as community United Order cooperatives. Some of them lasted for a year or two, but most of them continued until Young's death and then slowly fell apart because of natural disasters and the lack of strong leadership caused by the persecutions and incarcerations of most of the bishops and other local leaders under the 1882 Edmunds Act and 1887 Edmunds-Tucker Act. These antipolygamy and antitheocracy acts placed hundreds of local leaders in jail and removed them from the operation of church enterprises.

When Smith first taught Young the principle of plural marriage in 1843, Young was repulsed. But he soon came to see the divinity and social advantages of the practice in that moment of trial, and he married several wives. Some had been plural wives of Smith, others were family dependents or employees, still others were daughters of prominent church officials. Some were older than he, others younger. At least sixteen of these were connubial marriages. With fifty-seven children, Young had one of the largest families in America. Forty-three of his children lived to maturity. One of his sons, Willard Young, became a colonel in the Corps of Engineers, and a daughter, Susa Young, became an officer in the International Council of Women. Young staunchly defended "the principle" and was often pilloried in the eastern press as a lustful man. He was tried for bigamy in 1871 but not convicted. Hundreds of Young's letters to his children after their maturity have survived and show a surprisingly close personal relationship.

In central Salt Lake City Young built, in 1854, the "Beehive House," a large, two-story adobe house faced with cement with a tower surmounted by a golden beehive. This was his official residence as governor and president of the church. In 1856 he built a three-story adobe structure, the "Lion House," where several of his families lived. He later built homes in south Salt Lake City (now removed to the Pioneer Trail State Park), Provo, and St. George. Well-constructed and finely appointed, they have been visited by thousands of tourists.

In 1868, at the insistence of her parents, Young married the recently divorced Ann Eliza Webb. The marriage was not compatible, and they were divorced in 1876. She published a book about the marriage and polygamy, partly written by her press agent, and delivered lectures throughout the East excoriating Young and the plural marriage system. Her lectures added to the crusade against Mormonism and were influential in the federal antipolygamy legislation of 1882 and 1887.

The abundant source materials suggest that Young was sincere in trying to establish friendly relations with Indians, had a reverence for animal life and for nature, constantly admonished settlers to develop wholesome and harmonious communities, and left a legacy of colorful doctrinal statements frequently quoted by Latter-day Saints. He was also occasionally self-deprecating, used humor and hyperbole in his ser-

mons and letters, and seldom lost his temper. He had a warm sympathy for the problems of the poor and disabled.

Usually portrayed as an organizer and political leader, Young was also a vigorous sermonizer, prayerful in making decisions, and insistent upon religious principles. He completed the picturesque temple in Nauvoo to provide a sacred place for ordinances in preparation for the trek west, and he supervised the construction of the St. George and Salt Lake temples and the Salt Lake Endowment House for a similar purpose. He helped with the design and planning for the famous tabernacle on Temple Square in Salt Lake City. He carefully instructed local bishops to look after orphans, widows, and the old and infirm, and his sermons, usually delivered on Sunday afternoon in the Salt Lake tabernacle, contained religious messages along with practical instruction on making a living in the Great Basin. Not a systematic theologian, he preached from the Bible, Book of Mormon, and revelations of Smith about God, Jesus Christ, the Holy Ghost, the eternities, man's mission and responsibility, a godly society, practical religion, and the importance of learning and laboring for "the Kingdom."

Young died in Salt Lake City. He was replaced as Mormon prophet in 1880 by John Taylor, a native of England who had moved to Canada, then to Kirtland. Taylor became a Mormon in 1836, an apostle in 1838, and president of the Quorum of the Twelve Apostles in 1877.

• A massive collection of Young's diaries, letters, day-by-day histories, office journals, telegram books, and accounting ledgers—as much as 300,000 pages of manuscript material—is in the LDS Historical Department Library-Archives, Salt Lake City, Utah. Papers on his governorship are in the Utah State Archives, also in Salt Lake City. Biographies include Leonard J. Arrington, *Brigham Young: American Moses* (1985); Newell G. Bringhurst, *Brigham Young and the Expanding American Frontier* (1986); Susa Young Gates, *The Life Story of Brigham Young* (1930); and Eugene England, *Brother Brigham* (1980). Other helpful works include Dean C. Jessee, ed., *Letters of Brigham Young to His Sons* (1974); Susan Easton Black and Larry C. Porter, eds., *Lion of the Lord: Essays on the Life and Service of Brigham Young* (1995); and Ronald W. Walker and Ronald K. Esplin, "Brigham Himself: An Autobiographical Recollection," *Journal of Mormon History* 4 (1977): 19–34. The context of Young's activities is given in Arrington, *Great Basin Freedom: An Economic History of the Latter-day Saints, 1830–1900* (1958); James B. Allen and Glen M. Leonard, *The Story of the Latter-day Saints* (1992); Eugene E. Campbell, *Establishing Zion: The Mormon Church in the American West, 1847–1869* (1988); and Milton R. Hunter, *Brigham Young, the Colonizer* (1945).

LEONARD J. ARRINGTON

YOUNG, Buddy (5 Jan. 1926–5 Sept. 1983), football player and sports executive, was born Claude H. Young in Chicago, Illinois. His parents' names and occupations are unknown. He attended Wendell Phillips High School, where he was an outstanding athlete in both track and football. Young's success as a football player was remarkable because of his size; he was

5′5″ and weighed 165 pounds. Young entered the University of Illinois in 1944. Although as a black athlete he knew the sting of racial discrimination, Young believed that his small stature was an equal handicap—at least on the football field. Recalling his initial football season at Illinois, Young remarked, "I could never stop proving myself. I had to work harder, play better, block better than the big guys. . . . At my first practice they acted like I was some kind of sideshow, like I was supposed to go out with the band at halftime."

As a freshman at Illinois, Young became one of the most exciting wartime players. Playing halfback against Iowa in his first collegiate game, he ran 64 yards for a touchdown on the first play from scrimmage. On his second carry, Young sprinted 30 yards for another score. During that season he had touchdown runs of 93, 92, 74, 64, and 63 yards. Young averaged 8.9 yards a carry and scored 13 touchdowns, equaling the Big Ten Conference record set by Red Grange in 1924. Illinois coach Ray Eliot called Young "the best running back I have ever seen." After his first year of college football, Young was named to a number of All-America teams. In addition to his prowess on the gridiron, he was an outstanding sprinter. In 1944 he won the national collegiate championships in the 100- and 200-yard dashes and was the Amateur Athletic Union's 100-meter champion; he tied world records for the 45- and 60-yard dashes.

In January 1945 Young was drafted into the navy. After first reporting to the Great Lakes Naval Training Station, he was transferred to the naval base at Fleet City, California, where he played for the Fleet City Bluejackets football team, one of the best squads on the West Coast. The Bluejackets were made up of many college All-Americans and National Football League (NFL) players. In one of his greatest games, Young led Fleet City to a 45–28 victory over the El Toro, California, marines in the West Coast service championship game in 1945. Before 65,000 fans in Los Angeles, Young exploded for kickoff return runs of 94 and 88 yards for touchdowns and added another on a 30-yard run from scrimmage. El Toro coach Dick Hanley, who formerly coached at Northwestern, called Young "the greatest college back I've ever seen."

Despite rumors that he would turn professional after his service obligation was fulfilled, Young returned to the University of Illinois in the fall of 1946. He helped lead the Fighting Illini to their first Big Ten championship since 1928. In the Rose Bowl game on 1 January 1947, Illinois defeated the highly regarded UCLA team by a score of 45–14. Young rushed for 103 yards in 20 carries and scored two touchdowns in the game. The following summer Young was named the most valuable player in the College All-Star game, defeating the Chicago Bears 16–0 before more than 105,000 fans in Chicago. In 1946 Young married his high school sweetheart Geraldine (maiden name unknown); they had three children.

In 1947 the New York Yankees of the All-America Football Conference (AAFC) signed Young to a multi-year contract amid great fanfare. The previous year the AAFC had reintegrated big-time professional football, which had not included black players since 1933. In one of the early tests of fan reaction to pro football's integration, Young led the Yankees against the Cleveland Browns, which included African-American stars Bill Willis and Marion Motley. More than 70,000 fans, including 25,000 African Americans, turned out at Yankee Stadium on 24 November 1947 to watch the 28–28 tie. A number of commentators speculated that the game ensured that professional football owners would continue with the experiment in integration. During 1947 Young helped lead the Yankees to the AAFC Eastern Division title, but the New Yorkers lost the championship game to the Cleveland Browns, 14–3.

In addition to his tenure with the AAFC New York Yankees (1947–1949), after the league's demise Young played in the NFL for the New York Yanks (1950–1951), the Dallas Texans (1952), and the Baltimore Colts (1953–1955). He was best known for his sensational run-backs of kickoffs and punts, and he was rated as the best in this category during the 1950s. During his pro career, Young rushed for 2,727 yards and 17 touchdowns. He also caught 179 passes for 2,711 yards and 21 touchdowns. He averaged 27.7 yards per kickoff return. After his retirement as a player in 1955, Young became an assistant general manager of a radio station and worked as a public relations official for the Baltimore Colts. In 1964 Young became a special assistant to NFL commissioner Pete Rozelle, a position that made him the first African-American executive hired by a major sports league. In 1968 he was elected as a member of the College Football Hall of Fame. Young died in an automobile accident in Texas while on NFL business.

• Materials relating to Young's career are in the Professional Football Hall of Fame, Canton, Ohio. Also see *Who's Who among Black Americans* (1978); John McCallum and Charles H. Pearson, *College Football USA, 1869–1971* (1971); Roger L. Treat, *The Encyclopedia of Football* (1979); David S. Neft and Richard M. Cohen, *The Sports Encyclopedia: Pro Football, the Early Years, 1892–1959* (1987); Thomas G. Smith, "Outside the Pale: The Exclusion of Blacks from the National Football League, 1934–1946," *Journal of Sport History* 15 (Winter 1988): 255–81; and the *New York Amsterdam News,* 29 Nov. 1947. An obituary is in the *New York Times,* 6 Sept. 1983.

JOHN M. CARROLL

YOUNG, Charles (12 Mar. 1864–8 Jan. 1922), army officer, was born in Mayslick, Kentucky, the son of Gabriel Young and Armintie Bruen, former slaves. When he was nine years old, Young's family moved north to Ripley, Ohio. Young graduated from Wilberforce University, a black college in Xenia, Ohio, and then embarked on a career as a public school teacher. Inspired by Ohio native John H. Alexander, the second African-American to graduate from West Point, Young sought and won his state's nomination to the military academy in 1884. He graduated from West Point in 1889, despite an atmosphere of racial prejudice and the hostility of his fellow cadets.

On leaving West Point, Young was assigned as second lieutenant with the Tenth Cavalry. He was transferred to the Ninth Cavalry in 1889 and in 1894 was assigned to Wilberforce University as a professor of military science and tactics. This was one of a very small number of assignments available to black officers. While at Wilberforce, Young taught French, German, and mathematics and helped to run the University's drama group. His record at Wilberforce so impressed the president of nearby all-white Antioch College that Young was asked to teach a course in military training there. Young remained intellectually active throughout his career and displayed artistic talent in a number of areas. In addition to a collection of poetry and a monograph entitled "Military Morale of Nations and Races" (1912), Young wrote a play about the leader of the Haitian slave revolt, Toussaint L'Ouverture. As a musician he wrote numerous compositions and played the piano, harp, ukelele, and cornet. While in the Philippines he would add a proficiency in Spanish to the two languages he learned in college, German and French.

Young's primary calling, however, was in the military, and he devoted the bulk of his energy to climbing the ranks of the officer corps. Following the death of John H. Alexander in 1894, Young became the highest ranking black officer in the U.S. Army. He would own this distinction and the racial burden that accompanied it until his death. By the time the Spanish-American War broke out in 1898, he had been promoted to first lieutenant. As the only black commissioned officer in the army, he was assigned to command and oversee the training of the Ninth Ohio Battalion, a black volunteer unit. While Young's regular regiment, the Ninth Cavalry, saw action in Cuba, the Ninth Ohio Battalion never left the United States. In 1901 Young was promoted to captain, and for the following year he saw service with the Ninth Cavalry in quelling the Philippine insurrection. Young questioned the pervading view in the army that black troops could succeed only under the command of white officers, when he wrote in 1912 that the experience of the Spanish-American War and the Philippine Insurrection demonstrated clearly the ability of black officers to command their own men.

Young's race, however, continued to undermine his military assignments. Between 1904 and 1907 he served in Haiti as U.S. military attaché, a post for which the *Army and Navy Journal* believed black officers were best suited because they could deal better with the local population than their white counterparts. Also in 1904 he married Ada Mills of Xenia, Ohio; they would have two children. While in Haiti Young surveyed the military preparedness and the terrain of the island nation. According to the U.S. ambassador to Haiti, Young took great personal risk in his endeavors, traveling deep into previously uncharted territory. By the time he left the country, Young had completed a map of Haiti and written a monograph entitled "Handbook of Creole as Spoken in Haiti." His work would later prove invaluable to the U.S. Marines during their occupation of the Caribbean republic. In 1912 Young was promoted to the rank of major, and in the same year he was once again assigned as a military attaché, this time to the African Republic of Liberia. Young's assignment, as part of the 1912 loan agreement between the William Howard Taft administration and the Liberian government, was to oversee the training and reorganization of the country's defense forces, the Liberian Frontier Force. Although he saw himself as an adviser, leaving the day-to-day command to three African-American officers he appointed to assist him, Young was occasionally called on to command troops. In one incident, he led a force deep into the Liberian interior to rescue fellow American, Captain Arthur A. Browne. Browne and an attachment of Liberian troops were trapped by a group of native Africans, who were rebelling against the Americo-Liberian government, the descendants of freed American slaves who had founded the country and who monopolized power by excluding the African population from any form of political participation. Young's expedition succeeded in rescuing Browne, and during his tour of duty the Liberian Frontier Force succeeded in quelling numerous native rebellions. Young believed that Liberia was "a heritage" for all black people; so, it is ironic that his successful performance of duty there helped to perpetuate an oligarchy that for many years to come would remain ethnically exclusive.

Upon his return to the United States in 1915, Young was awarded the Spingarn Medal by the National Association for the Advancement of Colored People in recognition of his work in Africa. Young's success in the hostile racial environment of the early twentieth century made him a natural role model for the African-American community. In 1916 he reunited with the Tenth Cavalry to take part in General Pershing's Punitive Expedition to Mexico, where he distinguished himself by leading the rescue of a unit of the Thirteenth Cavalry at Parral. During his tour of duty in Mexico he was promoted to lieutenant colonel. The racial question, however, was to bring a premature end to Young's career in the regular army. Fearing that U.S. entry in World War I in 1917 would result in Young's being given command of the Tenth Cavalry, the white officers in the regiment protested the prospect of serving under a black officer. Their protests were taken up by a number of U.S. senators, causing the War Department to force Young into early retirement, ostensibly for medical reasons. Young sought to demonstrate his health by riding his horse from his home in Ohio to Washington, D.C., but to no avail. He was retired in 1917 at the rank of colonel, the highest rank ever achieved to that date by an African-American officer. Although Young was recalled to train troops in the last days of the war, the actions of the War Department in 1917 cost him the prospect of promotion to brigadier general. Young returned to Liberia as U.S. military attaché in 1919, and while visiting Lagos, Nigeria, he contracted Bright's disease and died. His body was returned to the United States, and he was buried with full military honors at Arlington National Cemetery.

Young is a figure of historical significance, not just because of what he achieved but because of the manner and circumstance in which he achieved it. One generation removed from slavery, Young demonstrated tremendous courage in entering and graduating from the white-dominated world of the U.S. Military Academy. Young's determination to succeed despite the racial barriers that were placed in his path was tempered by his restraint in the face of racial hostility. His career is more remarkable for that fact that he rose to the rank of colonel during a period when prejudice against African Americans was worse than at any time since the Civil War. Although Young's determination to succeed was often resented by the black troops under his command, his achievements won him the respect of the African-American community at large. He remains a significant figure in the history of African-American people and their struggle against racism in the United States.

• Although there is no collection of Young's papers, the records of the U.S. War Department for this period and the records of U.S. State Department for Liberia and Haiti contain numerous materials by and pertaining to him. Abraham Chew, *A Biography of Colonel Charles Young* (1923), is a contemporary pamphlet that offers an overview and evaluation of Young's career. It also contains a record of service and a number of obituaries. Willard B. Gatewood, Jr., *"Smoked Yankees" and the Struggle for Empire; Letters from Negro Soldiers, 1898–1901* (1971), offers insight into Young's career during the Spanish-American War period. Marvin Fletcher, *The Black Soldier and Officer in the United States Army, 1891–1917* (1972), places Young's career into the larger context encompassed by the book's title, while Bernard C. Nalty, *Strength for the Fight: A History of Black Americans in the Military* (1986), does the same for a lengthier period.

DAVID P. KILROY

YOUNG, Charles Augustus (15 Dec. 1834–3 Jan. 1908), astronomer, was born in Hanover, New Hampshire, the son of Ira Young, professor of mathematics and natural philosophy at Dartmouth College, and Eliza Minot Adams. Young helped his father in scientific projects from a young age and entered Dartmouth at the age of fourteen. After receiving a B.A. in 1853, he spent a summer in Europe with his father, who had become professor of natural philosophy and astronomy and was planning the new Shattuck astronomical observatory at Dartmouth. The purpose of the trip was to visit foreign observatories and to obtain equipment.

From 1853 to 1855 Young taught classics at Phillips Academy in Andover, Massachusetts, and the next year he continued this work part time while studying theology at Andover Seminary, with the possible intention of becoming a missionary. Awarded an M.A. by Dartmouth in 1856, he accepted an appointment the next year as professor of mathematics, natural phi-

losophy, and astronomy at Western Reserve College in Hudson, Ohio. Also in 1857 he married Augusta S. Mixer; the couple had three children.

In 1862, during the Civil War, Young was captain for four months of the Eighty-fifth Ohio Volunteer Infantry, which was detailed to guard prisoners and escort a group of them for exchange. He returned to Western Reserve, where teaching left him little time for research. He set up a working system for Cleveland, Ohio, for determining exact time by astronomical methods. During several summers he was an astronomical assistant on a War Department program surveying what the department called "northern and northwestern lakes," which was chiefly the Great Lakes region. For this program he made telegraphic determinations of longitude.

In 1866 Young became professor of natural philosophy and astronomy at Dartmouth, in the same endowed professorship that had been held by his father from 1833 to 1858 and even earlier by his maternal grandfather, Ebenezer Adams. He taught physics and astronomy, and during several years he also gave lecture courses at schools for young women, including Mount Holyoke College.

At Dartmouth Young had time and equipment for research. About that time astronomers were beginning to use new equipment for studying the stars, and by 1859 they had concluded that dark lines in the solar spectrum resulted from gases above the sun's surface that could be used to reveal the chemical composition of the stars. Young observed the sun's chromosphere and prominences, which he illustrated with drawings and lithographed sketches in 1869. He presented the first observation by an astronomer of a sunspot with reversed lines in some of its elements, which were later identified as cooler spots in glowing gases. In 1870 he obtained the first known photograph of a protuberance on the sun, which, requiring an exposure of three and one-half minutes, was not sharp, but it illustrated the technique for photographing through a spectroscope. Especially adept at instrument design, he built an excellent solar spectroscope.

Young observed the solar eclipse of 7 August 1869 at Burlington, Iowa, with a group organized by the U.S. Naval Observatory. To establish the contact of the eclipse, he watched "the bright C line shorten under the approach of the moon" (Frost [1910]: p. 95), which allowed him to determine the time of contact within a second. From his observations of the prominences of the sun he established the gaseous nature and solar origin of the corona, which some had considered associated with the eclipsing moon. He confirmed this at the eclipse of 22 December 1870 in Jerez, Spain, when he also accurately located the position of the green corona line, which much later was found not to be the corona line of uncertain origin numbered 1474 by Gustave-Robert Kirchhoff in 1859. Also at the 1870 eclipse he described for the first time the flash spectrum of "hundreds and thousands" of bright colors for two or three seconds at the moment of complete sun cover (*The Sun*, p. 82). This observation was not believed by some other astronomers until similar observations were made during a later eclipse.

In 1872 Young traveled to Sherman, Wyoming, where, in the clear mountain air, he observed additional chromospheric lines of the sun and confirmed the presence of many reversed lines in the chromosphere and on the body of the sun. Over a few years he cataloged hundreds of bright lines in the chromosphere spectrum that identified the chemical elements in the sun. By comparing solar outbursts with magnetic records at Greenwich and Stonyhurst observatories in England, Young was among the astronomers who concluded that solar disturbances produce an immediate effect on the earth's magnetism. In 1876 he used for the first time a diffraction grating with his spectroscope and was able to measure accurately the rate of rotation of the sun.

In 1877 Young became professor of astronomy at Princeton University, where he obtained new equipment and established the best teaching observatory in the country of that time. He observed the eclipse of 29 July 1878 at Denver, Colorado. In 1883, by using a spectroscope attached to a 23-inch telescope at Princeton's Halstead Observatory, he was able to distinguish unusually fine dark lines on the sun.

In addition to his studies of the sun, Young observed the transit of Venus at Peking, China, in 1874 and at Princeton in 1882. He published on the spectra of several comets and of Venus, on the polar and equatorial diameter of Mars, on double stars, and on the planet Uranus.

Young exercised much influence through his widely accepted textbooks. These included *The Sun* (1881; eighth ed., 1905); *General Astronomy* (1888; rev. ed., 1898); a more elementary college text, *The Elements of Astronomy* (1890); *Lessons in Astronomy* (1891), for even younger students; and an intermediate text, *Manual of Astronomy* (1902).

Described as a man of "extreme modesty" (Poor, p. 219), Young made major contributions in solar astronomy at a time when new equipment and new concepts were creating significant advances in the emerging field of astrophysics. Much appreciated by his students, he was also popular as a public lecturer. He was elected to the National Academy of Sciences in 1872 and received the Janssen Medal of the French Academy of Sciences in 1891. After retiring from Princeton in 1905, he moved back to Hanover, New Hampshire, where he died.

• The library at Dartmouth College has archival material on Young, chiefly relating to astronomy and solar eclipses, donated by his family. Young published many of his solar observations in a series of papers under the heading "Spectroscopic Notes" in the *Journal of the Franklin Institute* from 1869 to 1872 and two more in *American Journal of Science* in 1880 and 1883. In all he published more than 130 papers, as well as the books cited above. Biographies are by John M. Poor in *Popular Astronomy* 16 (1908): 218–30; and Edwin B. Frost in *Science* 27 (1908): 136–39, *Astrophysical Journal* 30 (1909): 323–38, and National Academy of Sciences, *Biographical Memoirs* 7 (1910): 90–114, with bibliography. An obituary is in the *New York Times*, 5 Jan. 1908.

ELIZABETH NOBLE SHOR

YOUNG, Chic (9 Jan. 1901–14 Mar. 1973), cartoonist, was born Murat Bernard Young in Chicago, Illinois, the son of James L. Young, a shoestore proprietor, and Martha Techen, an artist. He completed high school in St. Louis—where the nickname "Chic" may have been applied to recall his city of origin—and went on to study art in Chicago, New York, and Cleveland. He created and drew the comic strip "The Affairs of Jane" for the Bell Syndicate in 1923 and shortly thereafter joined Hearst's King Feature Syndicate, with whom he remained for the next half-century. He created and drew "Dumb Dora" for King, beginning in 1924, and with it added a new simile to the language. He married Athel L. Lindorff in 1927, and they had three children.

Young's early comic strips owed much to the inspiration of the "flapper era" of the 1920s, and so did "Blondie," the strip he began for King in 1930. The title character was Blondie Boopadoop, a flighty gold digger whose boyfriend, Dagwood Bumstead, was the son of a railroad magnate. But as the depression deepened, flappers and rich boyfriends seemed less amusing than in flush times, and the strip lost readers. The wedding of Blondie and Dagwood in 1933 restored the audience and set the stage for Young's exploration of daily doings at home and work. Dagwood became an office worker when the elder Bumstead disowned him for marrying beneath his station; Blondie became a housewife and the mother of Alexander ("Baby Dumpling") and Cookie.

King Features held distribution rights to "Blondie," but Young retained ownership of the strip, and his fortunes rose with its popularity. In 1938 Columbia Studios released the first of a series of twenty-eight feature films starring Penny Singleton as Blondie and Arthur Lake as Dagwood; the same actors appeared in CBS radio's "Blondie," beginning in 1939. The strip and its attendant manifestations were cultural mainstays during World War II, representations of hearth and family indicative of the value system Americans believed they were fighting to defend. "Blondie and Dagwood are America's favorite," *Life* proclaimed (17 Aug. 1942). The last of the motion pictures appeared in 1950, but NBC offered "Blondie" television series in 1954 and 1958, and CBS television presented another in 1968. Young, who had begun his career as a $22-per-week artist, was reported to be earning $300,000 per year from the strip and subsidiary rights. By the early 1970s, "Blondie" was appearing in more than 1,600 newspapers in sixty countries in approximately two dozen languages.

The international appeal of "Blondie" derived from Young's decision to concentrate on four common aspects of life: eating, sleeping, maintaining a household, and making money. Dagwood, owing to his problems completing naps on the sofa or in the bathtub, the distinctive sandwiches that were his late-night snacks, and his relationship with his employer, was usually the center of attention. Blondie's life revolved around getting Dagwood up in the morning, dressed, fed, and to work on time, or, when he was not at work, urging him to perform long-neglected chores. The one-time flapper had become the levelheaded wife, the calming influence on an alternately slothful and frenetic husband. The Bumstead family never observed American holidays as Young believed it would have detracted from their universal appeal.

Young established his home and studio in Clearwater, Florida, and in 1963 his son Dean began scripting the strip. After Young's death in St. Petersburg, Florida, Dean Young and artist Tim Raymond (Young's assistant since 1934) continued "Blondie" and its formula without interruption. By 1990 "Blondie" was appearing in 2,000 newspapers in fifty-four countries and thirty-five languages.

• A good introduction to Young and his work is Dean Young and Rick Marshall, *Blondie and Dagwood's America* (1981). Coulton Waugh, *The Comics* (1947), establishes context, as does Maurice Horn, *Women in the Comics* (1977). Arthur Asa Berger, *The Comic-Stripped American* (1973), contains an early statement on gender issues suggested by the "Blondie" strip. An obituary is in the *New York Times*, 16 Mar. 1973.

WILLIAM W. SAVAGE, JR.

YOUNG, Cy (29 Mar. 1867–4 Nov. 1955), baseball player, was born Denton True Young near Gilmore, Ohio, the son of McKenzie Young and Nancy Mot Miller, farmers. His middle name was the surname of a soldier who had saved his father's life during the Civil War. The 6′2″ Young worked hard on the family farm until he was 23, developing strong arms, broad shoulders, a thick chest, and muscular legs. He pitched and played third base for several northeastern Ohio teams, for an independent Red Cloud, Nebraska, club, and in 1889 for the Tuscarawas County team. Young married his childhood sweetheart, Robba Miller, in 1892; they had no children.

Young's father wanted him to remain a farmer, but in 1890 Young tried out for the Canton, Ohio, team of the Tri-State League. The shy, gangly farm boy walked around the outside of the Canton ballpark six times before mustering enough courage to enter. Canton manager George Moreland, impressed with Young's size, gave him a tryout and signed him to a contract at $40 a month. When Young's fastballs battered the grandstand boards, a Canton catcher nicknamed Young "Cyclone." A sportswriter soon shortened it to "Cy," a popular term for the era's stereotypical stage rube.

Young's minor league career lasted only half a season because the Tri-State League disbanded in July 1890. The right-handed Young won 15 of 30 decisions, including his final five games. On 25 July he struck out 18 batters and held McKeesport hitless. Davis Hawley, secretary-treasurer of the Cleveland Spiders' National League club, signed Young for $300

in August 1890. Hawley, fearful that teammates might ridicule Young because of his outgrown clothes and undersized derby hat, purchased some new clothes for him.

Young usually pitched every other day for Cleveland. Excellent physical conditioning enabled him to need only 12 warm-up pitches before games. He finished the season with a 9–7 won-lost mark, becoming the Spiders' lone winning pitcher. Two of his victories came on 4 October in a doubleheader against the Philadelphia Athletics. In 1891, Young won 27 games and lost 20. His best season came in 1892 with a 36–11 record. That same season he led the National League in shutouts with 9. His repertoire included an excellent fastball, overhand and sidearm curveballs, and a "tobacco ball" delivered with consistent control. He allowed the fewest walks per nine innings in the National League in 1890. Overall, he led the National League in fewest walks eight other times.

Young spent nine years with Cleveland, through 1898, compiling a 239–134 won-lost record. Except for his rookie year, he had at least 21 victories each season and surpassed 30 wins in 1892, 1893, and 1895. He pitched the first of his three career no-hitters on 18 September 1897, blanking the Cincinnati Reds. Young recorded three victories in the five-game 1895 Temple Cup playoff series, helping the Spiders upset the Baltimore Orioles. The 1896 Temple Cup series, swept by Baltimore, saw Young lose his only decision.

In 1898, Spiders' owner Frank Robison acquired the St. Louis Cardinals, hoping to reap financial rewards by combining the best Cleveland and St. Louis players. He sent the better Cleveland players, including Young, to St. Louis for the Cardinals' worst players before the 1899 season. Young, whose $2,400 salary topped the National League, won 26 games in 1899 and 20 in 1900.

The American League, formed in 1901, started raiding National League clubs for players. Young, then 34 years old, joined the Boston Pilgrims (later the Red Sox) for $3,000 a year. Catcher Cy Criger accompanied him from St. Louis, maintaining one of baseball's best batteries. Young won 193 of 305 games for Boston from 1901 through 1908, leading the team in total innings, games started, complete games, victories, strikeouts, and shutouts. He paced American League pitchers in victories in 1901 (33), 1902 (32), and 1903 (28), leading the Pilgrims in 1903 to their first pennant. He pitched in the first modern World Series game in 1903, losing 7–3 to the Pittsburgh Pirates. Boston eventually upset the Pirates, five games to three, as Young won two games and relieved once.

Several outstanding individual games distinguished his Boston tenure. On 5 May 1904 he no-hit the Philadelphia Athletics, pitching the first American League and third major league perfect game in history. The same year he set major league records by pitching 23 consecutive hitless innings and 45⅔ consecutive scoreless innings. His crucial 1–0 decision over the New York Highlanders during the season's final week helped Boston win the 1904 title. On 4 July 1905,

Young dueled 20 innings with Philadelphia's Rube Waddell and did not walk any Athletics; Philadelphia scored twice in the twentieth inning to win. On 30 June 1908, Young pitched his third no-hitter, shutting out the New York Highlanders.

Young experienced his first losing seasons in 1905 and 1906 but surpassed 20 victories again in 1907 and 1908. In 1907 his 22 wins at age 40 gave the seventh-place Red Sox more than one-third of their wins. That year he declined a permanent managerial post, stating, "I believe I will have one of my best seasons this year. . . . I do not have the ability to manage the team. . . . I could not do justice to both positions."

In February 1909 the American League's Cleveland Indians acquired Young for $12,500. Although 42 years old, Young won 19 games for the sixth-place club. After Cleveland released him in August 1911, the Boston Braves signed him for the remainder of the National League season. Young took four of nine decisions, losing a 12-inning 1–0 heartbreaker in his final game to rookie Grover Cleveland Alexander of the Philadelphia Phillies. His last job in baseball came as manager of the Cleveland club of the independent Federal League in 1913.

Young dominated major league pitching as Ty Cobb ruled over batting and baserunning and Babe Ruth over slugging. His 511 wins spanned 22 major league seasons. Modern pitchers struggle to win 200 during a career. Other pitchers have enjoyed more spectacular seasons, but at the end of the twentieth century, none had approached his career wins. Walter Johnson, his closest competitor, won 416 major league games. Young's 313 setbacks also set a major league record. No other major league pitcher started (818) or completed (749) as many games. From 1891 to 1904 he had 13 20-victory seasons. He led his league 14 times in fewest walks allowed and issued under 1.5 walks a game over his career.

Young's exceptional physical condition kept him in the major leagues past his forty-fourth birthday. During the off season, he strengthened his legs through constant running and his arms and back by chopping wood and performing other chores. Teammates, opponents, and spectators admired him for his courtesy, and umpires never ejected the even-tempered pitcher from a game.

In 1912 he retired to a farm near Peoli, Ohio. Writers overlooked him as a charter member of the National Baseball Hall of Fame, but they selected him the next year, in 1937. On Young's eightieth birthday, owner Bill Veeck of the Cleveland Indians hosted an extravagant party and gave him an expensive automobile. Young died in Newcomerstown, Ohio. The town has honored him with a city park, statue, and museum. In 1956 Commissioner Ford Frick instituted the Cy Young Award, given annually to the best American League and National League pitchers.

• Some of Young's records before 1900 differ slightly among the most authoritative sources of baseball statistics; those records most generally agreed on have been used here. The National Baseball Library in Cooperstown, N.Y.; the Cy Young Museum, near Newcomerstown, Ohio; and the National Baseball Hall of Fame in Cooperstown have material on Young as well as some of his artifacts. The Ellery Clark, Jr., Red Sox Analytical Letter Collection in Annapolis, Md., contains correspondence of Young, Norwood Gibson, and Fred Parent. The Clark papers also include interviews with Young, Lou Criger, George La Chance, Kip Selbach, Gibson, and Parent. Ralph H. Romig, *Cy Young: Baseball's Legendary Giant* (1964), remains the only book-length biography, but its information about Young's life and times is inadequate. Young's statistical accomplishments are detailed in *The Baseball Encyclopedia*, 9th ed. (1993); *Daguerreotypes*, 8th ed. (1990); and John Thorn and Pete Palmer, eds., *Total Baseball* (1989). For Young's pitching feats, see *My Greatest Day in Baseball* (1945; a collection of reminiscences by 47 stars, as told to sportswriters), and John Thorn and John B. Holway, *The Pitcher* (1987). Young's roles with specific teams are described in Franklin Lewis, *The Cleveland Indians* (1949); Frederick G. Lieb, *The St. Louis Cardinals* (1945) and *The Boston Red Sox* (1947); Ellery H. Clark, Jr., *Boston Red Sox: 75th Anniversary History* (1975); and Harold Kaese, *The Boston Braves* (1948). Obituaries are in the *New York Times*, 5 Nov. 1955, and the *Sporting News*, 16 Nov. 1955.

DAVID L. PORTER

YOUNG, Donald Ramsey (5 July 1898–17 Apr. 1977), sociologist and foundation executive, was born in Macungie, Pennsylvania, the son of Jonas Francis Young and Mary Catherine Rems. After serving as a seaman in the U.S. Naval Research Force in World War I, Young completed a bachelor's degree (1919) at LaFayette College and then earned a master's degree (1920) and Ph.D. (1922) in sociology at the University of Pennsylvania. He later pursued postdoctoral studies at Rutgers, Princeton, and the Wharton School of the University of Pennsylvania. In 1925 he married Ada Wise; they had two children.

Young spent his entire academic career at the Wharton School, where he began as an assistant instructor in 1919 and became an assistant professor in 1923 and a professor in 1935. He served as secretary for fellowships and grants-in-aid for the Social Science Research Council from 1932 and 1945 and as its executive director from 1945 to 1948. In 1948 he became president of the SSRC for a brief period.

Young's early scholarly work involved the application of social scientific work to public affairs. His doctoral dissertation, *Motion Pictures: A Study in Social Legislation*, published in 1922, concluded that some degree of censorship of the motion picture industry by state agencies was necessary. His main interest, however, was minority and race relations, a field in which he is considered a pioneer. His *American Minority Peoples: A Study in Racial and Cultural Conflicts in the United States* (1932) was the first treatment of its kind. Although it contains racist overtones typical of the era—particularly in dealing with acculturation, assimilation, and "Americanization"—the work is a detailed and comprehensive overview of the situation of minorities in the United States at the beginning of the 1930s. In *Research Memorandum on Minority Peoples in the Depression* (1937), Young provides insights into how the depression affected minorities. Young also contributed to public understanding of social issues through a number of volumes that he edited for the *Annals of the Academy of Political and Social Science* between 1928 and 1942. He served as associate editor of the *Annals* from 1930 to 1945.

Perhaps Young's most notable contribution to the field of race and minority relations was the support that he gave to the Carnegie-sponsored study of American race relations undertaken by Gunnar Myrdal and published as *An American Dilemma* in 1944. Young assisted Myrdal in recruiting researchers, chaired the editorial committee, and sought to make Myrdal personally more aware of African-American life.

During World War II, Young was a special consultant on interracial relations to the secretary of war on the Joint Army and Navy Committee on Welfare and Recreation. Working closely with the Information and Education Division of the Army Research Board, he advised that body on how race relations could be improved in the armed forces and contributed to such educational initiatives as the film *The Negro Soldier*, the orientation series "Why We Fight," and the pamphlet *Command of Negro Troops*. He also helped write policy manuals for the improvement of race relations in branches of the American armed forces.

Following the war, Young took an active part as executive director of the SSRC in the ill-fated effort to have the social sciences included in the National Science Foundation. He became president in 1948 of the Russell Sage Foundation and laid the groundwork for its emergence as a major research foundation. He retired from the Sage Foundation in 1963 and in 1965 began to chair the National Academy of Sciences' Committee on Government Programs in the Behavioral Sciences. The committee's report, released in 1968, made wide-ranging recommendations for redefining relations between the government and the social sciences. In 1972 Young worked as a consultant to the government of Brazil.

During his long career as a foundation executive, Young established a reputation as a forthright and demanding administrator who "was very tough and gruff on the outside, but very empathetic and warm on the inside" (Riley, p. 117). His views on the nature and purpose of philanthropic management were published in *Trusteeship and the Management of Foundations* (1969), which he cowrote with Wilbert E. Moore. Proud of his Pennsylvania Dutch heritage, Young was fond of sprinkling his remarks with folk sayings from his Lehigh Valley upbringing. He died in Allentown, Pennsylvania.

• Some biographical material on Young is available at the University of Pennsylvania Archives. His oral history for the Carnegie Corporation, at Columbia University, provides insights into his career as a social science administrator. In "Limiting Factors in the Development of the Social Sciences," *Proceedings of the American Philosophical Society* 92 (1948): 325–35, Young gives his views on the state of the social sciences in the postwar period, and in "Sociology and the Practicing Professions," *American Sociological Review* 20 (1955): 641–48, he addresses the relevance of sociological research to applied fields. Young's contributions to the development of the social sciences in the United States are discussed in Gene Lyons, *The Uneasy Partnership: Social Science and the Federal Government in the Twentieth Century* (1969), and in Donald Fisher, *Fundamental Development of the Social Sciences: Rockefeller Philanthropy and the United States Social Science Research Council* (1993). John Riley provides a brief discussion of some of Young's postwar work with the SSRC in *The Nationalization of the Social Sciences*, ed. S. Klausner and V. Lidz (1986), and some of Young's contributions to improving race relations in the armed forces during World War II are discussed in Ulysses Lee, *The Employment of Negro Troops* (1966). An obituary is in the *New York Times*, 22 Apr. 1977.

WILLIAM J. BUXTON

YOUNG, Ella Flagg (15 Jan. 1845–26 Oct. 1918), educator, was born in Buffalo, New York, the daughter of Theodore Flagg, a workman in the sheet metal trades, and Jane Reed. Ella spent her early years being regarded as a delicate and sickly child; her mother kept her out of school and in fresh air and sunshine as much as possible. A curious child, she enjoyed visiting her father at the forge, where she sat for hours and asked questions about the work he was doing. By the age of nine, she had taught herself to read and began to read everything she could find. Two years later her parents allowed her to go to school, which she immediately enjoyed and in which she excelled. In 1858 the Flagg family moved to Chicago. Ella graduated from high school in 1862 and began her long professional journey as teacher/administrator. In 1868 she married a Chicago merchant and friend of the family, William Young; they did not have children. A good deal older than Ella, he died in 1873.

Young's career spanned that period of educational history when individual states tried to develop public school systems founded on the latest nineteenth-century pedagogical principles. This process involved expanding the curriculum from the traditional classical subjects to include more practical studies in manual arts and business; taking students' interests into account in order to make the material more meaningful; avoiding rote memory recitations; including practice teaching experience in teacher training; and organizing school administration into a bureaucracy with a superintendent in charge of local schools and a state superintendent to oversee the entire system. For twenty-five years Young witnessed many of these changes take place in the teaching profession in Chicago while serving as primary school teacher, sixth grade teacher, assistant principal teacher, supervisor of student teachers, high school math teacher, and principal of two elementary schools.

In 1887 Young became one of the assistant superintendents of the Chicago schools. In this capacity she visited the schools in her district and provided in-service teacher training in the latest pedagogical methods and theory. She also continued to broaden her own education. In 1895, when she was fifty years old, she enrolled at the University of Chicago and became the student of philosopher John Dewey. Under his direction she studied logic, ethics, metaphysics, and the philosophy of G. W. F. Hegel. She also helped Dewey formulate his pragmatic philosophy known as instrumentalism. He credited her with being a practicing pragmatist long before the philosophical system was ever in print. He said that he was constantly getting ideas from her: "More times than I could well say I didn't see the meaning or force of some favorite conception of my own till Mrs. Young had given it back to me" (quoted in Smith, p. 63).

In 1899 Young resigned as district superintendent to devote herself full-time to her graduate study and to teach education courses. In 1900 she received a Ph.D. from Chicago and continued to teach at the university. Her dissertation, which was published as *Isolation in the School* (1901), embodied the main elements of a pragmatic approach for curricular designs and school management. She was also a contributing author in the Contributions to Philosophy and Contributions to Education series that Dewey edited, which embraced his instrumental brand of pragmatism and were evaluated favorably by William James: "It appears now that under Dewey's inspiration, they have at Chicago a flourishing school of radical empiricism of which I for one have been entirely ignorant" (quoted in Smith, p. 74). In addition to her dissertation, Young's 1901–1902 contributions to the series were *Ethics in the School, Some Modern Types of Educational Theory*, and *The Scientific Method in Education*.

In general, Young's greatest educational and theoretical gift was her ability to infuse educational practice with philosophical principles. Dewey said that her mind did not separate theory and practice: "In my opinion what Mrs. Young got from her study of philosophy was chiefly a specific intellectual point of view and terminology (the two things can't be separated, for terminology with a person like Mrs. Young is a very real thing, not a verbal one) in which to clear up and express the practical outcome of her prior experience" (quoted in Smith, p. 107).

In 1904 both Young and Dewey left the University of Chicago; Dewey became a professor at Columbia University, and Young became principal of the Chicago Normal School. In 1909 she left that position to become superintendent of Chicago public schools. In this capacity she was the first female to head up a major U.S. school system. Her administration, though not without its political struggles, was a successful and progressive one at a time when Chicago teachers, especially women teachers, were striving to have more say in their professional lives. For the most part she was effective in mediating the demands of board authority with those of the teachers during her six years in office. The most vocal and political group in support of women teachers was the Chicago Teachers Federation (CTF) under the leadership of Margaret A. Haley. The CTF and the Chicago Board of Education were strong supporters of Young's successful campaign for president of the National Educational Association in 1909–1910. In 1914, however, when she failed to be reappointed by the Chicago school board, many blamed the failure on the plot of a few members who did not like the recognition that she gave to the CTF. Mass protest meetings were held all over the city so that in a matter of days the board had reinstated her as its superintendent.

In December 1915 Young retired at the age of seventy-three. She had planned to write a book about schools, but instead, when World War I broke out, she worked to fund it by selling bonds for the Liberty Loan Committee. She died in Washington, D.C.

Young is generally remembered for a progressive style that practiced a pragmatic and scientific approach to education and administration. Noted social reformer Jane Addams was familiar with her accomplishments and claimed that Young "had more general intelligence and character than any other woman I knew." Young's successor as principal of the Chicago Normal School said that if Young had been a man, she "would have directed a great corporation, managed a railroad, served as governor of a state, or commanded an army" (quoted in Smith, p. 231).

• There is no adequate collection of Young papers, although the presidential papers at the University of Chicago hold many pieces of important correspondence that relate to her years with Dewey. The Chicago Teachers Federation Files at the Chicago Historical Society are also an important source during her years as superintendent, as are her annual superintendent reports. The most complete assessment of her life and career can be found in Joan K. Smith, *Ella Flagg Young: Portrait of a Leader* (1979). An important but dated work by a former student is John T. McManis, *Ella Flagg Young and a Half-Century of the Chicago Public Schools* (1916). An obituary and related article are in the *Chicago Tribune*, 27–28 Oct. 1918.

JOAN K. SMITH

YOUNG, Ewing (1792?–Feb. 1841), fur trapper and trader, was born near Jonesboro, Tennessee, the son of Charles Young and Mary Rebecca Wilkins, farmers. Ewing received only primary education and apprenticed as a carpenter. He left Tennessee for the West where in January 1822 near Charitan, Missouri, he and a partner purchased farmland along the Missouri River. Four months later Young sold his stake in the farm to invest in and accompany William Becknell's second caravan to Santa Fe (the first to use wagons on the Santa Fe Trail). In Santa Fe, Young became involved in the fur trade when he formed a partnership with William Wolfskill to trap beaver on the Pecos River for the 1822 fall hunt.

The two partners trapped the region surrounding Santa Fe during 1823. The following year they turned their attentions to the San Juan River, where they harvested more than $10,000 in furs. Young invested his profits in the Santa Fe trade. He became heavily involved in the opening years of American trade with the Mexican settlements of Santa Fe and Taos (1825–1826), importing goods overland from St. Louis.

With license from Mexican governor Antonio Narbona, Young organized an expedition to trap various tributaries of the Colorado during the fall of 1826. The party included famous trappers such as Milton Sublette, Thomas L. "Peg Leg" Smith, Michel (Miguel) Robidoux, and James Ohio Pattie. While trapping the Gila and Salt rivers, the party feuded with the Papago and Mojave. The expedition trapped the Colorado to its headwaters, crossed the Continental Divide near Long's Peak, then veered south back into New Mexico. The new presiding Mexican governor, Manuel Armijo, who disliked Americans, promptly seized the trapper's furs at Tàos, and imprisoned Young for several days for violating laws intended to restrict American trappers.

After his incarceration, Young organized another trapping venture from Tàos in August 1829. Young planned to cross the Mojave Desert westward to Mission San Gabriel, California. Accompanying the expedition was a callow young Kit Carson on his first hunt. In California, Young hunted the San Joaquin and Sacramento rivers. As a sideline, Young assisted in recovering runaway natives for Mission San Jose. By September he had returned to New Mexico via Los Angeles with a large collection of beaver pelts. Young's first California expedition deserves credit as effectively opening overland trade with California.

Back in Tàos, on 11 May 1831 Young received baptism into the Catholic church by a Father Martínez but did not apply for naturalization. Planning to make Tàos his permanent home, Young entered into a common-law union with María Josepha Tàyfoya.

The following October Young set out again for California. This time his trapping force included a partnership with David E. Jackson and David Waldo. They intended to develop a horse and mule trade using California stock. Jackson accumulated more than 700 head with help from connections Young had fostered during his previous visit. In April 1832 Jackson began driving the herd to Santa Fe while Young remained to hunt sea otter. Sometime in the late summer Young returned to Tàos, where María Tàyfoya gave birth to their first child.

The following October Young was again in California trapping the interior valley as far north as the Sacramento River, where his party encountered Hudson's Bay trappers. One of the Hudson's Bay men, John Turner (one of three to have survived the attack on Jedediah Smith's company by the Umpqua in 1827), joined Young's party. Turner interested Young in trapping the most northerly areas of present-day California, but their efforts produced dismal results.

Discouraged by poor trapping and a failed attempt at lumbering, Young gave way to emigrant Hall J. Kelly's exhortations to settle in Oregon. On the way to Oregon Young faced unjustified charges of horse stealing by Governor José Figuero of Santa Clara Mission, who forwarded the charges to John McLoughlin, chief factor of Fort Vancouver. The situation later caused Young some hardship, as McLoughlin refused him any services or business dealings after settling in Oregon.

Young arrived in Oregon in October 1834 and settled in Chehalem Valley. In 1836 he erected a sawmill and a whiskey distillery. Both enterprises frustrated the virtual monopoly the Hudson's Bay Company held on everything—a control that kept American settlers dependent on the British. Young also helped organize the successful Willamette Cattle Company designed to bring cattle from California to the American settlements and eliminate yet another British monopoly. He later constructed a grist mill, acted as local banker for many settlers, and prospered as a leading citizen among the American settlers. Young's operations distinguished him as the first successful American competition to the British hold on the region and as a vanguard of the advancing American settlement that ultimately forced the retreat of the British fur trade from Oregon.

Ewing Young died at his Oregon homestead from an acute ulcer, aggravated by his customary remedy of acid for indigestion. Young was considered by W. H. Gray to be "a stirring ambitious man," "candid and scrupulously honest, . . . thorough going, brave and daring." His life personified the opening of the Southwest, California, and Oregon to American expansion and settlement.

• The most complete work on Young remains Kenneth L. Holmes, *Ewing Young, Master Trapper* (1967). A biographical essay on Young can be found in Le Roy R. Hafen, *The Mountain Men and the Fur Trade of the Far West*, vol. 2 (1965), pp. 379–401. Young's involvement in the Southwest is examined by Joseph J. Hill, "Ewing Young in the Fur Trade of the Far Southwest, 1822–1834," *Oregon Historical Quarterly* 24 (1923): 7. The most detailed examination of Young's involvement in the California horse trade is Vivian Talbolt, "Out of Obscurity: A Biography of David E. Jackson, Field Captain of the Rocky Mountain Fur Trade" (master's thesis, Brigham Young Univ., 1992). The best overall examination of the southwest fur trade and Young's involvement in it is David J. Weber, *The Taos Trappers: The Fur Trade in the Far Southwest, 1540–1846* (1971).

S. MATTHEW DESPAIN

YOUNG, Hall (12 Sept. 1847–2 Sept. 1927), missionary, was born Samuel Hall Young in Butler, Pennsylvania, the son of Loyal Young, a Presbyterian minister, and Margaret Johnston. The family home was a stop on the Underground Railroad. Young's sister provided his early education, after which he attended Witherspoon Institute. Graduating at seventeen, he passed a teachers' examination and began teaching at a rural school in Middlesex Township, Pennsylvania. In 1867 he moved to the Traverse region of Michigan and obtained a teaching post at a school near Glen Arbor. Although always a Christian, he experienced at age twenty a profound religious conversion and with it the realization of his call as a missionary. One year later he joined his family in Oak Grove on French Creek in West Virginia, where they had recently moved. In 1871 Young entered the College of Wooster in Ohio, graduating four years later. He attended Princeton

Theological Seminary for one year and then finished his degree in two more years at the Western Theological Seminary in Allegheny, Pennsylvania.

One year into his program at Western, Young heard a lecture given by Sheldon Jackson, who, like Young, had been considered too physically weak for demanding missionary work in remote regions. Determination and hard work, however, had earned Jackson responsibility for much of the missionary work for the Presbyterian church in the American West and won him the moniker "Rocky Mountain Superintendent." Inspired, Young volunteered to join the three Presbyterian missionaries stationed in Alaska when he graduated in 1878. He was ordained in June of that year and sent to Fort Wrangell, Alaska, despite the Presbyterian Board of Home Missions's reservations about his fragile health. At Fort Wrangell he began preaching and holding Sunday school classes. In December 1878 he married a fellow missionary, Fannie E. Kellogg; they had three children.

Missionary work was just beginning in Alaska, but already it was colored by heavy political infighting. A destructive rivalry grew between Jackson, who was now serving in Alaska, and Aaron L. Lindsey, the pastor of the First Presbyterian Church in Portland, Oregon. Although Young tried to remain neutral, he became associated with Lindsey, his wife's uncle. Jackson eventually proved to be the more powerful of the two senior missionaries and helped his protégé, Young's missionary colleague John G. Brady, obtain the governorship of Alaska; this turn of events was a source of frustration for Young. Another major problem that would recur for Young throughout his work with the Alaskan Indians was the destructive influence of hard liquor. In addition to preaching against the harmful effects of alcohol, Young physically destroyed several stills. His campaign was moderately successful.

In August 1879 Young founded the first Protestant and the first American church in Alaska. In the same year he accompanied John Muir on his exploration of Glacier Bay and was present at the discovery of the Muir Glacier in October 1879. One glacier in Endicott Arm is named Young in honor of the missionary. Their explorations were not without danger. During one climb, Young slipped and fell, dislocating both shoulders and hanging helplessly over a 1,000-foot cliff. Unable to climb back up himself, Young was saved by Muir. In 1880 the two discovered and mapped a new canoe route to Sitka, on Baranof Island. Their trips mixed exploration with missionary work; on the journey to Sitka, Young preached to many of the Hoochenoo Indians. Young also made several major exploratory journeys without Muir, on one occasion traveling south to the Tongass tribe on Cape Fox.

As secretary and organizer of the first Alaskan territorial convention in 1881, Young wrote an appeal to Congress for improved government. The convention was small and the appeal did not have immediate effect in Congress. However, by 1884 Young's continued political efforts contributed to the passage of a congressional act that established the district of Alaska and funded schools and the employment of civil officials. In 1884 the U.S. government leased some abandoned garrison buildings to Young free of charge to be used to establish a school for Alaskan Indians. Young and his wife set up the Tlinket Training Academy, buying a 1,500-acre farm to supply the institution with food. By the following year they had twenty-seven pupils, who spent half the day working on the farm and the other half receiving instruction in religion and English. However, the school could not achieve financial self-sufficiency. When U.S. Commissioner James Sheckley visited the school and decided it was no more than an "Indian boarding house of rather inferior grade," thereby ruling out any chances of monetary government support, the Youngs closed it down. Young also traveled across the United States to recruit missionaries for Alaska. His efforts contributed to a significant increase in missionary work: by 1888, when he left the state, all the major Indian tribes in southern Alaska had missionary representatives.

From 1889 to 1892 Young divided his time between Long Beach and Wilmington, California, and Chicago, Illinois. In 1892 he accepted a position as pastor of the Presbyterian Church in Cedar Falls, Iowa, where he remained for three years. He then served as pastor and instructor of biblical history at Wooster College from 1895 to 1897.

Returning to Alaska in 1897 at the peak of the Klondike gold rush, Young founded a church in the mining community of Dawson. He moved to Nome, Alaska, two years later, where he nursed typhoid sufferers. Contracting the disease in the course of his ministrations, Young became critically ill and was close to dying. Although he lived occasionally in Ithaca, New York, to avoid the harsh Alaskan winters, Young otherwise remained in the state and continued working as a missionary until 1910. In that year he was recalled by the National Missionary Board. He went the following year to the Yukon, where he lived until 1913. Young then moved to Bellevue, Washington, where he continued to serve Alaska through his position on the Home Mission Council as secretary for the state and on the Presbyterian Board of Home Missions as special representative for Alaska. During this time he also wrote three memoirs of his adventures in Alaska: *Alaska Days with John Muir* (1915), *The Klondike Clan* (1916), and *Adventures in Alaska* (1919).

Young returned to Alaska again in 1921, intending to reorganize the missionaries there and create a "United Evangelical Church of Alaska." Young retired in 1924. He died while vacationing in West Virginia, near Clarksburg, where he was hit by a trolley car.

• Young's autobiography, *Hall Young of Alaska* (1927), was published posthumously. As well as detailing his life, it contains anthropological descriptions of the Alaskan Indians, including a chapter on native mythology. For further information on Young, see Ted C. Hinckey, "Early Alaskan Ministry of S. Hall Young, 1878–1888," *Journal of Presbyterian History* 46 (1968): 175–96. An obituary is in the *New York Times*, 4 Sept. 1927.

ELIZABETH ZOE VICARY

YOUNG, Hugh Hampton (18 Sept. 1870–23 Aug. 1945), urologic surgeon, was born in San Antonio, Texas, the son of General William Hugh Young, a lawyer and real estate developer who had risen to the rank of brigadier general during the Civil War, and Frances Michie Kemper. Young attended public schools in San Antonio and then transferred to the San Antonio Academy. In 1888, at the age of eighteen, he was sent to study under his uncle at the Aspinhill School in Louisa County, Virginia. After his uncle accepted a professorship in Kentucky, Young spent a year at the Staunton (Va.) Academy. In 1890, after working for a summer with a surveyor, he enrolled in the University of Virginia, and three years later he was awarded simultaneously an A.B. and an A.M. A year later, in 1894, he obtained an M.D. from the University of Virginia.

Soon after Young had returned to San Antonio and set up a medical practice, a friend, who felt the old doctors of San Antonio were inadequate, persuaded him to operate on a lady with uterine tumors. Through polite maneuvers, Young enticed an experienced surgeon to perform the operation while he assisted. From this experience, Young realized that if he was to pursue surgery as a profession, he must obtain further training in a large city hospital and chose the new Johns Hopkins Hospital, which had opened only five years earlier.

On his arrival in Baltimore in 1894, Young worked under William D. Booker in pediatrics until the graduate school opened. Through Booker Young was able to obtain a position for graduate surgical training on the service of Dr. J. M. T. Finney, assistant to Chief of Surgery William Stewart Halsted. During the summer Young worked in the pathological and bacteriological laboratory of the Thomas Wilson Sanitarium in Baltimore. Young applied for and eventually obtained a position on the service of Halsted, who in 1897 persuaded Young to head the Department of Genito-Urinary Surgery, in spite of Young's inexperience in that area. Taking charge of the department in November 1897, young became the following year instructor in genitourinary diseases at the Johns Hopkins Medical School, where in 1914 he was appointed clinical professor of urology and in 1932, professor of urology. Young married Bessie Mason Coulson in 1901; they had four children.

When Young took charge of the department, its urological instrumentation consisted of two cystoscopes, developed by Max Nitze in 1876, which were crude instruments for looking into the bladder. Realizing that the center of progress in the growing field of urology was in Europe, Young spent two months in the Berlin clinic of Dr. Leopold Casper, who had developed a cystoscope useful for ureteral catheterization. While in Europe, Young constructed an improved Nitze cystoscope. Against the advice of his German comrade Casper, Young showed his cystoscope to Nitze, who rebuked him for his improvements.

On his return to Johns Hopkins, Young set about organizing a department that ultimately had a great influence on the development of urology. As Young's reputation grew, patients with difficult genito-urological problems came to him from all over the United States and the world. Young dealt with these complicated illnesses in ingenious ways: by designing a new cystoscope, modifying and making new instruments, and devising new operations. With these innovative techniques he successfully treated many complicated urological problems that had previously been poorly managed. Young's most famous innovations were his punch cystoscope (the Young punch), designed in 1913 for transureteral prostate resection, and the perineal prostatectomy, for management of benign hypertrophy and cancer of the prostate. Both procedures improved treatment of prostatic disease by allowing removal of prostatic tissue without opening the bladder or entering the peritoneum. These extraperitoneal approaches made prostate surgery much safer, a great advantage in the days before antibiotics.

Young was an excellent teacher and a tough taskmaster who demanded hard work from his interns and residents. Taking great interest in the future of those he trained, he found them academic positions and, frequently, personally aided them financially until they were established.

Young's most famous patient was James Buchanan "Diamond Jim" Brady, a manufacturer of steel railroad cars, who came to Young in 1912 with prostatic obstruction. Brady's case was difficult, for he was vastly overweight and suffered from diabetes, gallstones, high blood pressure, and coronary disease. Young successfully relieved his prostatic obstruction with his cold punch instrument under local anesthesia. As payment for Young's services, Brady gave him money to build a modern urologic clinic. The James Buchanan Brady Urological Institute of the Johns Hopkins Hospital opened in January 1915. This was a complete hospital and research unit with inpatient and outpatient facilities, X-ray equipment, clinical laboratories, research facilities, and a machine shop. For Young the machine shop was of particular importance, for it gave the staff of the Brady Institute the ability to build new instruments suitable for coping with the urological problems they encountered. Although Young managed many of the problems of the kidneys and ureters, such as tumors, obstructions, infections, and stones, his main field of expertise was diseases of the prostate. According to an anonymous contemporary source, "the prostate makes man old, but the prostate has made Hugh Young."

In 1917 Young volunteered for duty in the U.S. Army and went to France, where he organized the urological service, which under his direction significantly lowered venereal diseases in the Allied armies of World War I. Impressed by the immunologist Paul

Ehrlich's salvasan for the treatment of syphilis, Young upon his return to Baltimore in 1919 put a number of the members of his staff of the Brady Institute to work in finding antibacterial agents useful for treating genito-urinary diseases. In 1920 H. A. B. Dunning synthesized the water-soluble mercury compound mercurochrome (dibromooxymercuryfluoresceine) that had antibacterial activity and was not injurious to tissue. At first this antiseptic was only used topically for the treatment of surface infections. However, after Edmund Piper in Philadelphia found during the early 1920s that intravenous mercurochrome was of some benefit in the treatment of puerperal sepsis, the group at the Brady Institute began using it intravenously for treating septicemia. In the late 1930s Young pioneered the use of sulfonamide for the treatment of urinary infections.

Even with his busy clinical and teaching schedule, Young published numerous papers on various urological topics. In 1917 he founded the *Journal of Urology*, of which he remained an editor until his death.

An energetic man with a pleasing personality, Young also played a role in public affairs. In 1903, through the aid of an influential politician who was a patient, he secured passage of laws for the control of tuberculosis in Maryland. He served as chairman of the Maryland State Lunacy Commission (later the Board of Mental Hygiene). Being interested in aviation, Young was appointed chairman of the Maryland State Aviation Commission in 1929. Politically, Young was a Democrat, and in 1932 he led an unsuccessful attempt to obtain the presidential nomination for Maryland governor Albert C. Ritchie. Young died while still at work as a retired professor in the Brady Institute at the Johns Hopkins Hospital.

• An extensive collection of Young's papers, with a detailed index and description, is in the archives of the Johns Hopkins Medical School. Young's own account of his life is *Hugh Young: A Surgeon's Autobiography* (1940). Other accounts of his life are by Miley B. Wilson in the *Journal of Urology* 57 (1947): 203–8; and "The Clinic of Hugh Hampton Young," *British Journal of Surgery* 9 (1921): 272–80. An obituary is in the *Baltimore Sun*, 24 Aug. 1945.

DAVID Y. COOPER

YOUNG, John (17 Mar. 1744–17 Dec. 1835), seaman and adviser to King Kamehameha I of the Hawaiian Islands, was born in Liverpool, England. His parents' identities are not known. Young had little or no formal education. At an early age he went to sea and before the American Revolution was aboard merchant ships sailing out of New York and Philadelphia. In 1789 he joined the *Eleanora*, a brig of about 190 tons, as boatswain, sailing from New York on a fur-trading voyage to the American Northwest. Early in 1790, en route to China with a load of furs, the *Eleanora* reached the island of Maui in the Hawaiian Islands to pick up supplies. There they ran into trouble with the islanders. One of the ship's boats was taken at night and the guard aboard it killed. Captain Simon Metcalfe retaliated by luring many islanders to the side of his ship, ostensibly to trade, and when they were closely gathered at one side of the *Eleanora*, he fired a lethal volley from guns loaded with musket balls and nails, killing about 100 people.

The *Eleanora* then sailed off to Kealakekua Bay on the island of Hawaii. While there the companion ship, *Fair American*, captained by Metcalfe's son Thomas, having been delayed on the California coast, finally put into another port on Maui, not aware that the local chief, Kameeiamoku, harbored a grudge against all white traders because Simon had once struck him with a rope's end. Kameeiamoku had decided to vent his anger. The *Fair American* was captured, and Thomas and all but one of the crew of four were murdered. When news of the fate of the *Fair American* reached Kamehameha I, the high chief on Hawaii, John Young happened to be ashore. Young was immediately detained by Kamehameha to prevent news of the fate of the *Fair American* reaching Captain Metcalfe. After several days of futile appeals by Metcalfe for Young's return to his ship, the *Eleanora* sailed for China, leaving its boatswain behind.

From the beginning of Young's enforced sojourn on Hawaii, Kamehameha treated him with kindness. Young and a companion, Isaac Davis, the sole survivor of the *Fair American*, made only one attempt to escape. It was firmly thwarted by Kamehameha, and from then on they settled down on the island of Hawaii and became invaluable advisers to Kamehameha in handling foreign men, ships, and arms. In 1791 Young and Davis commanded Kamehameha's victorious artillery in a historic sea battle in the channel between Maui and Hawaii known as Kepuwahaulaula (the red-mouthed gun).

Lavishly rewarded for their work as trusted advisers to Kamehameha I, Young and Davis quickly adjusted to life as Hawaiian chiefs, enjoying grants of land, wives, and servants. Young established a home at Kawaihae, on the island of Hawaii, where its remains are still visible. In 1795 he married Namokuelua of the island of Oahu; they had two children. After her death he married Kaoanaeha in 1805; they had four children. Their only son, John (also known as Keoni Ana), served Kamehameha III as a close adviser and as prime minister and minister of the interior in the government of the kingdom. One of their daughters, Fannie, was the mother, and another daughter, Grace, was the adoptive mother of Queen Emma, consort of Kamehameha IV.

Captain George Vancouver, a British naval explorer who visited the islands in 1793–1794, gave a firsthand description of Young and Davis, whom he met when he arrived in the islands in 1793. The men had been in the islands for three years and he recorded in his journal that the two seamen were in Kamehameha's "most perfect confidence, attend him in all his excursions of business or pleasure, or expeditions of war or enterprise; and are in the habit of daily experiencing from him the greatest respect, and the highest degree of esteem and regard" (Vancouver, p. 823).

Vancouver gathered a great deal of his information about the islands, the chiefs, and the people from Young and Davis, apparently relying heavily on their opinions of the characters of the many chiefs in forming his own assessment of each chief's trustworthiness in writing his recommendations to the British navy and to other foreign seamen who came to Hawaii after him. Before leaving the islands in 1794, Vancouver offered Young and Davis passage home to England.

After mature consideration, they preferred their present way of life, and were desirous of continuing at Owhyhee (Hawaii); observing, that being destitute of resources, on their return home, . . . they must be again exposed to the vicissitudes of a life of hard labour for the purpose of merely acquiring a precarious supply of the most common necessaries of life; objects which, for some years past, had not occasioned them the least concern. (Vancouver, pp. 1190–91)

Throughout the king's life, Young was a trusted councilor to Kamehameha I, serving him in many different capacities. Between 1802 and 1812 Young served as governor of the island of Hawaii in the king's absence. Later, in 1816, when the Russians had been ousted from the islands, Young supervised the construction of a fort in Honolulu, begun as a fortified trading post by representatives of the Russian-American Company. In 1819 Young was one of the chiefs at the deathbed of Kamehameha I, and in due course he became an adviser to his son and successor, Kamehameha II.

When Young died (in Honolulu), he was buried in the royal tomb on the grounds of what is now the port city's Iolani Palace. In 1866 his remains, with those of the other chiefs, were moved to the newly built Royal Mausoleum. In his long lifetime, Young was an honest and intelligent adviser to the Hawaiian kings and chiefs and to the foreigners. He advocated tolerance and fair play in all involvements between the two sides and helped to create an atmosphere of mutual trust in which commerce between Hawaiians and foreigners could thrive.

• There are several firsthand accounts of John Young in the journals of explorers in the Pacific at the end of the eighteenth and beginning of the nineteenth centuries; the most exhaustive is that of Captain George Vancouver, *A Voyage of Discovery to the North Pacific Ocean and Round the World, 1791–1795*, ed. W. Kaye Lamb (1984), which includes an account of the *Eleanora/Fair American* affair as told to Vancouver by Young and Davis. In 1913 Bishop Henry B. Restarick cast doubt on the nationality of John Young in "John Young of Hawaii, An American," in *Hawaiian Historical Society's Annual Report for 1913*. The question was argued over the next few years and finally laid to rest by John F. G. Stokes in "Nationality of John Young, a Chief of Hawaii," in the *Hawaiian Historical Society's Annual Report for 1938*.

RHODA E. A. HACKLER

YOUNG, John (12 June 1802–23 Apr. 1852), politician, was born in Chelsea, Vermont, the son of Thomas Young and Mary Gale, who kept a public house and later owned a farm. When John was four, his family moved to Conesus, Livingston County, New York. He attended the common schools and read widely, seeking the classical education his family could not afford. He worked alternately at farm labor and teaching school until his twenty-first birthday, when he began the study of law in the office of Augustus A. Bennett in East Avon. He was admitted to the county bar in 1827 and to practice before the state supreme court in 1829. Self-confident, shrewd, and energetic, Young pursued his clients' interests vigorously, and he soon enjoyed a large and profitable practice.

In 1828 Young ran as a Jacksonian Democrat for county clerk but was defeated by an Anti-Mason. Party lines in New York were still quite fluid, and within a year Young had joined the Anti-Masons, who, like the Jacksonians, made strong appeals to the "common man." He was elected as an Anti-Mason to the state assembly in 1832, served competently, but won little notice. Opposition to the Fraternal Order of Masons was a narrow base for a permanent political organization, and Young, like many Anti-Masons, eventually drifted toward the recently organized Whig party. In 1836 he was elected to Congress as a Whig to fill a vacancy created by the resignation of Philo C. Fuller, but he did not seek reelection. In 1840 he was again elected to Congress. The Whig landslide of that year seemed to prove the Whigs' viability as a party, and the young lawyer hoped through aggressive support of its program to become one of its leaders. William Henry Harrison's death after only a month in the presidency elevated John Tyler (1790–1862), a southern states' rights Whig, to the White House. When the latter's independence on matters such as the tariff, bank, and the distribution of monies from the sale of the public lands threatened Whig party unity, Young helped to orchestrate the "regular" Whig opposition to Tyler in Congress, which culminated in a manifesto virtually reading the president out of the party.

Young's bid for party leadership and demands for party recognition in the form of patronage made him the rival of New York's Whig governor William Henry Seward and his powerful adviser, newspaper editor Thurlow Weed. Young returned to New York after his congressional term and ran for the state assembly in 1843, serving two terms in 1844 and 1845. Although Democrats held the majority of seats, Young demonstrated his political shrewdness by pushing through a Whig bill for a new constitutional convention. He achieved his majority by appealing to dissident Democrats and especially to Anti-Renters, who opposed the antiquated manorial system of landholding that still existed in several eastern counties. In 1845 he supported a bill abolishing the rents.

Likely support from the Anti-Renters in the closely divided state made Young an attractive gubernatorial candidate in 1846 against incumbent Democrat Silas Wright. Young won the significant election by a margin of 11,000 among over 400,000 ballots cast and promptly pardoned Anti-Renters convicted of various misdeeds on the grounds that their crimes had been political. This action shocked conservatives in the

Whig party. Young's refusal to accept Weed's suggestions for awarding the limited number of patronage positions still available under the newly adopted constitution of 1846 weakened Young's position further. His term (1847–1849) also coincided with the difficult issue of the Mexican War, regretted by some Whigs yet difficult for party members to denounce and still appear patriotic. The Wilmot Proviso also threatened to divide the party north and south over the extension of slavery to the newly acquired territory. Young hedged on these issues, satisfying no one and further confirming his enemies' image of him as devoid of principles. He wisely did not seek reelection.

In 1848, as a delegate to the Whig National Convention, Young supported Zachary Taylor, a southern slaveholder but also a nationalist, for the presidency. Despite vigorous opposition from Seward and Weed, he received a lucrative patronage appointment as assistant treasurer in New York City upon Taylor's election. Young used the position to award jobs to his supporters. He favored the Compromise of 1850 on slavery, disliked by Seward, and at the time of his death in New York City from tuberculosis, he had become the recognized leader of the anti-Seward Whigs. (He left no immediate family behind, having never married or had children.) Unable to master the diversity of perspectives within the party he longed to lead, Young was bitterly denounced as an unprincipled trimmer by many of the men who had helped elect him governor only six years previously.

• Young's papers are at the New York State Library, Albany. Some letters on N.Y. politics may also be found in the Burrows family papers at the University of Michigan. See also William P. Boyd, *History of the Town of Conesus, Livingston County, N.Y.* (1887); D. S. Alexander, *A Political History of the State of New York*, vol. 2 (1906); and James H. Smith, *History of Livingston County, New York* (1881). An obituary is in the *New York Times*, 24 Apr. 1852.

PHYLLIS FIELD

YOUNG, John Orr (25 June 1886–1 May 1976), advertising and public relations executive, was born in Leon, Iowa, the son of John Lewis, a farmer, and Elizabeth Woodbury. Young attended Lake Forrest College in Illinois from 1906 to 1908. In his memoir, *Adventures in Advertising* (1949), he claimed that while there he had learned almost nothing from books because he had taken on so many jobs to pay for his schooling that he had little time left for study.

After leaving college in 1908, Young worked for two years in the advertising department of the *Salt Lake Herald Tribune* and then moved to Chicago, where he took a copywriting position with one of the largest agencies in America, Lord and Thomas. There he worked under Claude Hopkins and Albert Lasker, two of the most prominent advertising thinkers of their era. Hopkins and Lasker believed that advertising should rely on copy rather than pictures, and so they barely tolerated Young's work for Sunkist, which featured images of juicy oranges. But his departure from Lord and Thomas was also speeded, Young re-

called in his memoir, by his circulating a parody of the company letterhead that read "Loud and Promise: Bad Advertising."

In 1913 Young joined Procter and Gamble as the Crisco division's advertising manager, a position he left in 1914 to become a partner at Young, Henri, Hurst. That same year he married Ethel Prague Butler, with whom he had three children before her death in 1942. Young worked briefly with two other agencies before joining N. W. Ayer & Son in Philadelphia in 1921 as an account executive. It was at Ayer that Young met Raymond Rubicam, a young copywriter. In 1923 they decided to leave Ayer and open their own agency. Young & Rubicam, as Young liked to point out, was literally founded on a shoestring, because the agency's first account was a device for making shoelaces at home.

Because of Young's business contacts and outgoing personality, his job at the agency was to attract new clients. Young's approach was not to ask for all of a potential client's business but only for its most difficult product. He assumed that if the agency succeeded, the client would send additional business his way. This approach led the group of companies that later became General Foods to give Young & Rubicam its first major assignment, Postum, a decaffeinated beverage with declining sales. The advertising revived the brand, won a Harvard-Bok Prize, and helped establish Young & Rubicam as a legitimate agency. As Young had predicted, success with Postum led to additional assignments from General Foods, and the agency soon agreed to open a New York office in order to work on such brands as Jell-O and Sanka coffee.

Concerned about its being labeled a "food shop," Young sought to diversify his agency's accounts, and he gradually helped add such clients as Rolls Royce, Johnson and Johnson, and Parke-Davis to the agency roster. But as Young & Rubicam grew increasingly successful, Young began to be plagued with health problems. He started taking extended vacations to try and regain his health. But he was also taking less and less part in the daily operations of the agency because he was bored. As he said in his memoir, he was "more interested in people than in establishing such colossal facts as the extreme crunchiness of Crunchos" (p. 130). Young's disinterest showed, and both employees and clients began to complain. Finally, in 1934 Young was forced out of the agency he had helped to found.

After leaving Young & Rubicam, Young sought to restore his health by traveling in Europe and collecting farms and antiques in Virginia, Connecticut, and Vermont. At the outbreak of World War II, he moved to Washington, D.C., and went to work for the War Production Board, Chemicals Division, where, among his other duties, he helped increase the production of alcohol, which was essential to the manufacture of synthetic rubber. In 1944 he married Lorna Holland Byrne. The couple was divorced in 1959, and shortly thereafter Young married Bernice Renner. He had no children with either wife.

At the end of World War II, Young returned to New York, where he opened a public relations agency, Young and Meyers, with Harold C. Meyers, former head of Institutional Relations. Young had grown increasingly interested in public relations because he felt that the times demanded a way to address not only sales but also a company's entire social contribution. In fact, it was this concern for larger social issues that caused him to take out ads in 1947 urging Republicans to nominate General Dwight D. Eisenhower for president. He had to halt the effort when Eisenhower refused to run.

In 1948 Young published *Adventures in Advertising*, which described his experiences and laid out his thoughts on the business. The volume, he said, was written on the train during his daily commute from his home in Westport, Connecticut, to his office in New York. Its publication was marked by a surprise party on the train given by eleven of his fellow commuters.

In later years, Young continued to live in Westport but maintained a two-person office on Park Avenue from which he helped top advertising agencies arrange mergers and evaluate campaigns. In fact, by the 1960s he had become something of an advertising elder statesman whose insights were so valued that R. W. Apple writing in the *New York Times* said Young had assumed the "same standing in certain executive suites that Bernard Baruch once had in the White House" (29 Jan. 1964). Young died in Westport.

• The most complete account of Young's life and thought is found in his memoir, *Adventures in Advertising* (1949). The work was serialized in alternate issues of *Printers Ink*, beginning 5 Mar. 1948. Carolyn Tripp provides a solid overview of Young's life and accomplishments in *Ad Men and Women: A Biographical Dictionary of Advertising* (1994). Although Stephen Fox's discussion of Young in *The Mirror Makers* (1984) is brief, Fox's access to manuscripts at Young & Rubicam enabled him to provide valuable insight into the reasons for Young's departure from that agency. An obituary is in the *New York Times*, 3 May 1976.

BRETT ROBBS

YOUNG, John Richardson (1782–8 June 1804), physician, was born in Hagerstown (then Elizabethtown), Maryland, the son of Samuel Young, a physician, and Ann Richardson. He attended the College of New Jersey (now Princeton University) and graduated in 1799; he then returned home to serve as an assistant to his father. After this apprenticeship, Young enrolled, in 1802, as a medical student at the University of Pennsylvania and graduated in 1803. The Pennsylvania medical faculty at that time included such notable figures as William Shippen, Benjamin Rush, and Benjamin Smith Barton, who became Young's friend and adviser, and to whom his famous inaugural dissertation for the M.D. was dedicated.

The dissertation, *An Experimental Inquiry into the Principles of Nutrition and the Digestive Process* (1803; repr. in Charles Caldwell, ed., *Medical Theses* [1805]), was also dedicated to Young's father. It described the results of a number of experiments that Young had made, including those on the big bullfrog (*Rana ocellata*), a creature with large esophagus. His procedure was to lower various foodstuffs, including small frogs, into the large frog's stomach and to extract them at intervals in order to study the process of digestion. He also used snakes in his experiments, emptying their stomachs so that he could investigate the breakdown of various materials. In addition, Young regurgitated the contents of his own stomach to see what happened in the human process. One of his friends from medical school, John Stevenson Mitchell, was his obliging coworker in this research and "frequently threw up the contents of his stomach for me."

Young was looking for the true nature of digestion, a topic about which there had been centuries of speculation with little or no real understanding. From ancient times, theories had been advanced that included an animistic doctrine; ideas of trituration, putrefaction, and solution; and a belief in a fermentation process. In the seventeenth century, new discoveries in anatomy such as the lacteals, the pancreatic duct, and the thoracic duct raised new questions—for example, what were the purposes of all of the ducts and absorbents "clustered for some puzzling but surely definite purposes around the mouth and the upper intestinal tract?" In the next century, investigators such as Reaumur and Spallanzani in Europe and Rush and Edward Stevens in America established beyond a doubt that digestion was a chemical process that involved a "gastric juice." None of these men identified it as an acid; Rush wrote that no "acid ferment" was necessary for digestion.

Young's contributions to an understanding of the digestive process included all of the following—rejection of theories of innate heat and vital spirits and of trituration, putrefaction, and fermentation; identification of the "gastric juice" as an acid (identified by Young as phosphoric acid—it is hydrochloric acid) secreted in the stomach; and demonstration that the acidic gastric juice checked putrefaction. He explained the digestive process as follows: "We would, therefore, explain this process in a few words. Aliment is dissolved by the gastric menstruum; it then passes into the duodenum and meets with bile and pancreatic liquor; after being united with these, a heterogeneous mass is formed called chyme, and from this, the lacteals secrete chyle." Young also noted that the flow of the gastric juice and that of the saliva were synchronous.

After he graduated, Young, who never married, joined his father in medical practice in Hagerstown for one year until his death there from tuberculosis. His only other writings were two letters published posthumously in the Philadelphia Medical and Physical Journal ([1804]), "A case of Tetanus Cured by Mercury" (pp. 47–51), and one on the use of saccharum saturni in three cases of uterine hemorrhage (p. 145). After his death, discovered among his effects was a manuscript on digestion, which was evidently intended for a general audience as it was written in nontechnical language.

Young was obviously a very gifted man. Contemporaries described him as possessing "uncommon talents and great industry," and in his short life he made a major contribution in establishing gastric physiology on a scientific experimental basis.

• Young's dissertation was reprinted in facsimile form in 1959 by the University of Illinois Press, Urbana. Biographical articles include Howard A. Kelly, "John R. Young: Pioneer American Physiologist," *Bulletin of the Johns Hopkins Hospital* 29 (1918): 186–91; Donald G. Bates, "American Therapeutics in 1804: The Case of John R. Young," *Bulletin of the History of Medicine* 38 (1964): 226–40, and "The Background to John Young's Thesis on Digestion," *Bulletin of the History of Medicine* 36 (1964): 341–61; and Stacey B. Day, "In Old St. John's Burying Ground on Mulberry Street," *Surgery* 69 (1971): 895–98. A work related to this subject is Day, *Edward Stevens: Gastric Physiologist, Physician and American Statesman* (1969).

ROBERT F. ERICKSON

YOUNG, Lester (27 Aug. 1909–15 Mar. 1959), jazz musician, was born in Woodville, Mississippi, the son of Willis Handy Young, a musician, and Lizetta (maiden name unknown). "Prez," or "the President," as Billie Holiday dubbed him in the 1930s, spent his early childhood in Algiers, Louisiana, across the river from New Orleans. When his parents divorced in 1919 he moved to Minneapolis with his father, who headed a family band that played in carnivals and vaudeville shows. Young played drums in the band, but he changed to the alto saxophone at age thirteen. Unwilling to tour the South and suffer the racist humiliations that accompanied such trips, he left the band in 1927. He played briefly with Walter Page's Blue Devils and Art Bronson's Bostonians, where he switched to the tenor saxophone. In 1931 he settled again in Minneapolis and then toured with the Blue Devils in 1932. When they disbanded he moved to Kansas City, traveling and playing with a variety of groups, including King Oliver's Band. He also was married for the first time in 1931, to a white, Jewish girl named Bess Cooper. They had one child, but shortly after giving birth his wife underwent surgery and bled to death. Young was grief-stricken. His constant traveling forced him to place his infant daughter with foster parents, but he always maintained close contact with her.

Early in 1934 Young joined the Count Basie band for several months, but he left in March to join Fletcher Henderson's band. One night he had come to hear Henderson's tenor player, Coleman Hawkins, but Hawkins failed to appear, and Young ended up replacing him for the evening. Henderson was impressed enough to hire Young as a replacement when Hawkins later left the band, but the job lasted only a few months. Young's style and tone were so different from Hawkins's that band members complained, and Henderson's wife spent hours playing the band's records for Young in an effort to teach him how to play like Hawkins. By 1936 Young was back with Basie.

He made his first recordings with a Basie-led group in November of that year, immediately producing several classic solos in tunes like "Lady Be Good," "Shoe Shine Boy," "Boogie Woogie," and "Evenin'." He had already created a fully developed style. Influenced by Jimmy Dorsey and especially by Frankie Trumbauer on C-melody saxophone and by Bix Beiderbecke, he had a light tone, almost without vibrato, a breathtaking sense of melodic beauty, rhythmically relaxed phrasing, and a linear approach to improvising that contrasted sharply with the more harmonic, chordal approach of Hawkins. He played in a ceaselessly variegated, sometimes flurrying, unexpectedly accented legato style that could be said to mark the beginning of modern jazz, and his solos unfolded in a daring, freshly logical, and strikingly balanced flow of ideas. Like all great jazz playing, his solos told a story, and there is a sense of inevitability and "rightness" in them that commands total attention.

Young also left a personal imprint on the jazz world. Musicians loved him, and he epitomized the sense of "hip" that characterized many black communities of the South and Southwest at that time. He specialized in giving other musicians nicknames (he named Billie Holiday "Lady Day"), and he invented a myriad of cryptic expressions that dotted his language; he had "big eyes," for instance, for things he liked, or "no eyes" for those he did not. He loved to play practical jokes, such as ringing a bell onstage when a band member made a mistake. But Young also was introverted, a shy man whose sensitivity and concern for the underdog endeared him to his colleagues and left him vulnerable to the pain and humiliation of the racist society he lived in. He spoke frequently of his anger at this racism, and he sought release in alcohol and marijuana, although he avoided hard drugs. Music was his real life, offering him the total escape he desired. Equally therapeutic was his close, platonic friendship with Holiday, whom he recorded with frequently during the late 1930s. His soft, tender accompaniments on tunes like "All of Me" reveals a profoundly empathetic artistic partnership.

Young stayed with the Basie band through the 1930s, touring and making several hundred recordings and live broadcasts. He also played clarinet occasionally during these years; even Benny Goodman expressed admiration for Young's skill on the instrument. The death of his friend and fellow saxophonist Herschel Evans in early 1939, however, affected him deeply, and business and artistic differences led him to leave Basie in 1940 to form a small band of his own. He later co-led a group with his brother Lee Young, a drummer, playing lengthy engagements in New York City and Los Angeles. He also freelanced widely until rejoining Basie by December 1943, and he recorded a series of widely influential sessions for Keynote Records in late 1943 and early 1944. He now began to attract wider public notice, winning the *Down Beat* poll for tenor saxophone in 1944. Beginning in 1942 his playing underwent the first of two major stylistic changes, as his sound became broader and heavier and his style more overtly emotional.

In September 1944 Young was drafted. Army discipline was antithetical to his personality, and he quickly alienated his superiors with his indifference. They confiscated his saxophone and refused to allow him to play in the jazz band at Fort McClellan, Alabama, where he was stationed. After being hospitalized for a minor injury, Young became addicted to painkillers. When a white officer discovered a picture of Young's second wife, Mary (who was white and whom he had married in 1937), he also found pain medication that Prez had obtained illegally. The army subsequently court-martialed Young, gave him a dishonorable discharge, and sentenced him to a year in the detention barracks at Fort Gordon, Georgia. The entire experience left him emotionally scarred.

After his discharge, Young made a series of recordings for the Los Angeles–based Aladdin company, producing classic performances on such tunes as "These Foolish Things." Starting in 1946 he toured almost annually with Norman Granz's well-paying "Jazz at the Philharmonic." He appeared often with groups of his own and as a guest with Basie's band, and his popularity rose dramatically. His domestic life became more settled. He was married for a third time, to another woman named Mary, in 1946; the two moved into a house in the Queens borough of New York and had two children. But Young also continued to drink and smoke heavily, and by now he was suffering from malnutrition, alcoholism, and cirrhosis of the liver. Although he kept his musical commitments, he grew suspicious and uncommunicative and increasingly uncomfortable around whites. As he noted in a Paris interview shortly before he died, "they want everybody who's a Negro to be an Uncle Tom, or Uncle Remus, or Uncle Sam, and I can't make it."

Some critics claim that Young's later recordings, particularly those made after 1950, were vastly inferior to those he made during the late 1930s. But while his style changed, it was not necessarily inferior. He continued to explore new musical conceptions; he preferred to work with younger musicians, and by the late 1940s his groups were playing in a more modern, bop-influenced style. His tone also became fuller and rounder, partly as a result of his use of a new mouthpiece and his temporary adoption of plastic reeds. Although his tone weakened after 1950, he often played with his old self-assurance. This was particularly true when he was surrounded by musicians of a similar aesthetic. The pianist John Lewis often played with Young in 1951 and 1952, and Lewis's light, linear style allowed Young to return to his light tone and float airily over the accompaniment. He found a similarly sympathetic partner in 1952 recordings with Oscar Peterson, and in two wonderful 1956 quartet sessions with Teddy Wilson on piano. His live sessions with a trio at Olivia's Patio Lounge in Washington, D.C., contain some of his best later work. But after 1953 Young's recordings were less consistent. He suffered from painful toothaches and sporadic epileptic attacks, and he was hospitalized several times for alcohol-related problems. He moved out of his home and into the Alvin Hotel, across the street from Birdland, where he often played in his later years. His last great moment came on the December 1957 television show, "The Sound of Jazz," in a poignant reunion with Lady Day. Young was so ill that the show's producers considered canceling his appearance, and they decided to allow him only a brief solo. When his time came, he rose and played an exquisite 45-note chorus on Holiday's classic "Fine and Mellow." The two never saw each other again.

Young seemed to recover a bit during the final year of his life, reducing his drinking and gaining weight, and in January 1959 he opened an engagement at the Blue Note Club in Paris. But he stopped eating and began to drink heavily again. Ill and in great pain, he returned to New York on 13 March and died two days later in his hotel room, of heart failure.

Lester Young once said that originality should be the goal of both life and art. He remains the most original, influential figure in the history of jazz between Louis Armstrong and Charlie Parker. He spawned dozens of imitators and complained that he could not go anywhere without hearing himself. His diatonic style pointed the way toward the bop era and even to the modal jazz of the 1950s and 1960s. His playing reflected his inner self. A kind, gentle man, he sought the same qualities in his music: "It's got to be sweetness, you dig?" And more than anything else, his playing reflected the essence of great jazz: "The blues? Great Big Eyes! . . . Everybody has to play the blues and everybody has them too . . . "

• We are fortunate to have several excellent studies of Young's career and music. The fullest biography is Frank Büchmann-Møller's superb *You Just Fight for Your Life: The Story of Lester Young* (1990). The most perceptive musical analysis is in Gunther Schuller, *The Swing Era: The Development Of Jazz, 1930–1945* (1989), pp. 547–62. Lewis Porter's outstanding *Lester Young* (1985) provides a thorough, readable biography and detailed analyses of Young's style and of a number of his solos. There are good, briefer analyses in Martin Williams, *The Jazz Tradition*, 3d ed. (1993), pp. 129–34, and James Lincoln Collier, *The Making of Jazz: A Comprehensive History* (1978), pp. 228–35. The quotations are from Young's interview with François Postif in Paris in 1959 for the *Jazz Review*, reprinted in Martin Williams, ed., *Jazz Panorama* (1962), pp. 139–44. Also see John McDonough, *Lester Young* (1980), a booklet for the Time-Life "Giants of Jazz" series; Leonard Feather, *From Satchmo to Miles* (1972), pp. 115–28; and Ira Gitler, *Swing to Bop* (1985), pp. 35–40, for brief comments by musicians on Young's life and music; and Lewis Porter, ed., *A Lester Young Reader* (1991).

RONALD P. DUFOUR

YOUNG, Mahonri Mackintosh (9 Aug. 1877–2 Nov. 1957), sculptor, teacher, and painter, was born in Salt Lake City, Utah, the son of Mahonri Moriancumer Young, the owner of a textile factory, and Agnes Mackintosh; he was a grandson of Brigham Young. The family lived on a farm near Salt Lake City. His fondest early memories were playing in the woods and using clay from the nearby riverbed to form art objects. "I cannot remember when I did not want to be a sculptor," reads the first line of his unfinished autobiography.

In 1884 Young's father died, and his mother moved the family to Salt Lake City, where he attended public schools. At the beginning of his freshman year in high school, however, he dropped out and took a job in a stationery store and later in a bicycle shop for $2.50 a week. This amount went to James T. Harwood of Salt Lake City for art lessons. Young also worked as a portrait and sketch artist for the *Salt Lake Tribune* and worked in its photoengraving shop. In 1899 he went to New York City to study at the Art Students League. By 1901 he had saved enough money to go to Paris, where he lived for the next four years. He studied drawing and painting with Jean Paul Laurens and modeling with Charles-Raoul Verlet at the Académie Julian and with Jean-Antoine Injalbert at the Académie Colarossi; he also studied at the Académie Delécluse. He visited Italy before returning to Salt Lake City in late 1905. In 1910 he moved to New York City.

In the early 1900s Young began using watercolors and increased his abilities as an artist. He worked in several media, including watercolors, sculpture, etching, and drawing. Basic to all his artistic endeavors was a love of and a strong ability for drawing.

In 1907 Young married Cecelia Sharp, daughter of a Mormon bishop. The couple had two children. His wife died in 1916. Several years later, in 1931, he married Dorothy Weir, a New York artist.

In 1911 Young completed the bronze statuette *Bovet Arthur—A Laborer*. The National Academy of Design awarded him the Helen Foster Barnett Prize, and he was later elected an Academician. Describing Young's bronzes, J. Lester Lewine, writing in *International Studio* (Oct. 1912), noted that "the natural endowment of talent, of which his work bears the unmistakable impress, entitles him to a commanding position in contemporary art."

In 1912 Young had a one-man show, held at New York City's Berlin Photographic Company; it was well received and included sculpture, watercolors, and drawings. The following year one of Young's most noted works, the *Sea Gull Monument*, was erected in Salt Lake City. The sea gulls depicted commemorate those who ate the grasshoppers that threatened the Mormons' first crops after their arrival in Utah. The Armory Show of 1913 in New York exhibited some of the relief panels from the *Sea Gull Monument*.

Young was known for his realism; his figures, animals, and landscapes were authentic because of his preparation and attention to detail. In this respect, he was well served by the time he spent in the American Southwest between 1912 and 1918. He made three trips to sketch the Hopi, Apache, and Navajo Indians, making many drawings. These drawings were praised by C. Lewis Hind in *International Studio* (Apr. 1918), and he described Young as "the artist of the actual, of movement, of adventure; he is the man to give the spirit of the appalling restlessness of the Western front."

The resulting sculptures were placed in the American Museum of Natural History in New York. Young's sculpture can be divided into two large categories: first, working men and men in action poses, for example, boxing, and second, scenes of the American West.

Significant other pieces include two large statues, *Agriculture* and *Industry*, in the Hall of Special Events at the New York World's Fair in 1939. Young won first prize for his sculpture *Knockdown* at the Olympic Games Exhibition in Los Angeles, California (1932). Fighters and pugilistic figures were always favorites of Young and are among his best work. *This Is the Place* was erected (near Great Salt Lake) at the entrance to Emigration Canyon in 1947. The title refers to Brigham Young's words upon seeing the valley of the Great Salt Lake for the first time. When Utah chose to honor Brigham Young by placing his statue in National Statuary Hall in the U.S. Capitol, Young received the commission. His grandfather's marble statue has stood in the Capitol since 1950, among the other honorees from the various states. Another measure of Young's versatility was his ability to execute this larger-than-life statue (seated 5′11″) and several monumental sculptures and yet be remembered particularly for his statuettes, many of which were only a few inches in height.

Young maintained a studio and apartment in New York City for many years; his country home and studio were in Ridgefield, Connecticut. He taught at the Art Students League in New York from 1916 to 1943 and also spent extended periods in Paris. He was a member of the American Academy of Arts and Letters (elected in 1947) and the National Sculpture Society. Young died in Norwalk, Connecticut.

Young is remembered for the great quantity of his work and for the several different media in which he worked. Lorado Taft in the 1923 supplementary chapter to his *History of American Sculpture* recognized Young's painting, teaching, and illustrating, and his "much interesting and virile sculpture." Young's interests included not only the actual execution of his work, but teaching students his skills, as well as writing about the process.

• The chief collection of Young's work is at Brigham Young University, Provo, Utah. Included are models, sculptures, drawings, paintings, etchings, maquettes, exhibition catalogs, and newspaper clippings. A biography is Thomas E. Toone, *Mahonri Young: His Life and Art* (1997). *Mahonri M. Young, Retrospective Exhibition*, a catalog of an exhibition at the Addison Gallery of American Art, Phillips Academy, Andover, Mass. (c. 1940), includes an article by Frank J. Mather, Jr., as well as parts of Young's incomplete autobiography titled "Notes at the Beginning." See also J. Lester Lewine, "The Bronzes of Mahonri Young," *International Studio*, Oct. 1912; Jane Watson, "News and Comments," *Magazine of Art*, Oct. 1940; and C. Lewis Hind, "Mahonri Young's Drawings," *International Studio*, Apr. 1918. An obituary is in the *New York Times*, 3 Nov. 1957.

PHILIP H. VILES, JR.

YOUNG, Milton Rueben (6 Dec. 1897–31 May 1983), U.S. senator, was born in Berlin, La Moure County, North Dakota, the son of John Young and Rachael Zimmerman, farmers. He attended public schools, North Dakota State Agricultural College, and Graceland College but did not receive a college degree. Young returned home to become a grain farmer. Winning election to the local school board in 1924, he never lost an election afterward. From 1932 to 1945 he was elected first to the North Dakota House and then the state senate as a Republican. In 1944 he played a key role in Fred Aandahl's election to the governorship. Aandahl rewarded him by appointing him to fill the unexpired term of U.S. senator John Moses on 12 March 1945. Young subsequently won election to the Senate for five full terms, in 1968 winning the highest percentage of the vote of any Republican senator who ran opposed that year. In 1974 opponents used his advanced age as an issue. Young responded with a television commercial showing him breaking a one-inch board with a karate chop, and he defeated William Guy by 200 votes. Young did not stand for reelection in 1980.

Young was a political conservative. In the first part of the twentieth century the liberal Nonpartisan League dominated his state's politics. After World War II Young and Aandahl used the Republican Organizing Committee to purge these liberal elements as well as the powerful Farmers Union (FU) of party influence. Yet when the state legislature began attacking the FU cooperatives, Young warned his fellow Republicans they must not become "purely a businessman's party." In 1961 he denounced the reactionary John Birch Society. On national and international issues he usually voted with the moderate wing of the Republican party.

Late in his career Young told a reporter that he was more proud of the federal pork he obtained for his state than any other achievement. Using his position on the powerful Senate Appropriations Committee, he obtained seven major water projects and several federal research laboratories for his state as well as the important air force bases at Minot and Grand Forks. Otherwise, he sponsored no legislation of note and was little known outside his state. His only other attainment in the Senate was longevity. By 1980 he had the longest continual service of any current Republican senator and had the most seniority of the minority party on the Appropriations and Agriculture committees. He also served as secretary of the Senate Republican Conference Committee from 1946 to 1971, the longest Senate leadership tenure in the twentieth century. His senatorial longevity was due to his philosophy concerning his farmer constituents: "You have to know farmers and stay close to them. They are loyal to a fault."

Young married Malinda V. Benson in 1919. They had three sons. She died in July 1969, and in December of that year Young married his secretary of twenty-four years, Patricia M. Byrne. He died in Sun City, Arizona.

• Young's papers are deposited at the University of North Dakota Library. The *Congressional Directory* and the *Biographical Directory of the United States Congress* have brief sketches of him. His role in modern state politics is mentioned in Robert P. Wilkins and Wyona Huchette Wilkins, *North Dakota* (1977). The *New York Times* carried a story of his career on 1 June 1983.

R. ALTON LEE

YOUNG, Owen D. (27 Oct. 1874–11 July 1962), lawyer, business leader, and public servant, was born in Van Hornesville, New York, the son of Jacob Smith Young and Ida Brandow, farmers. Enrolling in St. Lawrence University in 1890, he graduated in 1894. In 1896 he graduated from Boston University Law School cum laude, completing the three-year program in two years. From 1896 to 1903 Young taught evening classes in common-law pleading at the law school.

Young's main efforts, however, centered on the Boston law firm of Charles Tyler, which he joined in 1896 as a clerk and which became Tyler & Young in 1907. In 1898 he married Josephine Sheldon Edmonds; they had five children before she died in 1935. For Tyler, Young handled complicated cases involving the Union Pacific Railroad and the Canadian Grand Trunk Railroad. He became increasingly involved in the affairs of Stone and Webster, an engineering firm that pioneered in electric street utilities and electric lights. He represented their interests in Texas, Minnesota, and Washington State.

In 1913 Charles A. Coffin, president of the General Electric Company (GE), recruited Young as the firm's general counsel and vice president. At the time GE was concentrated in the fields of power, lighting, and electric railways. During World War I, Young settled strikes at GE plants in Erie, Pennsylvania, Lynn, Massachusetts, Schenectady, New York, and Fort Wayne, Indiana. An expert in patent law, he expedited licensing and patent exchange. In 1919 and 1920 he served on President Woodrow Wilson's Second Industrial Conference, which proposed a national industrial board to settle major disputes. In 1921 he was appointed to President Warren Harding's Unemployment Conference, chairing its Subcommittee on Business Cycles and Unemployment in 1922 and drafting the best study on industrial stabilization to that time. In 1922 he also chaired the American delegation to the International Chamber of Commerce's International Court of Arbitration, and from 1925 to 1928 he chaired the International Chamber itself.

During World War I, the British Marconi Wireless Company sought to secure exclusive rights to a high-frequency alternator, a device that had revolutionized long-distance wireless transmission and which was invented by GE scientist Ernst Alexanderson. Realizing that the transaction would give Britain control of the world's radio communication, President Wilson secretly asked Young in 1919 to join GE with Westinghouse, AT&T, and Western Electric to form a rival company. In response Young organized the Radio Corporation of America (RCA), becoming the first chairman of its board, and negotiated agreements pooling American radio technology while dividing radio equipment and transmitters. Under Young's leadership RCA became the largest radio company in the world. He also began engineering agreements with foreign companies that partitioned the world into radio zones and facilitated wireless communication. In 1929 Young relinquished the RCA board chairmanship and in 1933 left the chairmanship of its executive committee. In 1926 Young helped found the National Broadcasting Company and in 1928 the Radio-Keith-Orpheum movie chain.

When Coffin stepped down in 1922, Young became GE board chairman, and engineer Gerard Swope was appointed the firm's president. Until 1939 the two men formed one of the most famous collaborations in the history of American business, Young focusing on policy and Swope on operations. In 1924 Young and Swope sold GE's utility holdings and emphasized the manufacturing of consumer goods, which soon encompassed refrigerators, ranges, and radios.

Pioneers in the "welfare capitalism" that was such an earmark of the 1920s, Young and Swope fostered pensions, profit sharing, home mortgage loans, and company-sponsored life insurance and unemployment insurance plans. Young promoted the concept of a "cultural wage," one that bestowed enough income on the employee to develop the intellect. In an address to Harvard Business School in 1927, Young said: "I hope the day may come when these great business organizations will truly belong to the men who are giving their lives and their efforts to them. I care not in what capacity." He spoke of employees "buying capital as a commodity at the lowest price." At one time he said, "The old notion that the heads of business are the paid attorneys of stockholders, to exploit labor and the public in the stockholders' interest, is gone—I hope forever." No foe of trade unions, the GE management asked William Green, president of the American Federation of Labor, to organize its workers. Green, who believed solely in craft unions, refused. Highly publicized as an "industrial statesman," Young was *Time* magazine's "Man of the Year" in 1931. Ida M. Tarbell's eulogistic biography (1932) portrayed him in almost Lincolnesque tones.

In December 1923 Secretary of State Charles Evans Hughes appointed Young a member of the First Expert Committee on Reparations, headed by Chicago banker Charles G. Dawes. In the early twenties Germany had been experiencing economic paralysis, seeing its rich Ruhr region occupied by France and Belgium, undergoing ruinous inflation, and failing to make required reparations payments. During the committee meetings in Paris, Young showed himself to be the key figure in negotiating with the Germans. Early in 1924 the committee designed the Dawes Plan, which saved all Europe from financial collapse. No final figure was set for reparations, but a graduated series of annuities was proposed, beginning with $250 million the first year and rising over the next five years to a normal expectation of $625 million. American

bankers were to lend Germany $200 million in gold to stabilize the mark, which would possess a gold value of 23.8 cents.

The reparations experts unanimously accepted the plan in May 1924. That July and August, as unofficial adviser to the London Conference of Premiers, Young negotiated the compromises that led to the plan's general acceptance. He was perhaps the only figure involved who possessed the confidence of the four major prime ministers, those of Britain, France, Germany, and Belgium. From September to October he was chosen agent general for reparations payments, in charge of transfer payments, and he established an international bank to handle Germany's accounts and taxes.

Within five years the Dawes Plan had revealed certain technical defects, especially in transferring reparations payments from one nation to another. In February 1929 Young chaired the Second Expert Committee on Reparations, which met in Paris. Unlike the Dawes Plan, Young's proposal eliminated foreign supervision. Annual payments were reduced by one-third. The resulting Young Plan reduced Germany's total liability to just $8 billion, payable at 5.5 percent interest, and provided for the termination of reparations in 1988. In return the Allies floated a $3 million loan to Germany to aid the country in financing its initial payment. A Bank for International Settlements (BIS) was established to serve as a "trustee" for reparation payments, act as a clearinghouse for international accounts, facilitate exchange between central banks, and solve problems inherent in the gold exchange system. Unofficially annuities were linked to the Allied war debts owed the United States. In May 1930 the Young Plan and BIS were launched, but the advent of the Great Depression made Young's efforts irrelevant.

In 1929 President Herbert Hoover appointed Young to the Committee on Recent Economic Changes. In 1931 Hoover made him chairman of the Committee on Mobilization of Relief Resources of the President's Unemployment Relief Commission. Always a Democrat, Young was a dark horse for governor of New York in 1925, mayor of New York City in 1930, and president in 1928 and 1932.

Consistently excluded from policy making during the presidency of Franklin D. Roosevelt, Young had mixed feelings concerning the New Deal. While he endorsed farm supports, public works, and the Civilian Conservation Corps, he opposed the "torpedoing" of the London Economic Conference of 1933 and had misgivings over aspects of the National Industrial Recovery Act and the Tennessee Valley Authority. He believed that the Wagner Act of 1935 created the very adversarial relationships he had always sought to avoid, but he accepted the unionization of GE employees by the United Electrical Workers. From 1923 to 1940 he was a director of the Federal Reserve Bank of New York, serving as deputy chairman from 1927 to 1928 and chairman from 1938 to 1940. He strongly opposed the Banking Act of 1935 on the grounds that it weakened local Federal Reserve banks. In 1937 he married Louise Powis Clark, who had three children from previous marriages.

In 1939 both Young and Swope retired from GE, but from 1942 to 1944 the war brought both men back to their former posts. As Young had run up huge margin debts that fell due during the Great Crash of 1929, he labored into old age to avoid simple bankruptcy. His posts in public service included chairman of both the American Youth Commission (1936–1942) and the advisory board of the Transportation Study of the National Resources Planning Board (1940–1942). He was a member of the New York Regional Committee of the War Manpower Commission (1942–1945); Harry S. Truman's President's Advisory Committee on Foreign Aid (1947), which helped pave the way for the Marshall Plan; and the Hoover Commission on the Executive Branch of the Government. He chaired the New York Temporary Commission on the Need for a State University (1946), which designed the state's university system. In retirement he concentrated on dairy farming at his home in Van Hornesville, and in 1941 he helped settle a New York State milk strike. He also tended his plantation citrus grove, "Washington Oaks," twenty miles south of St. Augustine, Florida. He died in St. Augustine.

• The Young papers are deposited in the Van Hornesville Community Corporation, Van Hornesville, N.Y. For the definitive biography, see Josephine Young Case and Everett Case, *Owen D. Young and American Enterprise: A Biography* (1982). Ida M. Tarbell, *Owen D. Young: A New Type of Industrial Leader* (1932), is an uncritical popular account. Scholarly accounts of Young's diplomatic efforts are in Brady A. Hughes, "Owen D. Young and American Foreign Policy, 1919–1929" (Ph.D. diss.; Univ. of Wisconsin, 1969); and John M. Carroll, "Owen D. Young and German Reparations: The Diplomacy of an Enlightened Businessman," in *U.S. Diplomats in Europe, 1919–1941*, ed. Kenneth Paul Jones (1981). For Young at GE, see Kim McQuaid, "Young, Swope, and General Electric's 'New Capitalism'," *American Journal of Economics and Sociology* 36 (July 1977): 323–35, and "Competition, Cartelization and the Corporate Ethic: GE during the New Deal Era, 1933–1940," *American Journal of Economics and Sociology* 36 (Oct. 1977): 417–28. Scholarly work on the Dawes and Young plans includes Frank C. Costigliola, "The Other Side of Isolationism: The Establishment of the First World Bank, 1929–1930," *Journal of American History* 59 (1972): 602–20; Stephen A. Schuker, *The End of French Predominance in Europe: The Financial Crisis of 1924 and the Adoption of the Dawes Plan* (1976); and Melvyn P. Leffler, *The Elusive Quest: America's Pursuit of European Stability and French Security, 1919–1933* (1979). The formation of RCA is covered in Michael J. Hogan, *Informal Entente: The Private Structure of Cooperation in Anglo-American Economic Diplomacy, 1918–1928* (1977). Young's obituary is in the *New York Times*, 12 July 1962.

JUSTUS D. DOENECKE

YOUNG, Pierce Manning Butler (15 Nov. 1836–6 July 1896), army officer, congressman, and diplomat, was born in Spartanburg, South Carolina, the son of Robert Maxwell Young, a physician and planter, and Elizabeth Caroline Jones. In 1838 the family moved to Cartersville, Cass County (renamed Bartow County in 1861), Georgia. Young attended Georgia Military Institute (1852–1857) in Marietta, where he excelled in Thomas McConnell's cavalry class. Young entered the U.S. Military Academy at West Point in 1857. George A. Custer, a classmate, recalled that in the winter of 1860–1861 Young predicted: "Custer, my boy, we're going to have war. . . . And who knows but we may move against each other" ("War Memoirs," *Galaxy*, Apr. 1876, p. 451).

Young resigned on 11 March 1861, before his class of June 1861 graduated, and became a second lieutenant in the Confederate army on 16 March. After serving on the staff of General Braxton Bragg in Florida, Young returned to Georgia in July and became adjutant of Cobb's Legion, quickly advancing to major and then lieutenant colonel and commanding the legion's cavalry. Serving in Wade Hampton's brigade, Young was wounded at Burkittsville, Maryland, in August 1862 and again on 13 September 1862 near Middletown, Maryland. He was promoted to colonel on 1 November 1862.

At Brandy Station, on 9 June 1863, Young led a charge up Fleetwood Hill. He would later praise the Confederate Army of Northern Virginia and the Federal commanding general in characteristic remarks to the U.S. Congress on 27 February 1874. "But no man who did not serve in the army in which I had the honor to serve during the desperate campaign of Gettysburg," Young said of Union general George G. Meade, "can appreciate the vigor and ability with which he handled his army."

Young was wounded south of the Rappahannock River in August 1863 and was promoted to brigadier general to date from 28 September 1863. He led a brigade that included the First North Carolina, First South Carolina, Phillips's Legion, Cobb's Legion, and the Jeff Davis Legion. On 1 January 1864 the Confederate diarist Mary Boykin Chesnut recalled Young said, "I like fellows who fight and don't care what all the row's about." Young was wounded at Ashland (30 May 1864) but still went on the Hampton-Rosser cattle raid (16 Sept. 1864). He went to Georgia in November 1864 to get recruits and remounts, and he tried to help defend Augusta and Savannah from the attacks of General William T. Sherman. Promoted to major general to date from 30 December 1864, Young commanded a division under Hampton and fought Sherman in the Carolinas.

After the Civil War, Young returned to Cartersville and was elected to the U.S. House of Representatives in 1868. He was allowed to take his seat through the influence of the military governor of Georgia, General Meade, whose son was a friend of Young's from West Point. Meade's "magnanimity" was acknowledged by Young, who believed that, without Meade's letters of recommendation, he would have been refused his seat. Meade wrote to Ulysses S. Grant in a letter on 19 June 1868, "It is just such men as he we want down here, as their influence & example are most powerful. . . . I know he is loyal to the Union . . . as if the rebellion had never existed" (*Papers of Ulysses S. Grant*, vol. 18 [1991], p. 586).

Young first served from 25 July 1868 to 3 March 1869. The Forty-first Congress rejected the Georgia delegation in retaliation for the poor civil rights record of the Georgia General Assembly, which expelled its black members and did not ratify the Fifteenth Amendment. Young was elected to fill the resulting vacancy and was reelected to the Forty-second and Forty-third Congresses, serving from 22 December 1870 to 3 March 1875. In Congress, he became a symbol of national reconciliation. Even Benjamin F. Butler of Massachusetts, while debating with Young on 24 January 1871, referred to "his customary fairness." A conservative, or "Bourbon" Democrat, Young was a delegate to the Democratic National Conventions of 1872, 1876, and 1880. He advocated diversification in agriculture and industrialization for the New South. His vote for the "Salary Grab" Act of 1873, which increased congressional pay by 50 percent, brought criticism, and he withdrew as a candidate for renomination in 1874.

Although Young considered marrying Mattie Ould, a brilliant and compassionate Richmond belle, he never married. According to Stephen E. Ambrose, "In the grand southern tradition, the two most important things in Young's life were his mother and his debts." In 1874 Young was a member of the Board of Visitors of the U.S. Military Academy. He later wrote, "There is no doubt of the fact that the American army is officered by the best educated set of gentlemen of any army in the world today" (*Atlanta Constitution*, 19 Mar. 1893).

Young was a commissioner to the Paris Exposition of 1878. President Grover Cleveland appointed him consul general at St. Petersburg, Russia, where he served from 1885 to 1887. On 30 March 1893 he was appointed minister plenipotentiary to Guatemala and Honduras, and he arranged the Central American exhibit at the Cotton States and International Exposition in Atlanta in 1895.

The most important contribution of the former Confederate cavalry general who became a U.S. diplomat was to national reconciliation between North and South. The attitude of Young and other Confederate officers who became officials of the U.S. government partially accounts for the American Civil War not having as disastrous consequences as civil wars in some other countries. Young had seen foreign armies while serving in Russia and France, and he gave a remarkably accurate assessment of the future role of the U.S. Army, predicting the triumph of American arms in the twentieth century. Writing in the *Atlanta Constitution* (19 Mar. 1893), Young said, "The army of the United States is extremely small, really only a skeleton of an army. . . . But it is a nucleus around which an army of millions can be formed in a few months . . . the great republic will be more powerful than any force that can oppose her." On leave from his post in Guatemala, Young died in New York City. His body was taken back to Georgia for burial in Cartersville; his train was

met at Atlanta by Confederate veterans and the United Daughters of the Confederacy.

• Young's papers are in private hands. Young's reports are in *The War of the Rebellion: A Compilation of the Official Records of the Union and Confederate Armies* (128 vols., 1880–1901). For Young's views on agriculture, see his report on "Cotton Culture" in U.S. House, *U.S. Commission to the Paris Exposition, 1878, Reports*, vol. 3, 46th Cong., 3d sess., 1880, Exec. Doc. 42, pt. 3. Young wrote about West Point and the Civil War in the *Atlanta Constitution*, 12 and 19 Mar. 1893. A biography is Lynwood M. Holland, *Pierce M. B. Young: The Warwick of the South* (1964). The best book review is by Stephen E. Ambrose in *North Carolina Historical Review* 41 (Autumn 1964): 495–96. He is mentioned in C. Vann Woodward, ed., *Mary Chesnut's Civil War* (1981). For George G. Meade's influence on Young's congressional career, see *Congressional Record*, 27 Feb. 1874, p. 1841. For an evaluation of Young as cavalry leader, see Jeffry D. Wert, "Pierce Manning Butler Young," in *The Confederate General*, ed. William C. Davis (1991). Obituaries are in the *New York Times* and the *New-York Tribune*, 7 July 1896.

RALPH KIRSHNER

YOUNG, Plummer Bernard (27 July 1884–9 Oct. 1962), newspaper editor and publisher, was born in Littleton, North Carolina, the son of former slave Winfield Scott Young, a businessman, newspaper editor, and officeholder, and Sallie Adams. Young founded his own monthly paper the *Argus*, in 1904. He attended St. Augustine's College in Raleigh, North Carolina, at the same time that he taught printing and produced the school's publications. In 1906 he married Eleanor Louise White, the adopted daughter of the college's president, and went to work as foreman at his father's printing shop. The next year, after the birth of the first of their two children, the couple moved to Norfolk, Virginia's second largest city. There Young began work as plant foreman for the *Lodge Journal and Guide*, a weekly newspaper published by the Supreme Lodge Knights of Gideon, an African-American fraternal order of which his father was a member.

Young spent the rest of his life in the newspaper business in Norfolk. By 1909 he had become editor, and in 1910 he bought the paper from the Gideons and changed its name to the *Norfolk Journal and Guide*. Over the years Young built up the paper until it had the largest circulation of any black weekly published in the South. From a four-page paper with a circulation of about 1,000 at the time he took it over, he transformed it into an eight-page paper with a circulation of 4,000 by 1920 and a sixteen-page paper with a circulation of 28,000 by 1935. In the 1940s circulation topped 60,000. Young incorporated the business in 1913 and became president; his wife was treasurer, his brother Henry Cheatham Young was plant manager and then secretary, and his father was circulation manager. Young was publisher of the *Journal and Guide* for fifty-two years, from 1910 until his death, though he turned over most of the responsibility to his sons in 1946.

Young allied himself with Booker T. Washington in his early years in Norfolk and continued to take an accommodationist approach to civil rights after Washington's death in 1915. "Build up, don't tear down," he exhorted. But as times changed so did his approach to civil rights. In 1917 he organized a local chapter of the National Association for the Advancement of Colored People. Young came to politics as a committed Republican, a position he maintained into the 1920s. Then he exemplified the switch among African Americans to the Democratic party. The Republican party in Virginia adopted a "lily-white" hue, and in 1921 a group of black Virginians responded by running a "lily-black" slate for state office. The group offered Young the nomination for the lieutenant governorship, but Young had misgivings about the strategy, and he was also miffed that the gubernatorial nomination had gone to his rival, John Mitchell, editor of the *Richmond Planet*, so he declined, though he and the others later joined forces. Young served as a delegate to the 1924 Republican National Convention in Cleveland, but the party's near exclusion of black delegates from the 1928 convention in Kansas City led him to support Democrat Alfred E. Smith's candidacy that year. He supported Franklin D. Roosevelt in 1932, embraced the New Deal, and attended Roosevelt's second inaugural in 1936. Young served during World War II (1943–1944) on the Fair Employment Practices Committee, which President Roosevelt ordered established in 1941 in response to A. Philip Randolph's planned march on Washington.

Young entered into the civic life of his adopted city and state, as he promoted his newspaper as a voice for black Norfolk and the South. He and his wife joined the Grace Protestant Episcopal Church as soon as they arrived in Norfolk; he was elected to the vestry in 1910 and later served for many years on the board of trustees. At one time or another he served as vice president of the statewide Negro Organization Society, led the Negro Forward Movement as it pushed for improvements in Norfolk, presided over the board of the Norfolk Community Hospital, and chaired the advisory committee to the Norfolk Redevelopment and Housing Authority. Young served on the Howard University board of trustees for twenty-one years (1934–1955) and chaired it for six years (1943–1949). He was also a board member at Hampton Institute and at St. Paul's College.

Young used the *Journal and Guide* to campaign against many of the ills that beset black Virginians. Between the revival of the Ku Klux Klan in 1915 and passage in 1928 of a state antilynching law, he campaigned against lynching. He publicized a criminal proceeding in Norfolk in 1931 that led not only to the black defendant's being acquitted on the charge of rape but also to the imprisonment of his white accuser for perjury. From the 1920s into the 1940s he pushed for better housing, and he campaigned to pave dirt roads in black neighborhoods. He editorialized against the white Democratic primary in Virginia, until a court decision invalidated it in 1929 (*West v. Bliley et al.*), and against the poll tax as an impediment to black voting. Concerned about scant employment opportu-

nities for black citizens, by December 1916 Young was developing an approach that later emerged as the "double-duty dollar" or "buy where you work," a precursor to the "don't shop where you can't work" movement that swept many American cities in the 1930s. In 1941, though troubled by A. Philip Randolph's March on Washington Movement, Young campaigned to open defense jobs in the Norfolk area to black workers. Meanwhile, Young's home was a perennial meeting place for discussing strategy and ideology when James Weldon Johnson, Walter White, Roy Wilkins, and other NAACP leaders visited Norfolk, as well as when the National Urban League's Whitney Young did. Correspondents for his paper included Nannie Helen Burroughs, Gordon Blaine Hancock, and Carter G. Woodson.

Young hesitated to attack segregation directly, but he strived to secure greater equality within the framework of "separate but equal." On 21 June 1913 he editorialized about segregated streetcar transportation, "We do not object to separate cars, but we want equal accommodations." He was a founding member of the Southern Commission on Interracial Cooperation in 1919 and its successor organization, the Southern Regional Council, in 1944. In the 1930s he campaigned for such public facilities as parks, bathing beaches, and a new elementary school for black residents of Norfolk. During World War II he pushed successfully for the appointment of black police officers in Norfolk. He involved himself in the establishment of a black community college in Norfolk in 1935 (later Norfolk State University) and chaired its advisory board. In the 1930s and 1940s he publicized the inferior physical facilities and teachers' salaries that characterized black public schools, and he fostered the breakthrough court case *Alston v. Board of Education of the City of Norfolk*, which in 1940 secured the principle of salary equalization.

"Mr. P. B.," as he was called, edited a newspaper about which it was often said, "See what the *Guide* says about it." Tall and fair-skinned in appearance, grave and unemotional in demeanor, proud yet cautious in character, pragmatic yet prodding in politics, Young achieved prosperity, respect, and influence. He received numerous honors, and the National Newspaper Publishers Association named him Distinguished Editor of the Year in 1960. Eleanor Young died in 1946, and Young married Josephine Tucker Moseley in 1950. After he died in Norfolk, his sons carried on the family business.

• Henry Lewis Suggs supplies a full account of Young's life and career in *P. B. Young, Newspaperman: Race, Politics, and Journalism in the New South, 1910–62* (1988). Obituaries are in the *Richmond Times-Dispatch*, 10 Oct. 1962; the *Washington Post*, 11 Oct. 1962; the *New York Times*, 12 Oct. 1962; and the *Norfolk Journal and Guide*, 13 Oct. 1962.

PETER WALLENSTEIN

YOUNG, Rida Johnson (28 Feb. 1875–8 May 1926), playwright and lyricist, was born Rida Louise Johnson in Baltimore, Maryland, the daughter of William A.

Johnson and Emma Stuart. According to the *Chicago Examiner* (3 Apr. 1910), her late father had been "well known as a prominent resident of Baltimore." Young attended Wilson College in Chambersburg, Pennsylvania, probably in the early 1890s, and evidence suggests that she also studied at Radcliffe College. An undated clipping in the Billy Rose Theatre Collection of the New York Library claims that Young was president of the Radcliffe Dramatic Society, which presented a play of hers.

Young wrote her first play when she was eighteen, and she persuaded her parents to allow her a short stay in New York to peddle it. There she took a job selling furniture polish for four dollars a week, making the rounds of the theatrical agencies in her spare time. When her efforts proved fruitless, she decided to send her play to a prominent actor. She selected E. H. Sothern. Although Young's sprawling epic about Omar Khayyam was evidently not producible, Sothern arranged to meet her. He promised her a part in his company and gave her a letter of introduction to producer Daniel Frohman, which resulted in an interview and a walk-on part in *The Three Musketeers*. Young's stint as an actress with Sothern's company came to an abrupt end during rehearsals for *The Song of the Sword* in 1899. When she was instructed to ward off the villain with a three-legged stool, she threw it, hitting the director in the face. Young was subsequently asked to resign from the company, and she did so with the full realization that her talent did not lie in acting. Soon she was earning twenty-five dollars a week as an extra.

Young's original ambition, to write for a living, came to fruition when she worked for two years (c. 1898–1900) for Witmark music publishers in New York, writing song lyrics to order. Her contributions included encore verses for vaudeville hits, songs to suit particular performers, and new words to existing music. Young's experience at Witmark served her well when she later wrote books for musical comedies. She left the publishing house when she was given the opportunity to tour with a company of young actors, playing opposite the handsome James Young, Jr., son of a Maryland senator. She had met him in Baltimore, where he was working on the staff of a local newspaper. For him, Young wrote *Lord Byron*, which the company produced in 1900, opening in Norfolk, Virginia. The couple were married later that year and settled in New York but were divorced in 1909 or 1910; they had no children. Young appeared onstage for the last time, under the name Louise Jansen, as Emelia in Viola Allen's 1904 production of *The Winter's Tale* at the Knickerbocker Theatre.

Young's first play produced in New York, *Brown of Harvard* (1906), starred Harry Woodruff, ran for five years, and made popular the genre of college plays. The play also launched one of her greatest hit songs, "When Love Is Young in Springtime." In 1907 G. P. Putnam published Young and Gilbert P. Coleman's novel based on the play. Young also recycled the material as a three-character farcical sketch, with two additional musical numbers, for the vaudeville stage,

where it was performed in 1908 by her husband, for whom she had originally conceived the popular comedy. Her next play, *The Boys of Company B* (1907), lasted two seasons on Broadway, with John Barrymore replacing Arnold Daly in the leading role for the second season. With *Glorious Betsy* (1908), which starred Mary Mannering, Young fully established herself as a commercially successful playwright.

Young made her first trip abroad in 1908, returning to New York in January 1909. Encouraged by producers Charles Frohman, Young returned to England a few months later, to study academic life at Oxford University and to write a play about it. She spent April and May soaking up the atmosphere and interacting with undergraduates and faculty. Although no play on the subject was ever performed on Broadway, the *New York Telegraph* (28 Jan. 1910) notes that a play of Young's about Oxford life was to be produced by Frohman in London.

In 1909 Young wrote *Ragged Robin* for the popular tenor Chauncey Olcott, and the success of that work led to an invitation from Victor Herbert to write the book for a romantic comic opera. Herbert and Young's collaboration resulted in *Naughty Marietta* (1910), which included some of her best-known songs: "I'm Falling in Love with Someone," "Ah, Sweet Mystery of Life," "Italian Street Song," and "'Neath the Southern Moon." Also for Olcott, Young wrote *Barry of Ballymore* (1911), with the enduring favorite "Mother Machree." Among Young's other hit musicals are *Maytime* (1917, with "Sweetheart"), *Sometime* (1918, starring Ed Wynn), and *The Dream Girl* (1924). She also contributed songs to musical comedies by other authors; among them are "A Song of Yesterday," from *The Sultan of Sulu* (1902), and "Dearie," from *Mam'selle Napoleon* (1903). In 1917 Young had both a comedy and a musical running on Broadway, and a second musical was in rehearsal. Her other successful plays include *Shameen Dhu* (1914), *Little Old New York* (1920), and *Macushla* (1920).

Young's long string of hit plays and musicals on Broadway brought her considerable wealth. By 1908 she had bought a summer home "in the millionaire's end of Greenwich, Ct." During the winter she lived, with her maid, at a fashionable New York hotel. Later she bought a summer home in Bellhaven, New York. During the 1910s Young's name appeared frequently in the theatrical and social news. Often described as a "handsome" woman, Young was also regarded as a fountain of youthful gaiety and optimism. In 1912 Young was sued by her friend Edith Ellis Furniss, who had directed Young's play *The Lottery Man* in 1909. Furniss felt entitled to a percentage of the royalties as a coauthor because she had made some changes and written some new lines in rehearsal. The state supreme court, however, ruled in favor of Young and the Shubert organization.

Young's working method was to shape her ideas in her head for twenty-four hours, preferably while indulging in her favorite activity—gardening. She considered her three hours at the typewriter each morning merely the measure of the work she had already accomplished. "You learn a lot about plays by writing in a garden," she told interviewer Helen Ten Broeck, "for the gentle art of pruning is an essential part of the dramatist's work, and you learn to develop situations, to weed out extraneous dialogue, to carefully tend and water the growing idea that is at once the seed and the fruit of your work—all these things you learn in a garden." Indeed, Young attributed her productivity as a writer to the "financial obligations" of her "expensive hobby."

Young capped her writing career with two novels, *Out of the Night* (1925) and *The Red Owl* (1927). She died of breast cancer at her home in Southfield Point, Connecticut. Although her name has been virtually forgotten, Young's work survives in popular culture. A number of her more than 500 songs are universally recognized. Her most popular musicals, *Naughty Marietta* and *Maytime*, were made into films starring Jeanette MacDonald and Nelson Eddy, and both remain classics of the 1930s cinema.

• Clippings in the Billy Rose Theatre Collection of the New York Public Library for the Performing Arts, Lincoln Center, are the major source of information on Young. A personality profile by Helen Ten Broeck, "Rida Young—Dramatist and Garden Expert," *Theatre Magazine*, Apr. 1917, pp. 202, 250, includes two photographs of Young. Much information about her early career is found in Helen Christine Bennett, "The Woman Who Wrote 'Mother Machree,'" *American Magazine*, Dec. 1920, pp. 34–35, 178–87. See also Shirley Burns's useful piece, "Women Dramatists," *Green Book Album*, Sept. 1910, pp. 634–35. An obituary is in the *New York Times*, 9 May 1926.

FELICIA HARDISON LONDRÉ

YOUNG, Robert Ralph (14 Feb. 1897–25 Jan. 1958), financier and railroad executive, was born in Canadian, Texas, the son of David Young, a local businessman who became president of the First National Bank of Canadian, and Mary Moody. As a teenager he attended Culver Military Academy in Indiana. He graduated first in his class in 1914, excelling in English and math. After graduating he enrolled at the University of Virginia but withdrew during his second year. At about the same time, in 1916, he married Anita O'Keeffe, sister of the painter Georgia O'Keeffe. The couple had one child, Eleanor Jane, who died in an airplane crash in 1941 at the age of twenty-three.

After leaving college, Young took a factory job at the E. I. du Pont de Nemours & Company powder plant in Carneys Point, New Jersey. He quit in 1920 when he inherited several thousand dollars, which he soon lost in the stock market. In 1922 he began working in the accounting office of General Motors and by 1928 was an assistant treasurer. He left GM the following year to serve as financial adviser to financier John J. Raskob. Young and Raskob soon parted because Raskob ignored Young's advice to sell shortly before the 1929 stock market crash. Young followed his own advice and made his first million. Young and Frank F. Kolbe, a former colleague at GM, formed a brokerage firm, Young, Kolbe & Company, which flourished during the 1930s, permitting Young to amass a fortune of several million dollars. Young, Kolbe & Company dissolved in the autumn of 1937 because of differences that developed between the partners during Young's successful attempt to enter the railroad industry.

After a brief retirement in 1937, Young and a group of investors purchased the Alleghany Corporation, a railroad holding company, for $4 million. The corporation owned stocks and securities in a dozen railroads, with 23,000 miles of track, coal mines, trucking companies, and orchards. Its most significant railroad interests were the Chesapeake & Ohio (C&O), the Nickel Plate, and the Pere Marquette. Acquisition of Alleghany marked the first cooperative venture between Young and Allan Kirby, who inherited a fortune his father made with F. W. Woolworth Company. The two complemented each other: Young was flamboyant, while Kirby was content to remain in the background. Their relationship was mutually beneficial, lasting until Young's death.

Acquisition of Alleghany made Young, who became the chair of the board, a prominent figure in the American railroad industry. Shortly after Young took over Alleghany, Thomas W. Lamont, a partner in J. P. Morgan & Company, summoned Young to his office. Morgan & Company had always had a voice within Alleghany Corporation, and Lamont informed Young that he expected the same courtesy. Young called the meeting a turning point in his life. He deeply resented the imposition and informed Lamont that he would not cooperate. Privately he pledged that he would make J. P. Morgan & Company a tenth-rate bank, a vow he later often repeated in public.

Conflict with the Morgan interests followed quickly. In the autumn of 1937 Guaranty Trust Company of New York, a Morgan-controlled institution, impounded all income and surplus cash of the C&O Railroad, because loan collateral the railroad had with the bank had dropped in value. Young now engaged in a proxy fight with Guaranty Trust for control of the C&O. In this fight Young first demonstrated his knack for succinctly summarizing issues and relating complex problems to small stockholders—the "Aunt Janes," as he referred to them. In May 1938 the two sides reached a compromise. Young and his slate of directors won positions on the board of C&O, and three candidates from Guaranty's slate were also seated on the new, larger board.

Young's victory was not complete. Not all the directors he placed on the board were loyal, and more important, the investment banking firms of Morgan, Stanley & Company, and Kuhn, Loeb & Company still held C&O bonds, which were due in the autumn of 1938. Representatives of the banking firms expected that renewal of the bonds on their terms would be a routine matter. Young secured a competing bid from Otis & Company of Cleveland, which he knew the others could not match. When the board indicated that it would ignore the Otis bid, Young threatened, as a stockholder in the company, to hold the directors personally responsible. Coming from Young, who had a reputation for legal challenges, the directors could not ignore the threat and acquiesced. Young had engineered a major defeat of the two dominant investment banking firms used by the railroads and laid the foundation for competitive bidding on bond issues.

As World War II drew to a close, Young undertook and lost an effort to purchase the Pullman Company. The government ordered the parent company, Pullman Inc., to sell one of its two subsidiaries because of antitrust violations. The board elected to sell the Pullman Company, which operated its sleeping cars. Because of the company's monopoly, it was impossible for passengers to cross the country without switching cars, which Young thought was absurd. Once again Young portrayed himself as a Wall Street outsider fighting for the small stockholder and the traveling public. The Interstate Commerce Commission (ICC) ultimately ruled against Young, but he firmly established himself in the minds of the public as a man interested in the average person's comfort and convenience.

As the battle for the Pullman Company neared its conclusion in the fall of 1946, Young shifted his attention to a far greater prize, the New York Central Railroad. He had implemented some of his ideas for improving passenger service, including a no-tipping policy, a method for collecting tickets on the train, a credit card system, and motion pictures on C&O trains, but they failed to capture public imagination because the C&O was not a large passenger carrier. The Central, however, had ample passenger traffic, and Young hoped to capitalize on its excellent network.

Word circulated that Young was buying Central stock in the autumn of 1946. By March 1947 Alleghany Corporation and C&O had acquired 400,000 shares of Central stock, making them the largest stockholders. Young demanded a seat on the Central's board of directors. The board gambled and granted his request, hoping that it would bring him into conflict with the ICC because he had not relinquished his positions with Alleghany Corporation or C&O. In May 1948 the ICC announced that Young could not take his seat on the Central's board. The confrontation and subsequent hearings before the ICC revealed the Central's weakened position. Its stock value fell, and its debt continued to rise after Young's takeover attempt.

Young lost the battle, but he continued the war. Alleghany Corporation and C&O continued to purchase Central stock, and secretly Young and Kirby began buying it for their personal accounts. They each bought 100,000 shares, making them the Central's largest stockholders; they also controlled 800,000 shares owned by Alleghany Corporation and C&O. In January 1954 Young attacked. To avoid the legal entanglement that caused his earlier defeat, he resigned his positions with Alleghany and C&O. Young demanded a seat on the board and the positions of chief executive officer and chief operating officer. When the Central refused, Young initiated a proxy fight.

Young attacked through the media, using open letters and advertisements. He defined the struggle as being between monopolistic Wall Street interests and himself, the champion of the small stockholder. Young won by more than one million votes and in July 1954 took over as chief officer of the railroad.

Although Young knew the road was struggling financially, he did not know the whole truth: he controlled a virtually bankrupt railroad. The struggle to put the Central on sound fiscal footing consumed the remainder of his life. He believed a merger with the Pennsylvania Railroad was the best solution to both roads' financial troubles. He did not live long enough to see the merger of the two great roads in 1968, for Young committed suicide by shooting himself in his mansion in Palm Beach, Florida.

Young left a contradictory legacy. He became a millionaire by playing the stock market yet became a public figure by championing the rights of "Aunt Janes" and by attacking the "goddamned bankers." Most Wall Street insiders viewed him as an irresponsible speculator all too ready to file a lawsuit, while to the small stockholders he was a defender of their interests who was also looking for ways to improve service.

• Young's papers were destroyed in the mid-1960s. The contemporary national media and railroad industry journals covered Young's activities extensively. Joseph Borkin, *Robert R. Young: The Populist of Wall Street* (1969), is an extensive study of Young's life. Young's tenure on the C&O is discussed in Charles W. Turner, *Chessie's Road*, rev. ed. (1993). The story of his death is in the *New York Times*, 26 Jan. 1958, and his obituary appeared on 28 Jan. 1958.

JON R. HUIBREGTSE

YOUNG, Ruth (30 Aug. 1916–4 Feb. 1986), labor union official, was born Ruth Youkelson in Chicago, Illinois, the daughter of Reuben Youkelson and Rose Zan, Jewish immigrants from Zhitomir, Ukraine (then part of Russia). When Ruth was born, her father worked in a cigar factory and was active in the Cigar Makers' Union and in the United Hebrew Trades; he later moved to New York where he joined the staff of the Yiddish Communist daily newspaper *Morgen Freiheit*. When Ruth was five years old her mother died of leukemia. After that, she lived for a few years with her aunt and her grandfather in Chicago, until she moved to New York to join her father, who had since remarried.

Her father and stepmother, Rebecca Kaplan, both were active in the Jewish left, and Young's first home in New York was in the Bronx "Coops," a cooperative housing project built in the 1920s and populated mainly by left-wing Jews. The family was poor; many years later she remembered having one skirt when she was in high school. As a teenager, she joined the Communist-affiliated Young Pioneers, where she met her first husband, Irving Charles "Charlie" Velson (born Israel Shavelson). His mother was Clara Lemlich Shavelson, a key leader of the massive 1909–1910 New York garment workers' strike. Ruth lived with Charlie, who was also active in the labor movement, for several years before they were legally married in January

1937. Her legal name then became Ruth Y. Velson, but both before and after this marriage, throughout her career in the labor movement, she was known as Ruth Young. She used that name (instead of Youkelson) when she first started working because "they weren't hiring Jews."

Young had already worked at various part-time jobs before she graduated from high school in 1932. She wanted to go to college, but there was no money to make that possible. She did win a scholarship to become a dental assistant, and completed the training, but she never worked in that field because it paid less than she could earn as an unskilled factory worker. By the time Young was self-supporting, her father had remarried and there was no room for her in his apartment. She worked in a series of factories and almost immediately became a union activist. She had already participated in her first strike, as a waitress at a summer resort in upstate New York. The first factory job she had was in a unionized shop, and she was soon elected a shop steward there, launching her long career in the labor movement. She became active in the Communist-led Trade Union Unity League, and then in the United Electrical, Radio and Machine Workers of America, known as the UE, part of the industrial union movement that emerged in the mid-1930s.

Young was elected as a delegate to every convention of the UE from 1937 until she left the union in 1950. By 1938 she had joined the UE's full-time staff. She was sensitive to the issue of bringing women into union activity from the outset. At the union's 1939 convention, for example, she implored, "We have to show the girls in our shops that there is not a position in our organization that is not open to them." She herself held a series of such positions. In 1940 she was the membership and educational director of UE District 4, which covered New York City and northern New Jersey. In this position she organized cultural, social welfare, and educational activities for the union's growing membership. She went on to become the membership activities director and by 1943 the executive secretary of District 4. She organized a large UE women's conference in October 1941, the first such effort directed specifically at the union's female membership. She also wrote a weekly column in the union's newspaper, the *UE News*, called "Work and Play."

After the United States entered World War II, when the ranks of women war workers swelled, the opportunities for women's leadership in the unions also grew. Young rose rapidly through the ranks of the UE to become in late 1944 a member of its highest executive body, the International Executive Board. She was the only woman to rise to this level in a major union during this period. Partly due to her efforts, the UE was especially advanced regarding women's issues during this period. She also served on the U.S. Women's Bureau Advisory Committee as a spokesperson on women workers' needs during World War II, and in 1944 she was appointed as an adviser to New York State's

industrial commissioner to help administer the state's new equal-pay law.

Throughout this period, Young was a member of the Communist party, like many UE leaders. Although her primary commitment was to the labor movement, she also participated in a variety of Communist-linked organizations. She was an instructor and trustee of the Jefferson School of Social Science, a delegate to the 1944 Congress of American-Soviet Friendship, and an officer of the Congress of American Women. She was also active in the American Labor party, and in 1944 she ran in the primary election for the position of delegate to that party's convention. She was also active in the 1948 presidential campaign of Henry Wallace.

In 1942 Young had her first child, and during her brief maternity leave the union hired two women to replace her. It was extremely unusual for women who were so active in public life to have children during this period. "Everyone was shocked that I did this," she later recalled. But she was very satisfied with her life. "I had everything. I was on the national board of the union, the first woman. I had a kid, which I wanted, a beautiful child. Well, I had everything except I didn't love my husband. But that wasn't important at the time."

It became more important to her in the postwar period, however. In 1950 she left the UE and the Communist party for a completely different life. She had fallen in love with another member of the union's executive board, Leo Jandreau, a French-Canadian Catholic. Jandreau was a skilled tool-and-die maker who since its founding in 1936 had been the leader of UE Local 301, which represented workers at the giant Schenectady, New York, General Electric plant, one of the UE's largest affiliates. Young and Jandreau divorced their spouses and married in August 1950. Ruth, who used the name Ruth Y. Jandreau from that time on, moved to Schenectady and became a full-time homemaker, abandoning her union career and silently watching as the UE and other left-wing unions were attacked by anti-Communists.

Whether or not Leo Jandreau was a Communist is unclear; although he was frequently accused of membership in press reports, he denied it. In 1954, at the height of McCarthyism, and soon after he was summoned before the House Committee on Un-American Activities, Jandreau led the twenty thousand members of Local 301 into the UE's rival, the anti-Communist International Union of Electrical, Radio and Machine Workers of America (IUE). This was a major blow to the UE and marked the end of its role as a major force in the electrical products industry. Young later recalled that in 1954 her former friends and associates from New York City, most of whom had not been in contact with her since she left the UE in 1950, "appeared out of the woodwork" to try to persuade her to help change Jandreau's mind.

Young had a child with Jandreau in the early 1950s, and they were married until his death in 1978. Ruth was active in a number of local volunteer and community activities in the 1950s and 1960s. She also joined the Unitarian church. After her children were grown, she learned to drive and to type and launched her second career. Starting in 1967, she worked in a series of administrative positions at local colleges. She also returned to school, attending the College of St. Rose, a small Catholic college in Albany, New York, where she earned a B.A. in Higher Education Administration in 1973 and an M.A. in Liberal Studies in 1980. In the 1980s she began giving public lectures on women's work and on women's labor history. She was the director of continuing education at the College of St. Rose from 1974 until her death in New York City. She lived just long enough to see the emergence of scholarly interest in women's labor history and to win some new recognition for her own crucial contribution to that history, a contribution that had been obliterated from public memory during the postwar decades.

• The U.S. Federal Bureau of Investigation collected extensive information on Young's activities. The FBI records and an oral history interview with Ruth Young Jandreau, conducted by Ruth Milkman and Meredith Tax on 29 Aug. 1985, are in the New Yorkers at Work Collection, Robert F. Wagner Labor Archives, Tamiment Library, New York University. There is no detailed biography of Ruth Young. An account of her early life is in Beryl Williams, *People Are Our Business* (1947). Her activities were frequently noted in the *UE News*, the *Daily Worker*, and in local newspapers in New York City and northern New Jersey during the 1940s. For her role in the labor movement in the 1940s, see Ruth Milkman, *Gender at Work: The Dynamics of Job Segregation by Sex during World War II* (1987). An obituary dealing mainly with her later years is in the *Schenectady Gazette*, 6 Feb. 1986.

RUTH MILKMAN

YOUNG, Samuel Baldwin Marks (9 Jan. 1840–1 Sept. 1924), commanding general of the U.S. Army, was born in Forest Grove, Pennsylvania, the son of Captain John Young, an army officer, and Hannah Scott. Young's reputation as an aggressive, dedicated soldier began in the American Civil War. After attending Jefferson College in Canonsburg, Pennsylvania, he joined a group of ninety-day volunteers in that state's Twelfth Infantry during the opening days of the conflict, in April 1861. When the regiment was mustered out of service in the summer, he returned home and raised his own company. Young received a commission and commanded this organization as its captain. It was later redesignated as a mounted unit, becoming a troop in the Pennsylvania Fourth Cavalry. In 1861 Young married Margaret McFadden. After a stint in the defenses of Washington, D.C., the captain and his troop were swept up in Major General George B. McClellan's ill-fated 1862 Peninsula campaign drive on Richmond. That fall Young became known for his courage and daring at the battle of Antietam, was promoted to the rank of major, and was given command of a squadron of cavalry. In 1863, at the cavalry contest with J. E. B. Stuart's Confederates at Brandy Sta-

tion, Virginia, the Pennsylvanian was seen fiercely wielding a saber with one arm while nursing a bloody wound in the other.

Young finished the war with considerable fame and valuable professional connections. Badly wounded in the fall of 1863, the cavalry officer returned after convalescence and resumed fighting. He was promoted to lieutenant colonel and then to full colonel in 1864, commanding both a regiment and a brigade before he once again was seriously wounded. In the war's last campaigns Young attracted the admiration of two important Union officers, Brigadier General J. Irving Gregg and Major General George Crook. In 1865 he led the regiment that captured the last battle flags taken from Robert E. Lee's Army of Northern Virginia before its surrender.

In July 1865 a disappointed Young found himself a civilian in the wake of the dissolution of the large Federal volunteer force. In May 1866, through the efforts of Crook and Gregg, Young obtained an infantry commission in the regular army as a second lieutenant. By that summer he was back in the cavalry as a captain.

From 1866 until the 1880s Young and his fellow officers mostly served in a series of Indian campaigns, living in the bare-bones environment of the American West. By the late 1860s he was at Fort Mohave, Arizona Territory, fighting the Walapais. A brief sojourn from Indian fighting came in 1870 along with a recruiting assignment in Chicago, a duty that was interrupted by policing tasks in the aftermath of the great fire that consumed much of the city in 1871. Cavalry life was resumed in 1874 along the Red River and later, under the command of Colonel Ranald Slidell Mackenzie, along the Rio Grande.

In the 1880s the frontier routine of the U.S. Army began to dissolve, and Young drew new assignments and experiences. In 1881, still a captain, he was posted to Fort Leavenworth, Kansas, as an instructor at the newly opened Infantry and Cavalry School. The next year Young was promoted to major and dispatched to California as a squadron commander of the Third Cavalry. When a violent labor disturbance broke out in California in 1894, Young and his men had the arduous duty of maintaining order. By 1896 Young and his horsemen were in Yosemite National Park fending off the encroachments of sheepherders. Young was appointed acting superintendent of that park and was named to the same position in Yellowstone National Park in 1897. In the latter place the major met and formed a lifelong friendship with one of the nation's foremost conservationists, Theodore Roosevelt.

Young's reputation in the 1898 Spanish-American War was much like the one he had earned in the Civil War. At the outbreak of the war with Spain, Young, having been promoted to full colonel in 1897, was in the nation's capital. Leading a cavalry brigade, the colonel and his troopers landed in Cuba and promptly initiated the first skirmish with the Spanish army. This action was described as an ill-considered, blundering move that was characterized by questionable American tactics. Nonetheless, the Spanish came off worse and retreated. By the summer of 1899 Young was in the Philippines fighting Filipino insurrectionists. There, in 1900, he was promoted to brigadier general in the regular army, and he became embroiled in a dispute with one of his superiors. Typically, the argument was about Young having taken too many tactical risks.

Whatever his renown for rash battle action, Young had established the connections that would lead him to attain the highest position in his service. As soon as Roosevelt became vice president in 1901, Young's career began to overshadow that of other U.S. Army generals. In February 1901 he rose to the rank of major general. In 1902 he assumed the duties of president of the War College Board, an early army war planning and staff agency in Washington. On 9 August 1903 he was catapulted to lieutenant general and was appointed to the position of commanding general of the U.S. Army. That title disappeared nine days later in an army reorganization, and Young then became the first officer to hold the position of chief of staff of the U.S. Army. Lieutenant General Young reached the mandatory retirement age in January 1904, and forty-two years of service came to a close. He served as superintendent of Yellowstone National Park from 1907 to 1908 and as president of the Soldier's Home from 1910 to 1920. He died in Helena, Montana.

General Young's long career was marked by numerous instances of personal bravery, but little evidence indicates he contributed to the broad improvement and professional development of the U.S. Army as an institution. The generation of officers that preceded Young's own and the one that followed his era had the opportunity to command large formations and manage diverse and complex establishments. Young, like all of his contemporaries, mainly experienced both battle and peacetime command with relatively small units and modest institutions. His fighting expertise and professional interests were thus confined to minor tactics, the routine on small posts, and constabulary-type problems of establishing or restoring peace. His rise to high rank was chiefly due to his personal connections with a succession of superiors in addition to his bravery in combat. Young's advancement was not founded on a demonstrated ability to manage a large-scale organization nor on his skill handling broad, policy-type responsibilities. His tenure at this level was too brief to be adequately assessed.

• Young's papers are at the U.S. Army Military History Institute in Carlisle, Pa., and mostly consist of official correspondence. Several descriptions of Young and his early service are recounted in George Crook, *General George Crook: His Autobiography*, ed. Martin F. Schmitt (1960). Later accounts depicting Young include John M. Gates, *Schoolbooks and Krags: The United States Army in the Philippines, 1898–1902* (1973), and William Thaddeus Sexton, *Soldiers in the Sun* (1939).

ROD PASCHALL

YOUNG, Stanley Paul (30 Oct. 1889–15 May 1969), mammalogist, wildlife biologist, and scientific administrator, was born in Astoria, Oregon, the son of Swedish immigrants Benjamin Youngquist and Christina Swanson. His father, who had been a cabin boy on the Confederate ship Alabama, later a member of the U.S. Merchant Marine, a sugar plant foreman, and owner of several Pacific coast fish canneries, changed the family name to Young when his son was a boy. Young's mother died when he was twelve, his father when he was twenty-two. He was raised by his older married sister Carol.

Young attended Astoria High School and was a letterman in football and track at the University of Oregon, from which he graduated in 1911 with a B.S. in mining engineering. He entered the University of Michigan with intentions of doing graduate work in geology, but he changed to biology and secured his M.S. in 1915. In the summer of 1917, while on his way to California, where he planned to look for a teaching position, Young visited an older brother in Arizona. There he was offered a ranger's position with the U.S. Forest Service, and he accepted. After several months he transferred to the U.S. Biological Survey, with which he would spend the rest of his working career. He first served as a professional hunter for two years, shooting predatory mammals, and was then briefly assigned to offices in Phoenix, Arizona, as an assistant inspector of predator control work. Young soon returned to several years of predator control activity in New Mexico. In 1921 he married Lydia Marie Acker; they had at least four children. That same year he was transferred to Denver, where he became biological survey agent in charge of predator control efforts for the states of Colorado and Kansas, remaining until 1927.

Young first went to Washington, D.C., as assistant head of the Division of Predatory Animal and Rodent Control (1927–1928). He then was named principal biologist in charge of Economic Operations for a period of six years, after which he served successively as chief of the Division of Game Management from 1934 to 1938 and as chief of the Division of Predator and Rodent Control from 1938 to 1939. Young's responsibilities for predator control were carried out in compliance with a congressional mandate first imposed on the Biological Survey in 1907.

The survey, and later the Fish and Wildlife Service, enjoyed strong support for these control programs from farmers and ranchers in the western states. There was, however, vigorous opposition from environmental organizations and individuals opposed to what was seen as an unnecessarily harsh regimen of shooting, trapping, and poisoning certain rodents and predators. Young defended these policies, insisting that circumstances sometimes necessitated their use. Wolves had in fact largely disappeared from the western United States by the early 1930s, and in consequence, coyotes and mountain lions increasingly became the focus of Young's concern. He was appointed senior biologist in the branch of Wildlife Research in 1939. In 1940 the Biological Survey was moved from the Agriculture to the Interior Department, where it was merged with the Fish Commission from the Commerce Department to form the U.S. Fish and Wildlife Service.

Young continued as senior biologist in wildlife research until 1957, when he was named director of the Fish and Wildlife Service's Bird and Mammal Laboratories at the U.S. National Museum (now the National Museum of Natural History). He enjoyed international standing as an expert on the life histories and habits of wolves, coyotes, pumas, and bobcats. Young was not entirely a desk-bound administrator, however, and he periodically spent time in the field. Various trips were taken to the West to photograph wolves, coyotes, or mountain lions, and Young became an authority on the self-photography of these animals in nature (a process in which trip wires, attached to rocks or vegetation, triggered the camera when animals walked over or into them, usually in hours of darkness). He also helped to uncover fossil remains of mammoths in Alaska.

In addition to some professional papers, Young authored a number of popular articles and books dealing with the larger North American predators. These included *The Last Stand of the Pack* (1929), with Arthur H. Carhart; *The Wolves of North America* (1944), with Edward A. Goldman; *The Puma, Mysterious American Cat* (1946), with Goldman; *Sketches of American Wildlife* (1946); *The Wolf in North American History* (1946); *The Clever Coyote* (1951), with H. H. T. Jackson; and *The Bobcat of North America* (1958). *Leloo, Last of the Loners* was published posthumously in 1970.

Young was presented with the Department of Interior's Distinguished Service Award in 1957. He was an honorary member of the Wildlife Society and of the American Society of Mammalogists (1964). Following his retirement in 1959, he became a collaborator of the Bureau of Sport Fisheries and Wildlife. Young died in Washington, D.C.

• Young's papers are in the Smithsonian Archives (Record Unit 7174). See also Bird and Mammal Laboratories, U.S. Fish and Wildlife Service, U.S. Department of Interior Records, Smithsonian Archives (Record Unit 7171); and Records of the U.S. Fish and Wildlife Service, Record Group 22, National Archives and Records Administration, Washington, D.C. Biographical sketches include obituaries by Clifford Presnall in *Journal of Wildlife Management* 33 (1969); Richard H. Manville in *Journal of Mammalogy* 51 (1970); and James B. Craig in *American Forests* 76 (1970). See also sketches in Elmer C. Birney and Jerry R. Choate, eds., *Seventy-Five Years of Mammalogy (1919–1994)* (1994), and by William A. Deiss in Keir B. Sterling et al., eds., *Biographical Dictionary of American and Canadian Naturalists and Environmentalists* (1997).

KEIR B. STERLING

YOUNG, Stark (11 Oct. 1881–6 Jan. 1963), writer, was born in Como, Mississippi, forty miles south of Memphis, the son of Alfred Alexander Young, a Confederate veteran and physician, and Mary Clark Starks. When Young was eight, his mother died, leaving her son and his younger sister to the care of his aunts and uncles, members of the large, close-knit, landed Mc-

Gehee family that spread over north-central Mississippi. His mother's death, his years with the McGehees, and his Como schooling conditioned Young's later preoccupation with family and southern life.

In 1895 Dr. Young married again and moved his family to Oxford, Mississippi. Two years later, Young entered the University of Mississippi. While a student he was strongly influenced by Sarah McGehee Isom, a gifted teacher of elocution and drama. In 1901 Young was graduated; the same year he entered Columbia University as a graduate student in English. Courses under Brander Matthews accentuated Young's interest in drama. After receiving the M.A. degree in 1902, he returned to Mississippi and taught briefly in a secondary school before joining the faculty of the University of Mississippi as an assistant in English.

While teaching at the University of Mississippi, Young published a volume of poetry, *The Blind Man at the Window* (1906), and a verse play, *Guenevere* (1906), the former dealing with classical and regional themes, the latter notable for its treatment of the trial scenes. From 1907 to 1915 Young taught at the University of Texas, where he founded and directed the Curtain Club, one of the first little theater organizations to gain national recognition. He also wrote a number of one-act plays, published as *Addio, Madretta and Other Plays* (1912), and founded the *Texas Review* (later *Southwest Review*), a successful scholarly and critical journal. In 1915 he became a member of the faculty of Amherst College. Always a popular teacher, Young began to contribute essays to such periodicals as the *New Republic*, the *Nation*, the *North American Review*, the *Yale Review*, and *Theatre Arts Magazine*, in which his first full-length play, *At the Shrine* (1919), was published. Near the end of Young's tenure at Amherst, Robert Frost seems to have circulated rumors about Young's sexual misconduct with students. Despite his homosexual proclivities, Young was absolved of these allegations.

In 1921, at the age of forty, Young moved to New York City as a freelance writer. Soon he became an editor of *Theatre Arts Magazine*, under Edith J. R. Isaacs, drama critic for the *New Republic*, edited by Herbert Croly, and a member of its editorial board. With the exception of the year 1924–1925, when he served as drama critic for the *New York Times*, Young held these positions until his retirement in 1947. In the 1920s Young's creativity brought him widespread fame as a playwright, drama critic, and director. His second full-length play, *The Queen of Sheba* (1922), appeared in *Theatre Arts Magazine*; *The Saint* (1925) was produced at the Greenwich Village Theatre; and *The Colonnade* (1924) was staged by the London Stage Society.

During these years, Young also wrote some of the finest drama criticism since that of Coleridge and Hazlitt. Throughout the Broadway season, Young reviewed the serious drama—he wrote little about musical comedy—in weekly essays in the *New Republic*. In 1948 many of his critiques were collected and published as *Immortal Shadows*. In these reviews and in

The Flower in Drama (1923), *Glamour* (1925), *Theatre Practice* (1926), and *The Theater* (1927) Young articulated his theory of drama.

Young's drama criticism owes much to his mastery of every facet of drama production as well as his grasp of the history of the theater. He saw the play as a unified whole to which every element—playwright, director, scene designer, costume maker, actor, and "props"—contributes. For him art and nature are never the same; for art translates actuality into its own terms and adds something that has not been there before. His criticism is primarily impressionistic, for it depends largely upon his sense of what was "right" in terms of theater. His standards were his own, but they were based upon an intensely sensitive awareness of dramatic sincerity and effectiveness. Young examined plays and acting in brilliant essays about such artists as Eleonora Duse, Sarah Bernhardt, Charlie Chaplin, Jacinto Benavente, Luigi Pirandello, Eugene O'Neill, Sherwood Anderson, Doris Keane, and the Lunts (Lynn Fontanne and Alfred Lunt). He was one of the few American critics to measure Broadway productions against the great achievements of the past. Young would have been the first to admit a certain southern coloring to his judgments, especially in his insistence that an actor must be a great person to be a great actor and his emphasis on southern values of living.

Between 1926 and 1934, Young wrote four novels about Mississippi: *Heaven Trees* (1926), *The Torches Flare* (1928), *River House* (1929), and *So Red the Rose* (1934). In them and in the essay he wrote for the conclusion of *I'll Take My Stand* (1930), Young defined his southern agrarian philosophy of life. The characters in these novels, for the most part, are fictional treatments of his relatives in the McGehee, Starks, and Young families. Through them Young endeavored to establish the values of family life, the virtues that come from the heart, and the wisdom to be gained from the land. Although he did not intend to develop his fiction chronologically, the novels span the years from 1850 to 1930. Throughout his novels Young contrasts southern life and values with those of the North, focusing upon the difference between rural agrarianism and urban industrialization. He was all too aware of the erosion of traditional southern life but also conscious of the depressing effects of northern industrialism. Although Young had no desire to resurrect the antebellum South, he wished to save what was worthwhile in southern culture: insistence upon self-control, fairness to others, obedience to law, and respect for the social order. The most forceful statement of his principles is embodied in *So Red the Rose*, certainly one of the best novels focusing on the Civil War. In it Young sought to show that northern society lacked a commitment to humanism and stressed material goods over moral values; the South, he believed, with all its deficiencies, placed its emphasis upon right living and man's responsibility to his fellow man.

Despite his successes, Young's own life during the 1930s and 1940s was beset by personal and professional troubles. After the death of Herbert Croly in 1930, the atmosphere at the *New Republic* changed markedly. Young was labeled "southern," and his work was often pushed aside. The sudden death of Young's nephew in 1936 saddened the remainder of his life. His final work for the theater, a musical entitled first *Belle Isle* and later *Artemise* (1942), was first accepted and then rejected by the Lunts. In addition, Young felt that the quality of plays and performers was declining. Embittered by these matters, Young turned to painting. He enjoyed some success with landscapes and flowers, several of his exhibitions receiving good reviews from art critics. In 1951 he published his autobiography, *The Pavilion,* an account of his life in Como and Oxford to age twenty-one. He traveled frequently in Europe with William M. Bowman, his companion for many years. In 1959 Young suffered a stroke from which he only partially recovered. He died in New York.

Stark Young's circle of friends extended throughout the fine arts. He was widely known for his wit, stimulating conversation, and sensitivity to creativity in all its forms. He will be remembered chiefly for his contributions to drama criticism and his success in defining the special qualities of the southern family, the southern land, and traditional southern values, as well as his protest against the materialism of an urban, industrial America. To an extraordinary degree he is representative of the art world of the 1920s and 1930s.

• Extensive collections of Stark Young's letters and related materials may be found in the university libraries of Mississippi, Chicago, Columbia, Princeton, Texas, Vanderbilt, Virginia, and Yale. The most complete bibliography is Bedford Thurman's Cornell dissertation, "Stark Young: A Bibliography of his Writings" (1934). Young's letters and biographical commentary may be found in John Pilkington's *Stark Young: A Life in the Arts, 1900–1962* (2 vols., 1975). The most modern critical analysis of Young's work is Pilkington's *Stark Young* (1985). For additional criticism see Eric Bentley, "Stark Young," *Theatre* (Yale) 14 (Winter 1982): 47–53; George Frank Burns, "Art and Society: Stark Young's Theory of Literary Form," *Southern Quarterly* 24 (Summer 1986): 55–67; and V. F. Gutendorf, "Stark Young: A Critic for All Seasons," *Southern Quarterly* 24 (Summer 1986): 41–54.

JOHN PILKINGTON

YOUNG, Trummy (12 Jan. 1912–10 Sept. 1984), jazz trombonist, was born James Osborne Young in Savannah, Georgia. His father (name unknown) was a railroad worker; his mother (name unknown), a schoolteacher and seamstress; his uncle, a trombonist who played with James Reese Europe's ragtime band. After moving to Richmond, Virginia, following his father's death in 1918, Young began playing trumpet and then trombone in the school band and took lessons from John Nick, a brass teacher from the Jenkins Orphanage Band. Young left school before graduation and moved to Washington, D.C., where he took a job as an elevator operator and began to play music professionally, first with Frank Betters and then with Booker

Coleman's Hot Chocolates. Young also played with the Hardy Brothers Orchestra and Elmer Calloway before joining the band of drummer Tommy Myles, who gave Young his nickname (likely a reference to the trombone, the only instrument he played after turning professional). In early 1933, while in Washington for an engagement, pianist Earl Hines heard the Myles group and was so impressed with its sound that he hired Myles's arranger and tenor saxophonist Jimmy Mundy for his own band. Once established, Mundy suggested that Hines also hire Young, who joined the band in October at their regular stand in Chicago.

Young remained with Hines through August 1937, although he also worked summers in the small groups of Albert Ammons and Roy Eldridge. After leaving Hines, he toured briefly with the Midwest band of Jimmy Raschel before joining the Jimmie Lunceford Orchestra in September. While with Lunceford he achieved his first widespread exposure on records, both as a high note specialist on trombone and as a singer of rhythm novelties. Young left Lunceford in March 1943 and spent the balance of the year with Charlie Barnet's racially mixed orchestra. In November 1943 Young briefly led his own group, but in early 1944 he began working as a sideman again for Tiny Grimes, Roy Eldridge, and Claude Hopkins as well as playing in the CBS staff orchestra of Paul Baron and occasionally appearing as a guest star on Mildred Bailey's radio show. Beginning in the summer of 1944 he worked for eight months in Boyd Raeburn's progressive jazz orchestra, and in February 1945 he joined Benny Goodman's band.

Young remained with Goodman until August, when he left to form his own sextet with young modernists Leo Parker, John Malachi, and Tommy Potter. In the fall of 1945 Young worked with the Tiny Grimes Sextet in New York City, where they accompanied Billie Holiday and played their own sets opposite the Art Tatum Trio. He then spent most of 1946 and the early part of 1947 touring with Jazz at the Philharmonic, after which he rejoined Claude Hopkins in mid-1947. In October he went to Hawaii with Cee Pee Johnson, a Los Angeles drummer whose band also included Gerald Wilson, Dexter Gordon, and Red Callender.

When the Johnson job ended Young decided to stay in Honolulu, where he married his second wife and worked locally with the Art Norkus Trio and his own groups. While on tour with his All Stars, Louis Armstrong heard Young play in Honolulu and asked him to replace his current trombonist, who was himself a temporary substitute for Jack Teagarden. Young accepted and in September 1952 joined the All Stars, a position he maintained until New Year's Day 1964, when he returned to Hawaii to resume his family life and local work. In September 1971 he appeared at a weekendlong all-star jazz party at the Broadmoor Hotel in Colorado Springs and worked with Hines at Disneyland. After a serious illness in 1975 Young continued to tour Europe, record, and lead his own groups in Hawaii. He died in San Jose, California.

Rejecting the older style of tailgate trombone, Young initially was impressed by the smooth tone and fluent, Armstrong-like improvisations of Jimmy Harrison and Benny Morton, but by the late 1930s he had adopted Armstrong himself as his primary model. He concentrated on developing a powerful upper register on trombone, and it was this technique, along with his softly intoned, highly rhythmic singing style, that made him such a valuable member of the Lunceford band. Of the records he made with Hines between October 1933 and February 1937, "Copenhagen," "Cavernism," "Disappointed in Love," and "Japanese Sandman" offer the best examples of his Morton-tinged style. However, he came into more prominence on the Lunceford records of November 1937 through June 1942. Here, his technically liberated, increasingly vocalized delivery surfaces on "Annie Laurie," "Margie," "'Tain't What You Do," "The Lonesome Road," "Blue Blazes," "Easter Parade," "Think of Me," "Dinah," "Battle Axe," and "Hi Spook," with several of these as well as others also featuring his singing. Young's only other recordings during the 1930s were with Mundy in March 1937 and Teddy Wilson in November 1938.

It was only after he left Lunceford that Young began to participate more regularly in small-band record sessions. In February 1944 he emerged for the first time as a major jazz stylist on "Blue Moon" and "Thru' for the Night" from a Cozy Cole septet date featuring Hines and Coleman Hawkins. On these titles his tone and phrasing suggest the growing influence of Dicky Wells and Vic Dickenson, especially in their use of unconventional timbres. Demonstrating his acceptance by younger, more modern jazzmen, in January 1945 he played on a Clyde Hart session with Dizzy Gillespie, Charlie Parker, and Don Byas, teamed once again with Byas on Gillespie's first leader date, and in February, along with Gillespie and Erroll Garner, recorded with Georgie Auld's modern big band.

Between February and August 1945 Young recorded only with Benny Goodman, but starting in 1946 he took part in sessions led by Benny Carter, Buck Clayton, Grimes, Illinois Jacquet, Lunceford, and Billy Kyle. Understandably, Young received more consistent exposure than ever before while he was a featured member of Armstrong's All Stars, but in deference to the more traditional style of the band, he also simplified his phrasing, broadened his tone, and deepened his range, as can be heard on the hundreds of studio and concert recordings and telecasts he made with Armstrong between October 1952 and December 1963. During this period, however, he also participated in a March 1954 Buck Clayton Jam Session date, a June 1957 Lunceford tribute album directed by Billy May, and an April 1958 All Stars session led by Armstrong-styled trumpeter Teddy Buckner. From 1953 on Young had also recorded with various European bands while on tour with the All Stars, but his last American sessions were with his own bands in Hawaii in the mid-1970s and a final tribute album to Armstrong with Peanuts Hucko and Billy Butterfield in

October 1983. Young also recorded several times as the leader of his own small groups between February 1944 and December 1955. During his years with Lunceford and as a freelancer on modern swing records in the mid-1940s, Young influenced an entire generation of younger trombonists, including Bill Harris, J. J. Johnson, Kai Winding, and Al Grey.

• Although Trummy Young apparently left no memoirs, an extended 1961 interview included in Stanley Dance, *The World of Earl Hines* (1977), touches on matters relevant to his early life and career. Other references to his background and milieu are in Dance, *The World of Swing* (1974); Albert McCarthy, *Big Band Jazz* (1974); and Dan Morgenstern, *Jazz People* (1976). His Armstrong period is touched on in James Lincoln Collier, *Louis Armstrong: An American Genius* (1983), as well as in many other documents dealing with Armstrong's career in the 1950s and 1960s. A short biographical entry is in John Chilton, *Who's Who of Jazz* (1985), and discographical listings are in Brian Rust, *Jazz Records, 1897–1942* (1982), and Walter Bruyninckx, *Traditional Jazz Discography, 1897–1988* (6 vols.), *Swing Discography, 1920–1988* (12 vols.), *Modern Jazz* (6 vols.), and *Modern Big Band* (2 vols.).

JACK SOHMER

YOUNG, Victor (8 Aug. 1900–10 Nov. 1956), motion picture composer, musical director, and arranger, was born in Chicago, Illinois, the son of William Young and Rose (maiden name unknown). He studied the violin beginning at age six, encouraged by his parents, who were both interested in music and pleased by having a child prodigy. When he was ten, Young went to Poland to live with his grandparents. There he continued his schooling and studied music with Roman Statlovsky in Warsaw. He also attended the Warsaw Conservatory, studied violin with Isidor Lotto, and received the Diploma of Merit from the Conservatory upon completing his studies. He made his concert debut with the Warsaw Philharmonic, but the outbreak of World War I interrupted the development of his career. At various points during the war he was interned by both the Russians and the Germans. At the war's end he returned to Chicago and made a successful American concert debut there before beginning his musical career in earnest as a violinist and concert director around 1920. After a brief move to Los Angeles, California, Young returned to Chicago and began to move away from classical music.

Young's attraction to popular songs and entertainments influenced his next several jobs, including a stint as concertmaster of the Central Park Theater, as violinist and arranger for Ted Fiorito's orchestra, and as musical supervisor for a number of vaudeville productions. He also began composing songs for musicals and radio shows, and he appeared on radio as an orchestra leader with Al Jolson, Don Ameche, and others during the 1930s. In this era he also became a musical director for Decca Records.

In 1935 Young began his long and distinguished career in Hollywood, first as an arranger and musical director for over a dozen mostly forgettable films, although a few, like *Anything Goes* (1936), *Rhythm on the Range* (1936), and *Double or Nothing* (1937), stand out. Young was particularly prolific during his first decade in Hollywood, when he composed scores and supplied the musical direction for numerous pictures, the best of which were *Maid of Salem* (1937), *Gulliver's Travels* (1939), *The Great Man's Lady* (1942), *The Story of Dr. Wassell* (1944), *Frenchman's Creek* (1944), and *The Great John L.* (1945).

Young's evocative scores were heard in dozens of outstanding motion pictures, including such diverse classics as *Golden Boy* (1939), *For Whom the Bell Tolls* (1943), *To Each His Own* (1946), *Golden Earrings* (1947), *State of the Union* (1948), *Samson and Delilah* (1949), *Sands of Iwo Jima* (1949), *Rio Grande* (1950), *The Quiet Man* (1952), *The Greatest Show on Earth* (1952), *Shane* (1953), *Three Coins in the Fountain* (1953), and *Johnny Guitar* (1954). He wrote numerous popular songs derived from his scores, with words by a variety of lyricists. The most popular among these were "Sweet Sue" (1928; lyrics by Will Harris), "Street of Dreams" (1933; lyrics by Sam M. Lewis), "A Hundred Years from Today" (1935; lyrics by Ned Washington), "Stella by Starlight" (1946; lyrics by Washington), "My Foolish Heart" (1949; lyrics by Washington), and "Around the World in Eighty Days" (1956; lyrics by Harold Adamson). The last became one of the leading hit songs of 1956.

Young impressively composed for every genre of motion picture, from musicals to westerns, and he was particularly effective at weaving familiar songs and traditional themes into his original scores as a way of capturing the feeling of the actual period in which the story was set. For example, his evocative score for John Ford's classic, *The Quiet Man* (1952), weaves traditional Irish folk music into a lush and romantic score; it is difficult to think of the film without recalling Young's insistent themes. Ford and Cecil B. DeMille were among the leading movie directors who favored Young's music for their films. However, creating film scores was a highly pressured existence. "Why, indeed," he once told an interviewer (as quoted by Tony Thomas), "would any trained musician let himself in for a career that calls for the exactitude of Einstein, the diplomacy of Churchill, and the patience of a martyr. Yet I can think of no other medium that offers this challenge and excitement, provided that your interest in the universe is unflagging and your knowledge of musical forms is gargantuan."

Throughout his career as a composer, Young continued to provide musical direction for many films. Beginning in the late 1930s he also supplied music with his own orchestra for popular recordings by such artists as Dick Powell, Eddie Cantor, Deanna Durbin, Helen Forrest, Frances Langford, Cliff "Ukelele Ike" Edwards, and the Boswell Sisters. Two of his outstanding sessions produced Judy Garland's commercial recording of "Over the Rainbow," the Oscar-winning song from her 1939 screen classic, *The Wizard of Oz*, and Bing Crosby's million-selling recording of "Too-Ra-Loo-Ra-Loo-Ral," from 1944's Oscar-winning best picture of the year, *Going My Way*, for which

Crosby also won a best actor Oscar. Although Young's output of movie scores slowed slightly after World War II, he was still remarkably prolific by any standards. His last decade featured outstanding scores for several films, including *The Searching Wind* (1946), *Two Years before the Mast* (1946), *I Walk Alone* (1947), *The Paleface* (1948), *The File on Thelma Jordan* (1950), *Appointment with Danger* (1951), *Scaramouche* (1952), *The Tall Men* (1955), and *China Gate* (1957; completed by Max Steiner after Young's death).

In the 1950s Young composed music for two Broadway musicals, *Pardon Our French* (1950) and *Seventh Heaven* (1955), although neither show was particularly successful. He died suddenly of a heart attack in Palm Springs, California. At the time of his death he was working on a score for a musical comedy based on the life of Mark Twain. Composer Ferde Grofé was tapped to try to complete the score, but the show was never produced.

It is for his numerous and frequently memorable compositions for films that Young is best remembered. He was nominated for an astonishing twenty-two Academy Awards for scoring or song, but he did not actually win an Oscar until 1956 for the all-star epic *Around the World in Eighty Days*, produced by Mike Todd. Unfortunately, the Oscar was awarded posthumously, as Young had died unexpectedly weeks before the ceremony. Young's prodigious output of scores for motion pictures can be matched by only a few of his contemporaries, such as Erich Wolfgang Korngold, Max Steiner, and Herbert Stothart, all of whom, like Young, labored within the Hollywood studio system in the golden age of American movies. Tony Thomas has written that Young's admiring contemporaries claimed that he "needed only to sit at the piano for the melodies to fall out of his sleeves."

• For information on Young's life and career, see Gian Carlo Bertolina, *Rivista del Cinematografo* (1981); David Ewen, *Popular American Composers* (1962); Alain Lacombe, *Hollywood* (1983); Tony Thomas, *Music for the Movies* (1973); Thomas, "Victor Young," *International Dictionary of Films and Filmmakers*, vol. 4 (1994); "Victor Young," *Music Journal*, Sept. 1956; and Mark White, *You Must Remember This . . . Popular Songwriters 1900–1980* (1983). An obituary is in the *New York Times*, 11 Nov. 1956.

JAMES FISHER

YOUNG, Whitney Moore, Jr. (31 July 1921–11 March 1971), social worker and civil rights activist, was born in Lincoln Ridge, Kentucky, the son of Whitney Moore Young, Sr., president of Lincoln Institute, a private African-American college, and Laura Ray, a schoolteacher. Raised within the community of the private academy and its biracial faculty, Whitney Young, Jr., and his two sisters were sheltered from harsh confrontations with racial discrimination in their early lives, but they attended segregated public elementary schools for African-American children and completed high school at Lincoln Institute. In 1937 Young, planning to become a doctor, entered Kentucky State Industrial College at Frankfort, where he

received a bachelor of science degree in 1941. After graduation he became an assistant principal and athletic coach at Julius Rosenwald High School in Madison, Kentucky.

After joining the U.S. Army in 1942, Young studied engineering at Massachusetts Institute of Technology (MIT). In 1944 he married Margaret Buckner, a teacher whom he had met while they were both students at Kentucky State; they had two children. Sent to Europe later in 1944, Young rose from private to first sergeant in the all-black 369th Anti-Aircraft Artillery Group. His experience in a segregated army on the verge of President Harry Truman's desegregation order drew Young to the challenges of racial diplomacy. In 1946 after his discharge from the army, he entered graduate study in social work at the University of Minnesota. His field placement in graduate school was with the Minneapolis chapter of the National Urban League, which sought increased employment opportunities for African-American workers. In 1948 Young completed his master's degree in social work and became industrial relations secretary of the St. Paul, Minnesota, chapter of the Urban League. In 1950 he became the director of the Urban League chapter in Omaha, Nebraska. He increased both the Omaha chapter's membership and its operating budget. He became skilled at working with the city's business and political leaders to increase employment opportunities for African Americans. In Omaha he also taught in the University of Nebraska's School of Social Work.

In 1954 Young became dean of the School of Social Work at Atlanta University. As an administrator, he doubled the school's budget, raised faculty salaries, and insisted on professional development. In these early years after the Supreme Court's decision in *Brown v. Board of Education of Topeka, Kansas*, Young played a significant advisory role within the leadership of Atlanta's African-American community. He was active in the Greater Atlanta Council on Human Relations and a member of the executive committee of the Atlanta branch of the National Association for the Advancement of Colored People (NAACP). He also helped to organize Atlanta's Committee for Cooperative Action, a group of business and professional people who sought to coordinate the social and political action of varied black interest groups and organized patrols in African-American communities threatened by white violence. He took a leave of absence from his position at Atlanta University in the 1960–1961 academic year to be a visiting Rockefeller Foundation scholar at Harvard University.

In January 1961 the National Urban League announced Whitney Young's appointment to succeed Lester B. Granger as its executive director. Beginning his new work in fall 1961, Young came to the leadership of the Urban League just after the first wave of sit-in demonstrations and freedom rides had drawn national attention to new forms of civil rights activism in the South. Among the major organizations identified with the civil rights movement, the Urban League was the most conservative and the least inclined to favor public demonstrations for social change. Young was resolved to move it into a firmer alliance with the other major civil rights organizations without threatening the confidence of the Urban League's powerful inside contacts. In 1963 he led it into joining the March on Washington and the Council for United Civil Rights Leadership, a consortium initiated by Kennedy administration officials and white philanthropists to facilitate fundraising and joint planning.

In his ten years as executive director of the Urban League, Young increased the number of its local chapters from sixty to ninety-eight, its staff from 500 to 1,200, and its funding by corporations, foundations, and federal grants. After the assassination of President John Kennedy, Young developed even stronger ties with President Lyndon Johnson's administration. Perhaps his most important influence lay in Young's call for a "Domestic Marshall Plan," outlined in his book, *To Be Equal* (1964), which influenced President Johnson's War on Poverty programs.

By the mid-1960s, however, the civil rights coalition had begun to fray. In June 1966 Young and Roy Wilkins of the NAACP refused to sign a manifesto drafted by other civil rights leaders or to join them when they continued the march of James Meredith from Memphis, Tennessee, to Jackson, Mississippi. Young continued to shun the black power rhetoric popular with new leaders of the Congress of Racial Equality and the Student Nonviolent Coordinating Committee. Simultaneously, in consideration of the vital alliance with the Johnson administration, he was publicly critical of Martin Luther King's condemnation of the U.S. pursuit of the war in Vietnam. At the administration's request, he twice visited South Vietnam to review American forces and observe elections there. Before leaving office in 1969, Lyndon Johnson awarded Young the Medal of Freedom, the nation's highest civilian citation.

After Richard Nixon's inauguration in 1969, however, Young modified his earlier positions, condemning the war in Vietnam and responding to the black power movement and urban violence by concentrating Urban League resources on young people in the urban black underclass. He continued to have significant influence, serving on the boards of the Federal Reserve Bank of New York, MIT, and the Rockefeller Foundation and as president of the National Conference on Social Welfare (1967) and of the National Association of Social Workers (1969–1971). Subsequently, Young's successors as executive director of the Urban League, Arthur Fletcher, Vernon Jordan, and John Jacob, maintained his legacy of commitment to the goals of the civil rights movement by sustained engagement with centers of American economic and political power.

In March 1971, while Young was at a conference on relations between Africa and the United States in Lagos, Nigeria, he suffered either a brain hemorrhage or a heart attack and drowned while swimming in the Atlantic Ocean. Former Attorney General Ramsey Clark and others who were swimming with him pulled Young's body from the water, but their efforts to revive him were to no avail.

• The Whitney M. Young, Jr., Papers are in the Rare Book and Manuscript Library of Columbia University; the National Urban League Papers are at the Library of Congress. The standard biography, Nancy J. Weiss, *Whitney M. Young, Jr., and the Struggle for Civil Rights* (1990), includes a helpful note on sources. On the National Urban League, see Guichard Parris and Lester Brooks, *Blacks in the City: A History of the National Urban League* (1971), and Jesse Thomas Moore, Jr., *A Search for Equality: The National Urban League, 1910–1961* (1981). An obituary is in the *New York Times*, 12 Mar. 1971.

RALPH E. LUKER

YOUNG, William Field (28 May 1821–18 Aug. 1900), labor reformer, was born in Burrillville, Rhode Island, the son of William Young and Abigail Smith. Little is known of Young's childhood, save that his father was "engaged in the cotton manufacturing business" in his native state of Rhode Island and moved the family to the farmlands of western and southern New Hampshire when William was a boy. Here, he attended schools in several small towns, including the Appleton Academy in New Ipswich.

Coming of age during the long depression that followed the panic of 1837, Young first tried his hand at farming, then briefly studied dentistry, and finally apprenticed in the harness-making trade. In 1843, after a short stint as a journeyman harness-maker in Nashua, New Hampshire, a growing manufacturing center, Young moved to the small mill town of Fitchburg, Massachusetts, where he began his career as a labor reformer, helping to establish the local Workingmen's Association there in late 1844. A general upsurge in working-class protest swept New England during these years, and Young and the association launched the *Voice of Industry* (1845–1848), a labor newspaper that quickly became the movement's mouthpiece. The following fall, Young moved the paper to Lowell, a major center of factory production and labor agitation, where he served as president of the local workers' organization, as an officer of the New England Workingmen's Association and other regional labor conventions, and as a traveling lecturer. During the late 1840s and early 1850s, he also played a leading role in the pro-labor New England Industrial League, the Massachusetts Ten Hour Conventions, and the New England Protective Union, a network of workers' cooperatives.

In 1853 Young gave up his work as a "crupper-stitcher" and became a salesman for a wholesale dry goods firm in Boston, probably as a result of his earlier work as manager of the Protective Union's store in the city. From 1866 to 1885, when he retired, he was a partner in a major Boston wholesale grocery business. During these years, living in Wakefield, Massachusetts, an industrial town north of Boston, he remained committed to the cause of labor reform, serving, for example, as Wakefield's delegate to conventions of the Knights of Labor in the late 1880s.

Young became a powerful voice for antebellum workers because his public life and worldview joined three of the most powerful impulses of his age: labor protest, social reform, and evangelical religion. His labor politics combined an advocacy of basic working-class demands (wages, hours, conditions) with a call for general social reform (antislavery, temperance, land reform, workers' cooperatives, utopian socialism, peace, women's rights, abolition of capital punishment, health reform), all as an explicitly Christian endeavor. Although apparently not a church member until after the Civil War, when he joined the First Universalist Society of Wakefield, Young's antebellum writings are suffused with biblical rhetoric (particularly from the Gospels) and have an unmistakably evangelical, sometimes explicitly millennial, style.

Young was married twice, in 1845 to Sarah Wright, who died in 1848, and in 1855 to Ada L. Taft, with whom he had three children. He died in Wakefield.

• Most of Young's significant writings appeared in the *Voice of Industry*. For the only modern analysis of his contribution as a labor reformer, see Jama Lazerow, "Religion and Labor Reform in Antebellum America: The World of William Field Young," *American Quarterly* 38 (Summer 1986): 265–86. Biographical material can be found in obituaries in the *Boston Globe*, 20 Aug. 1900; the *Boston Transcript*, 20 Aug. 1900; the *Daily Item* (Wakefield, Mass.), 20 and 22 Aug. 1900; and in *Biographical Sketches of Representative Citizens of the Commonwealth of Massachusetts* (1901).

JAMA LAZEROW

YOUNG, William Gould (30 July 1902–5 July 1980), organic chemist, was born in Colorado Springs, Colorado, the son of Henry A. Young, a stockbroker, and Mary Ella Salisbury. His father was an amateur golf champion, and Young played so expertly in his teens that he thought of making golf his career. At Colorado College he was the Rocky Mountain Conference champion. However, James Hollingsworth Smith, a Chicago Ph.D. in chemistry, aroused his scientific interests, and he majored in chemistry for his bachelor's and master's degrees in 1924 and 1925. In 1926 he married Helen Graybeal, a 1925 Colorado College graduate; they had no children. Smith recommended Young to another Chicago Ph.D., Herman Spoehr, at the Coastal Laboratory of the Carnegie Institution in Carmel, California. After serving as Spoehr's assistant from 1925 to 1927, he undertook doctoral studies at the California Institute of Technology with Howard Lucas, a third Chicago-trained chemist. He received the Ph.D. in 1929. Smith, Spoehr, and Lucas brought the Chicago emphasis on uniting physical and organic chemistry to the West, an approach decisive for Young.

In 1930 Young became an instructor of chemistry at the University of California in Los Angeles. At the time UCLA was a small college with only an undergraduate program, having been a teacher's college prior to becoming part of the University of California system. Young's effect on students seems to have been electric. He impressed the brightest students with the freshness of his outlook and grasp of organic chemistry. An exceptionally talented student was Saul Winstein, a sophomore in 1931 and a student in the first course on organic chemistry ever taught by Young. Young's ability to inspire and promote initiative and independent thought was immediately evident to Winstein. Young and Winstein collaborated, publishing eight papers by 1935 when Winstein received a master's degree in UCLA's new graduate program. These papers are now classics in organic chemistry. Winstein also went to Caltech for his Ph.D. under Lucas, returned to UCLA as a faculty member in 1942, and became one of the world's foremost physical organic chemists.

Young was department chair from 1940 to 1948, initiating a doctoral program and producing many Ph.D. students who became distinguished scientists and teachers. He consciously set out to build a strong research program in physical organic chemistry, in part because of the weakness of the field at the University of California in Berkeley. In 1947 he hired Donald Cram, another brilliant organic chemist and a future Nobel Prize winner. Physical organic chemistry gave UCLA with its new doctoral program an opportunity to excel, and with Young, Winstein, and Cram as a nucleus, UCLA became the world's foremost center for research on reaction mechanisms.

From 1946 to 1957 Young was dean of the Division of Physical Science, and from 1957 to 1970 he was vice chancellor of UCLA. He retired in 1970 but continued both to teach and do research. He was vice chancellor for planning and construction, and during his tenure he oversaw and coordinated a massive building program that resulted in forty-two new buildings or major additions.

Young's research focused on the preparation and structure of stereoisomers, reaction mechanisms, and molecular rearrangements. For three decades he intensively studied the allylic rearrangement. An allylic system refers to a three-carbon unit with a double bond. Highly reactive, it often reacts with a rearrangement involving no migration of atoms, and only the double bond appears in a different position. What led him to this topic was his doctoral thesis, an attempt to synthesize pure *trans*-2-butene by a simple sequence of well-established reactions. Instead, he obtained a complex mixture of products. In the 1930s, continuing investigations he began at Caltech, Young discovered with Winstein the existence of a reversible reaction, a rapid equilibration between isomeric substances. He unraveled the steps in the reaction sequence, including the allylic rearrangement, and developed methods to isolate each of the substances formed and an interpretation involving a reaction intermediate, the butenyl cation, capable of existing in several forms as a resonating carbonium ion. He used Linus Pauling's recent concept of resonance and electron delocalization in demonstrating this allylic rearrangement. The research not only established this type of carbonium ion and its resonance stabilization, but it also accustomed chemists to think of intermediates in organic reactions. The idea of a butenyl cation was novel in the 1930s, and the concept of resonance was new and difficult for organic chemists. Young's work was important in the development of chemical theory, organic synthesis, and chemical technology. The research subsequently appeared in most modern textbooks, having revealed the state of dynamic equilibrium in which some types of unsaturated carbon compounds exist. It became an important part of the material taught in organic chemistry. Traditional, hands-on organic chemists found that the knowledge of mechanisms and intermediates made possible the synthesis of substances difficult to prepare. Industrial chemists in the rubber, plastics, and petroleum-refining industries found that their work depended on new knowledge of unsaturated molecules provided by the fundamental studies of Young.

Young served the chemistry profession in yet another capacity. He was a member of the American Chemical Society's Committee on Professional Training from 1943 to 1959 and its chair for ten of those years. The ACS was disappointed with the educational standards prevailing in the 1930s and charged the committee with the development of minimum standards for departments of chemistry. Its members visited campuses, evaluated programs, and accredited departments all over the United States. It proposed major curriculum reforms and restructuring of courses. Young was very influential as committee chair. His success in prompting hundreds of chemistry departments to make the necessary changes in staffing, curriculum, and equipment was a testimony to his diplomacy, firmness of purpose, and persuasiveness.

Young's many honors include election to the National Academy of Sciences in 1951; the Priestley Medal, the highest honor in American chemistry, in 1968; and the Caltech Distinguished Alumnus Award in 1968. He was a soft-spoken, low-key person with a gentle wit. In his characteristically quiet and unassuming manner, he made an impact on organic chemistry as a teacher, research scientist, administrator, and educational reformer. He also maintained an active social and recreational life as an expert golfer and shared with his wife an enthusiasm for fishing, gardening, travel, and participation in UCLA dance groups. He died in Laguna Hills, California.

Young was important for promoting the acceptance of physical organic chemistry in the United States. The field was looked on with suspicion in the 1930s; it did not fit in with the needs of chemistry departments and the industrial laboratories, which wanted chemists trained in traditional synthetic organic chemistry. The institutional base was limited to a few places, such as Chicago and Caltech. Young expanded this institutional base at UCLA, and as the UCLA group revealed the relationships between organic structures, reactivity, pathways, and products, organic chemists in the postwar years saw that the field could reinvigorate organic chemistry, revolutionize organic synthesis, and produce practical results.

• The primary source on Young is a transcript of interviews conducted during 1969–1970 for the University of California Oral History Program (1984). Young reviewed his major area of research in "Organic Reaction Mechanisms with Allylic Compounds," *Journal of Chemical Education* 27 (1950): 357–64, and more broadly with R. H. DeWolfe in "Allylic Reactions," in *The Chemistry of Alkenes*, ed. Saul Patai (1964). Two brief accounts of his career are in *Chemical and Engineering News* 40 (2 Apr. 1962): 102, and 45 (24 July 1967): 56–57. See John D. Roberts, *The Right Place at the Right Time* (1990), an autobiography by Young's most famous Ph.D. student, on Young as a research director. See also Leon Gortler, "The Development of a Scientific Community: Physical Organic Chemistry in the United States, 1925–1950," in *Essays on the History of Organic Chemistry*, ed. James Traynham (1987), pp. 95–113, for Young's role in creating the physical organic program at UCLA. Obituaries are in the *Los Angeles Times*, 7 July 1980, and *Chemical and Engineering News* 58 (22 Sept. 1980): 43.

ALBERT B. COSTA

YOUNGDAHL, Luther Wallace (29 May 1896–21 June 1978), governor of Minnesota and federal judge, was born in Minneapolis, Minnesota, the son of John Carl Youngdahl, a grocer, and Elizabeth Johnson. The child of Swedish immigrants, Youngdahl was raised in a strongly Lutheran environment and remained an active member of that church throughout his life. After his college studies were interrupted by service in the army during World War I, Youngdahl received a B.A. from Gustavus Adolphus College in 1919 and a law degree from the Minnesota College of Law in 1921. He began his legal career by working as an assistant city attorney in Minneapolis from 1921 to 1923. In the latter year, he married Irene Annet Engdahl. The couple had three children.

From 1923 to 1930 Youngdahl maintained a private law practice in Minneapolis and became active in Republican party politics. He then began a state judicial career that took him from municipal judge in Minneapolis from 1930 to 1936, to judge of the district court for Hennepin County from 1936 to 1942, and ultimately to the position of associate justice on the Minnesota Supreme Court from 1942 to 1946.

In 1946 Youngdahl stepped down from the bench and won election to the first of three terms as governor of Minnesota. As governor, he attacked gambling syndicates controlled by organized crime several years before the televised Kefauver Committee hearings brought this issue to national attention. Youngdahl was also ahead of most reformers in working to replace the Minnesota mental health system's emphasis on physical restraint with the goal of treatment. He dramatized the latter program in 1949 by personally setting fire to a collection of straitjackets and manacles outside of a state hospital. He also supported efforts to combat juvenile delinquency through prevention and rehabilitation as opposed to harsher measures.

Youngdahl came to the attention of President Harry S. Truman in April 1951, when he publicly supported the president's decision to fire General Douglas MacArthur. Later that year Truman appointed Youngdahl to the U.S. District Court for the District of Columbia. He resigned the governorship to accept the post.

Youngdahl became nationally prominent as a judge when the government brought perjury charges against Owen J. Lattimore, a university professor and expert on Asia. The indictment claimed that Lattimore, a target of Senator Joseph R. McCarthy's anti-Communist campaign, had lied when he testified before a Senate Committee that he was not a sympathizer or promoter of Communist interests. In 1953 Youngdahl dismissed the key portions of the indictment on grounds that the charges were too vague and that the prosecution would limit free speech. "The First Amendment," the judge wrote, "protects an individual in the expression of ideas though they are repugnant to the orthodox. Communism's fallacy and viciousness can be demonstrated without striking down the protection of the First Amendment of discourse, discussion and debate."

This decision made Youngdahl himself a target of criticism from the supporters of Senator McCarthy. After the federal court of appeals upheld the judge's dismissal of the key counts in the indictment, the government secured a new set of charges against Lattimore and then petitioned to have Youngdahl remove himself from the case on grounds of prejudice. Youngdahl denied the petition and then, in 1955, dismissed the government's new indictment, again citing the First Amendment. When the court of appeals affirmed, the government dropped the case.

Following the Lattimore case, Youngdahl continued to serve as a federal judge until his death in Washington, D.C. His career as governor and judge placed him in the tradition of progressive Republicans who saw government as limited by the Constitution but capable of attacking social problems.

• A collection of Youngdahl papers is at the Minnesota Historical Society. Youngdahl himself collected many of his speeches, including excerpts from his inaugural addresses, in his *The Ramparts We Watch* (1961). As with all federal judges, Youngdahl's published opinions are collected in the federal reporter system; his rulings dismissing the indictments against Lattimore may be found at 112 F. Supp. 507 (D.D.C. 1953) and 127 F. Supp. 405 (D.D.C. 1955). For biographical details, see Robert Esbjornson, *A Christian in Politics: Luther W. Youngdahl* (1955). A thorough description of Youngdahl's involvement in the Lattimore case is in Robert P. Newman, *Owen Lattimore and the "Loss" of China* (1992). The most extensive obituary is in the *Washington Post*, 22 June 1978.

STEVEN GOLDBERG

YOUNGER, Cole (15 Jan. 1844–20 Mar. 1916), outlaw, was born Thomas Coleman Younger in Lee's Summit, Missouri, the son of Henry Washington Younger, an affluent plantation owner who served at one time as a county judge and also as mayor of Harrisonville, Missouri, and Bursheba Fristoe. Younger grew up experiencing at close hand the violent conflicts between antislavery factions in nearby Kansas and proslavery groups in Missouri prior to the Civil War. The war intensified these conflicts, as the region experienced numerous atrocities carried out by rival guerrilla bands.

Younger was a prominent lieutenant in William Clarke Quantrill's band of Confederate guerrillas and participated in the Lawrence, Kansas, massacre of about 150 unarmed pro-Union men. He later joined the regular Confederate army. Younger's father opposed secession and remained neutral during the war. Nevertheless, on 20 July 1862 he was ambushed, robbed, and murdered by Union soldiers. Cole Younger's family home was burned by Federal troops, and his sisters were jailed.

After the Civil War, Younger and his three brothers, Jim, John, and Bob, participated with former guerrilla comrades Frank and Jesse James in a series of robberies. In March 1874 John Younger was killed in a gunfight with Pinkerton agents. Cole Younger published a moving letter in the *St. Louis Republican* proclaiming his brother's innocence and condemning the Pinkertons who "hunted him down like a wild beast" (30 Nov. 1874).

For the next ten years the Youngers and other ex-Confederates were lauded by the press and politicians of the Confederate wing of Missouri's Democratic party. The prominence of the Younger family and injustices done to the boys' parents by Union troops during the war were frequently recounted. Newspaper editor John Newman Edwards was the prime force in shaping a Robin Hood image for the James-Younger gang through numerous editorials and in the book *Noted Guerrillas* (1877). In one essay Edwards described the brigands as "men who might have sat with Arthur at the Round Table, ridden in tourney with Sir Lancelot, or won the colors of Guinevere" (*Kansas City Times*, 29 Sept. 1872).

Edwards served as an able "campaign manager" for the James-Younger gang, but these outlaws also had a shrewd sense of how to construct a good public image. Besides writing letters to newspapers claiming innocence and condemning the ruling Radical Republicans, the bandits dramatized their robberies in meaningful ways, fostering a Robin Hood image tinged with postwar politics.

All these public relations efforts culminated in an amnesty resolution proposed by the Confederate wing of the Democratic party in Missouri before the Missouri House of Representatives on 17 March 1875. The resolution described the James and Younger brothers as men who were driven into crime by Missouri Republicans and characterized them as men too brave to be mean, too generous to be revengeful, and too gallant and honorable to betray a friend or break a promise. It further suggested that most, if not all, the offenses with which they have been charged were committed by others, and perhaps by those pretending to hunt them. With every ex-Confederate in the legislature supporting it, the resolution narrowly missed the two-thirds majority needed to pass.

Attempts to revive the resolution were dashed by the attempted robbery of the Northfield, Minnesota, bank on 7 September 1876, during which a cashier was killed and another wounded as he gave the alarm. In the confusion that followed, several robbers also were killed or wounded. The three Younger brothers wandered lost in the unfamiliar landscape for two weeks. On 21 September they were captured by a posse after a spirited gunfight. All Younger brothers were severely wounded. Only two bandits escaped, presumably Frank and Jesse James.

The Younger brothers were taken by wagon through Madelia, Minnesota, where a crowd gathered. Cole Younger, despite eleven bullet wounds, managed to stand and bow to the women. Surprisingly, the captured bandits were treated kindly and regarded with curiosity. Numerous citizens and reporters met with the celebrities once they arrived at the Faribault, Minnesota, jail. The press interviewed the brothers at length and presented a picture of decent and courageous men united by bonds of love, honor, and compassion. These were also men who were quite adept at manipulating public sentiment. Younger told of his family and spoke of his religious background, often quoting from the Bible and expressing deep regret for his crimes. William Settle noted that Younger "was able to touch some of his audience, and when they wept, he allowed tears to roll down his cheeks. Then the visitor would usually reach a 'wipe' through the bars for him to use in drying the tears" (1966, p. 93). All three brothers pled guilty to robbery and murder and were sentenced to life in Stillwater Penitentiary.

Bob Younger died in prison in 1889. Cole and Jim Younger were paroled in 1901 but were required to live in Minnesota. Jim Younger committed suicide in 1902. Cole Younger received an official pardon in 1903 and eventually joined Frank James in a touring Wild West show. To his death in Lee's Summit, Missouri, Younger refused to reveal the identity of the two robbers who escaped from Northfield. He never married or had children.

Younger's fame was eclipsed by fellow gang member Jesse James, arguably America's most noted criminal. However, like James, Younger received widespread adulation both in his own lifetime and for following generations. His notoriety resulted from several factors. First, he was supported through the media and in other ways by powerful friends in Missouri politics. Second was his identity as an ex-Confederate soldier from a respectable Missouri family. And third was the social context that made extralegal symbols of justice marketable to a broad audience; in addition to the turmoil of Reconstruction politics, there was an economic depression in the 1870s throughout the West that was widely blamed on banks, railroads, and land monopolies—the victims of outlaws of the time such as the James-Younger gang, Billy the Kid, and Sam Bass. Newspapers and dime novels found outlaw tales to be quite profitable.

• A good place to begin examining the life of Younger is his autobiography, *The Story of Cole Younger, by Himself* (1903). Other books of note on the subject include John Newman Edwards, *Noted Guerrillas* (1877), and Augustus Appler, *The Guerrillas of the West; or, the Life, Character, and Daring Exploits of the Younger Brothers* (1875). William A. Settle, Jr., *Jesse James Was His Name* (1966), provides the definitive account of the James-Younger gang and includes a twenty-page descriptive bibliography analyzing works about the outlaw band. Paul Kooistra, *Criminals as Heroes: Structure, Power, and Identity* (1989), explains how certain mass murderers and habitual criminals like Younger have come to be glorified rather than uniformly condemned. The most recent work is Carl Breihan, *Ride the Razor's Edge: The Younger Brothers Story* (1992). Younger's life has been dramatized in several films, including *Cole Younger, Gunfighter* (1958), *The Great Northfield Raid* (1972), and *The Long Riders* (1980).

PAUL G. KOOISTRA

YOUNGER, Maud (10 Jan. 1870–25 June 1936), labor and women's rights activist, was born in San Francisco, California, the daughter of William John Younger, a socially prominent dentist, and Anna Maria Lane. Born into wealth, she enjoyed a life of privilege during her early years. Upon her mother's death, twelve-year-old Maud and her four siblings inherited the considerable fortune amassed by Anna Lane's father. Maud completed her formal education at boarding and finishing schools in San Francisco and New York.

In 1901 circumstances and her own desire for a purposeful life transformed Younger from a socialite to a social activist. While on a stopover in New York City on the way to Europe, she visited the New York College Settlement, founded in 1889 by graduates of Smith, Wellesley, Vassar, Bryn Mawr, and Radcliffe colleges. Said Younger, "I went to see it, stopped for a week, and stayed five years" ("Along the Way").

The years at the settlement molded Younger into an advocate of working-class women. It also made her impatient with reformers who treated their clients with condescension. She later expressed regret regarding "the artificial relation between settlement worker and the neighborhood. For however warm the friendships, we were there as a favored class on a basis of superiority" ("Along the Way"). Her dissatisfaction with the limits of settlement work fueled her conversion to trade unionism and to her involvement in the New York Women's Trade Union League (NYWTUL).

Younger jumped feet first into labor activism. She investigated the work lives of New York City waitresses firsthand by securing jobs at several restaurants. At the end of the experience, she joined the New York Waitresses' Union. Younger documented her career in this service trade in "The Diary of an Amateur Waitress: An Industrial Problem from the Worker's Point of View" (*McClure's Magazine*, Mar.–Apr. 1907, pp. 542–52, 665–77). In the NYWTUL she served as chair of the Waitresses' Committee and represented the Waitresses' Union on the NYWTUL executive board. Referring to the variety of jobs that she took on in the NYWTUL, Younger dubbed herself "a maid of all work."

The San Francisco earthquake in April 1906 brought Younger back to the city of her birth. She paid a visit to Waitresses' Union Local 48 and presented her union card, hoping to establish contact with the women unionists there. Initially they gave her the cold shoulder. However, when the business agent announced that a waitress was needed to fill a position, Younger took the post. This job qualified Younger as a Local 48 member, and the "millionaire waitress," as she was popularly called, soon became a vital member of the union and the San Francisco movement. Local 48 members elected her union president for one term and delegate to the San Francisco Central Labor Council for three terms.

At the same time, Younger's activism also included suffrage work. She and Local 48 official Louise LaRue were instrumental in the founding of the San Francisco Wage Earners' Suffrage League (WESL) in September 1908. Organized to represent the interests of wage-earning women in suffrage campaigns, the WESL was originally organized in reaction to mainstream suffragists who refused to honor a boycott of a streetcar line during a violent strike in 1907.

Younger and LaRue agitated up and down the state for the vote for wage-earning women. Younger argued that "the wage-earning woman needs the ballot because her every gain in the past has come through her own effort, and every future victory she must win for herself" (*San Francisco Call*, 4 July 1909). Officially sanctioned by the San Francisco Labor Council, the WESL gave working-class women and their allies a distinct way to address working-class male voters and lobby for the vote in their own community, as well as participate in the suffrage coalition on their own terms. California women won the suffrage in October 1911, and the WESL contributed significantly to that effort.

Younger and other WESL activists also successfully lobbied the California legislature for an eight-hour workday law for women in March 1911. When the opponents of the measure challenged its constitutionality in court, Younger financed a legal defense through 1915, when the U.S. Supreme Court upheld the law, earning herself the accolade "Mother of the Eight-Hour Day for Women."

Following the victory of woman suffrage in California, Younger continued her labor and suffrage activism. In 1913 she picketed during a New York City garment workers' strike and campaigned for the retrial of members of the Industrial Workers of the World convicted of murder during the Wheatland Riot in northern California. In 1914 Younger joined with Nevada suffragists in their successful effort for the ballot.

A year later Younger met the charismatic Alice Paul of the Congressional Union. The Congressional Union broke with the National American Woman Suffrage Association in 1913 because Paul and her followers favored militant acts as the means to win woman suffrage on a national level. Younger joined the group, which eventually changed its name to the National Women's party (NWP) in 1916, and served as chair of the Lobby Committee. NWP activists such as Younger used White House picketing as well as conventional lobbying to pressure the president and Congress to approve a woman suffrage amendment to the U.S. Constitution.

After the ratification of the Nineteenth Amendment in 1920, Younger and her NWP cohorts promoted the Equal Rights Amendment (ERA) to the U.S. Constitution, which would mandate equal protection under the law for men and women. In order to advocate the ERA, Younger had to renounce her support of gender-based labor legislation such as eight-hour day laws for women. In doing so, she severed her relationship with the trade-union movement. Younger spent the last years of her life fighting for legal equality for women and actively opposing the laws she had formerly championed. She supported the wording of the National Industrial Recovery Act of 1933, which she believed gave women "industrial equality" with men. Younger died at her ranch in Los Gatos, California.

Younger acted as a bridge between labor activists and those advocating women's rights, bringing elements of each movement to the other. She kept issues of women and work at the center of her political activity throughout her life.

• The most fruitful location for Younger's papers is the National Women's Party Papers at the Library of Congress, which includes her unpublished autobiography, "Along the Way." Other letters and sources can be found in the Jane Norman and Inez Haynes Irwin Papers at the Schlesinger Library; the Alice L. Park Papers at the Huntington Library; the Francis Noel Papers at the Special Collections Department, UCLA University Research Library; the Ann Martin and Keith-McHenry-Pond Papers at the Bancroft Library, University of California at Berkeley; and the Suffrage–U.S. Biography Collection in the Sophia Smith Collection at Smith College. The most comprehensive treatments of Younger's life can be found in Susan Englander, *Class Conflict and Class Coalition in the California Woman Suffrage Movement, 1907–1912: The San Francisco Wage Earners' Suffrage League* (1992), and April McDonald, "Maud Younger, 1870–1936: A California Woman as Labor Reformer, Suffragist, and Activist" (M.A. thesis, California State Univ., 1994). Younger's publications are listed in these sources. See also Susan Becker, *The Origins of the Equal Rights Amendment: American Feminism between the Wars* (1981), for her role in the National Women's party. An obituary is in the *New York Times*, 28 June 1936.

SUSAN ENGLANDER

YOUNG MAN AFRAID OF HIS HORSE (1850?–1894), chief of the Sioux tribe of Oglala Tetons, was the son of Old Man Afraid of His Horse. His birthplace and the name of his mother are not known. His Indian name was Tashunka-Kokipapi. The names of his wife and children are unavailable to this author. He was a lifelong comrade-in-arms and friend of famous Oglala chiefs such as Red Cloud, Crazy Horse, and American Horse and Cheyennes such as George Bent (who initiated Young Man into his Crooked Lances clan in 1865). Later in his life Young Man became an "agency Indian" and dedicated his life to keeping peace between and among the Oglalas and the whites on the Pine Ridge Reservation in South Dakota. Several times he rescued whites from hostilities and unsuccessfully attempted to prevent bloodshed during the Ghost Dance movement, sometimes with the help of

Indian police. Recognized for his influence among the Oglalas, Young Man Afraid of His Horse participated in treaty sessions and traveled to Washington, D.C., to confer with the president and the commissioner of Indian affairs.

By the eighteenth century the Teton Sioux, one of three branches of Plains Sioux, had separated from the eastern Santee Sioux in order to live on the Great Plains, where they acquired horses and arms from the French and interacted with the Cheyennes, the Pawnees, the Crows, and other indigenous groups. Entering the area of Minnesota first, the invading Sioux pushed the indigenous Omahas, Otos, Missouris, and Iowas south- and westward.

Born into the Oglala tribe, one of seven comprising the Teton Sioux, Young Man Afraid of His Horse spoke Lakota, a language with many soft consonants reminding whites of French. He grew up during the peak of the Plains Indian buffalo-oriented economy and horse-centered culture. At the time of his birth there were about 25,000 western Sioux who were represented at the large gathering of 10,000 Indians at the Fort Laramie treaty conference in 1851. This was the height of Teton Sioux power.

Little is known about Young Man Afraid of His Horse's youth except that he distinguished himself in the Platte River fight of 1865 and successfully participated in the great diplomatic triumph of the Sioux Treaty of 1868, which promised the Oglalas the Black Hills in perpetuity unless three-fourths of Sioux men voted in favor of abrogating it. One month after the conclusion of this treaty Young Man Afraid of His Horse was formally inducted as chief. In a ceremony for himself and four others (Crazy Horse, American Horse, He Dog, and Man That Owns Sword) the new chief was given a beaded buckskin outfit, an eagle feather, a pipe, and a tobacco bag. Young chiefs were chosen for their outspokenness, bravery, ambition, honesty, and kindness to all creatures. Young Man Afraid of His Horse inherited this warrior name, which is more accurately translated as "They Even Fear His Horse," from his father. The name indicated outstanding bravery, making enemies fear the mere sight of his horse.

By the late nineteenth century the Lakotas had become the romanticized and enduring stereotype of "wild Indians" wearing buckskins, engaging in constant warfare, and riding horses. Such images were immortalized by innumerable white artists, reporters, and fiction writers, and these Indians were depicted as heroes by traveling "Wild West shows" all over the eastern United States and Europe. Although never a participant of any Wild West show, Young Man Afraid of His Horse was such a "mounted warrior of the Great Plains." He also saw the cruel decline of his people's lifestyle.

Because of the decline of the buffalo herds and the discovery of gold resulting in the increasing numbers of whites in the Black Hills, the strength of the Sioux gradually withered. In 1874 General George Armstrong Custer and the Seventh Cavalry made an "expedition" into the Black Hills, officially still in possession of the Oglalas, and oversaw the ensuing gold rush. Meanwhile the United States began to assign Indians to reservations.

Never belligerent, Young Man Afraid of His Horse and his father became known among whites as friendly agency Indians, sometimes dubbed "progressives." Father and son continued to exert their influence on the reservation by mitigating more militant factions in order to prevent bloodshed of white officials and the excessive "punishment" by whites that would surely follow.

In October 1874 father and son rescued a company of twenty American soldiers under Lieutenant Emmet Crawford, who had constructed a fortified stockade against Oglala chief Red Cloud's express will. When hostile Indians attacked the soldiers on their way to the stockade, Young Man Afraid of His Horse and his father dissuaded the attackers from burning the stockade down and led a group of Indian police to escort the soldiers to safety.

In September 1875 Young Man Afraid of His Horse demonstrated his circumspect leadership when he prevented bloodshed involving a group of seven white treaty commissioners who angered the Sioux by trying to pressure them into selling the Black Hills. This botched negotiation drew thousands of Sioux warriors, with many making demonstrations of power and military strength. Crazy Horse's followers were most adamant in their opposition. Young Man Afraid of His Horse and a group of unofficial Indian police removed militant envoys of Crazy Horse and allowed the commissioners to reach safety at nearby Camp Robinson. The commission's scaled-down treaty offer for mineral rights in the Black Hills was rejected, yet peace was kept.

Following the unsuccessful 1875 treaty commission, the United States embarked on a crackdown focusing on the subjection of nonreservation Indians. However, all Indians, including agency Indians such as Young Man Afraid of His Horse, suffered. A new treaty was forced on the Red Cloud agency in 1877 (immediately after the embarrassing defeat of General Custer at the Little Bighorn) to relinquish the Black Hills and Powder River country. Of the original 2.5 million, only 43,000 square miles remained in Oglala hands (twentieth-century courts upheld the Sioux Treaty of 1868 and declared the taking of the Black Hills illegal).

In 1877 Young Man Afraid of His Horse was part of a delegation of Oglala chiefs (including Red Cloud, Spotted Tail, American Horse, He Dog, and Little Big Man) to see President Rutherford Hayes in Washington and protest the treaty, which was finalized without the required approval of three-fourths of the Oglala men.

Following the Treaty of 1877 American soldiers removed even agency Indians' guns and horses. Militant leaders such as Sitting Bull went into exile in Canada or were assassinated, like Crazy Horse. During this so-called war period of 1876 to 1881, many Oglalas in fact stayed on their reservations, including Young Man Afraid of His Horse.

There he was the leader of the "progressives," along with American Horse and other notable warriors of former days. Their way of life had changed dramatically. Oglala institutions such as warrior societies crumbled. They were replaced by official Indian police (headed by George Sword) and the personal abilities and ambitions of individual leaders such as Young Man Afraid of His Horse, who cooperated with Indian agents.

During the 1880s and 1890s the buffalo hunt disappeared completely, only halfheartedly replaced by the U.S. government's insistence that the Indians farm the sandy South Dakota soil in the area's harsh climate. Because of the government's emphasis on farming, few stock animals were raised by the Oglalas. Episcopal missionaries banned the Sun Dance and young men's vision quest, thereby stifling the Oglala's habits, activities, customs, and values. A new, syncretistic religion sprang up: originally from Nevada, the Ghost Dance movement (combining Indian and Christian religious symbols) was embraced by many disenchanted Sioux, some of whom saw it as a spiritual fortification for a final, victorious battle against whites. In 1889 Young Man Afraid of His Horse, American Horse, and four others warned Oglala Ghost Dancers that they were outnumbered by white soldiers and settlers. The chief tried to persuade Little Big Man's party to stay on the reservation, advice they failed to heed. White hysteria about the Ghost Dance movement resulted in the killing of Sitting Bull and the massacre at Wounded Knee in 1890.

Conditions on the Sioux reservations deteriorated. Indians were starving, and Indian agents even withheld rations as "punishment" for minor transgressions. In the spring of 1891 Young Man Afraid of His Horse traveled to Washington in a large delegation of Teton Sioux for a meeting with Commissioner of Indian Affairs Thomas J. Morgan. Morgan promised relief for their suffering, especially increased and better food rations.

Young Man Afraid of His Horse died of a heart attack on his way to visit the Crow Indians of Montana, near Edgemont, South Dakota, and Newcastle, Wyoming. Among Indians he was remembered as a wise and compassionate leader.

• Accounts of Young Man Afraid of His Horse and his participation in treaty negotiations are in Dee Brown, *Bury My Heart at Wounded Knee: An Indian History of the American West* (1971); Robert A. Clark, ed., *The Killing of Chief Crazy Horse* (1976); Alvin M. Josephy, Jr., *The Patriot Chiefs: A Chronicle of American Indian Resistance*, chap. 8 (1958); Edward Kadlecek and Mabell Kadlecek, *To Kill an Eagle: Indian Views on the Last Days of Crazy Horse* (1981); Robert H. Lowie, *Indians of the Plains* (1954); and Robert M. Utley, *The Indian Frontier of the American West, 1846–1890* (1984).

KATJA MAY

YOUNGS, John (baptized 10 Apr. 1623–12 Apr. 1698), political agitator and public official, was born at Southwold, England, the son of John Youngs, a Puritan minister, and Joan Herrington. Although forbidden to leave England in May 1637, the elder Youngs was in Salem, Massachusetts, with his family in December of that year and in the New Haven colony in 1638; in 1640 he founded the town of Southold at the east end of Long Island. The younger John Youngs acquired and developed land throughout Southold. In 1653 he married his stepsister, Mary Gardner, and they had five children. She died in 1689, and about 1691 he married Hannah (Wines) Tooker, a widow.

Several colonies, including New Netherland, New Haven, and Connecticut, claimed title to eastern Long Island. In 1654 Youngs attempted to raise a garrison at Southold in defiance of New Haven, which had denied him a voice in choosing his militia officers. At about the same time he tried to raise a force to attack New Netherland. This quixotic adventure resulted in his arrest by the Dutch as a pirate and bandit. He escaped but soon surrendered and was released under bond. Shortly thereafter he appeared at New Haven to apologize for his words and actions against that colony.

In 1656 he was engaged by the United Colonies of New England to sail Long Island Sound and prevent Narragansett Indians from crossing over and attacking Long Island Indians. He apparently had acquired some Algonquian language skills, being called to a meeting at Montauk in 1658 as interpreter.

Youngs, who resented interference by New Haven in Southold's local affairs, in 1661 reluctantly accepted office under New Haven as magistrate of Southold. A year later New Haven was absorbed into the soundly administered Connecticut, whose jurisdiction he accepted enthusiastically. The general assembly in 1662 called him a gentleman of quality, accepted him as deputy from Southold, and reappointed him as magistrate. He informed the English towns on western Long Island that Long Island was annexed to Connecticut, which elicited a sharp letter from New Netherland to Connecticut. In 1663 the Connecticut General Assembly appointed Youngs a commissioner for Southold and one of four magistrates for Long Island, another being Captain John Scott, the self-proclaimed president of Long Island. In January 1664 Scott, backed by Youngs's militia, rallied the western English towns to his cause of uniting the English towns of Long Island and exercising control of the Dutch ones, resulting in a confrontation with Dutch officials. An incidental brawl over the refusal by a Dutchman, the younger Marten Creiger, to take off his hat for the royal (English) flag led Youngs to threaten to burn some houses. Connecticut in May ordered the arrest of Scott for attempting to claim Long Island for the duke of York, despite having a commission to pursue Connecticut's interests there, but elected Youngs to the governor's council.

In August 1664 the King's "Commissioners for Setling Boundarys between Neighbouring Colonyes" conquered New Netherland with support from Captain Youngs and various New England militia. Youngs argued Connecticut's claim to Long Island but was unsuccessful, the commissioners awarding it to New

York. Nowhere did he indicate whether his antipathy toward New York was due to the government's Royalist origin, the established Church of England, or the duke of York's Catholicism, but all three are likely. Youngs was ordered to collect taxes on Long Island for New York, without result. New York governor Richard Nicolls doubted that Youngs was the organizer of this tax revolt: "I believe Capt. Young is a bad Instrument, but if I am not mistaken, hee hath not Braines to carry on such a businesse."

When a Dutch fleet reconquered New York in 1673, Youngs petitioned Connecticut to protect Southold from the Dutch and was appointed commissioner and magistrate. A year later, when New York, again an English colony, reclaimed eastern Long Island, Youngs petitioned Connecticut once more for protection. New York governor Edmund Andros summoned Youngs and forced him to submit. In 1676 he and six others accepted a new patent for Southold as a town within New York. Following Andros's departure for England, Deputy Governor Anthony Brockholes appointed Youngs high sheriff of Yorkshire (Long Island, Staten Island, and Westchester) in 1681, an office he held until the division of Yorkshire into five counties in 1683. Governor Thomas Dongan then appointed him to a commission to settle the boundary between New York and Connecticut and in 1684 promoted him to lieutenant colonel of a cavalry troop on Long Island.

He also was appointed, probably in 1683, to the Council of New York, which shared power with the governor. Living far from New York City, however, he seldom attended meetings, except when the agenda was of particular interest to eastern Long Island. Dongan attempted to remove him from the council in 1685, giving three reasons, none of them true: that he was very ancient, a person of no estate, and living 150 miles from New York City. Perhaps under pressure from London, Dongan reinstated Youngs in 1686. Youngs supplied Dongan with another excuse in 1687: ordered to send one-tenth of his militia to Albany to defend against invasion from French Canada, Youngs had sent men unfit for service, for which Dongan suspended him from the council.

Upon the fall of James II and the succession of William and Mary, government in New York collapsed. Jacob Leisler established an ad hoc administration that Southold and the rest of Suffolk County did not recognize. They sought once again to join Connecticut, which this time refused to intervene. Two years later Youngs was one of the judges who tried Leisler for treason and sentenced him to death.

Under royal instructions Governor Benjamin Fletcher (whose tenure ran from 1692 to 1698) appointed Youngs to his council. Within a year Fletcher had suspended Youngs as commander of Suffolk County militia for repeatedly neglecting to send reinforcements to defend Albany. Later reinstated, Youngs in 1695 again had to be prodded to send troops. Fletcher's successor, Lord Bellomont, was instructed to reappoint Youngs to the council. However,

Youngs died ten days after Bellomont's arrival (presumably in Southold). His tomb is in the cemetery of the First Presbyterian Church at Southold.

Youngs was an ardent supporter of Connecticut's rights to Long Island, hostile to New Haven over some perceived slights, and an implacable opponent of New York rule, whether Dutch or Anglican Royalist. He was apparently very popular in Southold and the rest of Suffolk County, and well regarded in Connecticut, none of which would have recommended him to the king, the duke of York, or New York's governors. Nevertheless, they valued his leadership abilities and intelligence and granted him numerous appointments. He is memorable as a central figure in the disputes between New York and Connecticut for territory, and between the Netherlands and England for trade, and as a representative of those Puritans who chose an American field to oppose royal authority in government and episcopal jurisdiction in church. Both admirers and detractors could agree that he was almost unswerving in his devotions, cooperative only when there was no other choice.

• Highly favorable articles appear in Epher Whitaker, *History of Southold, L.I.* (1881), and Selah Youngs, *Youngs Family* (1907). The principal documentary sources include the *New York Historical Manuscripts* series, begun in 1974 and continuing; E. B. O'Callaghan and Berthold Fernow, *Documents Relative to the Colonial History of the State of New York*, vols. 2–4 (1853–1858), and vol. 14 (1883); J. Wickham Case, ed., *Southold Town Records* (1882–1884); J. Hammond Trumbull, *The Public Records of the Colony of Connecticut*, vols. 1–2 (1850–1852); and C. J. Hoadly, ed., *Records of the Colony and Plantation of New Haven*, vol. 2 (1858). Unpublished manuscripts in the New York State Archives are described in E. B. O'Callaghan, ed., *Calendar of Historical Manuscripts*, vol. 2 (1866), and Berthold Fernow and A. J. F. van Laer, eds., *Calendar of Council Minutes, 1668–1783* (1902). Material in the Public Record Office, London, is described in J. W. Fortescue, *Calendar of State Papers, Colonial Series, America and West Indies*, vols. 12–13 (1899–1901).

PETER R. CHRISTOPH

YOUNT, George Concepción (4 May 1794–5 Oct. 1865), fur trapper and farmer, was born in Dowden Creek, North Carolina, the son of Jacob Yount and Amarilla (maiden name unknown), farmers. George's grandfather changed the family name from Jundt, its original German spelling, when he immigrated from Alsace in 1731. The Yount family moved often during George's early years and left North Carolina to settle eventually in the White River region of southwestern Missouri. Young George received no formal education but became well versed in frontier living. He fought in the War of 1812, after which he started his own farm. In 1818 he married Eliza Wilds from Kentucky. Ill feelings developed between Yount and his father-in-law after a neighbor took Yount's savings—his father-in-law believed him less than competent as a husband. In an effort to recoup his fortune and reputation, Yount joined a Santa Fe caravan as a teamster (the same caravan with which young runaway Kit Carson was traveling) and arrived in New Mexico in the fall of 1826.

That same fall, Yount joined Ewing Young's trapping expedition to the Gila and Salt rivers. The party included not only Young but other noteworthy figures such as Milton Sublette, Thomas L. "Peg Leg" Smith, James Ohio Pattie, and Michel (Miguel) Robidoux. The party had confrontations with both the Papago and Mojave Indians, and some trappers were killed. Yount continued trapping with Young on the Colorado River, near the Grand Canyon, and on to the river's headwaters. While in the central Rockies, the expedition crossed the Continental Divide near Long's Peak. The party then pushed south and arrived back in Taos, New Mexico, only to witness the confiscation of their year's work by the Mexican governor, Manuel Armijo, who harbored a great distaste for Americans.

The next fall (1827) Yount organized his own venture to trap the lower Gila River. Yount's party joined forces with Sylvester Pattie, but the joint venture suffered internal conflict, leading ultimately to its division. Pattie's group pushed on to California. Yount's detachment trapped the Colorado River down to its delta and then back up the river to the Mojave villages. The Mojave had recently destroyed part of Jedediah Smith's brigade, and they forced Yount to leave. Yount quickly turned toward Taos via the Hopi and Zuni villages. Yount earned enough from his furs at Taos to pay his debts and organize another venture for the coming fall hunt.

Yount's new expedition headed north out of Taos to the middle branches of the Colorado. He trapped the Green River and then pushed farther north to the Great Salt Lake, where his party survived one of the worst winters on record. Extreme snow depths thwarted travel and forced the party to winter in Bear Valley in present-day Idaho. After winter's thaw Yount's party remained in the region to trap through the year (1829) and spent the following winter in the same vicinity.

Yount returned to Taos in the spring of 1830. There he learned from notices in the Missouri papers that his wife had divorced him. While at Taos he also combined forces with William Wolfskill as joint leaders of a trapping expedition bound for California in the fall. The party pioneered the route known as the Old Spanish Trail, linking Santa Fe with Los Angeles.

In California, Yount initially turned to hunting sea otters near Santa Barbara and around Santa Cruz Island but soon settled down on the land. While visiting Sonoma he made himself a useful hand to the missionaries and the local authority, General Mariano Guadalupe Vallejo. His assistance secured for him a large land grant near the head of Napa Valley. Legal title to the land, however, required Mexican citizenship and conversion to the Catholic faith. He received the baptismal name George de la Concepción Yount, though he rarely used his middle name. As a Mexican citizen and landowner he assisted in the defense of the northern frontier by participating in a punitive expedition

against the "Jota" band in Pope Valley, where he narrowly escaped death.

Back at his Napa ranch Yount built an impressive Kentucky-style house. He constructed a sawmill and a flour mill—the first of their kind in the region. He raised stock, grew grain, and became a well-respected vineyardist as well as a pioneer fruit and berry farmer. George Yount became the first American developer in the Napa Valley.

Yount took no part in California's Bear Flag revolt against Mexico, but he continued to hold the respect of the local American settlers. His home became a place of refuge for weary hunters and settlers, including survivors of the Donner Party tragedy. Many believed he helped expedite the rescue of that fated party when snowbound in the Sierra Nevada. In 1855 Yount was remarried, to Mrs. Eliza Gashwiler, who helped manage his growing business affairs. The influx of settlers, however, brought problems for Yount. Squatters invaded his land, thieves stole stock and fruit, and the primitive legal system in place offered little redress.

George C. Yount died at his ranch. He was in the vanguard of the American expansion into the Southwest and California. The town of Yountville, California, carries his name. A prominent man of that community, he donated the plot for the Yountville cemetery and contributed much to the area's growth. Of all the celebrated pioneers of Napa Valley and Sonoma, Yount must be recognized as first and foremost.

• The most complete work on Yount's life remains his own memoirs dictated to the Reverend Orange Clark in the 1850s and later edited by Charles L. Camp in "The Chronicles of George C. Yount," *California Historical Society Quarterly* 2 (1923): 2–66, and still later published in book form as *George C. Yount and His Chronicles of the West* (1966). Camp also wrote a short biographical essay on Yount for Le Roy Hafen, *The Mountain Men and the Fur Trade of the Far West*, vol. 9 (1972), pp. 411–20. Yount's involvement in opening the Spanish trail is best detailed in Hafen, *Old Spanish Trail* (1954), pp. 139–53. The best overall examination of the southwest fur trade and Yount's involvement in it is David J. Weber, *The Taos Trappers: The Fur Trade in the Far Southwest, 1540–1846* (1971).

S. MATTHEW DESPAIN

YOURCENAR, Marguerite (8 June 1903–17 Dec. 1987), author, was born Marguerite Antoinette Jeanne Marie Ghislaine Cleenewerck de Crayencour in Brussels, Belgium, the daughter of Michel de Crayencour and Fernande de Cartier de Marchienne, both members of wealthy and influential families. Her Belgian mother died shortly after childbirth and Marguerite inherited the French citizenship of her father, who assumed responsibility for her upbringing. She was raised at "Mont-Noir," the family home near Lille, and traveled extensively as a child between Paris and the south of France. Her education was supervised at home by her father, who encouraged Marguerite at an early age to pursue her literary interests. In 1921 he arranged for the private publication of her first book,

Le Jardin des chimères, a dramatic adaptation of the Icarus legend. This was followed a year later by a collection of poems, *Les Dieux ne sont pas morts*. Her father also assisted in the invention of her anagrammatical pseudonym, which in 1947 she adopted as her legal name.

After her father's death when Yourcenar was twenty-four, she decided to devote herself exclusively to travel, study, and literature. She began to contribute poetry and critical essays to a variety of literary periodicals and in 1929 published her first novel, *Alexis; ou, Le Traité du vain combat*, revised in 1965 and translated as *Alexis* in 1984, which earned for her critical as well as popular attention. This was followed by a second novel in 1931, *La nouvelle Eurydice*. Her emerging literary reputation was further enhanced by the publication in 1934 of *Denier du rêve*, revised and expanded in 1959 and translated in 1982 as *A Coin in Nine Hands*. Set amidst the rise of Fascism in prewar Italy, the novel is atypical of Yourcenar's fiction in utilizing a contemporary setting and an ensemble cast rather than a single, dominant protagonist. It is nonetheless characteristic of thematic concerns that accentuate Yourcenar's distinct artistic vision, notably the exploration of self, the mystery of human emotion, and the fusion of dream and reality.

Following the favorable reception of *Denier du rêve* and illustrative of her versatility as a writer, Yourcenar published a sequence of lyrical prose pieces titled *Feux* in 1936, revised in 1974 and translated as *Fires* in 1981; a collection of short stories, *Nouvelles orientales*, in 1938, revised in 1963 and 1975 and translated as *Oriental Tales* in 1985; and a novel titled *Le Coup de grâce* in 1939, translated in 1957 as *Coup de Grâce*. Having completed the novel while living in Italy, Yourcenar returned to Paris shortly before the outbreak of World War II. Disheartened by the imminent invasion of France, Yourcenar left Europe for the United States at the invitation of Grace Frick, an American friend who would become her lifelong companion. The decade that followed was disappointing artistically for Yourcenar; compelled by economic necessity, she turned to translating and teaching as a means to earn her livelihood. In 1942, while living in Hartford, Connecticut, Yourcenar and Frick began to summer in Maine, where in 1950 they purchased what became their permanent residence in Northeast Harbor, on Mount Desert Island. It was during this time, in 1947, that Yourcenar became a naturalized U.S. citizen.

The turning point of Yourcenar's literary career was her decision to resume work on a character study of the Roman Emperor Hadrian, a creative impulse that evolved into *Mémoires d'Hadrien*, published in 1951 and translated as *Memoirs of Hadrian* in 1954, the novel generally acknowledged to be her most significant achievement. Described by Yourcenar as "a psychological novel and meditation on history," *Memoirs of Hadrian* was the first of Yourcenar's works to be published in the United States. Written in the form of a letter to his adopted grandson and future heir, Marcus Aurelius, the novel explores the boundaries of human experience, allowing the protagonist to ruminate on the circumstances of his life while confronting the inevitability of death. In composing what constitutes a self-analytical autobiography as well as a philosophical treatise, Hadrian is addressing his own mortality while orchestrating the transfer of authority and experience. As noted by Louis Auchincloss in the *New York Times Book Review* the importance of the novel "lies in the sense conveyed of the essential loneliness of the man who has gained the supreme power and learned to use it humanely" (10 Jan. 1988).

The critical reception of *Memoirs of Hadrian* established Yourcenar as an author of international stature. This was solidified by the publication in 1968 of *L'Oeuvre au noir*, translated as *The Abyss* in 1976. Similar in context and methodology to *Memoirs of Hadrian*, *L'Oeuvre au noir* is set in northern Europe in the mid-sixteenth century. The protagonist of the novel is the fictitious Zeno, a physician-alchemist-philosopher in search of enlightenment in an age dominated by repression. Inviting comparison to Hadrian, Zeno was described by Frank Kermode in the *New York Review of Books* as "the second deity in this author's cult of the full man, endlessly inquiring, ever skeptical, considerate of the body as of the spirit, of the future as well as the present" (14 Oct. 1976).

The death of Grace Frick after a long illness in 1979 was a tremendous personal loss for Yourcenar. Her companion for over fifty years, Frick was both a source of creative inspiration to Yourcenar and her collaborator, translating all of her major works into English. It was shortly after Frick's death that Yourcenar's nomination for membership to the Académie Française was proposed by Jean d'Ormesson, novelist and former editor of *Le Figaro*. Although her nomination generated heated debate over admission of a woman to the all-male institution, she was elected on 6 March 1980 and inducted on 22 January 1981. Largely the result of becoming France's first *académicienne*, the demand for her work in the United States prompted publication in English of her earlier fiction as well as *Comme l'eau qui coule* (1982), translated as *Two Lives and a Dream* (1987). In addition, her early collection of criticism *Sous bénéfice d'inventaire* (1962), was translated as *The Dark Brain of Piranesi and Other Essays* (1984). This was followed in 1986 by *Mishima: A Vision of the Void*, first published in 1980 as *Mishima, ou la vision du vide*, a critical study of the Japanese writer Yukio Mishima. A second collection of criticism, originally published in 1983 as *Le Temps, ce grand sculpteur*, was translated as *That Mighty Sculptor, Time* and published in Great Britain in 1987 and in the United States in 1992. *Souvenirs pieux*, the first volume of her semi-autobiographical work titled "Le Labyrinthe du monde," was published in 1973 and translated as *Dear Departed* in 1991. The second volume, *Archives du Nord*, was published in 1977 and translated as *How Many Years* in 1995, and the final volume, published in 1988 as *Quoi? l'Eternité*, was left unfinished.

The recipient of numerous honors throughout her career, Yourcenar was elected to the Académie Royale Belge de Langue et Littérature Françaises and the American Academy of Arts and Letters. In France, she was awarded the Prix Femina-Vacaresco for *Mémoires d'Hadrien*, the Prix Combat, the Prix Femina for *L'Oeuvre au noir*, the Grand Prix National des Lettres from the French Ministry of Culture, and the Grand Prix de l'Académie Française. She won the prestigious Erasmus Award in 1983 and in 1986 received both the National Arts Club's Medal of Honor for Literature and the Medal of the Commander of the French Legion of Honor.

Yourcenar enjoyed a prolific and diversified career and as the first woman to be inducted into the Académie Française is ensured a lasting legacy as an author. She possessed a unique and enduring artistic voice. Merging the past with the present, her fiction evokes a sense of agelessness as well as timely significance. She died at her home in Northeast Harbor, on Mount Desert Island, Maine. In response to the announcement of her death, Roger W. Straus, the president and chief executive officer of her American publisher, Farrar, Straus and Giroux, issued a statement that assessed the magnitude of her achievement, "Marguerite Yourcenar was without question or doubt one of the great writers of the twentieth century. She is a great loss to the literary community, but her words will be read and remembered forever."

• A selection of Yourcenar's letters, manuscripts, and memorabilia is in the library of Bowdoin College, Brunswick, Maine; some of her correspondence with Natalie Barney is in the Bibliothèque Littéraire Jacques Doucet in Paris; the remaining correspondence is in the Houghton Library, Harvard University. The first full-length biography is Josyane Savigneau, *Marguerite Yourcenar: Inventing a Life* (1993), first published as *Marguerite Yourcenar: l'invention d'une vie* in 1990. The most complete critical assessment is Joan E. Howard, *From Violence to Vision: Sacrifice in the Works of Marguerite Yourcenar* (1992). See also C. Frederick Farrell and Edith R. Farrell, *Marguerite Yourcenar in Counterpoint* (1983), and Deborah Trustman, "France's First Woman 'Immortal,'" *New York Times Magazine*, 18 Jan. 1981, pp. 18–22, 24–25, 42, 44. An obituary is in the *New York Times*, 19 Dec. 1987.
STEVEN R. SERAFIN

YULEE, David Levy (12 June 1810–10 Oct. 1886), politician and businessman, was born David Levy on St. Thomas in the Virgin Islands, the son of Moses Elias Levy, a timber dealer and merchant, and Hannah Abendanone. The young Levy studied at the Norfolk Academy in Virginia but was forced in 1827 to move to Florida, where his father had acquired large tracts of land in hopes of founding an agricultural colony for European Jews. The elder Levy had decided his children should support themselves, a condition apparently met by his son's taking up residence on a plantation the father owned in Micanopy. David Levy subsequently read law in St. Augustine and, after being admitted to the bar in 1832, practiced there for several years.

By the mid-1830s the young lawyer had entered territorial politics. He was elected to Florida's legislative council in 1836 and to its constitutional convention in 1838. A Jacksonian Democrat, he did battle with the banks, opposing the support and privileges the territorial government had extended to certain institutions. Levy's hostility to government activism of that sort did not prevent him, as territorial delegate to Congress in 1841, from seeking federal funding for river and harbor improvement and railroad surveys in Florida. After Florida became a state in 1845, Levy was elevated by the legislature to the U.S. Senate, thus becoming America's first Jewish senator. He did not remain Jewish for very long, though. After marrying Nancy Wickliffe in 1846, a union that produced at least three children, he converted to Christianity (though he remained the subject of anti-Semitic slurs). The same year he changed his name to David Levy Yulee, adopting a name his Moroccan forebears had used.

In the Senate, Yulee continued to solicit federal aid for Florida, ranging from grants of public land to the sponsorship of exploration in the Everglades. He also backed the acquisition of Cuba by the United States. However, he refused to countenance any exercise of federal power that might encroach on the prerogatives of southern slaveholders. Yulee himself prospered as a planter through the 1840s and 1850s, and by the end of that period he had about eighty slaves on his sugarcane plantation near Homosassa. Willing to contemplate secession from a Union his state had only recently joined (with his ardent support), he declared against restrictions on slaveholding in the territories, even restrictions that might arise under the doctrine of popular sovereignty. In the tortured deliberations in 1850 over disposition of the land won from Mexico, Yulee was prepared to yield only to the extent of extending to the Pacific the Missouri Compromise line that divided slave from free. He opposed California's admission as a free state and the abolition of the slave trade in the District of Columbia, while voting for the Fugitive Slave Laws.

Many Floridians were more enthusiastic about the Compromise of 1850 than was Yulee, but disenchantment with his states' rights militancy does not entirely explain his failure to be returned to the Senate the following year. Yulee fell victim not only to his Whig opposition but also to the parochial enmities that his interest in building a railroad across northern Florida had generated among Democrats from South Florida and those allied with rival transportation interests. Yulee chartered the Florida Railroad in 1853, intending to build a transpeninsular line that by means of steamship connections at Tampa and Cedar Key would channel the trade of the Mississippi Valley, the Gulf of Mexico, and even the Pacific (via the Central American isthmus) through Florida to Fernandina, a town on the Atlantic coast north of Jacksonville. Yulee secured generous government aid for his private enterprise, including state guarantees of company bonds, tax exemptions, vast federal land grants, and mail contracts. Even so, Yulee had to turn an increasing share of his road over to Yankee businessmen to secure adequate financing. Only in 1861 was the 155-mile line completed—chiefly by slave labor—between Fernandina and Cedar Key (to Tampans' distress, Yulee's railroad did not reach them).

In the meantime, with Democrats resurgent in Florida in the wake of the Kansas-Nebraska Act, Yulee returned to the Senate in 1855. Perhaps because of his dependence on northern capital and his ambitions for a far-flung trading empire, he behaved with more circumspection in regard to sectional issues during his second term. Yulee supported Stephen Douglas's candidacy late into the campaign of 1860, implying that he was willing to accept the proposition that settlers themselves might effectively bar slavery from their territories. After Abraham Lincoln's election, Yulee seemed to blow hot and cold on secession; his more heated statements, however, attracted more attention. He resigned from the Senate in January 1861 after Florida left the Union. Once war had begun, Yulee did not seem willing to invest much in the Confederate effort. He fought a protracted battle to keep the authorities from using iron from his railroad to construct lines that might be more militarily useful after Fernandina had fallen into Union hands. He also haggled with Confederate officials who confiscated sugar grown on his plantation.

Though not a model Confederate citizen, Yulee was held by federal authorities at Fort Pulaski for almost a year after the war ended because he had recommended, early in the secession crisis, the seizure of federal installations in Florida. Eager to get back to the business of railroading in the company of Yankee investors, he nevertheless counseled sectional reconciliation (though he seems not to have been entirely reconciled to black freedom, being of the opinion that some system would have to be substituted for slavery to again compel black people to work). He was courted by conservative Republicans but remained a Democrat, never again holding elective office but intruding into the political arena as necessary to protect his interests. He was well served through Reconstruction and afterward by both Democratic and Republican officials. Tattered by warfare and unable to meet its obligations, Yulee's railroad was sold by the state in 1866; the buyers, however, were the existing ownership, thus relieving the company of financial burdens while keeping Yulee and his associates in control. This transaction eventually involved the state in litigation with the company's injured creditors. Transpeninsular service was reestablished, shipping connections made with New Orleans, Mobile, and Havana, and track extended toward Tampa. Nevertheless, Yulee's road—reorganized in 1872 as the Atlantic, Gulf and West India Transit Railway Company—never made a profit for him, owing to competition from other Gulf shippers and Jacksonville rivals as well as a sour economy. Yulee increasingly concentrated on marketing the real estate he had accumulated, although he remained on the board of what became the Florida Transit Railway when it came under the control of British financiers in 1881. That same year, Yulee moved to Washington, D.C. He died in New York City five years later.

• There is a large collection of Yulee papers at the P. K. Yonge Library of Florida History at the University of Florida at Gainesville and a smaller one at the American Jewish Historical Society, Waltham, Mass. For treatments of Yulee's career, see Arthur W. Thompson, "David Yulee: A Study of Nineteenth Century American Thought and Enterprise" (Ph.D. diss., Columbia Univ., 1954), and Joseph Gary Adler, "The Public Career of Senator David Levy Yulee" (Ph.D. diss., Case Western Reserve Univ., 1973). There is also useful material in Arthur W. Thompson, *Jacksonian Democracy on the Florida Frontier* (1961); Jerrell Shofner, *Nor Is It Over Yet: Florida in the Era of Reconstruction, 1863–1877* (1974); Edward C. Williamson, *Florida Politics in the Gilded Age, 1877–1893* (1976); Charlton W. Tebeau, *A History of Florida* (1971); Robert L. Clarke, "The Florida Railroad Company in the Civil War," *Journal of Southern History* 19 (1953): 180–92; and Dudley S. Johnson, "The Florida Railroad after the Civil War," *Florida Historical Quarterly* 47 (1968–1969): 292–309. On Yulee's family background, see Joseph Gary Adler, "Moses Elias Levy and Attempts to Colonize Florida," in *Jews of the South*, ed. Samuel Proctor et al. (1984), pp. 17–29.

PATRICK G. WILLIAMS

YUNG Wing (17 Nov. 1828–21 Apr. 1912), educator and diplomat, was born near Macao, China, the son of Yung Ming-kun and Lin Lien-tai. He was educated in schools that had been established by western missionaries in Macao and Hong Kong. In 1847 Yung's teacher Samuel Robbins Brown brought him and two other Chinese students to the United States, where their education continued at Monson Academy near Springfield, Massachusetts. He entered Yale and in 1854 became the first Chinese person to graduate from an American college. During his seven years in the United States he became a Christian and an American citizen. But the biblical text, "If any provide not for his own, and specially for those of his own house, he hath denied the faith, and is worse than an infidel" (1 Tim. 5:8), haunted him, and he resolved to devote most of his life to the modernization of China.

Yung returned to China in 1854 and became a protégé of the important regional leader Zeng Guofan. Zeng sent him to the United States to purchase machine tools to equip a modern Chinese arsenal. While there he volunteered for the Union army but was not accepted. Upon his return to China with the equipment, he was given an appointment in the Chinese bureaucracy even though he had neither a traditional Confucian education nor taken the imperial examinations based upon it. In 1870 he proposed that a number of young Chinese men be sent to the West for education, a project he had conceived while at Yale. The resulting Chinese Educational Mission, established in 1872, sent thirty teenagers a year to the United States for four successive years. The students were to study in America for fifteen years, be allowed to travel for another two years, and then return to serve China. Yung, who was second in command of the mission, first established it in Springfield and later in Hartford,

Connecticut. But the educational mission was opposed from the start by cultural conservatives in China and was aborted in 1881. In the meantime Yung had become a Chinese diplomat, serving as assistant minister to the United States between 1875 and 1881, and in that capacity had written a harshly condemnatory report on the coolie trade that was conducted with Peru. In 1875 he married an American, Mary Louise Kellogg; they had two children.

After 1881 Yung traveled extensively and was involved in a number of unconsummated Sino-American ventures, including a railway company, and at one time had the Gatling gun concession for all of China. In 1898, when he sought the assistance of the American minister to China, that official was instructed by Secretary of State John Sherman (1823–1900) that the State Department "does not feel that it can properly recognize [Yung] as a citizen of the United States." Despite the Chinese Exclusion Act, Yung returned to the United States in 1902. He died in Hartford and is buried there. His autobiography, *My Life in China and America* (1909; repr. 1978), a detailed account of his educational and political experience, is the first autobiography of a Chinese American published in English.

• Yung's papers, at Yale's Sterling Library, are available on microfilm. There is no biography of Yung. The best account is Edmund H. Worthy, Jr., "Yung Wing in America," *Pacific Historical Review* 39 (1985): 265–87. For a contemporary Chinese view, see William Hung, "Huang Tsun-hsien's Poem 'The Closure of the Educational Mission in America,'" *Harvard Journal of Asiatic Studies* 18 (1955): 50–73. Y. C. Wang, *Chinese Intellectuals and the West, 1872–1949* (1966), examines the education of Chinese in several western countries including the United States. Also useful is the chapter on Yung Wing in K. Scott Wong, "Encountering the Other: Chinese Immigration and Its Impact on Chinese and American Worldviews. 1875–1905" (Ph.D. diss., Univ. of Michigan, 1992).

ROGER DANIELS

YURKA, Blanche (18 June 1887–6 June 1974), actress, was born in St. Paul, Minnesota, the daughter of Anton Jurka, a teacher, and Karolina Novak. When she was thirteen, the Jurka family (she later changed the spelling of her last name for professional reasons) left St. Paul because her father had taken a position with the Czech Benevolent Society. As a child, perhaps influenced by her father's enthusiasm for theater, Yurka became interested in the world of the stage.

In New York Yurka began singing lessons and soon decided on a career in opera. She made her debut in 1901 singing the lead in the Czech Sokol Singing Society's production of *The Bohemian Girl*. She was awarded a two-year scholarship (1903–1905) to the Metropolitan Opera School; however, her voice, strained by overuse, did not develop properly, and the scholarship was not renewed. Deeply disappointed but determined, between 1905 and 1907 Yurka pursued her dream at the Institute of Musical Art (now the Juilliard School of Music). Again her injured voice failed her,

and she was advised to focus her dramatic talents on a career in the theater.

After months of fruitless knocking on Broadway doors (during which she earned $5 each Sunday singing at St. Bartholomew's Church under choirmaster Leopold Stokowski), Yurka finally was signed by David Belasco in 1907 as a general understudy at $25 per week. A few weeks later she had a walk-on role in *Grand Army Man*; eventually there were small parts in *The Warrens of Virginia* (1907) and *An Old New Yorker* (1911) and a lead in a comedy, *Is Matrimony a Failure?* (1909). These were followed by long periods of no work at all. Learning her craft, she took roles in summer stock and road companies. A commitment to acting took over her life. Gradually her efforts and talent were rewarded with increasingly important roles. Yurka played everything from light comedy to Shakespeare to Greek tragedy. She was Gertrude to John Barrymore's Hamlet, the nurse to Katharine Cornell's Juliet. She played in *Goat Song* (1926) with the Lunts, *The Squall* (1926), *Lysistrata* (1930), *Electra* (1932), *Jane Eyre* (1958), *The Corn Is Green* (1961), and *Dinner at Eight* (1966).

Her interpretations of Henrik Ibsen characters became legendary, particularly Hedda in *Hedda Gabler* (1929), which she also directed and about which *New York Times* critic Brooks Atkinson wrote, "Miss Yurka is an actress of great depth of emotion blessed with a voice of almost eerie timbre." Her universally acclaimed portrayal of Gina in *The Wild Duck* (1925) was praised by *New York Tribune* critic Percy Hammond: "But the best performance is probably that of Blanche Yurka as the patient, ageless Gina. It dominates the whole piece, even in the moments when she is not on stage."

Over her long career, Yurka appeared in more than sixty roles on Broadway, in stock, and on the road. She made twenty-one films, among them *A Tale of Two Cities* (1935), in which her Madame Defarge was widely acclaimed and about which she said, "I never had another picture to equal it." Some of her other films were *Escape* (1940), *Keeper of the Flame* (1942), *The Song of Bernadette* (1943), and *The Bridge of San Luis Rey* (1944). She also played in a number of television productions, including "Alice in Wonderland" (1954).

Yurka created a repertory of one-woman programs based on scenes from great plays and performed in cities and towns from Maine to Hawaii from 1935 to 1938 and again in 1959. She played in *Prometheus Bound* at the 1957 Greek Drama Festival in Athens, marking the first time an American actress had appeared on the 2,000-year-old Herod-Atticus stage.

Yurka also lectured and wrote about theater. Her book, *Dear Audience: A Guide to the Enjoyment of Theatre* (1959), shares her "thrills, excitement and moving experiences during a lifetime of theatre on both sides of the curtain." She was an organizer and outspoken member of Actor's Equity. As an early enthusiast for a national theater in the United States, she was involved in the founding of the American National Theatre (ANTA) and served as a director for many years.

In 1970 Yurka produced and starred in a revival of *The Madwoman of Chaillot* at the Sokol Theatre, where she had made her New York stage debut in *The Bohemian Girl* some seventy years earlier. On closing night she announced her retirement, bringing her stage life full circle. The same year Yurka wrote her autobiography, *Bohemian Girl*. In the book's afterword, Brooks Atkinson commented on her particular significance as an actress: "It is because of thoughtful interpretations and sensitive performances that Blanche Yurka is and always has been a total actress. . . . her commitment to the theatre remained total . . . giving the public a good performance takes precedence over everything."

Yurka was honored by Actor's Equity with an honorary life membership on its council, and ANTA awarded her its Anniversary Award, a gold medal given only once every five years. Yurka married actor Ian Keith in 1922; they had no children. The couple separated in 1925 and were divorced in 1928. Yurka died in New York City.

• The Billy Rose Theatre Collection and the Robinson Locke Scrapbooks in the New York Public Library for the Performing Arts, Lincoln Center, include important sources of historical and critical material from newspapers, periodicals, and playbills. There is also a file on her in the Harvard University Theatre Collection. Articles on Yurka include Louis Sheaffer's interview in the *New York Times*, 6 Nov. 1955; a review in *Opera News*, 3 Apr. 1971, pp. 12–13; and Arthur William Row, "A Star Who Is a Luminary," *Poet Love* (Spring 1928): 132–33. *Contemporary Authors* (1965) provides helpful details. Obituaries in the *New York Times*, 7 June 1974, and *Variety*, 12 June 1974, are also useful.

ADELE S. PARONI

Z

ZABLOCKI, Clement John (18 Nov. 1912–3 Dec. 1983), congressman, was born in Milwaukee, Wisconsin, the son of Matthew Zablocki, a laborer, and Mary Jankowski. Zablocki's parents were immigrants from Poland, and he grew up on Milwaukee's predominantly Polish south side. He earned a bachelor of philosophy degree from Marquette University in 1936 and did graduate work in education at that institution. After college he taught high school and worked as a church organist and choir director. In 1937 he married Blanche M. Janic, with whom he had two children.

Zablocki, a Democrat, entered politics at the state level. In 1942 he won election to the Wisconsin Senate from the Third District, and he was reelected in 1946. In 1948 he defeated Republican John C. Brophy for Wisconsin's Fourth Congressional District seat. His election that year was one of many that contributed to the rejuvenation of the Democratic party in Wisconsin. When Zablocki entered Congress, he was one of only two Democrats in Wisconsin's eleven-member congressional delegation, but by the time of his death the Democrats held a majority. Congressman Zablocki aspired to even higher office. After the death of Wisconsin senator Joseph R. McCarthy in 1957, Zablocki sought the Democratic nomination for McCarthy's vacated seat. In the Democratic primary, William Proxmire defeated him handily, although Zablocki won Milwaukee and Portage counties, both of which contained considerable Polish populations.

On his arrival in Washington, D.C., in 1949, Zablocki was assigned to the House Foreign Affairs Committee, where he remained throughout his congressional career. Between 1955 and 1969 he chaired the House Subcommittee on Asian and Pacific Affairs and became a widely recognized expert in East Asian affairs. He traveled extensively throughout the region and edited a scholarly book, *Sino-Soviet Rivalry: Implications for U.S. Policy* (1966), which included essays by notables such as Zbigniew K. Brzezinski, Bernard B. Fall, and George F. Kennan.

Zablocki became known for his strong anti-Communist views and was one of the most prominent Cold War hawks in the Congress. He often gave speeches in Polish over Voice of America radio and was a defender of Nationalist China. The congressman was also a staunch supporter of America's war effort in Vietnam during both the Lyndon B. Johnson and Richard Nixon administrations. By the early 1970s his support for the war led to some disgruntlement in his district but never put his political career in serious jeopardy. "I think my constituents are a little more conservative than some of my Democratic colleagues," he once said. "They're supportive of a strong national defense and are fiercely anti-Communist, and in that respect I reflect their views to a T."

Zablocki was a strong advocate of congressional participation in foreign affairs. In 1962, for example, he sponsored the Berlin Resolution, a reaffirmation of U.S. determination to protect West Berlin, stating, "The only voice that has not yet been heard on this issue is the voice of the U.S. Congress." Perhaps Zablocki's most notable legacy was his House sponsorship of the 1973 War Powers Act, a measure designed to increase congressional influence in foreign affairs by limiting the president's claimed authority to deploy military forces overseas. Congress overrode President Nixon's veto to enact the measure, and presidents from Nixon onward proclaimed the law to be an intrusion into their constitutional powers. However, in the law's first major test, the 1983 peacekeeping operation in Lebanon, Zablocki negotiated a compromise with President Ronald Reagan that set a time limit on the mission, forcing the president to acknowledge, albeit tacitly, the validity of the legislation.

During his years on the Foreign Affairs Committee, Zablocki gained a reputation for seeking a bipartisan consensus on foreign policy, an increasingly difficult task in the years during and after the Vietnam War. In 1977 Zablocki was elected chair of the House Foreign Affairs Committee, despite opposition from liberals who opposed his hawkish positions on foreign policy issues.

In domestic affairs, Zablocki also reflected the concerns of his blue-collar Democratic constituency. A strong supporter of labor unions, he favored increased funding for education and veterans' benefits but voted against busing to achieve racial integration in schools. Zablocki also favored prayer in school and vehemently denounced pornography. His domestic record suited his constituents, reflected in his winning eighteen consecutive terms to Congress, more than any previous congressional representative in Wisconsin history. At the time of his death, only two other House members had more seniority.

Zablocki was a key player in U.S. diplomatic history during the Cold War. He personified the ethnic, working-class Cold War hawk but was also a learned expert in East Asian affairs. The *Milwaukee Journal* described him as "a kielbasa man, but a caviar man, too." Zablocki died in Washington, D.C.

• Prior to his death, Zablocki bequeathed his papers to his alma mater, Marquette University. A helpful biographical sketch of Zablocki is Margaret Carpenter's *Clement J. Zablocki: Democratic Representative from Wisconsin* (1972) in the Ralph Nader Congress Project's Citizens Look at Congress series. For more on his role in Wisconsin politics, see Richard C. Haney, "A History of the Democratic Party of Wisconsin since World War Two" (Ph.D. diss., Univ. of Wisconsin, 1970); Stephen Leahy, "Polonia's Child: The Public Life of Clement J. Zablocki" (Ph.D. diss., Marquette Univ., 1994); and William F. Thompson, *The History of Wisconsin*, vol. 6: *Continuity and Change, 1940–1965* (1988). Aside from congressional proceedings and articles in Milwaukee area newspapers, little has been written about Zablocki's thirty-four years in Congress, though his name appears in the indexes of numerous scholarly works on Cold War diplomacy and politics, especially where Asia is concerned. On the Berlin Resolution, see *Congressional Quarterly's Guide to Congress*, 4th ed. (1991). For Zablocki's role and influence in the War Powers Act and its subsequent application, see "Controversy over the War Powers Act," *Congressional Quarterly* 62 (Nov. 1983); Michael Rubner, "The Reagan Administration, the 1973 War Powers Resolution, and the Invasion of Grenada," *Political Science Quarterly* 100 (Winter 1985–1986); and U.S. Congress, House Committee on Foreign Affairs, *The War Powers Resolution: A Special Study of the Committee of Foreign Affairs* (1982). A comprehensive yet concise obituary is in the *New York Times*, 4 Dec. 1983.

MARK D. VAN ELLS

ZACCHINI, Hugo (20 Oct. 1898–20 Oct. 1975), circus daredevil, was born in Peru, the son of Idebrando Zacchini and Nina Dal Paos, Italian circus performers. Zacchini was born while his family was on tour, and he and his eight siblings performed in the circus, most of them, eventually, as human cannonballs. The oldest son, Edmundo, was first a famous clown, known throughout Italy and North Africa as *Pagniotta* or "Little Loaf of Bread." That was before his father told him about an act he envisioned in which an acrobat would be catapulted by some sort of mechanism onto a trapeze. While serving in the Italian army during World War I, Edmundo was haunted by his father's dream and eventually conceived of a person being shot from a cannon. Upon his return to the family circus after the war, Edmundo was commissioned by his father to build such a device. It was to have debuted in Cairo, in November 1922, but in a test flight Edmundo's leg was shattered to such an extent that he remained physically handicapped for the rest of his life.

Undaunted, Edmundo perfected the design of his mechanism while recuperating. When the revised cannon was ready, Hugo volunteered as the new cannonball. Edmundo was within view nearby as an example of what could happen if the cannon misfired, and more than a little foolhardiness was obviously required of the next man to insert himself into the cannon's mouth. Hugo was just such a person. He, too, had served in the Italian army during the war, where also he volunteered for the most dangerous duty, the Arditi, an assault unit known as *La Squandra de la Morte* (The Death Squadron).

Although Hugo survived the test shot without injury, all agreed that further modifications in the cannon were required. It was at this time, however, that the family circus fell on hard times, and a lack of funds prevented Edmundo from completing his work. The original cannon was abandoned in Barcelona in 1924 when the family was unable to pay its transportation costs. Two years later, once again on a sound financial basis, the family chose to construct a new cannon rather than rebuild their circus. When the second cannon was ready, the act was offered to the directors of Spain's Olympia Circus, who rejected it and dismissed Edmundo as a lunatic. The only solution was for the Zacchinis to put together a circus of their own once again, featuring the Great Hugo being shot from a cannon.

The act caused such a sensation that offers began pouring in from all over the world. With much improved finances, a third cannon was readied, one that could shoot its human projectile even farther, as far as 200 feet. It was built in Turin, Italy, and first used in 1927. Soon thereafter the second cannon was revamped, and a second troupe, this one featuring brother Victor, took to the road. Also in 1927 Hugo married Elsa Walker; they adopted two children.

While Hugo and brother Bruno were working their version of the act in Copenhagen's Tivoli Park, they were seen by the American circus impresario John Ringling, who contracted with them to make their American debut with Ringling Bros. and Barnum & Bailey Circus in 1929.

Hugo never returned to Europe, and he was joined in the United States the following year by several of his brothers. By 1932 the entire family had settled in Tampa, Florida. With so large a family and so many of them participating in the family business of being shot from cannons, they eventually became known as the Tanbark Barrymores.

Despite the uniqueness of their act, the family found American circus audiences continually demanding greater and greater thrills. In 1933 Ringling asked for a new gimmick to be added: a second cannonball. The repeating cannon, with brother Mario as the second "bullet," was inaugurated in 1934.

Although the human projectiles appear to be "shot" from the cannon, they are actually propelled by a coiled spring and compressed air. The smoke and retort are simply theatrical effects. Nonetheless Hugo and all the Zacchinis who performed this act reported that they were often knocked momentarily unconscious by the jolt.

Zacchini had a taste for danger and continued to perform his act for forty years, but he had another, more sedentary aspect to his character. Like his father, his real passion, he often told reporters, was art. Although he had little or no formal education as a youngster, he laid claim to having graduated from the Rome Art Academy at the age of twenty-one. Whether or not this is true, it is an indisputable fact that he used every available opportunity to paint the people he saw around the circus lot. After his retirement from performing, he taught art at Chaffey College in Alta Loma, California. He died in San Bernadino, California.

Two other Hugo Zacchinis carried on the family act, Hugo's adopted son and a nephew, the son of Edmundo, but Hugo the elder will always be the first and therefore the greatest daredevil of them all.

• Like many other noteworthy circus performers, Hugo Zacchini was often interviewed by reporters and writers, but he was actively careless about the details of his life, often inventing, enlarging, or dramatizing events to create what he assumed would be a greater effect. Much of what has been written about him and his family must therefore be carefully considered and compared with other accounts of the same events. Clipping files may be found at the Billy Rose Theatre Collection of the New York Public Library for the Performing Arts, Lincoln Center, the research library of the Circus World Museum in Baraboo, Wis., and the Hertzberg Circus Museum in San Antonio, Tex. The most truthful account is the subject's own story of his family, which has never been published but can be examined at the Circus World Museum library in Baraboo. An obituary is in the *New York Times*, 21 Oct. 1975, and *Variety*, 22 Oct. 1975.

ERNEST ALBRECHT

ZACH, Max (31 Aug. 1864–3 Feb. 1921), conductor and violist, was born Max Wilhelm Zach in Lemberg, Galicia (now L'vov, Ukraine), the son of Heinrich Zach and Julia Deim. His early education was in the lower and middle schools of Lemberg and Vienna. His first musical instruction was with Czerwinski in piano and Bruckmann in violin. He studied at the Vienna Conservatory from 1880 to 1883: piano with Joseph Edler, violin with Siegmund Bachrich and Jacob Grün, harmony with Robert Fuchs, and counterpoint and composition with Franz Krenn. His compulsory military service was satisfied from 1883 to 1886 by playing violin for three years in the band of the thirty-first Regiment of the Austrian Army, in which he attained the rank of sergeant. He was solo violinist with the regimental orchestra and acted as conductor on various occasions.

Engaged by Wilhelm Gericke, conductor of the Boston Symphony Orchestra, Zach in 1886 immigrated to the United States to be the principal violist in that orchestra. He served in that capacity for twenty-one seasons (1886–1907) and was also the violist in the Adamowski Quartet (1890–1906). He married Blanche Going of Boston in 1891; they had four children. After conducting several of his own compositions (for example, "Harlequin en Voyage," "Waldgeist," "Oriental March," "Austrian March") to much success, from 1895 to 1902 and then from 1905 to 1907 he conducted (with others) the Boston "Pops" concerts. He organized and conducted a chamber orchestra for summer concerts at Keith's Theater in Boston. Along with Emil Mollenhauer, he conducted the Boston Band at the Louisiana Purchase Exposition in St. Louis (1904).

When the orchestra of the St. Louis Choral-Symphony Society became a professional orchestra in 1907, Zach was invited to become its conductor. During Zach's first season the orchestra (later renamed the Saint Louis Symphony Orchestra) increased in size from fifty-two to sixty-four players. Zach created a disciplined ensemble through strenuous section rehearsals and developed the players' skills to a high degree of technical and artistic proficiency. The number of subscription concerts was also increased. Zach was a mas-

ter program builder, and he included many modern works in the orchestra's concerts, among them forty-five symphonic compositions by twenty-six American composers. This number included some American and world premiere performances. Zach's presentation of the complete cycle of Beethoven's symphonies during the 1909–1910 season was the first in St. Louis and among the first in the United States. He died of septic pneumonia in St. Louis, Missouri. He is buried at Forest Hills, Massachusetts.

• Information about Zach's time in Boston is included in M. A. DeWolfe Howe, *The Boston Symphony Orchestra: An Historical Sketch* (1931; repr. 1978). See also Ernst C. Krohn, "The Development of the Symphony Orchestra in St. Louis," in *Papers and Proceedings of the Music Teachers National Association* (1924). Richard E. Mueller, *A Century of the Symphony* (1979), and Katherine Gladney Wells, *Symphony and Song: The Saint Louis Symphony Orchestra* (1980), give more recent discussion. Carl Engel, "Max Zach As He Worked and Lived," the *Boston Evening Transcript*, 5 Feb. 1921, summed up his career. Obituaries are in the *Boston Evening Transcript*, 3, 4 Feb. 1921, and the *St. Louis Post-Dispatch*, 3 Feb. 1921.

JAMES M. BURK

ZACHARIAS, Ellis Mark (1 Jan. 1890–28 June 1961), naval officer, was born in Jacksonville, Florida, the son of Alron Zacharias, a tobacco farmer, and Theresa Budwig. A graduate of the U.S. Naval Academy in 1912, Zacharias began a four-decade-long career in which he distinguished himself as an intelligence officer and as one of the navy's foremost authorities on Japan. Zacharias's interest in Japanese language and culture began at the academy and led to his appointment to Tokyo in 1920 as assistant naval attaché. During his three-year tour in Japan Zacharias became fluent in Japanese. He also became an enthusiastic student of the craft of intelligence. Although most officers preferred sea duty or other staff positions to service in the Office of Naval Intelligence (ONI), Zacharias eagerly pursued a career as an intelligence specialist.

After a brief assignment as a communications intelligence officer on the USS *Huron* (Nov.–Dec. 1923), he served in several unrelated posts at sea and on shore in Latin America and with the Asiatic Fleet. In 1924, while he was on duty in the Panama Canal Zone, he met and married Clara Evans Miller, an aviator. They had two sons, both of whom served in the navy. In 1928 he returned to a brief but controversial tour in Tokyo. Accused by the naval attaché of trying to usurp his authority during a temporary illness, Zacharias returned to the United States to become chief of the Far Eastern Division of ONI until 1931. Following two years of sea duty Zacharias completed the senior course at the Naval War College and returned to ONI as head of the Far East Division (1934–1936). Following more sea duty he resumed his intelligence work, this time as district intelligence officer in the Eleventh Naval District, San Diego (1938–1940). Zacharias commanded the heavy cruiser USS *Salt Lake City* during the early months of the war against Japan and earned a Letter of Commendation for the bombardment of Wotje Island in the Marshall Islands. In June 1942 he left the Pacific to become deputy director of ONI, an assignment he believed to be a preliminary to his appointment as director.

By this time Zacharias had built a reputation as the navy's best intelligence officer, but he had his detractors as well. Impatient with those who did not share his vision for ONI, Zacharias feuded with colleagues and ran afoul of J. Edgar Hoover, director of the Federal Bureau of Investigation (FBI). Zacharias's difficulties with other intelligence officials probably explain his being passed over for the coveted director's position in favor of the inexperienced but bureaucratically competent Captain Harold Train.

Disappointed by this turn of events, Zacharias nevertheless continued his efforts to reinvigorate the navy's sluggish intelligence agency. Emphasizing aggressive action, he moved ONI into the areas of propaganda, psychological warfare, counterespionage, and operational intelligence. Of particular significance was the Special Warfare or "W" branch, which produced the successful Commander Norden broadcasts aimed at demoralizing German U-boat crews. Zacharias's efforts to reform ONI once again brought him into conflict with his fellow officers, including Captain Train, who believed that Zacharias was after his job. Zacharias was removed as deputy director in August 1943. He spent the next year in the Pacific as commander of the battleship USS *New Mexico* and returned to the states as chief of staff to the commandant of the Eleventh Naval District in October 1944.

In April 1945 Secretary of the Navy James Forrestal brought Zacharias to Washington for what was to be his most controversial assignment. Working out of the Office of War Information, and identifying himself as an official spokesman of the U.S. government, Zacharias made fourteen broadcasts, in both Japanese and English, in which he attempted to convince the Japanese high command to surrender. In the twelfth of these, Zacharias implied that if the Japanese surrendered the emperor would be spared. Although many U.S. officials had privately concluded that they would need to use the emperor to ensure the surrender of Japanese troops, President Harry S. Truman opposed any public modification of the unconditional surrender formula. Consequently, Zacharias was instructed to drop the words "official spokesman" from his remaining broadcasts.

The impact of Zacharias's broadcasts on Japan's surrender is difficult to assess. Nevertheless, the controversial Zacharias maintained that the Japanese could have been persuaded to surrender without the use of the atomic bombs. In 1946 he published *Secret Missions*, a memoir of his intelligence exploits, and retired with the rank of rear admiral. In retirement he wrote *Behind Closed Doors: The Secret History of the Cold War* (1950), a plea for a more aggressive psychological warfare campaign in the Cold War, and contributed articles to *United Nations World*, *Readers Digest*, and *Saturday Evening Post*. He supported the United Nations and criticized reports that it was being used as a cover for hundreds of foreign agents operating in the United States, and he opposed supporting any dictatorship in China, whether Nationalist or Communist. He died in West Springfield, New Hampshire.

• There is no biography of Zacharias, but Jeffery M. Dorwart, *Conflict of Duty: The U.S. Navy's Intelligence Dilemma, 1919–1945* (1983), contains the most authoritative secondary account of his intelligence career. See also Robert J. C. Butow, *Japan's Decision to Surrender* (1954), and Marc Gallicchio, *The Cold War Begins in Asia: American East Asian Policy and the Fall of the Japanese Empire* (1988). An obituary is in the *New York Times*, 29 June 1961.

MARC GALLICCHIO

ZACHARIAS, Jerrold Reinach (23 Jan. 1905–16 July 1986), physicist and science educator, was born in Jacksonville, Florida, the son of Isadore Zacharias, a lawyer, and Irma Kaufman, a violin teacher. After completing high school in Jacksonville, he entered Columbia University as a pre-engineering student at the age of seventeen. At Columbia University he met a graduate student, Isidor I. Rabi, who influenced his decision to major in physics; this relationship resulted in a lifelong professional association and friendship. Zacharias received a bachelor's degree in 1926, a master's degree in 1927, and a doctorate in 1933, all in physics, from Columbia. During his junior year he met Leona Hurwitz, a biology major at Barnard College; they were married in 1927 and had two daughters.

From 1931 to 1941 Zacharias was first an instructor and later an assistant professor at Hunter College. During this period he conducted research under Rabi at Columbia, developing new methods of molecular beam magnetic resonance. (In 1944 Rabi won the Nobel Prize in physics for the work done with his group on the magnetic properties of atomic nuclei.)

Zacharias was a key figure in the cadre of physicists who came to prominence during World War II and dominated American science and technology policy for the next thirty years. In 1940 he became head of the division of radar transmitter components of the Radiation Laboratory at the Massachusetts Institute of Technology (MIT). In 1945 he went to Los Alamos, New Mexico, to direct the ordnance engineering division of the Manhattan Project, which developed the atomic bomb. He returned to MIT in 1946 as professor of physics and director of the Laboratory for Nuclear Science and Engineering, which he headed for ten years. His association with Rabi continued when both turned to war technology perfected in the radiation laboratory at MIT. He continued investigations he had started at Columbia on the radio frequency spectra of atoms. In addition to yielding information on the shapes of atomic nuclei, his research resulted in the development of the first commercially available atomic frequency standard or clock. While others had invented various kinds of atomic clocks, Zacharias's advance in the field was a cesium clock that could be manufactured. His clock was correct to approximately five seconds over 300 years, the most accurate and stable clock of its kind. Atomic clocks revolutionized the measurement of time throughout the world.

In a 1948 study of nuclear-powered flight, known as Project Lexington, Zacharias served as associate director; this was the first of a series of summer investigations in which he became involved. He is credited with leading the first successful "summer study" for the U.S. Navy in 1950, a model for academic input into military policy for more than a decade afterward. He was director of Project Hartwell, dealing with undersea warfare, in 1950, associate director of Project Charles on air defense in 1951, and associate director of Project Lincoln in 1952; out of the last came the MIT Lincoln Laboratory and the SAGE air defense system. He helped to initiate and then headed the 1952 summer study on the Distant Early Warning Line that led to automatic radar detection of aircraft. In 1954–1955 he was technical director of Project Lamp Light, which dealt with continental air defense by the U.S. Navy.

Zacharias was a member of the President's Science Advisory Committee between 1952 and 1964. A respected and prolific experimenter with a record of managing innovative technical projects, he was part of the scientific elite, with friendships among members of the "secret war" as well as generals and government officials. He was awarded the President's Certificate of Merit in 1948 and the Department of Defense Certificate of Appreciation in 1955—the highest civilian honor given by the Department of Defense.

In 1956, a year before Russia launched its Sputnik satellite, Zacharias alerted physicists and physics educators to the outmoded methods of teaching physics in America's secondary schools. He convinced physicists in universities that they must work with high school physics teachers to reshape the curriculum. He formed the Physical Science Study Committee (PSSC) to develop a new method of physics instruction in high schools. With grants from the National Science Foundation, the Ford Foundation, and the Alfred Sloan Foundation, the PSSC-designed course was field-tested in eight high schools in 1957 and 1958. The PSSC curriculum was adopted by 360 secondary schools in 1958, and by 1970 it was being used by more than 200,000 students in 5,000 schools. In 1958 Educational Services, Inc. (ESI), a nonprofit corporation, was formed to carry on the work of the PSSC; Zacharias served as ESI's director of academic affairs. In 1967 he led a merger of ESI and the Institute of Educational Innovation to form the Education Development Center, Inc. (EDC) in Newton, Massachusetts.

Awards given to Zacharias included the Oersted Medal of the American Association of Physics Teachers (1961) and the National Science Teachers Association Citation for Distinguished Service to Science Education (1969). He was a fellow of the American Association for the Advancement of Science and of the Institute of Electrical and Electronic Engineers, and a member of the National Academy of Sciences, the American Academy of Arts and Sciences, the American Physical Society, and the American Association of Physics Teachers.

In 1966 Zacharias was named Institute Professor at MIT, a designation reserved by its faculty for colleagues of special merit and distinction. In 1968 he became director of MIT's Education Research Center, a position he held until 1972. He retired from the MIT faculty in 1970. EDC, with Zacharias as a founding trustee and vice president, became involved with more than twenty course-content improvement projects.

Throughout the 1970s Zacharias worked steadfastly at EDC, leading several national and international mathematics and science curriculum improvement projects for all grade levels. He died at his home in Belmont, Massachusetts.

• A collection of Zacharias's papers is in the Archives of the Massachusetts Institute of Technology, Cambridge. A biography is Jack S. Goldstein, *A Different Sort of Time: The Life of Jerrold R. Zacharias, Scientist, Engineer, Educator* (1992). See also National Academy of Sciences, *Biographical Memoirs* 68 (1995): 435–99; and "Jerrold Zacharias Dies at 81," *Tech Talk* (MIT), 23 July 1986.

NORMAN F. RAMSEY

ZACHOS, John Celivergos (20 Dec. 1820–20 Mar. 1898), educator and author, was born in Constantinople, Turkey, the son of Nicholas Zachos, a prosperous merchant and an interpreter in the sultan's court, and Euphrosyne (maiden name unknown). His father became an officer in the Greek army during the Greek war of independence and was killed in battle in 1825. His mother, a well-educated woman who subsequently married Nicholas Silivergos (apparently the source of Zachos's middle name), sought better educational opportunities for Zachos than were available in wartime Greece. She arranged for American philhellene Samuel Gridley Howe to transport him to America. Zachos left Greece in November 1827; he never returned to Greece or saw his mother or sister thereafter. His mother was able to support his education for a few years, until Silivergos exhausted the family fortune. Thereafter, Zachos received support from the Greek community in Boston for a few years, then supported himself.

Zachos entered Mt. Pleasant Classical Institute in Amherst, Massachusetts, in early 1828 and studied there until it closed in 1833. After working briefly as a printer's boy, he made his way to Bristol, Pennsylvania, and entered the Bristol Manual-Labor College, where he spent two years. There he gained the mechanical training that would prove valuable to him many years later when he invented the stenotype. In 1836 he enrolled in Kenyon College in Gambier, Ohio, and graduated with honors in 1840. He began teaching grammar school in Cincinnati, Ohio, that same year. He studied for three years (1842–1845) with Reuben Mussey, a member of the faculty of the Medical College of Ohio, but abandoned medicine in 1845 to devote himself fully to education. Kenyon College awarded him an M.A. in 1843.

By 1848 Zachos was professor of mathematics in an academy founded in Cincinnati by the former head of Bristol Manual-Labor College, Chauncey Colton. Zachos married Harriet Tomkins Canfield in 1849. They had six children. The same year he was principal and co-owner, with Margaret Coxe, of Cincinnati Female Seminary. In 1850 he became coprincipal, again with Coxe, of Cooper Female Seminary in Dayton, Ohio, where he remained until 1854 when Horace Mann convinced him to join him at Antioch College in Yellow Springs, Ohio, as principal of the preparatory school. He remained three years at Antioch, until struggles between Mann and the college trustees forced Zachos to resign in 1857. He returned to Cincinnati to teach, lecture, and write.

Along with his work as teacher and principal in these years, Zachos moved into educational reform. He was active in the Ohio State Teachers Association, organized the Association for the Advancement of Female Education, worked in teachers' institutes, and spoke frequently on topics in spelling reform, phonics, and women's education. He edited the first two volumes of the *Ohio Journal of Education* (1852–1853).

Simultaneously, Zachos began a literary life. He was one of a dozen young men who founded the Literary Club of Cincinnati in 1849. A well-known speaker, his first publication was *The New American Speaker* (1851), a 500-page textbook on elocution that was in its fourth edition within three years. In the following decade he published *Introductory Lessons in Reading and Elocution* (1852), *Analytic Elocution* (1861), and articles on literature and literary criticism. Throughout his teaching and literary endeavors, he expressed a commitment to democracy and to the use of education to achieve greater democratic ends.

The outbreak of the American Civil War drew Zachos out of Ohio and into new educational arenas. He was one of three dozen women and men selected to enter the Sea Islands at Port Royal, South Carolina, in March 1862 to superintend plantations abandoned by their owners and to teach the former slaves freed by the Union forces. Acting on his belief in democracy and education, he devoted two years to creating schools for and teaching the freedpeople on Parris Island and to preparing a reading textbook, *The Phonic Primer and Reader* (1864), for use in the freedmen's schools and other adult education settings.

In 1864 Zachos returned to the North and was ordained as a Unitarian clergyman. He served churches in West Newton, Massachusetts (1864–1866), Meadville, Pennsylvania (1866–1868), and Ithaca, New York (1868–1870). While in the latter two assignments, he taught sacred rhetoric at Meadville Theological Seminary and lectured at Cornell University. However, he was drawn back to secular education when philanthropist Peter Cooper invited him to New York City to become professor of literature and curator of Cooper Union Institute. Cooper Union was a remarkable experiment in adult education and vocational training for women. Zachos remained with the institute, teaching, writing, and administering its edu-cational programs, until his death in New York City over a quarter-century later. During the Cooper Institute years he wrote *The Political and Financial Opinions of Peter Cooper, with an Autobiography of His Early Life* (1877), *Our Financial Revolution: An Address to the Merchants and Professional Men of the Country, without Respect to Parties* (1878), and *The Fiscal Problems of All Civilized Nations* (1881), the latter two under the name "Cadmus." He also found time to invent the stenotype, a device for high-speed printed reporting, taking out patents in 1876, 1883, and 1886.

John Zachos is no longer well known, yet he was a champion of the education of women, African Americans, and adults. He spoke passionately for, and acted on behalf of, enlarged educational opportunity for democratic ends. He was not merely a spokesperson for educational reform but an activist who taught, trained teachers, wrote textbooks, and developed curriculum.

• Zachos's papers have not survived. His major publications, beyond those mentioned above, include *The Primary School Speaker: A Collection of Pieces, Colloquies, and Dialogues, Designed for Children in Schools, from the Age of Six to Twelve* (1858), *The High School Speaker* (1858), *The Analytic and Phonetic Word-Book* (1859), and *A Sketch of the Life and Opinions of Mr. Peter Cooper* (1876). Eva Catafygiotu Topping, "John Zachos: Cincinnatian from Constantinople," *Cincinnati Historical Society Bulletin* 34 (Spring 1974): 46–69, though parochial, provides an adequate overview of his life, correcting errors that have been repeated in other sources. Obituaries are in the *New York Daily Tribune* and the *New York Times*, both 21 Mar. 1898.

RONALD E. BUTCHART

ZAHARIAS, Babe Didrikson. *See* Didrikson, Babe.

ZAHM, John Augustine (14 June 1851–10 Nov. 1921), Catholic educator and author, was born in New Lexington, Ohio, the son of Jacob M. Zahm and Mary Ellen Braddock, farmers. After elementary classes in an Ohio log school and also at Saints Peter and Paul School in Huntington, Indiana, Zahm enrolled at the University of Notre Dame in 1867. He received his A.B. in philosophy in 1871 and in that year also entered the novitiate of the Congregation of the Holy Cross at Notre Dame. Two years later he received a master's degree, and in 1875 he was ordained for the priesthood at Notre Dame.

As a professor of physics and an administrator at Notre Dame from 1875 to 1892, Zahm delighted students and Indiana audiences with popular lectures and experiments on sound transmission with Helmholtz and Lissajores machines, static electricity, optics, electromagnetism, and phonograph machines. His research and studies on the physical sciences would end in 1892 when he published his first book, *Sound and Music*.

Attracted to the popular debates on contemporary philosophical topics, Zahm soon became fascinated by the relationship between religion and science, especially Catholic dogma and modern science. His popular American and international lectures together with his books on this relationship brought him international publicity—and also a specific warning from the Vatican for his advanced interpretations on Christianity and evolution. Zahm believed that theistic evolution was possible, that God created the universe with the potential of becoming fully developed. For example, he wrote in his book *Bible, Science and Faith* (1894) that the evidence of embryology favors the view "of a God who inaugurates the era of terrestial life by the creation of one or more simple organisms, unicellular monads . . . and causing them, under the action of His Providence, to evolve in the course of time into myriad, complicated, specialized and perfect forms which now people the earth." Moreover, he believed that the human body could have been created indirectly; the soul, however, was created directly by God.

Two other books, *Scientific Theory and Catholic Doctrine* (1896) and *Evolution and Dogma* (1896), presented additional explanations for understanding modern science and its relationship to Catholic dogma. In the foreword to *Evolution and Dogma*, Zahm described the new scientific environment:

I have been criticized for holding views which are hostile to religion. But the old views can no longer be held. They are good enough to explain during the middle ages questions which are still in controversy and which are not "of faith," but the researches of modern science have made a thousand discoveries in biology, paleontology, archaeology, which throw new light on these questions and suggest solutions which never could have occurred to medieval scientists.

With characteristic enthusiasm he predicted that "the twentieth century will not be very old before nine out of ten thinkers and students will be evolutionists, as opposed to believers in a special creation."

Awarded an honorary doctorate by Pope Leo XIII in 1895, Zahm enjoyed growing public acclaim during his lecture tours to America and Europe; he also became the target of religious and lay critics of his interpretations, especially his views concerning evolution. He was notified confidentially in 1898 that the Vatican's Sacred Congregation of the Index had decided to decree that further circulation of *Evolution and Dogma* in all its translations was prohibited. Zahm, in a letter for the Congregation of the Index, promptly submitted to the decision, but despite his hopes that the decree would not be published, reports of the condemnation and submission were published in the *New York Daily Tribune* on 2 July 1899 (provided by the Rome correspondent of the *Freeman's Journal*). Zahm not only submitted to the Congregation's decision, but he published no further studies on the relationship between religion and science.

Zahm and his friends believed that the Vatican decision had resulted in large measure from his close association with Cardinal James Gibbons, Archbishops John Ireland (1838–1918) and John Keane, and Bishop Denis O'Connell, liberal American Catholic leaders who wanted to Americanize the church in the United States and who approved of Zahm's efforts to reexamine Scripture through the lens of evolutionary theory. In 1895 Zahm had established Holy Cross College, a house of graduate studies at the newly founded Catholic University of America in Washington, D.C., and as procurator general (1896–1898) and then American provincial (1898–1906) of the Congregation of the Holy Cross at Notre Dame, Zahm continued to emphasize the absolute necessity of providing graduate studies for the community's seminarians and priests.

In 1907 Zahm returned to a very successful career of critical writing and extensive travel. Fascinated by South American culture and history, he traveled to that continent, and over the next decade, in residence at Holy Cross College, he published a trilogy, *Following the Conquistadores*, under the pseudonym H. J. Mozans. These volumes, acclaimed by Theodore Roosevelt (1858–1919) and other historians, recounted the history of these lands, especially the missionary work of the Jesuits, Dominicans, and Franciscans. The first volume, *Up the Orinoco and Down the Magdalena*, appeared in 1910; the second volume, *Along the Andes and Down the Amazon*, the following year. After traveling through Brazil, Uruguay, Argentina, and Paraguay with former president Theodore Roosevelt's expedition, Zahm wrote *Through South America's Southland* (1916). The next year, he published the last of his Hispanic American studies, *The Quest of El Dorado*. Two other books, *Woman in Science* (1913) and *Great Inspirers* (1917), the latter an account of the four women who inspired St. Jerome and Dante, praised the scholarly accomplishments of women. He did not live to complete his final book, *From Berlin to Bagdad and Babylon* (1922), before his death in Munich.

Zahm's vision and extensive program for developing a truly superior university at Notre Dame together with his extensive critical writings on science, religion, and Latin America advanced American Catholic education beyond the "bricks and mortar" phase. As the earliest and most popular American Catholic apologist to address these popular topics with intensive and scholarly research, he provided significant new interpretations for understanding the role of religion in higher education.

• Zahm's papers are in the Archives of the University of Notre Dame, Notre Dame, Ind. The only biography is Ralph E. Weber, *Notre Dame's John Zahm* (1961). Thomas T. McAvoy, *The Great Crisis in American Catholic History, 1895–1900* (1957) and *The Americanist Heresy in Roman Catholicism, 1895–1900* (1963), describe the severe tensions between Rome and liberal Catholic leaders in America. Gerald P. Fogarty, *The Vatican and the Americanist Crisis* (1974) and *The Vatican and the American Hierarchy from 1870 to 1965* (1982), explain the extensive differences between religious conservatives and liberals. Patrick Carey, ed., *American Catholic Religious Thought* (1987), and George M. Marsden, *Religion and American Culture* (1990), provide important perspectives on Catholicism in a pluralistic America.

RALPH E. WEBER

ZAHNISER, Howard Clinton (25 Feb. 1906–5 May 1964), editor and conservationist, was born in Franklin, Pennsylvania, the son of Archibald Howard McElrath Zahniser, a clergyman, and Bertha Belle Newton. Zahniser worked on several newspapers while attending Greenville College in Illinois. He completed his bachelor's degree in 1928 and briefly taught high school English before joining the Department of Commerce as an editorial assistant in 1930. While in Washington, D.C., Zahniser also attended graduate school at American University and George Washington University.

The Department of Agriculture's Bureau of Biological Survey hired Zahniser in 1931, and he edited, wrote, and broadcast on behalf of wildlife research, management, and conservation for that agency and its successor, the Interior Department's Fish and Wildlife Service, until 1942. From 1942 to 1945, he performed similar duties for the Bureau of Plant Industry, Soils, and Agricultural Engineering in the Department of Agriculture. In 1936 Zahniser married Alice Bernita Hayden, the daughter of Moses Hayden, an Alexandria, Virginia, minister, in Frederick, Maryland. The Zahnisers had four children—two daughters and two sons.

Deeply concerned with the preservation of wilderness areas, Zahniser became, in 1945, executive secretary (executive director after 1962) of the Wilderness Society, formed ten years earlier by Robert Marshall, Aldo Leopold, and several other prominent conservationists. In addition to his administrative obligations, he edited the organization's magazine, *The Living Wilderness*. In 1946 Zahniser aided in the organization of the Natural Resources Council of America. In addition, he was a member of the Advisory Committee on Conservation to the secretary of the interior from 1951 to 1954, an honorary vice president of the Sierra Club, a book editor and essayist for *Nature* magazine, and an author of wilderness and wildlife articles for the *Encyclopedia Britannica*.

Zahniser and the Wilderness Society were intimately involved in the successful effort to prevent the construction of a dam as part of the ambitious Colorado River Storage Project within Dinosaur National Monument in the early 1950s. The persuasive efforts of wilderness advocates like Zahniser and the Sierra Club's David Brower reflected an oftentimes fractious shift from utilitarian to aesthetic priorities within the conservation movement. Zahniser showed the film *Two Yosemites* to members of Congress to remind them of the controversy over damming the Hetch Hetchy Valley within Yosemite National Park forty years before. Brower pointed out embarrassing errors in Bureau of Reclamation calculations on evaporation at the dam site. An aroused public, not only concerned with the potential loss of scenery but also worried about recreational opportunities, flooded Congress with protest letters on several occasions. In 1955 the Eisenhower administration dropped the proposed dam from the project.

The greatest concern of Zahniser and wilderness advocates after the Dinosaur National Monument victory lay in establishing a national system of wilderness preservation. Zahniser initiated discussion of a wilderness system at the Sierra Club's First Biennial Wilderness Conference in 1949, then made a formal proposal at the second conference in 1951. By 1955 a consensus among conservationists in support of wilderness legislation had emerged. Zahniser wrote the bulk of the bills introduced by such congressional supporters as Senator Hubert H. Humphrey and devoted the remainder of his life to lobbying and testifying for a wilderness act on behalf of the National Wilderness Council.

He based the proposed system on New York State's constitutionally sanctioned Forest Preserve, which dated to 1885. In articles, speeches, and testimony before state legislative and congressional committees, Zahniser enunciated the recreational, spiritual, educational, and scientific needs that wilderness areas satisfied. Further, he argued that wilderness provided a palliative to the frustrations of coping in an urban, industrial, mechanized society.

The first of sixty-six wilderness bill drafts was introduced in Congress in 1956. In nine separate Congressional hearings between 1957 and 1964, Zahniser and other wilderness supporters sparred with lumber, oil, grazing, and mining interests, professional foresters, federal bureaucrats, and several powerful western congressmen and senators, particularly Colorado's Wayne Aspinall. Multiple-use proponents claimed that a wilderness bill would lock up necessary resources and lock out most Americans from enjoying more recreational opportunities. However, as with Dinosaur, public sentiment was strongly behind preservation, and when Zahniser secured the support of Senator Clinton P. Anderson of New Mexico, Senator Frank Church of Idaho, and President John F. Kennedy the wilderness bill gathered momentum.

Zahniser suffered a heart attack just days after testifying in the final round of congressional hearings on the wilderness bill and died at his home in Hyattsville, Maryland. On 3 September 1964, four months after his death, President Lyndon B. Johnson signed the Wilderness Act of 1964, guaranteeing permanent protection of wilderness areas. Zahniser's eloquent definition of wilderness—"an area where the earth and its community of life are untrammeled by man, where man is a visitor who does not remain" (Public Law 577, 88th Cong., 2d sess. [3 Sept. 1964], 891)—provided the philosophical foundation for the establishment of the National Wilderness Preservation System. More than thirty years later that system represents Zahniser's most enduring legacy.

• Zahniser's public career can be traced in the collections of the Wilderness Society in Washington, D.C.; the Sierra Club in San Francisco, California; and both the Interior and Agriculture Departments in the National Archives in Washington, D.C. Howard Zahniser, *Where Wilderness Preservation Began: Adirondack Writings of Howard Zahniser*, ed. Ed Zahniser (1992), relates Zahniser's exertions on behalf of wilderness protection from New York's Adirondacks to the Wilderness Act. Lawrence Hott and Diane Garey, *Wild by Law* (1991), a film in the American Experience series, briefly considers the origins of the 1964 Wilderness Act through examinations of the careers of Robert Marshall, Aldo Leopold, and Zahniser. Roderick Nash, *Wilderness and the American Mind*, 3d ed. (1982) offers good overviews of the Dinosaur fight and the Wilderness Act process. Obituaries are in the *Washington Post* and the *New York Times*, both 6 May 1964.

FRANK VAN NUYS

ZAKRZEWSKA, Marie Elizabeth (6 Sept. 1829–12 May 1902), physician and early advocate of women's entry into the medical profession, was born in Berlin, Germany, the daughter of Ludwig Martin Zakrzewski, a Prussian civil servant, and Caroline Fredericke Wilhelmina Urban, a midwife. The Zakrzewski family, once Polish nobility, lost their property to the Russians during the second partitioning of Poland in 1793, at which time Marie's grandfather fled to Prussia. Her mother's family could be traced to the Gypsy tribe of the Lombardis and numbered several medical practitioners, including her grandmother, who was a veterinary surgeon. Marie's father lost his job as a Prussian military officer in the early 1830s, presumably because of his liberal views, although he soon landed a position in the civil service. Still, his meager salary could not support his family, and his wife went to work, training as a midwife at the Royal Charité hospital in Berlin. By the age of thirteen, Marie had left school and was occasionally assisting her mother on her rounds. By the age of twenty, after repeated attempts (she was turned down twice because of her youth), she too was studying midwifery at the Charité. She immediately became the protégé of Joseph Hermann Schmidt, professor of obstetrics and director of the hospital's school of midwifery, who succeeded in promoting her—over the objections of many of his colleagues—to the position of head midwife in 1852, shortly after her graduation. However, intrigues against her led her to leave this position after only six months to go to the United States to study medicine.

Zakrzewska (pronounced Zak-shef´-ska) arrived in New York City in March 1853, accompanied by a younger sister, and was soon joined by other siblings. After a difficult first year, in which she received little encouragement from male physicians to pursue a medical career, she met Elizabeth Blackwell, the first woman in America to earn the M.D. Blackwell immediately took the young immigrant under her wings and managed, by the fall of 1854, to enroll Zakrzewska in Western Reserve College in Cleveland, a traditionally all-male medical school. The college had opened its doors briefly to women in the 1850s, offering Marie, along with five other women, the rare opportunity to earn the M.D. in a coeducational setting. After twenty months of study, and with the help and financial support of several organizations, including the Physiological Society of Cleveland (under the presidency of

Caroline M. Severance, a prominent reformer), Zakrzewska received the M.D. in March 1856.

A woman with an M.D. was an anomaly in the 1850s, and Zakrzewska, who had returned to New York City, had a difficult time setting up practice. However, she and Elizabeth Blackwell, joined by Blackwell's physician sister, Emily, soon decided to establish a small hospital for the training and treatment of women. On 12 May 1857, after six months of fundraising activities, they opened the New York Infirmary for Indigent Women and Children. Zakrzewska worked there as resident physician for two years, supervising the daily activities, providing medical care, and offering clinical training to female medical students. In March 1859 she left for Boston, accepting a position as professor of obstetrics at the New England Female Medical College, with the charge of organizing a new clinical department. She made this move, she explained, in order to advance further "the cause of the medical education of women," especially since the New York Infirmary was financially secure and firmly in the hands of the Blackwell sisters. Tensions with the Blackwells may also have contributed to her decision, not surprising given the strength of all their personalities.

Much later in life Zakrzewska remarked that another reason for her move was to follow a close friend, the German émigré Karl Heinzen, who had recently settled in Boston with his wife and child. Heinzen, whom Zakrzewska had met in New York in 1856, had played a central role as propagandist in the German Revolution of 1848, being forced to flee his native land when the revolution failed. As Zakrzewska explained, their friendship was "based not simply on affinity by nature but also on principle," which included a commitment to the abolition of slavery, women's rights, and radical democracy. Zakrzewska shared her Boston home with Heinzen and his family for twenty years. This unusual living arrangement also included another sister of Zakrzewska, as well as Julia A. Sprague, a founding member of the New England Women's Club and Zakrzewska's friend and traveling companion for more than forty years. During these years in Boston, Zakrzewska joined and supported several political organizations, but her most important work was in the education of women physicians.

Early in the summer of 1862 Zakrzewska left the New England Female Medical College over disagreements with its founder, Samuel Gregory, whom she had failed to convince that instruction in microscopy, thermometry, and dissection belonged in the curriculum. She also left because she had the opportunity to start her own hospital. In July 1862, with the support of several of Boston's leading liberal reformers, including Ednah Cheney, Lucy Goddard, and William Lloyd Garrison, Zakrzewska founded the New England Hospital for Women and Children. Under her leadership, the hospital grew into an important symbol of the nineteenth-century American women's movement. Not only did it offer female practitioners clinical experience at a time when most medical schools and hospitals remained closed to them, it also provided medical care to women (and their children) by practitioners of their own sex. Zakrzewska functioned as resident physician of the hospital for a brief period, as attending physician until 1887, and then as advisory physician until her retirement in 1899, but for all intents and purposes she ran the hospital during this entire period—according to some, with an iron fist. Strong-willed, ambitious, and fiercely independent, she won the respect of her colleagues, male and female alike; she also impressed some of the younger physicians in her hospital as dogmatic and set in her ways. She died in Boston.

Zakrzewska stood out among her female contemporaries for her strong commitment to scientific medicine. At a time when most women physicians promoted an image of themselves as uniquely caring and nurturing, Zakrzewska insisted that women pay greater attention to their scientific training. For her outspoken views, and for the large number of interns and residents who trained in her hospital, Zakrzewska earned a reputation as one of the most prominent female physicians in nineteenth-century America.

• The richest source available on Zakrzewska's life is *A Woman's Quest: The Life of Marie E. Zakrzewska, M.D.*, ed. Agnes Vietor (1924; repr. 1972). The first part of this book is basically a reprint of an autobiographical sketch Zakrzewska wrote in 1860, which was published under the title *A Practical Illustration of "Woman's Right to Labor,"* ed. Caroline H. Dall (1860). For subsequent years, Vietor relied on letters and manuscripts Zakrzewska left her for the explicit purpose of writing Zakrzewska's biography; these papers have not been located. See also the memoir published by the New England Hospital for Women and Children, *Marie Elizabeth Zakrzewska: A Memoir* (1903), and Zakrzewska's *Introductory Lecture Delivered . . . before the New England Female Medical College* (1859). Also important is Virginia G. Drachman, *Hospital with a Heart: Women Doctors and the Paradox of Separatism at the New England Hospital, 1862–1969* (1984), a book about the New England Hospital for Women and Children in which Zakrzewska figures prominently. Other sources that include more than a brief mention of Zakrzewska are a chapter in Mary Roth Walsh, *Doctors Wanted: No Women Need Apply: Sexual Barriers in the Medical Profession, 1835–1975* (1977), and two articles in *Sickness and Health in America*, ed. R. L. Numbers and J. W. Leavitt, 2d ed. (1985), one by Drachman, "Female Solidarity and Professional Success: The Dilemma of Women Doctors in Late 19th-Century America," and the other by Regina Morantz-Sanchez, "The 'Connecting Link': The Case for the Woman Doctor in 19th-Century America." Extensive obituaries are in the *Boston Herald*, 16 May 1902, and the *Woman's Journal*, 24 May 1902.

ARLEEN MARCIA TUCHMAN

ZANE, Arnie (26 Sept. 1948–30 Mar. 1988), dancer and choreographer, was born in the Bronx, New York, the son of Orlando Zumpano, at various times an upholsterer, a store manager, and a factory worker, and Edith Zacklin, a retail shop owner. His father, of Italian parentage, and his mother, from a Lithuanian family of Orthodox Jews, synthesized their own last name. Zane entered the State University of New York at Binghamton in the spring of 1966, intending to study science, but graduated in 1970 as an art history major. He then moved to Europe, where he lived on a houseboat in Amsterdam, found work in a medical publishing company, and began to take photographs with a borrowed camera.

After a year Zane returned to Binghamton and immediately met a new student of theater and dance, Bill T. Jones. In an oral history interview conducted in 1987, Zane recalled Jones as "very dashing, very exciting. We met, and we became friends and formed an intimate relationship." Zane urged that a better education was available by just living in Europe, so Jones dropped out of school after his first semester, and they went to Amsterdam. Zane continued with his photography, while Jones took classes in a jazz ballet studio. They lived in a tiny apartment, endlessly discussing politics and ideas "about what art should or should not look like."

They soon returned to Binghamton, where Jones reentered the university, but he was developing a serious interest in dance, and the next semester they transferred to the state university campus at Brockport, which offered a stronger dance program. Jones persuaded Zane that both of them should sign up for a summer workshop in contact improvisation taught by Lois Welk and Jill Becker, who were visiting from San Francisco. Contact improvisation is a movement technique of partnered duets based on giving and receiving another person's full physical weight. The form would remain a signature element for Zane and Jones as their theatrical work developed. Dance critic Jennifer Dunning, in a *New York Times* review (11 Dec. 1985), commented on "the interest inherent in their partnering of each other in the dances—Mr. Jones being tall, intense, and black; Mr. Zane being short, a little zany, and white."

Zane remembered, "It was a great form. I had a real taste for dance that was opening. Suddenly my life was open, and before me was a new range of possibilities." Zane had earlier resisted dance technique classes, considering them offensively authoritarian, but now he started to study with dancer and musician Richard Bull and modern dance choreographer Erin Martin. Around 1973 Jones and Zane decided to try living in San Francisco, where Jones continued as Zane's mentor in physical techniques, including yoga, and encouraged him to choreograph. Zane's first dance was *Self Portrait* (1973), a mixed-media solo that used movement, an operatic aria, and slide projections of his drawings.

After several months Jones and Zane and Welk and Becker decided together to return to New York state. They rented a studio in Binghamton, where they operated as a collective called American Dance Asylum, teaching classes and creating a laboratory company for performances. They began touring in New York state, received funding from the state arts council, and invited guest artists to Binghamton. In July 1976 Jones performed his solo *Everybodyworks!* in New York City and received excellent reviews; he was invited to repeat it the next summer at the New York Dance Festival in Central Park. This success convinced the couple that it was time to move closer to the artistic mainstream of New York City, and they found a cottage in the Hudson Valley. There Jones and Zane collaborated on a trio of pieces inspired by their new house, *Monkey Run Road* (1979), *Blauvelt Mountain* (1980), and *Valley Cottage* (1981), which were performed at Dance Theatre Workshop in New York City and established them as new stars of "downtown" dance. On tour in Europe, *Blauvelt Mountain* won the German Critics Award for 1980.

During the same period, both artists created concerts with other groups of dancers. Zane presented *Pieman's Portraits* in 1980 and *Cotillion, New Hero*, and a collaboration with choreographer Johanna Boyce, *Garden*, in 1981. Zane also assisted Jones in his work *Social Intercourse: Pilgrim's Progress* for the 1981 American Dance Festival, which was then presented at City Center in New York City.

Jones and Zane formed their company as an official entity, Bill T. Jones/Arnie Zane and Company, in 1982. Zane remarked in his oral history interview that "by combining our forces we [created] organizational strength. Our talents are very different." The Brooklyn Academy of Music's Next Wave Festival commissioned their first company work, *Intuitive Momentum* (1983), performed as an improvisatory collaboration with drummer Max Roach, on a set by artist Robert Longo, which received international attention. *Freedom of Information* (1984) premiered at the Théâtre de la Ville in Paris. *Secret Pastures*, with sets by painter Keith Haring and costumes by fashion designer Willi Smith, was performed in 1984 at the Brooklyn Academy of Music. *Secret Pastures* could be seen as a form of protest art: iconoclastic statements on sexual and racial politics, spoken texts, an intense performance style, and a combination of dance technique and other physical languages. Paradoxically, critics also wrote of the work's "warmth" and "tenderness." In Zane's oral history interview, he said of his contributions, "My approach to building movement is to integrate, shape, and change it. . . . For me, the passion in dance-making is with the movement itself—how it's spaced on the stage." Zane continued to create his own works for the company, including a duet, *The Black Room* (1985), as well as continued collaborating with Jones on *The Animal Trilogy*, commissioned for the 1986 Biennale de la Danse in Lyons, France. The two dancers won a "Bessie" (New York Dance Performance Award) in 1986.

In the mid-1980s acquired immunodeficiency syndrome (AIDS) began to affect Zane's health. He was among the first gay creative artists to speak openly of his AIDS infection. Of his 1987 work, *The Gift/No God Logic*, he said, "I thought it was going to be the last dance that I was making, and I went into the studio and I was angry. . . . I felt it was like the last gift I was giving." At the time of Zane's death from AIDS-related lymphoma at his home in Valley Cottage, New York, he was working on another collaboration with Jones, *The History of Collage*, which their company premiered two months later in New York.

• An oral history recording of Arnie Zane with Lesley Farlow, 23 Dec. 1987, in the Dance Collection of the New York Public Library, is a principal source, together with Elizabeth Zimmer and Susan Quasha, eds., *Body against Body: The Dance and Other Collaborations of Bill T. Jones and Arnie Zane* (1989). Extensive reviews and videotapes also are in the Dance Collection. For additional information see interviews by Connie Kreemer, ed., *Further Steps: Fifteen Choreographers on Modern Dance* (1987), and by Burt Supree, "Any Two Men on the Planet," *Village Voice*, 18–24 Mar. 1981. Obituaries are in the *New York Times*, 1 Apr. 1988, and *Dance Magazine*, June 1988.

MONICA MOSELEY

ZANE, Betty (1766?–1831?), patriot, was born Elizabeth Zane in either Berkeley or Hardy County, in the Potomac River valley of western Virginia (now West Virginia), the daughter of William Zane and his wife (whose name is unrecorded, though it may also have been Elizabeth). The Zanes were of Danish descent and traditionally members of the Society of Friends (Quakers) but, according to family lore, William Zane—either because his personality clashed with the tenets of his religion or because he married outside of it—moved his family from the Philadelphia–New Jersey area (where Betty's grandfather, William's father, had originally settled in 1677) to the western Virginia wilderness. Betty Zane was the only daughter and the youngest of five children. The birthdate of her eldest brother, Ebenezer, was recorded as 7 October 1747, but there is no confirmed date for Betty's birth (although Betty's son stated it was 1766). However, given the number of siblings who preceded her, and Ebenezer's appearing to be a decade or more older than she, a birthdate in the late 1750s would be the earliest feasible one.

William Zane's adventurous spirit carried on in his children. The Zane brothers—three of whom survived kidnapping by Indians when they were children—were frontiersmen who explored the Kentucky–Ohio–western Virginia borderlands and were known for their skill in Indian warfare. In 1770 Ebenezer Zane founded a settlement on Wheeling Creek, at the end of the Cumberland Road from Maryland, which would later become Wheeling, West Virginia. This location became of strategic importance in the Indian wars and the American war for independence, though those conflicts restricted full initial development of a community at the time. Along with establishing a small settlement of homes, in 1774 Ebenezer and his brothers helped build Fort Fincastle (named after Lord Dunmore, who was also Viscount Fincastle and the royal governor of Virginia, the westernmost county of which was also called Fincastle). In just two years the fort was renamed Fort Henry, in honor of the revolutionary Patrick Henry. As the American Revolution grew in intensity, Ebenezer was granted the rank of colonel in the Virginia militia, and Fort Henry became a principal supply base for the western campaigns of the revolt.

At the time the colonies declared independence from Britain at a gathering in Philadelphia, Betty Zane was in that city also, apparently living with an aunt and finishing her schooling. Whether Betty's fateful year was 1777, one year after the Declaration of Independence, or 1782, one year after Yorktown and one year before the American Revolution officially ended, is still open to speculation because accounts differ widely. Both years saw major sieges against Fort Henry, as did 1781, with the siege of 1782 often being credited as the last major campaign of the war—and it was at the siege of Fort Henry (whichever one) that Betty Zane's name grew into legend.

First made public in 1891 by her nephew Ebenezer Zane Clark, a Zane family story about Betty prior to her arrival at Fort Henry contains intimations of her future mythic status. Around 1781 Betty was staying with friends in Chester County, Pennsylvania. A troop of British soldiers stopped at the house for a meal. The soldiers' horses were apparently all tied together, with one bridle rein thrown over the next, and only one horse actually hitched to the post. Betty got on the hitched horse, unhitched it, and then, while the British ate their meal in happy ignorance, led the whole string of horses off to George Washington's army. This feat of course made staying in Pennsylvania unadvisable for Betty, so she went to visit her brother at Fort Henry. Though apocryphal and impossible to confirm, this possibly tall tale fits with the fearless Betty of the "gunpowder exploit" at Fort Henry and with how she came to be regarded by posterity.

Most of the stories of Betty Zane and the siege of Fort Henry do agree on several points (keeping in mind that agreement does not equal factual confirmation): Betty had just returned from school in Philadelphia to her family in Wheeling Creek; the fort was under attack by the British and their Indian allies; the majority of the settlers had taken refuge in the fort; and the fort's defenders had ammunition but were running low on gunpowder. There was apparently a sufficient supply of gunpowder at Colonel Zane's house, but the problem was getting it to the men in the fort. It was clear that someone had to try to get the gunpowder, which basically meant running a sixty-yard gauntlet through a hail of musketfire. Each man bravely volunteered to make the suicidal run, but the youngest Zane, the schoolgirl from Philadelphia, convinced them all that she should do it: she was small, she was swift of foot like her brothers, and she was expendable, the fort needing every soldier it had but having little use for a girl, except in this instance. Whatever her argument really was—whatever really happened (Betty might not have even bothered waiting for approval but simply seized the opportunity)—it was decided that Betty would run for the gunpowder.

There is some question as to whether Betty was in the fort or her brother's home outside the compound. If she was in the fort, that means she had to cover the distance twice. Some accounts have her running, others say she "walked at her utmost speed" (Ellet, p. 279) or "swiftly glided" (Kiernan, p. 310). Some stories say the attackers were too astounded to shoot at her; others grant a certain level of chivalry to the Wyandotte and Shawanee Indians and British who would not fire at a girl; and yet others say the shock had worn off the attackers by the second time Betty appeared and that she heroically outran and outdodged the bullets. In whichever case, and by either carrying a keg of gunpowder in her arms or the loose gunpowder tied in a tablecloth around her waist, Betty Zane succeeded in her heroic dash. The gunpowder she retrieved was enough to support the ammunition and allowed the defenders to hold off the fort's attackers until relief came from Virginia. The British and Indians were routed.

Fort Henry was possibly the most famous frontier fort of the time, and it had withstood numerous Indian onslaughts even before the Revolution and the subsequent joint British-Indian attacks. The siege of September 1777, known as the year of the "Bloody Sevens" and the date historian George Kiernan associates with Betty, was a major attack, but the fort survived. Another attack in 1781 was similarly fierce. In September 1782 the siege went on for several days and is remembered and commemorated as the final battle of the American Revolution. Kiernan (1843), Elizabeth Fries Ellet (1848), and *Appleton's Cyclopaedia* (1889) place Betty Zane at the 1777 siege; most other commentaries put her in 1782. But whether Betty charged into history in 1777 or in 1782 matters very little. Although *exactly* what she did on one dangerous day is not completely clear or fully documented, she did do *something* that was extremely brave, brave enough to become a legend.

What Betty Zane did after that day, though, does not generally lend itself to florid embellishments and patriotic exultation but is brave in its own way. She went on to marry and have children and be part of the settlements that would expand the new country. Betty's first husband was John (or Henry) McLaughlin (although the spelling of his name varies), and with him she had five daughters. McLaughlin died, and Betty eventually remarried. Her second husband was Jacob (or John) Clark, and they had two children. With Clark, Betty moved from Wheeling Creek to a farm near St. Clairsville and Martin's Ferry, Ohio. It was there that she died, sometime in 1831 at the age of sixty-five, according to her son (Draper manuscripts, 19 Jan. 1891 letter), or perhaps earlier in 1828 (Schneider and Farley, p. 12) or maybe in the 1840s (Ellet, p. 280).

The mystery—or, at least, confusion—surrounding the date of her death (as well as her birth and which siege she was in) is consistent with the story and legend of Betty Zane. Little can be said with certainty. Indeed, in 1849 an alleged eyewitness to one of the sieges of Fort Henry said that Betty Zane was still in school in Philadelphia when the attack occurred and that another girl, Molly Scott, carried the gunpowder from the fort to the Zane house (rather than the other way around) (De Hass, pp. 280–81). But contradicting that account was Molly Scott's own grandson, who said that Molly always said that Betty had saved the day (Galbreath, pp. 595–96). What is certain is that Betty Zane's name came to mean heroism and patriotism. And in honor of her and of those ideals, her portrait hangs in the Wheeling State House, two poems have been written about her (one by Thomas Dunn English and the other by John S. Adams for *St. Nicholas*, the popular children's magazine), a World War II Liberty ship was named for her, and a memorial statue marks her grave in Walnut Grove Cemetery, Martin's Ferry, Ohio, not too far from Wheeling and the site of her gallantry.

• There are two full-length accounts of Betty Zane's life. *Betty Zane* (1903), is a fictionalized, melodramatic version by her descendant Zane Grey, the popular novelist. Grey, in a prefatory note, alleges that "the main facts" of the story came from an old, faded notebook (whereabouts now unknown) written by his great-grandfather, Colonel Ebenezer Zane, Betty's brother. The other work is an attempt at factual biography titled *Betty Zane: Heroine of Fort Henry* (1969) by Norris F. Schneider and G. M. Farley. Because records for the period are sketchy at best, because Betty Zane's exploit has become myth, and because there was more than one Elizabeth Zane and more than one siege at Fort Henry, sources of information and dating can be confusing and contradictory. Useful resources relating particularly to the 1777 and 1782 sieges of Fort Henry (which often get confused with each other) include George Kiernan (or McKiernan), "Siege of Fort Henry," *American Pioneer* 2 (1843): 302–14, which states that Betty's exploit took place in 1777; the Draper Manuscripts Collection at the State Historical Society of Wisconsin, Madison, in which are contained letters from Wilbur C. Brockunier (great-grandson of Colonel Ebenezer Zane) to Lyman C. Draper; Wills De Hass, *History of the Early Settlement and Indian Wars of Western Virginia* (1851), which argues for the 1782 siege as the one in which Betty ran for the powder; and, for a different interpretation, Alexander S. Withers, *Chronicles of Border Warfare* (1895), who presumably drew on notes (now lost) made by Noah Zane, Betty's nephew, for a biography of his famous aunt. See also Elizabeth Fries Ellet, *The Women of the American Revolution* (1848); Gibson L. Cranmer, ed., *History of Wheeling City and Ohio County, West Virginia, and Representative Citizens* (1902); C. B. Galbreath, "Unveiling of Memorial to Elizabeth Zane," *Ohio Archaeological and Historical Quarterly* 37, no. 3 (July 1928): 592–98, which gives Zane's birth and death dates as 1759 and 1847, contrary to her son's recollection; and Adelaide M. Cole, "Did Betty Zane Save Fort Henry?" *DAR Magazine* 114 (1980): 672–75.

E. D. LLOYD-KIMBREL

ZANE, Charles Shuster (3 Mar. 1831–29 Mar. 1915), lawyer and judge, was born in Tuckahoe, New Jersey, the son of Andrew Zane and Mary Franklin, farmers. As a young man, he moved to Illinois and worked on his brother's farm. In 1852 Zane began three years of study at McKendree College in Lebanon, Illinois. After a short interlude he studied law with James Conkling in Springfield. Admitted to the Illinois bar in 1857, Zane opened a law office in Springfield, which was above the office of Abraham Lincoln and his partner William H. Herndon. All three were actively involved in the new Republican party. In April 1859 Zane married Margaret Maxcy, a niece of Herndon's; they had nine children.

When Lincoln was elected president, Zane succeeded him in partnership with Herndon. Their firm lasted until Herndon's dwindling interest in law impelled Zane into a two-year stint as a solo practitioner. In 1870 Zane joined Shelby Cullom's firm, leaving it in 1873 on his election to a six-year term as a state circuit judge. He was reelected once but resigned when, at the suggestion of then senator Cullom, President Chester Alan Arthur appointed Zane as chief justice of the Utah Territory on 5 July 1884. He served in that position until 1893, with only one break between 1888 and 1889. In 1896, however, he returned to the bench as the first chief justice of the state of Utah, having been elected with support from all religious groups. His election is a measure of Zane's reputation as a territorial judge, a reputation that may have been enhanced because his well-known agnosticism kept him out of religious disputes.

Zane was part of a large contingent of federal officials sent to Utah to eradicate polygamy. Their chief weapon was the 1882 Edmunds Act, which banned unlawful cohabitation, disenfranchised polygamists, and barred them from jury service. Although as chief justice he bore the brunt of criticism by Mormons for this "war" against them, Zane's opinions were no more significant than those of the other federal judges. He joined them in an intentionally broad interpretation of the Edmunds Act, agreeing that proof of cohabitation did not require evidence of a sexual relationship. He also concluded that a continuous polygamous relationship could be the basis for multiple indictments—each six-month period could support separate charges. (The U.S. Supreme Court accepted the first interpretation but rejected the second.) For Zane, the statute and its interpretation were appropriate responses to "a scandal to society and a menace to the lawful marriage."

Even in his moral rectitude, Zane's approach was more one of following a sense of justice than of exacting vengeance. In one case, for example, he dissented when he could find no evidence that a defendant and his lawful wife had any contact during a year in which they were charged with cohabiting. Likewise, as a trial judge (supreme court judges also sat as trial judges during the territorial period), he suspended the sentence of defendants who publicly promised to obey the law; those who refused received the maximum sentence. Most important of all was Zane's immediate acceptance of the declaration by Wilford Woodruff, president of the Church of Jesus Christ of Latter-Day Saints, that all members should adhere to the laws prohibiting plural marriages. Zane gave national prominence to his acceptance in an article in the November 1891 issue of *The Forum*, "The Death of Polygamy in Utah." He also signed a petition asking that the president pardon those convicted of polygamy.

Zane treated other statutes much the same as he did the antipolygamy laws. He applied the law with little reference to precedent. The period was one of rapid development in Utah—water systems were being built, mines were being explored, and railroads were bringing both progress and injury. Yet Zane showed little interest in articulating a vision for the future; he seemed little inclined to bring his decisions within any developing body of American common law. He did, though, have a sense of a community of interest shared by all in Utah. Thus, he held that the legislature could regulate the hours worked in a mine just as a municipality could control the distribution of water as long as the actions were fair and just. He was content to rely on the apparent certainty of treatises and on phrases such as "justice and the public good" and "reason and principle" even when it meant that he disagreed with a significant body of state court precedent.

Zane failed to gain reelection, due to his opposition to the free coinage of silver. In 1899 he joined his son in private practice in Utah. He retired in 1914 and died the next year in Salt Lake City.

• Zane's opinions as chief justice are reported in *Utah Reports*, vols. 4–9 and 13–18. For a discussion of some of those cases as well as some of his trials, along with references to contemporaneous sources, see Thomas G. Alexander, "Charles S. Zane . . . Apostle of the New Era," *Utah Historical Quarterly* 34 (1966): 290, and Orma Linford, "The Mormons and the Law: The Polygamy Cases," *Utah Law Review* 9 (1964–1965): 308, 543. For an appreciation by Zane's son, who had been reporter of the Utah decisions as well as his law partner, see John M. Zane, "A Rare Judicial Service," *Journal of the Illinois State Historical Society* 19 (1926): 31. An obituary is in the *Deseret Evening News*, 29 Mar. 1915.

WALTER F. PRATT, JR.

ZANE, Ebenezer (7 Oct. 1747–19 Nov. 1812), pioneer, was born in what is now Moorefield, Hardy County, West Virginia, the son of William Zane and his wife (name unknown). Nothing is known of his parents' occupations or his early education. In late 1768 Zane went on a hunting expedition with two brothers and some friends in what is now northern West Virginia. The next year he explored the upper Ohio River Valley and, in 1770, brought his wife, Elizabeth McCulloch (whom he had probably married in 1768 and with whom he had twelve children), her relatives, and several other families to live along the Ohio River. Over the next decade, Zane gained title through surveying claims to 2,700 acres in and around a town that he would later call Wheeling. He also claimed land west of the Ohio River and owned some 10,000 acres in what is now Wood County, West Virginia. Zane had no interest in developing his land, preferring to hold on to it until prices rose with the demand created by new settlers. He waited until 1793 before he laid out the town of Wheeling and began to sell lots in it. Between 1795 and 1805, he may have earned as much as $2,000 per year from sales of his property.

By the late 1780s Zane's settlement had become an economic, military, and social center for travelers and settlers in the upper Ohio River Valley. While his principal occupation was hunting, he and his wife operated an inn, a general store, and a ferry. Elizabeth became well known for her medical abilities and her devout Methodism, although most of her time was undoubtedly given over to raising their children.

As a colonel in the Virginia militia, Zane oversaw the construction of Fort Fincastle (later Fort Henry) in 1774 and defended it against sieges by Native Americans in 1777 and 1782. In peacetime, however, Native Americans were frequent visitors at the Zanes's settlement. Indeed, some observers thought that the Zanes lived like Indians. In 1789 a New England merchant, while admiring Zane's hunting skills, complained about his failure to develop his property: Zane made "money Verry fast but live[d] poor"; even after two decades, his "plantation" was still a "fronttear" (Smith, p. 135).

Zane was never concerned with elaborate projects for the improvement of his land. Despite his strong temper, he was an exceedingly practical man. When his seventeen-year-old daughter, Sarah, married 35-year-old John McIntire, Zane went off angrily on an extended hunting trip, but McIntire soon became one of his closest associates. Similarly, Zane supported ratification of the Constitution as a member of the 1788 Virginia convention, largely because he thought a stronger national government would cause a rise in land sales by offering greater protection from Native Americans and by improving transportation.

Zane's faith in the potential benefits of a federal government was not misplaced. He marked the 1795 signing of the Treaty of Greenville, by which Native Americans ceded southern Ohio to the United States, by planning what he called "a good waggon Road" from Wheeling to Limestone (Maysville), Kentucky (Carter, p. 551). He theorized that the road would be shorter and more reliable than the Ohio River, which was subject to floods, ice, and wind. An eager Zane began construction of the trace before he petitioned Congress for permission to do so on 25 March 1796. He was less interested in federal authorization than in insuring that he would have title to tracts of land at the points at which travelers would have to cross the Muskingum, Hock-hocking, and Scioto rivers. Zane asked to locate military warrants at these places; this was the only "compensation" or "reimbursement" he sought (Carter, p. 551). On 17 May, Congress granted his petition, with the provisos that the road be open by 1 January 1797, that Zane operate ferries on the three rivers, that he pay for his three tracts with federal bounty warrants, and that he finance the surveying of his three tracts.

Accompanied by a Native American guide, Zane and his brother Jonathan marked out the route of the trace, often incorporating existing Indian trails. A ragged road when finished in 1797, Zane's Trace was wide enough to accommodate people on horseback but not in wagons. Meanwhile, Zane's nephew William McCulloch had started a ferry across the Muskingum River in 1797 and had opened a tavern nearby. Two years later, Zane and McIntire established the town of Westbourne, which was renamed Zanesville in 1801. Zane also laid out the town of Lancaster at the point at which his trace crossed the Hock-hocking River and sold the tract on the Scioto River, which was near the existing settlement of Chillicothe.

Zane never left the Wheeling area, where he died. He proudly left his land to his children and grandchildren "for and in consideration of the natural love and affection" that he and Elizabeth felt for them. When those who knew him best buried him in Martins Ferry, Ohio, they recorded on his tombstone that "He died as he had lived, an honest man."

• There are no Zane papers. The only detailed account of his life is John Gerald Patterson, "Ebenezer Zane, Frontiersman," *West Virginia History* 12 (1950): 5–45. See also Norris F. Schneider and Clair C. Stebbins, *Zane's Trace* (1973). More general works include J. A. Caldwell, *History of Belmont and Jefferson Counties, Ohio* (1880); Joseph Doddridge, *Notes on the Settlement and Indian Wars of the Western Parts of Virginia and Pennsylvania, from the Year 1763 until the Year 1783 Inclusive* (1824); and W. H. Hunter, "The Pathfinders of Jefferson County," *Ohio Archaeological and Historical Society Publications* 6 (1898): 96–313. Zane's contract with the federal government is in Clarence E. Carter, ed., *Territorial Papers of the United States*, vol. 2 (1934). Some comments on the Zanes may be found in Dwight L. Smith, ed., *The Western Journals of John May* (1961).

ANDREW CAYTON

ZANUCK, Darryl F. (5 Sept. 1902–22 Dec. 1979), motion picture producer and film studio head, was born Darryl Francis Zanuck in Wahoo, Nebraska, the son of Frank Zanuck, a hotel manager, and Louise Torpin. Zanuck dropped out of high school and, just one day short of his fourteenth birthday, lied about his age and joined the army. He served briefly on border detail in New Mexico, then in France during World War I. His letters home were printed in the local newspaper and later in the army newspaper *Stars and Stripes*. After the war Zanuck, still in his teens, ended up in Los Angeles. He tried, unsuccessfully, to write short stories for pulp magazines. He did sell stories (basic stories, not screenplays) to the movies, working for a variety of film companies before landing at Warner Bros. In 1924 he married actress Virginia Fox. They had three children, one of whom, Richard, became a highly successful film producer.

Jack Warner later insisted that Zanuck was hired as a screenwriter because he was so good at acting out the part of the studio's dog star Rin Tin Tin in story conferences. Zanuck was a fast writer, and in order that his name not appear on too many of the company's films, he used three pseudonyms: Melville Crossman, Mark Canfield, and Gregory Rogers. Zanuck moved up from writing to supervising the production of films, most notably the first talking film, *The Jazz Singer* (1927). In the late twenties Zanuck was made head of production at Warner Bros. He specialized in developing musicals, historical films, and most notably gangster films such as *Public Enemy* and

Little Caesar (both 1931). The 1932 film *I Am a Fugitive from a Chain Gang* was based on a true story and, like the gangster pictures, was the sort of film that Zanuck described as "torn from today's headlines." These were vivid, contemporary motion pictures about current social problems, the type of film that Zanuck's reputation rests on. Zanuck thought that these pictures could illuminate the world and affect people's lives for the better by exposing social problems. While one of his motivations was to improve society, another was commercial; he recognized early in his career that the public controversies over such films could help make them financially successful.

In 1933 Zanuck left Warner Bros. and with producer Joseph Schenck (1878–1961) founded a small company they called Twentieth Century Pictures. The company worked out of rented studio space, but by 1935 it was so successful that a merger was arranged with the larger Fox Film Corporation. Fox owned its own studios and theaters, but its bosses simply were not good enough producers to make enough successful pictures to keep their theaters full. At Zanuck's insistence, Twentieth Century got top billing, and the company was called Twentieth Century-Fox. Zanuck remained as head of production from 1935 until 1956.

At Fox, Zanuck continued to produce some of the types of films he had made at Warner Bros., although he was aware of the life and death of film cycles, once telling screenwriter Marvin Borowsky that Borowsky's baseball story was "too late for the last baseball cycle and too soon for the next one." There were historical films such as *In Old Chicago* (1938), musicals such as *Alexander's Ragtime Band* (1938), and Shirley Temple vehicles such as *Wee Willie Winkie* (1937), but he temporarily stopped making social comment pictures to focus on more obviously commercial genres until the studio was more solvent.

Unlike the heads of other studios, Zanuck was more interested in developing stories than in creating stars. At Metro-Goldwyn-Mayer and Warner Bros. the stories were fitted to the stars, but at Fox the stars were adjusted to the stories, so that Fox stars such as Tyrone Power and Alice Faye did not develop as distinctive star personalities as did the other studios' stars, with Shirley Temple and perhaps later Betty Grable and Marilyn Monroe being the exceptions, although Zanuck's professional interest in Monroe was limited.

Zanuck spent much of his effort working with writers in long afternoon story conferences. Screenwriter Ben Hecht recalled in his autobiographical *A Child of the Century* (1954) that Zanuck "was sharp and quick and plotted at the top of his voice, like a man hollering for help." Screenwriter Nunnally Johnson thought "Zanuck had a Geiger counter in his head" that told him "exactly where it [the script] wasn't moving right." Zanuck would dictate notes on the scripts and often suggest dialogue, although the writers understood that they should not use Zanuck's "dialogue" verbatim but improve on it. Once, when a scene came back to Zanuck exactly the way he had dictated it, his next note said it was "the worst scene I ever read in my life." Once a script was completed, Zanuck insisted it be shot as written. He almost never went on the set while a director was shooting a film.

In the evening Zanuck would run completed pictures in his projection room, along with the dailies, the material shot each day at the studio. Zanuck was ruthless in editing films, cutting out directors' favorite touches if he felt they slowed the story. Director Joseph Mankiewicz complained to writer Philip Dunne after he had completed both *A Letter to Three Wives* (1949) and *All about Eve* (1950) that Zanuck had cut both films to incoherence, but Mankiewicz won Academy Awards for writing and directing *both* films.

In 1940 Zanuck returned to "stories torn from the headlines" with his production of John Steinbeck's novel of Okies coming to California, *The Grapes of Wrath*, one of the most powerful social comment films in American cinema history. The following year he produced *How Green Was My Valley*, which retained from the novel the social issue of the struggle between the coal miners and the mine owners while also providing a nostalgic view of family life in Wales. After a brief period in the army (where he volunteered to produce documentaries for the U.S. Army Signal Corps), Zanuck returned to Fox where he produced *Wilson* (1944), a biography of Woodrow Wilson about which Deems Taylor noted, "The public was more interested in seeing films of World War II than the story of the man who tried to prevent it."

During the promotion for *Wilson*, Zanuck said that if it was not a box office success he would never make another picture without Fox musical star Betty Grable and her famous legs. While he did continue to make Grable musicals (often simply remaking the same story with new settings and new songs; having found a story he liked, he stuck with it), in the immediate postwar era he produced a series of striking films on social issues, beginning in 1947 with *Gentleman's Agreement*, based on Laura Z. Hobson's novel of genteel anti-Semitism. While there was a low-budget film that year on the same subject, Zanuck gave his film a big budget and an all-star cast including Gregory Peck, John Garfield, and Celeste Holm. The picture won an Academy Award for best picture.

The following year Zanuck made *The Snake Pit*, a film about conditions in mental institutions, which he later claimed caused twenty-six states to change their laws governing such institutions (although there has been no research to show if the changes were made and, if they were made, whether they were in direct reaction to the film). In 1949 Zanuck produced *Pinky*, the story of a light-skinned black woman who decides she should no longer pass for white. He was criticized for casting a white actress in the lead, but the film was the second-highest-grossing picture of the year and helped change attitudes within the black community about passing for white.

In 1953, to help fight the growing impact of television, Zanuck and Fox introduced the wide-screen system CinemaScope, which became one of the standard wide-screen systems of the fifties. The system, however, was better for spectacle films than for the kind of films Zanuck was best at, and he turned down such projects as *On the Waterfront*, which was made by another studio, on the grounds that it was not spectacular enough for color and CinemaScope. Such CinemaScope box office successes as *The Robe* and *How to Marry a Millionaire* did help the studio financially.

By 1956 Zanuck found he had to spend more time negotiating with writers, stars, and directors than working on films. He left Fox and became an independent producer. His independent productions were generally unimpressive, with the exception of the last one, *The Longest Day* (1962), a re-creation of the World War II Allied landings on D Day. Zanuck worked with the five writers and the three credited directors of the film, and he claimed that his job was harder than General Dwight D. Eisenhower's had been in the original landings because, unlike Eisenhower, he had to locate equipment for both sides of the battle. Zanuck's skill at story construction and editing makes the film much more coherent than many similar films.

By 1962 Fox was in financial difficulties caused primarily by the lavish production of *Cleopatra* (1963). Zanuck, to protect the release of *The Longest Day* and his Fox stock, came back to head the company as president. He installed his son Richard as head of production. The company had some financial success in the sixties, most notably with *The Sound of Music* (1965), but attempts to duplicate the success of that film resulted in large-budget disasters such as *Dr. Doolittle* (1967) and *Star!* (1968).

In December 1970 Zanuck, working with the board of directors of Fox, forced his son Richard to resign from the company, even though several of his own expensive productions, such as *Tora! Tora! Tora!* (1970), were more responsible for Fox's weakened condition than his son's hits, such as *MASH* (1970). Richard went on to become a successful independent producer, and Darryl was shifted to a more honorary position as chairman of the board. Zanuck's days of active involvement in the company were ending, at least partially because of ill health. He died in Palm Springs, California.

At a time when Hollywood films were held in disregard by the intellectual establishment, Zanuck not only produced light entertainment, but many intelligent and powerful films about contemporary social issues.

• Zanuck's papers are not collected in a single location, although libraries at both the University of California at Los Angeles and the University of Southern California have extensive collections of material from the Twentieth Century-Fox story files, which include Zanuck's working memos. Rudy Behlmer, *Memo from Darryl F. Zanuck* (1993), is a collection of Zanuck's memos, which give a good account of his professional approach to making films. Mel Gussow, *Don't Say Yes Until I Finish Talking* (1971), is the best biography of Zanuck, based on interviews with him, although it does not include his later years. Marlys J. Harris, *The Zanucks of Hol-*

lywood (1989), is more about Zanuck as a family man, but it does include material from legal documents about his professional activities. Leonard Mosley, *Zanuck* (1984), is riddled with errors. Zanuck appears in works by and about his collaborators, most notably Philip Dunne, *Take Two: A Life in Movies and Politics* (1980; rev. ed., 1992), and Tom Stempel, *Screenwriter: The Life and Times of Nunnally Johnson* (1980).

TOM STEMPEL

ZAPPA, Frank (21 Dec. 1941–4 Dec. 1993), musician, was born Francis Vincent Zappa in Baltimore, Maryland, the son of Francis Vincent Zappa, an army scientist, and Rose Marie (maiden name unknown). He grew up amid bizarre circumstances and dislocations, a factor that would decisively influence his music. The son of a Sicilian immigrant of Arab-Greek extraction and a first-generation Italian mother, Zappa's early childhood was spent in the army housing facility in Edgewood, Maryland, where the senior Zappa was involved in a chemical warfare project. Owing to the nearby storage tanks of mustard gas, the family kept a rack of gas masks on hand in case of emergency. Zappa used his as a make-believe space helmet at first and later took it apart to find out exactly how it worked. These two sides to his nature—the dramatic and the experimental—defined his career as a musician. Subsequent moves to Florida (where his father was involved in ballistics) and California (his father had a position at the naval postgraduate school teaching metallurgy) allowed Zappa relief from the chronic health problems that had plagued him in Maryland. He attended Antelope Valley High School in Lancaster, California, graduating in 1958. Almost immediately after graduating, Zappa turned to the life of the independent original musician, which he embraced with unbroken fidelity until the day he died. In 1959 he married Kay Sherman. The couple had no children and were divorced in 1964.

Zappa's youth was not uneventful musically. As he relates in his autobiography, *The Real Frank Zappa Book* (1989), his first intimation of his future came in 1957, when he read in *Look* magazine of a record salesman named Sam Goody, who could sell anything, even an album by Edgard Varèse titled *Ionisation*. "The article," remembered Zappa, "went on to say something like: '*This album is nothing but drums—it's dissonant and terrible; the worst music in the world*.' Ahh! Yes! That's for me!"

Before he could begin his career as an experimental composer, however, Zappa had to establish himself as a professional musican. He appeared in 1960 on the Steve Allen show playing a "bicycle concerto" on the spokes and handlebars. He played in cocktail lounges and planned movies. He co-wrote with Ray Collins the doo-wop song "Memories of El Monte" (1963), the royalties of which bailed him out of jail, where Zappa had landed for delivering a tape of faked grunting to an undercover policeman.

Inevitably he gravitated toward the "freak scene" in underground Los Angeles, and it was there that he founded the Mothers of Invention, with whom he re-

corded the seminal *Freak Out!* album in 1966. Although the double album sold poorly and was largely ignored by the mainstream music industry, Zappa's distinctive style and social libertarianism showed themselves in songs such as "Who Are the Brain Police?" and "You're Probably Wondering Why I'm Here." The following year he married Adelaide Gail Sloatman.

Subsequent years produced a consolidation of the essential Zappa style. Complicated production techniques mingling montage, improvisational odysseys, noise, sound effects, complex rhythms, sampled compositions by Igor Stravinsky and Varèse, witty (if uneven) lyrics, and his own contagious pop melodies informed 1967's *Lumpy Gravy* (recorded with a fifty-piece orchestra), *Cruising with Ruben and the Jets* (1968; a doo-wop theme album), and *We're Only in It for the Money* (1968), a caustic parody of the Beatles' *Sgt. Pepper's Lonely Hearts Club Band* and the hippie genre generally. This style, coming as it did in albums with names such as *Weasels Ripped My Flesh* (1970) and *Burnt Weeny Sandwich* (1970), seemed highly psychedelic in flavor to many admirers and detractors alike, a fact that pained Zappa, a lifetime abstainer from both drugs and alcohol.

Over the next decade Zappa continued to tour on and off with the Mothers, as well as composing and performing his own modern orchestral compositions whenever possible. He and Gail had four children: Dweezil, Moon Unit, Diva, and Ahmet Rodin. In this period, a fertile one even by Zappa's standards, he was responsible for dozens of albums, hundreds of songs ranging from the scatological to the socially didactic, a film (*200 Motels* [1971]), and a performance of his music with Zubin Mehta in the Hollywood Bowl, as well as a number of European symphony orchestras. These last experiences were so frustrating to Zappa that all of his later compositions were composed on the electronic synthesizer.

The 1980s brought Zappa a number of artistic rewards. In 1984 modern composer Pierre Boulez released *Boulez Conducts Zappa/The Perfect Stranger*, one of the most popular and well-received classical music albums of the year. The following year Zappa, a lifetime free-speech advocate, became the most prominent critic of the Parents' Music Resource Center (PMRC), a political organization of Washington, D.C., wives dedicated to the reform of the music industry. Zappa appeared on numerous news and interview shows and spoke before Congress to protest against the PMRC and to propound his claim that it was in fact a smokescreen to divert attention from a new tax on blank cassettes lobbied for by the recording industry. Although the PMRC did win the battle, Zappa found himself with a new career as social critic. From then until the end of his life, he was an occasional guest on television talk shows to discuss issues ranging from the Moral Majority to the AIDS epidemic.

In 1991, on the eve of Zappa's Universe, a tribute concert to be held in New York City, Moon Unit and Dweezil Zappa announced that their father had been diagnosed with prostate cancer. Over the next two years Zappa continued working at an uninterrupted pace. Before his death in Los Angeles, he completed a sequel to *Lumpy Gravy* titled *Civilization Phase III*; a new orchestral work, "The Yellow Shark"; and an album of Varèse works, *The Rage and the Fury: The Music of Edgard Varese*.

One of the least classifiable of all modern musicans, Zappa was simultaneously a composer of "serious" avant-garde music and an icon of the extravagant West Coast rock scene of the 1960s. His flamboyant, Dada-esque compositions and performances gave him and his band, the Mothers of Invention, countercultural immortality. Zappa was a rarity in American music, a sui generis figure who, like Orson Welles in film, remained true to his artistic aspirations, financing what he knew would be unpopular works with the proceeds from more conventional efforts. Although Zappa's work was probably far too idiosyncratic to be of much use to cultural historians looking to uncover his era's zeitgeist, the complexity of his career and the valor with which he pursued it ought to be remembered in any discussion of the artist and society in postwar America.

• What personal papers Zappa may have had are currently in the possession of the Zappa family. Probably the best primary source widely available is Zappa's autobiography, from which much can be learned about Zappa's life and career, although not with rigorous exactitude. The chapter on music is especially useful. Entries in the *Rolling Stone Encyclopedia of Rock and Roll* (1983; rev. ed., 1995) and Irwin Stambler, *Encyclopedia of Pop, Rock, and Soul*, rev. ed. (1990), provide useful overviews; the former is a little more extensive. Zappa was an inveterate writer of occasional prose; his liner notes, speeches, and miscellaneous writings are uncollected but of great value to students of his life and work. An obituary is in the *New York Times*, 6 Dec. 1993.

JOSHUA OZERSKY

ZARISKI, Oscar (24 Apr. 1899–4 July 1986), mathematician, was born in Kobrin, Russia, the son of Bezalel Zaritsky, a Talmudic scholar, and Hannah Tannenbaum. His father died when he was two, and he was raised by his mother, who opened a small general store, and his older brother, who taught him mathematics and encouraged him to leave the Pale of Settlement for the wider world of secular schools. He left home for a Gymnasium in Vladimir-Volynskiy when he was ten and went on to study algebra and number theory at the University of Kiev from 1918 to 1920.

The following year, seeking to escape the chaos of the Russian Revolution, he entered the University of Rome, the most important center of algebraic geometry in the world at that time. More interested in "geometric intuition" than in the rigor of their proofs, the Italians had taken algebraic geometry in exciting new directions. Zariski's talent was quickly recognized by the three mathematicians whose names now symbolize classical algebraic geometry: Guido Castelnuovo, Federigo Enriques, and Francesco Severi.

When Zariski finished his thesis in 1924 on a problem of solvability by radicals, Castelnuovo, his adviser, encouraged him to emigrate to the United States in order to take advantage of the new possibilities for rigor offered by topology. In 1927 Zariski accepted a postgraduate fellowship from Johns Hopkins University and settled comfortably into life in Baltimore, Maryland, with his wife, Yole Cagli, whom he had married in 1924; they had two children. Zariski's attack on topological problems in algebraic geometry during this period led to a series of papers on fundamental groups that marked innovations in topology as well as in algebraic geometry.

In 1932, during the writing of *Algebraic Surfaces* (1935)—a definitive account of the classical theory of algebraic surfaces—Zariski realized that "the whole structure must be done over again by purely algebraic methods." He taught himself the new commutative algebra developed in Göttingen by Emmy Noether, whom he met in 1933–1934 on a fellowship to the newly formed Institute for Advanced Study at Princeton. Contrasting himself with Noether, he later suggested that he was not "mentally made for purely formal algebra, formal mathematics. I have too much contact with real life," he said, "and that's geometry" (quoted in Parikh, p. 76).

A short note in the *Proceedings of the National Academy of Sciences* in 1937, "Some Results in the Arithmetic Theory of Algebraic Functions of Several Variables," is often regarded as the first step toward what gradually became the complete transformation of classical algebraic geometry into modern algebraic geometry. To the algebraic concept of the integral closure of a ring, announced here, Zariski would, over the next fifteen years, add general valuation rings and the completion of a local ring, and he would use these three powerful algebraic tools to develop an abstract theory of algebraic geometry valid over an arbitrary ground field. He began with the problem of the resolution of singularities of surfaces and higher dimensional varieties, which he later called a "godsend" because it gave him "ideas in general about many things." One of these ideas, which became known as Zariski's Main Theorem, is a stability result that gives a general structure theorem for birational maps and shows that a normal point cannot be modified without being destroyed. His later extension of his Main Theorem to a general connectedness theorem helped to create a valuable instrument for modern algebraic geometers.

Another important series of results that he saw as "a natural outgrowth" of his work on the resolution of singularities began with his concept of special rings and their completion, later known as Zariski rings, which he worked out in letters and conversations with André Weil, the French-born mathematician who shared his interest in rebuilding algebraic geometry on a purely algebraic basis. These results formed the beginning of a series of papers on holomorphic functions, which is often regarded as Zariski's most original work.

His work in this fruitful period was widely recognized. In 1937 Johns Hopkins promoted him to full professor, and two years later he won a Guggenheim fellowship. The National Academy of Sciences elected him to membership in 1942, and he received the Cole Prize from the American Mathematical Society in 1944.

In 1947 Zariski accepted a professorship at Harvard University, where he remained for the rest of his life, influencing the course of algebraic geometry through both his teaching and his research. Forceful and demanding, he trained a number of students who continued the work of transformation he had begun. Among them were Shreeram Abhyankar, Michael Artin, Robin Hartshorne, Heisuke Hironaka, Steven Kleiman, Joseph Lipman, David Mumford, and Maxwell Rosenlicht.

In the early 1950s, eager to test his new algebraic tools, Zariski led a small group of students in an attack on the theory of linear systems that lay at the heart of Italian geometry; together they freed it from dependence on the complex ground field and extended it to characteristic p. In the late 1950s he led another group through what remained of the classical Italian corpus in the world of characteristic zero and extended these results, too, into characteristic p. Although he never learned the radical techniques of Alexander Grothendieck that threatened to replace his own, he welcomed Grothendieck's "great generalization of the field." In 1960 he became the Dwight Parker Robinson Professor of Mathematics at Harvard.

In the early 1960s Zariski again took up the problem of singularities. He pursued "the elusive concept of equisingularity" for the next twenty years with characteristic single-mindedness. The insights he gained enabled him to give new proofs for results in his hardwon theory of surfaces, although he was still not able to discover a canonical process for the resolution of singularities in higher dimensions. Bernard Tessier, one of the many algebraic geometers who were attracted to Zariski's ideas during this period, described his work on resolution as "like a cathedral: beauty locally everywhere, directed towards a single global purpose, and a feeling of awe" (quoted in Parikh, p. 165).

In 1965 Zariski received a National Medal of Science from President Lyndon B. Johnson. In 1969 he became an emeritus professor.

During his final years, although he was plagued by tinnitus, Zariski was able to take refuge in mathematics. When he became aware of the weakening of his creative powers, his despair was eased by the devotion of his family and by the small group of former students who continued to meet with him in weekly seminars. In 1982, Israel honored him with the Wolf Prize for "harnessing the power of modern algebra to serve the needs of algebraic geometry."

Zariski died in Brookline, Massachusetts.

• Zariski's papers can be found in his *Collected Papers* (1972), which include his own description of the three main phases of his work as well as a discussion of each phase by his students.

Carol Parikh, *The Unreal Life of Oscar Zariski* (1991), presents his work in the context of his life and includes a complete bibliography.

CAROL PARIKH

ZATURENSKA, Marya Alexandrovna (12 Sept. 1902–19 Jan. 1982), poet, was born in Kiev, Russia (Ukraine), the daughter of Avram Alexander Zaturensky, a tailor, and Johanna Lupovska Zaturenska. The Zaturensky family immigrated to the United States in 1909, settling in New York City and becoming naturalized citizens in 1912. At the age of fourteen, to help support the family, Zaturenska began working odd jobs in a publishing house and at Brentano's bookstore, sometimes taking in embroidery work. She went to high school at night. During the little time she had to herself she would go to the still new Forty-second Street Library and read everything she could. Within the library's otherworldly dark wood and marble confines she discovered modern poetry by way of *The New Poetry: An Anthology* (1917), the collection put together by Harriet Monroe and Alice Corbin Henderson. Monroe was the founder of the influential literary magazine *Poetry* and an advocate of new and struggling writers. Zaturenska's first published poems appeared in *Poetry* in 1920, initially under the name "Zaturensky" (the Americanized and Russian-masculine form of her family name), and in *Harper's*. In 1922 she received *Poetry*'s John Reed Memorial Prize. Monroe and Zaturenska also formed a long-standing friendship. Zaturenska's scholastic abilities were similarly recognized in the literary world: Willa Cather secured her a fellowship to Valparaiso University, and Monroe was influential in Zaturenska's being awarded the Zona Gale Scholarship at the University of Wisconsin at Madison. She graduated from Wisconsin in 1925, after spending her last two years in the university's library school, expecting to become a librarian and thereby find a shelter in which to write poetry.

After graduation Zaturenska returned to New York and worked briefly as a newspaper reporter, but her true energies were devoted to poetry. Her friendship with Monroe also connected her to the young literary and artistic aspirants in New York's intellectual circles at the time. One of those young writers was Horace Gregory, a poet and soon-to-be critic and reviewer. Gregory had also been a student at Wisconsin. Zaturenska had not met him there, but she had heard about him from a mutual friend and teacher, the imposing and influential William Emery Leonard, "from whom she learned scattered legends of [Gregory's] erratic behavior" (Gregory, p. 163). Zaturenska and Gregory finally met in New York in the summer of 1925, introduced to each other by another joint friend, poet Kenneth Fearing. Gregory recalled that "all I saw was a slight, dark-haired, beautiful girl in a fluttering lilac-tinted organdy dress, who was as passionately devoted to poetry as I was" (Gregory, p. 163) and who was a fellow denizen of the Forty-second Street Library both as refuge and resource. On 21 August 1925 they were married. Gregory later noted that "only the most romantic and courageous of young women would have taken the chance of marrying me" (Gregory, p. 163). Their marriage would produce two children and would remain strong and loving until the end of their lives.

At the beginning, though, the young couple faced significant financial hardships—the writing life is seldom lucrative. For the rest of the 1920s, the Gregorys struggled. While taking care of their first baby, Joanna, Zaturenska kept up her writing, including her diaries; Gregory wrote his poetry as well as real estate descriptions, copy for trade journals, and book reviews, making just enough money to keep going. The one advantage to their lean lifestyle was that the stock market crash of 1929 and subsequent depression had little effect on them. Their one indulgence came on Sundays when they journeyed from their Brooklyn walk-up to the 100th Street home of poets Luis Muñoz Marín (later governor of Puerto Rico) and Muna Lee Marín. At the Marins they mixed with a crazy quilt of guests that could include explorers, diplomats, writers, dilettantes, artists, revolutionaries, and mercenaries. The Gregorys eventually moved to Sunnyside, a model housing development for low-income families near Long Island City, where they became friends with writer Lewis Mumford and literary critic Van Wyck Brooks. At Sunnyside they also acquired something approaching domestic stability, although financial stresses forced Gregory into writing book reviews virtually full-time.

Although poor, Zaturenska and Gregory were both making names for themselves as writers; they also had a large and empathetic support group. One beneficial result of overlapping acquaintances was that literary critic Malcolm Cowley secured them a three-month stay at Yaddo, the artistic enclave in Saratoga Springs, New York, in 1932. At Yaddo they had time for leisure and for writing, as well as childcare for Joanna and her younger brother, Patrick.

In 1934 the Gregorys were invited by "Bryher"—the pseudonym of Winifred Ellerman, a friend of Harriet Monroe and a writer and patron of the arts who was interested in getting to know the two writers—to spend the summer in Britain, all expenses paid. Zaturenska and Gregory's sojourn in England and Ireland was both relaxing and stimulating. They met and formed ties with most of the prominent writers of the day, including H.D., T S. Eliot, and Dorothy Richardson. The level of intellectual stimulation did sometimes become overwhelming, as when, in Dublin, Zaturenska declined the opportunity to visit William Butler Yeats and instead stayed in with the children (while Gregory went to visit).

Also in 1934, Zaturenska became formally established as a poet with promise. Her first poetry collection, *Threshold and Hearth*, published by Macmillan, received the Shelley Memorial Prize. The literary and classical allusions and mysticism in her work bore stylistic affinity to the work of Christina Rossetti and Algernon Swinburne as well as Robert Herrick and Sir Philip Sidney. In a sense, her poetry was "old-fash-

ioned," or, more accurately, "beyond fashion." Her language, though rounded and technically formal, was no less sharp in observation, possessing a poetic voice at once traditional and singular.

Her second book, *Cold Morning Sky*, was awarded the Pulitzer Prize in 1938. Her diary entry for 5 May 1938, the day Columbia University announced the winners, reads: "Wild excitement—telephones—telegrams—champagne and roses. . . . " Louis Untermeyer called her poems "a combination of delicate observation and modern vision, of sharp personality and shadowed allegory" (Barrows, p. 202). From that collection "The Lunar Tides" in particular gives a sense of some quintessential elements of Zaturenska's work, not least of which is her unique mysticism, which embraced both her Jewish heritage and her adopted High-Church Episcopalianism.

In receiving the 1938 Pulitzer Prize, Zaturenska won out over both Wallace Stevens (*Man with the Blue Guitar*) and Allen Tate (*Selected Poems*). Some literary critics, in retrospect, have questioned the wisdom of the selection committee's decision (see Hohenberg, pp. 164–65). But at its best the Pulitzer Prize committee has been as concerned with encouraging younger talented writers as it has been with recognizing established ones.

Since September 1934 Gregory had been teaching English at Sarah Lawrence College in Bronxville, New York, where he would stay until his retirement in 1960. The academic life provided the couple with both security and space: a home for their children, first in New York City and later in an old, comfortable house in Palisades; time for both Gregory and Zaturenska to write; and a haven and gathering place for the many vibrant writers and thinkers—many famous, many who would be—who were their friends.

Zaturenska's poetic output was careful and steady; she did not rush. Her lyric style, with its rhymes and controlled metrics, was contrary to modern blank verse. Her subjects, too, held onto an older objective; they addressed (sometimes coolly) personal grief, loss, decay—and joy. She had an audience; even reviewers critical of her style acknowledged her skill. Her poetic voice was constant, and she stayed with it, with no regard as to whether it was in the mainstream. She also used that voice to make accessible other poetry: not the least significant of her works are her translations from the Italian of Tasso and Stampa and Lorenzo di Medici. These verses, which have yet to be published, display both her technical proficiencies and her affinity for restrained intensity of feeling.

Two more books of original poetry followed, in 1941 and 1944. Then Zaturenska turned to prose and coauthored with Gregory *A History of American Poetry, 1900–1940* (1946), an exemplar of sound scholarship, astute criticism, and personal style (the Gregorys shared the writing equally). *A History* was critically praised and became a standard text. Zaturenska and Gregory's formal critical and editorial partnership would continue through three more collaborations.

Zaturenska's most critically acclaimed work was not a book of poetry, however, but rather a biography of the poet whom she most admired. *Christina Rossetti: A Portrait with Background* (1949) is a graceful and appreciative consideration of a poet whose reputation had diminished unjustly over time. Although her more exuberant claims for Rossetti's poetry are open to argument, and though some of the biographical sources she used were less than fully reliable, Zaturenska demonstrated a powerful skill for narrative and a sensitivity of analysis. Her "portrait" did much to resurrect Rossetti from obscurity and to open up her work to new critical discoveries and debate.

Despite this success, Zaturenska's main discipline continued to be poetry, and with the exception of her sympathetic and knowledgeable introduction to the reprint of Swinburne's *Love's Cross Currents*, she did not venture much further into prose work on her own. In 1954, five years after *Christina Rossetti*, her next book of poems was published, this time a selection of what had come before. Zaturenska was painstaking in her compositions; that, combined with the distractions of family life and the collaborations with Gregory, slowed her output—three collections in fourteen years. Her final collection, titled *The Hidden Waterfall* (1974), deliberately recalled T. S. Eliot's *Four Quarters*. In these last poems she poignantly faced the prospects of old age, most gently in "Another Snowstorm." More deeply and directly personal than her previous poems, these new ones were revenants, recalling small moments made important by time and sharing.

Following Gregory's retirement from Sarah Lawrence in 1960, he and Zaturenska settled down to a life filled with writing and reading and friends. In 1977 she was awarded an honorary doctorate from the University of Wisconsin, which pleased her greatly. And, although she did not publish any more books of poetry, she kept writing—many poems (four of which were published in *Modern Poetry Studies* in 1978, along with an illuminating interview) and always her diaries. But she had developed diabetes, and her health was failing. By the late 1970s it was sadly evident that the Gregorys could no longer live on their own. They moved in 1980 to The Anchorage, a large, airy, rambling, and estatelike retirement and nursing home outside of Shelburne Falls, Massachusetts. Their room there looked out onto the changing seasons of the lush mountainside that backed the house. Here, at the edge of the Berkshire Mountains, Alzheimer's disease began its insidious encroachment into her mind. She would try to write, and then forgetfulness and fury would take over. The change was heartbreaking. When she was herself, she would look to Gregory for assurance, which he always gave her. He had promised her that they would go everywhere together. Zaturenska died of cardiovascular disease at The Anchorage. Her husband died seven weeks later, of pneumonia.

Marya Zaturenska was the first foreign-born American poet to receive the Pulitzer Prize. In her writing, English—her second language—is meticulously and precisely wrought. Zaturenska is an important minor poet in the way that Herrick and Herbert are minor poets. Her Rossetti biography was a significant contribution to literary study and women's literature. In the 1970s she forcefully refused inclusion in a collection of women poets, being of a generation that fought hard for equal standing with men and would not be segregated, no matter the cause. Because she followed an older, traditional poetic style, her work sometimes has been viewed as anachronistic. And her influences, particularly the more florid of the Pre-Raphaelite and Decadent poets, have led some critics to devalue her work. Yet a close reading makes it clear that Zaturenska's work was not derivative; rather, she was a better writer than most of those she emulated. The lyric, with touches of religion and Romanticism, sensuousness and sound, was her decided voice; sometimes she changed her timbre but never her form—it was her own brand of independence.

She said of herself, "I am a pure, I hope, lyric poet. There are few of us around these days. I write my poems as if I were writing a song" (Phillips, "The Real Thing," p. 36). In instances where the music of the words seems to obscure the meaning, Zaturenska's work is a precursor to Dylan Thomas's "sound over sense" approach to poem building. In a way, her poems are more like settings than single gems. They need to be read in groups, as some critics have rightly observed, for their full effect. As her husband lovingly observed: "Poetry was part of her sense of being alive. . . . Her poems haunted the imagination and the soul, and her lyricism was that of music sounding through a dream" (Gregory, p. 164).

• A substantial collection of Zaturenska's letters, manuscripts, and memorabilia are in the Marya Zaturenska and Horace Gregory Collection at the Syracuse University Library. Other papers remain with the Gregory family. The annual "memory books," consisting of photos, notes, and other ephemera compiled by and about the residents of The Anchorage, are still at The Anchorage in Shelburne Falls, Mass. A brief selection from her diaries was published as "Marya Zaturenska's Depression Diary, 1931–1932," with an introduction by Mary Beth Hinton, in *Syracuse University Library Associates Courier* 31 (1996): 125–52. Robert Phillips, "The Real Thing: An Interview with Marya Zaturenska," along with four previously unpublished poems, appears in *Modern Poetry Studies* 9, no. 1 (Spring 1978): 33–50. Zaturenska's other poetical works include *The Listening Landscape* (1941), *The Golden Mirror* (1944), *Selected Poems* (1954), *Terraces of Light* (1960), and *Collected Poems* (1965). She also edited the *Collected Poems of Sara Teasdale* (1966) and the *Selected Poems of Christina Rossetti* (1970). Her other collaborations with Gregory are *The Mentor Book of Religious Verse* (1957), *The Crystal Cabinet* (1962), and *The Silver Swan: Poems of Romance and Mystery* (1966). A recording of Zaturenska reading six of her poems at a New York City poetry reading in 1949 is included on the Library of Congress phonodisc *Poets Reading Their Own Poems* (1954). Poetry recitations by her and Gregory can be heard on the ABC Studios (New York) tape recording *Poems. Selections* (1948). Horace Gregory's keenly observed and elegantly written autobiography, *The House on Jefferson Street: A Cycle of Memories* (1971), covers his and Zaturenska's life together up through the summer of 1934.

Reviews of her work include Babette Deutsch, *Poetry in Our Time* (1952; rev. ed., 1963); Kenneth Fields, "Review of *Collected Poems*," *Southern Literary Review* 5, no. 2 (Spring 1969): 577–78; Robert Phillips, "A True Lyric Poet," *Ontario Review* 2 (Spring/Summer 1975): 98–100; Robert B. Shaw, "Courtly Music," *Poetry*, May 1975, pp. 100–102; and E. D. Lloyd-Kimbrel, "Christina Rossetti," in *St. James Guide to Biography* (1992). See also Marjorie Barrows, comp., *Pulitzer Prize Poems* (1941), and John Hohenberg, *The Pulitzer Prizes: A History of the Awards in Books, Drama, Music, and Journalism, Based on the Private Files over Six Decades* (1974). Obituaries are in the *New York Times*, 21 Jan. 1982, and the *Bookman's Weekly*, 22 Feb. 1982.

E. D. LLOYD-KIMBREL

ZAVALA, Lorenzo de (3 Oct. 1788–15 Nov. 1836), politician in Mexico and Texas, was born Manuel Lorenzo Justiniano de Zavala y Sáenz in Tecoh, Yucatán, near Mérida, the son of José Anastasio de Zavala y Velázquez, a notary, and Bárbara Sáenz y Castro. He received a classical education in Mérida but rejected the priesthood. He joined a band of liberal intellectuals who read forbidden copies of John Locke, Voltaire, and Jean-Jacques Rousseau smuggled into Mexico, and Zavala wrote and circulated revolutionary political tracts. The Spanish Inquisitors ordered him to report to Mexico City, but the political turmoil caused by the Mexican independence movement saved him from trial in 1812.

Zavala edited the first newspaper ever published in Mérida in 1813 and was elected a delegate to the Spanish Cortes, but the restoration of King Ferdinand VII to the Spanish throne in 1814 ended the brief reform movement in Spain and its colonies. Zavala was imprisoned in the notorious fortress of San Juan de Ulúa in the harbor of Veracruz from 1814 to 1817 for his revolutionary activities. With other political prisoners he became a Freemason and mastered English and medical books available to him. After his release he became a physician and with the aid of powerful men returned to Mérida, where he supported his family by his medical practice. Although under surveillance of the Crown, Zavala initiated like-minded men into the forbidden order of Freemasons and urged the creation of a constitutional monarchy.

When the Spanish Constitution of 1812 was reinstituted in Spain in 1820, Zavala returned to journalism and was chosen a deputy to represent Yucatán in the Cortes in Spain. By the time he reached Madrid in January 1821, he was convinced that Yucatán must be independent from Spain. When the session closed in June, deputies from the American colonies were discouraged, but the question was moot for Zavala because Mexican independence had been achieved. Zavala took his seat in the newly formed Mexican constituent congress in March 1822 and assisted Stephen F. Austin, who arrived in Mexico City at that time seeking confirmation of the colonization contract issued to his father in the final days of Spanish Mexico. Zavala was president of the congress in 1824, when the Republic of Mexico adopted its constitution, and also served as senator from Yucatán.

Political ambition caused Zavala to move to the state of Mexico, where he served as governor from 1826 to 1829, instituting, among other reforms, free higher education and establishing public libraries. In 1829 he became minister of finance under President Vicente Guerrero, the second president. The following year a coup by the conservative centralist faction that favored a strong central government in opposition to the federalist party that had crafted the constitution of 1824, which permitted strong states and a weak central government, deposed Guerrero. In June 1830 Zavala fled to New York, where his only son, Lorenzo, Jr., was attending school. He left his ill wife, Josefa Teresa Correa y Correa, whom he had married in 1813, and a daughter in the care of friends. His wife died in 1831.

While in New York, Zavala sold his interest in his 1829 colonization contract (to settle families in southeastern Texas) to a group of New York speculators in October 1830. The Galveston Bay and Texas Land Company also acquired two other contracts covering all of eastern Texas, but the project, of doubtful legality, was unable to recruit sufficient European settlers as specified by a recent law in spite of Zavala's efforts in Europe in 1831. While in Paris, in 1831, he published volume one of his *Ensayo Histórico de las Revoluciones de Mégico desde 1808 hasta 1830* (Historic essay of Mexican Revolutions from 1808 until 1830). Volume two was published in New York in 1832.

A federalist revolt led by General Antonio López de Santa Anna in 1832 resulted in the general's election as president the following year. Zavala returned to Mexico in August 1832 and reoccupied his seat as governor of the state of Mexico in October. He worked feverishly during early 1833 to have the legislature pass reforms limiting the powers of the established elites: the church, the military, and the wealthy landowners. He also took a seat in the national congress briefly from October to December 1832 and served as president of the chamber of deputies.

In November 1832 President Santa Anna named Zavala minister plenipotentiary to France, and he sailed for New York with his second wife, Emily West (whom he had married in 1831 and with whom he had three children), and their children, including Lorenzo, Jr., who served as his father's secretary. The family reached Paris in April 1834. While there, in 1834, he published his *Viaje á los Estados-Unidos del Norte de América* (Journey to the United States of North America). However, disenchanted with Santa Anna's turn toward centralism, Zavala resigned his post in August and returned to New York City.

Zavala wrote to friends in May 1835 that he planned to move to Texas to develop his land speculations in order to support his family. On his way he paused in New Orleans, where he met with other Mexican federalist refugees to plot the overthrow of Santa Anna. While others aroused federalist support in the states along the Rio Grande, Zavala rallied disaffected Anglo Texans to the federalist cause. He bought a home on Buffalo Bayou opposite what became the San Jacinto battleground, and his family arrived from New York in December. Santa Anna ordered Zavala's arrest because of his revolutionary activities in Texas, but local civil authorities refused to carry out the order, and the Anglo Texans captured the military garrison at Anahuac. However, by the close of 1835, the majority of the Anglo Texans preferred severing ties with Mexico, and Zavala faced the dilemma with characteristic pragmatism.

Zavala's neighbors elected him a delegate to the convention to be held at Washington-on-the-Brazos in March 1836. Faced with the inevitable, Zavala, along with two native Tejanos, signed Texas's declaration of independence. Just before adjourning on 17 March, amid untrue rumors that Santa Anna's army was approaching, the delegates elected Zavala vice president of the interim government of the Republic of Texas.

The new government met at Harrisburg near Zavala's home, but on 13 April word reached the community that Santa Anna was crossing the Brazos intent on capturing the Texan officials. The Zavalas fled with the others to Galveston Island while young Lorenzo joined Sam Houston's army. After the Texan victory on 21 April, scouts captured the Mexican president and brought him into General Sam Houston's camp, where Lorenzo, Jr., served as translator. Zavala arrived at the battleground by steamer on 23 April and discovered that his house was being used as a hospital for wounded Texans and Mexican officers. Zavala met with Santa Anna who, to save his life, had already agreed to order his troops on the Brazos River to retreat.

After treaties were signed between Santa Anna and the Texas government on 14 May, Zavala agreed to accompany Santa Anna to Veracruz, where he was to use his influence to secure the recognition of an independent Texas. But a revolt by newly arrived volunteers from the United States prevented the Texas government from fulfilling its arrangement to send Santa Anna home. The weak and bickering interim government, unable to control the volunteer army, disgusted Zavala, and he retired to his home in June, ill with fever. He gradually regained his strength but took no further role in Texas politics when the election was called in September to choose permanent officers. While crossing Buffalo Bayou with his small son in November 1836, the boat capsized, throwing the pair into the cold water. Saving the boy taxed Zavala's strength and led to his death a few days later at home at Zavala Point (now Harris County, Tex.).

• Zavala documents written after July 1835 are in John H. Jenkins, ed., *The Papers of the Texas Revolution* (10 vols., 1973). Zavala family papers are at the Center for American History, University of Texas at Austin; first deposited in Galveston in the 1870s, the documents were replevied, some lost, before being sent to the university. A detailed Zavala genealogy appears in Jose Maria Valdes Acosta, *A Traves de las Centurias*, vol. 2 (1926). Zavala's published works are useful, and his *Journey to the United States of North America* was translated and published in 1980. The best study of Zavala's political career is Raymond Estep, "Lorenzo de Zavala" (Ph.D. diss., Univ. of Texas-Austin, 1942); it was subse-

quently published in Spanish in 1955. María de la Luz Parcero López, *Lorenzo de Zavala: fuente y origen de la reforma liberal en mexico* (1969), published by the Instituto Nacional de Antropolgía e Historia, is a scholarly work concentrating on Zavala's contributions as a liberal reformer; except for in Yucatán, his native state, Zavala is usually viewed as a traitor for joining the Texans in 1836. For additional information on Zavala, consult Margaret Swett Henson, *Lorenzo de Zavala: The Pragmatic Idealist* (1996).

MARGARET SWETT HENSON

ZECKENDORF, William (20 June 1905–30 Sept. 1976), real-estate developer, was born in Paris, Illinois, the son of Arthur Zeckendorf, a hardware merchant and shoe manufacturer, and Bertha Rosenfield. When he was three years old, his family moved to Cedarhurst on Long Island, where his father joined Jacobs & Sons, an early mass producer of shoes for mail-order retailers. In 1917 the family moved to a large apartment in the Darrleton at Seventy-first and Broadway, an area attracting an increasing number of well-to-do Jewish families. Zeckendorf attended DeWitt Clinton High School; thoroughly bored with classes, he enrolled at Clark's School for Concentration to cram for regent's exams. He skipped his senior year of high school and enrolled at New York University at the age of seventeen.

Zeckendorf enjoyed many aspects of college—playing football, partying with his fraternity, watching "delightfully giddy flappers"—but not the classes required for his major in commerce. He quit in his third year and went to work for his uncle Sam Borchard in real estate, doing "housekeeping"—collecting rents, dealing with tenant complaints, buying supplies. But Zeckendorf had no interest in that end of the business; he wanted to be in sales. He kept asking for a chance. So when Borchard was leaving for Europe on a family trip, he gave Zeckendorf the challenge of filling a half-empty office building at 32 Broadway. He did. But Borchard, upon returning, gave Zeckendorf small credit for his accomplishment; Zeckendorf quit in anger and went to work for Leonard Gans, a well-established New York real-estate broker. With his first successful deal for Gans, he married Irma Levy in Sept. 1928, and the couple sailed to Europe for their honeymoon.

During the depression years Zeckendorf made his living in two ways. He negotiated for owners trying to salvage their properties from foreclosure from banks and insurance companies. He also tried to ferret out the few buyers still active for the properties the banks and insurance companies were holding and anxious to unload. In this work Zeckendorf was reasonably successful, but he drifted apart from his wife, with whom he had two children. In 1934 they divorced.

In 1938 Webb & Knapp, a "reputable if not very profitable firm," offered Zeckendorf a partnership. In 1937 he had brokered the sale of an office building to Webb & Knapp. After losing several major tenants the next year, they asked Zeckendorf to find new ones. When he quickly succeeded, the partnership offer followed. The firm, which had long been very conservative, had little capital to work with until 1940. Then a young cousin of the senior partner Eliot Cross joined and put $400,000 in the firm's coffers. This permitted Zeckendorf—by far the most aggressive partner—to expand significantly Webb & Knapp's activities. The most notable purchase was of a building on Fifty-fourth and Madison that housed what appeared to be a very successful nightclub. Appearances deceived; soon Zeckendorf had responsibility for a nightclub, one which he transformed into a highly successful club that netted half a million before it was sold in 1948. In 1940, Zeckendorf's private life changed again; he met Marion Griffin when he saved her poodle from an attacking bull dog. He was enchanted with the attractive, vivacious woman from Waycross, Georgia; they married in December.

In 1942 Webb & Knapp got the big break that would make it, for a time, perhaps the world's largest real-estate company and launch Zeckendorf on his spectacular career in real-estate development. Vincent Astor had been called to active duty; he wanted to put management of his extensive properties into professional hands. Because Astor's attorney was a close friend of Eliot Cross, Webb & Knapp was invited to submit a proposal for managing the properties. Astor had properties worth more than $50 million, debt-free, but producing no profit. When Zeckendorf met Astor, he dismissed the usefulness of soliciting competing management proposals; he then told Astor his assessment of Astor's holdings: "For the most part, Commander, they stink; they are outmoded." Zeckendorf then laid out his ideas about what properties to sell, how to sell them, and what to buy in their place. In June 1942, Webb & Knapp became the exclusive consultants for reorganizing the Astor holdings. The next morning, the story was front page news in the *New York Times*; overnight Webb & Knapp were the best known real-estate firm in America. When completed in 1945, the Astor reorganization had taken 152 transactions, increased aggregate value by a third, and was generating a steady profit of $2.5 million. And the publicity had brought dozens of offers to the firm, giving Zeckendorf the opportunity to unleash his enormous energy and creativity in dozens of new ventures.

In 1946 Zeckendorf completed what he himself considered his most important real-estate transaction. He had a vision of "creating value" by developing "inventive, original, and eminently sensible use" for core areas in a city, similar to what Columbia University had achieved with the land that became Rockefeller Center. Along the east side of Manhattan's midtown stretched a huge complex of Swift and Wilson slaughterhouses and cattle yards. In 1946 Webb & Knapp was offered the entire area, but at a steep price. Zeckendorf finally agreed, and then, working through other brokers, bought seventy-five adjacent parcels at very low prices. He turned to Wallace Harrison for a grand design of office towers and apartments for the nearly seventeen acres of "X City." By December 1946, Zeckendorf was ready to launch this project.

But then a crisis developed around the siting of the United Nations. Unable to find a suitable location in the city, the UN was considering moving to Philadelphia. On 6 December Zeckendorf offered part of his parcel; eight days later Nelson Rockefeller called to confirm that his father would buy it for the UN. Zeckendorf told his wife Marion, "We have just moved the capital of the world."

Two years later, after Zeckendorf bought out his partners to become the sole owner of Webb & Knapp, he determined to bring modern design to his large projects. With the help of Nelson Rockefeller, he hired Dick Abbott from the Museum of Modern Art to interview architects; Abbott soon brought Ieo Ming Pei, then a professor at Harvard's Graduate School of Design, to Zeckendorf. Soon Pei was on board; Zeckendorf then built a large creative staff around Pei.

Zeckendorf soon embarked on a series of enormous urban projects, beginning with Mile High City in Denver in 1953. He then initiated similar landmark projects such as Place Ville-marie in Montreal, L'Enfant Plaza in Washington, D.C., Century City in Los Angeles, Kips Bay Plaza in New York City, and Society Hill in Philadelphia. Because of such projects, arguably no twentieth-century developer has had so significant an impact on the revitalization and—because of his insistence on giving gifted young architects like Pei a lead role—on the design of major downtown centers in the United States and Canada. In addition, Zeckendorf bought and sold vast tracts of land from Canada through most of the Americas, constantly looking for opportunities to convert the land to new uses or exploit opportunities, even in oil and minerals. He also financed more than thirty Broadway shows and was a major benefactor to Long Island University, which opened a new health sciences center named for him in 1995.

Along with the completed projects, Zeckendorf had as least as many that he trumpeted but that never got off the drawing board. He was nearly always overextended, commonly borrowing at usurious rates, leveraging his properties to the maximum by selling or mortgaging every component, and selling properties prematurely, failing to recoup his investment, all to try to maintain a cash flow to sustain current expenses. His largest single failure was probably his Freedomland Amusement Park, built on a 300-acre parcel in the Bronx. It crashed; on that site Co-op City then rose in the 1960s.

In 1965 Zeckendorf's zeal to make every deal brought him down; Marine Midland Bank forced Webb & Knapp into Chapter 10 bankruptcy. In 1968, soon after his wife died in a tragic airline crash, Zeckendorf himself declared personal bankruptcy. In 1970 he suffered the first of a series of strokes. He did remarry twice more, to Alice Bache in 1972, from whom he was soon divorced, and to Louise Betterly Malcolm in 1975, who survived him. In April 1976, a grand jury handed down two indictments against Zeckendorf for tax evasion; they were unresolved when he died in his Park Avenue apartment in New York City.

• There are apparently no Zeckendorf papers extant. However, he wrote an engaging and revealing, if self-serving autobiography, which conveys a sense of both his creativity and recklessness: *The Autobiography of William Zeckendorf*, with Edward McCreavy (1970). Also see Elliott Bernstein, "Real Estate's Humpty-Dumpty: Bill Zeckendorf after the Fall," *New York*, 23 Sept. 1968, pp. 28–31; "Awesome Mr. Z," *Look*, 11 June 1957, pp. 102–4, 113; and "Businessmen in the News," *Fortune*, Oct. 1957, p. 72. An obituary is in the *New York Times*, 2 Oct. 1976.

ELDON BERNSTEIN
FRED CARSTENSEN

ZEISBERGER, David (11 Apr. 1721–17 Nov. 1808), Moravian missionary, was born in Zauchtenthal, Bohemia, the son of David Zeisberger and Rosina (maiden name unknown), freeholders. Followers of the United Brethren (Moravian church), they moved in 1726 to Herrnhut, Saxony; in 1736 the parents went with the Moravians to Georgia. Zeisberger, after a brief indenture, joined them in 1737. The family moved to Pennsylvania in 1740, settling at Bethlehem in 1741. There Zeisberger began his study of American Indian languages in preparation for his vocation as a missionary.

In the midst of King George's War and seeking to learn an Iroquoian language, Zeisberger visited the Mohawk chief Hendrick at Onondaga, the central fire of the Six Nations, in 1745. Amid rumors that Catholic and foreign agents were operating among the Iroquois, Zeisberger was arrested and jailed by New York on suspicion of treason. His refusal on grounds of conscience to take an oath of loyalty to the king delayed his release; he was freed in March 1746 thanks to the intercession of Pennsylvania governor Thomas Penn and the Indian agent Johann Conrad Weiser. Zeisberger then undertook active work in mission towns of the Susquehanna and Lehigh valleys. After a trip to Germany, England, and Holland in 1750–1751, Zeisberger resumed his study of Iroquois languages at Onondaga from 1752 to 1755. In 1758, during the Seven Years' War (1754–1763), Zeisberger attended the great Indian treaty conference at Easton, Pennsylvania, at which the eastern Delawares made peace with the British and promised to help bring the western Delawares of the upper Ohio Valley to peace. After the war Zeisberger returned to his missionary labors among eastern Delawares in the Susquehanna Valley. In 1767 he ventured to the upper Ohio Valley. There, among the western Delawares, Zeisberger became the most successful Protestant missionary to independent Indian peoples of the colonial and revolutionary eras. Working at a distance from Euroamerican settlements, he allowed the persistence of certain native economic arrangements and kept council with neighboring Indian leaders. In what is now Ohio, on the Muskingum River, Zeisberger gathered a Delaware following at Schoenbrunn in 1772 and directed the work of John Heckewelder, who led the establishment of Gnadenhütten that year. Some 400 converts filled these and several other "Moravian Indian" villages.

Zeisberger and the Delaware Christians confronted a revitalizing Delaware Indian religion. Indian "prophets," particularly Wangomend, challenged Zeisberger's spiritual authority and threatened to attract the Christians. Indeed, prophetic missionaries of the revitalized religion defeated Zeisberger's efforts to spread Christianity to the Shawnee. Zeisberger recorded the contests in his diaries and discussed them in his "History of the North American Indians" (1779–1780).

The American Revolution further confounded his efforts. Most of the region's Indian peoples allied with Great Britain, while Delawares divided and Moravian Indian communities remained nominally neutral. On a brief visit to Bethlehem, Zeisberger married 37-year-old Susan Lecron on 4 June 1781; she accompanied him back to the Ohio Country. Quietly pro-American, he and other missionaries sent intelligence to Americans at Pittsburgh and Fort Laurens. Suspecting this, anti-American Wyandots and Delawares arrested the missionaries, carrying them to be interrogated by Detroit's British commander, Arrent De Peyster, in 1781. Zeisberger skillfully satisfied De Peyster, but before he could return to Schoenbrunn and Gnadenhütten, American militiamen under David Williamson captured and executed the majority of their inhabitants on 8 March 1782. Until now pro-American, Zeisberger remained with refugee Delawares until 1792 among other British-allied Indians near either Detroit or the shores of Lake Erie, preaching at various sites. In 1792 Zeisberger led the formation of a Delaware mission at New Fairfield, Ontario. Although American troops under William Henry Harrison destroyed the town in 1813, the Delawares rebuilt it, and the mission lasted until 1903. This is not Zeisberger's only lasting mark; he also left a wealth of ethnographic and linguistic material in his writings. Much of George Henry Loskiel's *History of the Missions* (1792) is appropriated from Zeisberger's "History."

In 1798, with the support of Congress and such prominent Americans as Rufus Putnam, Zeisberger returned to Schoenbrunn and established the new mission town of Goshen, Ohio. When he died there, the mission had only twenty-two inhabitants.

• Zeisberger's papers, diaries, and other manuscripts, generally in an archaic German script, are at the Moravian Archives of Bethlehem, Pa. Many have been microfilmed and published, with extensive translations by William Nathaniel Schwarze, as Carl John Fliegel et al., eds., *Records of the Moravian Mission among the Indians of North America from the Archives of the Moravian Church, Bethlehem, Pennsylvania* (40 reels, 1970). In print, Zeisberger's writings include Eugene F. Bliss, ed. and trans., *Diary of David Zeisberger: A Moravian Missionary among the Indians of Ohio* (2 vols., 1885); P. S. Du Ponceau, trans., *Essay of a Delaware-Indian and English Spelling-Book* (1776); *Grammar and Language of the Lenni Lenape or Delaware Indians* (1827); Archer Butler Hulbert and William Nathaniel Schwarze, eds. and trans., "The History of the North American Indians," *Ohio Archaeological and Historical Society Publications* 19 (1910): 1–173; Hulbert and

Schwarze, eds. and trans., "Diary of David Zeisberger and Gottlieb Senseman, Journey to Goschgoschunk on the Ohio and Their Arrival There, 1768," *Ohio Archaeological and Historical Society Publications* 21 (1912): 42–69; and *Zeisberger's Indian Dictionary* (1887).

His biographies are Edmund De Schweinitz, *The Life and Times of David Zeisberger* (1870); Elma E. Gray, *Wilderness Christians: The Moravian Mission to the Delaware Indians* (1956); and Earl P. Olmstead, *Blackcoats among the Delaware: David Zeisberger on the Ohio Frontier* (1991). See also John Heckewelder, *A Narrative of the Missions of the United Brethren among the Delaware and Mohegan Indians, from Its Commencement, in the Year 1740 to the Close of the Year 1808* (1820); and George Henry Loskiel, *History of the Missions of the United Brethren among the Indians of North America*, trans. Christian Latrobe (1794).

GREGORY EVANS DOWD

ZEISEL, Hans (1 Dec. 1905–7 Mar. 1992), legal scholar and statistician, was born in Kaaden, in the present-day Czech Republic, the son of Otto Zeisl, a lawyer, and Elsa Frank, a journalist. (Zeisel added a second *e* to his family name after he emigrated to the United States.) Zeisel's family moved to Vienna, Austria, when he was an infant, and the intense cultural and political atmosphere of prewar and interwar Vienna did much to form his character. He studied at the University of Vienna, receiving a law degree in 1927 and a doctorate in political science in 1928. He practiced law, but his most enduring experience in Vienna was his association with the mathematician-turned-psychologist Paul F. Lazarsfeld. They became leaders of the young socialist movement at the university, and Zeisel served as a researcher at a small social research institute that Lazarsfeld had established. They remained colleagues and friends until Lazarsfeld's death in 1976. In 1938 Zeisel married Eva Stricker, an internationally known ceramics designer; they had two children.

Zeisel's association with Lazarsfeld set the course for his professional career. The first enduring product was a 1930s study of unemployed workers in the village of Marienthal, near Vienna, undertaken by Lazarsfeld's research institute and published in 1933 as *Die Arbeitslosen von Marienthal: Ein soziographischer Versuch über die Wirkungen langdauernder Arbeitslosigkeit*, coauthored by Marie Jahoda, Lazarsfeld, and Zeisel. An English translation, *Marienthal: The Sociography of an Unemployed Community*, was published in 1971. Methodologically, it is notable for its eclectic use of interviewing techniques, participant observation, life history analysis, and a variety of unobtrusive measures, such as changes in the frequency of reading library books and newspapers. Substantively, it is important for its analysis of the worker apathy and alienation that presaged the rise of National Socialism. In addition to directing the field work in Marienthal, Zeisel took the photographs for the book and wrote a bibliographical appendix on the international status of community studies.

Three months after the 1938 Anschluss, Zeisel was forced to leave Austria, and he emigrated to New York. Lazarsfeld had arrived in New York five years earlier, and he assisted Zeisel—as he assisted many other refugees—in finding a position in the relatively new field of market research, an activity at which they both had become skilled in Vienna. Zeisel was highly successful in this field in New York City, becoming first the manager of media research at the McCann-Erickson advertising agency (1943–1950) and subsequently an executive at the Tea Council (1950–1953).

Zeisel's next major publication was his distinctive and influential text on the analysis and reporting of survey data, *Say It with Figures* (1947), which has subsequently been published in six English-language editions and has been translated into six foreign languages. It is notable for its clear presentations of a theory of causation, of the construction of statistical tables, and of regression and reason analysis. At the 1976 memorial service for Lazarsfeld, Zeisel modestly described the book as "the expanded codification of what we had learned from Paul."

A crucial turning point in Zeisel's career was his appointment in 1953 as a professor at the University of Chicago Law School. For four decades his teaching and research were almost entirely devoted to the use of empirical social research to clarify questions of law. His long association with Lazarsfeld had prepared him for this new career, but he brought to it a brilliance and an originality of his own. One of his principal associates during the Chicago years was the legal scholar and law professor Harry Kalven, Jr. Together, with financial support from the Ford Foundation, they applied social research procedures and perspectives to the empirical study of the American jury system. *Delay in the Court* (1959), written with Kalven and Bernard Buchholz, is a study of court congestion in civil litigation and the jury's role in it. "The law's delay" has been decried at least since Hamlet's famous complaint; Zeisel and his associates ascertained the length and circumstances of delay for different kinds of cases and examined the efficacy of various administrative proposals for reducing it. *The American Jury* (1966), written with Kalven, is a study of 3,576 criminal jury trials held in the United States during the 1950s. The researchers learned through interviews that judges disagreed with the jury verdict in only 22 percent of the cases studied. A conclusion was drawn that the evidence produced in court, rather than the values of the jury members, is the most important determinant of verdicts.

After the death of Kalven in 1974, Zeisel collaborated for more than a decade with psychologist Shari Seidman Diamond. They jointly published a series of research papers related to the efficacy of different procedures in the court system. The topics examined included sentencing disparities between judges, the effectiveness of specially appointed sentencing councils, the merits of twelve-member juries versus smaller ones, the effects of peremptory challenges by trial lawyers on the outcome of trials, and the frequent inconsistencies regarding the death penalty. Inconsistencies stemming from inadequate instructions to juries by judges was a problem Zeisel was conducting research on at the time of his death. In *The Limits of Law Enforcement* (1983), Zeisel examined the frequent failure of both laws and the police to prevent felonies and misdemeanors and concluded that changing the social environment offers the best hope. *Prove It with Figures: Empirical Methods in Law and Litigation* (1997) is a methods text written for practitioners, law teachers, and their students. It is in effect a summary of what Zeisel had learned during a lifetime of using empirical research to illuminate and solve practical problems in the law. Unfinished at Zeisel's death, the manuscript was completed and brought to publication by his longtime associate, legal scholar David Kaye.

Like his mentor and friend Paul Lazarsfeld, Zeisel was primarily a methodologist, but he had passionate views on a number of substantive topics. For example, he expressed his disapproval of capital punishment by collecting evidence suggesting that capital punishment not only fails to serve as a deterrent to murder and other capital crimes but also discriminates unfairly against blacks accused of murdering whites. He acted on his belief in the importance of constitutional rights by his 1965 support of a lawsuit against the House of Representatives Un-American Activities Committee, pointing out that many of the committee's questions violated the witnesses' constitutional rights.

Zeisel was a fellow of the American Academy of Arts and Sciences, the American Statistical Association, and the American Association for the Advancement of Science; he was a consultant to the Rand Corporation and many other research institutes; and he was a member of the governing board of the *Bulletin of the Atomic Scientists*. In 1967 the American Association for Public Opinion Research awarded him its highest honor, the AAPOR Award for Exceptionally Distinguished Achievement. In 1992 the American Sociological Association honored him with its Paul F. Lazarsfeld Award for his contributions to quantitative social research. In his entry in *Who's Who in America*, Zeisel described himself simply as "scientist." He died in Chicago, Illinois.

• A collection of Zeisel's books and papers is in the library of the University of Chicago Law School. Zeisel's collaboration with Shari Seidman Diamond on the effects of jury selection is reflected in their "The Jury Selection in the Mitchell-Stans Conspiracy Trial," *American Bar Foundation Research Journal* 1 (1976): 151–74; on sentencing disparities between judges see "Sentencing Councils," *University of Chicago Law Review* 43 (1975): 109–49, and "Search for Sentencing Equity," *American Bar Foundation Research Journal* 2 (1977): 883–940; on twelve-member versus smaller juries see "'Convincing Empirical Evidence' on the Six Member Jury," *University of Chicago Law Review* 41 (1974): 281–95; on peremptory challenges see "The Effect of Peremptory Challenges on Jury and Verdict," *Stanford Law Review* 30 (1978): 491–531; and on inconsistencies in the use of the death penalty see Diamond's "Instructing on Death," *American Psychologist* 48 (1993): 423–34. Two of Zeisel's publications on capital punishment are "The Deterrent Effect of the Death Penalty: Facts and Faith," in *Supreme Court Review*, ed. Philip B. Kurland (1976), pp. 317–43, and "Race Bias in the Administration of

the Death Penalty: The Florida Experience," *Harvard Law Review* 95 (1981): 456–68. His analysis of the testimony given to the House Un-American Activities Committee is in Zeisel and Rose Stamler, "The Case against HUAC—The Evidence: A Content Analysis of the HUAC Record," *Harvard Civil Rights—Civil Liberties Law Review* 11 (1976): 263–98. Obituaries are in the *New York Times*, 11 Mar. 1992; American Sociological Association, *Footnotes* (May 1992); and *Public Opinion Quarterly* 56 (1992): 536–37. A Festschrift was published as a special issue of the *University of Chicago Law Review* 41 (1974): 209–96.

DAVID L. SILLS

ZEITLIN, Solomon (31 May 1892 ?–28 Dec. 1976), historian and scholar of religion, was born in Tshashaniki, Russia, the son of Yale Zeitlin and Levitt Zeitlin. He studied in Russia with Rabbi Joseph Rozin Rajoslover. He then studied at the University of Paris, where he received a D.Th. He was ordained a rabbi at the École Rabbinique in Paris. In 1915 he immigrated to the United States and went on to graduate in 1917 with a Ph.D. from Dropsie College in Philadelphia, Pennsylvania, where he spent the remainder of his career as a professor of Jewish history (1918–1925) and rabbinical literature (1925–1976). Zeitlin also served on the faculties of the Jewish Theological Seminary and Yeshiva University in New York and in 1919 was among the founders of the American Academy for Jewish Research. He was the longtime editor of and a regular contributor to the *Jewish Quarterly Review*. Never married, he lived all his adult life in a bachelor apartment at the Drake Hotel in Philadelphia.

Zeitlin spent most of his academic career defending his convictions about Jewish history. The annotated bibliography of his works enumerates 406 books and articles. His prolific scholarly output started with *Megillat Taanit* (1922), a book on Jewish chronology in the Hellenistic and Roman periods, but his first claim to a scholarly breakthrough came with the publication of *The Slavonic Josephus and Its Relation to Josippon and Hegesippus* (1929), in which he proves that the so-called Slavonic Josephus is a medieval work written in Old Russian.

Zeitlin advocated a scientific approach to the study of history as opposed to a dogmatic one. He held the opinion that a credible historian should not attempt to concentrate authoritatively on more than one epoch in history or on more than one facet of that epoch. Yet, this belief did not deter him, an inter-Testamental specialist, from writing a biography of Maimonides (1935), studies on Jewish identity and education, and numerous articles on other wide-ranging contemporary Jewish issues.

In the early 1950s Zeitlin began what was to become a lifelong polemic concerning the authenticity and dating of the Dead Sea Scrolls, refuting their antiquity and claiming that they had no value for studies in early Christianity or the origins of normative Judaism. Denouncing the results of carbon-14 tests and paleography, he was convinced that the scrolls were composed between the seventh and twelfth centuries of our era by "semiliterate" messianic Jews of Karaitic descent.

The main points of his controversial position are found in *The Dead Sea Scrolls and Modern Scholarship* (1956), a collation of previous articles on the subject. Zeitlin was widely challenged and harshly criticized for these contentions, from which he never withdrew. The French scholar A. Dupont-Sommer remarked bluntly: "Zeitlin's theory is no longer credited in the scientific world and for good reasons, but the author continues to complain bitterly that his arguments have not been refuted" (*The Essene Writings from Qumran* [1961]).

In *Who Crucified Jesus?* (1942), Zeitlin contributed to New Testament scholarship and advanced arguments toward the eradication of anti-Semitism. In a period when most textbooks still carried the accusation that the Jews were solely responsible for the death of Jesus, he maintained that the Romans and their collaborators, the high priests, carried out the crucifixion.

Zeitlin's main contribution to the history of the Second Commonwealth was his narrative history of the period, *The Rise and Fall of the Judean State: Studies in the History of Early Judaism*, published in four volumes (1962–1978), which repudiated the theories of the German theologians who had previously dominated scholarship in the field. At the time, this work filled a gap in the history of the inter-Testamental period. Committed to the principles of text reconstruction and the pivotal role of the Jewish Halakhah, Zeitlin fought for the recognition of rabbinic sources as equal in status to other non-Jewish sources of the Second Commonwealth. In addition, he contended that no serious scholar should treat that history without a thorough knowledge of Jewish law. His ongoing debate with Arnold Toynbee, who supported Arab claims for Palestine, reflected Zeitlin's concern for the young Jewish state. He argued a Jewish claim for Palestine based on title.

Despite his extensive rabbinic training, Zeitlin was critical of Orthodox Judaism. He urged contemporary rabbis to change and modernize the law and frequently spoke of what he considered to be the stagnation of the Israeli rabbinate. However, he is chiefly remembered as an innovative historiographer, whose views on the halakhic differences between the Pharisees and Sadducees represent a major breakthrough in the interpretation of the history of the Second Commonwealth. Unfortunately, his reputation has been damaged through a perceived intractability with respect to his views on the Dead Sea Scrolls. He died in Philadelphia, having incorporated a personality of a true Zealot who fought fiercely for a better understanding of the Jewish sources of the Second Commonwealth.

• Zeitlin's writings are listed in Sidney B. Hoening, *Solomon Zeitlin: Scholar Laureate—An Annotated Bibliography, 1915–1970 with Appreciation of His Writings* (1971). For specific writings on the inter-Testamental period see *Studies in the Beginnings of Christianity* (1924), *Josephus on Jesus* (1931), and *Sadducees and Pharisees* (1936). An obituary is in the *New York Times*, 30 Dec. 1976.

DINA RIPSMAN EYLON

ZENGER, John Peter (1697–28 July 1746), printer, was born in the German Palatinate, the son of Johanna Zenger (his father's name is unknown). In 1710 his family was part of a company of Palatine refugees whose migration to New York by way of England was financed by the British Crown. He arrived with his mother, a younger brother, and a younger sister; his father had died on the voyage. Governor Robert Hunter, who assumed the care of many of the newly arrived Palatine boys for assignment to apprenticeships, signed the articles apprenticing Zenger to William Bradford, at that time New York's only printer, on 26 October 1710. Zenger's mother ratified the articles of indenture the following year.

Zenger, free from his indenture to Bradford in 1718 at the age of twenty-one, married Mary White in Philadelphia in 1719 and opened a printing business in Chestertown, Maryland, where he sought to become the colony's official printer. Both his first printing enterprise and his first marriage turned out to be short-lived. Mary Zenger died, and Zenger returned to New York, where he married Anna Catharina Maulin in 1723. In 1725, the year Bradford founded the city's first newspaper, the *New-York Gazette*, he took Zenger into a printing shop partnership that lasted only until the younger man set up on his own in 1726.

Now in competition with his former partner and master, Zenger struggled for a living. Between 1726 and the end of 1731, he produced but twenty-one books, pamphlets, and broadsides, compared with Bradford's fifty-four imprints and newspaper. He found a small niche for himself in Dutch-language sermons and religious tracts, which accounted for eight of his seventeen imprints before 1731. He also printed Peter Venema's Dutch-language *Arithmetica* of 1730, the first arithmetic text printed in the colony. This small specialty, however, was not enough to sustain a competitive printing business. In 1732 his fortunes began to change because of the mutual discovery of New York's opposition political faction and Zenger's very available printing press.

The arrival in August 1732 of a new governor, William Cosby, set off a chain of political events that shaped Zenger's immediate future and secured his place in history. Among other unpopular acts, Cosby claimed half the salary of his acting predecessor, Rip Van Dam. When Cosby decided to facilitate his suit against Van Dam by conferring equity jurisdiction on the supreme court, the wealthy and influential chief justice Lewis Morris protested loudly and was forthwith dismissed from his post. Thus Morris became the focus of a powerful opposition party, whose tracts Zenger now printed, bringing his production of imprints in 1732 actually higher than Bradford's in that year. The alliance between the Morrisite party and Zenger's press continued through 1733, culminating in the founding of the *New-York Weekly Journal*, which Zenger printed over his own name under the silent sponsorship of the Morrisite leaders and the effective editorship of James Alexander, a lawyer and member of the provincial council. The first number of the *Weekly Journal* appeared, under the misprinted date of 5 October, on 5 November 1733. From its beginning, the paper specialized in essays ranging from abstract statements of libertarian philosophy, often copied from the opposition press in Britain, to more specific attacks on Cosby and his associates. For several weeks the administration tried to ignore the *Journal*, but finally began to respond with counterattacks in Bradford's *Gazette*, marking the beginning of a "paper war," a new feature of the factionalized political culture of New York.

The province council ordered four numbers of Zenger's *Journal*—nos. 7 (17 Dec. 1733), 47 (23 Sept. 1734), 48 (30 Sept. 1734), and 49 (7 Oct. 1734)—to be publicly burned as seditious. On 17 November 1734, eleven days after the burning order was carried out, Zenger was imprisoned on a warrant from the council charging him with seditious libel. Unable to meet the bail set by the court, Zenger spent eight and one-half months in jail, though the *Journal* continued to appear, until he came to trial in the supreme court of the province on 4 August 1735. The grand jury having refused to indict him, he was tried on Attorney General Richard Bradley's "information" that he had published "false, scandalous, malicious, and seditious" libels in numbers 13 (28 Jan. 1734) and 23 (8 Apr. 1734) of the *Journal*.

As all parties understood, Zenger's trial was really more a political than a legal exercise. During the pretrial proceedings, Chief Justice James De Lancey had disbarred Alexander and William Smith, who were to have represented Zenger, and appointed another attorney, John Chambers, in their place. Alexander, however, recruited his friend Andrew Hamilton of Philadelphia, who appeared on the day of the trial to take over the defense. Hamilton's address to the jury asserted the right of the jury to determine matters of law as well as of fact and held that the truth of an utterance could be upheld as a defense against a charge of libel. Both assertions were contrary to the common law that then prevailed, but it took the jury only a few minutes of deliberation to return a verdict of innocent. Hamilton was immediately hailed as a popular hero and Zenger as a symbol of the free press as a bulwark against tyranny. The case attracted great interest in both England and America, especially after the publication of the proceedings in 1736 and its republication in many editions over the rest of the century. In reality, the Zenger case changed nothing in the law in the short run, and its direct influence on later changes in both British and American libel law along the lines argued by Hamilton was apparently negligible. However, the significance of the Zenger case has been a matter of great interest and debate by successive generations of historians.

After Zenger's acquittal, the *New-York Weekly Journal* became simply another newspaper, in rivalry but no longer in open political warfare with Bradford's *New-York Gazette*. The occasion for the close participation of its former Morrisite sponsors had run its course, and Cosby died in 1736. In 1737 Zenger was appointed official printer for New York and, in 1738, for New Jersey as well. He continued his printing business and his newspaper until his death when he was succeeded by his widow who owned and operated the business until his eldest son, John, one of the six children who survived him and apparently the only child of his first marriage, succeeded to the business in December 1748. The specific place where Zenger died is not known; it presumably was in New York.

• Historical and biographical interest in Zenger has focused almost entirely on his trial of 1735. *A Brief Narrative of the Case and Trial of John Peter Zenger*, written by James Alexander and published originally by Zenger in 1736, is readily accessible in two twentieth-century editions, both accompanied by helpful scholarly supplements. Livingston Rutherford's *John Peter Zenger: His Press, His Trial and a Bibliography of Zenger Imprints* (1904) contains a reprint of Alexander's narrative and is introduced by useful biographical information, some of which is not readily accessible elsewhere. Stanley Nider Katz's carefully edited and annotated edition of *A Brief Narrative* (1963; repr. 1989), which can now be taken as the standard scholarly edition and for most purposes the most useful one, is introduced by a thorough interpretive account of the episode and is accompanied by other documents not originally included. Other important interpretations of the Zenger case include those in Stephen Botein, *"Mr. Zenger's Malice and Falshood"*: Six Issues of the New-York Weekly Journal, 1733–1734* (1985); Leonard W. Levy, *Emergence of a Free Press* (1985), a revision of his earlier *Legacy of Suppression: Freedom of Speech and Press in Early American History* (1960); Levy, "Did the Zenger Case Really Matter? Freedom of the Press in Colonial New York," *William and Mary Quarterly*, 3d ser., 17 (1960): 35–60; and Michael Warner, *The Letters of the Republic: Publication and the Public Sphere in Eighteenth-Century America* (1990). Some discussion of Zenger's early career and the founding of the *New-York Weekly Journal* can be found in Charles E. Clark, *The Public Prints: The Newspaper in Anglo-American Culture, 1665–1740* (1994). Early sources on Zenger's career and the Zenger case include Isaiah Thomas, *The History of Printing in America* (1810; repr., ed. Marcus A. McCorison, 1970); and Cadwallader Colden, "History of William Cosby's Administration . . . ," New-York Historical Society, *Collections* 68 (1935). Irving G. Cheslaw combines a thorough narrative and biographical treatment of Zenger with an interpretation of the case in *John Peter Zenger and "The New-York Weekly Journal"* (n.d.).

CHARLES E. CLARK

ZÉSPEDES Y VELASCO, Vicente Manuel de (1720–21 July 1794), military officer and governor and captain-general of Spanish East Florida, was born in southern Castile, Spain, where his father (name unknown), a member of the lesser nobility, held the rank of *hidalgo*. (His mother's identity is unknown.) Zéspedes entered military training in 1734. Beginning active duty in 1737, he spent thirty months at Oran, a north African port, then transferred to garrisons in Spanish America: Cartagena de Indias, in present-day Colombia (1740); Santiago de Cuba (1741), where he became a lieutenant in the *Piquets de Victoria*; and finally to Havana as secretary of government for Governor and Captain-General Francisco de Cagigal de la Vega from 1747 to 1754.

After rising to captain of the grenadiers, an elite unit of the Havana Regiment, Zéspedes commanded two companies sent in 1761 to defend Pensacola (Fla.), which was under siege by British-supported Creek Indians. Sorties against the Indians over a period of seven months achieved peace. In June 1762 the appearance of a British naval squadron at Havana revealed the surprising news that England had declared war on Spain the previous December. For the grenadiers' efforts in prolonging the siege until August, Zéspedes received a royal citation when his regiment returned briefly to Spain following the surrender of Havana.

By terms of the Treaty of Paris in 1763 ending the globally fought Seven Years' War, Spain lost Florida—a Spanish province since 1513—to Great Britain but regained Havana and acquired New Orleans and Louisiana Territory west of the Mississippi River from France. When New Orleans residents opposed Spanish occupation in 1768, Zéspedes accompanied the expedition to suppress insurrection as battalion executive officer. In 1770 he commanded forces sent to Santiago de Cuba, where attack from Jamaica was feared at the time of the crisis with the British concerning possession of the Falkland Islands. After Spain declared war on England in 1779, he became inspector of troops, and as colonel of the Havana Regiment he directed mobile units patroling the north coast of Cuba. He went to Santiago for the third time in 1782 to become interim provincial governor.

Following the second Treaty of Paris in 1783, which returned the Floridas to Spain as well as granted independence to thirteen British colonies, Zéspedes in December was appointed governor and captain-general of East Florida with a promotion to the rank of brigadier in the Spanish army. He arrived at St. Augustine on 26 June 1784 with an occupation force of 1,500 persons, including 500 troops, administrative personnel, and dependents. Evacuation of British Loyalists was completed in September 1785.

Zéspedes's primary concern was the defense of the province at the eastern end of Spain's colonial claims in North America, in 1784 stretching to the Pacific Ocean. To assure peace on the Indian frontier, he held his first Indian congress on 30 September 1784 with both Spanish and British officials present to indicate continuity of Indian policy despite the change in governments. A larger congress took place in the town plaza on 8 December, when leaders of the Lower Creek towns in Georgia as well as the nearby Seminoles stated that they no longer opposed the return of Florida to Spanish sovereignty. Zéspedes granted the Scots firm Panton, Leslie and Company a monopoly privilege to continue supplying British merchandise for the Florida Indian trade, although he did not receive royal permission for this exception to Spanish trade regulations until March 1786. Undetected by American authorities, the governor supplied ammunition for Creek warriors protecting hunting grounds on the Georgia frontier.

Zéspedes's domain in East Florida was restricted by a 1765 British Indian treaty to an area about ninety miles along the Atlantic coast south of the Georgia-Florida border, the St. Mary's River, extending inland about twenty-five miles to the St. John's River valley. He took charge of a diverse civilian population, including approximately 1,000 of European and 500 of African heritage, free and enslaved. Although a few British planters remained and several former Florida families returned from Cuba, the core of the civilian population in St. Augustine became the 470 Minorcan survivors of a British colonizing project that had arrived at New Smyrna in 1769. The garrison personnel, comprising Spanish, Cuban, and Irish military units, formed an integral part of St. Augustine society. The northern district of the province, still inhabited by a few hundred British sympathizers, remained a law-defying border zone kept under constant surveillance.

In governing East Florida, Zéspedes followed his experienced and flexible view of "the good of the royal service" rather than the letter of the law. Obtaining pesos from Mexico and provisions from American ports posed major problems. To inculcate Spanish Catholic values, Zéspedes established an integrated school for all boys in St. Augustine taught by a hospital chaplain. The governor's family was drawn into administrative and hospitality service. Sublieutenant Vicente Domingo and Cadet Antonio had special assignments as members of their father's regiment in Florida. Two older sons, Thomas and Fernando, who had served in Bernardo de Galvez's West Florida campaigns, were with regiments in Spain.

The first important visitors to Zéspedes's home were General Nathanael Greene, who had acquired a Loyalist plantation on Cumberland Island, and Benjamin Hawkins, recently appointed American emissary to the Creeks. In March 1785 they were charmed by Zéspedes's wife, Doña Concepción de Aróstegui, member of a wealthy Havana family, and the Zéspedeses' daughters, Dominga and Josepha, who both married officers in Florida. In a letter to his wife, Greene remarked, "The Governor who is rather corpulent has a good share of natural benevolence and is more remarkable for politeness than understanding." Zéspedes disapproved of "republican" government.

Zéspedes forwarded information to Diego de Gardóqui, the Spanish ambassador in New York, concerning American conspiracies to acquire Spanish territory, beginning with the suspicious appearance of Kentuckian James Wilkerson in New Orleans in 1785. Through Captain Carlos Howard, his English-speaking secretary of government, Zéspedes corresponded with Creek spokesman Alexander McGillivray and British and American informants. Although he discouraged Americans from coming to East Florida, he admitted Catholics requesting services of a priest, since there were none in the southern states.

The high point of Zéspedes's regime was the celebration of Charles IV's ascent to the throne, elaborately observed in St. Augustine on 2–4 December 1789. When portraits of the new monarchs were unveiled, the governor flung into the crowd specially minted silver medals. In the spring of 1790, learning that McGillivray was going to New York to make a treaty with the American government, he dispatched Captain Howard to intercept McGillivray and accompany him to New York and remain throughout negotiations. On 15 July 1790 Zéspedes sailed for Havana, where he lived until his death there. He had firmly reestablished Spanish rule and set the course for governing East Florida, a province that became American territory in 1821. He was promoted to *mariscal del campo* and named governor of Yucatan, but he was unable to serve.

• The only study of Zéspedes's career is Helen Hornbeck Tanner, *Zespedes in East Florida, 1784–1790* (1963), which contains most source material. Other publications by the same author that provide pertinent information are "Zespedes and the Southern Conspiracies," *Florida Historical Quarterly* 37 (1959): 15–28, and *General Greene's Visit to St. Augustine in 1785* (1964).

HELEN HORNBECK TANNER

ZEUNER, Charles (20 Sept. 1795–7 Nov. 1857), composer, organist, and pianist, was born Heinrich Christoph Zeuner in Eisleben, Saxony, Germany. No information is available about his parents. He studied in Weimar with Johann Nepomuk Hummel, who had studied with Mozart. Zeuner also studied in Erfurt with Michael Gotthard Fischer, who had been a pupil of Johann Christian Kittel, one of the last students of Johann Sebastian Bach. During the 1820s Zeuner published a set of piano variations and four polonaises in Erfurt, a piano rondo in Frankfurt, and *Fantaisie pour le pianoforte sur un air de la petite Russie*, op. 7 in Leipzig. He apparently served for a time as a court musician near his birthplace and as a military musician, since at his death he possessed medals given by Napoleon's generals.

Although some reports claim that Zeuner emigrated to Boston in 1824, it was more probably in 1830. The impetus may have been enquiries from the Handel and Haydn Society, since Zeuner's Missa no. 3 in E-flat, signed "H: C: Zeuner" and therefore probably composed in Germany, is dedicated to the society. On 13 February 1830 he made his American debut as organist, pianist, and vocalist in a program that included his *Grand Fantasie* for organ (based on a theme of Handel), piano variations on "Hail Columbia," and variations on "[Home,] Sweet Home" for horn. The following September Zeuner became organist for the Handel and Haydn Society. He was elected president of the society on 28 May 1838. During his years in Boston, he served as organist at three successive churches and also taught organ, theory, and singing. In 1831 Zeuner became president of the Musical Professional Society, which presented ten concerts of instrumental works before its demise.

Because of chronic absences from meetings of the Handel and Haydn Society, Zeuner was forced to resign on 7 February 1839. His opposition to Boston musician Lowell Mason's practice of adapting secular tunes for hymn tunes may have been involved in the conflict. Zeuner moved to Philadelphia and became organist at St. Andrew's Episcopal Church, where he remained from 1840 to 1845; he subsequently served as organist at the Old Arch Street Presbyterian Church. He applied for U.S. citizenship in November 1856; it is not clear whether or not he actually obtained citizenship. He had a stormy temperament and was described in *Dwight's Journal of Music* as "testy and sensitive" (17 Jan. 1861). Symptoms of mental instability became increasingly evident, and he committed suicide in Philadelphia.

Zeuner composed many songs and piano works that were published as sheet music, some advertised in the *Board of Music Trade Catalogue* (1870). Of his many hymn tunes, "Hummel" and "Missionary Chant" may still be found in modern hymnbooks. Zeuner also wrote larger works, beginning with Missa Solemnis no. 1 in C moll, published in Leipzig by Breitkopf und Härtel probably in 1826. His compilations of church music published in Boston include *Church Music* (1831), *The American Harp* (1832; later printings to 1844), *The Ancient Lyre* (1833; twenty editions to 1857), and *The New Village Harmony* (1833; 2d ed., 1835). Zeuner composed and arranged music for a wide variety of media, including organ, piano, chorus, orchestra, band, chamber ensemble, and solo instrument or voice with orchestra. His larger works are in the early nineteenth-century German tradition, imaginative and well crafted.

Zeuner is credited with writing the first concertos in the United States: his two "Grand Organ" concertos were premiered 21 November 1830 and 18 May 1834, respectively. He also composed the first collection of organ music published in the United States, *Voluntaries for the Organ* (1830), dedicated to the Handel and Haydn Society. This and his second such publication, *Organ Voluntaries* (1840), contain useful service music. Of the Zeuner manuscripts at the Library of Congress, one containing twenty fantasies and fugues, all are marked "für die Orgel" except for two, which are evidently for pianoforte. His cantata *Praise Ye the Lord* for choir, tenor solo, and orchestra was performed by the Handel and Haydn Society on 4 July 1838. His oratorio *The Feast of Tabernacles*, performed eight times in its entirety by the Boston Academy of Music in 1837, is the first large-scale work of its kind composed in the United States; the libretto is by the Reverend Henry F. Ware, Jr., of Harvard.

Zeuner was not the first professional German composer to emigrate to the United States, but he was the first of such high quality. His first decade in the United States was his most prolific. Reports of his superb performing abilities and examination of his manuscript scores reveal that he was the best-trained and most talented composer-performer in the United States in the 1830s and early 1840s. He is responsible for raising American musical standards to new levels.

• Most of Zeuner's manuscript and printed scores are in the Newland/Zeuner Collection at the Library of Congress; other materials are at the Free Library of Philadelphia. The most extensive study on Zeuner is William George Bigger, "The Choral Music of Charles Zeuner (1795–1857), German-American Composer, with a Performance Edition of Representative Works" (Ph.D. diss., Univ. of Iowa, 1976). His organ music is discussed in J. Bunker Clark, *The Dawning of American Keyboard Music* (1988). New information concerning his life, with a valuable list of works, is in Karl Loveland, "The Life of Charles Zeuner, Enigmatic German-American Composer and Organist," *Tracker* 30, no. 2 (1986): 19–28. His "Grand Centennial March, as Performed by the Boston Bands" (1830), is in Clark, ed., *Anthology of Early American Keyboard Music, 1787–1830* (1977). The following are in the series Three Centuries of American Music: "The Soft Bugle: A Romance" (1830), in Nicholas Tawa, ed., *American Solo Songs through 1865*, vol. 1 (1989); "Variations on Yankee Doodle" (1830s), in Clark, ed., *American Keyboard Music through 1865*, vol. 3 (1990); *The Fall of Zion*, for bass voice and orchestra (undated), ed. Sam Dennison, in Philip Vandermeer, ed., *American Sacred Music*, vol. 7 (1991); and *Variations pour le cor* (dated c. 1840 but probably from the 1820s) in Dennison, ed., *American Orchestral Music, 1800 through 1879*, vol. 9 (1992). Barbara Owen, ed., *A Century of American Organ Music* (4 vols., 1975–1976; 1983–1991), contains several solo organ works by Zeuner, but those labeled *Fuga* 1, 3, 4, and 14 are actually by Zeuner's teacher Michael Gotthard Fischer. Zeuner's first organ concerto is available in Betty Pursley, "Charles Zeuner's Concerto No. 1 for Organ and Orchestra: An Edition and Commentary" (D.M.A. diss., Univ. of Kansas, 1988).

J. BUNKER CLARK

ZEVIN, Israel Joseph (31 Jan. 1872–6 Oct. 1926), writer, was born in Gorki, Mogilov district, Belorussia, the son of Judah Leib Zevin (occupation unknown) and Feige Muravin. He grew up in the Pale of Settlement, receiving a traditional Jewish-Orthodox education.

In 1889 he immigrated to New York City, where he tried to make a living at various of the typical immigrant jobs. First he was a peddler; then he graduated to selling candy and other wares from a stand. In his spare time he wrote stories that were published in the *Yidisher Tageblatt* (*Jewish Daily News*). These proved so popular that in 1893 he was employed as a staff member, starting a professional affiliation that was to last until his death (with the single interruption of a short period in 1894 when he worked for the Philadelphia *Yidishe Presse* [*Jewish Press*]).

The *Tageblatt* was until the turn of the century the dominant Yiddish daily paper in New York; its circulation increased tenfold in the 1890s, reaching 40,000 in 1900. The paper's conservative policy was determined by its Orthodox owner Kasriel Sarasohn, and its sensationalist slant was the work of editor John Paley. Zevin's humorous stories about the problems that Orthodox immigrants encountered in the New World contributed to the popular appeal of the *Tageblatt* and conformed to the paper's traditionalist line. His character monologues aptly gave voice to the experiences of the baffled immigrants for whom he was writing. Zevin brought to his stories, most of which were published under the pen name Tashrak and collected in *Y. Y. Zevin's Geklibene Shriften* (1906), *Geklibene*

Shriften (1909), and *Tashrak's Beste Ertsehlungen* (4 vols., 1910), a great warmth of understanding that inspired sympathetic laughter, earning him the appellation "the Yiddish Mark Twain." He was unable, though, to offer his readers either the pragmatic advice or the imaginative and stylistic challenges that his contemporary Abraham Cahan blended into his own more enduring writing. Although Zevin and his colleagues at the *Tageblatt* (Zevin for a time as editor in chief after the death of Paley in December 1907) managed to increase the circulation of their paper to 69,000 by 1911, Cahan's policy on the *Vorwaerts* (*Jewish Daily Forward*) secured a far greater share of the ever-growing Yiddish-reading market, selling more than 122,000 copies a day in the same year.

Zevin was nevertheless a widely read journalist and author. In 1905 he had started to publish in English, undertaking the translation of some of his stories for the English-language section of the *Tageblatt* and for the *American Hebrew*. During the period 1914–1917 he regularly wrote for the Sunday edition of the *New York Herald*, contributing more than eighty vignettes of New York Jewish life. His stories and sketches featured such stock characters as Shulem the Shadchen (marriage broker), Joe the Waiter, and Katzenellenbogen the Newspaper Critic. Of uneven quality, these pieces usually work up effectively to a humorous point that is often fairly predictable. In "Shulem the Shadchen Tells of Clubbing for a Husband," four sisters, working at low-paid jobs, decide to share one good-quality hat, dress, etc., in order to win an adequate husband; as the title indicates, the girls are eventually forced to chip in even for a dowry but just for one of them. The weakest of these sketches are rather awkwardly composed of a few unrelated tales; the strongest feature schlemiel-like characters whose bad luck could have haunted them anywhere, in the Old World or the New. Thus "Katzenellenbogen Pays the Bill" relates how a group of men, meeting regularly in a restaurant for conversation over tea, decide that he will pick up the tab who fails to obey "his wife's first order on his coming home" that night. It turns out that all the men comply except for Katzenellenbogen, who recounts the next day:

When I came near the house I saw that . . . my wife was waiting for me. I made up my mind to do everything she'll tell me. Once for all I must show that I am a man of courage. But think of it what she told me to do! As I opened the door . . . she got up to meet me halfways and, standing in the centre of the room, she cried: "Shame! How can you look straight in my eyes? Aren't you ashamed to come home at this hour of the night? You ought to take a rope and hang yourself!" I thought I'd rather pay the bill than take my wife's order.

Zevin's English-language work did not interrupt the steady flow of his Yiddish writing: *Hayim der Kostromer Pedler* (1917) was followed by a volume of children's tales *Maaseh'lech Far Kinder* (1919), based on the bedside stories he told the two daughters he had with Sophia Berman, whom he had married in 1908. While he continued to contribute widely to the press (from 1924 he even wrote for the *Tageblatt*'s conservative competitor the *Morgen Journal* under the pen names of Dr. A. Adelman and Meir Zonenshayn), Zevin devoted his spare hours to anthologizing and translating into Yiddish a wealth of stories from the talmudic and rabbinic literature (*Ale Agadoth fun Talmud* [3 vols., 1922], *Der Ozar fun Ale Midroshim* [4 vols., 1926]) and the parables of the eighteenth-century preacher Yankev Krantz (*Ale Meshalim fun Dubner Magid* [1925]).

His own work became the subject of similar adaptation when Irving Meites published *The Marriage Broker, Based on the Stories of Shulem the Shadchen by Tashrak* in 1960. Zevin died in New York. A posthumous novel, *Fun Achzehn bis Dreisig*, appeared in 1929.

The popularity Zevin enjoyed as a humorist, journalist, and anthologist during his lifetime has not translated itself into any lasting impact. His name is rarely recalled in the present-day histories of Yiddish-American culture.

• The most comprehensive discussion of Zevin occurs in Zalmen Reisen, *Leksikon fun der Yidisher Literature*, vol. 4 (1929). Sol Liptzin, *A History of Yiddish Literature* (1972), has a paragraph on Zevin's writing. An obituary is in the *New York Times*, 7 Oct. 1926.

GERT BUELENS

ZHITLOWSKY, Hayim (1865–6 May 1943), philosopher and theoretician of Jewish socialism, diaspora nationalism, and Yiddish culture, was born in Uschatchi, a small town near Vitebsk, Russia, the son of Yosef Zhitlowsky, a successful flax merchant, and Hava Hasia Weinstein. His father, a child prodigy, combined rabbinical learning with hasidic pietism and business acumen with devotion to modern Jewish enlightenment. Zhitlowsky disliked the traditional Jewish elementary education he received in *heder*, so when the family moved to Vitebsk, his parents provided him with two tutors—for Hebrew and religious studies and for Russian and secular studies. He entered Gymnasium at age fourteen and became converted to the revolutionary Russian movement known as the People's Will. Zhitlowsky left school, assumed a Russian name, and went to Tula to propagate socialism. After a year and a half he returned to Vitebsk, deciding "to remain true to my two-fold duty as a Jewish intellectual" to serve socialism and the Jews.

By the time Zhitlowsky settled in the United States in 1908 he had completed a full career as a Russian revolutionary, Jewish socialist, and philosopher of diaspora nationalism. His first publication, *Thoughts on the Historical Destiny of Jewry* (1887), written in Russian and funded by his father, contrasted the moral superiority of Jews in ancient times to their current degradation due to unrelenting poverty and persecution, concentration in nonproductive middleman occupations, and estrangement of the Jewish intelligentsia from the masses. Like his subsequent Russian pamphlet, *A Jew to Jews* (1892), it generated sharp criticism from Jewish intellectuals. Zhitlowsky argued for the independence of the Jewish people and the need for Jewish intellectuals to fight for Jewish national and not just civic equality. He also saw a close connection between socialism and nationalism and thus between the Russian revolution and Jewish liberation. Zhitlowsky developed his ideas in Switzerland, first in Zurich, where he went to university in 1887, and then in Bern, where he received his Ph.D. in philosophy in 1892 with a thesis on "Abraham Ben David and the Beginning of the Aristotelian Period in Jewish Religious Philosophy." In 1893 he joined six other expatriates to found the Union of Social Revolutionaries abroad, the nucleus of the future Russian Social Revolutionary party, and he coedited its journal.

Zhitlowsky opposed Marxism because he rejected scientific socialism, specifically economic determinism, dialectical materialism, and historical teleology; he thought socialism and nationalism were compatible and saw the interests of workers and peasants as being in accord. He understood socialism to mean that all peoples were equal, none were chosen; similarly, internationalism meant all peoples were brothers. He argued that Jews were a nation scattered among many states, and increasingly he saw Yiddish as the cultural and spiritual embodiment of the Jewish nation. In 1898 he published "Zionism or Socialism" in the *Jewish Worker*, the Yiddish paper of the General Jewish Workers' Union, or Bund, organized in 1897 in Russia by Jewish socialists. In this article he attacked Zionism for its bourgeois and clerical associations and argued for the creation of a Jewish socialism grounded in Yiddish culture. The essay provided the intellectual rationale for the Bund's program of cultural autonomy. Zhitlowsky had attended the first Zionist Congress in 1897 in Basle as a journalist, but not until the devastating Kishinev pogroms in 1903 did he add the Zionist idea of autonomous Jewish settlement or territorialism to his program. His family life also disintegrated in 1903. He had married Vera Lokhova, a Russian revolutionary who was not Jewish, in 1888, and they had had six children. Zhitlowsky's first marriage, which had been arranged for him at a young age, had previously ended in divorce. In 1903 he abandoned his family after discovering that his wife had had an affair. He subsequently married a third time, also to a non-Jewish woman (name unknown) and with her had three more children.

Zhitlowsky first visited the United States in 1904 on a lecture and fundraising tour. His ideas about Jewish socialism and the importance of Yiddish attracted positive responses among intellectuals. In the United States he edited *Das Folk* (The People), a socialist territorialist organ, and lectured on such subjects as "The Jew and the Man" and "The Future of Nationalities in America." The latter, in English, argued that the United States would be a model, the first international nation made up of peoples from all over the world. In "The Jewish People and the Yiddish Language" he compared how Jews were denied status as a nation because they lacked land with how Yiddish was denied status as a language because it lacked grammar—yet Jews were a nation and Yiddish was a language. Zhitlowsky returned to Europe and ran for the second Russian Duma in 1906. By the time his election was confirmed, the Duma dissolved.

In 1907 Zhitlowsky helped Dovid Pinski and Nathan Birnbaum organize the first international conference on Yiddish culture held in Czernowitz in Bukovina, Austria, in 1908. That year he finally immigrated to the United States, where he focused his energies on propagating Yiddish language and culture. In 1909 he worked to establish the first national radical Jewish school in New York City that combined instruction in Yiddish language and literature with socialist teachings and became a model for Yiddish schools established both by the socialist Workmen's Circle and the Zionist Jewish National Workers Alliance. In 1910 he published *Philosophy: What It Is and How It Developed*, a two-volume philosophical treatise that Zhitlowsky hoped would introduce Yiddish readers to the history of philosophy and "help create an intelligentsia that writes and thinks in Yiddish." From 1912 to 1919 he published his collected works in ten volumes. Zhitlowsky gave a resounding "no" to the question "Should We Build Our Culture Here in English?" (1931), arguing that voluntary spiritual unity required a common culture in Yiddish. Yiddish was "a raft which can save us from drowning," he wrote; without land, Jews need language as a substitute to prevent assimilation.

Zhitlowsky joined many Jewish organizations in America. In 1915 he supported an American Jewish Congress. After the Balfour Declaration in 1917 he joined the Labor Zionists, wrote for their daily, and championed recruitment for the Jewish Legion to fight in World War I. He edited *Dos Naye Lebn* (The New Life) from 1908 to 1913 and again in 1922 when it was revived. In 1914 he joined the staff of the Yiddish paper *Der Tog* (The Day), writing for it with few breaks until his death. In 1931 he helped establish the Jewish Culture Society and contributed to its monthly, *Yidish*. He also wrote for *Tsukunft*, including a series of articles popularizing Albert Einstein's theories of relativity.

The 1929 riots in Palestine discouraged Zhitlowsky about Zionism's future. After Hitler's rise in Germany he turned to the Soviet Union as an antifascist ally of Jews. In 1937 he helped found the left-wing Yidisher Kultur Farband, a communist-oriented association devoted to preserving and furthering Yiddish culture through an arts section, writers groups, reading circles, and publications. Although he opposed Marxism, he became a fellow traveler except during the years of the Nazi-Soviet pact. In 1941, overlooking Stalin's many murders and injustice, he chaired the pro-Soviet Committee of Jewish Writers and Artists. Zhitlowsky died in Calgary, Canada, while on a lecture tour for the Jewish section of the communist-affiliated International Workers Order. His funeral in New York City on 12 May 1943 drew both communist and noncommunist Jewish writers. Perhaps they

agreed with a contemporary Yiddish writer who observed on the occasion of Zhitlowsky's seventieth birthday celebration that "We all live in Dr. Zhitlowsky's territory" (Epstein, p. 317).

Because relatively few of Zhitlowsky's writings have been translated from Yiddish his ideas have slipped into obscurity. Yet his concept of a Yiddish diaspora and his commitment to a humanist socialism influenced later intellectuals such as Irving Howe as well as such contemporary thinkers as Daniel and Jonathan Boyarin, and their relevance continues to be felt in the United States, a nation of immigrants.

• Zhitlowsky's papers can be found at the YIVO Institute for Jewish Research, New York. In addition to his *Collected Writings* (Yiddish), which appeared in three editions (1912–1919, 1929–1932, 1945–1951), a *Zhitlowsky Zamelbuch* (Yiddish), which contains a memoir and biography, was published in 1929 in honor of his sixtieth birthday. Zhitlowsky published a three-volume autobiography, *Recollections of My Life* (1935–1940), but it does not get beyond his years in Switzerland. Much less has been published in English. Melech Epstein, *Profiles of Eleven* (1965), includes a biography of Zhitlowsky. Emanuel S. Goldsmith, *Architects of Yiddishism at the Beginning of the Twentieth Century* (1976), focuses on the development of Zhitlowsky's thought in a biographical context. An essay by Israel Knox, "Zhitlowsky's Philosophy of Jewish Life," was published in *Contemporary Jewish Record* 8, no. 2 (Apr. 1945): pp. 172–80. Irving Howe and Eliezer Greenberg translated two of Zhitlowsky's essays in *Voices from the Yiddish* (1975), the autobiographical "The Jewish Factor in My Socialism" (pp. 126–34) and the philosophical "Moses Hess—Socialist, Philosopher, Jew" (pp. 169–84). An obituary is in the *New York Times*, 7 May 1943.

DEBORAH DASH MOORE

ZIEGFELD, Florenz (21 Mar. 1867–22 July 1932), theatrical producer, was born in Chicago, Illinois, the son of Florenz Ziegfeld, Sr., a music teacher and music school administrator, and Rosalie de Hez. He was christened in the Catholic church of his mother despite the protests of his Lutheran father. His father, the founder of the Chicago Musical College, wilted his children's love of classical music through his austere studio discipline. Young Ziegfeld remembered being severely punished by his father for playing popular music on the piano. He also had a four-year-old's memories of the destruction of the family home by the Chicago fire of 1871.

Ziegfeld's formal education never progressed beyond the public schools of Chicago. At age sixteen he had his first taste of show business when he appears to have won a marksmanship contest and an invitation to join Buffalo Bill's Wild West Show. His father put a quick end to his early infatuation with show business by dragging him home. He also attempted to get into show business in 1889 with an act featuring dancing chickens. However, the act was closed down by the Society for the Prevention of Cruelty to Animals when it discovered that to make the birds dance Ziegfeld had electrified the grid on which they performed.

When Ziegfeld was twenty-five, his father sent him to Europe to book legitimate musical acts to perform during the Chicago World's Columbian Exposition of 1893. He returned home with a number of popular variety acts that did not please his father; however, Ziegfeld, Sr., was eventually impressed with the substantial money his son made from one of the variety acts that he had booked. The Great Sandow, a strongman in skin-tight briefs, was Ziegfeld's first major success in the world of promotion. After the Chicago fair, he traveled with Eugene Sandow on a world tour for two years and made large sums of money.

Ziegfeld applied some of his newly acquired wealth to making the transition into the legitimate theater. While in England in 1896 he hired the popular French actress Anna Held for $1,500 a week to appear in New York in *A Parlor Match*. Acting as her press agent and manager, he cleverly generated large quantities of favorable press by asking celebrities such as Diamond Jim Brady and Lillian Russell to meet Held on a yacht in the New York Harbor. Probably Ziegfeld's most effective ploy for publicity was the manner in which he promoted Held's special milk baths. She did not actually use milk in her bath, but the story captured media attention. When the public's interest in the story waned, Ziegfeld created additional coverage by suing an innocent dairy for delivering what he alleged was spoiled milk. He also generated considerable free press when he purchased Lillie Langtry's old railroad car for Held's use on the nationwide tours they would take following a successful play's run in New York.

Ziegfeld and Held had an unofficial marriage ceremony in the spring of 1897 and continued to produce a succession of successful light musical farces for the next seven years: *The Gay Deceivers* (1898), *The French Maid* (1899), and *Festival of Flowers* (1899). From 1899 to 1906 they fell into the annual pattern of producing a New York show for a limited run in the fall and taking it on a U.S. tour before summering in Paris. In 1906 Ziegfeld lost 2.5 million francs gambling in Biarritz, France. In desperate straits, he sold Held's contract to his archcompetitors, the Shubert brothers, for the price of his casino bill. This questionable business transaction, plus the possibility that he staged a bogus heist of Held's jewels for insurance purposes, marked the beginning of the end of their relationship.

The *Follies* of 1907 began as a unique summer offering at the New York Theatre Roof in New York City. Actual producers of this first edition of the *Follies* were Marc Klaw and Abraham Erlanger (of Theatrical Syndicated fame), and Ziegfeld was hired for $200 a week to mount this trend-setting American revue. During the next few editions, Ziegfeld began to take more control and developed the structure of the *Follies* that came to be known internationally, and his name became a permanent part of the show's title in 1911. Small "in-one" acts were followed by large musical production numbers featuring numerous beautiful women in gorgeous costumes. At appropriate points in the entertainment, comedians were added to the bill to change the rhythm of the evening. The material covered a wide range of tastes, from glittering "girlie" show to clever dance satirizing topics such as Aubrey Beardsley's illustrations for *Salome*. In his desire to have something for all tastes, Ziegfeld even incorporated elements of the German cabaret theaters; Will Rogers's act consisted of the humorist commenting on the events in the evening papers. Not only did this give the performance a topical nature, but it also produced a distinctly American satiric comedy.

Based loosely on the Parisian *Folies-Bergère*, Ziegfeld pushed his *Follies* to the edge of controversy with the use of nudity on stage. Knowing that he could not get away with the dancing nudes of his Parisian counterpart, he instructed Ben Ali Haggin, a well-known society portrait painter, to pose the nearly naked "girls" in what they referred to as "living tableaux." These seminude women could, in their frozen stillness, be thought of as respectable "art." Ziegfeld had cleverly clouded the line between art and soft pornography, a fact that no doubt was partially responsible for his box-office success. Ziegfeld enumerated the qualities that he believed his "girls" should have: native refinement, poise, health, strength, symmetry, spirit, style, appeal to both sexes, femininity, and glory. In addition to these attributes, he created a specific look and walk that he required of women: a slightly open mouth and a hesitation step with a casual dragging of the back foot. He created a man's ideal fantasy of a visit to a harem.

Part of the audience's fascination with the *Follies* was the sheer display of extravagant wealth. Ziegfeld spent money excessively on scenery and costumes, knowing not only that it would achieve a richness of texture on stage but also that his spending habits would be a press agent's delight. Columnists loved to write gushingly or critically of the vast sums of money either lavished or squandered on the latest Ziegfeld production. He honestly did not care which way they wrote about his shows as long as they mentioned at which theater the shows were playing.

During the succeeding twenty-one editions of the *Follies* (no *Follies* were mounted in 1926, 1928, 1929, or 1930, despite what a number of sources say, owing to Ziegfeld's involvement in other musical productions), Ziegfeld hired some of the best talent in the American theater. Joseph Urban, one of the finest designers in the twentieth century, did most of his New York work for Ziegfeld. He designed the settings for twelve of the last thirteen editions of the *Follies* (Norman Bel Geddes designed the other edition). Urban's pointillistic style of using color like the neo-impressionists permitted the audience's eye to actually mix small daubs of pure color that it perceived from a distance as mixed hues. This clever use of color, coupled with the new lighting effects, allowed Urban and Ziegfeld to create a lush richness previously unseen on the stage.

Costume designs for many of the editions were done by such luminaries as Erté of Paris and Haggin. Ziegfeld sought out the day's leading composers, Jerome Kern, Irving Berlin, Victor Herbert, Rudolf Friml, and others, to write for the *Follies*. Many standards of the American popular music repertoire were written for the *Follies*, including "Shine on Harvest Moon," "By the Light of the Silvery Moon," and "A Pretty Girl Is Like a Melody." Although Ziegfeld was usually generous with his performers' salaries, he was almost always miserly when it came to paying royalties to his authors and composers. Major comedians kept the shows moving, among them Rogers, Eddie Cantor, W. C. Fields, Fanny Brice, Bert Williams, and Eddie Dowling.

It was the "Glorification of the American Girl," however, for which the *Follies* were best known. This glorification was so complete in its influence that Hollywood accepted Ziegfeld's theatrical standard of beauty as its own. Many of the *Follies* stars went on to careers in film: Olive Thomas, Marion Davies, Irene Dunne, Mae Murray, Martha Mansfield, Barbara Stanwyck, and Paulette Goddard. Other notables whom Ziegfeld either discovered or gave significant employment were Maurice Chevalier, Fred Astaire and his sister Adele Astaire, Billie Burke, Nora Bayes, Marilyn Miller, Sophie Tucker, Sigmund Romberg, George Gershwin, and Richard Rodgers.

In addition to the *Follies*, Ziegfeld produced a number of successful comedies and musicals, including *Sally* (1920), *Show Boat* (1927), *Bitter Sweet* (1929), and *Rio Rita* (with which he opened the Ziegfeld Theatre on 2 February 1927). *Show Boat* was the consummation of all that Ziegfeld believed about the musical theater. Fast-moving and kaleidoscopic, Kern's music and Oscar Hammerstein's lyrics flowed naturally and gracefully out of the action. The spectacle and comedy were integrated into a fluid seamlessness that make *Show Boat* one of the best examples of American musical theater.

Urban designed the Ziegfeld Theatre, located on Sixth Avenue near Central Park. It was a state-of-the-art facility designed in the art deco style and furnished with the best technical equipment and the richest decorative materials. This house of spectacle was reduced to a motion-picture theater shortly after Ziegfeld's death and was finally razed in 1969.

After his divorce in 1913 from Held (New York law recognized common-law marriages after a period of seven years), Ziegfeld in 1914 married Billie Burke, with whom he had his only child. He reportedly had numerous affairs with performers in his productions.

Ziegfeld's personal style has had an indelible effect on the way the public perceives the profession of theatrical producer. Beyond the stereotypical look of cigar and fedora, he was the master of the lengthy telegram. He was fond of dictating ten-page telegrams when a phone call or a letter would have proved just as effective. The fact that a telegram was more expensive than a letter and had a special theatrical effect was not lost on this inveterate showman. Contributing to the myth surrounding his life was the cinematic success of *The Great Ziegfeld*, which won the Academy Award for best picture in 1936. When he died in Hollywood, Ziegfeld was attempting to transfer his theatrical magic onto the silver screen. Unfortunately, his past ex-

cesses caught up with him and he left his family with nearly a half-million-dollar debt. It would be seven years before Hollywood made the kind of musical Ziegfeld envisioned—*The Wizard of Oz*. Ironically, it was in this classic that Burke made her most lasting performance as Glenda, the good witch. At last, the filmed musical had the color, sound, and mobility that Ziegfeld would have wanted.

Without question, Ziegfeld was a consummate promoter, a less-than-honorable husband, a flamboyant spender, and a skinflint when it came to paying royalties to his writers. His hiring of Urban to bring visual class and beauty to the *Follies* and his groundbreaking work on *Show Boat* remain among Ziegfeld's most important theatrical contributions. It became apparent only after he died and others tried to reproduce a Ziegfeld spectacle that he had indeed possessed a special gift. It was not his sensitive eye or his acute ear that informed his productions as much as it was his ability to hire good people and bring them together for a communal expression of his vision of fantasy and beauty.

Ziegfeld was one of the first musical producers to make a distinctive stylistic mark in the American theater. Most of his working career took place between the Chicago World's Columbian Exposition of 1893 and the crash of the New York stock market in 1929. Within this 36-year period his career rose, bloomed, and began to decline. He began his career by promoting peripheral entertainments for the Chicago fair and ended it as a producer of glossy New York shows. Once a sideshow hustler, the name and fame of Ziegfeld grew to become inexorably linked with American beauty and opulence.

• The Theatre Collection of the New York Public Library for the Performing Arts has an uncataloged collection of photographs, unpublished manuscripts, news clippings, correspondence, and programs. The 1993 publication of *The Ziegfeld Touch* by Ziegfeld's cousin Richard Ziegfeld and his wife, Paulette Ziegfeld, is a major new contribution to material related to the showman. Of lesser value but still worthwhile are Charles Higham, *Ziegfeld* (1972), and Randolph Carter, *The World of Flo Ziegfeld* (1974). Marjorie Farnsworth, *The Ziegfeld Follies: A History in Text and Pictures* (1956), reproduces many of the Joseph Urban designs unavailable elsewhere. Ziegfeld's own thoughts can be read in "Stars in the Making," *Theatre Magazine*, Nov. 1926, pp. 9, 64.

MIKE A. BARTON

ZIEGLER, David (13 July 1748–24 Sept. 1811), revolutionary army officer and pioneer settler of Ohio, was born in Heidelberg, Germany, the son of Johann Heinrich Ziegler, a hatmaker and innkeeper, and Louise Friedericka Kern. He spent six years (1768–1774) in the Russian army before migrating to Pennsylvania in 1774. Within a year he had joined a military company in Lancaster County as a third lieutenant. His successful command of a party escorting ammunition to General George Washington's army gained him the post of adjutant in Colonel William Thompson's battalion of sharpshooters. When this unit was incorporated into the First Regiment of Continental Infantry on 1 June 1776, Ziegler was promoted to second lieutenant.

By summer's end Ziegler was involved in the battle of Long Island, in which he was wounded. After a year's convalescence, he rejoined the army at Valley Forge, Pennsylvania, where his European military experience was helpful in training the Continentals. In 1778 his distinction at the battle of Monmouth Court House brought General Arthur St. Clair's recommendation for his promotion to captain. From that advancement came new opportunities, first as brigade inspector of the Pennsylvania Brigade, Department of the South, and then as commissary general of the Department of Pennsylvania. By 1782 he was pleased to return to the field when his company moved south to join General Nathanael Greene's army.

Following his retirement from the Continental army in 1783 at the end of the revolutionary war, Ziegler briefly operated a store in Carlisle, Pennsylvania. In 1784 he accepted a captaincy in Pennsylvania's First American Regiment, commanded by Lieutenant Colonel Josiah Harmar. Ziegler's company was ordered west; their task was defending the Ohio River frontier by staffing outposts (that would later become Marietta, Cincinnati, and Louisville), as well as trying to evict illegal settlers from American Indian lands.

In the West Ziegler was admired as a dependable commander whose troops were noted for their spit and polish. Like most units, Ziegler's company had its share of difficulties; one soldier was whipped for selling government shoes, while one of his sergeants called the captain a rogue, an infraction punished by fifty lashes and a reduction in rank. Despite the army's harsh living conditions and brutal discipline, Ziegler successfully recruited new levies, especially among German-speaking communities in Pennsylvania.

Because of Ziegler's reputation for calm leadership, his company was chosen to escort an official delegation of Indian diplomats from Fort Pitt to Fort Harmar on the Muskingum River in 1788. Included in the party were fifty Seneca, led by the venerable chief known as Cornplanter. Ziegler's commander, Harmar, knew that his subordinate would protect the Indians from frontier vagabonds like the Wheeling settlers who had threatened to kill any Native Americans who passed.

Ziegler found time despite his duties for personal interests. His service as a revolutionary war officer brought him membership in the Society of the Cincinnati in 1785. Ziegler's post at Fort Harmar was just across the Muskingum River from Marietta, a settlement established in 1788 by a speculative group known as the Ohio Company of Associates. Among the pioneers was Lucy Anne Sheffield, from Rhode Island, whom Ziegler married in February 1789. They had no children. Fortunately for the newlyweds, Ziegler was left in command of the post at Fort Harmar when the majority of the garrison was ordered west on Indian duty in December. In 1790, however, increasing frontier tensions brought instructions for Ziegler's company also to move west.

Both generals charged with guarding the western frontier, Harmar and his successor, St. Clair, desperately needed the stability of soldiers like Ziegler's company, who could follow orders under fire. The numerous militia units were not dependable; many deserted before the battles began. As a member of the staff serving under both Harmar and St. Clair, Ziegler witnessed the insubordinate militia, inferior equipment, and ineffective supply system that confounded American operations against the Native Americans in the Ohio country. Although Ziegler could not prevent the disasters that befell the two commanders, he testified on their behalf during official inquiries into the failed campaigns of 1790 and 1791.

General St. Clair thought so highly of Ziegler that he had promoted him to major in 1790; ultimately he left him to command the entire army in the West when St. Clair returned east to seek exoneration for the 1791 disaster. Nevertheless, Ziegler had found the jealous intrigues and petty disputes of his fellow officers disturbing. Faced with such unpleasantness, Ziegler resigned his commission on 5 March 1792 and cast his lot with the business of the growing frontier.

Ziegler's observation of economic development along the Ohio River convinced him that Cincinnati was a settlement with great promise. After he and his wife relocated there, he tried both farming and storekeeping but found neither profitable. A supporter of Thomas Jefferson, he found greater success in politics. He was the first person elected president of the council in Cincinnati and was chosen a second time as well, serving from 1802 to 1804, but declined a third term. He was successively appointed first marshall of the Ohio District in 1804, adjutant general of Ohio in 1807, and, finally, collector and inspector of the port of Cincinnati in 1809. Evidently he achieved some prosperity, for shortly after his death his wife had three servants in the household. Ziegler's long life of public service came to an end when he died in Cincinnati.

Like Lear's Kent, Ziegler was one of those absolutely dependable soldiers and public servants to whom the new country owed a great debt. Throughout his career, he had fulfilled responsibility in the most exemplary manner. Whether escorting ammunition to General Washington, carrying a flag of truce to enemy lines, guarding Native American diplomats, or standing fast in the face of enemy fire amid hysterical militia in retreat, Ziegler was ever the calm, loyal professional.

• Ziegler's life is sketched in George A. Katzenberger, "Major David Ziegler," *Ohio Archaeological and Historical Quarterly* 21 (1912): 127–74. There are references to Ziegler in Ebenezer Denny, *The Military Journal of Major Ebenezer Denny* (1859); William Feltman, *The Journal of Lieutenant William Feltman of the First Pennsylvania Regulars, 1781–82* (1853); Arthur St. Clair, *A Narrative of the Manner in Which the Campaign against the Indians in 1791 Was Conducted, under the Command of Brigadier General Arthur St. Clair* (1812); Winthrop Sargent, "Winthrop Sargent's Diary While with General Arthur St. Clair's Expedition against the Indians,"

Ohio State Archaeological and Historical Quarterly 33 (1924): 237–73; and the manuscript journal of General Joseph Buell, 20 Sept. 1785–29 June 1789, which is available in typescript in Special Collections, Dawes Memorial Library, Marietta College, Marietta, Ohio. There are also references to Ziegler in Wiley Sword, *President Washington's Indian War: The Struggle for the Old Northwest, 1790–1795* (1985). Information about the servants in the Ziegler household is in Marie Dickore, *Census for Cincinnati, Ohio, 1817, and Hamilton County, Ohio Voters Lists* (1960), p. 78.

JAMES H. O'DONNELL III

ZIEHN, Bernhard (20 Jan. 1845–8 Sept. 1912), music theorist and teacher, was born in Erfurt, Germany, the son of Johann Wilhelm Robert Ziehn, a journeyman shoemaker, and Friederike Schadt. Erfurt enjoyed a lively musical culture, and Ziehn was a precocious and successful autodidact. His education consisted of attendance at the local church school and teachers' seminary and had no special musical component. The seminary had a strong musical tradition, however, having originally grown out of the local high school music department. Ziehn passed his final examination at the seminary in September 1865 and on 22 September applied for a teaching position in a boys' school in Mühlhausen, equivalent to the American junior high school level, to which he was provisionally appointed. He arrived there on 7 October and became the youngest person on the faculty, remaining until 1868. He was called for military duty in 1866, during the Austro-Prussian War (1866–1888), which he fulfilled as a reservist during a six-week school break.

Ziehn left Germany for the United States when the war ended. He is said to have felt hemmed in and probably shared the political animus of many of his compatriots in regard to the Prussian expansion. (At the time Ziehn left there was a large general emigration from Thuringia and Saxony to the United States.) His first job in the United States was at a German Lutheran school in Chicago, where he taught music theory, history, and higher mathematics. Around 1870 he married Emma Trabing, about whom nothing else is known; they had a daughter who died early and a son. During the 1870s Ziehn made a living teaching theory and piano privately. His piano pedagogy resulted in a series of publications for piano study, including *System der Übungen für Klavierspieler* (1876), *Lehrgang für den ersten Unterricht* (1881), and *Alten Klavierstücke* (1883), which contains his ornamentation tables. He developed scale exercises in which the two hands moved in symmetrical inversion, a technique he also applied to composition.

He had finished his most significant work, *Harmonie- und Modulationslehre*, in 1866 (it was not published until 1887 but was subsequently reprinted in 1888 and 1910). Ziehn's theoretical work was strongly influenced by Carl Weitzmann, whose prize-winning articles were published in 1860 and with whom he either studied prior to leaving Germany or by whom he was at some time influenced. Ziehn's 1906 article "Ueber neuere und neueste Harmonielehre" harshly criticizes all the major theorists but is complimentary to Weitzmann, and many examples in *Harmonie- und Modulationslehre* are credited to Weitzmann. More to the point, the origin of most of Ziehn's ideas can be found in Weitzmann's; they shared numerous interests, particularly in canons, and they addressed many of the same issues. Ziehn wrote numerous articles, and in 1907 he published a revised, somewhat abridged English translation of his major work as *Manual of Harmony*. Ziehn believed that modern music could not be explained by theoretical systems. He is known for his ridicule of all musical systems, focusing his attacks on logical arguments based on speculation and brutally attacking theory's most prestigious practitioners; in his own theoretical works Ziehn eschewed system building. In *Harmonie- und Modulationslehre* he was the ultimate empiricist, using charts, lists, and numerous examples. His methodology consisted of identifying different types of simultaneities (chords) in music, categorizing them, placing them in short progressions, and showing them in their original musical contexts. He classified types of chordal configurations with only the sparsest annotations. His goal was to identify all conceivable types of chords and progressions, particularly of examples from a broad spectrum of musical literature, from the Renaissance through Anton Bruckner (barely known even in Germany at that time) and including Franz Liszt and Richard Wagner. He also was known for having disputed the authenticity of the ascription of the *St. Luke Passion* to J. S. Bach, a position shared by numerous scholars.

Ziehn was a highly respected and accomplished teacher whose students included some fine musicians and composers. He exerted a formidable cultural influence on the German emigrés in Chicago, who gathered and published his articles after his death (Goebel, ed., 1926–1927). Among his students were the musicologist Wilhelm Middelschulte, the composer John Alden Carpenter, and the pianist Fannie Bloomfield Zeisler. The composer-pianist Ferruccio Busoni praised him as "a theoretician who points to the possibilities of undiscovered lands—a prophet through logic. As a master of harmony he stands alone" (*Signale* [1910]). An article by the critic Winthrop Sargeant titled "Bernhard Ziehn, Precursor" touts his accomplishments as a "true prophet," anticipating and formulating in theoretical terms the compositional methods of forward-looking composers (*Musical Quarterly* 19 [1933]: 170–71). The extravagant nature of the claims made about Ziehn and his ensuing reputation were largely symptomatic of the crisis in music theory at that time, whereby current theory could not account for innovations in musical composition. Ziehn died in Chicago.

• Ziehn's papers were destroyed in a fire. His articles were gathered together and published in Julius Goebel, ed., *Jahrbuch der Deutsch-Amerikanischen Historischen Gesellschaft von Illinois*, vols. 26 and 27 (1927), which also contains bibliographic material in English. Hans Joachim Moser, *Bernhard Ziehn: Der Deutsch-Amerikanische Musiktheoretiker* (1950), is a biographical study that discusses Ziehn's work. Ziehn's work is treated in a historical context in Carol K. Baron, "At the Cutting Edge: Three American Theorists at the End of the Nineteenth Century," *International Journal of Musicology* 2 (1993): 193–247. A more detailed bibliography exists in the entry on Ziehn in David Damschroder and David Russell Williams, *Music Theory from Zarlino to Schenker: Bibliography and Guide* (1990).

CAROL K. BARON

ZIFF, William Bernard (1 Aug. 1898–20 Dec. 1953), publisher, editor, and author, was born in Chicago, Illinois, the son of David Ziff and Libby Mary Semco, farmers. A first-generation American—his father had been born in Bavaria and his mother in Lithuania—Ziff early displayed ambition. After being designated class artist at Crane Technical High School (where he was succeeded by young Walt Disney) he determined to become a portrait painter and worked at manual labor and sales jobs in order to finance two years of study (1915–1917) at the Art Institute of Chicago. Upon graduating he worked briefly as a commercial artist and as a cartoonist for the *Chicago Daily News* before World War I interrupted. Ziff served in the U.S. Army's 202d Aero Observation Squadron, fostering what would become his lifelong interest in military aviation.

Drawing on his knowledge of the newspaper business, Ziff organized a successful advertising agency in Chicago in 1920. He was married in 1923 to Denea Fischer—with whom he would have one daughter—and then settled into the publishing and writing career that would consume the rest of his life. He became head of the E. C. Auld Company, a local publishing house, and immediately created *Ziff's Magazine*, a humorous periodical that he illustrated and wrote almost entirely himself. *Ziff's* was quite successful. When the magazine was staffed by new creative talents and had its name changed to *America's Humor*, Ziff retained its editorship (1928–1930).

By the end of the decade Ziff's personal and professional circumstances changed again. After divorcing his first wife, in 1929 he married Amelia Mary Morton; together they would have three children, one of whom—William Bernard Ziff, Jr.—followed his father as head of the family publishing firm. At work Ziff devoted his energies to new pursuits, publishing and editing *Aeronautics*, a magazine that supported his view that the United States needed to aggressively develop a single, capable air force. Ziff wrote many articles arguing for this policy, allying himself with authorities such as Edward Rickenbacker, Alexander de Seversky, and, especially, General William "Billy" Mitchell—whose provocative articles on air power were frequently featured in *Aeronautics*.

Ziff also interested himself in civic matters. During 1928–1931 he briefly chaired the Interracial Society, a culturally diverse group of Chicago editors and publishers, and in 1932 he unsuccessfully sought the Republican nomination for Congress from his district. By 1933 he was immersed in private business again,

founding the Popular Aviation Corporation. Two years later this firm became Ziff-Davis Publishing, with which he was to remain associated for the rest of his life. Within a decade Ziff and his partner, Bernard G. Davis, were successfully publishing a dozen magazines, including "pulps" such as *Amazing Stories* and semitechnical "slicks" such as *Flying*.

His fortune established, Ziff turned to writing books devoted to foreign policy and military affairs. He became president of the Zionist Revisionist Organization in 1935 and wrote *The Rape of Palestine* (1938), a devastating critique of British treatment of the Jews in the Holy Land. (Ziff retained a special interest in the creation of a Jewish homeland even in his later internationalist writings.) Despite his criticisms, the British Air Ministry—recognizing Ziff's potential influence on the American public—flew him across the Atlantic in 1942 to survey the aftermath of the Nazi bombardment of England. This journey resulted in his most popular work, *The Coming Battle of Germany* (1942), a prescient analysis of the role of air power in any Allied victory. Ziff convincingly argued that air transport should become the preferred means of military supply—nullifying the Nazi U-boat threat—and the bomber the preferred weapon in offensive strategy. His exhortation was that "if we strike now, placing our last ounce of skill, determination and resource into that crowning tribute to American combat genius, the invincible Armada of the Air, Hitler must fall and drag with him the island citadels of the Mikado" (p. 274). The book not only was a bestseller but also became required reading in military staff schools; it earned Ziff a position as a special consultant to the Department of Justice's Economic Warfare Division and the opportunity to testify as an expert before the Military and Foreign Affairs committees of the House and Senate.

By 1944 Ziff was already turning to analysis of the postwar world. Broadening the scope of his interests even further, in *The Gentlemen Talk of Peace* (1944) he suggested that "the little nation of today is an anachronism. . . . The world must be regrouped into large federations capable of meeting the needs of a modern manufacturing and distributing economy." His insights were considered keen by reviewers and drew on a generally realistic analysis of contemporary economic and political facts. He continued his argument in *Two Worlds* (1946), suggesting that the United States and the Soviet Union oversee the restructuring of the world into five well-balanced federations.

Ziff had acquired great wealth from his endeavors and used it to maintain homes in Chicago, New York City, Florida, and Washington, D.C. A physically vigorous man, he also maintained a farm in Maryland that catered to his interests in cattle raising and the outdoors. He dabbled in poetry, publishing a brief volume, *He, the Maker* (1949)—his last book—four years before his death in New York City. Though his early magazines and his last books seem little but quaint curiosities in retrospect, his creation of *Aeronautics*—a timely and popular forum for many proponents of combat aviation—and his enormously influential *Coming Battle of Germany* make him significant in the history of the development of military air power in the United States and the world at large.

• Ziff's article "The Jew as Soldier, Strategist, and Military Advisor," in *The Hebrew Impact on Western Civilization*, ed. Dagobert Runes (1951), is an interesting blend of Ziff's views on military affairs, Zionism, and the international scene. The *Current Biography Yearbook* of 1946 contains a lengthy biographical sketch. An obituary is in the *New York Times*, 21 Dec. 1953.

W. FARRELL O'GORMAN

ZIMBALIST, Efrem (9 Apr. 1889–22 Feb. 1985), violinist, was born in Rostov-on-the-Don, Russia, the son of Alexander Zimbalist, a musician, and Maria Litvinoff. When he was seven, Efrem began studying the violin with his father, the conductor of the Rostov Opera Orchestra. He made rapid progress, and two years later he played in his father's orchestra and performed a Ludwig Spohr violin concerto in public. At age twelve Efrem enrolled at the St. Petersburg Conservatory for study with the great violin teacher Leopold Auer. Zimbalist quickly became a star pupil. He graduated with a gold medal and the Anton Rubinstein prize of 1,200 rubles. Across his certificate was written "incomparable."

After graduation Zimbalist received an invitation from a leading German concert manager. In those days it was customary for managers to underwrite the promotion of young talent as part of a contract (this is generally no longer true; now it is more common for the start-up costs of a career to be covered by the artist or by a third party). Zimbalist's Berlin debut, on 7 November 1907, was an immediate success. On invitation from an English manager he played his London debut on 9 December. In the following years Zimbalist appeared in many cities throughout Europe. His rich tone and brilliant technique rapidly established Zimbalist as one of the foremost violinists of his generation.

Zimbalist's quick rise to fame in Europe did not immediately lead to engagements in the United States. The New York impresario J. F. Francke tried early in 1908 to arrange an American tour for Zimbalist, but not until the 1911–1912 season could a sufficient number of concerts be arranged. His American debut took place on 27 October 1911; Zimbalist played the American premiere of the Glazunov Violin Concerto with the Boston Symphony Orchestra under the direction of Max Fielder. His New York debut occurred on 2 November; he performed the Glazunov Concerto with the New York Philharmonic, Josef Stransky conducting. Zimbalist appeared again with the New York Philharmonic on 5 November, playing the Tchaikovsky Concerto; a Carnegie Hall recital followed on 10 November. Zimbalist's success in the United States was such that he decided to immigrate in 1911, as had two other students of Auer, Misha Elman and Jascha Heifetz, who also had brilliant careers.

In 1914 Zimbalist married Alma Gluck, the famous Roumanian-born soprano. The couple had two children. After they were married, their individual careers reinforced each other. During the 1914–1915 season they performed together a number of times. They used two different program formats. In one Zimbalist acted as accompanist for his wife. In the other they both appeared as soloists, each with his or her own accompanist, and they would join together in arrangements of folksongs that Zimbalist made for soprano, violin, and piano. The joint appearance of two soloists was a well-established concert format in the late nineteenth and early twentieth centuries. Zimbalist and Gluck's programs were generally light in style, attracting huge audiences. Their long tours were financially very rewarding.

Substantial earnings enabled Zimbalist and Gluck to give generously to aid victims of World War I. In addition to being wealthy and famous, they moved in important social circles. The list of those who visited their large townhouse at 100 East Seventy-second Street in New York City reads like a veritable "Who's Who" in music.

Gluck retired from the concert stage in 1925. Three years later Zimbalist was appointed head of the violin department at the Curtis Institute in Philadelphia. He remained in constant demand as soloist, playing regularly with the New York Philharmonic. He made tours of the Orient and served as a judge at competitions.

Zimbalist's playing was characterized by a full, big tone, and his technique, while not as flamboyant as Heifetz's, was flawless. He was especially admired for his artistic insight and the honesty and nobility of his style; he was called a poet on the violin. During the final decades of romanticism in music, until about 1930, a period replete with overpersonalized excesses, the time was ripe for simple, true-to-the-score interpretation. Zimbalist fit perfectly with this new style.

In 1941 Zimbalist became director of the Curtis Institute, a post he held until his retirement in 1968. Alma Gluck had died in 1938, and in 1943 he married Mary Louise Curtis Bok, who had founded the Curtis Institute in 1924. She endowed the institute and served as its president from its inception until her death in 1970. (This second marriage produced no children.) Following her death, Zimbalist moved to Reno, Nevada, where he lived until his death there.

Zimbalist composed many songs and arrangements, principally for his first wife. He wrote works for violin and piano for his own use, including *Suite in Old Form* and *Three Slavic Dances* (1911); *Fantasy on Motives of Rimski-Korsakov's "Le Coq d'Or"*; Sonata in G Minor (1926); and *Sarasateana*, a suite of Spanish dances. For orchestra he composed *American Rhapsody* (1936; rev. ed., 1943); *Portrait of an Artist*, a symphonic poem (1945); and three concerti, for violin (1943), piano (1959), and cello (1969). He wrote one opera, *Landara* (1956), and a musical comedy, *Honeydew* (1920), which was successfully performed in many cities in the United States. He also composed String

Quartet in E Minor (1938), an exercise book for violinists, and transcriptions of Jewish airs.

Zimbalist's music is generally well constructed, and his style is basically romantic, utilizing traditional harmonic concepts. His violin music is idiomatically written, but it is rarely played. Zimbalist's major contributions to the world of music are his high standards of performance and interpretation that influenced many violinists, especially those at the Curtis Institute.

• The best account of Zimbalist's life and work is in Boris Schwartz, *Great Masters of the Violin* (1983). Gdal Saleski, *Famous Musicians of Jewish Origin* (1949), gives a detailed account of Zimbalist's life up to that year. An obituary is in the *New York Times*, 23 Feb. 1985.

KEES KOOPER

ZIMBALIST, Mary Louise Curtis Bok (6 Aug. 1876–4 Jan. 1970), founder and president of the Curtis Institute of Music, Philadelphia, and philanthropist, was born in Boston, Massachusetts, the daughter of Cyrus H. K. Curtis and Louisa Knapp. When she was an infant the family moved to Philadelphia, where her father became an eminently successful publisher of newspapers and periodicals. Her parents were gifted musical amateurs, and music became one of her principal subjects when she received her formal education at the Ogontz School for Young Ladies in Abington, Pennsylvania—a school to which she contributed generously in later years. Her studies in piano and music theory were ably supervised by her mother, with whom she began extensive travels to Europe at the age of thirteen. In 1893 she became engaged to Edward Bok, who had entered her father's publishing firm, and they were married in 1896. The couple had two children.

In 1910 Mary Louise Curtis Bok began her career as an administrator and major supporter of the Philadelphia Settlement School of Music, then recently established and to which her interest was drawn by friends. The first director of the school was Johann Grolle, a member of the Philadelphia Orchestra. In consultation with him, Leopold Stokowski, and Josef Hofmann, Mrs. Bok conceived the idea of a conservatory branch of the school for the professional training of exceptionally gifted students; and in 1924 she was able to invest the family fortune in such an institution, henceforth separated from the Settlement Music School and named the Curtis Institute of Music.

How Mary Bok (as she used to sign herself in early Curtis Institute days) dealt with the institute's transition from a local charitable institution to one that was to become world famed is characteristic both of her uncompromising standards and of her munificence. Initially the two schools shared one building, but the Curtis Institute was relocated within a year to two mansions bordering Philadelphia's downtown Rittenhouse Square. Grolle served as director of both for one year, after which he was replaced at the institute by William E. Walter, an experienced administrator who held a two-year term to set up the institute's sound

business basis; Grolle, embittered, withdrew to his duties at the Settlement School, closing its doors tightly to Mrs. Bok, who never ceased to pay for the maintenance of the school and who provided a pension for him when he retired in 1957. He was succeeded at the Settlement School by Sol Schoenbach, a distinguished member of the Philadelphia Orchestra and a member of the Curtis Institute faculty for many years.

The Curtis Institute of Music and Mary Bok's presidency rose to their true stature with the directorship (1927–1938) of Josef Hofmann. Hofmann, a student of Anton Rubinstein and Eugen d'Albert and one of the most celebrated pianists of his time, established the features that lent uniqueness to the school: a faculty recruited from the most illustrious artists of the time, a student body admitted on scholarship basis only, subsidy of concerts and tours in the United States and abroad for students and graduates, and provision of the best instruments, rent free, for students to use at home. Mrs. Bok supported the professed principle of excellence in numerous ways. She used her own funds to raise the institute's endowment from $5 million to over $12 million. She saw to it that lecture series and academic instruction rounded out the educational program. She established one of the most outstanding music libraries in the United States, including autographs by Bach, Mozart, and Brahms, as well as the Ileborgh Tablature, a famed medieval manuscript of keyboard music. She purchased the Burrell Collection of Wagneriana, with autograph sources for *Tannhäuser*, *Rienzi*, *Lohengrin*, and *Der Fliegende Holländer*; and she funded such significant scholarly projects as *Les Chansonniers des troubadours et des trouvères*, published by the medievalist Jean Baptiste Beck, who served on the Curtis faculty from 1924 to 1938.

Examples of Mrs. Bok's largesse are legion. She gave thirty artists, including the composers Gian-Carlo Menotti and Samuel Barber, annual living stipends until her death. Her support allowed Igor Stravinsky to concentrate on his creative work for a period early in his career. She contributed generously to the Berkshire Music Center, the Spoleto Festival, the Philadelphia Grand Opera Company, and a later small but excellent Philadelphia Opera Company. She donated a theater to Rollins College in Orlando, Florida, and there is no end of civic and cultural causes to which she richly contributed.

She guided the Curtis Institute of Music through the years of the Great Depression, rendered doubly difficult through the death of her husband (1930) and her father (1933) as well as Hofmann's resignation under the rising pressure of administrative duties (1938). But the same years saw the flourishing of a Curtis summer colony in both Camden and Rockport, Maine, communities that she had largely restored. In 1939 she faced the challenge of providing new direction for the institute with the choice of a highly cultivated candidate, Randall Thompson, then the young American composer whose work had received the widest response. Yet the choice met with a clash of traditions. The acknowledged place of the American composer was in the university rather than the conservatory, and Thompson's professed leaning toward the humanities brought about his replacement two years later by the brilliant violinist Efrem Zimbalist, who had joined the Curtis Institute faculty together with his teacher Leopold Auer in 1928. Mary Bok and Zimbalist were married in 1943; he would serve the cause of her life's work for over forty years.

After a long and successful tenure as director, Mary Bok Zimbalist was succeeded by a colleague whose appointment represented a reconciliation of the two schools of thought. In 1968 Rudolf Serkin, a performer who placed equal emphasis on virtuosity and learning, assumed the institute's directorship. The institute's founder was able to witness the promise of a new era; she died in Philadelphia two years after Serkin's appointment. She had completed six decades of a life marked equally by material wealth and the wealth of a noble, unbendingly positive spirit. Innumerable honors were bestowed on her. She received the Knight's Cross of the Austrian Order of Merit and of the Polish Order of *Polonia Restituta*. Though in 1932 she had declined an honorary degree from Rollins College, saying that she did not want "any more alphabetical decorations," she was subsequently awarded honorary doctorates from a number of universities. But her truest reward is characteristically suggested in a few words of her last address to Curtis Institute's students: "You're all my children, in a way. I've kept track of you more closely than any of you realize, and with the greatest affection."

• The manuscript and printed sources of Mary Louise Curtis Bok Zimbalist's biography are preserved at the library of the Curtis Institute of Music. A comprehensive bibliography is contained in Elza Ann Viles, "Mary Louise Curtis Bok Zimbalist: Founder of the Curtis Institute of Music and Patron of American Arts" (Ph.D. diss., Bryn Mawr College, 1983); Viles was the head librarian of the Curtis Institute library from 1975 to 1980. An obituary is in the *New York Times*, 6 Jan. 1970.

ALFRED MANN

ZIMMERMAN, Zim (25 May 1862–26 Mar. 1935), cartoonist, was born Eugene Zimmerman in Basel, Switzerland, the second son of Joseph Zimmerman, a baker, and Amelie Klotz, who died in childbirth two years later. Unable to care for his three children and earn a living, Joseph Zimmerman placed his children with relatives, sending Eugene to an aunt and uncle in Thann, Alsace. In 1867 Joseph emigrated to America with his oldest son, settling in Paterson, New Jersey. Anxious to protect their nephew from the dangers of the looming Franco-Prussian war, Eugene's relatives sent him to America in 1869. He stayed with another aunt and uncle in New York City for several months before going to live and work with his father in a bakery in Paterson. He attended Old Van Houten School, but his chores in the bakery took priority over education. He also served as part-time office boy for a real

estate broker and began to develop his artistic skills by lettering signs that advertised the properties his employer managed.

At age twelve Zimmerman deserted the city to become a chore boy on a farm in nearby Totowa, where he earned three meals a day and a room in the attic but had little or no time for school. Two years later he left that farm for a wine merchant's farm at neighboring Haledon, again as chore boy (and at the same "pay"); he often worked from dawn to midnight, and he slept in the barn with the horses. In about 1877 his lettering on the wine merchant's store windows attracted the attention of a passing sign painter, who offered him an apprenticeship for three meals a day, a room, and used clothes. Zimmerman seized the opportunity, and in 1878 he and the sign painter moved to Elmira, New York, where he stayed until 1880 when he was hired, for a salary of $9 a week, by another sign painter in nearby Horseheads.

By this time Zimmerman had seen copies of *Puck*, the weekly humor magazine that had started in 1877, and had decided that he wanted to be a comic artist. On a visit to New York City in late 1882, Zimmerman left a portfolio of his work with relatives who arranged for Joseph Keppler, editor of *Puck*, to see the samples. Keppler hired Zimmerman the following May. His salary, initially $5 a week, was quickly raised to $10, which Zimmerman supplemented with drawings for advertisements commissioned by local businessmen, increasing his weekly earnings to as much as $80 a week in two years.

Under Keppler, Zimmerman mastered the lithograph stone and crayon and began to develop the exaggerated style that later distinguished his work. The *Puck* staff, however, included many noted cartoonists, and Zimmerman soon realized that the work of a young newcomer like him would not be featured in the magazine. Moreover, as *Puck* began to list from political independence to Democratic partisanship, Zimmerman, a Republican, felt increasingly uncomfortable doing the occasional political cartoon demanded of him. Thus, when, in late 1885, *Judge* magazine, a Republican-leaning comic weekly, offered him a position with comparable pay as well as an opportunity to draw the all-important centerspread cartoon occasionally, Zimmerman left Keppler at the urging of Bernhard Gillam, another *Puck* cartoonist of Republican stamp (who had become art editor of *Judge*), and began an association with *Judge* that lasted nearly thirty years.

Now signing his work simply "Zim," the cartoonist courted Mabel Alice Beard of Horseheads. They married in 1886 and moved to Brooklyn; they had one child. Two years later, Zimmerman, probably exhausted from overwork, suffered a nervous collapse, and he and Mabel went to Florida for a few months to recuperate. When they returned, they took up permanent residence in Horseheads, Zimmerman spending every other week in New York at the *Judge* office. In Horseheads he was a genuine hometown dignitary, and throughout his residence there, he donated time and drawings to scores of civic enterprises. He joined the volunteer fire-fighting Acme Hose No. 2 during his first sojourn in town in 1881 and remained a member until his death. He served as alderman from 1891 to 1893 and organized a town band that was active from 1897 to 1900 and again from 1909 to 1916. In 1911 he wrote *Zim's Foolish History of Horseheads*, following it with a similar book about Elmira. The Horseheads Historical Museum remembered the cartoonist, who lived and died in its town, with its special "Zim Room," the walls of which were hung with his drawings.

In 1905 Zimmerman produced a "how to" book of cartooning, *This and That about Caricature*. Recalling its success when he retired from active cartooning for *Judge* in 1913, he launched a cartoon correspondence course that continued into the next decade, providing ample income. He also freelanced illustrations for books and advertising, sold occasional cartoons to major magazines, produced a newspaper comic strip called *Louie and Lena*, and wrote a monthly column, "Homespun Phoolosophy," for *Cartoons Magazine* from 1916 to 1918. In 1926 he served as the first (and only) president of the American Association of Cartoonists and Caricaturists, which expired the next year when *Cartoons Magazine* withdrew its support.

In a virtual enactment of the American dream, Zimmerman rose from a youth of poverty to fame and fortune through diligent application of his talent. In the last decades of the nineteenth century, he was among the most noted of his profession. In his 1926 autobiography, *This Is the Life!*, cartoonist Walt McDougal called Zimmerman "the greatest cartoonist of the [1880s]"; the *Chicago Tribune* said he was "the funniest cartoonist now living." And *Munsey's Magazine* in 1904 reported that he stood "alone in the point of originality of conception and treatment. . . . Careful scrutiny of his work will reveal the truth behind his grotesque exaggerations."

Zimmerman was among the first cartoonists to draw in what eventually was regarded as the "cartoon manner"—simple linework depicting exaggerated anatomy and lively movement. When he began, most of his colleagues were illustrators, not cartoonists; they drew realistically, but Zim drew flamboyantly, deploying a juicy liquid line that waxed and waned to limn his comically capering creations. In the spirit of humorous exaggeration, during his heyday Zimmerman frequently employed the crude racial stereotypes that were the common coin of comedy in his time—his big-nosed Jews were parsimonious; his simian-faced Irishmen, drunk; and his liver-lipped blacks, lazy. Writing his autobiography in the 1930s, Zimmerman realized that "only the most stupid publishers" would publish then the kinds of racist cartoons that were common at the turn of the century. "Forty or fifty years ago," he explained, "the comic papers took considerably more liberty in caricaturing the various races than they do today. Jews, Negroes, and Irish came in for more than their share of lambasting because their facial characteristics were particularly vulnerable to caricature" (Brasch, p. 96). A cartoonist looking for comedy,

Zimmerman found it where the show business of his age found it: in vaudeville and minstrel shows, blacks, Jews, and Irishmen were figures of fun. In exaggerating for graphic comedy, Zimmerman developed cartoon-style drawing.

• Zimmerman's papers and much original art are maintained at the Zim House Museum, once the cartoonist's home in Horseheads. Most of Zimmerman's artwork for *Judge*, however, was destroyed in a fire in the magazine's office in 1908. Virtually all of the readily available biographical information about Zimmerman is contained in *Zim: The Autobiography of Eugene Zimmerman* (1988), a compilation by Walter M. Brasch of Zimmerman's several autobiographical musings and drafts. In addition to the twenty-volume *Zim's Correspondence Course in Cartoons and Caricatures* (c. 1913), Zimmerman's works include *A Jug Full of Wisdom: Homespun Phoolosophy* (1916), *Fire: Heroic Deeds for the Dingville Fire Department* (1922), *Foolish History of Elmira and Its Environs* (1912), *Language and Etticket of Poker* (1916), and *In Dairyland* (1914). He illustrated *Bill Nye: His Own Life Story* (1926) and Nye's *Wit and Humor, Poems and Yarns* (1900), as well as *Railway Guide* (1888) by Nye and James Whitcomb Riley.

ROBERT C. HARVEY

ZINSSER, Hans (17 Nov. 1878–4 Sept. 1940), bacteriologist, was born in New York City, the son of German immigrants August Zinsser, a chemist, and Marie Theresia Schmidt. Zinsser's early education included a year of schooling in Wiesbaden, Germany, together with more formal training at Julius Sach's private German school in New York City and the benefits of periodic trips to Germany, France, and Italy. He entered Columbia College in 1895. While in college, the Spanish-American War broke out, and in 1898 Zinsser enlisted in Squadron A of the New York City Cavalry. Although he did not encounter fighting, he learned firsthand of the "unbelievably miserable sanitary supervision of the [army] camps." This experience, along with the influence of Columbia biologists Edmund Beecher Wilson and Bashford Dean, turned Zinsser from majoring in poetry and literature to science. He received an A.B. in 1899 and an A.M. in 1903, with a thesis on the early embryology of the mouse. Also in 1903, Zinsser received an M.D. from Columbia University's College of Physicians and Surgeons.

Zinsser then interned at Roosevelt Hospital in New York City, where he served as bacteriologist from 1905 to 1906. During this time he also acted as bacteriologist at Columbia University's College of Physicians and Surgeons, where he became instructor of bacteriology and hygiene from 1907 to 1910. From 1906 to 1910 Zinsser also acted as assistant pathologist to New York's St. Luke's Hospital. He married Ruby Handforth Kunz in New York City in June 1905; they had two children.

In 1910 Zinsser traveled to Stanford University and there established a department of bacteriology, serving as its professor from 1911 to 1913. Recalled by Columbia, Zinsser returned and accepted the university's professorship in bacteriology and the position of bacteriologist at Presbyterian Hospital in New York City. In 1923 Zinsser was appointed Charles Wilder Professor of Bacteriology and Immunology at Harvard Medical School, a position he retained until his death. In the Boston area, Zinsser served as a consulting bacteriologist and later chief of bacteriology at the Children's Hospital, consulting bacteriologist to Peter Bent Brigham and the Infants Hospitals, and a trustee of the Massachusetts General Hospital.

Zinsser was truly a student of disease. In the words of his colleague John F. Enders, "what can be more happily exciting than to study a disease in all its natural manifestations?" (Mueller, p. 750). In 1915 Zinsser witnessed the "mass misery" of typhus for the first time as part of the Red Cross Typhus Commission in Serbia. Zinsser characterized the typhus epidemic there as being "as terrifying and tragic an episode as has occurred since the Middle Ages" (Bayne-Jones, p. 272). He retained particular interest in the control of this disease and, in 1923, went to Russia as sanitary commissioner for the Health Section of the League of Nations.

When the United States entered the First World War, Zinsser was commissioned as a major in the U.S. Army Medical Corps in 1917, and he was promoted to lieutenant colonel the following year. He served in France as sanitary inspector of the First Corps and later of the Second Field Army of the American Expeditionary Force. This experience generated publication of his *Sanitation of a Field Army* in 1919. For his exceptional medical services, Zinsser received the U.S. Army's Distinguished Service Medal in 1922, the Order of St. Sava from Serbia, and, in 1935, France's Legion d'Honneur in the rank of chevalier. He was posthumously awarded the Sedgwick Memorial Medal of the American Public Health Association in 1940.

Zinsser published some 275 professional articles, attracting collaborators and students from around the world. Early in his career, in 1908, he published "Experimental and Clinical Studies on the Curative Action of Leucocyte Extracts in Infections—A Series of Papers," the first of his collaborative investigation with Philip Hanson Hiss, Jr., on the effects of leukocyte extracts in treating infection; and a translation of Rudolph Schmidt's *Pain, Its Causation and Diagnostic Significance in Internal Diseases*. While at Stanford, Zinsser demonstrated his avid interest in the growing field of immunology and published a series of papers on the nature and mechanism of antigen-antibody interactions as part of the immune reaction. He concluded that all antibodies were of similar nature, their differentiation in immune reactions resulting from different antigens. Together with J. Howard Mueller and others, Zinsser determined that the "residue" of bacterial extracts was only partially antigenic in that it could react with antibodies and produce local effects, but it could not provoke a complete immune response. He discussed many of his early studies in *Infection and Resistance* (1915). Recognized by his peers as an authority on anaphylaxis and bacterial hypersensitivity, he further collaborated with Hiss, and later Stanhope

Baynes-Jones, in preparing *A Textbook of Bacteriology*, which first appeared in 1910 and quickly became the standard in the field, going through eight revised editions and multiple translations during Zinsser's life.

In addition to laboratory studies, Zinsser also worked in the public health arena, attempting to control the spread of bacteria and viruses in human populations. War conflicts brought him face-to-face with outbreaks of typhus, influenza, and encephalitis. His postwar international investigations in Mexico (1931) and China (1938), and subsequent publications on typhus and related rickettsial organism diseases were recognized for their "world wide importance." Zinsser "patterned the methods of study of rickettsial disease throughout the world" (Bayne-Jones, p. 279). Zinsser received eponymic remembrance for demonstrating that Brill's disease—a common disorder among immigrants in New York City then commonly thought to be a type of murine, endemic typhus—was actually a recrudescent form of epidemic typhus that sufferers had actually contracted in Europe. His efforts in elucidating the immunology and epidemiology of this disease were recorded in "Varieties of Typhus Virus and the Epidemiology of the American Form of European Typhus Fever (Brill's Disease)" (*American Journal of Hygiene* 20 [1934]: 513–31). Zinsser reported his successful isolation of the bacteria causing typhus in 1936, and in January 1940 he announced his development of a human vaccine against this disease. This investigative work later led to the renaming of this disease as Brill-Zinsser disease.

In addition to the recognition brought about by his professional writings, Zinsser gained wide acclaim for *Rats, Lice and History* (1935), a "biography of the life history of typhus." The regular reprinting of this history and its use in many college courses has helped sustain Zinsser's name and work among the general public. Zinsser's work became further popularized with the publication of his semi-autobiographical, Book-of-the-Month-Club bestseller, *As I Remember Him: The Biography of R.S.* (1940). The "R.S.," his own "Romantic Self," publicly identified him as the poet whose works occasionally appeared in *Atlantic Monthly*. A book of his sonnets, *Spring, Summer, and Autumn*, was posthumously published in 1942.

Zinsser received numerous awards and honorary degrees and served as president of the New York Pathological Society in 1915, the American Association of Immunologists in 1919, and the Society of American Bacteriologists in 1926. He was a member of the National Academy of Arts and Sciences, the National Research Council, and many other professional societies, including the Society of Experimental Biology and Medicine, Association of Pathologists and Bacteriologists, American Association of Experimental Pathology, American Public Health Association, and American Epidemiological Society. Typical of his indefatigable courage and verve, Zinsser continued daily lab work for two years after being diagnosed with lymphatic leukemia in June 1938. He died in New York City.

• Among Zinsser's works of lasting importance are "Studies on the Tuberculin Reaction and on Specific Hypesensitiveness in Bacterial Infection," *Journal of Experimental Medicine* 34 (1921): 495–524; "On the Significance of Bacterial Allergy in Infectious Diseases," *Bulletin of the New York Academy of Medicine* 2d ser., 4 (1928): 351–83; "Studies in Ultrafiltrations," *Journal of Experimental Medicine* 47 (1927): 357–78, with Fei-fang Tang; "On the Possible Importance of Colloidal Protection in Certain Phases of the Precipitin Reaction," *Journal of Experimental Medicine* 17 (1913): 396–408, with Stewart Young; and "The Bacteriology of Rheumatic Fever and the Allergic Hypothesis," *Archives of Internal Medicine* 42 (1928): 301–9. Together with J. G. Hopkins and Reuben Ottenburg, Zinsser prepared *A Laboratory Course in Serum Study* (1916). His *Infection and Resistance* (1915) was revised, and appeared in a fifth edition in 1939, with John F. Enders and LeRoy D. Fothergill, under the title *Immunity: Principles and Applications in Medicine and Public Health*. Simeon Burth Wolbach appended a full bibliography to his memoir of Zinsser in National Academy of Sciences, *Biographical Memoirs* 24 (1947): 323–60. Other useful biographical sketches by contemporaries include Stanhope Bayne-Jones, "Hans Zinsser, M.D., 1878–1940," *Archives of Pathology* 31 (1941): 269–80, and J. Howard Mueller, "Hans Zinsser 1878–1940," *Journal of Bacteriology* 40 (1940): 747–53. For his work on typhus, see P. K. Olitsky, "Hans Zinsser and His Studies on Typhus Fever," *Journal of the American Medical Association* 116 (1941): 907–12.

PHILIP K. WILSON

ZINZENDORF, Nikolaus Ludwig von (26 May 1700–9 May 1760), Lutheran theologian and count, was born in Dresden, Saxony, the son of George Ludwig, Count von Zinzendorf, a privy counselor of the Saxon court, and Charlotte Justine von Gersdorf. Zinzendorf's father died when Zinzendorf was only six weeks old, and in 1704 his mother married a Prussian field marshal. She left Zinzendorf in the care of her mother, the baroness von Gersdorf, in her castle, "Gross-Hennersdorf." Philipp Jakob Spener, who in 1675 had inaugurated the Pietist movement with the publication of *Pia desideria*, was selected as one of Zinzendorf's godfathers at his baptism. Zinzendorf was raised on Pietist principles, which stress religious experience and a reformation of life, and from a very early age demonstrated a predilection for the religious life. "In this childlike way I associated with him [Jesus] for many years [and] conversed for hours together with him, as one friend to another" (Spangenberg, p. 27). At the age of ten, he was sent to Francke's Pietist school at Halle, where he studied until he was sixteen and entered the University of Wittenberg. Although Zinzendorf would later repudiate Halle, it is undeniable that Pietism was the dominant influence in his formative years.

Once Zinzendorf came of age he purchased the estate of "Berthelsdorf" from his grandmother. In 1722 he married Erdmuth Dorothea von Reuss, with whom he had twelve children, only four of whom survived childhood. In that same year a small group of Protestant refugees fled their homeland in Catholic Moravia and sought refuge on Zinzendorf's estates. They claimed to be members of the Unitas Fratrum, an old Hussite church that was nearly defunct. Many leaders of Pietism admired the Unitas Fratrum for its dedication to living the Christian life; therefore it is not surprising that Zinzendorf allowed these refugees to establish a village, which they named Herrnhut (Lord's Watch). In 1727 he and his wife moved their residence to Herrnhut, where he "gave himself completely to the service of the poor exiles" (Spangenberg, p. 406). In 1732 he inspired the Brethren in Herrnhut to send out foreign missionaries to St. Thomas. Soon he was the head of a vigorous, international Christian fellowship known as the Brüdergemeine. Zinzendorf's willingness to receive religious refugees, particularly from Moravia and Bohemia, resulted in his exile from Saxony in 1736.

Zinzendorf made two trips to the New World. The first was to the mission field of St. Thomas in 1739. His second trip was to North America, where he stayed for about eighteen months. He arrived in Philadelphia on 10 December 1741, and a week later he met with Henrich Antes, an unlicensed lay preacher. They agreed on a plan to unite all of the German sects and churches into a single synod. Antes invited representatives of the various German-speaking churches and sects in Pennsylvania to participate in the first ecumenical synods in America. This attempt at establishing a "Church of God in the Spirit" initially showed promise, but many participants were suspicious about Zinzendorf's theology and motives. Gradually the synods dwindled to only those persons who claimed some type of allegiance to the Moravian church. Of equal or greater interest to Zinzendorf were his visits to the Native American tribes. He made three visits to the wilderness of Pennsylvania to meet with representatives of the nations. The first was 24 July–7 August 1742 when he made a covenant with the Six Nations and received a wampum belt. His third and longest trip to the wilderness was 21 September–8 November when Conrad Weisser, his German wilderness guide, took Zinzendorf to Shawnee country.

Zinzendorf left the newly founded Moravian town of Bethlehem for Europe on 1 January 1743. He was convinced of the need for evangelical missions to both the natives and the German settlers in Pennsylvania. Bethlehem became the center of this mission enterprise, and the Moravians became the most effective Protestant missionaries to the native peoples, in part because of the applicability of Zinzendorf's "theology of the heart" to tribal and nonliterate cultures. In 1746 and 1747 the king of Saxony reconsidered the case of Zinzendorf and Herrnhut, and in October 1747 he ordered that Zinzendorf's banishment be removed. In 1749 the English Parliament recognized the Moravians as "an ancient and episcopal church." The remainder of Zinzendorf's career was spent traveling throughout Europe directing his international religious movement. He died in Herrnhut.

Zinzendorf was a controversial figure in his time and remains so today. Some have viewed him as one of the greatest Lutheran theologians since the Reformation, but others have seen his "heart religion" as a perversion of Christianity. His work, however, had a profound influence on German literature and theology through Novalis (Friedrich von Hardenberg), Johann Wolfgang von Goethe, and Friedrich Schleiermacher. He was one of the first theologians to directly confront the challenges of modern rationalism, and his alternative thought form attracted thousands of adherents during his lifetime. Zinzendorf published several volumes of sermons and hymns but no systematic theology. He was deeply suspicious of attempts to make Christian thought conform to a theological system. Instead he advocated a "religion of the heart" that viewed the Christian life in terms of personal experience rather than creedal adherence. As he said in his *Gemein Reden* (1748–1749), "There should not be a Christian religion in the sense that one only adopts a certain system . . . rather his [Christ's] death and suffering must be buried in the heart." Among his more controversial propositions were that Christ, not God the Father, is the Creator and that the Holy Spirit is the mother of all souls. Most importantly, the suffering and death of Christ was the focal point of his theology. Although his ecumenical activity in America was doomed to failure, his efforts have inspired later church-union efforts. His most enduring legacy, though, has been his worldwide mission activity. The mission to the Native Americans faltered after the massacre of ninety Moravian converts by an American militia in Ohio in 1781; however, the missions to Central America, the Caribbean, and Africa grew into vibrant churches.

• The Moravian Archives in Bethlehem, Pa., contain an excellent collection of Zinzendorf manuscripts relating to America as well as many of his publications. Most of his published works have been reproduced by Erich Beyreuther and Gerhard Meyer, eds., in the series Zinzendorf, *Hauptschriften in sechs Bänden* and the companion series *Ergänzungsbände zu den Hauptschriften* (1962–1966). The only modern translation of any of Zinzendorf's works is *Nine Public Lectures on Important Subjects in Religion Preached in Fetter Lane Chapel in London in the Year 1746*, trans. George W. Forell (1973). There are two biographies of Zinzendorf available in English. John R. Weinlick, *Count Zinzendorf* (1956; repr. 1989), gives the major outline of Zinzendorf's life, but the lack of footnotes makes it difficult for the scholar. A. J. Lewis, *Zinzendorf: The Ecumenical Pioneer* (1962), was written in the midst of the ecumenical fervor of the 1950s but unfortunately was confined largely to English-language sources. Most of the German and French biographies are derivatives of August Gottlieb Spangenberg, *Leben des Herrn Nikolaus Ludwig Grafen von Zinzendorf und Pottendorf* (1773–1775), which is reproduced in Beyreuther, ed., *Nikolaus Ludwig von Zinzendorf, Materialien und Dokumente* (1971). The best modern biography of Zinzendorf is by Beyreuther, *Der junge Zinzendorf, Zinzendorf und die sich allhier beisammen finden*, and *Zinzendorf und die Christenheit* (3 vols., 1957, 1959, 1961), which was recently republished *Die große Zinzendorf Trilogie* (1988). Jacob John Sessler, in his study of the Bethlehem community, *Communal Pietism among Early American Moravians* (1933), gives a detailed and very unsympathetic account of Zinzendorf's activities in America. An older but still useful presentation of Bethlehem and Zinzendorf's American activities is found in Joseph Levering, *A History of Bethlehem, Pennsylvania, 1741–1892* (1903).

CRAIG D. ATWOOD

ZIRBES, Laura (26 Apr. 1884–9 June 1967), educator, was born in Buffalo, New York, the daughter of William Jacob Zirbes, a Baptist minister, and Louisa Volk. During her childhood years her family lived frugally in Sheboygan, Wisconsin, then moved to Cleveland while Laura was in high school. There she completed normal school at nineteen and began her career as an elementary school teacher, at times having as many as fifty-six immigrant children in her class. From her first year as a teacher she experimented with new ways of teaching to make learning more meaningful to her students.

These experiments led to articles in the *Elementary School Journal* in 1918 and 1919 and an invitation in 1920 to join the staff at the Lincoln School in New York City, a hotbed of experimentation in the new progressive educational philosophy. There she conducted seminal research in individualizing education and pioneered new audiovisual techniques. Meanwhile she enrolled in Teachers College at Columbia University, working with such diverse thinkers as John Dewey, William Kilpatrick, E. L. Thorndike, and William Bagley. She obtained her bachelor's degree in 1925, her master's in 1926, and her doctorate in 1928 with a dissertation comparing reading practices.

In 1928 she accepted a job at Ohio State University where she established the elementary teacher education program. She displayed a genius for making change happen, often saying, "It's never too tight to wiggle, and wiggling widens the wedge" (A. L. Meyer, "Laura Zirbes: In Memoriam," *ACEI Branch Exchange* 36, no. 1 [1967]: 36i). Knowing that teachers needed to see progressive philosophy in practice before they could teach it, she also established a summer demonstration school and a laboratory school.

Zirbes understood a critical precept: teachers teach as they were taught. Therefore she taught her own classes using discussion, not lecture; inquiry, not information poured into the students' heads; application, not memorization; integrated learnings, not discrete skills. Her attitude toward traditional education is reflected in the story she told of the seven-year-old who said, "Our teacher *don'ts* us a lot but she doesn't let us *do* much!" (*Guidelines to Developmental Teaching*, p. 8).

Zirbes abhorred the practice of using the same reading book for all children, and in fact she turned down an offer to help write the Scott-Foresman basal reading program, though it would have made her wealthy and famous. She preferred that children read real books, recalling the first grader who was asked by his aunt, "How are you getting along at school?" He replied, "Well, not so good. We just go over and over things in a lesson book. How many of those do you have to read before you get a book with real stories in it?" ("That All Children May Learn WE Must Learn," p. 52). For beginning readers, she helped pioneer the Language Experience approach in which children's own experiences, related in their own language, are recorded and become stories for them to read.

Zirbes was active in the Progressive Education Association (PEA), on whose executive committee she served from 1930 until 1942. She was in the mainstream of progressive thinking, vigorously opposing those on the left who let children "do as they please." But when the PEA collapsed after World War II because of McCarthyism and a "back to the basics" movement, Zirbes kept developing new ideas. She was an early leader in the Action Research movement, urging teachers to experiment in their classrooms just as she had done thirty-five years earlier.

Everything Zirbes learned she eagerly shared with her colleagues. She wrote more than two hundred articles and books during her career, and in 1947 she was named chair of the board of editors of *Childhood Education*. She became a popular speaker for two organizations, the Association for Childhood Education International (ACEI) and the Association for Supervision and Curriculum Development (ASCD). Teachers flocked to hear her speak because her observations about children were so perceptive, and her speeches and writings were rich with anecdotes. Zirbes loved these organizations in return because of their child-centered philosophy and because they were not narrow, subject-centered groups. She enjoyed the fellowship of classroom teachers, principals, and professors all mixed together with the single concern of improving teaching.

In 1952 Zirbes and a small group of Ohio State professors started discussing how to foster and study creativity. Zirbes had been interested in creativity all her life, from the time her first-grade teacher had thrown her painting of a cosmos flower into the trash can because it looked wilted. The teacher had wanted a row of pretty paintings to make a border along the top of the blackboard. Years later those misplaced priorities still burned, and Zirbes told the story, asking teachers, "Are we making border designs or are we releasing creative potential in children?" ("Creative Teaching for Creative Thinking and Living," *Educational Leadership* 14 [1956]: 21). Zirbes became a national leader on teaching for creativity with that speech to ASCD in 1956 and with her best book, *Spurs to Creative Teaching* (1959).

Among her many contributions Laura Zirbes was foremost, as Harry Truman said, "a teacher of teachers." In 1948 she received the Woman of the Year award from President Truman and the National Woman's Press Club. ACEI chose her for its honor roll; Ohio State put her in the top rank of its Education Hall of Fame. Zirbes taught for sixty-one years, never marrying. She was a pathbreaking woman, winning respect through sheer competence, clear principles, knowledge of children, courage, and her insistence on being heard. But by the 1960s she was often considered old-fashioned by younger educators who, startled by Sputnik, favored a subject-centered approach instead of an interdisciplinary philosophy. Zirbes stopped giving workshops after 1964 but kept pondering new problems, such as how to liberate education from quantitative research. Shortly before her death in Columbus, Ohio, she wrote to a friend, "I am still a pioneer!"

• Zirbes destroyed her personal papers so only a thin biofile is available at Ohio State University. The ACEI Archives at the University of Maryland include many tape recordings of her speeches. Tony Reid taped interviews with eighteen colleagues and acquaintances of Zirbes; these, plus more than 250 Zirbes letters from the period 1954–1967, are at the University of South Carolina's Museum of Education. Zirbes's *Practice Exercises and Checks on Silent Reading in the Primary Grades* (1925) is still cited as one of the earliest studies on individualizing education. Her "Social Studies in a New School" (coauthored with Lou La Brant) *Progressive Education* 11 (1934): 88–94, describes the curriculum at her laboratory school. "The Experience Approach in Reading," *Reading Teacher* 5 (1951): 1–16, places Zirbes among the early advocates of Language Experience. "That All Children May Learn WE Must Learn," *Childhood Education* 34 (1957): 50–54, is a stirring call for professional development. *Spurs to Creative Teaching* (1959) and *Guidelines to Developmental Teaching* (1961) are good exemplars of her philosophy and her gift for anecdotes. The only biography of Zirbes is Tony Reid, "Towards Creative Teaching: The Life and Career of Laura Zirbes" (Ph.D. diss., Univ. of South Carolina, 1993). David Moore, "Laura Zirbes and Progressive Reading Instruction," *Elementary School Journal* 86 (1986): 663–71, discusses her approach to teaching reading. Reid, "Laura Zirbes: Forerunner of Restructuring," *Childhood Education* 68 (1991): 98–102, surveys her life and how she antedated many later reforms. See also a bibliography by Ruth Seeger, *The Writings of Laura Zirbes* (1954). An obituary by Leland Jacobs is in *Childhood Education* 44 (1967): 210–17.

TONY REID

ZITKALA-SA. *See* Bonnin, Gertrude Simmons.

ZNANIECKI, Florian (15 Jan. 1882–23 Mar. 1958), sociologist, was born Florian Witold Znaniecki near the town of Swiatniki, in German-occupied Poland, the son of Leon Znaniecki and Amelia Holtz. His father was an estate manager, the family having lost their land following the Franco-Prussian war through Bismarck's Prussification policies. Znaniecki obtained an education in philosophy at the Universities of Geneva and Zurich and at the Sorbonne. One of his adventures of that time was a fake suicide and enlistment in the French Foreign Legion. After gaining an honorable discharge, he edited a newspaper in Marseilles and worked as a librarian at the Polish National Museum in Rapperswil, Switzerland. He also returned to Paris to attend lectures by a number of prominent sociologists.

Znaniecki finally obtained his Ph.D. at the Jagiellonian University in Cracow, Poland, in 1910 and then published in Polish *The Question of Value in Philosophy* (1910), *Humanism and Knowledge* (1912), and a translation of Henri Bergson's *Creative Evolution* (1913). Unable to obtain a position at a Polish university for political reasons, he became the director of the Polish Emigrant Protective Association and editor of its publications, including the *Polish Emigrant* (in Polish). The extensive data he collected in that position resulted in lengthy reports to the czarist government and numerous articles. At the Emigrant Association he met W. I. Thomas, a sociologist from the University of Chicago, who was seeking material for a study of Poles because of the large numbers of Polish immigrants in the United States. Znaniecki provided him with background material and was in turn invited to the United States to assist with the collection and analysis of personal documents of the immigrants. He and his wife, Emilia Szwejkowska, whom he married when both were students at the University of Geneva, took the last train out of Poland before World War I, leaving a son, Juliusz Znaniecki, with her relatives because of the danger of the trip. The young Polish scholar brought with him not only knowledge of Polish society but also a philosophical perspective, with an emphasis on culture and especially values. Znaniecki was familiar with English, having published an article in the *Philosophical Review* in 1915.

At the University of Chicago, Znaniecki assisted Thomas in writing *The Polish Peasant in Europe and America*, published in five volumes between 1918 and 1920. Besides being the junior coauthor, Znaniecki wrote the introductions and methodological note. In the overall plan, *The Polish Peasant* was to be part of an extensive analysis of Polish society, including the intelligentsia and the bourgeoisie. Frustrated over the impossibility of including all his ideas in *The Polish Peasant*, Znaniecki wrote *Cultural Reality*, published by the University of Chicago Press in 1919. After his first wife died unexpectedly, Znaniecki married in 1915 an American lawyer, Eileen Markley, who left her job at the Legal Aid Society to help with *The Polish Peasant* and continued to assist her husband throughout his life. The extended project on the Poles of other social classes fell through when Thomas left the University of Chicago.

Znaniecki returned to Poland in 1920 at the invitation of the University of Poznan, which agreed to convert for him a professional chair in philosophy into one in sociology. The new faculty member organized the Polish Institute of Sociology and established with students the *Sociological Review*, the first sociological journal in that part of the world. The institute collected autobiographies of peasants and workers obtained through national competitions, resulting in numerous manuscripts. Many of the students, collectively known as the "Znaniecki school," contributed to making Polish sociology prominent in Europe, despite the break in its activities during the Stalinist years, when the subject was forbidden.

Znaniecki published numerous books during his Polish period (1920–1939), including *The Laws of Social Psychology* (1925), *The Method of Sociology* (1934), and *Social Actions* (1936) in English. His major Polish books include *Upadek Civilizacji Zachodniej* (The Fall of Western Civilization, 1921), *Wstep do Sociologii* (Introduction to Sociology, 1922), *Sociologja Wychowania* (Sociology of Education; 2 vols., 1928–1930), *Miasto w Swiadomosci Jego Obywateli* (The City in the Consciousness of Its Citizens, 1931), and *Ludzie Terazniej-si a Ciwilizacja Przyszlosci* (People of Today and the Civilization of Tomorrow, 1935).

Znaniecki maintained contact with American sociologists, teaching at Columbia University in 1931–1933 and again in the summer of 1939. His wife and daughter, Helena, born in 1925, accompanied him on the first trip but stayed in Poland the second time, thus being present during the Nazi invasion. After a stint in a concentration camp, they joined him at the University of Illinois at Urbana-Champaign where he accepted a position, having been stopped in England on the way to Poland. Because he was blacklisted by both the Communists and the Nazis, he was fortunate in not being able to return to his homeland. (Znaniecki's son by his first marriage was less fortunate. The younger Znaniecki's participation in the Warsaw uprising resulted in his internment at Dachau. Although he was released by the American liberating forces, the poet and novelist was unable to develop a new creative life in the United States and finally committed suicide.)

Znaniecki continued his academic work at the University of Illinois, publishing *The Social Role of the Man of Knowledge* (based on his Columbia lectures in 1940), *Modern Nationalities* (1952), and *Cultural Sciences* (1952). He was elected president of the American Sociological Association in 1954. At the time of his death in Urbana, he was in the process of writing his magnum opus, to be called *Systematic Sociology*. The completed part was published posthumously in 1965 as *Social Relations and Social Roles*.

In addition to his development of sociology in Poland, Znaniecki made several major contributions to sociological theory. One of these is the concept and methodology of "the humanistic coefficient," or the importance of understanding human behavior through the viewpoint of the participants. Toward the end of the twentieth century, his emphasis on culture as the basis of human action became of major interest to sociologists. Znaniecki's concept of a social role as a set of patterned, interdependent, social relations between a social person and a social circle, involving duties and rights, began to replace a view of that role as a set of expectations.

• Biographical information appears in Helena Znaniecki Lopata's introduction to Znaniecki, *Social Relations and Social Roles* (1965), and in Lopata, "Florian Znaniecki: Creative Evolution of a Sociologist," *Journal of the History of Behavioral Sciences* 12 (1976): 203–15. See also Znaniecki, *On Humanistic Sociology*, ed. Robert Bierstedt (1969); Zygmund Dulczewski, *Florian Znaniecki, Zycie i Dzielo* (Florian Znaniecki, Life and Work, 1984); Andrzej Kwilecki and Bohdan Czarnocki, eds., *The Humanistic Sociology of Florian Znaniecki: The Polish Period, 1920–1939*, trans. Czarnocki (1989); and Harold Orbach, "Znaniecki's Contribution to *The Polish Peasant*," paper presented at the International Seminar on the Contribution of Florian Znaniecki to Sociological Theory, Trento, Italy, 24–25 Oct. 1990.

HELENA Z. LOPATA

ZOLLARS, Ely Vaughn (19 Sept. 1847–16 Feb. 1916), Disciples of Christ minister, author, and college president, was born near Lower Salem, Washington County, Ohio, the son of Abram Zollars, a blacksmith and farmer, and Caroline Vaughn. His paternal grandfather, Frederick Zollars, emigrated from Germany or Holland between 1730 and 1740. Zollars was named for his maternal grandfather, Ely Vaughn (sometimes spelled Vaughan).

Abram and Caroline Zollars emphasized education, and three of their four sons received college degrees. Zollars attended private school in Marietta and completed a college preparatory course at Marietta College, but in 1865, at age eighteen, he married Hulda Louise McAtee, who was nineteen. In 1866 a daughter was born. Zollars abandoned plans to attend college and settled on a small farm purchased by his father. For six years he farmed and taught school during the winter, but in 1871 he sold his land and enrolled in Bethany College in West Virginia.

Abram Zollars had been an early Ohio convert to the Disciples of Christ religious movement, leading his family to unite with the church and his son to choose to attend the college established by Disciples patriarch Alexander Campbell in 1840. Though Campbell died in 1866, Bethany College remained the premiere educational institution among the Disciples of Christ, and it trained a generation of church leaders in the last half of the nineteenth century. Zollars excelled as a student; after he graduated in 1875 he remained for a year as an adjunct professor of ancient languages and completed a master's degree. Because he displayed conspicuous skills as a fund-raiser, the college employed him a second year as a "financial agent," and he was quite successful in securing pledges.

In 1877 Zollars accepted the presidency of Kentucky Classical and Business College located in North Middletown, Kentucky, and for seven years headed the small community school. For one year he served as the president of Garrard Female College in Lancaster, Kentucky, before accepting a position as minister of the First Christian Church in Springfield, Illinois, in 1885. The church was fifty-two years old when Zollars became its minister; it was one of the largest and oldest in the Disciples of Christ movement. During the three years Zollars served as its minister, the church nearly doubled in size to around 600 members.

In 1888 Zollars resigned his ministerial post in Springfield to become president of Hiram College in Hiram, Ohio, a position he held for fourteen years. Hiram opened in 1850 and among Zollars's predecessors as president were the only Disciples minister to become president of the United States, James A. Garfield, and Burke A. Hinsdale, who subsequently served as superintendent of schools in Cleveland and professor of education at the University of Michigan. During his tenure as president, Zollars stressed the relationship between the college and the churches; Hiram trained scores of Disciples ministers and missionaries. The Student Volunteer Movement and the Young Men's Christian Association (YMCA) flourished at Hiram during Zollars's presidency, and he encouraged the establishment in 1896 of a pioneering set-

tlement house in Cleveland—Hiram House. Zollars tried unsuccessfully to merge Hiram and Bethany College, and his efforts contributed to increased dissatisfaction among some supporters of the college.

While president of Hiram College, Zollars became acquainted with T. W. Phillips and his family. Phillips was a wealthy oil developer and a loyal Disciples of Christ layman who contributed to many church projects.

In 1902 Zollars accepted the presidency of Texas Christian University (TCU), which was then located in Waco. The school had originally been a private religious school named Add-Ran University, but in 1895 it was deeded to the Disciples of Christ in Texas and moved to Waco. At TCU Zollars once again proved to be an effective fund-raiser and attempted to rally the churches of the state to support the school. In 1905 a bitter dispute with the faculty over salaries led to Zollars's resignation and left him without a position.

Zollars immediately approached the Christian Missionary Society in the Oklahoma Territory with a plan to launch a Christian college in Oklahoma. He persuaded T. W. Phillips to underwrite a fund-raising effort that led to the opening of Oklahoma Christian University in Enid in 1907. Phillips died in 1912 and the name of the school was changed first to Phillips Christian University and later to Phillips University. The Phillips family continued to be major benefactors. Zollars was sixty years old when Oklahoma Christian University opened, but he remained president of the institution until deteriorating health forced him to resign in 1915. He retired to Warren, Ohio, where he died.

Zollars was a voluminous writer; his articles appeared regularly in church papers, particularly in the Cincinnati-based *Christian Standard*. Between 1895 and 1913 the Standard Publishing Company published ten books written by Zollars. His two most widely known books were *The Great Salvation* (1895), a basic outline of Disciples' theology, and *The Holy Book and the Sacred Day* (1914), a series of lectures delivered over a twenty-year period beginning in the 1890s. Zollars's books were mostly restatements of the basic beliefs of the Disciples of Christ movement; his biographer Ronald Osborn noted that "he himself held that truth needs to be repeatedly restated." His writing placed him squarely on the side of those Disciples leaders who felt threatened by the rise of Darwinian thought and the spread of higher criticism.

Zollars contributed in many ways to the organizational development of the Disciples of Christ. He appeared on scores of convention programs and preached from hundreds of pulpits in addition to writing unrelentingly for church publications. He was a conspicuous leader in early efforts to coordinate Disciples higher education; in 1910 he initiated a plan that led to the establishment of the Association of Colleges of the Disciples of Christ. More than any other man, Zollars created what his biographer called an "educational conscience" in the Disciples of Christ movement.

• The best treatment of Zollars's life and career is Ronald E. Osborn, *Ely Vaughn Zollars* (1947). A contemporary sketch is in John T. Brown, *Churches of Christ* (1904). See also Henry K. Shaw, *Buckeye Disciples* (1952); Francis M. Green, *Hiram College and Western Reserve Eclectic Institute* (1901); and Frank H. Marshall, *Phillips University's First Fifty Years* (1957). An obituary is in the *Christian Standard*, 19 Feb. 1916.

DAVID EDWIN HARRELL, JR.

ZOLLICOFFER, Felix Kirk (19 May 1812–19 Jan. 1862), journalist and politician, was born in Maury County, Tennessee, the son of John Jacob Zollicoffer, a planter, and Martha Kirk. The boy grew up in comfortable circumstances but under firm parental discipline. He attended local schools and in 1833 had a term of classical studies at Jackson College, Columbia, Tennessee. An avid reader, he was largely self-taught.

In 1827 Zollicoffer was apprenticed to a printer. Two years later he became editor and part owner of the Paris *West Tennessean*. After it failed in 1831, he worked as a printer in Alabama and Tennessee until his debts were paid. In 1835 he married Louisa Pocahontas Gordon; they had thirteen children, six of whom (all girls) were living at her death in 1857. From 1835 to 1840 Zollicoffer edited and published the *Columbia Observer* except for a year in 1836–1837 when he served as a first lieutenant in the Second Seminole War. A staunch Whig from that party's inception, the editor became one of the party's powerbrokers in the state.

While recovering from a serious illness, Zollicoffer was asked to assist with the Whigs' major state newspaper, the Nashville *Republican Banner*. An associate editor in 1841, he became editor the next year and was credited with helping reelect Whig governor James C. Jones over Democrat James K. Polk. During the Jones administration Zollicoffer was appointed state adjutant general and was elected comptroller of the treasury by the legislature. In 1849 the Whig voters of Davidson County elected him to the state senate where he served until 1851. He resumed the editorship of the *Republican Banner* in 1850 and helped elect William B. Campbell governor in 1851.

A delegate to the national Whig convention in 1852, Zollicoffer loyally supported Winfield Scott for president, although Millard Fillmore had been his first choice. Scott carried Tennessee but lost the election to Franklin Pierce. During the heated campaign Zollicoffer and Democratic editor John Leake Marling engaged in a gun battle on a city street on 20 August. Although hit first on his shooting hand, Zollicoffer inflicted a severe facial wound on his opponent. Aggressive, quick-tempered, and courageous, Zollicoffer was also noted for his sense of honor and his fairness. Unionist William G. "Parson" Brownlow said that the only mean thing Zollicoffer ever did was to join the Confederacy.

Zollicoffer abandoned editing to serve three consecutive terms (1853–1859) representing Nashville in the national House of Representatives. A Democrat described him as "tenacious in debate, logical in argument, and perfectly fearless; he was a formidable adversary at all times." Although he was a slaveowner, Zollicoffer deplored talk of secession but was nonetheless convinced that southern rights were being ignored. One of his major addresses defended the 1854 Kansas-Nebraska Act.

When the Whig party disintegrated in the 1850s Zollicoffer turned to the Know Nothing (American) party. During the 1860 campaign he supported John Bell and the Constitutional Union party as the best hope of preserving the Union. Even after Abraham Lincoln's election, he hoped that secession could be avoided. If it came, he believed that it should be done collectively after a convention of all the slave states. A delegate to the National Peace Conference in February 1861, Zollicoffer was disappointed by its failure to resolve the crisis. Through his speeches, letters, and articles he helped hold Tennessee in the Union until the war started in April.

In May Zollicoffer was commissioned a brigadier general in the Provisional Army of Tennessee; on 9 July he received the same rank in the Confederate army. Later that month he was ordered to eastern Tennessee, where Union sentiment was strong.

When Kentucky's neutrality ended in early September, Zollicoffer moved to hold the key mountain passes between the two states. Offensive minded, he invaded Kentucky in October 1861 with 4,500 men but was checked at Rockcastle Hills on 21 October by a Federal force commanded by Brigadier General Albin Schoepf. When Zollicoffer decided that the main Union thrust would come west of Cumberland Gap, he left detachments to hold the passes but shifted most of his troops westward. On 29 November they arrived at the village of Mill Springs on the south bank of the Cumberland River between Somerset and Monticello.

Despite orders to the contrary, Zollicoffer moved much of his command to the northern side of the river and entrenched at Beech Grove. He reasoned that on the north side they presented a greater threat to Union forces than they would if south of the river. When Major General George B. Crittenden arrived on 3 January 1862 to assume command, the Cumberland was in flood, and he could not immediately withdraw them. By 17 January Brigadier General George H. Thomas had a Federal army at Logan's Crossroads, some eight miles north of Beech Grove, and Schoepf was moving from Somerset to join him. The Confederates decided to attack Thomas before Schoepf arrived.

Zollicoffer's brigade led the advance on a cold, rainy Sunday morning, 19 January 1862. They surprised the Union camp shortly after daybreak. His men made initial progress, and Zollicoffer actively pushed their attack. Nearsighted and wearing a raincoat that covered his uniform, he rode into the ranks of Colonel Speed S. Fry's Fourth Kentucky Infantry, USA. Thinking that they were his troops, Zollicoffer ordered Fry to cease firing on a Confederate unit. Fry obeyed, but then an aide galloped up to the Confederate general, shouted, "It's the enemy, General!" and fired at Fry.

Fry shot at Zollicoffer and ordered his troops to resume fire. Hit several times, Zollicoffer was killed instantly. After the Confederates retreated three hours later, the Federals escorted the body to Bowling Green, and the Confederates sent it to Nashville where Zollicoffer was buried on 2 February.

Zollicoffer was an influential Whig editor and a power in the Whig party in the upper South. He displayed some talent and initiative during his brief military career, but his judgment in crossing the Cumberland River has been questioned. Since Zollicoffer became a hero in death, Crittenden shouldered the blame for the loss at Mill Springs (or Logan's Crossroads), the first break in the long defense line the Confederates had established across southern Kentucky.

• Zollicoffer's personal papers are scattered. Numerous references to his military career are in *The War of the Rebellion: A Compilation of the Official Records of the Union and Confederate Armies* (128 vols., 1880–1901), especially ser. 1, vols. 4, 7, and 52. Raymond E. Myers, *The Zollie Tree* (1964), is the most complete account of Zollicoffer's life; a good brief sketch is Edwin C. Bearss, "Felix Kirk Zollicoffer," in *The Confederate General*, vol. 6, ed. William C. Davis (1991). His career as a journalist and politician is examined in James C. Stamper, "Felix K. Zollicoffer: Tennessee Editor and Politician," *Tennessee Historical Quarterly* 28 (1969): 356–76, while Edd Winfield Parks, "Zollicoffer: A Southern Whig," *Tennessee Historical Quarterly* 11 (Dec. 1952):346–55, concentrates on his years as a Whig politician. His brief Civil War service is discussed in Thomas L. Connelly, *Army of the Heartland: The Army of Tennessee 1861–1862* (1967), pp. 44–45, 86–99, and in R. Gerald McMurtry, "Zollicoffer and the Battle of Mill Springs," *Filson Club History Quarterly* 29 (Oct. 1955): 303–19. C. David Dalton, "Zollicoffer, Crittenden, and the Mill Springs Campaign: Some Persistent Questions," *Filson Club History Quarterly* 60 (1986): 463–71, defends Zollicoffer's decisions at Mill Springs.

LOWELL H. HARRISON

ZOOK, George Frederick (22 Apr. 1885–17 Aug. 1951), educator, was born in Fort Scott, Kansas, the son of Douglas Zook and Helen Follenius, farmers. He earned his bachelor's (1906) and master's (1907) degrees at the University of Kansas, driving a hearse to pay for his education. He then went to Cornell University for doctoral study, on an assistantship. After traveling in Europe on a fellowship and returning to Cornell to complete his studies, he earned a Ph.D. in European history in 1913. Zook married Suzie Gant in 1911; the couple had no children.

From 1912 to 1920 Zook was a professor at Pennsylvania State University, taking a leave of absence in 1918 to work with the Committee on Public Information. In 1919 Zook accepted the position of associate director of the Savings Division of the U.S. Treasury and also published the book *The Company of Royal Adventurers Trading into Africa*. In 1920 he moved to the U.S. Bureau of Education, where he was chief of the Higher Education Division until 1925.

In 1925 Zook became president of the University of Akron. He had hoped to make the university eminent, but the financial pressures of the Great Depression proved too overwhelming. While at Akron he continued to serve the federal government as a member of President Herbert Hoover's National Advisory Committee on Education (1929–1931). In 1933 President Franklin Delano Roosevelt appointed Zook as U.S. commissioner of education.

But Zook was not to hold that post long; in 1934 he accepted the position of director of the American Council on Education. He stayed at the council for the remainder of his career, eventually becoming the chair and then the president. He was a prominent, if not the most prominent, lobbyist for higher education, actively promoting a variety of projects. Of particular interest to Zook were the issues of federal aid to education, junior colleges, vocational education, and international exchanges.

As both commissioner of education and as the head of the American Council on Education, Zook urged that junior colleges be viewed as terminal institutions of vocational training and general education rather than as pathways to four-year colleges and universities. Although students and their parents preferred to use two-year colleges for preparation for the baccalaureate, Zook considered the institutions more appropriate for educating large numbers of students in basic studies apart from the university.

From 1946 to 1951 Zook was the U.S. national commissioner for UNESCO, and he served in the foundation of the International Association of Universities (1950). He was also active in the restructuring of education in Germany and Japan following World War II.

Zook's annual presidential reports, published in the *Educational Record*, reveal exacting detail and extensive coverage of the association's activities. He was known as serious and deliberative, yet personal descriptions of him inevitably remark on his strong sense of humor. He was successful at the American Council on Education because of his connections to the White House and to foundations, and the latter provided innumerable grants to the council over the years. Under his leadership, the America Council on Education grew from 269 members in 1934 to 1,118 at his retirement. His major sustaining work, however, was as chair of the President's Commission on Higher Education, which published its report in 1947. Addressing issues such as universal access at the level of junior colleges and the need for federal financial support of academic programs and infrastructure, the 1947 report defines the relationship between higher education and the federal government, specifying ways in which colleges and universities can meet federal and national needs.

His writings cover a wide range of topics in higher education, the most notable being *Higher Education for Democracy* (1947). He also coauthored *Principles of Accrediting Higher Institutions* with Melvin E. Haggerty (1936). In 1947 his work *Japan and Germany: Problems in Reeducation* was published. Zook died in Arlington, Virginia.

• Useful works include George Knepper, *New Lamps for Old: One Hundred Years of Urban Higher Education at the University of Akron* (1970); and an unpublished history of ACE, "Leadership and Chronology, 1918–1968" (1968). Obituaries include those in *Educational Record* 32 (Oct. 1951) and 33 (Apr. 1952), and the *New York Times*, 19 Aug. 1951.

PHILO A. HUTCHESON

ZORACH, William (28 Feb. 1889–15 Nov. 1966), sculptor, was born Zorach Samovich in Eurberich, Lithuania, then a part of czarist Russia, the son of a flaxmaker and barge keeper. His father's name was probably Orchick Samovich; his mother's was probably Toba Getal. In 1892, when Zorach's father and oldest brother fled to the United States to avoid the persecution of the Jews, the family lost its inherited land and home and assumed the name Finkelstein. A year later, Zorach, five siblings, and his mother emigrated from Russia. Two additional siblings were born in Port Clinton, Ohio, where the immigrant family lived until 1896, when they moved about seventy miles east to Cleveland. Zorach's name was changed circa 1898 to William Finkelstein by a grade school teacher who found Zorach Finkelstein too difficult. He left school after the seventh grade (c. 1902) and worked at several menial industrial jobs because his family needed his wages. Determined to find a more creative occupation, he became an apprentice with the W. J. Morgan Lithograph Co., where he worked from 1902 to 1908, the summers of 1909 and 1910, and most of 1912.

From 1905 to 1908 Zorach studied drawing and painting in night classes at the Cleveland School of Art (now called the Institute of Art) with Henry Keller and others. During the academic years 1908–1910 he studied traditional drawing and painting techniques in New York City at the National Academy of Design and briefly at the more progressive Art Students League with George Bridgman. Arriving in Cherbourg, France, in December 1910, he traveled to Munich before settling in Paris. There he studied painting at a small school of modern painting, called La Palette, where he met his future wife, the California artist Marguerite Thompson, who became his mentor for vanguard art venues in Paris. When they were married in New York City on 24 December 1912, he changed his legal name to William Zorach and his birthdate from 1889 to 1887. The couple spent half of each year in New York (on West Tenth Street in Greenwich Village from 1913 to 1935 and thereafter at 276 Hicks Street in Brooklyn Heights) and half at artists' colonies or country sites (Chappaqua, N.Y., 1913–1914; Randolph and Plainfield, N.H., 1915, 1917, 1918; Provincetown, Mass., 1916, 1921; Stonington, Maine, 1919; Yosemite Valley, Calif., 1920; and Georgetown Island, near Bath, Maine, for the rest of their lives). They had two children, a son, Tessim, and a daughter, Dahlov, herself an artist who had a solo exhibition at the Museum of Modern Art in 1935.

The Zorachs were among a handful of American artists who between 1905 and 1915 began in Paris a modern tradition based on inventive spontaneity, the use of saturated expressionist color, and simplification and distortion of observed forms. They also were part of an enlightened inner circle of avant-garde artists and writers in New York and New England. The Zorachs collaborated on designs for painted scenery for the Provincetown Players during its initial seasons in Provincetown and New York. Both artists exhibited paintings in vanguard shows, including the Salon d'Automne, Paris, 1911 and 1913; the Armory Show, New York, 1913; and the Forum Exhibition of Modern American Painters at the Anderson Galleries, New York, 1916.

In 1917 Zorach carved his first sculpture in wood and, in 1921, his first sculpture in stone. Although in 1922 Zorach switched his primary medium from oil painting to sculpture, he painted watercolors and was a prolific draftsman for the rest of his life. In 1968 Donelson F. Hoopes organized an exhibition at the Brooklyn Museum of seventy-three of his pictorial works executed between 1911 and 1922 that demonstrated his experimentation with cubism, fauvism, expressionism, and primitivism. From 1929 to 1959 Zorach taught sculpture classes at the Art Students League and more informally and sporadically at his summer home and studio in Maine.

Zorach and the French-born Robert Laurent were the first Americans to focus on the special qualities of sculptures carved directly in stone and wood as opposed to modeling designs in clay and having them cast or carved in other materials. Both were inspired by sculptures by African and Oceanic ethnic groups, American folk carvings, and the primitivist carvings of the French postimpressionist painter Paul Gauguin. Zorach found it fascinating that rocks are concretions evolved over thousands of years and that carved stones exhibit a constant interchange between recognizable human or animal images and the natural material as stone. In *Woman of Mars* (1924, private collection), for example, Zorach left parts of the block rough and emphasized the large mica and quartz crystals of Maine granite (his signature material), which then metamorphosed before the viewer's gaze to a representation of a human head and then back to the qualities of color and form inherent in the dense, hard medium. The title and the rough textures engender the idea of the sculpture as an archaeological fragment. Between 1917 and 1966 Zorach carved 230 sculptures directly.

Simultaneous to working out ideas in his pioneering sculptures, Zorach began to develop his aesthetic philosophies in essays published in *The Arts*, a magazine founded (1920), owned, and edited by the critic, collector, and painter Hamilton Easter Field. In "The New Tendencies in Art" (Oct. 1921), "The Sculpture of Edgar Degas" (Nov. 1925), "The Sculpture of Constantin Brancusi" (Mar. 1926), and "The Child and Art" (Feb. 1930), Zorach advocated freedom of expression, the direct involvement of the artist in the entire process of creating sculpture, the abstraction of forms, and the importance of the spiritual content of children's, tribal, and folk art. He was especially interested in coaxing out the richness of the color, texture, and grain inherent in tropical woods and in stone by carving directly into the material of the finished sculpture. In contrast, contemporary academic sculptors had assistants or artisan/craftsmen transfer designs modeled in clay to bronze casts or to white marble. In later decades, sculptors identified with academies of art adopted many of Zorach's ideas, which were avant-garde in the second decade of the twentieth century. After 1930 Zorach combined modern and traditional ideas in both his direct carvings and in sculpture composed by modeling clay.

Zorach's works were regularly on view in both one-man and group exhibitions. Important lifetime exhibitions in New York of Zorach's sculpture include solo shows at Kraushaar Galleries in 1924 and 1928 and at Edith Gregor Halpert's Downtown Galleries in 1931, 1932–1933, 1936, 1943, 1947, 1951, and 1955–1956. The Whitney Museum of American Art (New York) organized a major retrospective in 1959.

Zorach is represented in more than one hundred museums internationally. His *Mother and Child* (Spanish rosa marble, 1927–1930) was purchased by the Metropolitan Museum of Art in 1952. A week before Zorach's death in Bath, Maine, he completed his last stone carving, *Wisdom of Solomon* (1963–1966, Brooklyn Museum, gift of Mr. and Mrs. Avnet), which depicts two women and the disputed child in a compact, blocky composition typical of his multifigured groups. Major public commissions include *Spirit of the Dance* (aluminum, 1932) for Radio City Music Hall, New York; *Benjamin Franklin* (pink Tennessee marble, 1936–1937) for the Post Office Department, Washington, D.C.; and *Man and Work* (bronze, 1952–1953) for the Mayo Clinic, Rochester, Minnesota.

Large retrospective memorial exhibitions of his two- and three-dimensional works were organized at the National Collection of Fine Arts (now called the National Museum of American Art), Smithsonian Institution, in 1967; Danenberg Galleries, New York, in 1968; the American Academy of Arts and Letters, New York, in 1969; and for ten museums of art in Maine in 1968–1969. Zabriskie Gallery in New York has represented his estate since 1974.

• Key works for biographical information and critical analysis of the art of both Marguerite and William Zorach are Roberta K. Tarbell, "Catalogue Raisonné of the Carved Sculpture of William Zorach" (Ph.D. diss., Univ. of Delaware, 1976) and *Marguerite Zorach, the Early Years: 1908–20* (1973), both based on the Zorach papers (11,000 items, Manuscript Division of the Library of Congress; on microfilm at the Archives of American Art, Smithsonian Institution) and the large study collections of two- and three-dimensional works at the National Museum of American Art, Smithsonian Institution. His other writings include *Art Is My Life: The Autobiography of William Zorach* (1967), *Zorach Explains Sculpture: What It Means and How It Is Made* (1947), and the foreword to *Contemporary American Sculpture* by C. Ludwig Brummé (1948). Zorach collaborated with Paul Wingert in cataloging his early works: *The Sculpture of William Zorach* (1938). John I. H. Baur and Donelson F. Hoopes wrote important essays in catalogs for retrospective exhibitions at the Whitney Museum of American Art (*William Zorach* [1959])

and at the Brooklyn Museum (*William Zorach: Paintings, Watercolors and Drawings, 1911–1922* [1968]), respectively. The innovative contributions of the Zorachs in New England were the focus of Marilyn Hoffman's *Marguerite and William Zorach: The Cubist Years* (1987) and Tarbell's *William and Marguerite Zorach: The Maine Years* (1980). The couple's integral role in the history of early twentieth-century modern art is assessed in William I. Homer, ed., *Avant-Garde Painting and Sculpture in America, 1910–1925* (1975); Joan M. Marter, Tarbell, and Jeffrey Wechsler, *Vanguard American Sculpture, 1913–39* (1979); Peter Morrin et al., eds., *The Advent of Modernism: Post-Impressionism and North American Art, 1900–1918* (exhibition catalog, High Museum of Art, Atlanta, Ga., 1986); and Ilene S. Fort, ed., *The Human Figure in American Sculpture: The Question of Modernity, 1890–1945* (1995). An obituary is in the *New York Times*, 17 Nov. 1966.

ROBERTA K. TARBELL

ZOUBERBUHLER, Bartholomew (1719–10 Dec. 1766), clergyman, was born in St. Gall, Switzerland, the son of the Reverend Bartholomew Zouberbuhler; his mother's name is unknown. He was educated probably at the Gymnasium in St. Gall, as well as by his father, and certainly by private study in America. He apparently was not married. (His last name is spelled several different ways in the literature.) Zouberbuhler's family moved to Purrysburg, South Carolina, in 1737, four years after the founding of Georgia; his father was the minister to the new settlement of Swiss there. The elder Zouberbuhler died in late 1738. The younger Bartholomew, then nineteen, began preaching at Purrysburg in his father's place. The Reverend John Martin Bolzius, Lutheran pastor of the German settlers of Ebenezer in Georgia, across the Savannah River from Purrysburg, said in 1741 that Zouberbuhler had neither a divine calling to the ministry nor ordination yet he baptized and married people. This he undoubtedly did as there was no one else in Purrysburg to do these things.

Zouberbuhler asked James Oglethorpe, the founder of Georgia, to make him preacher to the Calvinistic people in Savannah, but Oglethorpe did not make the appointment since Bolzius refused to recommend Zouberbuhler, saying that he did not know him well enough. Zouberbuhler attracted the attention of Alexander Garden, South Carolina commissary of the bishop of London, who urged him to study for holy orders in the Church of England. After study in Charles Town, South Carolina, Zouberbuhler went to England, where he was ordained deacon by the bishop of London on 22 September and priest on 20 October 1745.

Zouberbuhler was assigned to the Anglican parish in Savannah, then vacant, and arrived there in January 1746. On his voyage to Georgia there was an epidemic on board the vessel; thirteen died, including the captain. Zouberbuhler took over the navigation of the ship until the mate recovered enough to take charge.

Zouberbuhler served parishioners in Savannah for the next twenty years until his death. He conducted services in English, German, and French as there was a call for services in all of these languages. As Anglican missionary in Savannah, Zouberbuhler was promised a salary of £50 per year plus two indentured servants to cultivate his glebe. In March 1746 the Georgia Trustees, the government of Georgia in London, decided to employ the Reverend John J. Zubly, a Swiss Calvinist, as Zouberbuhler's assistant to preach to the Germans at Vernonburg, a settlement outside Savannah. Zubly was to be paid £10 a year from Zouberbuhler's salary, and Zouberbuhler was to receive a third indentured servant. Zouberbuhler objected to this, saying he could hardly live on the £50 salary and that the work of his servants did not produce enough to feed himself. Zubly declined the offer. By 1747 Zouberbuhler was looking for a position elsewhere, and the trustees became concerned that he might leave Georgia. So in 1749 he was granted 500 acres of land as an inducement to remain in Georgia.

In 1750 Zouberbuhler saw to the building of Georgia's first Anglican church in Savannah, which was enlarged in 1765 with additional pews and a gallery for an organ. He was diligent in parish duties, visiting the sick and conducting services in settlements near Savannah and down the coast at Frederica on St. Simon's Island. He also promoted education, bringing back from England in 1749 a library purchased by the Georgia Trustees. In addition, he encouraged the Savannah school and helped to raise funds to build a schoolhouse and a house for the schoolmaster.

The Church of England was established as the official church in Georgia in 1758 by action of the colony's legislature. While Zouberbuhler does not seem to have directly participated in the passage of the legislation, the positive impressions of his personality and services to the colony undoubtedly helped the church's proponents. He was thenceforth rector of Christ Church, the Savannah parish.

Zouberbuhler encouraged the work of Joseph Ottolenghe, who arrived in 1751, as catechist to the slaves in and near Savannah. Zouberbuhler left a considerable part of his estate to be used after his death to support a teacher for his own slaves as well as the work in Savannah. He also encouraged slaves to attend his services in Savannah.

In Georgia he became a planter who owned more than 2,000 acres of land and forty-two slaves by the time of his death. He also manufactured bricks for sale in Georgia. Zouberbuhler's health declined, and he would have liked to have retired several years before his death. A satisfactory successor could not be found, however, so he continued to serve. He died in Savannah after a long and painful illness.

Zouberbuhler brought stability to the Church of England in Georgia after a succession of unsatisfactory priests. He was a practical person who realized the limits of what he could do and did not attempt too much in this new and small colony. He was a conciliator who got along well with other clergymen, government officials, and his parishioners, who loved him deeply. He was clearly the most practical Anglican clergyman in colonial Georgia and served longer than any other Anglican priest in the colony.

• There is no collection of Zouberbuhler papers. The most complete treatment of Zouberbuhler is Edgar Lee Pennington, "The Reverend Bartholomew Zouberbuhler," *Georgia Historical Quarterly* 18 (1934): 354–63. See also Roger K. Warlick, *As Grain Once Scattered: A History of Christ Church Savannah, Georgia* (1987); Henry T. Malone, *The Episcopal Church in Georgia, 1733–1957* (1960); Harold E. Davis, *The Fledgling Province, Social and Cultural Life in Colonial Georgia, 1733–1776* (1976); Reba Carolyn Strickland, *Religion and the State of Georgia in the Eighteenth Century* (1939); Allen D. Candler et al., eds., *The Colonial Records of the State of Georgia* (1904–); George Fenwick Jones et al., eds., *Detailed Reports of the Salzburger Emigrants Who Settled in America . . . Edited by Samuel Urlsperger* (1968–); *Abstracts of Colonial Wills of the State of Georgia, 1733–1777* (1962; repr. 1981); and Gilbert P. Voigt, "Swiss Notes on South Carolina," *South Carolina Historical and Genealogical Magazine* 21 (1920): 93 104.

KENNETH COLEMAN

ZUBER, Paul Burgess (20 Dec. 1926–5 Mar. 1987), attorney and educator, was born in Williamsport, Pennsylvania, the son of Paul A. Zuber, an employee of the U.S. Post Office, and Jennie Baer. Zuber served in the Quartermaster Corps, special services branch, during World War II from 22 June 1945 to 13 February 1946. He received his B.S. from Brown University in 1949, having concluded the premedical program. In 1950 Zuber was drafted for service during the Korean War. He was the chief of psychological testing at the Murphy Army Hospital in Waltham, Massachusetts, until 1952. While directing this service, he began to recognize the damage caused by racial and other forms of discrimination in the United States. An examination of his life from 1952 on illustrates his growing commitment to the struggle of Americans of African origin in dealing with discrimination.

In 1953 Zuber married Barbara Johnson; they had one son and one daughter. Because of his financial needs and the length of time necessary to prepare for a medical career, Zuber decided to pursue the study of law. He entered the Brooklyn School of Law and was granted an LL.B. in 1956. After passing the state bar examination, Zuber began his law practice in New York City in 1957, devoting his attention to civil rights litigation.

Zuber's interest in civil rights was caused partly by his experience of living in Harlem and by the events surrounding the courting of his wife. Disappointed in the quality of education offered their daughter, her parents had removed her from the local public school and sent her to a private school to complete her education. Zuber recognized how an inferior education results in an individual failing to develop his or her potential and skills; consequently, poorly educated people attain inferior and low-paying positions when they become adults.

Realizing the high quality of both his wife's and his own education, Zuber began a crusade for quality education for all Americans. He used his adult experiences as a veteran of two wars, a student and practitioner of the law, and a witness of the trauma in American schools to build public attention concerning the national deficiency in equal and quality education. Zuber's affiliation in 1958–1959 with the 359th Infantry Veterans Association in Harlem, an organization of African Americans who had served in World War II, culminated in his acceptance of the chairmanship of its Educational Committee for 1960–1961. He viewed the committee's purpose as opposing the doctrine of "separate but equal education" as enunciated by the U.S. Supreme Court's decision in *Plessy v. Ferguson* (1896). This doctrine was reversed by *Brown v. Board of Education* (1954). The original case, *Plessy*, rose out of a Louisiana state statute dealing with public accommodation and stated that if the facilities were "equal" for the separate races there was no denial of due process protection. Only with modern scientific techniques were civil rights advocates such as Zuber able to stress the psychological damage illustrated by adherence to such theories. *Brown I*, with Chief Justice Earl Warren issuing the opinion in opposition to the Louisiana statute, stated that racial discrimination in public education is unconstitutional and that all provisions of federal, state, and local law requiring or permitting the same are illegal.

Zuber recognized that advocates of segregation were moving to a new front in maintaining racial separation: de facto segregation in housing and education. One of Zuber's early responses to unconstitutional violations of due process and the denial of civil rights occurred in New Rochelle, New York, with the Lincoln School issue. The Lincoln School was sixty-two years old, and a 1960 school bond referendum called for its demolition and replacement with a new structure in the same area. Many Americans of African descent favored the demolition but not the reconstruction of the Lincoln School in the same location if it resulted in more de facto segregation. Zuber's opposition to this plan led to discussions with John J. Theobald, superintendent of New Rochelle's school system, in 1960. Theobald supported gerrymandering, a "legal" method of creating boundaries without any valid rationale so that Lincoln students in the new school district would be again confined to an area with 94 percent African-American representation.

In *Taylor et al. v. Board of Education of City School District of City New Rochelle* (1961), the Court found that the Lincoln School was attended only by Americans of African descent; that the educational background and length of experience of the school's teachers was inferior to that of teachers in white schools; that the curriculum offered at Lincoln was inferior to that offered in white schools; and that the plaintiff children and other children attending this racially segregated school did not achieve their intellectual potential when compared to children in white schools.

The New Rochelle experience was one of Zuber's first legal battles concerning the guarantee of civil rights for all American children. He became involved in litigation challenging educational systems' gerrymandering in courts throughout the state of New York. He led the prosecution in *The Matter of Skipwith* (1958), proving to the satisfaction of Judge Justice Polier that the defendant, the Board of Education of the City of New York, and more specifically Junior High School No. 136, was providing an inferior education for the predominately Puerto-Rican and African-American student clientele. As a result of the proceedings, Polier determined that the parents of the aggrieved children need not obey the law and could refuse to send their children to a school that was racially unbalanced and whose facilities were deteriorating.

Zuber also represented parents in other desegregation cases in Chicago, Harlem, and Newark, New Jersey, after 1962. He began his struggles without financial or moral support. Although the National Association for the Advancement of Colored People (NAACP) did eventually assist with funding, the above cases were fought initially without the organization's financial support.

Zuber's dedication to civil rights and the Constitution of the United States led him to pursue a policy of aiding litigants throughout the United States. Peggy Olsen, a former editor of *Intersections*, described Zuber's commitment to equality in American education and quoted one of his many supporters, who said that Zuber had "arrived in New Rochelle at a critical moment of our fight to desegregate the Lincoln School and threw himself into the fray with gusto and fury. He did not let up until the Supreme Court vindicated us in the first northern struggle against segregation. We shall always remember him, and the New Rochelle fight will be one of the many monuments to his unceasing struggle for equal justice for all" ("A Tribute to Dr. Paul B. Zuber," *Intersections* 11 [1987]).

Zuber had a wide range of arenas in which to display his concerns and responsibilities, believing that the battle of equality had many fronts; he used radio, television, and active memberships in many organizations, professional and civic, to further his cause. In 1986 he turned his attention to the absence of African Americans in the managerial levels of the hotel industry, viewing participation on this level as a vital opportunity for qualified people regardless of their race or other characteristics.

After leaving the law in 1972, Zuber devoted himself to continuing the struggle for educational equality in the less confrontational venue of higher education at Rensselaer Polytechnic Institute in Troy, New York. He became an adjunct professor, focusing on academic education. Having obtained his degree from Brown University and having gained a wide range of litigation experience, he realized that a proper and well-rounded education was the key to economic and political advancement and success in America. He established the Center for Urban Environmental Studies upon arriving at Rensselaer and remained as its head until his death in Troy.

Zuber recognized the outdated judicial decision of the *Plessy* case and its inconsistency with the democratic ideal. His professional career, whether in law or education, was dedicated to the eradication of mere semblances of educational equality. He strove to eliminate prejudice under the cloak of de facto or de jure law. The most odious application of law was the attempt by some to adopt gerrymandering as a rationalization for "legal" segregation. The concept that legislators could create school districts for purposes contrary to constitutional intent in order to protect a pressure group and create an artificial majority was an anathema to him and a violation of democratic principle.

• The most valuable sources illustrating the violence of the times and the struggles under which Zuber operated in defending the Constitution of the United States can be found in the *New York Times* for the period from the 1950s through the 1980s, especially 9, 11, 13, 16–19, and 25 Sept. and 11 Nov. 1958; 22 Sept. and 1 Nov. 1959; 25 Jan., 12 Feb., and 9 Dec. 1961; 1 and 24 Feb. 1962; and 20 Sept. 1963. A discussion of his relations with the NAACP may be found in Peter M. Bergman, *The Chronological History of the Negro in America* (1969).

ARTHUR K. STEINBERG

ZUBLY, John Joachim (27 Aug. 1724–23 July 1781), clergyman, politician, and pamphleteer, was born in St. Gall, Switzerland, the son of David Zubly, a Reformed minister, and Helena (maiden name unknown). After completing his studies at the Gymnasium there, he followed his father to London and was ordained at the German Church in London on 19 August 1744. That same year he joined the Swiss German migration to Purrysburg, South Carolina, settling with his father and other Zubly family members who had removed there in 1736. Zubly preached among Swiss-, German-, and English-speaking settlers in South Carolina and Georgia and assisted the Reverend Bartholomew Zouberbuhler in Savannah in 1745, before they parted ways over personal and theological differences. In 1746 Zubly met George Whitefield and began a lifelong friendship. Zubly traveled to Pennsylvania and New Jersey to preach and raise money for Whitefield's Bethesda, Georgia, orphanage, but his strong style and contentious manner embroiled him in congregational disputes during his northern sojourn. During a brief stint at Purrysburg, in November 1746 Zubly married Anna Tobler, with whom he had three children before her death in 1765. In 1747 he began a successful thirteen-year ministry at Wando Neck, South Carolina. He then accepted a call from the Independent Presbyterian Church in Savannah. He remained there from 1760 until his death, except for a brief exile to South Carolina.

In Savannah Zubly rose rapidly in wealth and influence. Through shrewd investments in land and slaves, he amassed a comfortable fortune. His wealth placed him among the most prominent members of Savannah society, several of whom were members of Zubly's congregation of Protestant dissenters. Zubly's learning—fluency in several languages, ownership of one of British North America's largest libraries, theological training and discourse—brought him into the wider world of American colonial intellectual life. He corresponded with Ezra Stiles and other northern divines, and the College of New Jersey (Princeton) recognized Zubly's intellectual standing by conferring A.M. and D.D. degrees on him.

Zubly's reputation derived from his vigorous and abundant publications. He was a frequent contributor of religious and political items to the *Georgia Gazette*, and his early writings focused especially on Christian death. In 1756 he brought out his widely read book, *The Real Christians Hope in Death*, that extolled the beauty and glory of mortal death for Christians—a theme he continued in his funeral sermons and letters. By the mid-1750s Zubly had given up writing in German in favor of English and had moved away from his earlier Continental pietism toward a sturdy Calvinism. He became Georgia's chief defender of dissenters and their rights and opened his church to enthusiasts of revivalist preaching. He held several minor civil offices, such as clerk of Christ Church parish, and was a friend of Governor James Wright. Close to civil power without really exercising it, Zubly became a student of government.

From 1765 to 1775 Zubly emerged as one of colonial America's most significant pamphleteers. His fierce independence was bolstered by the virtual congregational autonomy of his church, and Zubly was quick to move against any claims to authority by distant powers. His own estate and personal contacts among the Savannah elite further made him jealous in defense of local interest. In a series of pamphlets—*The Stamp-Act Repealed* (1766), *An Humble Enquiry* (1769; repr. as *Great Britain's Right to Tax Her Colonies* [1774]), *A Letter to the Reverend Samuel Frink* (1770), *Calm and Respectful Thoughts* (1772), and *Law and Liberty* (1775; repr. as *A Sermon on American Affairs* [1775 and 1778])—Zubly fused the Puritan theme of America as a new Canaan, its people chosen by God for a special mission, with the English Commonwealthman theme of virtue residing in simplicity. He argued for "actual" over "virtual" representation, the right of assemblies to control their own members and policies, and the contractual basis of government. In his *Letter to the Reverend Samuel Frink*—an angry blast at the rector of Christ's Church parish in Savannah who had insisted that dissenters pay him fees for burial rites and bell tolling charges in the parish, even though a dissenting minister performed the services—Zubly alleged an Anglican conspiracy to force a bishop on America. Through such pamphlets Zubly echoed the arguments of northern divines about dark Anglican and Crown designs of tyranny, thereby pulling southward debates about colonial polity and British authority.

Zubly was more than a southern listening post for ideas generated elsewhere. He added to the debate by his forceful insistence that the colonial assembly had inviolable rights much like Parliament and that local rule, of church and government, was the best safeguard for liberty. He also cautioned his readers to respect law. Liberty demanded order. He feared concentrated power in any form, arguing that a constitution—the sum of natural rights, law, custom, and history—worked best when it divided power through function. Like many pamphleteers, Zubly vested sovereignty in the legislature, but the contradiction of divided sovereignty between Parliament and colonial assemblies troubled him. He drew back from proclaiming the collected people, standing outside government, alone as sovereign. Zubly feared the demagogue too much to trust the democracy. His arguments, however, pushed him and his readers where many feared to go—toward independence and democratic political participation.

Until 1775 Zubly's much-discussed and reprinted writings moved apace with, even guided, the process of political and constitutional maturation in the colonies—so much so that Zubly was among the first Georgia delegation sent to the Continental Congress in 1775, by the Georgia provincial congress that had seized power from the royal governor. At the Congress Zubly's essential conservatism surfaced. Although John Adams found Zubly a "warm and zealous Spirit" who spoke fervently and voted for military preparations, Zubly recoiled from any break with England. More radical elements in the Congress, such as Samuel Chase, labeled him a traitor for allegedly maintaining a secret correspondence with Governor Wright and conspired to undo him when he returned to Georgia in 1775. The Revolution rushed past Zubly in Georgia. His misgivings were read as opposition as the colony marched toward independent statehood. He was arrested twice in 1776, and Georgia confiscated his property and banished him to South Carolina for treason in 1777. These actions led Zubly to publish *To the Grand Jury of the County of Chatham* (1777), pointing to the new tyranny rising in the form of majority oppression among the revolutionaries. Zubly returned to Savannah in 1779, after the British occupied the city. In 1780 he vented his rage in a series of essays, published under the pseudonym "Helvetius" in the *Royal Georgia Gazette*. Drawing on the history of the Swiss, he argued for forbearance rather than revolution as the best means to prevent rebellion from degenerating into civil war and warned that the patriots' confiscation of property threatened ever more extreme violations of natural rights. Like other Americans who had defended American colonial rights before 1775 but drew back from independence, Zubly saw only ruin coming from violence. In the end, preached Zubly, God would judge those who violated the unity of his moral order.

Although tarred by contemporaries and subsequent historians as an unalloyed Loyalist, Zubly stood for colonial rights while opposing independence. He provided no services to the British, retiring to his home to scratch out angry private letters about past injustices while confining his public activities to his pastorate. Zubly's Loyalist complicity was his Whig constitutional bias toward restraint and discipline. The war drained Zubly physically, emotionally, and financially. His own children divided in their loyalties, and "after a long and painful illness" a broken Zubly died

quietly in Savannah, a revolutionary in thought who remained too conservative in action.

• Zubly's letters are scattered in many collections. The most revealing sustained correspondence is in the Ezra Stiles Papers at Yale University library. The Georgia Historical Society has a small collection of extracts of Zubly letters and the journal he kept in its Zubly papers. Also see Lilla Mills Hawes, ed., *The Journal of the Reverend John Joachim Zubly A.M., D.D. March 5, 1770 through June 22, 1781*, Georgia Historical Society *Collections*, vol. 21 (1989). For a critical study of Zubly's life and work, including reprints of his revolutionary era writings and a bibliography of all of Zubly's books and pamphlets, see Randall M. Miller, *"A Warm & Zealous Spirit": John J. Zubly and the American Revolution* (1982). See also Roger A. Martin, "John J. Zubly: Preacher, Planter, and Politician" (Ph.D. diss., Univ. of Georgia, 1976); William E. Pauley, Jr., "Tragic Hero: Loyalist John J. Zubly," *Journal of Presbyterian History* 54 (Spring 1976): 61–81; and Marjorie Daniel, "John Joachim Zubly—Georgia Pamphleteer of the Revolution," *Georgia Historical Quarterly* 19 (Mar. 1935): 1–16. An obituary is in the *Royal Georgia Gazette*, 26 July 1781.

RANDALL M. MILLER

ZUGSMITH, Leane (18 Jan. 1903–13 Oct. 1969), novelist and short story writer, was born in Louisville, Kentucky, the daughter of Albert Zugsmith, a businessman, and Gertrude Appel. Following a conflicted divorce—in which her mother's parents sided with her father and her mother was denied any further contact with her children—Zugsmith and her younger brother Albert, Jr., lived alternately with her mother's parents and her father, attending school in Louisville and Atlantic City.

After high school Zugsmith attended Goucher College and the University of Pennsylvania, each for one year. Finding nothing to hold her, she moved to New York, studied writing for one summer at Columbia, and landed a job as a copyeditor with Street & Smith. Soon she began reading widely and writing fiction. From Street & Smith, she moved up to the firm of Putnam and then on to Horace Liveright, where she wrote advertising copy. Vivacious and intelligent, she formed lasting friendships with several people, including Isidor Schneider, who became a colleague in radical politics; Alfred Kreymborg, who encouraged her to become a writer; and Saxe Commins, who later persuaded Random House to recruit Zugsmith as one of its writers. Having worked two years in New York, she convinced her father to help her go to Europe, where she spent a year living in Paris and traveling in Germany, Holland, and Italy, socializing as well as reading and writing.

When Zugsmith returned to New York, she had in mind her first novel, *All Victories Are Alike* (1929), which is built around two contrasting stories—one involving a cynical writer named Page Trent, who pounds out "careless damnation and careless praise" on his typewriter knowing that he has traded the noble intentions with which he began for the glitter of New York's social-literary life; and one involving a woman named Myra Bingham who, deserted by Trent, escapes the false world that destroys him. Later, Zugsmith expressed regret about publishing both her first novel and her second, *Goodbye and Tomorrow* (1931). But her first novel received the good notices that launched her career, and it disclosed a skepticism about the social-literary life of New York that her second novel developed. Emmy Bishop, a patron of the arts, is the central figure of *Goodbye and Tomorrow*. Through Bishop's circle of friends, Zugsmith exposes the false cleverness and petty jealousies of a world in which literature, art, and music are exploited by artists and patrons as well as the hangers-on and the sycophants who prey on them.

As Zugsmith became increasingly estranged from New York's literary-social scene, her interest in its social and political problems grew—a development that was reinforced by her relationship with Carl Randau, a midwesterner who had fought in World War I and been decorated by the French government. He had then worked as a journalist in Paris, Washington, D.C., and, after 1926, in New York, where he became a prominent investigator of the corruption of public officials and the problems of the poor. Living and working together in the 1930s, Zugsmith and Randau became increasingly active in reform politics. "As to my political convictions," Zugsmith wrote in the early 1940s, in a biographical sketch prepared for *Twentieth Century Writers* (1942), "I am anti-Fascist and for democracy, not merely a political democracy but also an economic democracy."

Two stories and a novel from the early 1930s—"Appointment at Five" (1931); "The Picture" (1932); and *Never Enough* (1932)—signaled a change in Zugsmith's writing. The first recounts the ill-fated efforts of a woman who wanders alone through a city, trying to get an illegal abortion on a cold rainy day. The second focuses on a lonely child whose mind is filled with Hollywood-inspired images of a perfect home and beautiful parents but whose life is dominated by an angry, uncaring father and a half-defiant, half-resigned, uncaring mother. And the third is a novel organized as a series of stories about eight embittered people, scattered in ten sections, each bearing an ironic title, such as "Back to Normalcy" or "Don't Sell America Short."

Together, these works marked Zugsmith's move into social fiction and defined both the thrust of her mature work and the central concerns of her life. "I think that writing should, first of all, be about human beings," she wrote in her *Twentieth Century Writers* sketch. But, she observed, "it seems to me to be increasingly difficult to write illuminatingly about human beings without regarding their social circumstances." Her next novel, *The Reckoning* (1934), took her back to New York's slums and the haunts of juvenile criminals who, reared in poor, abusive homes, are too damaged to be saved, even by the best efforts of reformers. The following April she and Randau attended the famous American Writer's Congress of 1935, where she heard Malcolm Cowley, Edward Dahlberg, and Kenneth Burke speak and where she saw her old friend Isidor Schneider.

A year later she published a novel she had been preparing to write for several years. *A Time to Remember* (1936), one of the classic "strike" novels of the Great Depression, is based on the long, bitter strike of retail and clerical workers against Ohrbach's department store that began in 1928 and ended in 1936. In the novel, Ohrbach's is replaced by Diamond's Department Store, which is owned and run by "Uncle" Sigmund Diamond. And though the conflicts surrounding the strike demoralize some characters and hurt others, dividing friends and even families, they also revitalize some people by giving them a cause to believe in. Published by Random House, promoted by a radical organization called Book Union, and reviewed favorably by the *New York Times* and the *Christian Science Monitor*, *A Time to Remember* helped to establish its author as one of the 1930s' representative writers.

A year later Zugsmith published a collection of stories, *Home Is Where You Hang Your Childhood* (1937), and in 1938 she published her sixth and last novel, *The Summer Soldier*, as well as a book called *L Is for Labor: A Glossary of Labor Terms*. In 1940 she and Randau were married, and in 1942 they coauthored *The Setting Sun of Japan*. But in the years that followed, as McCarthyism rose, while their energies declined and their health failed, the roles they had played with courage, conviction, and flair no longer seemed to matter. Zugsmith died alone at her home in Connecticut, a few weeks after her husband had died there of a stroke. But she left behind a body of work that has continued to play an important part in the literature of social protest and, more recently, has earned the attention of feminist critics and historians.

• Collections of Zugsmith's letters are held by the Van Pelt Library of the University of Pennsylvania, the Pattee Library of the Pennsylvania State University, and the Newberry Library of Chicago. Zugsmith's papers are in the possession of her family. The biographical sketch that Zugsmith wrote for *Twentieth Century Writers*, ed. Stanley J. Kunitz and Howard Haycraft (1942), pp. 1573–74, is of considerable interest, and Abe C. Ravitz, *Leane Zugsmith: Thunder on the Left* (1992), provides a short, valuable, sympathetic treatment of her life's work. An obituary is in the *New York Times*, 14 Oct. 1969.

DAVID MINTER

ZUKOFSKY, Louis (23 Jan. 1904–12 May 1978), poet and critic, was born in New York City, the son of Pinchos Zukofsky, a pants presser, and Chana Pruss. His parents were Orthodox Jews, but he did not follow their religious practices. Raised in the Yiddish-speaking community of the Lower East Side, he learned English in school. In January 1920 he entered Columbia University, where his first poems appeared in the *Morningside*, a student literary periodical. His student circle included Lionel Trilling, Meyer Schapiro, Mortimer Adler, and Whittaker Chambers, who, in the 1920s, arranged an interview for Zukofsky with the Communist party. Although he never joined, Zukofsky remained interested in Marxism and incorporated passages from Marx into the ninth section of *"A"*, his major poetical work.

Zukofsky received his M.A. in English in 1924 for a thesis later published in *Prepositions* as "Henry Adams: A Criticism in Autobiography." In 1933 he met Celia Thaew, whom he married in 1939. Their son Paul, a conductor and virtuoso violinist, was born in 1943. Paul's early career is the subject of Zukofsky's novel *Little: For Careenagers* (1970). Zukofsky wrote in his *Autobiography*, "My wife Celia and son Paul have been the only reason for the poet's persistence."

Zukofsky initiated an important correspondence in 1927 when he sent "Poem beginning 'The'" to Ezra Pound, who published it in *The Exile* in 1928. In a letter, Zukofsky called the work "a direct reply to T. S. Eliot's *The Waste Land*." Pound served as a mentor, offering advice and encouragement while Zukofsky worked on *"A"*, which he began in early 1927 but did not complete until 1974. By 1928 he already had its structure planned. *"A"* has been compared to Pound's *Cantos* and William Carlos Williams's *Paterson*, but unlike them, Zukofsky avoids myth, relying instead on structural patterns for unity. *"A"* consists of twenty-four movements that weave together a half-century of national and world events, including the depression and the war, with his private life, including his Jewish heritage, his art, and his love for his wife and son.

In 1928 Zukofsky met Basil Bunting; Pound later dedicated *Guide to Kulchur* (1938) to these two "strugglers in the desert." Although Zukofsky enjoyed the friendship and respect of Pound and Williams, whom he met in 1928, he was ignored by academic critics and the general reading public for most of his life. Zukofsky had a brief flirtation with fame when, through Pound's efforts, Harriet Monroe invited him to edit the February 1931 issue of *Poetry*, which included, along with *"A"*-7, poems by Williams, Bunting, Kenneth Rexroth, and, most importantly, the Objectivists: George Oppen, Carl Rakosi, and Charles Reznikoff. Zukofsky said he used the word *objectivist* only because Monroe insisted that he "must have a movement." He also wrote two essays for the issue: "Program: 'Objectivists' 1931" and "Sincerity and Objectification." The group agreed on the importance of form and the need for a language that could register particular details of the real world. The Objectivists were an important link between the early modernists and postwar experimental poetry.

Zukofsky served as editor for Oppen's To Publishers (1931–1932), which published works by Williams and Pound, as well as Zukofsky's *An 'Objectivists' Anthology* (1932), which received unfavorable reviews. When To failed, Zukofsky, Oppen, Reznikoff, and Williams started the Objectivist Press, which published volumes by Oppen, Reznikoff, and Pound as well as Williams's *Collected Poems 1921–31* (1934), edited and arranged by Zukofsky. He also edited Williams's *The Descent of Winter* (1928) and *The Wedge* (1944), which is dedicated to "L.Z." Zukofsky paid tribute to Williams in *"A"*-17 (1963).

In 1933 Zukofsky visited Europe, stopping in Rapallo to visit Pound. He saw Pound on only two more occasions, briefly in 1939 in New York and in 1954 at St. Elizabeths Hospital. This last visit is recounted in *Little*, where Pound appears as RZ Draykup.

After writing scripts for the WPA (1934–1942), teaching in New York City high schools (1942–1943), and editing technical manuals (1943–1947), Zukofsky became an instructor of English at Polytechnic Institute of Brooklyn (1947–1966). Zukofsky continued to write, publishing *55 Poems* (1941), *Anew* (1946), and *Some Time* (1956) with small presses. Except for favorable reviews by friends, such as Williams and Lorine Niedecker, Zukofsky was either ignored or dismissed as derivative of Pound and Williams until the mid-1960s, when he received recognition from younger poets, though critics still accused him of being obscure and pretentious.

In exchange for donating his correspondence with Pound to the University of Texas, its Ark Press published Zukofsky's major critical work, *Bottom: On Shakespeare* (1963). It is a personal study of Shakespeare's definition of love and the preeminence of the eye over the mind, two dominant themes in his own poetry.

Zukofsky found his first commercial publisher in 1965, when Denise Levertov accepted for W. W. Norton *All: The Collected Short Poems, 1923–1958*, which was followed in 1966 by *All: The Collected Short Poems, 1956–1964*. He retired from Polytechnic in 1966, after which he served as guest professor at the University of Connecticut. In his final years he published with commercial presses and enjoyed a considerable reputation for the music of his verse, his innovations in form, verbal precision, and intellectual range. Unfavorable reviews still continued, particularly for his experimental translation, *Catullus (Gai Valeri Catulli Veronensis Liber)*, done in collaboration with his wife Celia (1969).

In 1976 Zukofsky received a $3,000 award from the National Institute of Arts and Letters. In his last years he completed *"A"* and a work condensing all of his previous writings, *80 Flowers*, eighty, eight-line poems (plus a prologue). He died in Port Jefferson, Long Island, just as this volume and the University of California edition of the complete *"A"* were going to press.

Zukofsky has been called by Kenneth Rexroth "one of the most important poets of my generation." His influence as a theorist and practitioner has been acknowledged by such poets as Robert E. Duncan and Robert Creeley, along with other members of the Black Mountain school, and by the L=A=N=G=U=A=G=E poets. His reputation rests primarily with poets and critics who find in him a model in the avant-garde tradition of Pound and Williams.

• Zukofsky's papers are in the Humanities Research Center, University of Texas at Austin; see Marcella Booth, *A Catalogue of the Louis Zukofsky Manuscript Collection* (1975). In addition to *"A"*, the University of California Press has published an expanded edition of *Prepositions: The Collected Critical Essays* (1981) and *Bottom* (1987). *The Collected Poetry*

(1991) reprints *All, Catullus,* and *80 Flowers.* The *Collected Fiction* (1989) brings together *Little, It Was, Ferdinand,* "A Keystone Comedy," and "Thanks to the Dictionary." Other publications include an anthology textbook, *A Test of Poetry* (1948), and *Autobiography* (1970), a selection of poems from *All* set to music by Celia Zukofsky with some brief biographical statements. Still unpublished in English is *The Writing of Guillaume Apollinaire,* which appeared in France as *Le Style Apollinaire* (1934).

No biography is available, but accounts of his life can be found in Carroll F. Terrell, ed., *Louis Zukofsky: Man and Poet* (1979), which reprints a 1969 interview conducted by L. S. Dembo for *Contemporary Literature.* It also includes an interview with Celia Zukofsky, memoirs by poets who knew him, bibliographies, and essays of criticism. An important source of information is Barry Ahearn, ed., *Pound/Zukofsky: Selected Letters of Ezra Pound and Louis Zukofsky* (1987). A bibliography of secondary criticism (1932–1985) by Alvin R. Baily is in *Sagetrieb* (Spring and Fall 1991). Barry Ahearn, *Zukofsky's "A": An Introduction* (1983), and Michele J. Leggott, *Reading Zukofsky's "80 Flowers"* (1989), provide essential information concerning source material, manuscripts, and his method of composition. Valuable brief discussions of his work are available in Hugh Kenner, *A Homemade World: The American Modernist Writers* (1975), and Joseph M. Conte, *Unending Design: The Forms of Postmodern Poetry* (1991). An obituary is in the *New York Times,* 14 May 1978.

JOSEPH G. KRONICK

ZUKOR, Adolph (7 Jan. 1873–10 June 1976), movie producer and studio executive, was born in Ricse, Hungary, the son of Jacob Zukor, a farmer/storekeeper, and Hannah Liebermann, both of whom died by the time Zukor was eight years old. Zukor then lived with his uncle Kalman Liebermann, a dedicated Talmudist, but he eschewed rabbinical study. After a brief apprenticeship in a store Zukor sailed alone for the United States at the age of sixteen.

Zukor spent the next three years residing on New York's Lower East Side, boxing, attending night school, and apprenticing to a furrier. He then struck out on his own, moving to Chicago and creating the Novelty Fur Company in 1893, which achieved considerable success. Joining Kohn and Company, a larger firm, and gaining some sales experience, Zukor prospered, especially after marrying his partner's niece, Lottie Kaufman, in 1897 (with whom he had two children), relocating to New York around 1900, and specializing in red fox fur.

Successful but always looking for new ventures, in 1903 Zukor and Kohn opened Automatic Vaudeville, a successful penny arcade featuring kinetoscopes (sixteen- to sixty-second films viewed through a peepshow viewer), located on 14th Street east of Broadway. Zukor and his partners expanded into other cities, invested unsuccessfully in Hale's Tours (imitation train rides with moving picture footage that functioned as passing scenery), and transformed the space over Automatic Vaudeville into the Crystal Palace, a nickelodeon theater where patrons could watch projected, rather than peepshow, images.

Zukor grew even more excited about the future of the movies and nickelodeons after viewing Edwin S. Porter's *The Great Train Robbery* (1903). He converted the failed Hales' Tours into the thriving ten-cent Comedy Theater around 1906 and invested in entrepreneur Marcus Loew's vastly successful Theatrical Enterprises (a chain of upscale, small, and bit-time vaudeville theaters). He then studied movie making for several years. In 1910 he acquired the New York rights to the film *Passion Play,* and in 1912 he secured the American rights to *Queen Elizabeth,* the French Film D'Art version starring Sarah Bernhardt.

This latter film provided the key to Zukor's primary means of success in film production: famous actors in celebrated plays, his most persuasive tool for elevating the social stature of the parvenu movies in the eyes of established cultural arbiters. At a period during which many filmmakers believed that audiences would never sit still through feature-length movies, Zukor cajoled theater impresario Daniel Frohman to join his company. He subsequently also became partners with leading playwright-director-producer David Belasco and Frohmann's older brother Charles, another successful theater producer. The Famous Players Film Company was incorporated in 1912.

Henceforth, Zukor was able to secure matinee idols and film rights to new and classic plays for his lowly movies. He embarked on a series of static, abbreviated silent film versions of stage plays, including *The Prisoner of Zenda* starring James Hackett, *The Count of Monte Cristo* with James O'Neill, and *Tess of the D'Urbervilles* with Minnie Maddern Fiske. By 1918 Zukor had taken full advantage of the burgeoning star system; he had under contract Mary Pickford, Douglas Fairbanks, Wallace Reid, Marguerite Clark, Harold Lockwood, and William S. Hart, all regarded as the top box office stars of the year.

Zukor had shifted from the showing of motion pictures to their production, seeing in filmmaking the primary means of achieving profit and social acceptance for the movies and for himself personally. By the mid-teens he was a dominant force in the film industry. The breakup of the monopolistic Motion Picture Patents Company provided Zukor with further opportunity to expand.

Zukor's films were handled by Paramount, the first national distribution company in the country. Paramount took productions from many different companies and rented them to theaters, giving producers a flat fee and 65 percent of the profits from the films, if any. Zukor recognized that he could accrue more income if he ran the distribution arm of Paramount while remaining active in production. By mid-summer 1916 he had joined forces with former vaudeville performer and impresario Jesse Lasky to create the Famous Players–Lasky production company, and he had successfully taken over Paramount. The result was a company that dominated the production and distribution of motion pictures for the rest of the decade, producing anywhere between 70 and 104 films a year. The company collected 30 percent of *all* the movie rentals in the country.

Zukor, as president of the new entity, relied not only on corporate muscle, but he also developed distribution tactics such as block booking. This required theater managers to agree to rent Famous Players–Lasky's entire annual schedule of films, regardless of their quality and star appeal (or lack thereof). Theater managers agreed in order to ensure access to those few movies that featured the most popular stars and guaranteed high ticket sales.

Theater managers' resentment of Zukor's ruthless booking policies resulted in the formation of an exhibitors' coalition, First National, which entered the realm of production to avoid ruinous rental rates. When the coalition succeeded in wooing actor Charlie Chaplin from the Mutual Film Corporation and Pickford from Famous Players–Lasky, Zukor was determined to counter. In 1919 he persuaded Otto Kahn's Wall Street firm Kuhn, Loeb and Company to float a $10 million issue in preferred stock to finance the construction and/or purchase of fifty first-run movie theaters, and to secure major shares in several hundred others.

Zukor recognized that his company did not need to own a majority of the movie theaters in major cities in order to dominate the business. Instead he targeted first-run theaters. Located in downtown business areas, these larger houses could seat thousands of movie lovers who were willing to pay higher prices for the pleasure of seeing the latest movies (they would otherwise have had to wait a month or more to see the same film in a second-run theater). The owners of such theaters collected the lion's share of the income any film earned.

Kuhn's company recognized that, construction costs aside, large theaters did not cost much more to own and operate than did medium-sized theaters. With Wall Street's approval, Zukor's company had within two years acquired 303 mostly first-run theaters and could thereby guarantee the showing of all its films on screens in major markets around the country. Within another two years Samuel Goldwyn, Loew's, Inc., the Fox Corporation, and the newly formed Warner Bros. all followed Zukor's example. In 1926, with the acquisition of the Balaban & Katz chain of ninety-three theaters in and around Chicago, Zukor had taken over First National's largest member and had interests in over 1,000 theaters, organized into the Publix Theaters Corporation. With the depression, however, the Publix chain became a major liability, and Paramount was forced into bankruptcy in 1933. Lasky was forced out, and the company was reorganized in 1935, with Zukor as chairman of the board.

Zukor had expanded his company into a vertically integrated firm—one that owned and controlled the production, distribution, and exhibition of films in order to minimize its investment risks. He established the foundation by which the five biggest Hollywood studios (MGM, Warner Bros., 20th Century–Fox, and RKO) constructed their financial security and the oligopoly of the industry. The great studios held the bulk of their assets and received the bulk of their income from their theaters. Making movies was simply the means of ensuring that moviegoers buy tickets. Paramount was subjected to constant inquiry in the 1920s, and an antitrust suit was filed against the studio in 1938. When the Justice Department persuaded the Supreme Court in 1948 that the studios operated in violation of antitrust laws, Paramount was the first defendant named in the case.

Comfortably positioned as president of Paramount, Zukor remained in place even after new executives (such as Sam Katz) had joined the firm in the late twenties. He received a special Academy Award in 1949 for his "contribution to the industry." In 1953 he published a ghostwritten autobiography, *The Public Is Never Wrong* (coauthored with Dale Kramer), and he remained in Hollywood until his death there.

A stern, strict man who nevertheless enjoyed the luxuries that success afforded him, as a studio executive Zukor was comparatively detached from the business of movie making from the 1920s on. For him the triumph of the movies appears to have been their social acceptance by the mass audience and eventually by the intelligentsia. Having come to America as a poor orphan from Hungary, he seemed to personify the Horatio Alger hero, realizing the American Dream. Zukor's business schemes and aggressive behavior provided the backbone for the artistic achievements that the Hollywood industry realized between 1920 and 1960. With the assurance of paying customers in their theaters, the major studios were able to build huge production plants with specialized technicians and performers who honed their craft. With the need to change programs frequently, studios became specialists in different genres. Owing largely to Zukor's vision and his competitive strategies, the Hollywood studio system became the dominant force in American popular culture from the 1920s until the advent of television.

• A valuable interview with Zukor appears in Bernard Rosenberg and Harry Silverstein, *The Real Tinsel* (1970). See also Will Irwin, *The House that Shadows Built: The Story of Adolph Zukor and His Circle* (1928); Neal Gabler, *An Empire of Their Own: How the Jews Invented Hollywood* (1988); Richard Koszarski, *An Evening's Entertainment* (1990); Douglas Gomery, *The Hollywood Studio System* (1986); and Philip French, *The Movie Moguls* (1969). Obituaries are in the *New York Times*, 11 June 1976 and *Variety*, 16 June 1976.

MATTHEW BERNSTEIN

ZUNSER, Eliakum (28 Oct. 1836–22 Sept. 1913), poet and composer of Yiddish songs, was born in Vilna (later Vilnius), Russia, the son of Feive Zunser, a carpenter, and Etta Kayle. His family name probably came from Zunse, a nearby village. His father died when Eliakum was eleven, and the family moved into the home of his mother's sister. Zunser's formal education was limited by his boyhood apprenticeship to an embroiderer, where he learned to sew gold thread on civil and military uniforms, but he read Hebrew and studied the Talmud in his spare time.

Zunser left home in 1855 to work in the town of Bobruisk, where he was seized the next year for military service. There, living with other youths snatched from their homes, Zunser wrote one of his first songs, "Child Recruits or Judged and Found Guilty" (Die Poimanes oder Geshtanen zum Mishpot un Herois Shuldig), and trained a barracks choir to sing it. The song, which does not survive, dealt with the Babylonian captivity of the Jews but hinted at parallels with life under the czar.

Unlike his brother, Akiba, who was forced to perform nearly a quarter-century of Russian military service, Eliakum was freed after five weeks. The new czar, Alexander II, responding to the end of the Crimean War, revoked the military regulations that had placed heavy quotas on Jewish impressment. Zunser celebrated by writing and performing new songs, including "Salvation" (Die Yeshua).

Crowds were thrilled by his talent and by his choice of Yiddish. Scholars and serious poets preferred Hebrew and looked down on Yiddish as a "jargon," but Zunser's adoption of the language of the common folk was a popular innovation. His first collection of songs, Shirim Khadoshim, was published in 1861.

Zunser, acclaimed for his abilities as a composer, singer, and playwright, enjoyed a lucrative career as a badchen, or bard. In the Jewish settlements of Eastern Europe, the familiar badchen sang spontaneous compositions at weddings and other festivities. Most of Zunser's wedding verses never were recorded, but he wrote hundreds of poems and songs. Many were collected in his Ale Werk (1920). Zunser's wedding compositions contained little romantic love, which was not a requirement among the arranged marriages of the era. According to Sol Liptzin's biography, Eliakum Zunser: Poet of His People (1950), Zunser believed "a marriage based upon romantic infatuation was more likely to lead to tragic consequences."

Zunser's work undoubtedly was influenced by the horrors that befell his marriage to his first cousin Rochel, whom he married in 1862. They had ten children, five of whom survived birth. Of the five, the first was killed by a wolf; the other four died in an outbreak of cholera in 1871. Rochel died of tuberculosis after giving birth to stillborn twins. The tragedy of his children's deaths prompted Zunser to write his well-known dirge "The Postman's Bell" (Der Potshtover Glekel). In it, he likened the inexorable march of time to a postman bringing news:

Where are the people of yore? Where are their pride, their splendor, their wisdom of an hour? Time has flooded all who were: the head that bore a crown, the conqueror who ravaged the cities of men, the discoverer of isles unknown, the artist, the poet, the stargazer, the philosopher. What if they are remembered for a space? And what of the millions of heroes whose monuments the years have choked up with earth? Forgotten their books and their graves. We too shall fare no better.

After Rochel died in early 1872, Zunser married eighteen-year-old Hinde Feigel in September of that year in Minsk. They had eight children.

Zunser's creativity rose during the era of new freedoms for Russian Jews after the emancipation of the serfs in 1861. The prospect of assimilation, coupled with a backlash against the Jews in the 1880s, helped radicalize Zunser's work and shaped his moral tone. He became an early advocate of Zionism after the pogroms of 1881–1884. His popularity as a bard drew the suspicion of the Russian police, and in 1889 Zunser and his family emigrated to the United States. En route, he lauded the New World by composing the song "Columbus und Washington," the two names foreigners most often associated with the new land.

Zunser toured the United States, giving a series of concerts, before settling in New York City, where he opened a printing shop on East Broadway in the mid-1890s. His songs became staples of the Jewish ghettos, familiar to millions on both sides of the Atlantic. Liptzin said a writer arriving in New York in 1891 reported hearing the melody of Zunser's "The Peddler" (Der Pedler) coming from everywhere, including the harmonica of a Chinese laundry worker.

Although he began to concentrate on issues of labor, class, and religion, Zunser's work lacked the passion of Jewish firebrands such as Morris Winchevsky. His more radical compositions were embraced by socialists, anarchists, and Zionists, while the lyrical works he produced as bard enjoyed broad acceptance in the ghetto. Many Jews sympathized with his songs, whether they praised American institutions or—as in "The Golden Land" (Das Goldene Land)—expressed a growing disillusionment. He died at his home in New York City. Zunser's obituary in the New York Times quoted followers who called him the "man without an enemy."

Journalist Hutchins Hapgood, who visited Zunser at his print shop, gave a fitting assessment in his book The Spirit of the Ghetto (1902): "His melancholy is common to all Jewish poets. There is a constant reference to his race, too, a love for it, and a sort of humble pride. . . . Zunser has a fresh lyric quality which has gone far to endear him to the people. Yet in spite of his sweet birdlike speed of expression, Zunser's is a poetry of ideas although the ideas are simple, fragmentary, and fanciful, and are seldom sustained beyond what is admissible to the lyric touch."

• Much of Zunser's work remains in the original Yiddish. Ale Werk (1920) includes nearly all of his published poems, a play, Mekhiras Yosef, and his autobiography. For a bibliography of his publications, see Zalman Reisen, Lexikon fun der Yiddisher Literature, Presse, un Filologye (1929). For melodies, see Selected Songs (1928), arranged for voice with piano. An abridged English translation of Zunser's autobiography appeared in A Jewish Bard: Being the Biography of Eliakum Zunser (1905). More readily available in libraries is Liptzin's readable biography. Also useful are Harvard professor Leo Wiener's The History of Yiddish Literature in the Nineteenth Century (1899); Hapgood's book; and Ronald Sanders's The Downtown Jews (1969), which characterizes Zunser as a "sweatshop poet." An obituary appeared 23 Sept. and a report on Zunser's funeral 25 Sept. 1913 in the New York Times.

MICHAEL S. SWEENEY

ZUPPKE, Robert Carl (2 July 1879–22 Dec. 1957), football coach, known as Bob, was born in Berlin, Germany, the son of Franz Simon Zuppke, a jeweler, and Hermine Bocksbaum. In 1881 Zuppke's family came to the United States, settling in Milwaukee, Wisconsin. After attending Milwaukee Normal School and participating on its debate and basketball teams for two years, in 1901 Zuppke entered the University of Wisconsin, from which he received a bachelor of philosophy degree in 1905; he remained interested in philosophy all of his life. During his college years he was a reserve on the football team and excelled at basketball, winning a varsity letter as a member of the school's Western Conference championship team.

In 1905 Zuppke rejected an offer to coach football at local Madison High School and instead pursued his lifelong interest in drawing and painting by taking a job as a commercial artist in New York City. The position did not last long, for, as Zuppke explained, "the lions I was supposed to draw looked more like house cats." A short stint as a dress designer also ended in failure. In 1906 he returned to the Midwest, first as an artist in a Grand Rapids, Michigan, advertising agency, then in Muskegon as a history teacher, athletic director, and football coach at Hackley Manual Training School. He married Fanny Tillotson Erwin in 1908 and in 1910 accepted a teacher-coach position at Oak Park High School in Illinois. After leading three unbeaten Oak Park teams, Zuppke weighed offers from Northwestern University, Purdue University, and the University of Illinois. He finally contracted to become head football coach at Illinois in 1913.

In 1914 and 1915 Zuppke drew national attention by guiding Illinois to Western Conference championships. He later said that the 1914 squad, led by quarterback George "Potsy" Clark and halfback Harold Pogue, was the best he ever coached. As Zuppke's reputation grew, Illinois attracted a number of talented athletes, including Harold "Red" Grange, perhaps the most renowned running back in college football history. Zuppke's Fighting Illini became known for upset victories over heavily favored teams. In 1916 Illinois toppled a mighty University of Minnesota team, 14–9; in 1921, winless Illinois registered a 7–0 victory over undefeated Ohio State; and in 1924, in the game for which Illinois football is most famous, Grange scored five touchdowns as the Illini broke Michigan's twenty-game winning streak.

Zuppke was a play innovator. He has received credit for the development of the spiral pass from center (1906), the screen pass (1910), various trick plays (including the flea-flicker, 1910), the onside kick (1917), and the offensive huddle before the ball is put into play (1921). Although other coaches copied his original plays, he downplayed their importance. "Plays don't win," he insisted. "It's the men who carry out the plays." He is also credited with originating spring football practice sessions.

Illinois won or shared seven conference titles during Zuppke's career. He also led the fundraising drive to build War Memorial Stadium, which opened in 1924

on the Urbana campus. His later years at Illinois produced no championships and were punctuated by athletic director Wendell Wilson's effort to remove him as coach in 1938. Aroused alumni, led by Grange, persuaded the university's board of trustees to retain Zuppke. After a winless 1941 season, Zuppke finally retired. His career at Illinois lasted twenty-nine seasons, a longevity at a single institution surpassed only by Amos Alonzo Stagg's forty-one years at the University of Chicago. Zuppke's teams won 131 games, lost 81, tied 12, and were selected as national champions in 1923 and 1927 by the Helms Athletic Foundation.

In retirement, Zuppke concentrated on his talent for painting, and he raised livestock on his farm outside Champaign. He was sometimes referred to as the "Rembrandt of the Prairies," and he had his works displayed in New York, Chicago, Milwaukee, and other places. Bridging his various interests, he observed: "Football is not the only physical expression of a mental exercise; the great singer, the great pianist, violinist, the painter all express their thoughts physically." Noted for his humor, he once said: "We don't care how big or strong our opponents are, as long as they are human."

Zuppke's first wife died in 1936, while Zuppke was still coaching; the couple had no children. He was elected to the National Football Foundation Hall of Fame in 1951, and in 1956 he married Leona Ray. He died in Champaign.

• The Robert C. Zuppke Papers are located at the University of Illinois in Urbana. He wrote two books: *Football Technique and Tactics* (1922) and *Coaching Football* (1930). There are no full-length biographies, although Grange wrote an anecdotal remembrance, *Zuppke of Illinois* (1937). Profiles outlining Zuppke's life and contributions are included in Tim Cohane, *Great College Football Coaches of the Twenties and Thirties* (1973); Richard Whittingham, *Saturday Afternoon: College Football and the Men Who Made the Day* (1985); Allison Danzig, *The History of American Football* (1956); and Edwin Pope, *Football's Great Coaches* (1955). An obituary is in the *New York Times*, 23 Dec. 1957.

MARC S. MALTBY

ZWEMER, Samuel Marinus (12 Apr. 1867–2 Apr. 1952), pioneer missionary to and scholar of the Muslim world, was born in Vriesland, Michigan, the son of Adriaan Zwemer, a Reformed minister, and Catherina Boon. The Zwemers had migrated from Holland in 1849, lived briefly in Rochester, New York, and then joined the Dutch community in western Michigan, where Adriaan Zwemer had studied at Hope College and, ten years before Samuel's birth, accepted a ministerial appointment at Vriesland. Naturally studious, Samuel Zwemer, the thirteenth of fifteen children, learned three languages as a child and spent much time reading in his father's study; the latter inclination led his brothers to refer to him as "Lazy Sam." He studied at Hope Academy and College, earning an A.B. degree in 1887.

At home, school, and in church Zwemer had heard about the virtues of missionary service. His father at one time had hoped to serve in Africa, and when Samuel was an infant his mother prayed that he might be a missionary. A sister, Nellie, became a forty-year career missionary in China. Persuaded by the preaching of Robert Wilder, he joined the Student Volunteer Movement for Foreign Missions (SVM) while a senior at Hope College; throughout his years at New Brunswick Seminary in New Jersey (1887–1890) and later he was closely associated with the SVM. After he graduated from seminary in 1890, the Reformed Classis of Iowa ordained him as a missionary.

Motivated by word of the death of the first modern Christian missionary to Arabia, the Scotsman Ian Keith Falconer, Zwemer and fellow seminarian James Cantine committed themselves to succeed him in establishing a mission in what Zwemer called "the hardest country, the hardest climate, the hardest language, the hardest everything on earth." Officials of the Dutch Reformed church, aware that Islamic countries were the most difficult ones in which to win converts, turned down Zwemer and Cantine's initial funding request. Undaunted, they formed their own mission, The American Arabian Mission, and raised their own funds. After studying Arabic in Beirut they, with the help of Zwemer's younger brother, Peter, who arrived in 1892, established stations in Al Basrah, Iraq, in 1891, the Bahrain Islands in 1892, and Muscat, Oman, in 1893. In 1894 the Dutch Reformed church assumed sponsorship for the mission.

When in 1895 the Church Missionary Society (Anglican) brought two young women missionaries from Australia to Iraq, Cantine and Zwemer were asked to accompany them from Al Basrah to Baghdad. A year later Zwemer married one of the two women, Amy Elizabeth Wilkes, an English nurse, and they settled in Bahrain; they had six children.

During the next decade, Zwemer and Cantine evangelized the Persian coast region from Al Basrah to Muscat. This period of focused pioneer work ended for Zwemer in 1905 when he returned to the United States and began to promote and publicize missions in general, especially those in Muslim countries. Captivating and compelling as a speaker, he attracted recruits and funds in the United States. He accepted invitations to serve as traveling secretary for the SVM and as field secretary for the Reformed Board of Foreign Missions. In 1906 he organized and chaired the first general missionary conference on Islam, which met in Cairo, Egypt. Five years later he led a similar general conference in Lucknow (northern India) and founded the journal *Moslem World* (later the *Muslim World*), which for many of his thirty-seven years as editor served the West as its principal source of knowledge of Muslim culture and Christian missions to the Islamic world.

In 1912, at the request of several missionary societies, Zwemer was assigned to Cairo, the intellectual center of the Muslim world. There he taught in the theological seminary of the Arabian Mission and the Cairo Study Center, interacted regularly with Muslim students, preached extensively in Arabic and English, and worked with the Nile Mission Press in preparing Christian literature for Muslims. From Cairo he traveled widely to lead and participate in mission conferences; solicit funds and missionary recruits in the United States, Europe, and South Africa; encourage and inspire Christian missionaries in Muslim countries; establish missions to Muslims in India, China, Indochina, Iran, Iraq, and Malaysia; and stimulate interest everywhere in Muslim missions.

In 1929 he accepted an appointment as professor of Christian missions and history of religion at Princeton Theological Seminary. President John A. Mackay later noted that Zwemer had "made the missionary movement a thrilling reality on campus." Every student enrolled in his classes in missionary principles and methods and the history of religion. His wife died in 1937, also the year that he reached the mandatory retirement age of seventy. After retiring from Princeton, he moved to New York City, was remarried, to Margaret Clarke, in March 1940, and continued his teaching career at the Biblical Seminary of New York (three years), the Nyack Missionary Training Institute (seven years), and the Winona Lake (Ind.) School of Theology, a summer seminary. He died in Port Chester, New York.

Zwemer was the most influential Christian missionary to the Muslim world since the Middle Ages. A complex person, he was evangelical yet ecumenical, forthright yet respectful, a fervent believer in the supremacy of Christ over Mohammed yet an ardent student of Islamic culture—historian Carl Becker once described him as "the world's leading authority on popular Islam." He was also highly successful in recruiting Christian missionaries; indeed, according to missionary statesman John R. Mott, Zwemer "probably inspired more young people to offer themselves for mission service than any other man." Yet, like nearly all missionaries to Islamic countries, he was able to win very few—probably fewer than a dozen—Muslims to Christianity. Nevertheless, he gained wide respect among both Christians and Muslims and well deserved his popular title, "Apostle to Islam."

• Most of the Zwemer papers are located in the Hope College (Mich.) Archives. Zwemer authored or coauthored fifty books, including major studies on Islamic culture, Christian missionary strategy, and Christian meditation. The first and longest of these is *Arabia: The Cradle of Islam* (1900). *The Law of Apostasy in Islam* (1923) discusses why so few Muslims convert to Christianity. Both *Islam, a Challenge to Faith* (1907) and *The Cross above the Crescent* (1941) were widely read by college students considering a call to missionary service. Major devotional works include *Taking Hold of God* (1936) and *It Is Hard to Be a Christian* (1937). The only major biography of Zwemer is J. Christy Wilson, *Apostle to Islam: A Biography of Samuel M. Zwemer* (1952). Also see "Samuel Zwemer" in Sherwood Eddy, *Pathfinders of the World Missionary Crusade* (1945), pp. 240–47. Memorial notes of significance at the time of his death include John A. Mackay, "Dr. Samuel M. Zwemer: In Memoriam," the *Princeton Seminary*

Bulletin, Oct. 1952, pp. 25–27; "Faculty Memorial Minute: Samuel Marinus Zwemer," the *Princeton Seminary Bulletin*, Jan. 1953, pp. 34–35; and "Samuel M. Zwemer: In Appreciation," *International Review of Missions*, July 1952, pp. 357–58. An obituary is in the *New York Times*, 3 Apr. 1952.

WILLIAM C. RINGENBERG

ZWICKY, Fritz (14 Feb. 1898–8 Feb. 1974), astrophysicist and space scientist, was born in Varna, Bulgaria, the son of Fridolin Zwicky, a Swiss merchant, and Franziska Wrcek. Zwicky's early talent for science convinced his father to let him train for engineering rather than commerce. Accordingly, Zwicky moved to Zürich, Switzerland, where he attended the Eidgenössische Technische Hochschule. There Zwicky soon evinced a more abstract bent, switching from engineering to physics and mathematics in 1918. To obtain his teaching diploma in 1920, he wrote for the mathematician and mathematical physicist Hermann Weyl an essay on reflection in an inhomogeneous stratum. In 1922 he received his doctorate in theoretical physics, and his dissertation on the theory of ionic crystals was supervised by Peter Debye and Paul Scherrer. He stayed on until 1925 as a research assistant to Scherrer, working on X-ray cristallography, when he was offered a Rockefeller scholarship for research in the United States.

The two years Zwicky spent at the California Institute of Technology as a research fellow changed the course of his career. He had come for the mountains, fresh from climbing exploits in the Alps. When he asked about the closest peaks, he was shown Mount Wilson (elevation 1,700 meters) and reportedly replied "*Ja*, I see the foothills." He became assistant professor of theoretical physics at Caltech in 1927, and associate professor in 1929. Yet, his career in physics, in which he produced papers on thermodynamics, gaseous ionization, and solid state questions, was brief.

In 1928 the Rockefeller Foundation awarded Caltech the funds for a major new observatory. Zwicky willingly switched his allegiance to astronomy and helped to plan the new observatory on Palomar Mountain. In 1928–1929 he turned his attention to novae, producing a couple of papers on cosmology. Between 1928 and 1939, Zwicky and Walter Baade, a Caltech colleague after 1931, laid the foundations for the modern understanding of novae, supernovae, and neutron stars in a series of speculative papers. They then used an eighteen-inch Schmidt camera—a new kind of telescope built for Palomar at Zwicky's urging—to collect data and place their speculations on a firmer footing. During the first run, from 1936 to 1940, twelve supernovae were discovered, allowing for the study of their spectra and light-curves. The results of these observations would clearly demarcate ordinary novae from the much brighter supernovae, which were estimated to happen once per 300 to 400 years in a given galaxy. The survey of galaxies entailed by the supernova hunt yielded Zwicky's six-volume *Catalogue of Galaxies and of Clusters of Galaxies*, with E. Herzog, Paul Wild, and others (1961–1968) and the *Catalogue of Selected Compact Galaxies and of Post-Eruptive Galaxies*, with Margit A. Zwicky (1971).

In 1942 Zwicky became full professor of astrophysics. After his 1932 marriage to Dorothy Vernon Gates and their 1941 divorce, in 1947 he married Anna Margarita Zürcher; they had three daughters. In recognition of his work, Zwicky was appointed astronomer at the Mount Wilson and Palomar Mountain observatories in 1947. Invited to give the 1948 Halley Lecture at Oxford University, he chose to speak more on the subject of morphology than on astronomy. His morphological approach was concerned with the totality of all the possible aspects and solutions of any given problem. His 1957 monograph, *Morphological Astronomy*, reflected the same inclination in its discussion of galactic research.

Zwicky's astronomical interests also encompassed such subjects as the nature of the redshift (the shift toward longer wavelengths of light emitted by cosmic objects), the variability of fundamental "constants," intergalactic matter, "dark matter" (matter that may comprise most of the Universe's mass but that is undetectable except through gravitational effects), compact galaxies (galaxies of such concentrated brightness that they were almost indistinguishable from stars in normal photographs), and Humason-Zwicky objects (faint blue stars). He retired from Caltech's faculty in 1968 and was awarded the Gold Medal of the Royal Astronomical Society in 1972. Zwicky was working on a catalogue of all known supernovae when he died of a heart attack in Pasadena, California.

Although as a Swiss citizen living abroad, Zwicky was not called to arms during World War II, he nevertheless worked for victory over the Axis. He served as director of research for the Aerojet Engineering Corporation in Azusa, California (1943–1949), which was engaged in jet and rocket propulsion research for the U.S. military; on the Scientific Advisory Board of the Army Air Forces; and as one of the board's technical representatives sent to evaluate wartime jet propulsion research in Japan and Germany (1945–1946).

His propulsion research led to plans for making "artificial meteors," for launching the same pellets into space, and for bombarding the Moon with them on the dark side of the terminator, the dividing line between the bright and dark sides of the Moon. Over the course of fifteen years, Zwicky and Joseph F. Cuneo, former patent attorney at Aerojet Engineering, launched many "artificial meteors" from the ground or high-flying balloons, obtaining results outlined in *Morphology of Propulsive Power* (1962). However, they managed only two attempts at launching their coruscative pellets into interplanetary space. The first, off a captured V-2 rocket, in 1946, failed utterly. The second, from a U.S. Air Force Aerobee rocket, on 16 October 1957, apparently succeeded, marking the first time a human-made object had escaped Earth's gravity, but, happening twelve days after Sputnik, the achievement was thoroughly eclipsed, especially as the Air Force embargoed news of their success for several months. The

Moon shot they had dreamed of was never tried due to a lack of confidence on the part of the requisite U.S. agencies, which stemmed from the failure in 1946 and from adverse reviews by other scientists. Nevertheless, from the 1948 Halley lecture on, Zwicky was an ardent advocate of space exploration and colonization, calling for the development of space law.

Zwicky's dedication to humanitarian causes dates back to his days in Zürich. He particularly admired the work of Fridtjof Nansen, a pioneer of refugee relief. From 1946 to 1962 he was a member of the Pestalozzi Foundation, which financed war orphan villages. Locally, he denounced the smog that already plagued Los Angeles and proposed a tax on cars occupied by lone drivers. His most impressive initiative involved him in a decade-long effort when, realizing how World War II would ravage intellectual resources, he founded the Committee for Aid to War-Stricken Scientific Libraries. Starting in 1941, the committee gathered scientific publications and provided them free of charge to libraries abroad. Institutions in France, Germany, Japan, the Philippines, South Korea, and Taiwan were among its beneficiaries. For his many contributions, Zwicky received in 1949 the Presidential Medal of Freedom from President Harry S. Truman—in spite of Zwicky's criticism of the United States's bombings of Hiroshima and Nagasaki, Japan.

Zwicky sought to make his mark as a thinker by propounding a new heuristic methodology, which he termed the morphological approach. The fallibility of even his own trained mind often perplexed him, and he wished to understand the source of his insights. Still, however much he tended to credit his better ideas to the morphological approach, it is doubtful that it had any prescriptive value.

It is a measure of Zwicky's vision that it is still impossible in many cases to say with complete certainty whether he was right or wrong. In the light of later research, Baade and Zwicky were essentially correct when they related cosmic rays and neutron stars to supernovae. Zwicky was also one of the first to take seriously the idea of black holes. His almost unanimously disbelieved suggestion, that the Hubble redshift could be due to gravitational drag, has remained a subject of debate. Depending on the specialty considered, he will probably be remembered either as the discoverer of compact galaxies, the galactic surveyor, or the author of an enduring supernova paradigm.

• The papers of Zwicky, including 10,000 letters, are at the Landesbibliothek, 8750 Glarus, in Switzerland. Caltech's Astrophysics Library holds a complete listing of his 559 publications, and the Rockefeller Archive Center in North Tarrytown, N.Y., preserves materials bearing on Zwicky's International Education Board fellowship and his early years at Caltech. Many of his most important scientific papers appeared in the *Proceedings of the National Academy of Sciences*; these include "On the Red Shift of Spectral Lines through Interstellar Space" 15 (1929): 773–79; with Baade, "On Super-Novae" 20 (1934): 254–59; and "Cosmic Rays from Super-Novae" 20 (1934): 259–63. Other major papers include "Photographic Light-Curves of the Two Supernovae in IC 4182 and NGC 1003," with Baade, *Astrophysical Journal* 88

(1938): 411–21; "Types of Novae," *Reviews of Modern Physics* 12 (1940): 66–85; the landmark "On the Frequency of Supernovae, II," *Astrophysical Journal* 96 (1942): 28–36; and "On the Masses of Nebulae and Clusters of Nebulae," *Astrophysical Journal* 86 (1937): 217–46. For Zwicky's views on aeronautics and space science, see his "Report on Certain Phases of War Research in Germany" (1 Oct. 1945) in the Caltech Archives, and "A Stone's Throw into the Universe: A Memoir," published by NASA in *Essays on the History of Rocketry and Astronautics, II* (1977). His books *Discovery, Invention, Research through the Morphological Approach* (1969) and *Jeder ein Genie* (1971) best illustrate his personal outlook. For a thoughtful remembrance of the man, see Cecilia Payne-Gaposchkin, "A Special Kind of Astronomer," *Sky and Telescope* 47 (1974): 311–13.

JEAN-LOUIS TRUDEL

ZWORYKIN, Vladimir Kosma (30 July 1889–29 July 1982), scientist and television pioneer, was born in Murom, Russia, the son of Kosma A. Zworykin, a wealthy businessman, and Elaine Zworykin, a distant cousin of her husband. As a child, Zworykin spent his summers horseback riding, hunting, and spending time in his favorite hiding places along the banks of the Oka River, but when it came time for school he enrolled in the local Gymnasium and *realschule*, where by all accounts he was an excellent student with a special aptitude for science.

This talent enabled Zworykin to enroll in 1906 at the St. Petersburg Institute of Technology, where he studied under Boris Rosing, whose experiments with cathode-ray tubes would later enormously influence Zworykin. In 1912 he graduated and studied X-ray technology with physicist Paul Langevin at the College de France in Paris; he had planned to continue his studies in Berlin, but when World War I began he returned to Russia and enlisted in the army. With his engineering background, he was assigned to the signal corps and was soon promoted to lieutenant. In the army he also met Tatiana Vasilieff, whom he married in April 1916; the marriage was a troubled one (she stayed in Berlin while he was in the army), but they did have two children. After the war came the Russian Revolution. At first Zworykin was excited about the changes taking place, but when events turned violent and dangerous he decided to leave, settling in New York City with Tatiana in August 1919.

Since he was almost broke and spoke little English, Zworykin took a job as an adding machine operator at the procurement division of the Russian embassy and began to study English. In 1920 he was offered a job, at about half of his then-current salary, at the Westinghouse Electric Corporation in Pittsburgh. About a year later he resigned because of dissatisfaction with his pay and took a job in Kansas City, Missouri, but in 1923 Westinghouse rehired him with a substantial raise and gave him his own lab.

In 1924 Zworykin became a naturalized American citizen and that same year was accepted into the Ph.D. program in physics at the University of Pittsburgh; he earned his degree in 1926, and his dissertation on photoelectric cells later became one of six books he coauthored. The next several years were some of the most important and productive in Zworykin's life.

At Westinghouse, Zworykin built cathodes for radios and worked on photoelectric cells, but he is best remembered for the development of electronic television. He had designed and applied for a patent on a crude but workable television system as early as 1923 (the patent was granted in 1938), but it was only after a trip studying television research in Europe in 1929 that he perfected a device that would become one of the most important in the history of technology. Unlike other mechanical television tubes of the period, this one had no moving parts; it projected electrons onto a magnetically coated surface of a cathode-ray tube and presented clear images under normal lighting conditions. Zworykin presented a paper about his new device, which he called the kinescope, or picture tube, to the Institute of Radio Engineers (IRE) in Rochester, New York, on 28 November 1929.

One of those present that day was David Sarnoff, another Russian immigrant who was at that time vice president of the Radio Corporation of America. He was so impressed with Zworykin and his idea that he hired him, and within a few months Zworykin was in charge of his own lab at the RCA headquarters in Camden, New Jersey. By 1933 he had perfected the iconoscope, or camera tube, which was an improvement upon his own 1923 device and that of Philo T. Farnsworth, another television inventor whom Zworykin had visited in 1930 in San Francisco. (The influence on Zworykin by Farnsworth, who had developed a workable, all-electronic television system by 1930, has generated considerable controversy surrounding the advent of television.) The concept for this device he had learned from nature. In the human eye, light passes through the iris, then through the lens, and then focuses on the retina. This new invention performed this function electronically. On 28 April 1933 Zworykin presented his findings to the IRE. With these two inventions, Zworykin had ushered in the age of modern television and earned for himself the title "the father of television."

Zworykin now turned his attention to other pursuits, including early development of the electron microscope and the Superscope and Sniperscope night-vision equipment used during World War II and other military operations. During World War II, he served on the National Defense Research Committee and helped Army Air Force General H. H. "Hap" Arnold develop radar and missile-guidance systems.

A number of significant personal and professional changes occurred in Zworykin's life after the war. In 1947 Sarnoff named Zworykin a vice president and technical consultant at RCA. In June 1951 his wife filed for divorce, which became final on November 13; the next day Zworykin married Katherine Polevitsky, a widow whom he had been seeing for some time. In 1954, when Zworykin turned sixty-five, he was forced to retire from RCA but was named an honorary vice president. He soon became the director of the Medical Electronics Center at Rockefeller Institute (later Rockefeller University); he also lectured extensively in America and abroad and spent his winters in Miami, where he was a visiting professor at the University of Miami. In 1967 President Lyndon Johnson awarded him the National Medal of Science; in 1977 he was inducted into the Inventors Hall of Fame. Zworykin died at Princeton Medical Center.

With more than 120 patents to his name, Zworykin is deservedly credited with many of the electronic gadgets we take for granted today, including the one of which he is most proud—television. While he was unabashedly pleased with the technology of his invention, he seldom watched his own 27-inch color model because of the violence and inanities that the networks regularly showed. He perhaps best expressed his disappointment when he told the *New York Times* on 31 July 1974 that his greatest contribution to television was the "off" switch.

• Books published by Zworykin are *Photocells and Their Application* (1930), with E. D. Wilson; *Television: The Electronics of Image Transmission* (1940), with G. A. Morton; *Electron Optics and the Electron Microscope* (1945), with Morton et al.; *Photoelectricity and Its Applications* (1949), with E. G. Ramberg; *Television: The Electronics of Image Transmission in Color and Monochrome* (1954), with Morton; and *Television in Science and Industry* (1958), with Ramberg. A biography of Zworykin is Albert Abramson, *Zworykin: Pioneer of Television* (1995). Brief biographical sketches of his life and career are in Orrin E. Dunlap, *Radio's 100 Men of Science* (1944); *McGraw-Hill Modern Men of Science* (1966); David E. Fisher and Marshall John Fisher, *Tube: The Invention of Television* (1996); and Horace Newcomb, ed., *Museum of Broadcast Communications' Encyclopedia of Television* (1997). For further information on the development of television see Abramson, *A History of Television, 1880–1941* (1987). Obituaries are in the *New York Times*, 1 Aug. 1982, and the *Washington Post*, 31 July 1982.

ROGER A. SCHUPPERT

INDEX OF SUBJECTS

Feinstein, Moses
Feis, Herbert
Feke, Robert
Felix, Robert Hanna
Fell, John
Feller, William
Fellig, Arthur
Fels, Joseph
Fels, Samuel Simeon
Felsenthal, Bernhard
Felton, Cornelius Conway
Felton, Rebecca Latimer
Fendall, Josias
Fenger, Christian
Fenichel, Otto
Fenn, Wallace Osgood
Fenn, William Wallace
Fenneman, Nevin Melancthon
Fenner, Arthur, Jr.
Fenner, Charles Erasmus
Fenner, Eramus Darwin
Fenno, John
Fenollosa, Ernest
Fenton, Joseph Clifford
Fenton, Reuben Eaton
Fenwick, Benedict Joseph
Fenwick, Edward Dominic
Fenwick, George
Fenwick, John
Ferber, Edna
Ferebee, Dorothy Boulding
Ferguson, Elizabeth Graeme
Ferguson, Elsie
Ferguson, Homer
Ferguson, James Edward
Ferguson, John Calvin
Ferguson, Katy
Ferguson, Margaret Clay
Ferguson, Miriam Amanda
Ferguson, Richard Babbington
Ferguson, William Jason
Ferguson, William Scott
Fermi, Enrico
Fern, Fanny
Fernald, Charles Henry
Fernald, Merritt Lyndon
Fernandez, Royes
Fernow, Bernhard Eduard
Ferrel, William
Ferrer, Jose
Ferrin, Mary Upton
Ferris, Benjamin
Ferris, Jean Leon Gerome
Ferris, Theodore Parker
Ferriss, Hugh

Fessenden, Reginald Aubrey
Fessenden, Thomas Green
Fessenden, William Pitt
Festinger, Leon
Fetchit, Stepin
Fetter, Frank Albert
Feuchtwanger, Lion
Few, Ignatius Alphonso
Few, William
Fewkes, Jesse Walter
Feynman, Richard Phillips
Ficke, Arthur Davison
Fiedler, Arthur
Field, Cyrus West
Field, David Dudley, Jr.
Field, Erastus Salisbury
Field, Eugene
Field, Jessie
Field, Joseph M.
Field, Kate
Field, Marshall
Field, Marshall, III
Field, Rachel Lyman
Field, Ron
Field, Sara Bard
Field, Stephen Johnson
Fielding, Temple Hornaday
Fields, Annie Adams
Fields, Benny
Fields, Dorothy
Fields, Joseph Albert
Fields, Lew
Fields, W. C.
Fieser, Louis Frederick
Filene, Edward Albert
Fillmore, John Comfort
Fillmore, Millard
Fillmore, Myrtle, and
  Charles Sherlock Fillmore
Filson, John
Finch, Peter
Finck, Henry Theophilus
Findlay, James
Findley, William
Fine, Benjamin
Fine, Henry Burchard
Fine, Larry
Fink, Albert
Fink, Mike
Finlay, Carlos Juan
Finletter, Thomas Knight
Finley, James Bradley
Finley, John Huston
Finley, Martha
Finley, Moses

Finley, Robert
Finley, Samuel
Finn, Francis James
Finney, Charles Grandison
Finney, John Miller Turpin
Firestone, Harvey Samuel
Firth, Roderick
Fischer, Irwin
Fischer, John
Fischer, Louis
Fischer, Ruth
Fish, Carl Russell
Fish, Hamilton (1808–1893)
Fish, Hamilton (1888–1991)
Fish, Marian Graves Anthon
Fish, Nicholas
Fish, Stuyvesant
Fishback, William Meade
Fishbein, Morris
Fishberg, Maurice
Fisher, Ada Lois Sipuel
Fisher, Alvan
Fisher, Dorothy F. Canfield
Fisher, Fred
Fisher, Frederic John, Charles
  Thomas Fisher, William Andrew
  Fisher, Lawrence P. Fisher,
  Edward Francis Fisher, and
  Alfred Joseph Fisher
Fisher, Frederick Bohn
Fisher, George Park
Fisher, Ham
Fisher, Irving
Fisher, Mary
Fisher, M. F. K.
Fisher, Rudolph
Fisher, Sydney George
Fisher, Vardis
Fisher, Walter Lowrie
Fisher, William Arms
Fisk, James
Fisk, James Brown
Fisk, Wilbur
Fiske, Bradley Allen
Fiske, Daniel Willard
Fiske, Fidelia
Fiske, Harrison Grey
Fiske, John (1744–1797)
Fiske, John (1842–1901)
Fiske, Minnie Maddern
Fitch, Asa
Fitch, Clyde
Fitch, James
Fitch, John
Fitch, Thomas

Wallace, Hugh Campbell
Wallace, Irving
Wallace, Lew
Wallace, Lila Bell Acheson
Wallace, Lurleen Burns
Wallace, Sippie
Wallack, James William
(1795?–1864)
Wallack, James William
(1818–1873)
Wallack, Lester
Wallenstein, Alfred
Waller, Emma
Waller, Fats
Waller, Frederic
Waller, John Louis
Waller, Judith Cary
Waller, Thomas MacDonald
Walling, William English
Wallis, Hal B.
Wallis, Severn Teackle
Walls, Josiah Thomas
Walls, William Jacob
Waln, Robert, Jr.
Walsh, Benjamin Dann
Walsh, Blanche
Walsh, David Henry
Walsh, David Ignatius
Walsh, Edmund Aloysius
Walsh, Edward
Walsh, Frank P.
Walsh, Henry Collins
Walsh, James Anthony
Walsh, Joseph Leonard
Walsh, Raoul
Walsh, Stella
Walsh, Thomas James
Walsh, Thomas Joseph
Walt, Lewis William
Walter, Bruno
Walter, Cornelia Wells
Walter, Eugene
Walter, Thomas
Walter, Thomas Ustick
Walters, Alexander
Walthall, Edward Cary
Walthall, Henry Brazeale
Walther, Carl
Walton, George
Walton, Samuel Moore
Walworth, Clarence Augustus
Walworth, Ellen Hardin
Walworth, Jeannette Ritchie
Walworth, Reuben Hyde
Wambaugh, Sarah

Wampler, Cloud
Wanamaker, John
Wanamaker, Rodman
Waner, Paul
Wang, An
Wanger, Walter
Wanless, Harold Rollin
Wanton, John
Wanton, Joseph
Wanton, William
Wapahasha I
Wapahasha II
Wapahasha III
Warbasse, James Peter
Warburg, Felix
Warburg, James Paul
Ward, Aaron Montgomery
Ward, Archibald Burdette
Ward, Artemas
Ward, Frederick Townsend
Ward, Geneviève
Ward, Harry Frederick
Ward, Henry Augustus
Ward, Henry Baldwin
Ward, Henry Dana
Ward, Herbert Dickinson
Ward, Holcombe
Ward, Hortense Sparks
Ward, James Edward
Ward, James Harmon
Ward, James Warner
Ward, John Montgomery
Ward, John Quincy Adams
Ward, John William
Ward, Joshua John
Ward, Lester Frank
Ward, Lydia Arms Avery Coonley
Ward, Maisie
Ward, Nancy
Ward, Nathaniel
Ward, Samuel (1725–1776)
Ward, Samuel (1814–1884)
Ward, Samuel Ringgold
Ward, Theodore James
Ward, Thomas Wren
Warde, Frederick Barkham
Warde, Mary Frances
Warden, David Bailie
Ware, Caroline Farrar
Ware, Harold
Ware, Henry
Ware, Henry, Jr.
Ware, Nathaniel A.
Ware, Wilbur Bernard
Ware, William

Warfield, Benjamin Breckinridge
Warfield, Catherine
Warfield, David
Warfield, Solomon Davies
Warhol, Andy
Waring, Fred
Waring, George Edwin, Jr.
Waring, James
Waring, Julius Waties
Warman, Cy
Warmoth, Henry Clay
Warne, Colston Estey
Warneke, Heinz
Warner, Albert
Warner, Anne Richmond
Warner, Charles Dudley
Warner, Edward Pearson
Warner, Harry
Warner, Jack L.
Warner, Jonathan Trumbull
Warner, Olin Levi
Warner, Pop
Warner, Seth
Warner, Susan Bogert
Warner, W. Lloyd
Warren, Austin
Warren, Caroline Matilda
Warren, Charles
Warren, Cyrus Moors
Warren, Earl
Warren, Edward
Warren, Elinor Remick
Warren, Gouverneur Kemble
Warren, Harry
Warren, Henry Ellis
Warren, Herbert Langford
Warren, Howard Crosby
Warren, James
Warren, John
Warren, John Collins (1778–1856)
Warren, John Collins (1842–1927)
Warren, Joseph
Warren, Leonard
Warren, Mercy Otis
Warren, Peter
Warren, Richard Henry
Warren, Robert Penn
Warren, Russell
Warren, Samuel Prowse
Warren, Shields
Warren, Stafford Leak
Warren, William Fairfield
Warren, William Whipple
Warrington, Lewis
Washakie

INDEX BY CONTRIBUTOR

LOVOLL, ODD S.
Peerson, Cleng

LOW, LENA
Brown, Lydia

LOWANCE, MASON I., JR.
Johnson, Edward (1599–1672)
Mather, Samuel (1706–1785)

LOWE, RICHARD
Lewis, John Francis
Pierpont, Francis Harrison
Smith, William
Walker, Gilbert Carlton

LOWE, ROBERT
Leonard, Sterling Andrus

LOWE, STEPHEN R.
Demaret, Jimmy
Travers, Jerome Dunstan

LOWENFISH, LEE
Barrow, Edward Grant
Burke, Michael
Ebbets, Charles Hercules
Gomez, Lefty
Ward, John Montgomery

LOWERY, CHARLES D.
Barbour, James
Barbour, Philip Pendleton
Bradley, Stephen Row
Cabell, Samuel Jordan
Chandler, John
Clay, Matthew
Dale, Samuel
Eppes, John Wayles
Floyd, John
Grigsby, Hugh Blair
Holmes, David
Moore, Andrew
Pierce, Benjamin
Rittenhouse, William
Smith, Israel
Sullivan, George

LOWITT, RICHARD
Cannon, Joseph Gurney
Cutting, Bronson Murray
Garst, Roswell
Gore, Thomas Pryor
Hatch, Carl Atwood
Steed, Thomas Jefferson

LOWOOD, HENRY
Durand, William Frederick
Kompfner, Rudolf
Noyce, Robert Norton
Webster, David Locke

LOY, R. PHILIP
Farnum, Dustin Lancy

LOZA, STEVEN
Perez Prado, Damaso

LUCAS, JOHN A.
Eagan, Eddie
Flanagan, John J.
Hahn, Archie
Hardin, Slats
Hayes, Johnny
Hoppe, Willie
Hubbard, William DeHart
McDonald, Babe
Morris, Glenn Edward
Myers, Lon
Osborn, Harold Marion
Pilkington, James
Rose, Ralph Waldo
Scholz, Jackson Volney
Sheppard, Melvin Winfield
Wefers, Bernard J.
White, Benjamin Franklin

LUCAS, MARION B.
Fee, John Gregg

LUCAS, M. PHILIP
Berrien, John Macpherson
Boyd, Linn
Grinnell, Josiah Bushnell
Wickliffe, Charles Anderson

LUEPKE, GRETCHEN
Day, David Talbot

LUHR, WILLIAM
Raft, George

LUKER, RALPH E.
Barber, Jesse Max
Blackwell, Randolph Talmadge
Bowen, John Wesley Edward
Bradford, Amory Howe
Buttrick, Wallace
Crosby, Ernest Howard
DeBerry, William Nelson
Douglass, Harlan Paul

LUKER, RALPH E. (cont.)
Flower, Benjamin Orange
Haley, Alex
Herberg, Will
Hillis, Newell Dwight
Hurston, Zora Neale
Johns, Vernon Napoleon
King, Martin Luther
Lyman, Eugene William
McConnell, Francis John
Murphy, Edgar Gardner
Proctor, Henry Hugh
Ransom, Reverdy Cassius
Sheldon, Charles Monroe
Shilts, Randy
Steiner, Edward Alfred
Steward, Theophilus Gould
Walden, Austin Thomas
Walters, Alexander
Wieman, Henry Nelson
Young, Whitney Moore, Jr.

LUMPKIN, ANGELA
Bundy, May Godfray Sutton
Connolly, Maureen Catherine
Larned, William Augustus
McLoughlin, Maurice Evans

LUNBECK, ELIZABETH
Myerson, Abraham
Southard, Elmer Ernest

LUNDE, ERIK S.
Greeley, Horace

LUNDQUIST, M. SUZANNE
EVERTSEN
Radin, Paul

LUNSFORD, MATTHEW
Knott, James Proctor

LUPTON, KENNIE
Hanks, Nancy
Saarinen, Aline Bernstein
Saarinen, Eero
Saarinen, Eliel

LURIA, SARAH
Walter, Cornelia Wells

LURIE, EDWARD
Agassiz, Alexander
Agassiz, Louis

SILBEY, JOEL H.
Cass, Lewis
Green, Duff
King, Preston
Ritchie, Thomas
Seymour, Horatio
Spinola, Francis Barretto
Tilden, Samuel Jones

SILET, CHARLES L. P.
Bitzer, Billy
Eddy, Nelson
Griffith, D. W.
Ince, Thomas Harper
Welles, Orson

SILK, LEONARD
Hoover, Calvin Bryce

SILL, GERTRUDE GRACE
Haberle, John

SILLITO, JOHN R.
Priest, Ivy Baker

SILLS, DAVID L.
Berelson, Bernard
Lazarsfeld, Paul Felix
Zeisel, Hans

SILVER, DAVID MARK
Montgomery, Isaiah Thornton

SILVER-ISENSTADT, JEAN
Nichols, Thomas Low

SILVERMAN, KENNETH
Houdini, Harry
Poe, Edgar Allan

SIMMONDS, ROY S.
March, William
O'Brien, Edward

SIMMONS, JAMES R., JR.
Calvert, George Henry
Carter, Robert (1819–1879)

SIMMONS, NANCY CRAIG
Davis, Rebecca Blaine Harding
Sill, Edward Rowland

SIMMONS, WALTER G.
Mennin, Peter
Persichetti, Vincent Ludwig

SIMMS, L. MOODY, JR.
Basso, Hamilton
Baylor, Frances Courtenay
Bradford, Roark
Bruce, Philip Alexander
Cawein, Madison Julius
Eggleston, George Cary
Harris, Corra
Holden, William
Hope, James Barron
Kober, Arthur
Lockridge, Ross Franklin, Jr.
Moore, John Trotwood
Page, Thomas Nelson
Preston, Margaret Junkin
Russell, Irwin
Ryan, Abram Joseph
Smith, Charles Henry
Southworth, E. D. E. N.
Swanson, Gloria
Thompson, Maurice
Thompson, William Tappan
Ticknor, Francis Orray
Walsh, Raoul

SIMÕES, ANA
Mulliken, Robert Sanderson

SIMON, JOHN Y.
Hancock, Winfield Scott
Logan, John Alexander
McClernand, John Alexander
Rawlins, John Aaron
Washburne, Elihu Benjamin

SIMON, LINDA
Stein, Gertrude
Strong, Charles Augustus
Wilder, Thornton

SIMON, MYRON
Lounsbury, Thomas Raynesford
Warren, Austin

SIMONELLI, FREDERICK J.
Aldrich, Winthrop
Benson, Ezra Taft
Milk, Harvey
Moscone, George Richard
Ritchie, Albert Cabell

SIMONS, WILLIAM M.
Friedman, Benny
Greenberg, Hank

SIMONS, WILLIAM M. (cont.)
Leonard, Benny

SIMPSON, BROOKS D.
Ames, Adelbert
Babcock, Orville Elias
Badeau, Adam
Carpenter, Matthew Hale
Chamberlain, Joshua Lawrence
Cobb, Howell
Creswell, John Angel James
Doubleday, Abner
Fish, Hamilton (1808–1893)
Harlan, James (1820–1899)
Jewell, Marshall
Johnson, Bob
Martin, Billy
Nast, Thomas
Porter, Horace
Smith, Charles Ferguson

SIMPSON, MARCUS B., JR.
Baldwin, William
Bickmore, Albert Smith
Boll, Jacob
Brewster, William (1851–1919)
Cory, Charles Barney
Curtis, Moses Ashley
Fraser, John
Garden, Alexander (1730–1791)
Griscom, Ludlow
MacNider, William de Berniere
Oberholser, Harry Church
Pearson, Thomas Gilbert
Pursh, Frederick
Stone, Witmer
Townsend, John Kirk
Walter, Thomas

SIMPSON, MICHAEL
Adams, Thomas (1871–1940)

SIMPSON, PAMELA H.
Grafly, Charles

SINCLAIR, CORY
Humiston, William Henry

SINGER, MILTON
Redfield, Robert

SINGLETARY, WES
Johnson, Robert Lee
Welch, Mickey

SMITH, MERRIL D.
Estaugh, Elizabeth Haddon

SMITH, MICHAEL D.
Couch, Darius Nash
Halleck, Henry Wager
Meade, George Gordon
Thayer, Sylvanus
Thomas, George Henry

SMITH, MICHAEL W.
Evans, Donald

SMITH, NOLA
Hopper, Edna Wallace
Vincent, Mary Ann

SMITH, R. ALLEN
Love, Alfred Henry

SMITH, RICHARD CÁNDIDA
Rodia, Simon

SMITH, RICHARD D.
Whitley, Keith

SMITH, ROBERT W.
Woods, George David

SMITH, RONALD A.
Berenson, Senda
Camp, Walter Chauncey
Haughton, Percy Duncan

SMITH, STEPHEN K.
Hofmann, Hans

SMITH, SUSAN L.
Ferebee, Dorothy Boulding
Underwood, Felix Joel

SMITH, THOMPSON R.
Charlot

SMITH, TIMOTHY H.
Lingelbach, Anna Lane

SMITH, W. BARRY
Turner, William

SMITH, W. CALVIN
Habersham, James

SMITH, WESLEY
Boardman, George Dana
Dow, Lorenzo

SMITH, WILLIAM ANDER
Stokowski, Leopold

SMITH, WILLIAM SHAWN
Adler, Luther

SMITH, WILSON
Haddock, Charles Brickett
Knox, Samuel
Reed, Philip Dunham
Wade, John Donald
Ward, John William

SMOCOVITIS, VASSILIKI BETTY
Ames, Oakes (1874–1950)
Anderson, Edgar
Arthur, Joseph Charles
Burrill, Thomas Jonathan
Campbell, Douglas Houghton
Clausen, Jens Christen
Coulter, John Merle
Jepson, Willis Linn
Sargent, Charles Sprague
Sax, Karl
Setchell, William Albert
Shull, George Harrison
Stadler, Lewis John
Wright, Sewall

SMOLLER, SANFORD J.
McAlmon, Robert Menzies

SMULYAN, SUSAN
Jordan, Jim, and Marian Jordan

SNAPP, J. RUSSELL
Dobbs, Arthur
Graffenried, Christoph
Tryon, William

SNAVELY, KATHRYN D.
Abernethy, George
Adams, Charles
Allen, Henry Watkins
Applegate, Jesse

SNAY, MITCHELL
Macon, Nathaniel
Rives, William Cabell

SNEIDER, ALLISON L.
Sewall, May Eliza Wright

SNOWBERGER, BETH A.
Ryan, Jack

SNOWBERGER, BETH A. (cont.)
Stanwyck, Barbara
Tom Thumb

SNYDER, EDWARD F.
Wilson, E. Raymond

SNYDER, LAWRENCE W.
Cheney, Ednah Dow Littlehale
Spencer, Anna Garlin
Wendte, Charles William

SNYDER, TERRI L.
Berkeley, Frances

SOCHEN, JUNE
Einstein, Hannah Bachman
Meyer, Annie Nathan
Nathan, Maud
Soss, Wilma Porter
Waller, Judith Cary

SOCOLOFSKY, HOMER E.
Capper, Arthur
Morton, Levi Parsons

SODERLUND, JEAN R.
Penn, Hannah Callowhill
Penn, William
Pugh, Sarah

SOGGE, PAUL
White, Theodore H.

SOHMER, JACK
Archey, Jimmy
Armstrong, Lil
Bailey, Buster
Bechet, Sidney
Bonano, Sharkey
Boswell, Connee
Braud, Wellman
Carey, Mutt
Davison, Wild Bill
De Paris, Sidney
De Paris, Wilbur
Dickenson, Vic
Dodds, Johnny
Elman, Ziggy
Johnson, Bill
Johnson, Budd
Marsala, Joe
McKenzie, Red
McPartland, Jimmy
Miley, Bubber

INDEX BY PLACE OF BIRTH
IN THE UNITED STATES

For indexing purposes, places of birth have been indicated by names of the fifty states
and the District of Columbia rather than by historical names of colonies and territories.

ALABAMA
Abernathy, Ralph David
Allen, Viola
Andrews, Mary Raymond
   Shipman
Bankhead, John Hollis
   (1842–1920)
Bankhead, John Hollis
   (1872–1946)
Bankhead, Tallulah
Bankhead, William Brockman
Belmont, Alva Vanderbilt
Big Warrior
Birney, David Bell
Birney, William
Black, Hugo Lafayette
Boswell, Henry
Bradford, Perry
Bridgman, Frederick Arthur
Brims
Brown, Johnny
Brown, Letitia Christine Woods
Bullard, Robert Lee
Carmichael, Oliver Cromwell
Cheeseekau
Clay, Clement Claiborne
Clayton, Henry De Lamar
Clemens, Jeremiah
Cole, Nat King
Comer, Braxton Bragg
Connor, Bull
Culberson, Charles Allen
Davis, Mary Evelyn Moore
Day, Caroline Stewart Bond
DeBardeleben, Henry Fairchild
Delmore, Alton
Delmore, Rabon
De Priest, Oscar Stanton
Duggar, Benjamin Minge
Durr, Clifford Judkins
Ernst, Morris Leopold
Europe, James Reese
Fitzgerald, Zelda
Fleming, Walter Lynwood
Flowers, Walter Winkler, Jr.

ALABAMA (*cont.*)
Folsom, James Elisha
Ford, James William
Francis, Josiah
Fulton, Robert Burwell
Gaillard, Slim
Garrett, Leroy
Garrett, Pat
Gorgas, William Crawford
Grant, James Benton
Gregg, John
Gresham, Newt
Hall, Grover Cleveland
Hamilton, Andrew Jackson
Hancock, John (1824–1893)
Handy, W. C.
Harding, William Proctor Gould
Harrison, Tinsley Randolph
Haynes, Elizabeth Ross
Heflin, James Thomas
Hill, Lister
Hitchcock, Ethan Allen
   (1835–1909)
Hobson, Richmond Pearson
Huie, William Bradford
Johnson, Andrew N.
Johnson, Bill
Jones, Bob
Jones, Samuel Porter
Julian, Percy Lavon
Keller, Helen
Kitchin, William Hodge
Kolb, Reuben Francis
Louis, Joe
Louvin, Ira
Manly, John Matthews
Manning, Joseph Columbus
Manush, Heinie
March, William
Maverick, Mary
Mayer, Arthur Loeb
McGillivray, Alexander
McGraw, Myrtle Byram
McIntosh, William
McQueen, Peter

ALABAMA (*cont.*)
Menewa
Millinder, Lucky
Mitchell, Arthur Wergs
Moore, John Trotwood
Morgan, John Hunt
Mortar
Murrah, Pendleton
Nixon, Edgar Daniel
Norris, J. Frank
Oates, William Calvin
O'Neal, Edward Asbury, III
Opothle Yoholo
Osceola
Owens, Jesse
Owsley, Frank Lawrence
Paige, Satchel
Parsons, Albert Richard
Pelham, John
Pepper, Claude Denson
Percy, Walker
Perry, Pettis
Pittman, William Sidney
Pope, Charles Alexander
Proskauer, Joseph Meyer
Rapier, James Thomas
Reid, Joseph Neel
Rich, Arnold Rice
Rives, Richard Taylor
Ross, John
Screws, William Wallace
Sewell, Joe
Sibert, William Luther
Simmons, William Joseph
Sloan, Matthew Scott
Smith, Holland McTyeire
Smith, Pine Top
Sparkman, John Jackson
Stewart, Bennett McVey
Stinson, Katherine
Street, J. C.
Sun Ra
Taylor, Lily Ross
Thach, Charles Coleman
Thornton, Willie Mae

GEORGIA *(cont.)*

Rivers, Thomas Milton
Robinson, Jackie
Robinson, Ruby Doris Smith
Root, John Wellborn
Rusk, Dean
Russell, Richard Brevard, Jr.
Rutherford, Mildred Lewis
St. John, Isaac Munroe
Sherwood, Thomas Adiel
Shutze, Philip Trammell, II
Simms, Willie
Smith, Charles Henry
Smith, Jabbo
Smith, Relliford Stillmon
Smith, Trixie
Speer, Emory
Spencer, Samuel
Stallings, Laurence Tucker
Stanley, Roba
Stephens, Alexander Hamilton
Stephens, Linton
Sydnor, Charles Sackett
Talmadge, Eugene
Tampa Red
Tanner, Gid
Tattnall, Josiah
Taylor, Charlotte Scarbrough
Terry, Bill
Ticknor, Francis Orray
Tilly, Dorothy Eugenia Rogers
Tobias, Channing Heggie
Tomochichi
Toombs, Henry Johnston
Toombs, Robert Augustus
Towers, John Henry
Trotti, Lamar
Turpin, Tom
Twiggs, David Emanuel
Vann, Joseph
Vinson, Carl
Wade, John Donald
Wailes, Benjamin
Walden, Austin Thomas
Walker, William Henry Talbot
Watie, Stand
Watson, Thomas Edward
Wayne, James Moore
Wheeler, Joseph
White, Walter Francis
Williams, Mary Lou
Wilson, Augusta Jane Evans
Wilson, Ellen Axson

GEORGIA *(cont.)*

Winship, Blanton
Wood, John Stephens
Woodruff, George Waldo
Woodsmall, Ruth Frances
Wright, Louis Tompkins
Wright, Richard Robert, Sr.
Yancey, William Lowndes
Young, Trummy

HAWAII

Alexander, William DeWitt
Armstrong, Samuel Chapman
Bingham, Hiram (1875–1956)
Bishop, Bernice Pauahi
Carter, Henry Alpheus Peirce
Castle, William Richards, Jr.
Dole, Sanford Ballard
Emma
Freeth, George Douglas
Gulick, John Thomas
Gulick, Luther Halsey
 (1828–1891)
Gulick, Luther Halsey
 (1865–1918)
Hillebrand, William Francis
Ho, Chinn
Ii, John Papa
Judd, Albert Francis
Kaahumanu
Kahanamoku, Duke Paoa
Kalakaua, David Laamea
Kamehameha I
Kamehameha II
Kamehameha III
Kamehameha IV
Kamehameha V
Kawananakoa, Abigail
Kealoha, Warren Daniels
Kuhio
Lathrop, George Parsons
Liliuokalani
Luahine, Iolani
Malo, Davida
Matsunaga, Spark Masayuki
Onizuka, Ellison S.
Opukahaia
Patterson, William Allan
Pukui, Mary Abigail
Thurston, Lorrin Andrews

IDAHO

Angleton, James Jesus

IDAHO *(cont.)*

Benson, Ezra Taft
Borglum, Gutzon
Boyington, Gregory
Church, Frank
Edmundson, Hec
Fisher, Vardis
Jardine, William Marion
Mourning Dove
Ollokot
Pound, Ezra
Rainwater, Leo James
Ross, C. Ben
Sacagawea
Tendoy
Turner, Lana
Wells, Edward Curtis
Wood, Robert D.

ILLINOIS

Abbott, Emma
Abt, Isaac Arthur
Adams, Cyrus Cornelius
Adams, Franklin P.
Addams, Jane
Ager, Milton
Ainsworth, Dorothy Sears
Albert, Abraham Adrian
Albright, Ivan
Alcorn, James Lusk
Alinsky, Saul David
Allen, Edmund Turney
Allison, Samuel King
American, Sadie
Ammons, Albert C.
Ammons, Gene
Andersen, Arthur Edward
Ardrey, Robert
Arends, Leslie Cornelius
Arvey, Jacob Meyer
Astor, Mary
Atteridge, Harold Richard
Atwood, Wallace Walter
Austin, Mary Hunter
Ayer, Harriet Hubbard
Bacon, Ernst
Bacon, Henry, Jr.
Badger, Richard McLean
Baker, James
Balaban, Barney
Bancroft, Frederic A.
Barnum, Gertrude
Barrow, Edward Grant

KANSAS *(cont.)*

Felix, Robert Hanna
Fisher, Dorothy F. Canfield
Fleeson, Doris
Frank, Tenney
Friganza, Trixie
Goff, Bruce Alonzo
Gregg, John Andrew
Hadley, Herbert Spencer
Hall, Eugene Raymond
Hamlin, Albert Comstock
Harrington, John Lyle
Hatch, Carl Atwood
H'Doubler, Margaret Newell
Heap, Jane
Hedberg, Hollis Dow
Henderson, Paul
Hibbs, Ben
Inge, William
Johnson, Hugh Samuel
Johnson, Osa
Johnson, Walter
Johnson, Wendell Andrew Leroy
Jones, Donald Forsha
Jones, William (1871–1909)
Keaton, Buster
Kellogg, Vernon Lyman
Kelly, Emmett
Kenton, Stan
Kuhn, Joseph Ernst
LaMer, Victor Kuhn
Latimer, Wendell Mitchell
Livingstone, Belle
Lookout, Fred
Lund-Quist, Carl Elof
Malcolm, Norman Adrian
Mangelsdorf, Paul Christoph
Masters, Edgar Lee
McAlmon, Robert Menzies
McCollum, Elmer Verner
McDaniel, Hattie
Meek, Walter Joseph
Menninger, Karl Augustus
Menninger, William Claire
Miller, David Louis
Mills, Enos Abijah
Murdock, Victor
Nichols, Ernest Fox
Nutter, Gilbert Warren
O'Hare, Kate Richards
Parker, Charlie
Peabody, Lucy Waterbury
Pemberton, Brock

KANSAS *(cont.)*

Pennell, Joseph Stanley
Petalesharo
Pulliam, Eugene Collins
Randolph, Vance
Red Cloud
Robison, Carson Jay
Runyon, Damon
Rupp, Adolph Frederick
Schabinger, Arthur August
Schellenberg, Theodore Roosevelt
Schoeppel, Andrew Frank
Shelton, Ev
Slosson, Edwin Emery
Smith, Harold Dewey
Soper, Fred Lowe
Starrett, Paul
Starrett, William Aiken
Stryker, Roy Emerson
Sutherland, Earl W.
Tinker, Clarence Leonard
Vance, Vivian
Vincent, John Carter
Voorhis, Horace Jeremiah
Walker, George
Walt, Lewis William
Wettling, George Godfrey
White, Paul
White, William Allen
White, William Lindsay
Whittaker, Robert Harding
Wilkerson, Vernon Alexander
Willebrandt, Mabel Walker
Woodring, Harry Hines
Wright, Henry
Zook, George Frederick

KENTUCKY

Adams, John Quincy (1848–1922)
Akeman, Stringbean
Allen, Henry Tureman
Allen, James Lane
Altsheler, Joseph Alexander
Anderson, Richard Clough, Jr.
Anderson, Robert
Anshutz, Thomas Pollock
Applegate, Jesse
Arnow, Harriette Simpson
Atchison, David Rice
Baker, Jehu
Barkley, Alben William
Bell, James Franklin
Bennett, Belle Harris

KENTUCKY *(cont.)*

Bent, Silas
Bernard, Luther Lee
Bibb, Henry Walton
Bingham, Barry
Birney, James Gillespie
Blackburn, Joseph Clay Stiles
Blackburn, Luke Pryor
Blair, Eliza Violet Gist
Blair, Francis Preston, Jr.
Blair, Montgomery
Bland, Richard Parks
Blanding, Sarah Gibson
Bledsoe, Albert Taylor
Bloch, Claude Charles
Boggs, Lilburn W.
Boyle, Jeremiah Tilford
Bramlette, Thomas Elliott
Brandeis, Louis Dembitz
Breckinridge, Clifton Rodes
Breckinridge, Desha
Breckinridge, John (1797–1841)
Breckinridge, John Cabell
Breckinridge, Madeline McDowell
Breckinridge, Robert Jefferson
Breckinridge, Sophonisba Preston
Bristow, Benjamin Helm
Bristow, Joseph Little
Bronner, Augusta Fox
Brooks, Cleanth
Brooks, Nona Lovell
Browder, George Richard
Brown, Benjamin Gratz
Brown, John Mason, Jr.
Brown, John Young
Brown, William Wells
Browning, Orville Hickman
Browning, Pete
Browning, Tod
Bryan, Anna E.
Bubbles, John
Buchanan, Joseph Rodes
Buckner, Simon Bolivar
Buckner, Simon Bolivar, Jr.
Buford, Abraham (1820–1884)
Buford, John
Caldwell, Mary Gwendolin Byrd
California Joe
Campbell, Walter Gilbert
Canby, Edward Richard Sprigg
Carlisle, Cliff
Carlisle, John Griffin
Carson, Kit

MICHIGAN

Adams, Pepper
Algren, Nelson
Allen, George Herbert
Atkinson, George Francis
Avery, Sewell Lee
Bachmann, Werner Emmanuel
Bacon, Leonard, Sr.
Bagley, William Chandler
Bailey, James Anthony
Bailey, Liberty Hyde
Baker, Ray Stannard
Barr, Alfred Hamilton, Jr.
Barrows, John Henry
Bates, Marston
Beach, Rex
Beal, William James
Bennett, Harry Herbert
Bigelow, Melvin Madison
Billington, Ray Allen
Binga, Jesse
Birkhoff, George David
Blaik, Red
Boeing, William Edward
Briggs, Lyman James
Briggs, Walter Owen
Briscoe, Benjamin
Brooks, Alfred Hulse
Brown, Olympia
Brucker, Wilber Marion
Brundage, Avery
Bueche, Arthur Maynard
Buffalo
Bunche, Ralph Johnson
Bundy, Harvey Hollister
Burnett, Leo
Butterfield, Kenyon Leech
Campbell, Douglas Houghton
Catton, Bruce
Cavanaugh, John Joseph
Chaffee, Roger Bruce
Chapin, Roy Dikeman
Chessman, Caryl Whittier
Child, Charles Manning
Cicotte, Eddie
Cole, Edward Nicholas
Collingwood, Charles
Comfort, Will Levington
Cooke, George Willis
Cooley, Charles Horton
Copeland, Royal Samuel
Corby, William
Corrothers, James David

MICHIGAN (cont.)

Corwin, Edward Samuel
Cowan, Clyde Lorrain, Jr.
Crosby, Elizabeth Caroline
Curtice, Harlow Herbert
Curtis, Heber Doust
Curwood, James Oliver
Custer, Elizabeth Clift Bacon
Cuyler, Kiki
Czolgosz, Leon F.
Darling, Jay Norwood
Davenport, Eugene
de Cleyre, Voltairine
de Kruif, Paul Henry
Desmond, Johnny
Dewey, Alice Chipman
Dewey, Thomas Edmund
De Witt, Lydia Maria
Diegel, Leo H.
Dinkeloo, John Gerard
Dodge, Horace Elgin
Dodge, John Francis
Dodge, Joseph Morrell
Donahue, Sam
Donner, Frederic Garrett
Dow, Alden Ball
Eaton, Daniel Cady
Elliott, Walter Hackett Robert
Ellmann, Richard
Fairchild, David Grandison
Farnsworth, Elon John
Ferber, Edna
Fisher, M. F. K.
Flaherty, Robert Joseph
Flanagan, William
Flint, Austin (1836–1915)
Folks, Homer
Ford, Edsel Bryant
Ford, Henry
Ford, Henry, II
Forsyth, Thomas
Gauss, Christian Frederick
Geddes, Norman Bel
Gehringer, Charlie
Gerber, Daniel Frank
Gingrich, Arnold
Gipp, George
Gougar, Helen Mar Jackson
Gould, Laurence McKinley
Graham, Ernest Robert
Green, Constance McLaughlin
Haley, Bill
Harley, Herbert Lincoln

MICHIGAN (cont.)

Hathaway, Starke Rosecrans
Haworth, Leland John
Hayden, Robert Earl
Haynes, Williams
Hayward, William Louis
Hill, Charles Andrew
Hill, Louis Clarence
Holley, Major Quincy, Jr.
Howard, Bronson Crocker
Howard, Timothy Edward
Hume, David Milford
Humphrey, George Magoffin
Hunt, Henry Jackson
Hurd, Henry Mills
Hutcheson, William Levi
Ingersoll, Royal Rodney
Irwin, George Le Roy
Jarvis, Gregory B.
Jeffries, Edward John, Jr.
Jenks, Jeremiah Whipple
Jones, Howard Mumford
Jones, Thad
Kearns, Jack
Kelland, Clarence Budington
Kelley, Truman Lee
Kellogg, John Harvey
Kellogg, Paul Underwood
Kellogg, W. K.
Ketchel, Stanley
Kidder, Alfred Vincent
King, Henry Churchill
Kirchwey, George Washington
Koch, William Frederick
Kohler, Max James
Krehbiel, Henry Edward
Lamb, Theodore Lafayette
Lansdale, Edward Geary
Lardner, Ring
Lathrop, John Howland
Leisen, Mitchell
Leuschner, Armin Otto
Leyda, Jay
Liggett, Louis Kroh
Lindbergh, Charles Augustus
Lindeman, Eduard Christian
Lipscomb, Big Daddy
Lovejoy, Owen Reed
Macomb, Alexander
MacPhail, Larry
Main Poc
Mayo, Mary Anne Bryant
McAndrew, William

NEW YORK *(cont.)*

Fosdick, Harry Emerson
Fowle, Elida Barker Rumsey
Fowler, Bud
Fowler, George Ryerson
Fowler, Lorenzo Niles
Fowler, Orson Squire
Fox, Dixon Ryan
Foy, Eddie
Foy, Eddie, Jr.
Fraenkel, Osmond Kessler
Frank, Jerome New
Frankel, Charles
Frantz, Virginia Kneeland
Frazier, Brenda Diana Duff
Frederic, Harold
Freeman, Cynthia
Freeman, Elizabeth
Freer, Charles Lang
Freneau, Philip Morin
Freund, Ernst
Friedlander, Leo William
Friedmann, Herbert
Friend, Charlotte
Friendly, Henry Jacob
Frisch, Frank
Frost, Holloway Halstead
Fuertes, Louis Agassiz
Funk, Wilfred John
Furman, Richard
Gage, Lyman Judson
Gage, Matilda Joslyn
Gaige, Crosby
Gale, Benjamin
Gale, George Washington
Gallagher, Ralph W.
Gallico, Paul William
Gannett, Frank Ernest
Gannon, Mary
Garacontié, Daniel
Gardner, Isabella Stewart
Gardner, John
Garfield, John
Garis, Howard Roger
Garnet, Sarah J. Smith Tompkins
Garroway, Dave
Gates, Frederick Taylor
Gavin, James Maurice
Gayler, Charles
Gaynor, William Jay
Gear, John Henry
Gehrig, Lou
Geismar, Maxwell David

NEW YORK *(cont.)*

Gellatly, John
Gemunder Family
George, Grace
George, Samuel
Gerard, James Watson
Gershwin, George
Gershwin, Ira
Geschwind, Norman
Gibbs, George (1815–1873)
Gibbs, Wolcott (1822–1908)
Gibbs, Wolcott (1902–1958)
Gifford, Sanford Robinson
Gilbert, Grove Karl
Gilbert, Rufus Henry
Gilder, Helena de Kay
Gilder, Jeannette Leonard
Gildersleeve, Virginia Crocheron
Gill, Irving
Gill, Theodore Nicholas
Gilman, Frank Patrick
Gilman, Lawrence
Ginter, Lewis
Gleason, Jackie
Gleason, James
Gleason, Kate
Gleason, Ralph Joseph
Godey, Louis Antoine
Godfrey, Arthur
Goell, Theresa Bathsheba
Goethals, George Washington
Goforth, William
Gold, Michael
Goldberg, Leo
Golden, John
Goldmark, Henry
Goldmark, Josephine Clara
Goldmark, Rubin
Goldsmith, Joel Sol
Goldstein, Herbert S.
Goldwater, Sigismund Schulz
Goodell, William (1792–1878)
Goodhart, Arthur Lehman
Goodman, Joseph Thompson
Goodman, Paul
Goodnow, Frank Johnson
Goodrich, Benjamin Franklin
Goodspeed, Thomas Wakefield
Goodwin, Charles Carroll
Gordon, Andrew
Gordon, Max
Gordon, Waxey
Goss, Albert Simon

NEW YORK *(cont.)*

Gottlieb, Adolph
Gould, George Jay
Gould, Jack
Gould, Jay
Gouldner, Alvin Ward
Granger, Gordon
Grant, Madison
Gray, Asa
Graziano, Rocky
Greatorex, Eleanor Elizabeth
Greeley-Smith, Nixola
Green, Abel
Green, Anna Katharine
Green, Johnny
Greenberg, Clement
Greenberg, Hank
Greene, Cordelia Agnes
Greenslet, Ferris
Gregg, Willis Ray
Gregory, Charles Noble
Gregory, William King
Griffes, Charles Tomlinson
Grinnell, George Bird
Griscom, John Hoskins
Griscom, Ludlow
Groesbeck, William Slocum
Grofé, Ferde
Gropper, William
Gross, Milt
Gross, Paul Magnus
Groves, Leslie Richard, Jr.
Gruening, Ernest Henry
Grumman, Leroy Randle
Guarnieri, Johnny
Guggenheim, Peggy
Guthrie, Joseph Hunter
Guyasuta
Hackett, James Henry
Hadden, Briton
Hagedorn, Hermann
Hagen, Walter Charles
Hagerty, James Campbell
Haggin, B. H.
Haight, Henry Huntley
Haley, Alex
Hall, Abraham Oakey
Hall, Adelaide
Hall, Charles Cuthbert
Halleck, Henry Wager
Halliday, John
Halsey, Frederick Arthur
Halsted, William Stewart

NEW YORK *(cont.)*

Hovey, Henrietta
Howard, Curley
Howard, George Elliott
Howard, Joe
Howard, Moe
Howard, Shemp
Howe, Irving
Howe, John Homer
Howe, Julia Ward
Howe, William Wirt
Howell, John Adams
Howland, Emily
Howland, John
Hoyt, Beatrix
Huebsch, B. W.
Hughan, Jessie Wallace
Hughes, Charles Evans
Hulbert, William Ambrose
Hull, Clark Leonard
Hume, James B.
Hunt, Ward
Hunt, Washington
Hunter, Glenn
Huntington, Daniel
Huntington, Edward Vermilye
Huntington, George
Huntington, Henry Edwards
Hurley, Roy T.
Husing, Ted
Hutchins, Robert Maynard
Hutton, Barbara Woolworth
Hutton, E. F.
Hyatt, John Wesley
Hyde, Henry Baldwin
Hyer, Tom
Hyman, Stanley Edgar
Ingalls, Marilla Baker
Ingersoll, Robert Green
Inman, Henry
Inness, George
Irish, Ned
Irving, Peter
Irving, Washington
Irving, William
Irwin, Elisabeth Antoinette
Irwin, William Henry
Iselin, Columbus O'Donnell, II
Isham, Ralph Heyward
Isherwood, Benjamin Franklin
Ives, Irving McNeil
Ives, James Merritt
Ives, Joseph Christmas

NEW YORK *(cont.)*

Jackson, James Caleb
Jackson, Samuel Macauley
Jackson, Sheldon
Jackson, William Henry
Jacobs, Hirsch
Jacobs, Mike
Jacoby, Oswald
Jaffe, Sam
Jaffee, Irving W.
James, Alice
James, Henry (1811–1882)
James, Henry (1843–1916)
James, Janet Wilson
James, Leon
James, William
Janeway, Charles Alderson
Janis, Sidney
Janssen, Werner Alexander
Jarvis, DeForest Clinton
Javits, Jacob Koppel
Jay, John
Jeffords, Thomas Jonathan
Jelliffe, Smith Ely
Jemison, Alice Mae Lee
Jenkins, Helen Hartley
Jervis, John Bloomfield
Jessel, George
Jessup, Philip C.
Johnson, Crockett
Johnson, David
Johnson, John
Johnson, Owen McMahon
Johnson, Samuel William
Johnson, William Woolsey
Johnston, John Taylor
Jones, Amanda Theodosia
Jones, George Heber
Jones, Jane Elizabeth
Jones, John (1729–1791)
Jones, Samuel
Jones, Susan Charlotte Barber
Jones, Thomas
Jordan, David Starr
Jorgensen, Christine
Josephson, Matthew
Judah, Samuel
Judd, Gerrit Parmele
Judd, Laura Fish
Judd, Norman Buel
Judson, Edward Zane Carroll
Judson, Emily Chubbuck
Judson, Harry Pratt

NEW YORK *(cont.)*

Kaiser, Henry John
Kallet, Arthur
Kalmar, Bert
Kane, John Kintzing
Kardiner, Abram
Kasner, Edward
Kaufman, Joseph William
Kaye, Danny
Kaye, Nora
Kearny, Philip
Keating, Kenneth Barnard
Keeler, Wee Willie
Keeley, Leslie Enraught
Keene, Thomas Wallace
Keep, Henry
Keith, Minor Cooper
Kellogg, Frank Billings
Kellogg, Samuel Henry
Kelly, John
Kelly, Michael
Kelly, Patsy
Kelly, Walter C.
Kelsey, Francis Willey
Kemper, Jackson
Kenedy, Patrick John
Kent, Charles Foster
Kent, James
Kent, James Tyler
Kent, Rockwell
Kenyon, Dorothy
Kenyon, Josephine Hemenway
Keppel, Francis C.
Keppel, Frederick Paul
Kern, Jerome
Kidder, Daniel Parish
Kieran, John Francis
King, Carol Weiss
King, Charles
King, John
King, Preston
King, Richard
King, Rufus (1814–1876)
King, Stanley
King, Thomas Starr
Kingsley, Clarence Darwin
Kingsley, Norman William
Kinzel, Augustus Braun
Kip, William Ingraham
Kiphuth, Robert John Herman
Kirchwey, Freda
Kirk, Edward Norris
Kirkland, Caroline Matilda

INDEX BY PLACE OF BIRTH
OUTSIDE THE UNITED STATES

ALBANIA
Nassi, Thomas

ARGENTINA
Parvin, Theophilus
Wrinch, Dorothy Maud

ARMENIA
Gorky, Arshile
Kazanjian, Varaztad
Mugar, Stephen Pabken

AUSTRALIA
Booth, Marian Agnes
Bridges, Harry Renton
Campbell, Persia Crawford
Clavell, James
Errol, Leon
Flynn, Errol
Grainger, Percy
Heggie, O. P.
Henry, Alice
Jacobs, Joseph
Kellerman, Annette
Kenny, Elizabeth
Lawrence, Marjorie
Mayo, George Elton
Orry-Kelly
Ritchard, Cyril
Sheed, Francis Joseph
Travis, Walter John

AUSTRIA
Adamson, Joy
Adler, Alfred
Artin, Emil
Baraga, Frederic
Baum, Vicki
Bayer, Herbert
Bemelmans, Ludwig
Berger, Victor Louis
Bergmann, Gustav
Berk, Fred
Bernays, Edward
Bettelheim, Bruno
Bibring, Grete Lehner
Bitter, Karl Theodore Francis

AUSTRIA *(cont.)*
Bloomfield, Maurice
Bluhdorn, Charles G.
Brill, Abraham Arden
Burns, Arthur Frank
Carnegie, Hattie
Cermak, Anton Joseph
Conried, Heinrich
Deutsch, Gotthard
d'Harnoncourt, René
Drexel, Francis Martin
Englander, Ludwig
Fall, Bernard B.
Feigl, Herbert
Fellig, Arthur
Fenichel, Otto
Fleischer, Max
Flesch, Rudolf Franz
Frank, Philipp G.
Frankfurter, Felix
Geiringer, Hilda
Gericke, Wilhelm
Gruen, Victor David
Gruenberg, Sidonie Matsner
Grund, Francis Joseph
Harris, Jed
Harteck, Paul
Heider, Fritz
Herbert, F. Hugh
Hertz, John Daniel
Herzfeld, Karl Ferdinand
Hess, Victor Franz
Homolka, Oscar
Ichheiser, Gustav
Jackson, Joe
Katzer, Frederick Xavier
Keppler, Joseph
Kober, Arthur
Kohut, Heinz
Kompfner, Rudolf
Kreisler, Fritz
Landsteiner, Karl
Lang, Fritz
Lazarsfeld, Paul Felix
Leinsdorf, Erich
Lenya, Lotte
Liebman, Max

AUSTRIA *(cont.)*
Lotka, Alfred James
Lowie, Robert Harry
Machlup, Fritz
Marek, George Richard
Massing, Hede Tune
Muni, Paul
Neugebauer, Otto Eduard
Neutra, Richard Joseph
Nordberg, William
Ottendorfer, Oswald
Padover, Saul K.
Pierz, Francis Xavier
Preminger, Otto
Pupin, Michael Idvorsky
Rank, Otto
Rasch, Albertina
Reik, Theodor
Rosenstein, Nettie
Roth, Henry
Sachs, Hanns
Sakel, Manfred Joshua
Schindler, Rudolph Michael
Schoenberg, Arnold
Schreiber, Frederick
Schumann-Heink, Ernestine
Schuschnigg, Kurt von
Schuster, Max Lincoln
Schutz, Alfred
Spiegel, Sam
Sporn, Philip
Steindler, Arthur
Steiner, Max R.
Sternberg, Josef von
Strasberg, Lee
Taussky-Todd, Olga
Trapp, Maria von
Urban, Joseph
von Mises, Richard Marten Edler
von Stroheim, Erich
Weiss, Paul Alfred
Wellek, René
Werner, Heinz

AZORES
Benavides, Alonso de

INDEX BY OCCUPATIONS AND
REALMS OF RENOWN

Many subjects of biographies had more than one occupation or achieved fame in several realms of renown. Their names will thus be found under various rubrics in this index.

AIR FORCE OFFICERS *(cont.)*
Stratemeyer, George Edward

AIRLINE INDUSTRY LEADERS
Braniff, Thomas Elmer
Chennault, Claire Lee
Coffin, Howard Earle
Damon, Ralph Shepard
Doole, George Arntzen
Frye, William John
Gorrell, Edgar Staley
Henderson, Paul
Hunter, Croil
Patterson, William Allan
Prescott, Robert William
Rickenbacker, Edward Vernon
Six, Robert Forman
Smith, Cyrus Rowlett
Trippe, Juan Terry
Woolman, Collett Everman

ALIENISTS. *See* Psychiatrists

ALLEGED ASSASSIN
Oswald, Lee Harvey

ALLEGED HERETICS
Bowne, Borden Parker
Crapsey, Algernon Sidney
Hutchinson, Anne

ALLEGED MURDERERS
Borden, Lizzie
Sacco, Nicola, and Bartolomeo
  Vanzetti

ALLEGED SLAVE REVOLT LEADER
Jeremiah, Thomas

ALLEGED TRAITORS
Bayard, Nicholas
Billy

ALLERGIST
Schick, Béla

ALMANAC MAKERS
Ames, Nathaniel (1708–1764)
Ames, Nathaniel (1741–1822)
Collins, Isaac
Foster, John
Franklin, Ann Smith
Franklin, Benjamin (1706–1790)
Gaine, Hugh
West, Benjamin (1730–1813)

ALUMINUM INDUSTRY LEADERS
Clapp, George Hubbard
Davis, Arthur Vining
Hall, Charles Martin
Hunt, Alfred Ephraim

AMBASSADORS. *See* Diplomats

**AMERICAN INDIAN ARTIFACTS
  COLLECTORS**
Lawson, Roberta Campbell
Mercer, Henry Chapman
Rindge, Frederick Hastings

AMERICAN INDIAN LEADERS.
  See also American Indian
  Religious Leaders
Abraham
Alligator
American Horse
Ann
Arapoosh
Atsidi, Sani
Attakullakulla
Ayres, Jacob
Big Warrior
Billy Bowlegs
Blackfish
Black Hawk
Black Hoof
Black Kettle (1807–1868)
Black Kettle (died c. 1698)
Blue Jacket
Brant, Joseph
Bright Eyes
Brims
Buckongahelas
Buffalo
Canonchet
Canonicus
Captain Jack
Captain Pipe
Charlot
Cheeseekau
Cloud, Henry Roe
Coacoochee
Cochise
Colbert, Levi
Colbert, William
Cornplanter
Cornstalk
Crazy Horse
Davis, Alice Brown
Dodge, Henry Chee
Doublehead
Dragging Canoe

AMERICAN INDIAN LEADERS *(cont.)*
Dunquat
Egushawa
Folsom, David
Frechette, James George
Gall
Garacontié, Daniel
Garry, Spokan
George, Samuel
Geronimo
Godfroy, Francis
Grass, John
Gray Lock
Guyasuta
Hagler
Harjo, Chitto
Hatathli, Ned
Hendrick
Hiawatha
Hole-in-the-Day
Hollow Horn Bear
Inkpaduta
Jones, Sam (?–1867)
Joseph
Juh
Kamiakin
Kekewepelethy
Keokuk
LeFlore, Greenwood
Leschi
Little Crow
Little Turtle
Little Wolf
Logan, James (1776?–1812)
Looking Glass
Lookout, Fred
Mangas Coloradas
Manuelito
Massasoit
Matchekewis
Mathews, John Joseph
Mazakutemani, Paul
McGillivray, Alexander
McIntosh, William
McQueen, Peter
Menewa
Miantonomo
Morgan, Jacob Casimera
Mortar
Moses
Mountain Chief
Mourning Dove
Mushalatubbe
Nampeyo
Nimham, Daniel
Oconostota

ANGLICAN BISHOP
Inglis, Charles

ANGLICAN CLERGY. *See also*
  Episcopalian Clergy
Bacon, Thomas
Bailey, Jacob
Banister, John
Blackstone, William
Boucher, Jonathan
Bowden, John
Bray, Thomas
Camm, John
Checkley, John
Coke, Thomas
Cooper, Myles
Eaton, Nathaniel
Evans, Evan
Evans, Nathaniel
Honyman, James
Inglis, Charles
Jarratt, Devereux
Johnson, Samuel
Le Jau, Francis
MacSparran, James
Odell, Jonathan
Ogilvie, John
Peters, Richard (1704?–1776)
Peters, Samuel Andrew
Smith, William (1727–1803)
Spencer, Archibald
Sterling, James
Zouberbuhler, Bartholomew

ANIMAL BREEDERS. *See* Cattle
  Raisers and Traders; Dog
  Breeders; Racehorse Breeders and
  Trainers; Ranchers

ANIMAL TRAINERS
Adams, Grizzly
Beatty, Clyde
Rarey, John Solomon

ANIMAL WELFARE ACTIVIST
Bergh, Henry

ANIMATORS. *See* Film Animators

ANTHOLOGISTS
Alger, William Rounseville
Asimov, Isaac
Auslander, Joseph
Bontemps, Arna Wendell
Braithwaite, William Stanley

ANTHOLOGISTS *(cont.)*
Brownson, Henry Francis
Burnett, Whit
Child, Francis James
Clarke, Mary Bayard
Coggeshall, William Turner
Conroy, Jack
Dannay, Frederic
Dunbar-Nelson, Alice
Foley, Martha
Gassner, John Waldhorn
Griswold, Rufus Wilmot
Hakluyt, Richard
Hall, James (1793–1868)
Hart, James David
Henderson, Alice Corbin
Kennedy, William Sloane
Kronenberger, Louis
Lawson, James
Moore, Milcah Martha
O'Brien, Edward
Sargent, Epes
Smith, Elihu Hubbard
Stoddard, Richard Henry
Teasdale, Sara
Tenney, Tabitha Gilman
Untermeyer, Louis
Zevin, Israel Joseph

ANTHROPOLOGISTS. *See also*
  Ethnographers; Ethnologists;
  Ethnomusicologists; Folklorists
Angel, John Lawrence
Ardrey, Robert
Bartlett, John Russell
Bascom, William Russel
Bateson, Gregory
Benedict, Ruth
Boas, Franz
Chamberlain, Alexander Francis
Cobb, William Montague
Coon, Carleton Stevens
Cushing, Frank Hamilton
Day, Caroline Stewart Bond
Dixon, Roland Burrage
Dorsey, George Amos
Dozier, Edward Pasqual
Drake, St. Clair, Jr.
Eiseley, Loren Corey
Emory, Kenneth Pike
Fairbanks, Charles Herron
Farabee, William Curtis
Fewkes, Jesse Walter
Fishberg, Maurice
Fletcher, Alice Cunningham
Goldenweiser, Alexander A.

ANTHROPOLOGISTS *(cont.)*
Hallowell, A. Irving
Heizer, Robert Fleming
Herskovits, Melville J.
Hewett, Edgar Lee
Hodge, Frederick Webb
Hooton, Earnest Albert
Hrdlička, Aleš
Hurston, Zora Neale
Kluckhohn, Clyde
Kroeber, Alfred Louis
La Farge, Oliver
La Flesche, Francis
Lewis, Oscar
Linton, Ralph
Lowie, Robert Harry
Malinowski, Bronislaw
McGee, William John
McNickle, D'Arcy
Mead, Margaret
Mooney, James
Morgan, Lewis Henry
Morton, Samuel George
Murdock, George Peter
Parsons, Elsie Clews
Powdermaker, Hortense
Powell, John Wesley
Primus, Pearl
Putnam, Frederic Ward
Radin, Paul
Redfield, Robert
Reichard, Gladys Amanda
Roberts, Jack
Sapir, Edward
Sheldon, William Herbert
Spier, Leslie
Steward, Julian Haynes
Swanton, John Reed
Todd, Thomas Wingate
Turner, Victor
Verrill, Alpheus Hyatt
Warner, W. Lloyd
Weltfish, Gene
White, Leslie Alvin
Wissler, Clark
Wyman, Jeffries

ANTIABORTION RIGHTS ACTIVIST
Storer, Horatio Robinson

ANTICOMMUNISTS
Budenz, Louis
Chambers, Whittaker
Cohn, Roy
Cvetic, Matthew C.
Fischer, Ruth

ARCHITECTURAL HISTORIANS. *See also* Architectural Critics
Brown, Glenn
Frothingham, Arthur Lincoln
Hamlin, Alfred Dwight Foster
Hitchcock, Henry-Russell
Kimball, Fiske
Kocher, A. Lawrence
Moore, Charles Herbert
Tallmadge, Thomas Eddy
Tuthill, Louisa
Warren, Herbert Langford

ARCHIVIST OF THE UNITED STATES
Connor, Robert Digges Wimberly

ARCHIVISTS. *See also* Librarians
Candler, Allen Daniel
Fitzpatrick, John Clement
Knight, Lucian Lamar
Leland, Waldo Gifford
McAvoy, Thomas Timothy
Rhees, William Jones
Schellenberg, Theodore Roosevelt

ARMS AND ARMOR COLLECTORS
Dean, Bashford
Riggs, William Henry

ARMS INDUSTRY LEADERS. *See* Firearms Manufacturers; Ordnance Manufacturers

ARMY AIR CORPS AND ARMY AIR FORCE OFFICERS
Arnold, Henry Harley
Eatherly, Claude Robert
Kelly, Colin Purdie
Kenney, George Churchill
Tinker, Clarence Leonard
Vandenberg, Hoyt Sanford

ARMY AIR SERVICE OFFICERS
Lufbery, Gervais Raoul Victor
Rickenbacker, Edward Vernon
Twining, Nathan Farragut

ARMY AVIATORS. *See* Army Signal Corps Aviators; Army Air Service Officers; Army Air Corps and Army Air Force Officers

ARMY CHIEFS OF STAFF
Craig, Malin
Hines, John Leonard
Johnson, Harold Keith
McNair, Lesley James
Ridgway, Matthew Bunker
Summerall, Charles Pelot
Wheeler, Earle Gilmore

ARMY ENGINEERS. *See* Military Engineers

ARMY OFFICERS. *See* Colonial Militiamen; Revolutionary Army Officers; Army Officers (1784–1860); Confederate Army Officers; Union Army Officers; Army Officers (1866–1995); Army Chiefs of Staff. *See also* British Army and Navy Officers; French Army and Navy Officers; Spanish Army and Navy Officers

ARMY OFFICERS (1784–1860)
Adair, John
Ainsworth, Fred Crayton
Armistead, George
Armstrong, John (1717–1795)
Armstrong, John (1755–1816)
Armstrong, John (1758–1843)
Beauregard, Pierre Gustave Toutant
Bedinger, George Michael
Benner, Philip
Bissell, Daniel
Bloomfield, Joseph
Bomford, George
Bonneville, Benjamin
Boyd, John Parker
Brown, Jacob Jennings
Campbell, Arthur
Carroll, William
Carson, Kit
Chandler, John
Childs, Thomas
Claghorn, George
Cocke, William
Connor, Patrick Edward
Cooke, Philip St. George
Cooper, Samuel (1798–1876)
Craik, James
Crawford, William
Crittenden, Thomas Leonidas
Croghan, George (1791–1849)
Crook, George

ARMY OFFICERS (1784–1860) *(cont.)*
Dearborn, Henry
Dodge, Henry
Doniphan, Alexander William
Eaton, William
Elliot, James
Emory, William Hemsley
Fannin, James Walker
Fanning, Alexander Campbell Wilder
Folsom, Nathaniel
Gadsden, James
Gaines, Edmund Pendleton
Gass, Patrick
Gilpin, William
Graham, James Duncan
Gridley, Richard
Hamtramck, John Francis
Hardin, John J.
Hardin, Martin D.
Harmar, Josiah
Harney, William Selby
Harrod, James
Hitchcock, Ethan Allen (1798–1870)
Hopkins, Samuel (1753–1819)
Howard, Benjamin
Howard, Oliver Otis
Ives, Joseph Christmas
Izard, George
Jackson, Andrew
Jesup, Thomas Sidney
Johnson, James
Johnston, Albert Sidney
Jones, Calvin
Kearny, Philip
Kearny, Stephen Watts
King, William
Lane, Joseph
Lane, Ralph
Leavenworth, Henry
Lee, Robert E.
Lewis, Andrew
Lewis, Meriwether
Logan, Benjamin
Long, Stephen Harriman
Lyon, Nathaniel
Macomb, Alexander
Mansfield, Joseph King Fenno
Mason, Richard Barnes
McClure, George
Meigs, Montgomery Cunningham
Miller, James
Miller, John
Mitchell, George Edward
Mordecai, Alfred

BOXERS *(cont.)*
Miller, Freddie
Molyneaux, Tom
Morrissey, John
Ortiz, Manuel
Robinson, Sugar Ray
Rosenbloom, Maxie
Ross, Barney
Ryan, Tommy
Sullivan, John L.
Tunney, Gene
Walcott, Jersey Joe
Walcott, Joe
Walker, Mickey
Wills, Harry

BREWERS
Brand, Virgil Michacl
Busch, Adolphus
Busch, August Anheuser, Jr.
Ruppert, Jacob
Vassar, Matthew

BRIDGE CHAMPIONS
Crawford, John Randolph
Culbertson, Ely
Jacoby, Oswald
Von Zedtwitz, Waldemar

BRIGANDS. *See* Outlaws

BRITISH ARMY AND NAVY OFFICERS
Abercromby, James
Amherst, Jeffery
André, John
Bouquet, Henry
Braddock, Edward
Bradstreet, John
Burgoyne, John
Butler, Walter
Coffin, Isaac
Coffin, John
Cornwallis, Charles
Cunningham, William
Fletcher, Benjamin
Forbes, John (1707–1759)
Gage, Thomas
Hall, Basil
Howe, George Augustus
Howe, William
Hunter, Robert (1666–1734)
Johnstone, George
Loring, Joshua (1716–1781)
Loudoun, Earl of
McIntosh, Lachlan

BRITISH ARMY AND NAVY OFFICERS *(cont.)*
Monckton, Robert
Morris, Roger
Nicholson, Francis
Parker, Peter (1721–1811)
Pitcairn, John
Robertson, James (1717–1788)
Ruxton, George Augustus Frederick
Sharpe, Horatio
Shute, Samuel
Skene, Philip
Tryon, William
Vancouver, George
Warren, Peter
Webb, Daniel
Wcbb, Thomas

BRITISH LEGISLATORS
Coote, Richard
Cruger, Henry, Jr.
Lyttelton, William Henry
Pownall, Thomas

BROADCASTING INDUSTRY LEADERS. *See* Radio and Television Industry Leaders

BROADCAST JOURNALISTS
Barber, Red
Beatty, Bessie
Blesh, Rudi
Clapper, Raymond
Collingwood, Charles
Cosell, Howard
Craig, Elisabeth
Cross, Milton
Davis, Elmer
Dean, Dizzy
Eisler, Gerhart
Eliot, George Fielding
Frederick, Pauline
Frick, Ford Christopher
Garroway, Dave
Gibbons, Floyd
Grange, Red
Hale, Arthur William
Hard, William
Harmon, Tom
Heatter, Gabriel
Heilmann, Harry Edwin
Howe, Quincy
Huntley, Chet
Husing, Ted
Kaltenborn, H. V.

BROADCAST JOURNALISTS *(cont.)*
Lewis, Fulton, Jr.
Lindstrom, Freddy
McBride, Mary Margaret
McCann, Alfred Watterson
McGee, Frank
McLendon, Gordon
McNamee, Graham
Murrow, Edward R.
Polk, George
Reasoner, Harry
Reynolds, Frank
Rice, Grantland
Robinson, Max
Samuel, Maurice
Savitch, Jessica
Schoenbrun, David
Scldcs, Gilbert
Sevareid, Eric
Shirer, William
Stern, William
Susskind, David
Thomas, Lowell
Thompson, Dorothy
van Loon, Hendrik
White, Paul
Winchell, Walter

BROTHELKEEPERS
Adler, Polly
Everleigh, Ada, and Minna Everleigh
Stanford, Sally

BUCCANEERS. *See* Pirates

BUDDHIST LEADERS
Olcott, Henry Steel
Trungpa, Chögyam

BUDDHIST STUDIES SCHOLARS. *See* Religious Studies Scholars

BUILDERS. *See* Architects; Carpenters; Civil Engineers; Construction Engineers; Construction Industry Leaders; Shipbuilders

BUILDING MATERIALS INDUSTRY LEADERS
Avery, Sewell Lee
Coxey, Jacob Sechler
Crown, Henry
Kelly, John Brendan, Jr.

CHEWING GUM INDUSTRY LEADERS
Adams, Thomas (1846–1926)
Wrigley, Philip Knight

CHIEF JUSTICES OF THE SUPREME COURT. *See* Supreme Court Chief Justices

CHIEFS OF NAVAL OPERATIONS
Coontz, Robert Edward
Eberle, Edward Walter
Pratt, William Veazie
Sherman, Forrest Percival
Standley, William Harrison
Stark, Harold Raynsford

CHILD DEVELOPMENT EXPERTS
Arbuthnot, May Hill
Gruenberg, Sidonie Matsner

CHILDREN'S BOOK WRITERS AND ILLUSTRATORS
Abbott, Jacob
Adams, Harriet Stratemeyer
Adams, William Taylor
Alcott, Louisa May
Alger, Horatio, Jr.
Altsheler, Joseph Alexander
Andrews, Jane
Arnold, Elliott
Austin, Jane Goodwin
Baum, L. Frank
Baylor, Frances Courtenay
Bee, Clair Francis
Bemelmans, Ludwig
Benchley, Nathaniel
Bontemps, Arna Wendell
Bouvet, Marie Marguerite
Brooks, Noah
Brown, Abbie Farwell
Brown, Margaret Wise
Burgess, Thornton W.
Burnett, Frances Hodgson
Carruth, Hayden
Clarke, Rebecca Sophia
Cox, Palmer
DeJong, David Cornel
Dodge, Mary Elizabeth Mapes
Eggleston, George Cary
Ellis, Edward Sylvester
Ets, Marie Hall
Field, Rachel Lyman
Finley, Martha
Fisher, Dorothy F. Canfield
Gág, Wanda

CHILDREN'S BOOK WRITERS AND ILLUSTRATORS *(cont.)*
Garis, Howard Roger
Geisel, Theodor Seuss
Goodrich, Charles Augustus
Goodrich, Samuel Griswold
Goulding, Francis Robert
Hale, Lucretia Peabody
Hale, Susan
Harris, Joel Chandler
Henderson, Alice Corbin
Herrick, Sophia
Irwin, Inez
James, Will Roderick
Jamison, Cecilia Viets
Janvier, Margaret Thomson
Johnson, Crockett
Johnson, Osa
Judson, Emily Chubbuck
Kelland, Clarence Budington
Kelly, Myra
Kent, Jack
Krapp, George Philip
Lathbury, Mary Artemisia
Leaf, Munro
McGinley, Phyllis
McIntosh, Maria Jane
Miller, Olive Beaupré
Montgomery, Elizabeth Rider
Moore, Clara
Nash, Ogden
Newcomb, Harvey
O'Hara, Mary
Orton, Helen Fuller
Parish, Peggy
Parrish, Anne
Parrish, Maxfield
Patten, Gilbert
Perkins, Lucy Fitch
Porter, Eleanor Hodgman
Prentiss, Elizabeth Payson
Pyle, Howard
Rey, H. A.
Richards, Laura
Sargent, Epes
Sawyer, Ruth
Scarry, Richard McClure
Scudder, Horace Elisha
Selden, George
Stratemeyer, Edward
Tunis, John R.
Very, Lydia
Wells, Carolyn
White, E. B.
White, Eliza Orne
Wibberley, Leonard

CHILDREN'S BOOK WRITERS AND ILLUSTRATORS *(cont.)*
Widdemer, Margaret
Wilder, Laura Ingalls
Woolsey, Sarah Chauncy

CHILD WELFARE REFORMERS.
See Social Reformers

CHIROPRACTORS
Palmer, Bartlett Joshua
Palmer, Daniel David

CHORAL DIRECTORS
Childers, Lulu Vere
Gilchrist, William Wallace
Hughes, Revella
Ives, George
Johnson, Hall
Lang, Benjamin Johnson
Luboff, Norman
Ritter, Frédéric Louis
Schreiber, Frederick
Tuckey, William
Waring, Fred

CHOREOGRAPHERS AND DANCE DIRECTORS
Ailey, Alvin
Albertieri, Luigi
Allan, Maud
Astaire, Fred
Balanchine, George
Beatty, Talley
Belcher, Ernest
Bennett, Michael
Berkeley, Busby
Bolm, Adolph
Borde, Percival
Bradley, Buddy
Camryn, Walter
Champion, Gower
Christensen, Lew
Cole, Jack
Costa, David
Dafora, Asadata
de Mille, Agnes
Dollar, William
Douvillier, Suzanne
Durang, John
Field, Ron
Fokine, Michel
Fort, Syvilla
Fosse, Bob
Fuller, Loie
Gould, Norma

CIVIL RIGHTS ACTIVISTS *(cont.)*
Remond, Charles Lenox
Rickard, Clinton
Robeson, Paul
Robinson, Ruby Doris Smith
Rosenberg, Anna Marie Lederer
Rustin, Bayard
Sanchez, George Isidore
Simmons, William James
Smith, Lucy Harth
Sparer, Edward V.
Spingarn, Arthur Barnett
Spottswood, Stephen Gill
Stanley, Sara G.
Stewart, Maria W.
Terrell, Mary Eliza Church
Tilly, Dorothy Eugenia Rogers
Tobias, Channing Heggie
Tourgée, Albion Winegar
Trotter, William Monroe
Tucker, Samuel Wilbert
Tureaud, Alexander Pierre
Turner, James Milton
Turner, Thomas Wyatt
Walden, Austin Thomas
Walling, William English
Waring, Julius Waties
Washington, Booker T.
Wells-Barnett, Ida Bell
Whipple, Henry Benjamin
White, Walter Francis
Wilkins, Roy
Williams, Aubrey Willis
Willkie, Wendell Lewis
Wilson, J. Finley
Winnemucca, Sarah
Wright, Louis Tompkins
Wright, Muriel Hazel
Young, Whitney Moore, Jr.
Zuber, Paul Burgess

CIVIL SERVANTS
Bulfinch, Charles
Clague, Ewan
Greenhow, Robert
McCarthy, Charles
O'Connor, William Douglas
Thornton, William
Tolley, Howard Ross

CIVIL SERVICE REFORMERS
Bonaparte, Charles Joseph
Wheeler, Everett Pepperrell

CIVIL WAR MILITARY OFFICERS.
See Confederate Army Officers;
Confederate Naval Officers; Union
Army Officers; Union Naval
Officers

CLARINETISTS
Bailey, Buster
Baquet, Achille
Baquet, George
Bechet, Sidney
Bigard, Barney
Burbank, Albert
Caceres, Ernie
Dodds, Johnny
Dorsey, Jimmy
Fazola, Irving
Goodman, Benny
Hall, Edmond Blainey
Herman, Woody
Jenkins, Edmund Thornton
Lewis, George
Lewis, Ted
Mezzrow, Mezz
Nicholas, Albert
Noone, Jimmie
Parenti, Tony
Picou, Alphonse
Procope, Russell
Robinson, Prince
Scott, Cecil
Sedric, Gene
Shields, Larry
Simeon, Omer
Tio, Lorenzo, Jr.

CLASSICISTS. *See also* Philologists
Anthon, Charles
Bonner, Campbell
Bonner, Robert Johnson
Bundy, Elroy Lorraine
Calhoun, George Miller
Capps, Edward
Carter, Jesse Benedict
Cherniss, Harold Fredrik
Edelstein, Ludwig
Felton, Cornelius Conway
Fränkel, Hermann Ferdinand
Friedländer, Paul
Gildersleeve, Basil Lanneau
Goodwin, William Watson
Hadas, Moses
Hamilton, Edith
Highet, Gilbert
Jaeger, Werner Wilhelm
Johnson, Allan Chester

CLASSICISTS *(cont.)*
Kelsey, Francis Willey
Lattimore, Richmond A.
Lewis, Charlton Thomas
Linforth, Ivan Mortimer
Loeb, James
Macurdy, Grace Harriet
Meritt, Benjamin Dean
Morgan, Morris Hicky
Nock, Arthur Darby
Oldfather, William Abbott
Parry, Milman
Pease, Arthur Stanley
Peck, Harry Thurston
Perry, Ben Edwin
Platner, Samuel Ball
Rand, Edward Kennard
Shorey, Paul
Short, Charles
Smith, Kirby Flower
Smyth, Herbert Weir
Sophocles, Evangelinus
    Apostolides
Tarbell, Frank Bigelow
Turyn, Alexander
Wheeler, Arthur Leslie
White, John Williams

CLEANING AIDS
MANUFACTURERS. *See also*
    Housewares and Household
    Appliance Manufacturers
Colgate, William
Fels, Joseph
Fels, Samuel Simeon
Fuller, Alfred Carl
Procter, William Cooper

CLERGY. *See* Anglican Clergy;
    Baptist Clergy; Congregational
    Clergy; Disciples of Christ Clergy;
    German Reformed Clergy; Jewish
    Clergy; Lutheran Clergy;
    Methodist Episcopal Clergy;
    Military Chaplains; Missionaries;
    Moravian Clergy; Presbyterian
    Clergy; Roman Catholic Clergy;
    Unitarian Clergy; *and other specific
    terms*

CLOCKMAKERS. *See also*
    Watchmakers
Bond, William Cranch
Thomas, Seth

CONFEDERATE LEGISLATORS AND GOVERNMENT OFFICIALS *(cont.)*

Randolph, George Wythe
Reagan, John Henninger
Seddon, James Alexander
Slidell, John
Staples, Waller Redd
Toombs, Robert Augustus
Trenholm, George Alfred
Vest, George Graham
Walker, Leroy Pope
Watson, John William Clark
Watts, Thomas Hill
Wigfall, Louis Trezevant
Yancey, William Lowndes

CONFEDERATE NAVAL OFFICERS

Brooke, John Mercer
Buchanan, Franklin
Jones, Catesby ap Roger
Kell, John McIntosh
Maffitt, John Newland
  (1819–1886)
Maury, Matthew Fontaine
Page, Thomas Jefferson
Parker, William Harwar
Semmes, Raphael
Tattnall, Josiah
Tucker, John Randolph
  (1812–1883)
Waddell, James Iredell
Wilkinson, John
Wood, John Taylor

CONGREGATIONAL CLERGY

Abbott, Lyman
Adams, John (1705–1740)
Alden, Timothy
Alvord, John Watson
Atwater, Lyman Hotchkiss
Austin, David
Bacon, Leonard, Sr.
Bacon, Leonard Woolsey
Baldwin, John Denison
Barnard, John
Bartlett, Samuel Colcord
Barton, James Levi
Beecher, Edward
Beecher, Henry Ward
Beecher, Lyman
Belknap, Jeremy
Bellamy, Joseph
Beman, Amos Gerry
Blackwell, Antoinette Louisa
  Brown
Bradford, Amory Howe

CONGREGATIONAL CLERGY *(cont.)*

Bradford, Ebenezer
Brattle, William
Brown, Charles Reynolds
Bulkeley, Gershom
Bulkeley, Gershom
Burton, Asa
Bushnell, Horace
Byles, Mather
Cardozo, Francis Louis
Chauncy, Charles (1705–1787)
Cheever, George Barrell
Clark, Francis E.
Colman, Benjamin
Cook, Russell Salmon
Cooper, Samuel (1725–1783)
Croswell, Andrew
Cutler, Manasseh
Davenport, John
Davis, Jerome Dean
Deane, Samuel
DeBerry, William Nelson
Dewey, Chester
Douglass, Harlan Paul
Dow, Daniel
Dwight, Louis
Dwight, Sereno Edwards
Dwight, William Theodore
Eastman, Annis
Eastman, William Reed
Edwards, Bela Bates
Edwards, Jonathan
Edwards, Jonathan, Jr.
Eliot, Jared
Emerson, Joseph
Emmons, Nathanael
Everett, Robert
Faulkner, William John
Flint, Timothy
Foxcroft, Thomas
Gay, Ebenezer
Gladden, Washington
Goodrich, Charles Augustus
Goodrich, Chauncey Allen
Goodrich, Elizur (1734–1797)
Gordon, George Angier
Green, Beriah
Griffis, William Elliot
Grinnell, Josiah Bushnell
Gunsaulus, Frank Wakeley
Haynes, Lemuel
Hemmenway, Moses
Hillis, Newell Dwight
Horton, Douglas
Hume, Robert Allen
Humphrey, Heman

CONGREGATIONAL CLERGY *(cont.)*

Hyde, William DeWitt
Kirk, Edward Norris
Langdon, Samuel
Lovejoy, Owen
Lyman, Mary Redington Ely
Magoun, George Frederic
Mather, Samuel (1706–1785)
Mayhew, Jonathan
McCulloch, Oscar Carleton
McKeen, Joseph
Moore, Zephaniah Swift
Morril, David Lawrence
Morse, Jedidiah
Moxom, Philip Stafford
Munger, Theodore Thornton
Nettleton, Asahel
Newcomb, Harvey
Ockenga, Harold John
Peet, Stephen Denison
Peloubet, Francis Nathan
Pennington, James William
  Charles
Phelps, Austin
Phillips, Channing E.
Pond, Enoch
Porter, Noah
Prince, Thomas
Proctor, Henry Hugh
Reed, Myron Winslow
Rogers, Daniel
Rogers, John Almanza Rowley
Saltonstall, Gurdon
Sanders, Daniel Clarke
Scofield, Cyrus Ingerson
Seccomb, John
Seccombe, Joseph
Sheldon, Charles Monroe
Smyth, Newman
Sperry, Willard Learoyd
Sprague, William Buell
Steiner, Edward Alfred
Stiles, Ezra
Stoddard, Solomon
Strong, Josiah
Sturtevant, Julian Monson
Taylor, Graham
Tennent, William, III
Thacher, Peter
Thacher, Thomas
Torrey, Reuben Archer
Tracy, Joseph Carter
Trumbull, Benjamin
Tufts, John
Tyler, Bennet
Walker, Timothy (1705–1782)

DENDROCHRONOLOGIST

Douglass, Andrew Ellicott

DENTISTS

Barber, Jesse Max
Bayne, Thomas
Delany, Annie Elizabeth
Evans, Thomas Wiltberger
Flagg, Josiah Foster
Freeman, Robert Tanner
Garretson, James Edmund
Greenwood, John
Harris, Chapin Aaron
Howe, Percy Rogers
Keep, Nathan Cooley
Kingsley, Norman William
McQuillen, John Hugh
Miller, Willoughby Dayton
Morton, William Thomas Green
Parmly, Eleazar
Taylor, Lucy Beaman Hobbs
Wells, Horace

DEPARTMENT STORE OWNERS

Altman, Benjamin
Avery, Sewell Lee
Bamberger, Louis
Filene, Edward Albert
Gimbel, Bernard Feustman
Hoving, Walter
Kaufmann, Edgar Jonas, Sr.
Kirstein, Louis Edward
Lubin, David
May, Morton Jay
Nelson, Donald Marr
Shedd, John Graves
Straus, Isidor
Straus, Jesse Isidor
Wanamaker, John
Wanamaker, Rodman
Whalen, Grover

DERMATOLOGISTS

Duhring, Louis Adolphus
Hyde, James Nevins
Morrow, Prince Albert
Pusey, William Allen
Schamberg, Jay Frank
White, James Clarke

DESERTERS. *See* Military Deserters

DESIGNERS. *See* Architects; Book
Designers; Costume Designers;
Fashion Designers; *and other*
specific terms

DESPERADOES. *See* Outlaws

DETECTIVES

Burns, William John
Horn, Tom
Hume, James B.
Means, Gaston Bullock
Pinkerton, Allan
Ruditsky, Barney
Siringo, Charles Angelo

DIARISTS

Andrews, Eliza Frances
Ballard, Martha Moore
Bentley, William
Breen, Patrick
Bridge, Horatio
Browder, George Richard
Burr, Esther Edwards
Carter, Landon
Chesnut, Mary Boykin Miller
Delano, Amasa
Doten, Alfred
Drinker, Elizabeth
Emerson, Mary Moody
Ferguson, Elizabeth Graeme
Fields, Annie Adams
Green, Ely
Grimké, Charlotte Forten
Harmon, Daniel Williams
Heaton, Hannah Cook
Hone, Philip
James, Alice
Johnson, William (1809–1851)
Jones, John Beauchamp
Knight, Sarah Kemble
Langford, Nathaniel Pitt
Larpenteur, Charles
Maclay, William
Manly, William Lewis
Marshall, Christopher
Mencken, H. L.
Merton, Thomas
Miller, David Hunter
Moran, Benjamin
Newcomb, Charles King
Nin, Anaïs
Ramsay, Martha Laurens
Robinson, Harriet
Sewall, Samuel
Smith, Elihu Hubbard
Smith, Richard
Strong, George Templeton
Thoreau, Henry David
Welles, Gideon
Wister, Sarah

DIME STORE OWNERS. *See* Variety
Store Owners

DIPLOMATS. *See also* Secretaries of
State; State Department Officials

Adams, Charles
Adams, Charles Francis
(1807–1886)
Adams, John (1735–1826)
Adee, Alvey Augustus
Allen, Elisha Hunt
Allen, George Venable
Allison, John Moore
Alvarez, Manuel
Anderson, Larz
Anderson, Richard Clough, Jr.
Andrews, Israel DeWolf
Angell, James Burrill
Armour, Norman
Austin, Warren Robinson
Bacon, Robert
Baker, Jehu
Bancroft, George
Barclay, Thomas
Barlow, Joel
Barnard, Daniel Dewey
Barrett, John
Barringer, Daniel Moreau
Bayard, Richard Henry
Bayard, Thomas Francis
Biddle, Anthony Joseph
Drexel, Jr.
Bigelow, John
Bingham, Robert Worth
Bliss, Tasker Howard
Blount, James Henderson
Blue Jacket
Bohlen, Charles Eustis
Boker, George Henry
Borland, Solon
Bowdoin, James (1752–1811)
Bowers, Claude Gernade
Bowles, Chester Bliss
Bragg, Edward Stuyvesant
Breckinridge, Clifton Rodes
Brewster, Kingman, Jr.
Briggs, Ellis Ormsbee
Bristol, Mark Lambert
Broadhead, James Overton
Brodhead, John Romeyn
Brown, Ethan Allen
Brown, James
Bruce, David Kirkpatrick Este
Bullitt, William Christian
Bunche, Ralph Johnson
Bunker, Ellsworth

DRAMATISTS *(cont.)*

Kennedy, Charles Rann
Klein, Charles
Kober, Arthur
Kummer, Clare
Langner, Lawrence
Lawson, James
Lawson, John Howard
Leonard, William Ellery
Lerner, Alan Jay
Lewis, Estelle
Lindsay, Howard
Logan, C. A.
Logan, Joshua
Long, John Luther
Luce, Clare Boothe
Ludlam, Charles
MacArthur, Charles
MacKaye, Hazel
MacKaye, Percy
MacKaye, Steele
MacLeish, Archibald
Mann, Klaus
Mann, Louis
Manners, John Hartley
Markoe, Peter
Marqués, René
Mathews, Cornelius
Mayo, Frank
Mayo, Margaret
McCord, Louisa
McCullers, Carson
Megrue, Roi Cooper
Miller, Alice Duer
Mitchell, Langdon Elwyn
Mitchell, Thomas
Moeller, Philip
Moody, William Vaughn
Morton, Martha
Munford, Robert, III
Muse, Clarence E.
Nichols, Anne
Noah, Mordecai Manuel
Nugent, Elliott
Odets, Clifford
O'Neill, Eugene
Osborn, Paul
Payne, John Howard
Peabody, Josephine Preston
Perelman, S. J.
Pollock, Channing
Porter, Charlotte
Potter, Paul Meredith
Raphaelson, Samson
Rice, Elmer
Riley, Alice

DRAMATISTS *(cont.)*

Rinehart, Mary Roberts
Rives, Amélie
Robinson, Harriet
Sackler, Howard Oliver
Saroyan, William
Sawyer, Lemuel, Jr.
Séjour, Victor
Sexton, Anne
Shaw, Irwin
Sheldon, Edward Brewster
Sherwood, Robert Emmet
Skinner, Cornelia Otis
Sklar, George
Smith, Betty
Smith, Elihu Hubbard
Smith, Richard Penn
Smith, William Henry
   (1806–1872)
Smith, Winchell
Spewack, Samuel, and
   Bella Spewack
Stallings, Laurence Tucker
Stone, John Augustus
Strong, Austin
Sturges, Preston
Tarkington, Booth
Taylor, Charles Alonzo
Teichmann, Howard
Thompson, Denman
Thompson, Eloise
Thurman, Wallace
Totheroh, Dan
Treadwell, Sophie
Tyler, Royall
Van Druten, John
Veiller, Bayard
Wallack, Lester
Walter, Eugene
Ward, Theodore James
Wexley, John
Wheeler, Hugh Callingham
Wilder, Thornton
Williams, Jesse Lynch
Williams, Tennessee
Wilson, Harry Leon
Woodworth, Samuel
Young, Rida Johnson
Young, Stark

DRESS REFORMERS

Austin, Harriet N.
Bloomer, Amelia Jenks
Hasbrouck, Lydia Sayer

DRUGGISTS. *See* Pharmacists

DRUGSTORE OWNERS

Liggett, Louis Kroh
Walgreen, Charles Rudolph

DRUMMERS. *See* Percussionists

DRY CLEANING BUSINESS EXECUTIVE

Burrell, Berkeley Graham

DUELISTS

Allen, Henry Watkins
Arnold, Benedict
Austin, William
Barron, James
Bennett, James Gordon
   (1841–1918)
Benton, Thomas Hart (1782–1858)
Broderick, David Colbert
Brooks, Preston Smith
Brown, Benjamin Gratz
Burk, John Daly
Burr, Aaron (1756–1836)
Cadwalader, John
Campbell, George Washington
Carey, Matthew
Carroll, William
Claiborne, William Charles Coles
Clark, Daniel (1766–1813)
Clark, John
Clay, Cassius Marcellus
Clay, Henry
Clingman, Thomas Lanier
Conway, Thomas
Crawford, William Harris
Daniel, Peter Vivian
Davis, Jefferson
Decatur, Stephen (1779–1820)
Denver, James William
Dudley, Benjamin Winslow
Flagg, Edmund
Foote, Henry Stuart
Garreau, Armand
Gates, Horatio
Gibbons, Thomas
Gist, William Henry
Goodman, Joseph Thompson
Gwinnett, Button
Hamilton, Alexander
   (1757?–1804)
Hamilton, James, Jr.
Hemphill, John
Hope, James Barron
Hughes, Robert William
Jackson, Andrew
Jackson, James (1757–1806)

DUELISTS *(cont.)*
Jackson, John George
Johnston, Albert Sidney
Laurens, Henry
Laurens, John
Lee, Charles (1731–1782)
Lee, Samuel Phillips
Leggett, William
Levy, Uriah Phillips
Livingston, Henry Brockholst
Marigny, Bernard
Marshall, Humphrey
Maverick, Samuel Augustus
McDuffie, George
McIntosh, Lachlan
Mitchell, David Brydie
Moore, Gabriel
Morgan, John Hunt
Nolte, Vincent Otto
Otero, Miguel Antonio
Pattison, Granville Sharp
Perry, Benjamin Franklin
Perry, Oliver Hazard
Pierce, Benjamin
Pike, Albert
Placide, Alexandre
Pleasants, John Hampden
Porter, Andrew
Porter, Peter Buell
Potter, Robert
Pryor, Roger Atkinson
Rowan, John
Slidell, John
Smyth, Alexander
Soulé, Pierre
Stanly, Edward
Tattnall, Josiah
Temple, John
Terry, David Smith
Van Rensselaer, Solomon
Waddell, James Iredell
Walker, William
Webb, James Watson
Wigfall, Louis Trezevant
Wilkinson, James
Wise, Henry Alexander
Wise, John Sergeant
Yancey, William Lowndes

DUTCH REFORMED CLERGY

Berg, Joseph Frederic
Bertholf, Guiliam
Bogardus, Everardus
Corwin, Edward Tanjore
Freeman, Bernardus

DUTCH REFORMED CLERGY *(cont.)*
Frelinghuysen, Theodorus
Jacobus
Griffis, William Elliot
Hardenbergh, Jacob Rutsen
Krol, Bastiaen Janszen
Livingston, John Henry
Megapolensis, Johannes
Michaelius, Jonas
Milledoler, Philip
Seelye, Julius Hawley
Selijns, Henricus
Talmage, Thomas De Witt
Van Raalte, Albertus Christiaan
Van Rensselaer, Nicholas
Verbryck, Samuel

EARLY CHILDHOOD EDUCATORS.

See also Child Development
Experts
Andrews, Jane
Arbuthnot, May Hill
Blaker, Eliza Ann Cooper
Bradley, Milton
Bryan, Anna E.
Cooke, Flora Juliette
Cooper, Sarah Brown Ingersoll
Dobbs, Ella Victoria
Fisher, Dorothy F. Canfield
Fuller, Sarah
Garrett, Mary Smith
Harrison, Elizabeth
Hill, Patty Smith
Huntington, Emily
Locke, Bessie
Marwedel, Emma
Mitchell, Lucy Sprague
Moten, Lucy Ellen
Neef, Francis Joseph Nicholas
Putnam, Alice Harvey Whiting
Schurz, Margarethe Meyer
Sharp, Zerna Addas
Ueland, Clara Hampson
Wheelock, Lucy
White, Edna Noble

EARTH SCIENTISTS. *See*

Geographers; Geologists;
Geophysicists; Meteorologists;
Oceanographers; Soil Scientists;
and other specific terms

EAST ASIAN STUDIES SCHOLARS

Fenollosa, Ernest
Holt, Claire
Jones, George Heber

EAST ASIAN STUDIES SCHOLARS
(cont.)
Lattimore, Owen
Morse, Edward Sylvester
Reischauer, Edwin Oldfather
Rockhill, William Woodville
Wright, Mary Clabaugh

ECCENTRICS

Andrews, Stephen Pearl
Brooke, Abraham
Calamity Jane
Fort, Charles Hoy
Grace, Charles Emmanuel
Green, Hetty
Jumel, Eliza Bowen
Pratt, Daniel (1809–1887)
Scott, Walter Edward
Williams, Eleazar

ECLECTIC PHYSICIANS

Beach, Wooster
Foote, Edward Bliss
King, John
Newton, Robert Safford
Scudder, John Milton

ECOLOGISTS. *See also*

Conservationists; Environ-
mentalists; Paleoecologists
Abbey, Edward
Allee, Warder Clyde
Cain, Stanley Adair
Carson, Rachel
Clausen, Jens Christen
Clements, Frederic Edward
Cowles, Henry Chandler
Forbes, Stephen Alfred
MacArthur, Robert Helmer
Morgan, Ann Haven
Sears, Paul Bigelow
Shelford, Victor Ernest
Vogt, William
Whittaker, Robert Harding

ECONOMIC REFORMERS

Baird, Henry Carey
Fels, Joseph
Harvey, Coin
Macune, Charles William
Warbasse, James Peter

ECONOMISTS. *See also* Economic

Reformers; Statisticians
Alexander, Sadie Tanner Mossell
Anderson, Benjamin McAlester

ENTREPRENEURS *(cont.)*
Saunders, Clarence
Savage, Edward
Savage, Henry Wilson
Scherman, Harry
Schultz, Dutch
Schuster, Max Lincoln
Smith, Francis Marion
Smith, Peter (1768–1837)
Smith, Venture
Sperry, Elmer Ambrose
Spotswood, Alexander
Sprague, Frank Julian
Sprunt, James
Stearns, Abel
Still, William
Stockton, Robert Field
Stratemeyer, Edward
Tabor, Horace Austin Warner
Tandy, Charles David
Tarascon, Louis Anastase
Thompson, J. Walter
Thompson, Lydia
Thompson, William Boyce
Torrence, Joseph Thatcher
Touro, Judah
Vann, Joseph
Vassall, John
Walker, C. J.
Walker, David (1796?–1830)
Walker, John Brisben
Walton, Samuel Moore
Wang, An
Ward, Henry Augustus
Washburn, Frank Sherman
Watson, Thomas Augustus
Wheelwright, William
Whipper, William
White, Eartha Mary Magdalene
White, Maunsel
Wilburn, Virgil Doyle
Worthington, Thomas
Yerkes, Charles Tyson

ENVIRONMENTALISTS. *See also*
Conservationists; Demographers;
Ecologists
Adams, Ansel
Douglas, William O.
Emerson, George Barrell
Fuller, R. Buckminster
Marsh, George Perkins
Marshall, Robert
Owings, Nathaniel Alexander

EPIDEMIOLOGISTS
Carter, Henry Rose
Chapin, Charles Value
Francis, Thomas, Jr.
Frost, Wade Hampton
Langmuir, Alexander Duncan
Lining, John
Lumsden, Leslie Leon
Paul, John Rodman
Potter, Nathaniel
Rosenau, Milton Joseph
South, Lillian Herreld

EPIGRAPHISTS
Gordon, Arthur Ernest
Morley, Sylvanus Griswold

EPISCOPALIAN BISHOPS
Brent, Charles Henry
Brooks, Phillips
Brownell, Thomas Church
Chase, Philander
Cheney, Charles Edward
Clark, Thomas March
Cobbs, Nicholas Hamner
Coxe, Arthur Cleveland
Cummins, George David
Doane, George Washington
Doane, William Croswell
Gailor, Thomas Frank
Grafton, Charles Chapman
Greer, David Hummel
Griswold, Alexander Viets
Hale, Charles Reuben
Hare, William Hobart
Hobart, John Henry
Holly, James Theodore
Hopkins, John Henry
Huntington, Frederic Dan
Ives, Levi Silliman
Kemper, Jackson
Kip, William Ingraham
Lawrence, William (1850–1941)
Madison, James (1749–1812)
Manning, William Thomas
McIlvaine, Charles Pettit
McVickar, William Neilson
Meade, William
Moore, Richard Channing
Nash, Norman Burdett
Onderdonk, Benjamin Tredwell
Onderdonk, Henry Ustick
Otey, James Hervey
Perry, William Stevens
Polk, Leonidas
Potter, Henry Codman

EPISCOPALIAN BISHOPS *(cont.)*
Provoost, Samuel
Quintard, Charles Todd
Ravenscroft, John Stark
Rowe, Peter Trimble
Satterlee, Henry Yates
Schereschewsky, Samuel
Seabury, Samuel (1729–1796)
Slattery, Charles Lewis
Smith, Robert (1732–1801)
Spalding, Franklin Spencer
Talbot, Ethelbert
Tuttle, Daniel Sylvester
Wainwright, Jonathan Mayhew
Whipple, Henry Benjamin
White, William
Williams, Channing Moore
Williams, Charles David
Wilmer, Richard Hooker

EPISCOPALIAN CLERGY. *See also*
Anglican Clergy
Allen, Alexander Viets Griswold
Auchmuty, Samuel
Blake, John Lauris
Bliss, William Dwight Porter
Brady, Cyrus Townsend
Bragg, George Freeman, Jr.
Breck, James Lloyd
Brooks, Phillips
Capers, Ellison
Cheney, Charles Edward
Coit, Henry Augustus
Colton, Calvin
Crapsey, Algernon Sidney
Crummell, Alexander
Curtis, Moses Ashley
Cutler, Timothy
De Koven, James
Dix, Morgan
Ewer, Ferdinand Cartwright
Ferris, Theodore Parker
Gallaudet, Thomas
Gavin, Frank Stanton Burns
Grant, Percy Stickney
Hare, George Emlen
Henry, Caleb Sprague
Hodges, George
Houghton, George Hendric
Huntington, William Reed
Ingraham, Joseph Holt
Jarratt, Devereux
Jones, Absalom
Jones, Edward
Langdon, William Chauncy
Lowell, Robert Traill Spence

FASHION DESIGNERS *(cont.)*
Ellis, Perry
Halston
Hawes, Elizabeth
Klein, Anne
Miller, Elizabeth Smith
Rosenstein, Nettie

FASHION INDUSTRY LEADERS. *See*
Clothing Industry Leaders

FASHION MAGAZINE EDITORS
Blackwell, Betsy Talbot
Chase, Edna Woolman
Long, Lois
Sheppard, Eugenia
Vreeland, Diana

FAST-FOOD BUSINESS LEADERS
Ingram, Edgar Waldo
Kroc, Ray
Sanders, Harland David

FEDERAL GOVERNMENT
OFFICIALS. *See also* Commissioners
and Superintendents of Indian
Affairs; Confederate Legislators
and Government Officials;
Diplomats; Municipal Government
Officials; State Government
Officials; *and other specific terms*
Abbott, Grace
Albright, Horace Marden
Alexander, Will Winton
Altmeyer, Arthur Joseph
Anderson, Joseph Inslee
Anderson, Mary (1872–1964)
Anslinger, Harry Jacob
Arnold, Thurman
Austin, Jonathan Loring
Ballantine, Arthur Atwood
Barnes, Julius Howland
Bennett, Henry Garland
Bennett, James Van Benschoten
Beyer, Clara Mortenson
Bissell, Richard Mervin, Jr.
Bradley, Abraham, Jr.
Brown, Walter Folger
Bullard, Arthur
Bundy, Harvey Hollister
Burgess, George Kimball
Burns, Arthur Frank
Cahill, Holger
Caldwell, Captain Billy
Calhoun, John

FEDERAL GOVERNMENT OFFICIALS
(cont.)
Caminetti, Anthony
Campbell, Walter Gilbert
Cary, William Lucius
Casey, William Joseph
Clinch, Charles Powell
Corcoran, Thomas Gardiner
Cotton, Joseph Potter
Creel, George Edward
Crèvecoeur, J. Hector St. John de
Daniels, Jonathan
Dean, Gordon Evans
Dennett, Tyler Wilbur
Dickinson, John (1894–1952)
Dodge, Joseph Morrell
Donovan, William Joseph
Douglas, Lewis William
Douglas, William O.
Du Bois, William Ewing
Eastman, Joseph Bartlett
Eccles, Marriner Stoddard
Edwards, Corwin D.
Eisenhower, Milton Stover
Elliott, Harriet Wiseman
Esch, John Jacob
Ewbank, Thomas
Ewing, Oscar Ross
Flagg, Edmund
Flint, Weston
Fly, James Lawrence
Ford, Guy Stanton
Fox, Gustavus Vasa
Frank, Jerome New
Gabrielson, Ira Noel
Gallagher, William Davis
Gardener, Helen Hamilton
Goldenweiser, Emanuel A.
Goodrich, Carter
Grant, Frederick Dent
Haas, Francis Joseph
Hanks, Nancy
Harding, William Proctor Gould
Harriman, W. Averell
Haworth, Leland John
Henderson, Leon
Hennock, Frieda Barkin
Henshaw, Henry Wetherbee
Hershey, Lewis Blaine
Hoey, Jane Margueretta
Hoffman, Paul Gray
Hopkins, Harry Lloyd
Howard, Oliver Otis
Hunt, Henry Alexander, Jr.
Hurley, Edward Nash

FEDERAL GOVERNMENT OFFICIALS
(cont.)
Jackson, Hartley Harrad
  Thompson
Johnson, Hugh Samuel
Jones, Jesse Holman
Judd, Gerrit Parmele
Kennedy, Joseph Patrick
Keyserling, Leon
King, Clarence Rivers
Kirlin, Florence Katharine
Knox, John Jay
Landis, James McCauley
Lane, Franklin Knight
Lawrence, David Leo
Lewis, George William
Lilienthal, David Eli
Lubin, Isador
MacDonald, Thomas Harris
Macy, John Williams, Jr.
Malone, Dudley Field
Maverick, Maury
McCabe, Thomas Bayard
McCone, John A.
McDill, James Wilson
Mead, Elwood
Mendenhall, Walter Curran
Merriam, Clinton Hart
Merriam, William Rush
Meyer, Eugene Isaac
Miller, James
Moore, John Bassett
Morgan, Arthur Ernest
Morrison, William Ralls
Murray, Thomas Edward
Myer, Albert James
Myer, Dillon Seymour
Nash, Philleo
Nelson, Donald Marr
Nelson, Edward William
Niles, David K.
Ohly, John Hallowell
Olds, Leland
Oliphant, Herman
Page, Charles Grafton
Page, Logan Waller
Patterson, Hannah Jane
Paulding, James Kirke
Peek, George Nelson
Pilling, James Constantine
Pope, Nathaniel
Post, Louis Freeland
Price, Byron
Prouty, Charles Azro
Raum, Green Berry
Rhees, William Jones

FICTION WRITERS *(cont.)*

Cahill, Holger
Cain, James M.
Caldwell, Erskine
Caldwell, Taylor
Calkins, Clinch
Calvert, George Henry
Campbell, Walter Stanley
Cannon, Charles James
Cannon, Cornelia James
Cantwell, Robert Emmett
Capote, Truman
Carr, John Dickson
Carrington, Elaine Sterne
Caruthers, William Alexander
Carver, Raymond
Cary, Alice
Caspary, Vera
Cather, Willa
Catherwood, Mary Hartwell
Chambers, Robert William
Chandler, Raymond
Chase, Ilka
Chase, Mary Ellen
Chateaubriand, François-René de
Cheever, John
Chesebrough, Caroline
Chesnutt, Charles Waddell
Chester, George Randolph
Chopin, Kate O'Flaherty
Churchill, Winston
Chute, Beatrice Joy
Clark, Walter Van Tilburg
Clavell, James
Clemens, Jeremiah
Coates, Robert Myron
Cobb, Irvin Shrewsbury
Cobb, Sylvanus, Jr.
Coffin, Charles Carleton
Cohen, Octavus Roy
Collens, Thomas Wharton
Collinge, Patricia
Comfort, Will Levington
Connell, Richard
Conroy, Jack
Cook, George Cram
Cooke, John Esten (1830–1886)
Cooke, Philip Pendleton
Cooke, Rose Terry
Coolidge, Dane
Cooper, James Fenimore
Corle, Edwin
Corrington, John William
Costain, Thomas Bertram
Cozzens, Frederick Swartwout
Cozzens, James Gould

FICTION WRITERS *(cont.)*

Crane, Anne Moncure
Crane, Stephen
Crawford, F. Marion
Cummins, Maria Susanna
Curtis, George William
Curwood, James Oliver
Cutler, Lizzie Petit
Daggett, Rollin Mallory
Dahlberg, Edward
Dana, Richard Henry, Jr.
Dannay, Frederic
Dargan, Olive Tilford
Davis, Clyde Brion
Davis, Harold Lenoir
Davis, Mary Evelyn Moore
Davis, Rebecca Blaine Harding
Davis, Richard Harding
Davis, Samuel Post
Davis, William Stearns
De Forest, John William
DeJong, David Cornel
Deland, Margaret
De Leon, Thomas Cooper
Dell, Floyd James
Deming, Philander
Denison, Mary Andrews
Derleth, August William
Digges, Thomas Attwood
Donn-Byrne, Brian Oswald
    Patrick
Dorr, Julia
Dorsey, Anna Hanson McKenney
Dorsey, Sarah Anne Ellis
Dos Passos, John
Douglas, Lloyd Cassel
Dreiser, Theodore
Dromgoole, Will Allen
Duganne, Augustine Joseph
    Hickey
Dunbar, Paul Laurence
Dupuy, Eliza Ann
Eastman, Mary Henderson
Eaton, Edith Maude
Edwards, Harry Stillwell
Eggleston, Edward
Eggleston, George Cary
Elder, Susan Blanchard
Eliade, Mircea
Ellin, Stanley Bernard
Elliott, George Paul
Elliott, Sarah Barnwell
Ellison, Ralph Waldo
Fante, John Thomas
Farrell, James Thomas
Faulkner, William

FICTION WRITERS *(cont.)*

Fauset, Jessie Redmon
Faust, Frederick Schiller
Fay, Theodore Sedgwick
Fearing, Kenneth Flexner
Ferber, Edna
Fern, Fanny
Feuchtwanger, Lion
Finley, Martha
Finn, Francis James
Fisher, Dorothy F. Canfield
Fisher, Rudolph
Fisher, Vardis
Fitzgerald, F. Scott
Flagg, Edmund
Flavin, Martin Archer
Fletcher, Inglis
Foley, Martha
Foote, Mary Anna Hallock
Forbes, Esther
Ford, Paul Leicester
Forester, C. S.
Foster, Hannah Webster
Fox, John, Jr.
Frank, Waldo David
Franken, Rose Dorothy
Frederic, Harold
Freeman, Cynthia
Freeman, Mary Eleanor Wilkins
French, Alice
French, Lucy Virginia Smith
Fuller, Henry Blake
Gale, Zona
Gallico, Paul William
Galt, John
Gardner, Erle Stanley
Garland, Hamlin
Gerould, Katharine Fullerton
Gerson, Noel Bertram
Gibbs, Arthur Hamilton
Gilman, Caroline Howard
Gilman, Charlotte Perkins
Glasgow, Ellen
Glaspell, Susan Keating
Gold, Michael
Gonzales, Ambrose Elliott
Gordon, Caroline
Grant, Robert
Green, Anna Katharine
Green, Asa
Greene, Sarah Pratt McLean
Grey, Zane
Grierson, Francis
Griffin, John Howard
Griggs, Sutton E.
Guthrie, A. B., Jr.

FICTION WRITERS *(cont.)*

Haldeman-Julius, Emanuel
Hale, Edward Everett
Hale, Nancy
Haley, Alex
Hall, James (1793–1868)
Hamilton, Alexander (1712–1756)
Hammett, Dashiell
Hammett, Samuel Adams
Harben, William Nathaniel
Harland, Henry
Harper, Frances
Harris, Corra
Harris, Frank
Harris, Miriam Coles
Harrison, Constance Cary
Harrison, Henry Sydnor
Harte, Bret
Hatton, Ann
Hawthorne, Julian
Hawthorne, Nathaniel
Hayes, Alfred
Heard, Gerald
Heath, James Ewell
Hecht, Ben
Heggen, Thomas
Heinlein, Robert Anson
Hemingway, Ernest
Hentz, Caroline Lee Whiting
Herbert, F. Hugh
Herbert, Frank
Herbst, Josephine Frey
Hergesheimer, Joseph
Herrick, Robert Welch
Hersey, John Richard
Heyward, DuBose
Hill, Grace Livingston
Hillyer, Robert Silliman
Himes, Chester Bomar
Hobart, Alice Tisdale
Hobson, Laura Z.
Hoffman, Charles Fenno
Holley, Marietta
Holmes, Mary Jane Hawes
Hopkins, Pauline Elizabeth
Hornblow, Arthur, Sr.
Hosmer, Hezekiah Lord
Hough, Emerson
Howard, Blanche Willis
Howe, Edgar Watson
Howe, Helen
Howells, William Dean
Hoyer, Linda Grace
Hughes, Rupert
Huie, William Bradford
Hurst, Fannie

FICTION WRITERS *(cont.)*

Hurston, Zora Neale
Huxley, Aldous
Ingraham, Joseph Holt
Ingraham, Prentiss
Irving, Washington
Irwin, Inez
Isherwood, Christopher
Jackson, Helen Hunt
Jackson, Shirley
James, Henry (1843–1916)
Jamison, Cecilia Viets
Janney, Russell Dixon
Jessop, George H.
Jewett, Sarah Orne
Johnson, James Weldon
Johnson, Owen McMahon
Johnston, Mary
Johnston, Richard Malcolm
Jones, James
Jones, James Athearn
Jones, John Beauchamp
Jordan, Elizabeth Garver
Judd, Sylvester
Judson, Edward Zane Carroll
Judson, Emily Chubbuck
Kantor, MacKinlay
Kelland, Clarence Budington
Kelley, Edith Summers
Kelly, Florence Finch
Kemp, Harry Hibbard
Kennedy, John Pendleton
Kerouac, Jack
Kerr, Sophie
Keyes, Frances Parkinson
Killens, John Oliver
King, Edward Smith
King, Grace Elizabeth
King, Susan Petigru
Kinzie, Juliette Augusta Magill
Kirkland, Joseph
Kober, Arthur
Kosinski, Jerzy
Krause, Herbert Arthur
Kronenberger, Louis
Kyne, Peter Bernard
La Farge, Oliver
Lamb, Martha Joanna R. N.
L'Amour, Louis Dearborn
Lanusse, Armand
Larsen, Nella
Lathrop, Rose Hawthorne
Latimer, Elizabeth Wormeley
Latimer, Margery Bodine
Leech, Margaret Kernochan
Le Gallienne, Richard

FICTION WRITERS *(cont.)*

Lennox, Charlotte Ramsay
Lewis, Alfred Henry
Lewis, Sinclair
Lewisohn, Ludwig
Libbey, Laura Jean
Lincoln, Joseph Crosby
Lincoln, Victoria Endicott
Lin Yutang
Lippard, George
Little, Sophia Louisa Robbins
Lockridge, Richard
Lockridge, Ross Franklin, Jr.
London, Jack
Long, John Luther
Loos, Anita
Lovecraft, H. P.
Lumpkin, Grace
Lumpkin, Katharine Du Pre
Lunt, George
MacDonald, John D.
Macdonald, Ross
MacInnes, Helen
Maclean, Norman
Magruder, Julia
Major, Charles
Malamud, Bernard
Maltz, Albert
Mann, Klaus
Mann, Thomas
March, William
Marquand, J. P.
Marqués, René
Marquis, Don
Marshall, Catherine
Martineau, Harriet
Mason, F. Van Wyck
Mathews, Cornelius
Mayo, William Starbuck
McAlmon, Robert Menzies
McCarthy, Mary
McCoy, Horace Stanley
McCrackin, Josephine
McCullers, Carson
McCutcheon, George Barr
McElroy, John (1846–1929)
McHenry, James (1785–1845)
McIntosh, Maria Jane
McKay, Claude
McKenney, Ruth
Melville, Herman
Mercier, Alfred
Metalious, Grace
Micheaux, Oscar
Miller, Alice Duer
Miller, Henry (1891–1980)

HISTORIANS *(cont.)*
Wharton, Anne Hollingsworth
White, Leonard Dupee
White, Solomon
White, Theodore H.
Whitehill, Walter Muir, Jr.
Whitmore, William Henry
Wiley, Bell Irvin
Willard, Emma Hart
Willard, James Field
Williams, George Washington
Williams, Mary Wilhelmine
Williams, Thomas Harry
Williams, William Appleman
Winthrop, John (1588–1649)
Wolfson, Harry Austryn
Woodson, Carter Godwin
Wright, Mary Clabaugh
Wright, Muriel Hazel
Wroth, Lawrence Counselman

HISTORIANS OF RELIGIONS. *See*
History of Religions Scholars

HISTORIANS OF SCIENCE
Barker, Jeremiah
Bass, Mary Elizabeth
Bolton, Henry Carrington
Bronowski, Jacob
Cajori, Florian
Coolidge, Julian Lowell
Corner, George Washington
Cushing, Harvey Williams
Deutsch, Albert
Draper, John William
Edelstein, Ludwig
Edwards, Everett Eugene
Ewbank, Thomas
Flick, Lawrence Francis
Fulton, John Farquhar
Garrison, Fielding Hudson
Goode, George Brown
Handerson, Henry Ebenezer
Long, Esmond
Major, Ralph Hermon
Miller, William Snow
Nixon, Pat Ireland
Osler, William
Packard, Francis Randolph
Rosen, George
Sarton, George Alfred Léon
Shryock, Richard Harrison
Sigerist, Henry Ernest
Smith, David Eugene
Stone, Witmer
Thorndike, Lynn

HISTORIANS OF SCIENCE *(cont.)*
White, George Willard
Wilder, Raymond Louis
Williams, Stephen West

HISTORICAL EDITORS. *See*
Documentary Editors

HISTORIC PRESERVATIONISTS
Appleton, William Sumner
De Zavala, Adina Emily
du Pont, Henry Francis
Meem, John Gaw
Onassis, Jacqueline Kennedy

**HISTORY OF RELIGIONS
SCHOLARS.** *See also* Church
Historians; Religious Studies
Scholars
Adams, Hannah
Eliade, Mircea
Evans-Wentz, Walter Yeeling
Moore, George Foot
Nock, Arthur Darby
Smith, Henry Preserved
Wach, Joachim
Warren, William Fairfield

HOCKEY PLAYERS. *See* Ice Hockey
Players

HOLOCAUST SURVIVORS
Bettelheim, Bruno
Friedländer, Paul
Kadar, Jan

HOME ECONOMISTS
Atwater, Helen Woodard
Campbell, Helen Stuart
Morgan, Agnes Fay
Norton, Alice Peloubet
Parloa, Maria
Richards, Ellen Henrietta Swallow
Richardson, Anna Euretta
Roberts, Lydia Jane
Talbot, Marion
Terhune, Mary Virginia Hawes
Van Rensselaer, Martha
White, Edna Noble
Woolman, Mary Raphael Schenck

HOME MISSIONARIES. *See*
Missionaries

HOMEOPATHIC PHYSICIANS
Dunham, Carroll
Gram, Hans Burch
Guernsey, Egbert
Hale, Edwin Moses
Hempel, Charles Julius
Hering, Constantine
Kent, James Tyler
Leach, Robert Boyd
Merrick, Myra King
Talbot, Israel Tisdale
Wesselhoeft, Conrad

HORN PLAYERS
Jones, Thad
Rogers, Shorty
Sullivan, Maxine
Watkins, Julius

HORSE BREEDERS. *See* Racehorse
Breeders and Trainers

**HORSE-DRAWN VEHICLE
MANUFACTURERS**
Studebaker, Clement
Studebaker, John Mohler

HORSE TRADER
Nolan, Philip

HORTICULTURISTS. *See also*
Foresters; Landscape Architects;
Plant Collectors; Plant
Pathologists; Seedsmen
Bailey, Liberty Hyde
Blackstone, William
Burbank, Luther
Callaway, Cason Jewell
Downing, Andrew Jackson
du Pont, Henry Francis
Fairchild, David Grandison
Garey, Thomas Andrew
Hansen, Niels Ebbesen
Logan, Martha Daniell
Longworth, Nicholas (1782–1863)
Marshall, Humphry
McFarland, J. Horace
Prince, William
Pursh, Frederick
Waugh, Frank Albert

HOSPITAL ADMINISTRATORS. *See*
Public Health Officials

INDUSTRIALISTS *(cont.)*
  Straus, Roger Williams
  Symington, Stuart
  Takamine, Jokichi
  Talbott, Harold Elstner
  Thomson, Elihu
  Tompkins, Daniel Augustus
  Vanderbilt, William Henry
  Vauclain, Samuel Matthews
  Washburn, Cadwallader Colden
  Weeks, Sinclair
  Weston, Edward (1850–1936)
  Wharton, Joseph
  Widdicomb, John
  Wilson, Charles Edward
  Wilson, Joseph Chamberlain
  Woodruff, George Waldo

INDUSTRIAL MANAGEMENT EXPERTS. *See* Organization and Management Theorists

INDUSTRIAL RELATIONS EXPERTS
  Bass, Robert Perkins
  Kellor, Frances Alice
  Slichter, Sumner Huber
  Williams, John Elias

INFORMANTS. *See also* Spies
  Bentley, Elizabeth Terrill
  Cvetic, Matthew C.
  Massing, Hede Tune
  Richardson, Ebenezer
  Valachi, Joseph

INNKEEPERS. *See* Hotel Owners and Managers

INSECT PATHOLOGIST
  Steinhaus, Edward Arthur

INSPECTORS GENERAL
  Croghan, George (1791–1849)
  Steuben, Friedrich Wilhelm von

INSPIRATIONIST LEADERS
  Heinemann, Barbara
  Metz, Christian

INSTITUTIONAL FOUNDERS AND BENEFACTORS
  Baldwin, Abraham
  Baldwin, John
  Berry, Martha McChesney
  Blair, James

INSTITUTIONAL FOUNDERS AND BENEFACTORS *(cont.)*
  Bliss, Daniel
  Bliss, Lillie P.
  Bolton, Frances Payne
  Bradley, Amy Morris
  Bradley, Lydia Moss
  Burr, Aaron (1716–1757)
  Burroughs, Nannie Helen
  Butler, Marie Joseph
  Cataldo, Joseph Maria
  Chafer, Lewis Sperry
  Cornell, Ezra
  Corson, Juliet
  Crandall, Prudence
  Damrosch, Frank Heino
  Davidge, John Beale
  Dickey, Sarah Ann
  Dobbs, Ella Victoria
  Drumgoole, John Christopher
  Durant, Henry Fowle
  Evans, William Thomas
  Farmer, Fannie Merritt
  Fee, John Gregg
  Ferguson, Katy
  Fitton, James
  Flanagan, Edward Joseph
  Folger, Emily Jordan
  Freer, Charles Lang
  Fuld, Caroline Bamberger Frank
  Gallatin, Albert Eugene
  Gardner, Isabella Stewart
  Graham, Isabella
  Gregory, Samuel
  Guggenheim, Solomon Robert
  Harvard, John
  Huntington, Henry Edwards
  Jolas, Maria
  Jones, Bob
  Kander, Lizzie Black
  Kent, Aratus
  Lange, Mary Elizabeth
  L'Esperance, Elise Strang
  Livermore, George
  Lyon, Mary
  Mannes, David
  Mayo, William James, and Charles Horace Mayo
  McGroarty, Julia
  Menninger, Charles Frederick
  Merrick, Samuel Vaughan
  Minor, Benjamin Blake
  Morais, Sabato
  Morrison, Nathan Jackson
  Mossell, Nathan Francis
  Palmer, Lizzie Pitts Merrill

INSTITUTIONAL FOUNDERS AND BENEFACTORS *(cont.)*
  Parkhurst, Helen
  Parks, Oliver Lafayette
  Passavant, William Alfred
  Peale, Charles Willson
  Phillips, John
  Phillips, Samuel, Jr.
  Pierce, Sarah
  Porter, Sarah
  Rice, John Holt
  Rice, William Marsh
  Rogers, John Almanza Rowley
  Sage, Henry Williams
  Schofield, Martha
  Scudder, Ida Sophia
  Seelye, Laurenus Clark
  Seymour, Mary Foot
  Sill, Anna Peck
  Smith, Sophia
  Spreckels, Alma
  Starr, Ellen Gates
  Surette, Thomas Whitney
  Thurston, Matilda Smyrell Calder
  Tompkins, Sally Louisa
  Van Rensselaer, Stephen
  Vassar, Matthew
  Vincent, George Edgar
  Warren, Herbert Langford
  Watteville, Henrietta Benigna von
  Webb, Electra Havemeyer
  Wheelock, Lucy
  Whitney, Gertrude Vanderbilt
  Wilbur, Earl Morse
  Willard, Emma Hart
  Willey, Samuel Hopkins
  Williams, Walter
  Yale, Elihu
  Zimbalist, Mary Louise Curtis Bok

INSTRUMENTALISTS. *See* Accordionists; Banjoists; Cellists; Clarinetists; Fiddlers; Flutists; Guitarists; Harpsichordists; *and other specific terms*

INSURANCE INDUSTRY LEADERS
  Batterson, James Goodwin
  Bulkeley, Morgan Gardner
  Bush, John Edward
  Cohen, Walter L.
  Delafield, John (1748–1824)
  Douglas, Lewis William
  Dryden, John Fairfield
  Fackler, David Parks

JURISTS *(cont.)*
Orr, Jehu Amaziah
Overton, John
Parke, Benjamin
Parker, Isaac
Parker, Isaac Charles
Parker, Joel (1795–1875)
Parker, John Johnston
Parsons, Theophilus (1750–1813)
Patterson, Robert Porter
Pecora, Ferdinand
Pendleton, Edmund
Peters, John Andrew
Philips, John Finis
Phillips, John
Pickering, John
Platt, Jonas
Poland, Luke Potter
Pope, Nathaniel
Proskauer, Joseph Meyer
Pryor, Roger Atkinson
Putnam, William LeBaron
Pynchon, William
Radcliff, Jacob
Raney, George Pettus
Ranney, Rufus Percival
Redfield, Isaac Fletcher
Reeve, Tapping
Rives, Richard Taylor
Roane, Spencer
Roberts, Oran Milo
Robinson, Moses
Root, Jesse
Rosellini, Hugh J.
Rosenman, Samuel Irving
Ross, Erskine Mayo
Rost-Denis, Pierre-Adolphe
Ruffin, George Lewis
Ruffin, Thomas
Rugg, Arthur Prentice
Ruggles, Timothy
Russell, Chambers
Ryan, Edward George
Saffin, John
Saltonstall, Richard
Sampson, Edith Spurlock
Saypol, Irving
Schaefer, Walter V.
Sebastian, Benjamin
Sedgwick, Theodore (1746–1813)
Settle, Thomas, Jr.
Sewall, David
Sewall, Samuel
Sewall, Stephen
Sharkey, William Lewis
Sharswood, George

JURISTS *(cont.)*
Shaw, Lemuel
Sherwood, Thomas Adiel
Shippen, Edward, IV
Shiras, Oliver Perry
Sirica, John Joseph
Slater, Duke
Smith, James Francis
Smith, Jeremiah
Smith, William (1697–1769)
Sobeloff, Simon E.
Speer, Emory
Spencer, Ambrose
Springer, William McKendree
Stallo, Johann Bernhard
Staples, Waller Redd
Stone, David
Stone, George Washington
Stone, Wilbur Fisk
Stuart, Archibald
Swan, Joseph Rockwell
Swift, Zephaniah
Symmes, John Cleves
Taft, Alphonso
Tappan, Benjamin
Taylor, Creed
Taylor, John Louis
Terry, David Smith
Thayer, Amos Madden
Thornton, Jessy Quinn
Tichenor, Isaac
Toulmin, Harry
Tourgée, Albion Winegar
Tracy, Benjamin Franklin
Traynor, Roger John
Trott, Nicholas
Trowbridge, Edmund
Trumbull, John (1750–1831)
Trumbull, Lyman
Tucker, Henry St. George (1780–1848)
Tucker, St. George
Tyler, Royall
Underhill, John
Underwood, John Curtiss
Upshur, Abel Parker
Vanderbilt, Arthur T.
Van Ness, William Peter
Van Ness, William W.
Varnum, James Mitchell
Von Moschzisker, Robert
Waddy, Joseph C.
Walden, Austin Thomas
Walker, David (1806–1879)
Walker, Robert Franklin
Walworth, Reuben Hyde

JURISTS *(cont.)*
Ward, Nathaniel
Waring, Julius Waties
Watkins, George Claiborne
Weare, Meshech
Weinfeld, Edward
Welch, John
Wentworth, John (1719–1781)
Wheeler, Royall Tyler
White, Albert Smith
Whitman, Ezekiel
Williamson, Isaac Halsted
Wolcott, Erastus
Woods, William Allen
Woodward, Augustus Brevoort
Wright, Jonathan Jasper
Wright, J. Skelly
Wythe, George
Wyzanski, Charles Edward, Jr.
Yates, Joseph C.
Yates, Robert
Yerger, William
Youngdahl, Luther Wallace
Zane, Charles Shuster

JUSTICES OF THE PEACE
Dana, Richard
Morris, Esther Hobart

**JUSTICES OF THE SUPREME
COURT.** *See* Supreme Court
Justices

KEELBOATMAN
Fink, Mike

KEYBOARD PLAYER
Sun Ra

KIDNAPPERS
Chessman, Caryl Whittier
Hauptmann, Bruno Richard

KILLERS. *See* Murderers

KINDERGARTEN TEACHERS. *See*
Early Childhood Educators

KU KLUX KLAN LEADERS
Forrest, Nathan Bedford
Gholson, Samuel Jameson
Gordon, John Brown
Simmons, William Joseph

LECTURERS *(cont.)*

Clarke, Lewis G.
Coffin, Charles Carleton
Conwell, Russell Herman
Cook, Joseph
Cooke, George Willis
Copway, George
Couzins, Phoebe Wilson
Craft, William
de Cleyre, Voltairine
Devine, Edward Thomas
Dickinson, Anna Elizabeth
Dods, John Bovee
Emerson, Ralph Waldo
Ende, Amalie von
Fine, Benjamin
Fiske, John (1842–1901)
Fuller, R. Buckminster
Gage, Frances Dana Barker
Gestefeld, Ursula Newell
Goldsmith, Joel Sol
Gougar, Helen Mar Jackson
James, Henry (1811–1882)
Johnson, Osa
Jones, Jane Elizabeth
Keller, Helen
King, Thomas Starr
Kinnersley, Ebenezer
Lowell, Amy
Mitchel, Ormsby Macknight
Morris, Robert (1818–1888)
Newman, Angelia
Newton, Joseph Fort
Pollock, Channing
Pratt, Daniel (1809–1887)
Rohde, Ruth Bryan Owen
Rukeyser, Merryle Stanley
Salter, William Mackintire
Sampson, Deborah
Sanford, Maria Louise
Sawyer, Ruth
Seton, Ernest Thompson
Sheed, Francis Joseph
Smith, Elizabeth Oakes
Spencer, Archibald
Stearns, Lutie Eugenia
Stefansson, Vilhjalmur
Stone, Horatio
Thompson, Clara Ann
Thompson, Oscar
Thompson, Priscilla Jane
Twain, Mark
Waisbrooker, Lois
Warner, Charles Dudley
Wattles, John Otis
Watts, Alan Wilson

LECTURERS *(cont.)*

Whipple, Edwin Percy
Williams, Fannie Barrier

LEGAL HISTORIANS

Bigelow, Melvin Madison
Curtis, George Ticknor
Howe, Mark De Wolfe
Warren, Charles

LEGAL SCHOLARS

Ames, James Barr
Angell, Joseph Kinnicutt
Armstrong, Barbara Nachtrieb
Baldwin, Simeon Eben
Battle, William Horn
Beale, Joseph Henry
Bickel, Alexander Mordecai
Bigelow, Harry Augustus
Bigelow, Melvin Madison
Bishop, Joel Prentiss
Borchard, Edwin Montefiore
Bouvier, John
Cahn, Edmond Nathaniel
Cary, William Lucius
Chafee, Zechariah, Jr.
Chamberlain, Joseph Perkins
Clark, Charles Edward
Cobb, Andrew Jackson
Cook, Walter Wheeler
Corwin, Edward Samuel
Crosskey, William Winslow
Dane, Nathan
Daniel, John Warwick
Dickinson, Edwin De Witt
Dickinson, John (1894–1952)
Du Ponceau, Pierre Étienne
Dwight, Theodore William
Fairman, Charles
Farrar, Timothy
Frank, Jerome New
Freund, Ernst
Gilmer, Francis Walker
Glueck, Sheldon
Goodhart, Arthur Lehman
Goodnow, Frank Johnson
Goodrich, Elizur (1761–1849)
Gray, John Chipman
Green, Leon
Greenleaf, Simon
Gregory, Charles Noble
Gridley, Jeremiah
Guthrie, William Dameron
Hastie, William Henry
Hilliard, Francis
Hoffman, David

LEGAL SCHOLARS *(cont.)*

Hohfeld, Wesley Newcomb
Holcombe, James Philemon
Holmes, Oliver Wendell
   (1841–1935)
Houston, Charles Hamilton
Hudson, Manley Ottmer
Jessup, Philip C.
Keener, William Albert
Langdell, Christopher Columbus
Legaré, Hugh Swinton
Livermore, Samuel (1786–1833)
Llewellyn, Karl Nickerson
Magruder, Calvert
McClain, Emlin
Medina, Harold Raymond
Mentschikoff, Soia
Minor, Raleigh Colston
Morawetz, Victor
Morgenthau, Hans Joachim
Nicolls, Matthias
Oliphant, Herman
Parker, Joel (1795–1875)
Parsons, Theophilus (1797–1882)
Paschal, George Washington
Patton, John Mercer
Pfeffer, Leo
Pomeroy, John Norton
Pound, Roscoe
Powell, Thomas Reed
Prosser, William Lloyd
Ransom, Leon Andrew
Redfield, Amasa Angell
Redfield, Isaac Fletcher
Reeve, Tapping
Robinson, Conway
Rodell, Fred
Sayles, John
Schaefer, Walter V.
Schiller, A. Arthur
Sedgwick, Theodore (1811–1859)
Sharp, Malcolm Pitman
Sharswood, George
Stockton, Charles Herbert
Story, Joseph
Taylor, Hannis
Thayer, James Bradley
Tiedeman, Christopher Gustavus
Tucker, Beverley
Tucker, Henry St. George
   (1780–1848)
Tucker, John Randolph
   (1823–1897)
Von Moschzisker, Robert
Walker, Timothy (1802–1856)
Ward, Nathaniel

LIBRETTISTS *(cont.)*
Harburg, E. Y.
Hobart, George V.
Klein, Charles
Lerner, Alan Jay
Ryskind, Morrie
Stein, Gertrude

LIGHTHOUSE KEEPER
Lewis, Ida

LIMNOLOGISTS
Birge, Edward Asahel
Juday, Chancey

LINGUISTS. *See also* Grammarians;
Interpreters; Language Theorists;
Lexicographers; Philologists
Alexander, Joseph Addison
Andrews, Lorrin
Avery, John
Bloomfield, Leonard
Bolling, George Melville
Brickman, William Wolfgang
Buck, Carl Darling
Crane, Thomas Frederick
Davis, Charles Henry Stanley
Deloria, Ella Cara
Fortier, Alcée
Gatschet, Albert Samuel
Goddard, Pliny Earle
Goodell, William (1792–1867)
Harrington, John Peabody
Harriot, Thomas
Hewitt, John Napoleon Brinton
Jakobson, Roman
Kellogg, Samuel Henry
Krapp, George Philip
Leonard, Sterling Andrus
Lin Yutang
Lounsbury, Thomas Raynesford
Marsh, George Perkins
Monis, Judah
Neumark, David
Pareja, Francisco
Pei, Mario Andrew
Percival, James Gates
Rice, Charles
Riggs, Stephen Return
Roback, A. A.
Sapir, Edward
Sequoyah
Townsend, William Cameron
Van Name, Addison
Viele, Aernout Cornelissen
Whitney, William Dwight

LINGUISTS *(cont.)*
Whorf, Benjamin Lee

LITERARY AGENTS
Hayward, Leland
Norris, Charles Gilman Smith

LITERARY CRITICS
Aiken, Conrad
Arvin, Newton
Babbitt, Irving
Bacon, Leonard
Baker, Carlos Heard
Beach, Joseph Warren
Blackmur, R. P.
Bodenheim, Maxwell
Bogan, Louise
Bourne, Randolph Silliman
Boyd, Ernest Augustus
Braithwaite, William Stanley
Brooks, Cleanth
Brooks, Van Wyck
Brownell, William Crary
Burke, Kenneth
Clifford, James Lowry
Cournos, John
Cowley, Malcolm
Cuppy, William Jacob
Dabney, Richard
Dahlberg, Edward
Dell, Floyd James
Dennie, Joseph
Dupee, F. W.
Eliot, T. S.
Ellmann, Richard
Foerster, Norman
Freeman, Joseph
Fuller, Hoyt William
Geismar, Maxwell David
Gilder, Jeannette Leonard
Goodman, Paul
Greenslet, Ferris
Gregory, Horace Victor
Harby, Isaac
Harris, Corra
Hayne, Paul Hamilton
Hicks, Granville
Highet, Gilbert
Hillyer, Robert Silliman
Hoffman, Frederick John
Hofstadter, Richard
Howe, Irving
Howells, William Dean
Hyman, Stanley Edgar
Jacobs, Joseph
James, Henry (1843–1916)

LITERARY CRITICS *(cont.)*
Jarrell, Randall
Kirkus, Virginia
Koch, Vivienne
Krutch, Joseph Wood
Lewisohn, Ludwig
Locke, Alain Leroy
Loveman, Amy
Lowell, Amy
Matthiessen, F. O.
McCarthy, Mary
McHenry, James (1785–1845)
Mencken, H. L.
Millett, Fred Benjamin
Moore, Marianne
Morley, Christopher
Newman, Frances
Noguchi, Yone
Otis, Brooks
Payne, William Morton
Poe, Edgar Allan
Pound, Ezra
Rahv, Philip
Ransom, John Crowe
Redding, J. Saunders
Richards, I. A.
Ripley, George
Rittenhouse, Jessie Belle
Schorer, Mark
Schwartz, Delmore
Scott, Evelyn
Scudder, Horace Elisha
Sherman, Stuart Pratt
Smith, Henry Nash
Spingarn, Joel Elias
Stedman, Edmund Clarence
Stoddard, Richard Henry
Taggard, Genevieve
Tate, Allen
Thompson, Maurice
Trent, William Peterfield
Trilling, Lionel
Trowbridge, John Townsend
Tuve, Rosemond
Van Doren, Carl
Van Doren, Mark
Warren, Austin
Warren, Robert Penn
Whipple, Edwin Percy
Wilson, Edmund
Winters, Yvor
Yourcenar, Marguerite
Zukofsky, Louis

MATHEMATICAL HISTORIANS. *See* Historians of Science

MATHEMATICIANS

Adrain, Robert
Albert, Abraham Adrian
Alexander, James Waddell
Artin, Emil
Bartlett, William Holms Chambers
Bateman, Harry
Bell, Eric Temple
Bergmann, Gustav
Bing, R. H.
Birkhoff, George David
Blichfeldt, Hans Frederik
Bliss, Gilbert Ames
Bôcher, Maxime
Bochner, Salomon
Bolza, Oskar
Bowditch, Nathaniel
Brauer, Richard Dagobert
Bronowski, Jacob
Brown, Ernest William
Buchanan, Herbert Earle
Byerly, William Elwood
Caldwell, Joseph
Chapman, Sydney
Chauvenet, William
Church, Alonzo (1903–1995)
Coble, Arthur Byron
Coffin, James Henry
Cole, Frank Nelson
Coolidge, Julian Lowell
Courant, Richard
Cox, Elbert Frank
Craig, Thomas
De Forest, Erastus Lyman
Dickson, Leonard Eugene
Eisenhart, Luther Pfahler
Ellicott, Andrew
Evans, Griffith Conrad
Feller, William
Fine, Henry Burchard
Forbush, Scott Ellsworth
Fuller, Thomas
Geiringer, Hilda
Gibbs, Josiah Willard (1839–1903)
Godfrey, Thomas (1704–1749)
Greenwood, Isaac
Grew, Theophilus
Halsted, George Bruce
Harish-Chandra
Hassler, Ferdinand Rudolph
Hill, George William
Hille, Einar

MATHEMATICIANS *(cont.)*

Hoffmann, Banesh
Huntington, Edward Vermilye
Jackson, Dunham
Johnson, William Woolsey
Kac, Mark
Kasner, Edward
Kellogg, Oliver Dimon
Kemeny, John George
Koopmans, Tjalling Charles
Lane, Jonathan Homer
Leeds, John
Lefschetz, Solomon
Lewy, Hans
Maddison, Isabel
Martin, Artemas
Maschke, Heinrich
Mason, Max
McClintock, Emory
McShane, Edward James
Miller, George Abram
Minto, Walter
Montroll, Elliott Waters
Moore, Clarence Lemuel Elisha
Moore, Eliakim Hastings
Moore, Robert Lee
Morley, Frank
Morse, Marston
Moulton, Forest Ray
Murnaghan, Francis Dominic
Neugebauer, Otto Eduard
Newton, Hubert Anson
Nicollet, Joseph Nicolas
Osgood, William Fogg
Patterson, Robert
Peirce, Benjamin
Peirce, Benjamin Osgood, II
Peirce, James Mills
Pierce, Joseph Alphonso
Pólya, George
Prager, William
Rademacher, Hans
Ritt, Joseph Fels
Rittenhouse, David
Robertson, Howard Percy
Robie, Thomas
Robinson, Julia Bowman
Runkle, John Daniel
Safford, Truman Henry
Scott, Charlotte Angas
Steenrod, Norman Earl
Stone, Marshall Harvey
Story, William Edward
Stringham, Irving
Strong, Theodore
Sylvester, James Joseph

MATHEMATICIANS *(cont.)*

Tamarkin, Jacob David
Taussky-Todd, Olga
Thaxton, Hubert Mack
Thomas, Tracy Yerkes
Ulam, Stanislaw Marcin
Van Vleck, Edward Burr
Veblen, Oswald
Venable, Charles Scott
von Mises, Richard Marten Edler
von Neumann, John Louis
Walsh, Joseph Leonard
Weaver, Warren
West, Benjamin (1730–1813)
Weyl, Hermann
Wheeler, Anna Johnson Pell
White, Henry Seely
Whitehead, Alfred North
Whitney, Hassler
Whyburn, Gordon Thomas
Wiener, Norbert
Wilczynski, Ernest Julius
Wilder, Raymond Louis
Wilson, Edwin Bidwell
Wright, Chauncey
Wright, Sewall
Wrinch, Dorothy Maud
Zariski, Oscar

MAYORS

Baker, Newton Diehl
Behrman, Martin
Cermak, Anton Joseph
Clinton, De Witt
Conrad, Robert Taylor
Couzens, James
Cruger, Henry, Jr.
Curley, James Michael
Curtis, Edwin Upton
Daley, Richard Joseph
DiSalle, Michael Vincent
Dow, Neal
Dunne, Edward Fitzsimmons
Fagan, Mark Matthew
Fargo, William George
Fitzgerald, John Francis
Gaston, William
Gaynor, William Jay
Grace, William Russell
Hague, Frank
Hall, Abraham Oakey
Hamtramck, John Francis
Hardin, William Jefferson
Harrison, Carter Henry
Harrison, Carter Henry, Jr.
Havemeyer, William Frederick

MEDICAL WRITERS *(cont.)*
Hutchinson, Woods
Hyde, James Nevins
Jacobi, Mary Corinna Putnam
Kelly, Aloysius Oliver Joseph
Lee, Charles Alfred
Lloyd, John Uri
Mumford, James Gregory
Palmer, Alonzo Benjamin
Smith, Elihu Hubbard
Smith, Homer William
Stitt, Edward Rhodes
Terry, Charles Edward
Thorek, Max
Wood, George Bacon
Youmans, William Jay

MEDIEVALISTS. *See* Historians

MEDIUMS. *See* Spiritualists

MEMBERS OF CONGRESS. *See*
Resident Commissioners;
Territorial Delegates; U.S.
Representatives; U.S. Senators

MEMOIR WRITERS. *See*
Autobiographers

MENNONITE BISHOPS
Boehm, Martin
Rittenhouse, William

MERCENARIES
Bouquet, Henry
Boyd, John Parker
Harlan, Josiah
Henningsen, Charles Frederick
Ingraham, Prentiss
Kalb, Johann
Loring, William Wing
Ward, Frederick Townsend

MERCHANT BANKERS. *See*
Capitalists and Financiers;
Financial Industry Leaders

MERCHANTS. *See also* Department
Store Owners; Shipping Industry
Leaders; Slave Traders; Traders
with Indians and Pioneers
Alexander, Mary Spratt Provoost
Allen, James
Allerton, Isaac
Alvarez, Manuel

MERCHANTS *(cont.)*
Aspinwall, William Henry
Bache, Richard
Bache, Theophylact
Bates, Joshua
Bayard, John Bubenheim
Bayard, Nicholas
Biddle, Clement
Bingham, William
Bowdoin, James (1752–1811)
Bowen, Henry Chandler
Brooks, Peter Chardon
Brown, Alexander
Brown, John (1736–1803)
Brown, Joseph
Brown, Moses
Brown, Nicholas
Brown, Obadiah
Calef, Robert
Carroll, Daniel
Carter, Henry Alpheus Peirce
Carter, Robert (1663–1732)
Chouteau, Pierre, Jr.
Claflin, Horace Brigham
Clark, Daniel (1766–1813)
Clarkson, Matthew
Clymer, George
Coffin, Levi
Coleman, William Tell
Collins, Edward Knight
Colman, John
Cope, Thomas Pym
Crowninshield, Benjamin
Williams
Crowninshield, George, Jr.
Cruger, Henry, Jr.
Cupples, Samuel
Cushing, John Perkins
Cushing, Thomas
Cutt, John
Cutts, Samuel
Davis, Alice Brown
De Berdt, Dennys
Delafield, John (1748–1824)
Delafield, John (1786–1853)
De Peyster, Abraham
Derby, Elias Hasket
Derby, Richard
de Vries, David Pietersen
Dexter, Samuel
Dexter, Timothy
Duer, William
Dugdale, Richard Louis
du Sable, Jean-Baptiste Point
Eaton, Theophilus
Ellery, William

MERCHANTS *(cont.)*
Evans, William
Faneuil, Peter
Farwell, Charles Benjamin
Fell, John
Field, Marshall
Findlay, James
Fiske, John (1744–1797)
Fitzsimons, Thomas
Fleete, Henry
Flint, Charles Ranlett
Folsom, Nathaniel
Forbes, John (1767–1823)
Forbes, John Murray
Forstall, Edmond Jean
Gadsden, Christopher
Gaines, George Strother
Galt, John
Garrett, Robert
Gillon, Alexander
Gilman, John Taylor
Girard, Stephen
Glover, John
Goodwin, Ichabod
Gorham, Nathaniel
Gould, Benjamin Apthorp
(1787–1859)
Gratz, Barnard, and
Michael Gratz
Gray, William
Green, John Cleve
Green, Joseph
Grim, David
Grinnell, Henry
Gwinnett, Button
Habersham, James
Habersham, Joseph
Hambleton, Thomas Edward
Hamilton, Andrew (?–1703)
Hamilton, John
Hammett, Samuel Adams
Hancock, John (1737–1793)
Hancock, Thomas
Hand, Daniel
Hanson, John, Jr.
Hazen, Moses
Heathcote, Caleb
Heco, Joseph
Henry, Alexander
Herrman, Augustine
Hiester, Joseph
Higgins, Frank Wayland
Higginson, Nathaniel
Hillegas, Michael
Holker, John
Hooper, Samuel

METHODIST EPISCOPAL LAY LEADERS
Bennett, Belle Harris
Dickins, John
Jacoby, Ludwig Sigismund
Meyer, Lucy Jane Rider
Newman, Angelia
Robinson, Jane Marie Bancroft
Willing, Jennie Fowler

METHODIST PIONEERS AND LAY LEADERS
Albright, Jacob
Bangs, Nathan
Embury, Philip
Gatch, Philip
Heck, Barbara
Strawbridge, Robert
Watters, William
Webb, Thomas
Williams, Robert

METHODIST PROTESTANT CLERGY
Apess, William
McCaine, Alexander
Shaw, Anna Howard
Shinn, Asa
Snethen, Nicholas

MICROBIOLOGISTS. *See also*
Geneticists
Alexander, Hattie Elizabeth
Burkholder, Paul Rufus
Dubos, René
Evans, Alice Catherine
Koplik, Henry
Novy, Frederick George
Poindexter, Hildrus Augustus
Smith, Theobald
Waksman, Selman Abraham

MICROSCOPISTS
Clark, Henry James
Leidy, Joseph
Riddell, John Leonard
Woodward, Joseph Janvier

MIDGET
Tom Thumb

MIDWIVES
Ballard, Martha Moore
Van Blarcom, Carolyn Conant

MILITARY ADVENTURERS. *See*
Filibusters; Mercenaries

MILITARY BANDLEADERS. *See*
Bandleaders

MILITARY CHAPLAINS
Colton, Walter
Duffy, Francis Patrick
Eastman, William Reed
Fithian, Philip Vickers
McCabe, Charles Cardwell
Plummer, Henry Vinton
Trumbull, Henry Clay

MILITARY DESERTER
Fagen, David

MILITARY ENGINEERS
Abbot, Henry Larcom
Abert, John James
Babcock, Orville Elias
Bailey, Joseph
Barnard, John Gross
Bernard, Simon
Casey, Thomas Lincoln
Chittenden, Hiram Martin
Comstock, Cyrus Ballou
Cone, Hutchinson Ingham
De Brahm, William Gerard
Derby, George Horatio
Ericsson, John
Foster, John Gray
Franklin, William Buel
Gaillard, David Du Bose
Gardiner, Lion
Gillmore, Quincy Adams
Goethals, George Washington
Graham, James Duncan
Gridley, Richard
Groves, Leslie Richard, Jr.
Gunnison, John Williams
Haupt, Herman
Humphreys, Andrew Atkinson
Isherwood, Benjamin Franklin
Ives, Joseph Christmas
Jadwin, Edgar
Lander, Frederick West
Lay, John Louis
L'Enfant, Pierre Charles
Long, Stephen Harriman
Loring, Charles Harding
Machin, Thomas
Mackellar, Patrick
Mahan, Dennis Hart
Mangin, Joseph François

MILITARY ENGINEERS *(cont.)*
McPherson, James B.
Meade, George Gordon
Meigs, Montgomery Cunningham
Melville, George Wallace
Milligan, Robert Wiley
Montrésor, James Gabriel
Montrésor, John
Mullan, John
Newton, John
Pick, Lewis Andrew
Rains, George Washington
Roberdeau, Isaac
Robert, Henry Martyn
Shreve, Henry Miller
Sibert, William Luther
Swift, Joseph Gardner
Swift, William Henry
Taylor, Harry
Totten, Joseph Gilbert
Turnbull, William
Warren, Gouverneur Kemble
Webster, Joseph Dana
Weitzel, Godfrey
Wheeler, George Montague
Wright, Horatio Gouverneur

MILITARY GOVERNORS
Cortina, Juan Nepomuceno
Mason, Richard Barnes
Riley, Bennet
Stanly, Edward
Washington, John Macrae
Wood, Leonard

MILITIAMEN. *See* Colonial
Militiamen

MILLENNIALIST
Husband, Herman

MILLERS. *See* Flour Milling
Industry Leaders

MILLINERS. *See* Hatters

MILLWORKERS. *See* Factory
Workers

MILLWRIGHT
Lucas, Jonathan

MIMES
Enters, Angna
Fox, George Washington Lafayette

PALEOECOLOGISTS
Edinger, Tilly
Gardner, Julia Anna

PALEONTOLOGISTS
Clarke, John Mason
Cope, Edward Drinker
Cushman, Joseph Augustine
Dall, William Healey
Dunbar, Carl Owen
Gabb, William More
Grabau, Amadeus William
Granger, Walter
Gregory, William King
Hall, James (1811–1898)
Harlan, Richard
Holland, William Jacob
Hyatt, Alpheus
Leidy, Joseph
Marsh, Othniel Charles
Mather, Kirtley Fletcher
Matthew, William Diller
Meek, Fielding Bradford
Merriam, John Campbell
Newberry, John Strong
Osborn, Henry Fairfield
Patten, William
Patterson, Bryan
Romer, Alfred Sherwood
Schuchert, Charles
Scott, William Berryman
Simpson, George Gaylord
Vaughan, Thomas Wayland
Wachsmuth, Charles
Walcott, Charles Doolittle
Wetmore, Alexander
White, Charles Abiathar
Whitfield, Robert Parr
Wieland, George Reber
Williston, Samuel Wendell

PAMPHLETEERS
Bishop, Abraham
Bollan, William
Callender, James Thomson
Carroll, Anna Ella
Carter, Landon
Dickinson, John (1732–1808)
Flower, Richard
Hay, George
Ingersoll, Charles Jared
Kennedy, Archibald
Knox, William
Lee, Arthur
Paine, Thomas
Pratt, Orson

PAMPHLETEERS *(cont.)*
Stewart, Maria W.
Van Ness, William Peter
Walker, David (1796?–1830)
Ward, Nathaniel
Zubly, John Joachim

PAN-AFRICANISTS. *See* Black
Nationalists

PANTOMIMISTS. *See* Mimes

PAPER INDUSTRY LEADERS
Chisholm, Hugh Joseph
Crocker, Alvah
Dennison, Henry Sturgis
McCabe, Thomas Bayard
Rittenhouse, William
West, George

PAPERMAKER
Hunter, Dard

PAPYROLOGISTS
Welles, Charles Bradford
Westermann, William Linn

PARAPSYCHOLOGISTS. *See also*
Occultists
Hyslop, James Hervey
Rhine, J. B.

PARASITOLOGIST
Ward, Henry Baldwin

**PARK COMMISSIONERS AND
SUPERINTENDENTS.** *See* National
Park Officials

PARLIAMENTARIANS
Cannon, Clarence Andrew
Robert, Henry Martyn

PATENT EXPERTS
Carlson, Chester Floyd
Ewbank, Thomas
Jones, Thomas P.
Langner, Lawrence
Leggett, Mortimer Dormer
Renwick, Edward Sabine
Selden, George Baldwin

PATENT MEDICINE MAKERS
Ayer, James Cook
Brandreth, Benjamin

PATENT MEDICINE MAKERS *(cont.)*
Cesar
Hartman, Samuel Brubaker
Koch, William Frederick
Perkins, Elisha
Pinkham, Lydia Estes

PATHOLOGISTS. *See also* Insect
Pathologists; Plant Pathologists;
Teratologists; Veterinary
Pathologists
Andersen, Dorothy Hansine
Biggs, Hermann Michael
Cone, Claribel
Councilman, William Thomas
Delafield, Francis
De Witt, Lydia Maria
Ewing, James (1866–1943)
Fenger, Christian
Flexner, Simon
Frantz, Virginia Kneeland
Fuller, Solomon Carter
Gardner, Leroy Upson
Gerhard, William Wood
Goldblatt, Harry
Hertzler, Arthur Emanuel
Hinton, William Augustus
Hurdon, Elizabeth
Kinyoun, Joseph James
Landsteiner, Karl
Larson, Leonard Winfield
L'Esperance, Elise Strang
Longcope, Warfield Theobald
MacCallum, William George
Mallory, Frank Burr
Martland, Harrison Stanford
Meyer, Karl Friedrich
Minot, George Richards
Murphy, James Bumgardner
Opie, Eugene Lindsay
Pearce, Richard Mills, Jr.
Prudden, Theophil Mitchell
Rich, Arnold Rice
Ricketts, Howard Taylor
Shope, Richard Edwin
Smith, Harry Pratt
Smith, Margaret Gladys
Smith, Theobald
Warren, Shields
Wells, Harry Gideon
Whipple, George Hoyt
Wolbach, S. Burt
Wollstein, Martha

PLASTIC SURGEONS. *See* Surgeons

PLAYBROKERS. *See* Theatrical Agents

PLAYWRIGHTS. *See* Dramatists

POETS

Adams, Charles Follen
Adams, John (1705–1740)
Aiken, Conrad
Ainslie, Hew
Aldrich, Thomas Bailey
Allen, Elizabeth Akers
Allen, Hervey
Allen, Paul
Appleton, Thomas Gold
Arensberg, Walter Conrad
Arrington, Alfred W.
Auden, W. H.
Auslander, Joseph
Bacon, Leonard
Banvard, John
Barlow, Joel
Barnitz, Albert
Barr, Amelia E.
Bates, Katharine Lee
Beach, Joseph Warren
Beers, Ethel Lynn
Bell, James Madison
Benét, Stephen Vincent
Benét, William Rose
Benjamin, Park
Bennet, Sanford Fillmore
Bennett, Gwendolyn
Berryman, John
Billings, William
Bishop, Elizabeth
Bishop, John Peale
Bissell, Emily Perkins
Blackburn, Paul
Blake, Mary Elizabeth
Bleecker, Ann Eliza
Bloede, Gertrude
Bodenheim, Maxwell
Bogan, Louise
Bolling, Robert
Bontemps, Arna Wendell
Boyd, James
Bradstreet, Anne
Braithwaite, William Stanley
Branch, Anna Hempstead
Bremer, Fredrika
Brooke, Henry
Brooks, Maria Gowen
Brooks, Walter Henderson

POETS *(cont.)*

Brown, Sterling Allen
Brown, William Hill
Brownell, Henry Howard
Bryant, William Cullen
Bukowski, Charles
Burgos, Julia de
Burt, Struthers
Bush-Banks, Olivia Ward
Byles, Mather
Bynner, Witter
Calkins, Clinch
Calvert, George Henry
Campbell, James Edwin
Cane, Melville Henry
Cannon, Charles James
Carman, William Bliss
Carmer, Carl Lamson
Carver, Raymond
Cary, Phoebe
Caulkins, Frances Manwaring
Cawein, Madison Julius
Chandler, Elizabeth Margaret
Channing, William Ellery, II
Chapman, John Jay
Chivers, Thomas Holley
Church, Benjamin (1734–1778?)
Ciardi, John
Clampitt, Amy Kathleen
Clarke, Joseph Ignatius Constantine
Clarke, Mary Bayard
Clarke, McDonald
Cliffton, William
Coffin, Robert Peter Tristram
Conkling, Grace
Cook, Ebenezer
Cooke, Philip Pendleton
Coolbrith, Ina
Corrington, John William
Corrothers, James David
Cotter, Joseph Seamon, Sr.
Crafts, William
Cranch, Christopher Pearse
Crane, Hart
Crane, Stephen
Crapsey, Adelaide
Cromwell, Gladys
Crosby, Fanny
Cullen, Countée
Cummings, E. E.
Dabney, Richard
Daggett, Rollin Mallory
Dale, Thomas (1700–1750)
Daly, Thomas Augustine
Dana, Richard Henry

POETS *(cont.)*

Da Ponte, Lorenzo
Dargan, Olive Tilford
Davidson, Donald Grady
Davidson, Lucretia Maria, and Margaret Miller Davidson
Davies, Samuel
Davis, Harold Lenoir
Dawson, William
De Casseres, Benjamin
Denby, Edwin (1903–1983)
Deutsch, Babette
Dickinson, Emily
Dinsmoor, Robert
Doolittle, Hilda
Dorr, Julia
Drake, Joseph Rodman
Duganne, Augustine Joseph Hickey
Dunbar, Paul Laurence
Dunbar-Nelson, Alice
Duncan, Robert Edward
Dwight, Theodore (1764–1846)
Edwards, Harry Stillwell
Eliot, Charlotte
Eliot, T. S.
Ellet, Elizabeth F.
Elwyn, Alfred Langdon
Evans, Donald
Evans, Nathaniel
Fairfield, Sumner Lincoln
Fauset, Jessie Redmon
Fearing, Kenneth Flexner
Fenollosa, Ernest
Ficke, Arthur Davison
Field, Eugene
Field, Sara Bard
Fitts, Dudley
Flagg, Edmund
Fletcher, Bridget Richardson
Fletcher, John Gould
Foss, Sam Walter
Freneau, Philip Morin
Frost, Robert
Gallagher, William Davis
Garrigue, Jean
Gay, E. Jane
Gibran, Kahlil
Gilder, Richard Watson
Giovannitti, Arturo Massimo
Godfrey, Thomas (1736–1763)
Goodwin, Ruby Berkley
Gould, Hannah Flagg
Grant, Percy Stickney
Grayson, William John
Green, Joseph

POLITICAL FIGURES *(cont.)*

Patton, John Mercer
Pease, Elisha Marshall
Peck, George Wilbur
Pendergast, Thomas Joseph
Penhallow, Samuel
Perez, Leander Henry
Perkins, George Walbridge
Perkins, Thomas Handasyd
Petigru, James Louis
Phelan, James Duval
Phelps, John Smith
Philipse, Adolph
Phillips, Samuel, Jr.
Pierce, William Leigh
Pinchback, P. B. S.
Pinckney, Charles
Pinckney, Thomas
Pinkney, William
Pitkin, Timothy
Platt, Jonas
Pledger, William Anderson
Poinsett, Joel Roberts
Poland, Luke Potter
Porter, Benjamin Faneuil
Pory, John
Posey, Thomas
Potter, Robert
Poydras, Julien
Prat, Benjamin
Price, Sterling
Pruyn, Robert Hewson
Purnell, William Henry
Pusey, Caleb
Pynchon, John
Quay, Matthew Stanley
Quezon, Manuel Luis
Quick, Herbert
Quitman, John Anthony
Rainey, Joseph Hayne
Randall, Henry Stephens
Randolph, Sir John
Ranney, Rufus Percival
Ransier, Alonzo Jacob
Raymond, Henry Jarvis
Rayner, John Baptis
Rayner, Kenneth
Reid, Whitelaw
Rhett, Robert Barnwell
Richmond, Dean
Ricord, Frederick William
Ripley, Eleazar Wheelock
Rives, William Cabell
Roberts, William Randall
Robinson, John
Robinson, Moses

POLITICAL FIGURES *(cont.)*

Rodney, Caesar
Romney, George Wilcken
Roosevelt, Alice Hathaway Lee
Roosevelt, Elliott
Roosevelt, Franklin Delano, Jr.
Roosevelt, Theodore, Jr.
Root, Joseph Pomeroy
Ross, C. Ben
Ross, Edmund Gibson
Rowe, John
Rowley, Thomas
Roye, Edward James
Ruby, George T.
Ruef, Abraham
Rush, Richard
Russell, Chambers
Russell, Jonathan
Russell, Richard Brevard, Jr.
Rutherford, Griffith
Rutledge, John
Schuschnigg, Kurt von
Schwellenbach, Lewis Baxter
Scott, Hugh Doggett, Jr.
Seguín, Juan Nepomuceno
Settle, Thomas, Jr.
Sevier, Ambrose Hundley
Shafroth, John Franklin
Shannon, Wilson
Sharkey, William Lewis
Sherburne, Henry
Sherwood, Isaac Ruth
Sherwood, Lorenzo
Shields, James
Shippen, Edward
Shouse, Jouett
Sickles, Daniel Edgar
Sigel, Franz
Simmons, Furnifold McLendel
Smallwood, William
Smith, Alfred E.
Smith, Ashbel
Smith, Charles Emory
Smith, Charles Perrin
Smith, Daniel
Smith, Harry Clay
Smith, Hoke
Smith, Melancton (1744–1798)
Smith, Richard
Snow, Wilbert
Southard, Samuel Lewis
Southwick, Solomon
Spinola, Francis Barretto
Steedman, James Blair
Stephens, Linton
Stevens, Isaac Ingalls

POLITICAL FIGURES *(cont.)*

Stimson, Henry Lewis
Stoughton, William
Strong, Caleb
Stuart, Alexander Hugh Holmes
Sullivan, James
Sullivan, John
Sullivan, Timothy Daniel
Sumner, Charles
Swanson, Claude Augustus
Sweeny, Peter Barr
Symmes, John Cleves
Taliaferro, William Booth
Tazewell, Littleton Waller
Teller, Henry Moore
Thomas, Philip Francis
Thompson, Richard Wigginton
Thurston, Lorrin Andrews
Tilton, James
Tocqueville, Alexis de
Toulmin, Harry
Tracy, Uriah
Tumulty, Joseph Patrick
Tweed, William Magear
Twitchell, Marshall Harvey
Tyler, Ralph Waldo
Upham, Charles Wentworth
Vallejo, Mariano Guadalupe
Van Buren, Hannah Hoes
Van Buren, John
Van Cortlandt, Philip
Van Cortlandt, Pierre
Van Dam, Rip
Van der Kemp, Francis Adrian
Van Dyke, Nicholas (1738–1789)
Van Ness, William Peter
Van Rensselaer, Solomon
Van Wyck, Charles Henry
Vardaman, James Kimble
Varick, Richard
Varnum, Joseph Bradley
Vaughan, Benjamin
Vroom, Peter Dumont, Jr.
Waddell, Alfred Moore
Wadsworth, James Samuel
Wadsworth, Peleg
Walderne, Richard
Waldron, Richard, III
Waldron, Richard, Jr.
Waller, John Louis
Washburn, Cadwallader Colden
Watson, Thomas Edward
Watterson, Henry
Weare, Nathaniel
Webb, James Watson
Webster, Daniel

POLITICAL FIGURES (cont.)

Weed, Thurlow
Wentworth, Mark Hunking
Wilkins, William
Williams, David Rogerson
Williams, Israel
Williamson, Hugh
Willkie, Wendell Lewis
Wilson, William Lyne
Wise, John Sergeant
Wisner, Henry
Wolcott, Erastus
Woodbridge, William
Woodbury, Levi
Wormeley, Ralph
Worthington, John
Worthington, Thomas
Wright, Jonathan Jasper
Yates, Joseph C.
Young, John (1802–1852)
Zavala, Lorenzo de
Zollicoffer, Felix Kirk
Zubly, John Joachim

POLITICAL SCIENTISTS

Adorno, Theodor
Beard, Charles Austin
Bentley, Arthur Fisher
Boudin, Louis Boudinoff
Breckinridge, Sophonisba Preston
Brunauer, Esther
Burgess, John William
Dunning, William Archibald
Fainsod, Merle
Follett, Mary Parker
Freund, Ernst
Gilpin, William
Kendall, Willmoore
Key, V. O.
Lasswell, Harold Dwight
Lieber, Francis
Mason, Alpheus Thomas
Merriam, Charles E.
Moley, Raymond
Neumann, Franz Leopold
Ogg, Frederic Austin
Pool, Ithiel de Sola
Simons, Algie Martin
Smith, James Allen
Sorge, Friedrich Adolph
Taylor, John (1753–1824)
Walsh, Edmund Aloysius
White, Leonard Dupee
Wildavsky, Aaron Bernard
Willoughby, Westel Woodbury

POLITICAL THEORISTS. See
Political Scientists

POLITICIANS. See Political Figures

POLLSTERS

Campbell, Angus
Cantril, Hadley
Gallup, George Horace
Roper, Elmo

POLO PLAYER

Rumsey, Charles Cary

POPULAR SINGERS. See also Blues
Musicians and Singers; Country
Musicians and Singers; Folk
Musicians and Singers; Gospel
Musicians and Singers; Jazz
Singers; Rhythm and Blues
Musicians and Singers; Rock
Musicians and Singers; and other
specific terms

Andrews Sisters
Armstrong, Louis
Bailey, Pearl
Baker, Belle
Baker, Josephine
Bayes, Nora
Bledsoe, Jules
Bordoni, Irene
Brice, Fanny
Broderick, Helen
Calloway, Cab
Cantor, Eddie
Carpenter, Karen
Chapin, Harry
Cline, Maggie
Cohan, George M.
Cole, Nat King
Columbo, Russ
Cooke, Sam
Croce, Jim
Crosby, Bing
Crosby, Bob
Daniels, Bebe
Darin, Bobby
Davis, Sammy, Jr.
De Angelis, Thomas Jefferson
Desmond, Johnny
Dietrich, Marlene
Downey, Morton
Dragonette, Jessica
Elliot, Cass
Etting, Ruth

POPULAR SINGERS (cont.)

Fields, Benny
Foran, Dick
Friganza, Trixie
Garland, Judy
Groody, Louise
Haley, Jack
Hall, Pauline
Held, Anna
Holman, Libby
Howard, Joe
Hughes, Revella
Jessel, George
Jolson, Al
Kaye, Danny
Lenya, Lotte
Lewis, Ted
Liberace
Lund, Art
Machito
MacRae, Gordon
Mana-Zucca
McCormack, John
McRae, Carmen
Mercer, Johnny
Mercer, Mabel
Merman, Ethel
Miller, Roger
Mills, Florence
Mills, Harry, and Herbert Mills
Mills, Irving
Miranda, Carmen
Monroe, Marilyn
Monroe, Vaughn
Olcott, Chauncey
Pastor, Tony
Ray, Johnnie
Robbins, Marty
Rooney, Pat
Russell, Lillian
Shore, Dinah
Smith, Kate
Speaks, Margaret
Stratton, Eugene
Tanguay, Eva
Taylor, Eva
Trapp, Maria von
Tucker, Sophie
Vallee, Rudy
Waller, Fats
Webb, Clifton
Williams, Bert, and
George Walker
Wilson, Edith Goodall

POSTAL OFFICIALS

Davis, William Augustine
Goddard, Mary Katherine
Holbrook, James
Kasson, John Adam
Vail, Theodore Newton

POSTMASTERS GENERAL

Barry, William Taylor
Blair, Montgomery
Burleson, Albert Sidney
Campbell, James
Cortelyou, George Bruce
Creswell, John Angel James
Dickinson, Donald McDonald
Farley, James Aloysius
Gresham, Walter Quintin
Habersham, Joseph
Hitchcock, Frank Harris
Holt, Joseph
Howe, Timothy Otis
Jewell, Marshall
Kendall, Amos
Key, David McKendree
Maynard, Horace
Meigs, Return Jonathan, Jr.
New, Harry Stewart
Randall, Alexander Williams
Reagan, John Henninger
Vilas, William Freeman
Walker, Frank Comerford
Wickliffe, Charles Anderson

POTTERS. *See* Ceramists and Potters

POWERBROKERS

Cohn, Roy
Moses, Robert

PRESBYTERIAN CLERGY. *See also*
Congregational Clergy

Adams, William
Alexander, Archibald
Alison, Francis
Anderson, Matthew
Armstrong, George Dod
Bacon, John
Baird, Charles Washington
Baker, Daniel
Balch, Hezekiah
Barnes, Albert
Barnhouse, Donald Grey
Barrows, John Henry
Beard, Richard
Beecher, Lyman
Beman, Nathan Sidney Smith

PRESBYTERIAN CLERGY (cont.)

Biederwolf, William Edward
Bishop, Robert Hamilton
Blackburn, Gideon
Blake, Eugene Carson
Boisen, Anton Theophilus
Bonnell, John Sutherland
Bourne, George
Breckinridge, John (1797–1841)
Briggs, Charles Augustus
Brookes, James H.
Burr, Aaron (1716–1757)
Caldwell, David
Campbell, William Henry
Carrick, Samuel Czar
Cattell, William Cassady
Cavert, Samuel McCrea
Chafer, Lewis Sperry
Chavis, John
Chew, Ng Poon
Coffin, Henry Sloane
Colton, Calvin
Cook, John Francis
Cornish, Samuel Eli
Corrothers, James David
Cox, Samuel Hanson
Cuyler, Theodore Ledyard
Dabney, Robert Lewis
Davenport, James
Davies, Samuel
Dickinson, Jonathan
Doak, Samuel
Donnell, Robert
Duffield, George
Erdman, Charles Rosenbury
Erdman, William Jacob
Ewing, Finis
Fee, John Gregg
Finley, Robert
Finley, Samuel
Gale, George Washington
Garnet, Henry Highland
Gibbs, Jonathan C.
Girardeau, John Lafayette
Goulding, Francis Robert
Green, Ashbel
Grimké, Francis James
Hall, Charles Cuthbert
Hatfield, Edwin Francis
Hewat, Alexander
Hillis, Newell Dwight
Hiltner, Seward
Hoge, Moses
Hoge, Moses Drury
Howe, George (1802–1883)
Jessup, Henry Harris

PRESBYTERIAN CLERGY (cont.)

Jones, Charles Colcock
Junkin, George
Kellogg, Samuel Henry
Kent, Aratus
Kirk, Edward Norris
Knox, Samuel
Linn, John Blair
Lovejoy, Elijah Parish
Macartney, Clarence Edward Noble
MacCracken, Henry Mitchell
Makemie, Francis
Matthews, Mark Allison
McBride, F. Scott
McCord, James Iley
McCorkle, Samuel Eusebius
McCormick, Samuel Black
McGready, James
Miller, Samuel
Morris, Edward Dafydd
Morrison, William McCutchan
Palmer, Benjamin Morgan
Parker, Joel (1799–1873)
Parker, Thomas
Parkhurst, Charles Henry
Pattillo, Henry
Peck, Thomas Ephraim
Pierson, Arthur Tappan
Plumer, William Swan
Prime, Samuel Irenaeus
Rice, David
Rice, John Holt
Roberts, William Henry
Robinson, Stuart
Roe, Edward Payson
Rogers, John Almanza Rowley
Ruffner, William Henry
Smith, Benjamin Mosby
Smith, Samuel Stanhope
Smyth, Thomas
Spencer, Ichabod Smith
Sprague, William Buell
Spring, Gardiner
Stelzle, Charles
Stone, John Timothy
Swing, David
Talmage, Thomas De Witt
Tennent, Gilbert
Tennent, William
Thompson, Ernest Trice
Thornwell, James Henley
van Dyke, Henry
Waddel, John Newton
Waddel, Moses
Wallace, Henry

PRESBYTERIAN CLERGY (cont.)

Willey, Samuel Hopkins
Wilson, Joshua Lacy
Wines, Frederick Howard
Witherspoon, John
Woodrow, James
Wright, Theodore Sedgwick
Wylie, Andrew
Yandell, Lunsford Pitts, Sr.
Zubly, John Joachim

PRESBYTERIAN LAY LEADERS

Adger, John Bailey
Bennett, M. Katharine Jones
Speer, Robert Elliott

PRESIDENTIAL ADVISERS

Aldrich, Winthrop
Bennett, John Charles
Blair, Francis Preston
Bloomingdale, Alfred Schiffer
Corcoran, Thomas Gardiner
Cutler, Robert
Dean, Arthur Hobson
Donelson, Andrew Jackson
Flynn, Edward Joseph
Goldman, Eric
Graham, John
Haldeman, H. R.
Harlow, Bryce
Hauge, Gabriel Sylfest
Heller, Walter Wolfgang
Hopkins, Harry Lloyd
House, Edward Mandell
Howe, Louis McHenry
Hughes, Emmet John
Kistiakowsky, George Bogdan
Lauritsen, Charles Christian
Loomis, Francis Butler
Moley, Raymond
Okun, Arthur Melvin
Rosenman, Samuel Irving
Rublee, George
Taylor, Maxwell Davenport
Walker, Frank Comerford
Wallace, Hugh Campbell
Warburg, James Paul
Wiesner, Jerome Bert
Young, Owen D.

PRESIDENTIAL CANDIDATES

Bryan, William Jennings
Cass, Lewis
Crawford, William Harris
Davis, John William
Debs, Eugene Victor

PRESIDENTIAL CANDIDATES (cont.)

Dewey, Thomas Edmund
Douglas, Stephen Arnold
Frémont, John Charles
Hancock, Winfield Scott
La Follette, Robert Marion
Landon, Alfred Mossman
Lemke, William Frederick
McClellan, George B.
Seymour, Horatio
Smith, Alfred E.
Stevenson, Adlai Ewing, II
Tilden, Samuel Jones
Weaver, James Baird
White, Hugh Lawson
Wirt, William
Woodhull, Victoria Claflin

PRESIDENTIAL PRESS SECRETARIES

Cortelyou, George Bruce
Early, Stephen Tyree
Hagerty, James Campbell
Ross, Charles Griffith
Short, Joseph Hudson, Jr.

PRESIDENTIAL SECRETARIES. *See* White House Staff

PRESIDENT OF THE CONFEDERACY

Davis, Jefferson

PRESIDENTS OF THE UNITED STATES. *See also* Presidential Candidates

Adams, John (1735–1826)
Adams, John Quincy (1767–1848)
Arthur, Chester Alan
Buchanan, James
Cleveland, Grover
Coolidge, Calvin
Eisenhower, Dwight David
Fillmore, Millard
Garfield, James A.
Grant, Ulysses S.
Harding, Warren Gamaliel
Harrison, Benjamin (1833–1901)
Harrison, William Henry
Hayes, Rutherford B.
Hoover, Herbert
Jackson, Andrew
Jefferson, Thomas
Johnson, Andrew
Johnson, Lyndon Baines
Kennedy, John Fitzgerald

PRESIDENTS OF THE UNITED STATES (cont.)

Lincoln, Abraham
Madison, James (1751–1836)
McKinley, William
Monroe, James
Nixon, Richard Milhous
Pierce, Franklin
Polk, James K.
Roosevelt, Franklin Delano
Roosevelt, Theodore
Taft, William Howard
Taylor, Zachary
Truman, Harry S.
Tyler, John
Van Buren, Martin
Washington, George (1732–1799)
Wilson, Woodrow

PRESS AGENTS. *See also* Literary Agents; Public Relations Business Leaders; Theatrical Agents

de Lima, Agnes Abinun
Hannagan, Stephen Jerome
Malkiel, Theresa Serber
Michelson, Charles
Redpath, James
Revell, Nellie McAleney
Scott, Emmett Jay
Tully, Jim
Ward, Herbert Dickinson

PRESS-CLIPPING SERVICE OWNER

Romeike, Henry

PRINTERS. *See also* Typographers

Aitken, Robert
Bailey, Francis
Bailey, Lydia R.
Bradford, Andrew
Bradford, John
Bradford, William (1663–1752)
Bradford, William (1722–1791)
Carter, John
Cassin, John
Collins, Isaac
Currier, Nathaniel
Dawkins, Henry
Day, Stephen
Dobson, Thomas
Donahoe, Patrick
Doolittle, Amos
Draper, John
Draper, Margaret Green
Draper, Richard

PRINTERS *(cont.)*

Duane, Margaret
Dunlap, John
Edes, Benjamin
Fleet, Thomas
Foster, John
Fowle, Daniel
Franklin, Ann Smith
Franklin, James
Gaine, Hugh
Gales, Joseph
Gill, John
Goddard, Mary Katherine
Goddard, Sarah Updike
Goddard, William
Goudy, Frederic William
Green, Anne Catharine
Green, Bartholomew
Green, Jonas
Green, Samuel
Greenleaf, Thomas
Hall, Samuel (1740–1807)
Hamlin, William
Hoen, August
Holt, John
Houghton, Henry Oscar
Hugo, E. Harold
Humphreys, James
Hunter, Dard
Ives, James Merritt
Jansen, Reinier
Johnson, Marmaduke
Johnston, Thomas
Keimer, Samuel
Kneeland, Samuel
Loudon, Samuel
Maxwell, William
McFarland, J. Horace
Mecom, Benjamin
Mein, John
Miller, Henry (1702–1782)
Munsell, Joel
Nash, John Henry
Nicholson, Timothy
Nuthead, William
Parker, James
Parks, William
Prang, Louis
Revere, Paul
Rind, Clementina
Rives, John Cook
Rivington, James
Robertson, James (1747–1816)
Rudge, William Edwin
Russell, Benjamin
Seaton, William Winston

PRINTERS *(cont.)*

Sholes, Christopher Latham
Sower, Christopher, II
Stevens, Alzina Ann Parsons
Tanner, Benjamin
Thomas, Isaiah
Timothy, Ann
Timothy, Elizabeth
Timothy, Lewis
Towne, Benjamin
Updike, Daniel Berkeley
White, Thomas Willis
Zenger, John Peter

PRINT JOURNALISTS. *See also*
Magazine and Journal Editors and
Publishers; Newspaper Editors
and Publishers; Photojournalists
Abell, Arunah Sheperdson
Adams, Franklin P.
Adams, Samuel Hopkins
Agee, James
Allen, Young John William
Alsop, Joseph
Alsop, Stewart
Alvarez, Walter Clement
Ames, Mary Clemmer
Anderson, Paul Y.
Antheil, George
Asbury, Herbert
Ayer, Harriet Hubbard
Bagby, George William
Baker, Ray Stannard
Balderston, John Lloyd
Barnes, Djuna
Barrett, John
Beatty, Bessie
Beebe, Lucius
Belden, Jack
Bennett, Gwendolyn
Bent, Silas
Bentley, William
Berger, Meyer
Bernstein, Herman
Bierce, Ambrose
Bigart, Homer
Birney, William
Bishop, James Alonzo
Black, Winifred Sweet
Blake, Lillie Devereux
Bleyer, Willard Grosvenor
Bliven, Bruce
Bly, Nellie
Bourne, Randolph Silliman
Bowers, Claude Gernade
Boyle, Hal

PRINT JOURNALISTS *(cont.)*

Braden, Carl James
Bradford, Roark
Brann, William Cowper
Brewer, Thomas Mayo
Brewster, Anne Hampton
Briggs, Emily
Brisbane, Arthur
Bromfield, Louis
Brooks, Erastus
Brooks, Noah
Brough, John
Broun, Heywood
Browne, Carl
Bruce, John Edward
Brucker, Herbert
Bryant, Louise
Buckley, James Monroe
Bugbee, Emma
Bullard, Arthur
Burnett, Alfred
Cable, George Washington
Cain, James M.
Calhoun, William Barron
Cardozo, Jacob Newton
Carpenter, Frank George
Carr, Joseph F.
Cash, W. J.
Cayton, Horace Roscoe
Cazneau, Jane McManus Storms
Chadwick, Henry
Chapelle, Dickey
Chester, Thomas Morris
Ciancabilla, Giuseppe
Clapper, Raymond Lewis
Clark, Charles Heber
Cobb, Irvin Shrewsbury
Coffin, Charles Carleton
Cogley, John
Collens, Thomas Wharton
Colman, Norman Jay
Comfort, Will Levington
Connelly, Marc
Considine, Bob
Cooper, Kent
Corrothers, James David
Coxe, Tench
Coy, Ted
Craig, Elisabeth May Adams
Creel, George Edward
Creelman, James
Croly, Jane Cunningham
Crouse, Russel
Curtis, Charlotte Murray
Dabney, Wendell Phillips
Daggett, Rollin Mallory

PRINT JOURNALISTS *(cont.)*

Lubell, Samuel
Lukens, Henry Clay
MacArthur, Charles
MacGahan, Januarius Aloysius
Mackenzie, Robert Shelton
Manning, Marie
Marcosson, Isaac Frederick
Marquis, Don
Marshall, S. L. A.
Martineau, Harriet
Mason, Walt
Masterson, Bat
Matthews, Herbert Lionel
Maxwell, Elsa
Maynard, Robert Clyve
Mayo, Katherine
McBride, Henry
McCann, Alfred Watterson
McCarroll, Marion Clyde
McClain, Leanita
McClellan, George Brinton
McCord, Louisa
McCormick, Anne Elizabeth
  O'Hare
McCrackin, Josephine
McIntyre, O. O.
McKay, Claude
McKinley, Carlyle
Mencken, H. L.
Michelson, Charles
Middleton, Drew
Millet, Francis Davis
Mitchel, John
Moore, John Trotwood
Morford, Henry
Morris, George Pope
Mowrer, Edgar Ansel, and
  Paul Scott Mowrer
Murdock, Victor
Nettleton, Alvred Bayard
Neuberger, Richard Lewis
Nevins, Allan
Niles, Hezekiah
Nye, Bill
O'Connor, Jessie Lloyd
O'Hare, Kate Richards
Olds, Leland
Osbon, B. S.
Otis, Eliza Ann
Ottley, Roi
Owen, Chandler
Paret, Jahail Parmly
Parker, Jane Marsh
Parsons, Louella
Pearson, Drew

PRINT JOURNALISTS *(cont.)*

Pegler, Westbrook
Perlman, Philip Benjamin
Phillips, David Graham
Pike, James Shepherd
Plumb, Preston B.
Polk, George Washington, Jr.
Pollard, Edward Alfred
Pollock, Channing
Poole, Ernest
Poore, Benjamin Perley
Porter, Sylvia
Prentice, George Dennison
Price, Byron
Pringle, Henry Fowles
Pryor, Roger Atkinson
Pyle, Ernie
Ramírez, Sara Estela
Randall, James Ryder
Rawlings, Marjorie Kinnan
Ray, Charles Bennett
Raynal, Guillaume
Redpath, James
Reed, John
Reed, Myrtle
Reed, Sampson
Revell, Nellie McAleney
Rice, Charles Allen Thorndike
Rice, Grantland
Ridge, John Rollin
Riis, Jacob August
Rinehart, Mary Roberts
Ripley, Robert LeRoy
Roberts, Kenneth Lewis
Robinson, Solon
Rodell, Fred
Rogers, Will
Root, Waverley
Ross, Charles Griffith
Ross, Ishbel
Round, William M. F.
Rovere, Richard H.
Royall, Anne Newport
Ruby, George T.
Ruggles, David
Rukeyser, Merryle Stanley
Runyon, Damon
Russell, Charles Edward
Ryan, Cornelius
St. Johns, Adela Rogers
Salazar, Ruben
Salisbury, Harrison Evans
Sandburg, Carl
Schiff, Dorothy
Scholte, H. P.
Schultz, Sigrid Lillian

PRINT JOURNALISTS *(cont.)*

Schuyler, George Samuel
Scott, Leroy Martin
Scovel, Sylvester Henry
Scripps, Ellen Browning
Seabury, Samuel (1801–1872)
Searing, Laura C. Redden
Seldes, Gilbert Vivian
Sevareid, Eric
Seward, Frederick William
Sheppard, Eugenia
Shilts, Randy
Shirer, William Lawrence
Short, Joseph Hudson, Jr.
Simmons, Roscoe Conkling
  Murray
Slosson, Edwin Emery
Smedley, Agnes
Smith, H. Allen
Smith, Red
Smith, William Henry
  (1833–1896)
Snelling, William Joseph
Snow, Edgar Parks
Spencer, Matthew Lyle
Spewack, Samuel, and
  Bella Spewack
Squier, Ephraim George
Stahel, Julius
Stanley, Henry Morton
Stanton, Elizabeth Cady
Stanton, Frank
Steffens, Lincoln
Stevens, Alzina Ann Parsons
Stevens, John Leavitt
Stillman, William James
Stoddard, Elizabeth Drew Barstow
Stolberg, Benjamin
Stone, I. F.
Strong, Anna Louise
Strout, Richard L.
Strunsky, Simeon
Sullivan, Ed
Sullivan, Frank
Sullivan, Mark
Swados, Harvey
Swope, Herbert Bayard
Tarbell, Ida M.
Taylor, Bert Leston
Taylor, Charles Henry
Thompson, Dorothy Celine
Thomson, Mortimer Neal
Tobenkin, Elias
Treadwell, Sophie
Truman, Benjamin Cummings
Turner, George Kibbe

PUBLIC PROSECUTORS
Cohn, Roy
Dewey, Thomas Edmund
Garrison, Jim
Jaworski, Leon
Rogge, O. John
Wilentz, David Theodore

PUBLIC RELATIONS BUSINESS LEADERS
Bernays, Doris Elsa Fleischman
Bernays, Edward
Fleischman, Doris E.
Harlow, Bryce
Hill, John Wiley
Husted, Marjorie Child
Lee, Ivy Ledbetter
Swope, Herbert Bayard
Young, John Orr

PUBLIC SPEAKERS. *See* Lecturers;
Orators

PUBLIC UTILITIES EXECUTIVES.
See also Electricity Industry
Leaders; Telephone Industry
Leaders
Copley, Ira Clifton
Cortelyou, George Bruce
Couch, Harvey Crowley
Dawes, Rufus Cutler
Insull, Samuel
O'Sullivan, James Edward
Sloan, Matthew Scott
Sporn, Philip
Willkie, Wendell Lewis

PUBLISHERS. *See* Book Editors and
Publishers; Magazine and Journal
Editors and Publishers; Music
Editors and Publishers;
Newspaper Editors and Publishers

PUPPETEERS
Henson, Jim
Tillstrom, Burr

PURE FOOD CRUSADERS. *See*
Health and Safety Reformers

PURITAN CLERGY
Bulkeley, Peter
Chauncy, Charles (1592–1672)
Cotton, John
Eliot, John

PURITAN CLERGY *(cont.)*
Harvard, John
Hiacoomes
Higginson, Francis
Higginson, John
Hoar, Leonard
Hooker, Thomas
Hubbard, William
Lothropp, John
Mather, Cotton
Mather, Increase
Mather, Richard
Mitchell, Jonathan
Morton, Charles
Norris, Edward
Norton, John
Oakes, Urian
Parris, Samuel
Peter, Hugh
Shepard, Thomas
Stone, Samuel
Taylor, Edward
Weld, Thomas
Wigglesworth, Edward
Wigglesworth, Michael
Willard, Samuel
Williams, Roger (1603?–1683)
Wilson, John (c. 1591–1667)

PURITANS
Brainerd, David
Brewster, William (1567–1644)
Davenport, John
Edwards, Sarah Pierpont
Leverett, John (1616–1679)
Vane, Henry

QUAKER CLERGY
Ashbridge, Elizabeth
Bean, Joel
Bowers, Bathsheba
Coffin, Charles Fisher
Comstock, Elizabeth L.
Fisher, Mary
Gurney, Eliza Paul Kirkbride
Hicks, Elias
Hoag, Joseph
Hume, Sophia Wigington
Jay, Allen
Jones, Rebecca
Jones, Sybil
Malone, John Walter
Pemberton, John
Russell, Elbert
Sands, David
Starbuck, Mary Coffyn

QUAKER CLERGY *(cont.)*
Updegraff, David Brainerd
Way, Amanda
Wilbur, John

QUAKERS
Barnard, Hannah Jenkins
Bates, Elisha
Brinton, Howard Haines, and
Anna Shipley Cox Brinton
Brown, Moses
Brown, Obadiah
Dyer, Mary
Eddy, Thomas
Evans, Jonathan
Evans, William
Ferris, Benjamin
Gibbons, William (1781–1845)
Hopper, Isaac Tatem
Jansen, Reinier
Keith, George
Kinsey, John
Lay, Benjamin
Lloyd, David
Maule, Thomas
M'Clintock, Mary Ann Wilson,
and Thomas M'Clintock
Murray, John (1737–1808)
Murray, Lindley
Murray, Robert
Nicholson, Timothy
Norris, Isaac (1671–1735)
Norris, Isaac (1701–1766)
Pemberton, Israel
Penington, Edward
Penn, William
Perry, Edward
Pickett, Clarence Evan
Pusey, Caleb
Rodman, Samuel
Rotch, William
Rotch, William, Jr.
Shippen, Edward
Wister, Sarah
Wood, James
Wood, L. Hollingsworth
Woolman, John

RABBIS. *See* Jewish Clergy

RACE CAR DRIVERS
Bettenhausen, Tony
Chevrolet, Louis
De Palma, Ralph
De Paolo, Peter
Milton, Tommy

RAILROAD INDUSTRY LEADERS
(cont.)
Sloan, Samuel
Smith, Alfred Holland
Smith, Francis Marion
Smith, John Walter
Spencer, Samuel
Sproule, William
Stanford, Leland
Stevens, Edwin Augustus
Stickney, Alpheus Beede
Stilwell, Arthur Edward
Strong, William Barstow
Swann, Thomas
Thaw, William
Thomson, J. Edgar
Tod, David
Vanderbilt, Cornelius
Vanderbilt, William Henry
Vanderbilt, William Kissam
Van Sweringen, Oris Paxton, and
   Mantis James Van Sweringen
Van Winkle, Peter Godwin
Villard, Henry
Westinghouse, George
Willard, Daniel
Wright, Charles Barstow
Young, Robert Ralph
Yulee, David Levy

RANCHERS. *See also* Cattle Raisers
   and Traders
Burt, Struthers
Cassidy, Butch
Chisum, John Simpson
Cortina, Juan Nepomuceno
Goodnight, Charles
Greene, William Cornell
Ivins, Anthony Woodward
Jones, Buffalo
King, Richard
Lasater, Edward Cunningham
Littlefield, George Washington
Marsh, John
McCrea, Joel
Parker, John Palmer
Ross, C. Ben
Stearns, Abel
Vallejo, Mariano Guadalupe
Warner, Jonathan Trumbull
Wolfskill, William

READING TEACHERS
Gray, William Scott, Jr.
McGuffey, William Holmes
Sharp, Zerna Addas

REAL ESTATE BUSINESS
LEADERS
Astor, John Jacob, IV
Billingsley, Sherman
Binga, Jesse
Binney, Amos
Church, Robert Reed, Jr.
Cooper, William
Corbin, Austin
De Witt, Simeon
Dillingham, Benjamin Franklin
Disston, Hamilton
Ford, Barney Launcelot
Garrard, Kenner
Haggin, James Ben Ali
Hascall, Milo Smith
Hastings, Serranus Clinton
IIo, Chinn
Houston, Henry Howard
Huntington, Henry Edwards
Kenedy, Patrick John
Lafon, Thomy
Lasater, Edward Cunningham
Levitt, William Jaird
McKinlay, Whitefield
Morgenthau, Henry
Nail, John E.
Newberry, Walter Loomis
Otis, Harrison Gray (1765–1848)
Palmer, Potter
Payton, Philip A., Jr.
Putnam, Gideon
Ruggles, Samuel Bulkley
Savage, Henry Wilson
Starrett, William Aiken
Sutro, Adolph Heinrich Joseph
Torrence, Joseph Thatcher
Van Sweringen, Oris Paxton, and
   Mantis James Van Sweringen
Wadsworth, James (1768–1844)
Woodward, George
Zeckendorf, William

REBELS. *See* Insurgents;
   Revolutionaries

RECORDING INDUSTRY LEADERS
Asch, Moses
Berliner, Emile
Blesh, Rudi
Drake, Pete
Edison, Thomas Alva
Feather, Leonard
Goldmark, Peter Carl
Hammond, John Henry, Jr.
Johnson, Eldridge Reeves

RECORDING INDUSTRY LEADERS
(cont.)
Kapp, Jack
Marek, George Richard
Pace, Harry Herbert
Peer, Ralph Sylvester
Robey, Don D.
Satherley, Uncle Art
Walker, Frank Buckley
Williams, Clarence

REFEREES. *See* Sports Officials

REFORMED CHURCH IN AMERICA
CLERGY
Peale, Norman Vincent
Schenck, Ferdinand Schureman

REFORMERS AND ACTIVISTS. *See*
   Abolitionists; Civic Leaders; Civil
   Rights Activists; Clubwomen;
   Educational Reform Advocates;
   Environmentalists; Health and
   Safety Reformers; Historic
   Preservationists; Internationalists;
   Political Activists; Relief Workers;
   Social Reformers; Temperance
   Movement Leaders; Women's
   Rights Advocates; *and other specific*
   terms

REGGAE MUSICIAN
Marley, Bob

REGICIDES
Bresci, Gaetano
Dixwell, John
Whalley, Edward

REGIONAL PLANNERS. *See* City and
   Regional Planners

RELIEF WORKERS
Billikopf, Jacob
Empie, Paul Chauncey
Hoge, Jane Currie Blaikie
Porter, Eliza Emily Chappell
Reed, Esther De Berdt
Wood, Carolena
Wormeley, Katharine Prescott

RELIGIOUS BROADCASTERS
Alamo, Susan
Ayer, William Ward
Barnhouse, Donald Grey

UNION NAVAL OFFICERS *(cont.)*

Jeffers, William Nicholson
Jenkins, Thornton Alexander
Jouett, James Edward
Kempff, Louis
Lee, Samuel Phillips
Loring, Charles Harding
Luce, Stephen Bleeker
Mahan, Alfred Thayer
McNair, Frederick Vallette
Meade, Richard Worsam, III
Mullany, James Robert Madison
Nicholson, James William
  Augustus
Palmer, James Shedden
Parker, Foxhall Alexander, Jr.
Parrott, Enoch Greenleafe
Pattison, Thomas
Paulding, Hiram
Porter, David Dixon
Preble, George Henry
Radford, William
Ramsay, Francis Munroe
Remey, George Collier
Ringgold, Cadwalader
Rodgers, George Washington
  (1822–1863)
Rodgers, John (1812–1882)
Rowan, Stephen Clegg
Sampson, William Thomas
Sands, Benjamin Franklin
Schley, Winfield Scott
Selfridge, Thomas Oliver, Jr.
Shufeldt, Robert Wilson
Sicard, Montgomery
Sigsbee, Charles Dwight
Smith, Joseph (1790–1877)
Smith, Melancton (1810–1893)
Stringham, Silas Horton
Thatcher, Henry Knox
Wainwright, Richard (1817–1862)
Walke, Henry
Wilkes, Charles
Winslow, John Ancrum
Wise, Henry Augustus
Worden, John Lorimer

UNION OFFICIALS. *See* Labor
  Organizers and Leaders

UNITARIAN CLERGY

Abbot, Francis Ellingwood
Alger, William Rounseville
Bancroft, Aaron
Barrows, Samuel June
Bellows, Henry Whitney

UNITARIAN CLERGY *(cont.)*

Bentley, William
Blackwell, Antoinette Louisa
  Brown
Blake, James Vila
Buckminster, Joseph Stevens
Channing, William Ellery
Channing, William Henry
Clarke, James Freeman
Collier, Price
Conway, Moncure Daniel
Cooke, George Willis
Cummings, Edward
Dall, Charles Henry Appleton
Davies, A. Powell
Dewey, Orville
Dietrich, John Hassler
Eliot, Frederick May
Eliot, Samuel Atkins
Eliot, Thomas Lamb
Eliot, William Greenleaf, Jr.
Ellis, George Edward
Emerson, William
Fenn, William Wallace
Francis, Convers
Freeman, James
Fritchman, Stephen Hole
Frothingham, Nathaniel Langdon
Frothingham, Octavius Brooks
Furness, William Henry
Gannett, Ezra Stiles
Gilman, Samuel Foster
Hale, Edward Everett
Harris, Thaddeus Mason
Hedge, Frederic Henry
Higginson, Thomas Wentworth
Hill, Thomas
Holley, Horace
Holmes, John Haynes
Jones, Jenkin Lloyd
Judd, Sylvester
Lathrop, John Howland
Longfellow, Samuel
MacCauley, Clay
May, Samuel Joseph
Mayo, Amory Dwight
Palfrey, John Gorham
Parker, Theodore
Peabody, Andrew Preston
Peabody, Francis Greenwood
Peabody, Oliver William Bourn
Potter, Charles Francis
Potter, William James
Reese, Curtis Williford
Ripley, Ezra
Savage, Minot Judson

UNITARIAN CLERGY *(cont.)*

Sears, Edmund Hamilton
Simmons, Henry Martyn
Simons, Minot
Sparks, Jared
Stearns, Oliver
Stebbins, Horatio
Sullivan, William Laurence
Sunderland, Jabez Thomas
Toulmin, Harry
Tuckerman, Joseph
Upham, Charles Wentworth
Vogt, Von Ogden
Ware, Henry, Jr.
Ware, William
Wendte, Charles William
West, Samuel
Wheelwright, John
Woolley, Celia Parker

UNITARIAN LAY LEADER
Jones, Susan Charlotte Barber

**UNITARIAN UNIVERSALIST
CLERGY**
Greeley, Dana McLean

UNITED BRETHREN CLERGY. *See*
  Moravian Clergy

**UNITED SOCIETY OF BELIEVERS
IN CHRIST'S SECOND
APPEARING.** *See* Shakers

UNIVERSALIST CLERGY
Ballou, Adin
Ballou, Hosea
Ballou, Hosea, 2d
Brown, Olympia
King, Thomas Starr
Kneeland, Abner
Miner, Alonzo Ames
Murray, John (1741–1815)
Newton, Joseph Fort
Skinner, Clarence Russell
Soule, Caroline Augusta White

UNIVERSALIST LAY LEADER
Winchester, Elhanan

UNIVERSITY ADMINISTRATORS.
  See Educational Institution
  Officials

VICE PRESIDENTS OF THE UNITED STATES. *See also* Vice Presidential Candidates

Barkley, Alben William
Breckinridge, John Cabell
Burr, Aaron (1756–1836)
Calhoun, John C.
Clinton, George (1739–1812)
Colfax, Schuyler
Curtis, Charles
Dallas, George Mifflin
Dawes, Charles Gates
Fairbanks, Charles Warren
Garner, John Nance
Gerry, Elbridge
Hamlin, Hannibal
Hendricks, Thomas Andrews
Hobart, Garret Augustus
Humphrey, Hubert Horatio
Johnson, Richard Mentor
King, William Rufus Devane
Marshall, Thomas Riley
Morton, Levi Parsons
Rockefeller, Nelson Aldrich
Stevenson, Adlai Ewing
Tompkins, Daniel D.
Wallace, Henry Agard
Wheeler, William Almon
Wilson, Henry

VICTIMS OF MURDER. *See* Murder Victims

VICTIMS OF SHIPWRECK. *See* Shipwreck Victims

VICTIMS OF SPACECRAFT DISASTERS

Challenger Shuttle Crew
Project Apollo Crew

VIGILANTES

Coleman, William Tell
Langford, Nathaniel Pitt
Lynch, Charles

VINTNERS. *See* Winegrowers and Vintners; Wine Merchants

VIOLINISTS. *See also* Fiddlers

Beck, Johann Heinrich
Braham, David
Bristow, George Frederick
Bull, Ole
Dickerson, Carroll

VIOLINISTS *(cont.)*

Elman, Mischa
Gilbert, Henry Franklin Belknap
Heifetz, Jascha
Herrmann, Eduard Emil
Hill, Ureli Corelli
Hommann, Charles
Hupfeld, Charles Frederick
Kreisler, Fritz
Lang, Margaret Ruthven
Loeffler, Charles Martin
Mannes, David
Milstein, Nathan
Musin, Ovide
Nance, Ray Willis
Petrides, Frédérique
Piron, Armand
Powell, Maud
Rice, Helen
Schneider, Alexander
Smith, Stuff
Sobolewski, Edward
Stoessel, Albert Frederic
Urso, Camilla
Venuti, Joe
Weems, Ted
White, Clarence Cameron
Zimbalist, Efrem

VIOLISTS

Primrose, William
Zach, Max

VIROLOGISTS

Enders, John Franklin
Francis, Thomas, Jr.
Horsfall, Frank Lappin, Jr.
Paul, John Rodman
Rivers, Thomas Milton
Sabin, Albert Bruce
Salk, Jonas Edward
Shope, Richard Edwin
Stanley, Wendell Meredith
Theiler, Max

VOLCANOLOGIST

Jaggar, Thomas Augustus, Jr.

WAGON MANUFACTURERS. *See* Horse-Drawn Vehicle Manufacturers

WAR CORRESPONDENTS. *See* Print Journalists

WAR HEROES. *See also* Congressional Medal of Honor Recipients

Allen, William Henry (1784–1813)
Bailey, Ann Hennis Trotter
Carney, William Harvey
Corbin, Margaret Cochran
Ellsworth, Elmer Ephraim
Flora, William
Hale, Nathan
Hart, Nancy
Jones, John Paul
Kelly, Colin Purdie
Lafayette, James
Logan, James (1776?–1812)
Miller, Dorie
Murphy, Audie
Pitcher, Molly
Ross, Betsy
Sampson, Deborah
Shelby, Isaac
Sisson, Jack
Tarrant, Caesar
Taylor, Zachary
Thompson, Robert George
York, Alvin Cullum
Zane, Betty

WAR RELIEF WORKERS. *See* Relief Workers

WATCHMAKERS

Bulova, Arde
Crosby, Sylvester Sage

WEAPONS MANUFACTURERS. *See* Firearms Manufacturers; Ordnance Manufacturers

WEAVER

Bresci, Gaetano

WESLEYAN METHODIST CLERGY

Lee, Luther

WESTERN SWING MUSICIANS

Cooley, Spade
McAuliffe, Leon
Wills, Bob

WHALING INDUSTRY LEADERS

Rodman, Samuel
Rotch, Joseph
Rotch, William
Rotch, William, Jr.
Russell, Joseph